TUTTLE
G U I D E   T O
THE SINGLE
EUROPEAN
MARKET

TUTTLE

GUIDE TO

THE SINGLE
EUROPEAN
MARKET

**A Comprehensive Handbook
by RICHARD OWEN and MICHAEL DYNES**

Charles E. Tuttle Company, Inc.
Boston • Rutland, Vermont • Tokyo

Published in the United States in 1992 by
Charles E. Tuttle Company, Inc. of Rutland, Vermont & Tokyo, Japan,
with editorial offices at 77 Central Street, Boston, Massachusetts 02109.

Library of Congress Cataloging-in-Publication Data

Owen, Richard, 1947-
    Tuttle guide to the single European market : a comprehensive
handbook / by Richard Owen and Michael Dynes.
        p.   cm.
    Rev. ed. of: The Times guide to 1992.
    Includes bibliographical references and index.
    ISBN 0-8048-1815-0 (pbk.)
    1. Europe 1992—Handbooks, manuals, etc. I. Dynes, Michael,
1957- . II. Title. III. Title: Times guide to 1992.
HC241.2.0944 1992
341.24'22—dc20   92-22219
                                                                       CIP

Typeset by Rowland Phototypesetting Limited, Suffolk, England
PRINTED IN THE UNITED STATES

CONTENTS

PREFACE

Since the first edition of *The Times Guide to 1992* was published in 1989 the world has changed out of all recognition—and with it the debate over the future of Europe. This *Guide to the Single European Market* builds on the earlier guide, which dealt with the formative stages of the 1992 programme for the internal market. The single market, which appeared relatively remote when conceived in 1985, is now upon us.

In keeping with the remarkable changes which have reshaped Europe, the new guide offers an updated account of the way business, finance, trade and politics will operate in the single market. It also discusses the impact on a frontier-free Europe of recent upheavals: the reunification of Germany, the democratization of Eastern Europe, the collapse of Communism in the Soviet Union after the failed coup of August 1991, the end of the Cold War and the creation of a European Economic Area through an EC–EFTA deal that gives EFTA nations (the European Free Trade Association) access to the single market (with soft EFTA loans and grants to the EC southern states), thereby creating a still wider European market of 380 million people. The entry of the pound into the European Monetary System's exchange rate mechanism and the departure of Mrs Thatcher—brought down, in no small measure, by the issue of Europe —to be succeeded as Prime Minister by John Major are also considered.

Nowhere has the debate about European unification been more fierce than in Britain. Some argue that the need to accommodate Eastern Europe is slowing down the pace of integration, making political and economic union—a federal Europe and a single currency—less desirable and less practicable. This, in effect, was the sub-text at the Maastricht summit of December 1991. If a Community of Twenty-four or Thirty rather than Twelve is no longer out of the question, the argument runs, then notions of a single currency, a European Bank (the 'Eurofed') and federal political institutions must be put on one side as impracticable. Instead of a united Europe centred around Brussels, there should be a broad free-trade area embracing both East and West Europe.

For others, by contrast, the opening up of Eastern Europe challenges the Twelve to proceed towards full integration at an even faster pace, so that the EC can consolidate political and monetary union while helping the East Europeans and, indeed, independent states formed from the former Soviet Union—including Russia—to develop democratic pluralism and free-market economies. Eventually, in this view, there will need to be new EC institutions, perhaps even a 'core' of EC nations organized along the lines of the United Nations Security Council, to govern a broader collection of states in a general pooling of sovereignty.

This debate has set 'wideners' against 'deepeners'. While it continues, the 1992 programme goes ahead, in an amended form—and it has fallen to Britain, after taking over the rotating EC presidency from Portugal in the second half of 1992, to preside over the final version of the single market.

The dilemmas posed by the challenge of responding to the new Eastern Europe and to EFTA arose just as the EC was dealing with the most difficult 1992 issues, such as car imports, border controls, the harmonization of company law and securities trading, and airline deregulation. The fact remains that scarcely a single area of political life is untouched by the European dimension, from taxation to defence, from transport to broadcasting. Similarly, almost every aspect of business and professional life will be affected by 1992, from accountancy to pharmaceuticals, from engineering to the law.

The Times can claim to have recognized earlier than most what the 1992 target date could mean for industry, commerce and finance, as well as for ordinary travellers and consumers, and ultimately for the UK's national sovereignty. This book draws on the work of *Times* home and foreign reporters on various aspects of 1992, as well as on our own experience and observation.

We owe thanks to Simon Jenkins, Editor of *The Times*, and Martin Ivens, the Foreign Editor. We have a debt, too, to Piers Akerman, former Deputy Foreign Editor, who as long ago as 1987 oversaw a week-long series on 1992 in *The Times* which provided the idea for the original *Times Guide to 1992*. As an Australian, and thus an 'outsider', he perceived perhaps better than many Europeans the significance of the integration process then taking shape.

Our thanks go, too, to Julia Owen for sustaining us since the beginning with encouragement and support.

Richard Owen and Michael Dynes
January 1992

INTRODUCTION

Why the single European market matters to you

Few Europeans have been able to understand why the emergence of a single European market of 320 million potential consumers, the largest advanced industrial market in the world, with a gross national product in excess of $5 trillion, has attracted so little attention in the US. Perhaps it is because US business executives are too occupied at present with the threat to US economic interests from Japan and the Far East to devote much time to Europe. Furthermore, the theory that the centre of gravity of world trade is shifting away from the Old World towards the Pacific Rim has gained much ground in the US.

American manufacturers and exporters, not to mention politicians, are certainly right to focus on Japan—hence President Bush's tour of Asia at the beginning of 1992. The Old World is, however, being revitalised as a result of the European Commission's drive for economic and political integration, the collapse of communism in eastern Europe, the reunification of Germany and the dissolution of the Soviet Union. Consequently, the 1990s herald a departure from the economic ailment US business executives once characterised dismissively as 'Eurosclerosis', and the creation of an unprecedented range of business opportunities for US exporters and multinational corporations. While it remains true that Europe, unlike the US, will never have a single language or culture, there is every prospect that it will have a single currency towards the end of the 1990s. Moreover, business practices are being streamlined and harmonised from Spain to Denmark, and Great Britain to Greece, in an attempt to boost the volume of economic activity between the 12 member states, and encourage the kind of industrial and commercial restructuring that will enable European companies to respond to the global competitive threat posed by US and Japanese enterprises.

This book offers an insider's guide to the new Europe now taking shape. With Germany, Britain and France at its heart, the European Community of 12 nations has forged a programme, now nearly complete, for the abolition of internal barriers to the free movement of capital, goods, people, and services. By the end of the century, the 12 may well have risen to 20 or even 30 as former communist nations such as Poland and Hungary are drawn in, along with major European industrial powers such as Sweden and Norway which stayed outside the EC for many years but now feel the magnetic attraction of the single market. A united Europe is already exercising increased influence with which the world has to reckon, as the US has discovered during its skirmishes with EC officials over the future framework of world trade in the Uruguay Round of the General Agreement on Tariffs and Trade (GATT).

There are growing anxieties, however, that as the EC moves beyond economic integration to political union, US companies could be confronted by what has been called a 'Fortress Europe', in which the benefits of closer economic and political co-operation are reserved for Europeans. The spectre of protectionism was raised during the early days of the US presidential election campaign by Patrick Buchanan, George Bush's foremost challenger within the Republican party. Buchanan campaigned on an 'America First' platform, and struck a chord with many Americans by inveighing against the recipients of US foreign aid, whom Buchanan accused of 'mainlining out of the US Treasury'. In the case of Europe, Buchanan's concerns centred on the extent of EC agricultural subsidies, an issue which has caused increasingly heated exchanges within GATT; new rules for the establishment of banking subsidiaries in Europe; and allegedly restrictive trade practices in a wide range of manufacturing sectors.

In February 1992 Vice-President Dan Quayle went so far as to warn Europe that lack of progress on GATT could lead the US to reconsider its commitment to the security of Europe, that is, the maintenance of thousands of US troops for European defence. Addressing a security conference in Munich, Germany, Quayle observed: 'GATT is absolutely critical to the security of Europe, to the security of the United States, and the security of Asia. There are many reasons why we have got to get on with it.' The danger, Quayle said, was that 'we have the Cold War behind us and yet no comprehensive understanding of how we start trade relationships'. This was immediately seen by some prominent Europeans, such as Hans van den Broek, the foreign minister of the Netherlands, as tantamount to an American ultimatum: 'agree on GATT or we leave NATO'. Senator William Cohen of Maine remarked at the same conference that there was a popular view in the US that NATO was 'no longer affordable . . . America First is being heard from Right and Left, and many would like to retreat into a continental cocoon and zip out the rest of the world.'

Two days later, in London, Quayle was at pains to stress that he had intended no direct link between GATT and NATO, and that the US military commitment to Europe was undiminished. But he told British Foreign Secretary Douglas Hurd that Congress was in 'belligerent mood' over trade talks, and that some senators and congressmen were ready to press for troop cuts in Europe if the GATT talks failed. In essence, Quayle's message was that the US presidential election was rapidly turning into a plebiscite on free trade, with the Bush administration's critics playing the card of economic nationalism. But if his outburst was an attempt to intimidate his European counterparts into making further concessions on the trade talks, it clearly backfired. European trade negotiators, emboldened by the growing power and influence which have flowed from recent moves towards economic and political union, held their ground.

Unlike the US, Europe has only had a few decades in which to make progress toward full integration. How far will European unification actually go? In April 1990 the German economist Heiko Thieme ventured predictions for 1992 and beyond: Mrs Margaret Thatcher, then the British Prime Minister and a world figure, would not fight the next British election, but President Bush would be re-elected. Within five years Moscow would again have a stock exchange and free economy. In Europe, within the same period, there would be full economic and monetary integration, with political union by the end of the century. Six months later, at the extraordinary EC summit in October 1990 in Rome, under the Italian presidency, Mrs Thatcher lost patience with EC attempts to set a timetable for a European Bank and a single currency, accusing her fellow leaders of living in 'cloud cuckoo land'. The following month she stood down after failing to overcome a leadership challenge, and was replaced by John Major. 1990 also saw German unification achieved at a pace few had anticipated. The following year, 1991, witnessed the end of communism in Europe and the break-up of the Soviet Union following a bungled hardline coup against President Gorbachov in August, setting Russia on the precarious path of reform and privatisation. Will Herr Thieme's forecasts of EC monetary and political union be similarly fulfilled, or have the upheavals of 1990–91 pushed 1992 off course?

Part of the answer came at the EC summit held in the Dutch town of Maastricht at the end of 1991. The 12 EC countries chair the Community for six months in turn, holding a summit at the end of their presidency. At the end of 1991 it was the turn of the Netherlands to chair the six-monthly summit and chart the way forward. In essence, the Maastricht treaties are the EC's blueprint for the future, and, therefore, the first attempt to define a new European post-Cold War order to which the US, and the rest of the world, will have to adjust (a summary can be found at the end of this book). The treaties point the way to a Europe with common citizenship, common defence and foreign policies, and a common currency, with laws made by the European Parliament as much as national parliaments, and a more equitable distribution of wealth, benefiting the poorer countries in the South, such as Spain. Indeed, some see Spain as the future location of sunbelt industries, a European equivalent of California. Britain, ever the EC maverick, reserved the right not to exchange the pound sterling for the European Currency Unit (ECU), the single currency, and also opted out of common social policies. But Maastricht was a milestone nevertheless.

Where did this bold plan for a single European market with the free movement of capital, goods, people and services come from? Its immediate origins can be traced to the Single European Act, which was ratified by the 12 in 1987. At its core lay a desire to bring down barriers to cross-border trade. But the act swiftly acquired a political dimension, with federalist-minded idealists seeing in the single market the beginning of the United States of Europe. The plan grew as a result of a unique combination of circumstances: the determination of leading EC figures to fulfil the promise of the Treaty of Rome, the EC's founding document, by taking the EC further toward union; and the perception that only a pooling of resources could both match the economic strength of the US and Japan on a global scale, and guarantee growth and jobs within an expanded EC market. For some, the resulting vision was an exhilarating 'Eurocause', for others, a disastrous slide toward the surrender of sovereignty.

Between the two extremes lies a third way which seems likely to dominate the European debate after Maastricht: continuing economic integration and the abolition of the barriers to trade, tempered by a more pragmatic attempt to overcome the obstacles to closer economic and political cooperation resulting from the integration process. The need to control the flow of illegal drugs, for example, is highlighted by a European Parliament report released just before the Maastricht summit, which points to the operations of Turkish and Chinese gangs in Europe, some of them taking advantage of eastern Europe's easier access to a united Germany. Attacks by IRA terrorists on British servicemen on the Continent also underline the difficulty of policing open frontiers. So, too, does the growing problem of immigration and asylum, with Britain concerned by the large numbers of refugees—economic and political—seeking asylum in the UK, and Germany and France alarmed by the social pressures and xenophobic violence sparked off by the large numbers of immigrants in their countries.

Demolishing the internal barriers to trade

Nonetheless, the heart of the internal market programme remains the removal of the physical, technical, and fiscal barriers to trade, which have impeded the economic development of the European Community for decades. In terms of everyday life and business the internal market programme seeks to ensure that the 320 million citizens of the EC are able to move around Europe without hindrance in an integrated transport network based on free competition; to work in any of the 12 member states on the basis of harmonised professional qualifications; to sell their goods in any other EC country as if it were their home market on the basis of harmonised product standards; to deposit and borrow money anywhere in the EC, perhaps with a European Central Bank to control the money supply; in short, to think, work and act as if Europe were one country.

The model for frontier abolition is the Schengen Agreement signed in June 1990 by France, Germany, Belgium, Netherlands, and Luxembourg. The accord (named after the small town in Luxembourg where it was first mooted) removes all border controls between the five nations, harmonises visa requirements for third parties, and spells out cross-border police procedures. These include the exchange of information on 'criminals, undesirables and missing persons,' common criteria for political asylum-seekers, and the right of 'hot pursuit' on each others territories. The Schengen Agreement cannot, however, be applied without modification to other EC states. Italy, which wanted to join, was excluded because of its exceptionally long coastline, which makes control of illegal immigration more difficult; Denmark did not qualify because of its passport-free travel arrangements with other Nordic countries; and Britain has special status as an island. Nonetheless, the abolition of frontiers remains the Commission's objective for all 12 member states.

Behind the Commission's grand vision of an economically and politically integrated Europe lurks a fear of what could happen if European leaders failed to grasp the opportunity to re-shape Europe's destiny. As Jacques Delors, the President of the European Commission, said:

'Japan is spinning its spider's web over large areas of the Pacific. The US and Canada are closing together in a free trade zone, doubtless with Mexico tomorrow—the world is beginning to build large regional assemblies. We have to move fast or Europe will become an archaeological site where the Americans and Japanese come to dig over defunct ways of life.'

Despite the substantial progress made since its inauguration, the single market programme has, however, fallen behind schedule. In its progress report on single market measures in June 1991, the European Commission reported that of the 282 measures needed to create the internal market, only 193 had been adopted by all member states, and many of them only half-heartedly. Some barriers to the free movement of goods, services and people had been removed, but obstacles remained in vital areas such as investment, shipping and road haulage. Of the 89 measures still to be approved, 26 were in the internal market area, 28 in economic and financial affairs, 28 in agriculture, 5 in transport, 1 in the environment and 1 in social affairs (see Appendix 8). Non-controversial measures have been passed relatively quickly, while many of the more difficult issues remain to be solved. In addition, a number of member states have fallen behind in their efforts to transpose the single market directives into national law, while many of those who have done so are frequently failing to comply with the new legislation. Single market rhetoric and single market reality do not always go hand-in-hand.

The onset of the economic recession has diluted the enthusiasm with which the internal market programme was originally embraced. As the 1992 ideal becomes tempered by a more realistic attitude towards what is possible, Martin Bangemann, the Internal Market Commissioner, has adopted the pragmatic approach which marked his time as German economics minister between 1984 and 1988. He dismisses the growing demand for protectionism from the automobile and electronics industries, arguing that European companies should be more confident about free competition. The Commission has drawn back from over-regulation, with Bangemann refusing to intervene in a dispute between Britain and Germany over, for example, fireproof standards for mattresses. Similarly, it has refused to set EC standards for free-range chickens. 'How much range does a chicken need to be free?', he asked a farmers delegation in Brussels, the Commission headquarters. 'The Commission has no business trying to answer such questions.' The underlying principle here is 'subsidiarity' (similar to the US principle of states' rights), which has its origins in the 1931 Papal encyclical which established that: 'It is an injustice, a grave evil and disturbance of right order for a larger and higher association to arrogate to itself functions which can be performed efficiently by smaller and lower societies.'

Despite such reassurances, Euro-sceptics continue to fear that the 'federalists' will in the end impose not only a single European currency but also a common European defence policy, and even a common European athletics team. Britain under John Major continues to resist attempts by the European Commission to extend its powers to new areas, notably in the field of industrial relations, known in Euro-jargon as the 'social dimension', which would include EC-wide laws on minimum wages, conditions of work, and part-time workers.

The pace of EC integration

Although the immediate origins of the 1992 process lie with the Single European Act, the internal market programme is in fact little more than a re-statement of the aims and objectives contained in the 1957 Treaty of Rome, which brought the European Community into being. 'Europe will not be created at a stroke or according to a single plan. It will be built through concrete achievements,' observed Robert Schuman, one of the EC's founding fathers, and the man still revered in Brussels—together with Jean Monnet—as the originator of the dream of a united Europe. During the 1960s and 1970s, however, the Schuman-Monnet vision became bogged down in a series of petty national economic and political rivalries, which many critics thought were destined to undermine the great European experiment. It was in this context that the European Commission, and the Council of Ministers, launched a long-overdue be little doubt that Commission officials have availed themselves of the instruments of neo-protectionism in their long-standing trade disputes with Japan, and that US interests have, occasionally, been caught in the cross-fire. The Commission's defence is that Europe, like the US, has reached the point of exasperation in its attempts to reduce its trade deficit with Japan, and very few of these techniques for 'managing' foreign trade have been declared illegal by the GATT. Likewise, Commission officials regard claims that Europe is in the process of erecting a giant industrial policy as equally specious. Examples of large amounts of government aid being used to promote particular industries, such as Airbus, are few and far between. Moreover, while some member states, notably France, have been calling for increased government aid to support key sectors of economic activity, such as the electronics industry, they have met with little success.

Indeed, the Commission is adopting an increasingly aggressive approach towards illegal subsidies sanctioned by national governments to promote favoured state industries. In a recent statement on industrial policy, the European Commission made clear its view that market forces should be allowed to determine the success or failure of a company, rather than domestic political pressures in favour of government intervention. As the US Chamber of Commerce report pointed out: 'A "get tough" stance on the use of public subsidies and a pro-competition industrial policy would be a positive development for US business. American companies would not have to compete against government supported European companies.' The one concern, however, is that in the face of the economic downturn domestic political pressures to protect endangered industries could override the Commission's free market instincts.

There are a variety of additional benefits that US exporters and multinational corporations are likely to obtain from Europe's move towards economic and political union, most notably in the fields of taxation, monetary union, financial services, and access to the new markets in the east. Admittedly, the harmonization of corporate taxation has never been a component of the internal market programme, although there have been calls for moves in this direction in an effort to eliminate the disparities that presently exist in the corporate taxation regimes of the Twelve, and at the same reduce the number of tax returns companies engaged in cross-border trade are required to file. Convergence of corporate taxation regimes is likely to be a more long-term development, but the harmonization of indirect taxation has been all but finalised, and should result in a considerable boost to cross-border trade, a reduction in the cost of collecting value-added tax and excise duties, and a reduction in the price of goods traded across frontiers (see chapter 12).

Comprehensive economic and monetary union, even after the historic Maastricht agreement, remains a distant objective with many formidable obstacles still to be overcome. Although the European Community as a whole is more or less committed to economic and monetary union as its ultimate goal, different member states have different priorities. Germany, for example, has insisted that economic and monetary union must be linked to political union. The southern states, such as Spain and Portugal, have warned that they will not participate in any move towards economic and monetary union until there has been a considerable transfer of financial resources from the wealthy north to the impoverished south, a proposal few northern states, particularly Germany and Britain, have yet showed much enthusiasm for. There can be little doubt, however, that the creation of a European central bank, and the introduction of a single European currency, if and when it does materialise, would help generate greater price stability, reduce transaction costs, and promote the kind of exchange rate stability corporations need for successful long-term planning (see chapters 8 and 9).

The liberalisation of the European financial services sector can be expected to provide US financial services companies with a substantial boost in business opportunities. This is already the case for US companies operating in the European banking sector, where the single market for banking is in place. The situation can be expected to be much the same for those companies operating in the investment and insurance sectors, once the new regulatory frameworks are in place. Finally, while the collapse of the communist dictatorships in eastern Europe and the former Soviet Union has tended to act as a brake on the European Community's momentum towards economic and monetary union, forcing EC officials to help stabilise the fledgling democracies with trade and aid accords, it is clear that unimpeded access to any huge trading bloc stretching from the Atlantic to the Urals will be of central importance to the long-term health of the American economy.

December 31, 1992: no voice from the heavens

It is a mistake to suppose—in the words of one EC official—that 'neon lights will flash in the sky' at midnight on December 31, 1992, and that a voice from the heavens will proclaim an integrated Europe on January 1, 1993. In aspects of commerce and daily life, the internal market programme will continue to develop in the years after 1992. The European Court will still act as the arbiter in disputes over 1992 directives, while the European Commission will, no doubt, devise new areas into which to extend its power and influence.

However, there can be no doubt that industry and the professions are gearing up for a major change in the way business is done. The trades unions, too, are making plans. After a record of hostility toward the EC, the British Trades Union Congress (TUC), and its European equivalent, the ETUC (which represents 44 million workers) now accepts the 1992 programme, and wants it to include the protection of employee rights. There may even emerge European unions to represent shop floor workers in amalgamated European companies—a development which would have an impact on some of the TUC's more old fashioned policies, such as its opposition to single union deals. It was this kind of antiquated approach to modern industrial relations which prompted Ford to locate a new electronics component factory in Cadiz, Spain, in 1988, rather than in Dundee, Scotland, and, more recently, to move the second stage of its programme for modernising engine manufacture from Bridgend, England, to Cologne, Germany.

Despite Commission President Delors' assurance that the Commission is 'not like Napoleon's Grand Army, it only intervenes when it must', many critics of the European Community's moves towards closer economic and political co-operation still suspect that the 1992 initiative is little more than a fig-leaf disguising attempts by Brussels to increase intervention in all aspects of daily life, from the environmental impact of the latest motorway proposal to the amount of remuneration retired people are entitled to from the state. Although such anxieties may not be without some foundation, they are somewhat behind the times. An ever-increasing number of business executives, employees, and consumers, are becoming accustomed to the realities of the new Europe, and the seemingly all-pervasive reach of Brussels. The same applies to holiday resort managers who have to abide by EC bathing water standards, garage owners who have to apply stricter exhaust emission standards to vehicles, and local government purchasers who must now ensure that large-scale contracts for goods and services have been subject to competitive international tendering. Despite the appeals of those calling for the preservation of traditional forms of national sovereignty, the EC has already acquired a say in many areas of activity once thought of as the exclusive preserve of national governments.

For those trying to rise to the challenges presented by the post-1992 era, whether from Europe, America, or Japan, flexibility and a willingness to adjust to new ways of doing things is likely to be a key to success. Take, for example, the difficulties presented by language. While it is true that English tends to be the language of international business, and is even used at EC summits where the official language is French (Helmut Schmidt, the former German Chancellor, and Giscard d'Estaing, the former French President, were said to converse in English in private), company marketing executives will soon find that it is a severe handicap not to be fairly conversant with at least one major European language, and preferably two or three. North Europeans, the Dutch, Germans, and Danes, tend to speak very good English as, increasingly, do business and professional people from southern Europe. Mastery of European languages can, therefore, be expected to be an important asset to small, medium, and large-scale companies seeking to be successful in the single European market.

For anyone interested in identifying key differences and similarities between the US and the EC, a direct comparison of the American and European internal markets is extremely instructive. If EC plans for the free movement of capital, goods, people, and services are fulfilled—and many already have been—the European single market could turn out to be more homogeneous than that of the US. The US has, as noted earlier, a single currency, a common history, and a single federal budget. But the individual states still have wide supervisory or regulatory powers, which they often use to restrict trade. Under a 1926 federal law, banks in one state may not open branches in other states—and attempts to reform the system have foundered in Congress. There are also tight state regulations on insurance broking, and there is no uniformity from state to state on income tax, sales taxes or corporate taxes. There are even state differences in the licensing of professional people.

The European internal market programme may contain lessons for the US in how to modernise and update a single market to meet the business requirements of the 21st century, even though the US has been operating a single market for 200 years. By contrast, Europeans are beginning to appreciate from the US experience that federalism, which concentrates power at the centre, can have drawbacks. Equally, because of US criticism, Europeans have become more conscious of the dangers inherent in any move towards protectionism and isolationism. Promoting 'Europeanness' is one thing: doing so by fomenting anti-Americanism and fanning resentment towards what some European critics have denounced as the 'Coca Cola and Big Mac' culture is quite another.

If the attempt to create a stable post-Cold War order between the New and the Old Worlds is to prove durable, the US and the EC must make some important adjustments. The US has to learn how to cope with a united Europe without retreating into a new era of isolationism. As *The Times* of London put it in an editorial on February 10, 1992, 'Americans have long complained of being forced to shoulder too large a burden of security on behalf of the rest of the world. Influential congressmen such as Sam Nunn and Mike Mansfield have for two decades lent their names to amendments calling for American troops in Europe to come home. Ever since George Washington cautioned 'beware of foreign entanglements' isolationism has been a trait of the American character . . . Americans may well refuse to pay the bill for the defence of a continent that appears not only ungrateful but an economic rival too.' *The Times* added: 'The danger is that Europeans, still elated by the downfall of communism and their progress toward union, will be deluded by their own propaganda into believing they can really take over their own defence. Europe still needs NATO's security umbrella, albeit reduced to match the lessened threat . . . American voters need to see a return on their investment in Europe's security, however. Europe must show, by resolving its objections to GATT, that it does not want to wage economic war on America —and for America's defence of their continent, Europeans should shout their thanks back across the Atlantic.' The first step in developing trans-atlantic economic and political relationships, as Europe enters an era of unification, is for Americans to come to terms with the wider forces that lay behind the creation of the European internal market.

Maastricht Postscript

The Danish decision to reject the Maastricht Treaty in a referendum in June 1992 plunged the EC into its worst crisis in almost 30 years. By expressing doubts about integration under the terms of the Maastricht Treaty, the Danes prompted a bout of introspection in other member states. The EC's political élites, particularly in Britain, Germany, and France, are now obliged to ask themselves whether they are too far ahead of their peoples in their enthusiasm for European integration. The Danish vote serves, therefore, as a timely reminder that the Community is an association of democratic states whose legitimacy stems from the consent of its peoples.

The decision, a few weeks later, by the Irish electorate to endorse the Maastricht Treaty supports aspirations for closer European union but does not dispel uncertainty about the Community's future. The Danish no-vote cannot be rescinded, and, because Article 236 of the Treaty of Rome requires unanimity before any changes to the EC's founding document can be implemented, the determination of the remaining member states to press ahead with the ratification process smacks somewhat of illegality.

Technically, Maastricht is dead. Politically, however, the treaty is still very much alive. After the Lisbon summit in June, the member states declared that the Community has no intention of jettisoning its commitment to increased economic and political cooperation, despite the Danish vote. It falls to Britain to salvage the situation after it takes over the EC's rotating presidency in July.

The British presidency presents John Major with a threat and an opportunity. The threat arises from Conservative Party rebels, inspired by Margaret Thatcher (now Baroness Thatcher of Kesteven), who wants a British referendum in the hope that the Maastricht Treaty will be rejected. The opportunity springing from the scope the British presidency provides for redrafting the EC agenda so that British concerns, such as the question of subsidiarity (calling for the maximum possible devolution of power away from the center), and the initiation of accession negotiations with the EFTA states, are given greater prominence.

At the same time, it falls to Major to find solutions to a range of other pressing EC issues, including the extent to which the EC budget should be increased, and how to find a way out of the impasse in the world trade talks. By defining strict limits to the Commission's powers, and diluting the federalist impulse by expanding the EC's membership, Major hopes he can encourage the Danes and their supporters to think again.

1 THE IMPACT OF 1992

Twelve ways the single market is changing your life

The people of one English town—St Helens on Merseyside—are in no doubt about the impact of the single market on their lives. In October 1991 Pilkington, the world's largest glassmaker, announced that it was moving its headquarters to Brussels. Pilkington had been operating in St Helens for 165 years, but the management had decided that it could not afford to be 'on the periphery of the single market'. St Helens has been left with branch factories only, and the town has lost 750 jobs at a stroke, leaving the local community in a state of shock and a great deal wiser about the effects of 1992. For some companies and communities, on the other hand, a successful preparation for 1992 on their home ground will lead to job creation rather than job losses. Either way, life after 1992 will not be the same.

Imagine you are marketing manager for an office equipment company in Manchester. Shortly after the completion of the European single market on 31 December 1992 you put in a bid with the City Council for a contract to supply high-tech office equipment. But German, Italian and French firms are competing with you on an equal basis—and the German bid is accepted. On the other hand, you have just returned from Ghent, where, to the chagrin of the local Belgian firms, your bid for a major contract was successful. You also have high hopes of a supply contract at Lyons in France. You are learning to operate within a home market of twelve countries.

To relax from business pressures, you take your family for a break through France to Spain, using your new burgundy-coloured Euro-passports and putting your car—with EC-controlled exhaust emissions—on the new Channel Tunnel rail link with the Continent. While in Spain you interrupt your holiday at an EC-approved pollution-free beach to call on your brother, an accountant who works for a newly integrated Euro-telecommunications company near Madrid. On the way back to Calais you stop at a Barclays–Crédit Lyonnais Euro-bank and use your 'smart' electronic Euro-card to draw Danish kroner for your next trip to Copenhagen. How much easier it will be when the Ecu is finally introduced as a single currency, you think, controlled from the newly established European Bank based in London and Frankfurt.

Back home in the UK, you tune in to a variety of television satellite channels to watch the Euro-weather forecast and business news. Next morning, your managing director contacts you on your EC-compatible car phone to warn you that you might have to go to Brussels to seek permission for the proposed merger with your firm's Dutch subsidiary —unless the Dutch take the firm over first. The prospect does not arouse any particular anxiety, beyond the economic viability of the deal. You think of yourself automatically as a Mancunian, an Englishman—and a European.

Twelve benefits of the single market

This, or something like it, is what the world of post-1992 integrated Europe is supposed to be like. The aim of 1992, as enshrined in the Single European Act—a legally binding document amending the Treaty of Rome —is to fulfil the original EC vision of a common market without obstacles to the free movement of goods, services, capital and people. Not all the Euro-developments projected above will come about, but 1992 will have a major impact on the way we live and work in Europe. Among other things it will mean:

- EASIER TRAVEL FOR PEOPLE. Frontier controls will be all but abolished at the EC's internal frontiers—though not at its external points of entry (if anything, external controls will be increased, to ensure that non-EC citizens do not find 'soft' entry points). Computer-read, single-format EC passports will cut down delays, and police and immigration forces will deal with crime more through discreet co-ordination than through frontier controls. Eventually, duty-free sales will disappear. This was originally scheduled to happen in January 1993, but Britain has asked for a delay of between ten and 15 years because of the adverse impact on shops at ports and airports.

- EASIER TRAVEL FOR GOODS. Frontier delays for goods vehicles— many trucks and lorries wait at borders for eight hours or more— cost an estimated £17 billion, according to the European Parliament. Restrictions on tendering for public contracts cost a further £60 billion. The abscence of customs procedures should spare companies the need to fill in the 60 million forms at borders every year. It has been estimated that such border delays and bureaucratic red tape cost British and European consumers 80p for every £10 they spend.

- BUSINESS BOOM. 320 million customers await the efforts of EC business from Britain and Denmark to Greece and Portugal, with all firms competing on equal terms in a large open market. One of the key provisions obliges public authorities to give enterprises from any EC nation an equal opportunity to win high-value contracts.

- JOB RECOGNITION. A teacher from Glasgow will be able to teach in Lyons or Copenhagen, and an accountant from Brighton could work in Naples or Frankfurt, all on the basis of mutually recognized qualifications and diplomas. Linguistic barriers will still cause problems—and will work against the British, since as a nation their grasp of Continental languages is still poor.

- FINANCIAL SERVICES. Restrictions on capital movements were lifted in 1990. EC citizens are now able to open bank accounts or take out mortgages anywhere in the Community, with some exceptions in southern Europe. Cross-border stockbroking is still being held up. But plans are well advanced for a European Bank, perhaps to be operational as soon as 1994, with a single currency shared by at least some EC members by 1997.

- CONSUMER PROTECTION. EC states are no longer able to block imports of foodstuffs or toys because they do not meet national labelling, health or safety standards. Broad criteria and common standards have been devised.

- FREE COMPETITION. Protectionist practices preventing free competition—including that in transport by road, sea and air—become illegal. The first stages of liberalization in aviation and road haulage are already in effect, preventing cartels and quotas and allowing smaller operators increased market access.

- VAT AND INDIRECT TAXES HARMONIZED. Britain successfully resisted plans for the abolition of Vat zero rating on basic goods such as food and childrens' clothes. But the basic principle of the 1992 programme is that, once border controls have gone, trade in the integrated market will be distorted if there are large differentials between Vat rates. A minimum floor of 15% has been agreed as the standard rate.

- TV AND BROADCASTING. Rules for satellite broadcasting across frontiers have been agreed. To prevent European TV being dominated by American or Australian soap operas, as much as 50% of programmes is to be of EC origin 'where possible'. The harmonization of technical standards for high-definition TV (HDTV) will mean improved picture quality and sound.

- THE TELECOMMUNICATIONS MARKET. This is being opened up following a decision to end the monopoly supply of customer terminal equipment and telecommunications services, including databases and electronic mailboxes. A similar move to break up the electricity and gas monopolies in the EC is under way. There is less hope, however, that electrical plugs and sockets will be standardized so that holidaymakers and business executives do not have to carry adaptors or change plugs. Similarly, there are still several incompatible types of cellular telephone systems throughout the EC, making it difficult to use mobile phones when crossing frontiers.

- QUALITY OF LIFE. As environmental protection increases, so quality of life should improve with it. Over 100 separate directives have been or will be implemented in the fields of energy efficiency, water purity and air pollution. This meets a growing demand for a change for the better in the environment.

- PENSIONS. The European Court of Justice has ruled that occupational pensions schemes must apply equal retirement benefits to men and women in cases of compulsory redundancy. Following a 1990 case brought by a male employee of Guardian Royal Exchange Assurance, the court ruled that a pension constituted 'pay' within the meaning of Article 119 of the Treaty of Rome, which prohibits discrimination between men and women.

Momentum of the single market

The momentum which produced this blueprint for change is partly political, partly economic. Much of the drive came from Lord Cockfield, for four years Britain's senior Commissioner in Brussels, with responsibility for the internal market. Formally speaking, the Single European Act and 1992 have their origins in a series of declarations by EC summits on the way forward, notably the Copenhagen summit of December 1982 ('We instruct the Council to decide . . . on priority measures to reinforce the internal market') and the Brussels summit of March 1985 ('We lay particular emphasis on . . . action to achieve a large single market by 1992, thereby creating a more favourable environment for stimulating enterprise, competition and trade'). The programme really began in 1985, with a European Commission White Paper, followed by the Single European Act agreed at Luxembourg in December the same year.

In 1985, 1992 seemed a pipedream to many, but in the seven years since then the single market legislation has been put in place piece by piece, to the point where it now increasingly governs our lives. As the programme's originator, Cockfield believed passionately in a Europe in which crossing from one country to another would entail no more formality for holidaymakers or lorry drivers than crossing from England to Scotland. The burgundy-coloured Euro-passports, now gradually replacing the blue, stiff-backed British ones of old, are part of this drive for a frontier-free Europe.

Lord Cockfield divided the internal market programme into over 300 specific proposals, or groups of proposals, which would then be presented to the Council of Ministers in a timetable geared to completion by

31 December 1992. The Commission has since reduced the number of measures to 282. It has been aided by a provision in the Single European Act which stipulates majority voting procedures in the Council of Ministers for internal market measures, thus effectively robbing individual nations of the power to veto proposals they found unpalatable. However, once passed by Council, the measures have to be incorporated into national law, and several countries (notably France, Greece, Portugal and Italy) have been slow in carrying this out. The Commission's sixth progress report on completion of the single market, issued in July 1991, criticized Italy in particular for adopting only just over half the agreed 1992 measures, and warned that it was turning its attention to rigorous enforcement of internal market legislation under powers given to it by the Treaty of Rome.

In the current Commission the Internal Market portfolio is held by Martin Bangemann of Germany, who, over the past four years, has pursued the 1992 programme with the same vigour as Lord Cockfield while observing the principle of 'subsidiarity': that the EC should only deal with matters best handled at European rather than national, regional or local levels.

Single market measures already in force

In the seven years since 1992 became more than a gleam in the eyes of Cockfield and Delors, the programme has continued steadily forward. Despite 'slippage', three-quarters of the 1992 measures have been passed into law—and EC law takes precedence over national law—with most of the remaining directives tabled and awaiting approval.

In other words, we are already being governed by 1992 directives in all four of the areas covered by the 1992 concept: people, goods, services and capital. Technical standards are being harmonized, with common standards for products from lawnmowers (and the noise levels they emit) to forklift trucks (including, for example, their forward and reverse gears). Some local authorities in the UK have begun to realize the implications. Bolton, in Lancashire, for example, has a 1992 action programme. Local surveys by the action group show a nearly 100% awareness of the single market—although 20% of local companies thought that it was irrelevant to them because they were 'not export orientated'. In fact, they and others like them could face competition on their home ground from elsewhere in the EC: the single market is a two-way process.

The idea of an integrated Europe may seem somewhat far-fetched if you are, say, an Englishman encountering obstacles when trying to buy a house in Italy, a Dutchman attempting in vain to settle a garage bill in France with a Eurocheque or a German infuriated at having to pay a motorway tax in Belgium. But under the 1992 process such irritations are beginning to be overcome. The process will be a long one, with many countries facing prosecution against outmoded protectionist practices in the European Court of Justice at Luxembourg. But the process *is* under way, for all that national governments often do their best to disguise it by presenting new EC laws as national legislation.

Take the problem of moving goods around the EC by road. In June 1988, after months of prevarication, EC transport ministers agreed to abolish all EC, bilateral and transit road haulage quotas by 1 January 1993. Ironically, this measure—a regulation, not a directive—was passed under German chairmanship, even though the Germans had been among the most vociferous opponents of free competition in road transport, fearing that their haulage companies would be at a disadvantage to more efficient Dutch or Belgian trucking ones—as indeed they may after 1992. To allay West German fears, the Commission, playing a role which is becoming increasingly common in controversial 1992 measures, agreed to undertake an informal review of lorry drivers' hours of work and rest, and to make tachograph inspections more strict. But the measure was passed, and is vital to the 1992 objective, given that over half of all internally traded EC goods are transported by road. Equally, 1992 involves the liberalization of air transport, inaugurating an era of greater competition and cheaper fares.

On the seas around Britain, British fishermen have found themselves obliged to compete with Spanish fishermen following a successful Spanish challenge to the 1988 Merchant Shipping Act which sought to stop Spanish-owned vessels taking up British EC fishing quotas by using 'brass plate' companies registered in the UK. To prevent this 'quota hopping', the Act had insisted that 75% of the ownership of such companies be vested in persons who were both UK nationals and resident in the UK. In July 1991 the European Court of Justice ruled that this was incompatible with EC law, which takes precedence over national law—the first time an Act of Parliament had been struck down by the EC. The government compromised by negotiating a deal with the Anglo–Spanish companies, under which they would have to land their catches in the UK and have properly registered UK agents. As *The Times* observed in an editorial, it seemed logical that 'those who flew the British flag should be the persons for whom the quotas were intended—the British'. On the other hand, the 1992 principle at stake was 'the right of any commercial company to set up in any EC member state'.

As another example, take the freedom of professional people to move around the EC as if it were one country. Shortly after the road haulage agreement by transport ministers, trade ministers met in Luxembourg to draw up common principles for the mutual recognition of diplomas by all twelve EC states. What this means is that after 1992, a surveyor from Birmingham will be able to practise in Barcelona without retaking surveyor examinations, and a lawyer from Leeds will be able to find employment in Frankfurt if he or she so wishes without resitting Bar Finals (although in some areas, such as the law and accounting, a local top-up test may be required to prove adequate knowledge of local law). The same, of course, applies in reverse—and Continental Europeans tend to speak far better English than British people speak European languages.

Another vital 1992 directive, on 'public procurement', obliges public authorities, including local government, to open up major public supply contracts to tender from any EC firm. If an Italian or Dutch company makes the best offer—as our imaginary office equipment supplier from Manchester found—it must be accepted, and the home-based British bidder will receive no sympathy. After 1992 there will also be intense competition between EC ports, especially once the Channel Tunnel is in place.

The challenge to Britain

In other words, much will depend on the confidence, energy and ability of British companies and professionals, and their willingness to meet the 1992 challenge both by facing competition from other EC nationals on their home ground and by trying to make inroads into domestic markets in the other eleven EC states. A CBI survey in 1988 showed that only 7% of companies had appointed an executive or team to prepare for 1992; the same percentage had introduced language training; 20% had carried out a 'strategy review'; 10% had done 1992 market research. Thirty-one per cent had done nothing at all. More recently a survey conducted by MORI in 1991 for the UK division of Epson showed that over half of the executives interviewed did not know who Jacques Delors was; under half knew what the letters CAP stood for, what the member states of the EC were, or in which city the European Commission headquarters was located. A remarkable 77% did not know what the letters ERM meant, and only one in three could say in German 'Good morning, my name is Mr Smith'. Fifty per cent still thought that 1992 would have little or no impact on their business.

Yet Britain stands to gain enormously from the single market, with the British economy perhaps best placed in the area of financial services. In July 1990 capital movements across EC borders were liberalized, despite earlier reservations on the part of the socialist government in France, which had argued that allowing EC citizens to move cash around the Community could only encourage tax evasion. In its now familiar role as honest broker, the Commission agreed to study ways of increasing tax inspection, thus overcoming French doubts and allowing the directive to go forward.

Coupled with a new 1992 banking directive allowing High Street banks to operate anywhere in the EC under a single licensing system, the capital movements directive means that EC citizens—including Britons—can deposit or borrow money anywhere in the Community, with exchange controls abolished (except, for a provisional period, in Greece, Spain, Portugal and Ireland). Whether National Westminster and

Barclays make more of an inroad into France than the Crédit Lyonnais or the Deutsche Bank in Britain will depend on the drive of the banks concerned. The same applies to insurance, where Britain also has a strong reputation.

There are, of course, drawbacks to these schemes. As Neil Hartley of National Westminster's 1992 policy unit points out, 1992 will mean job losses as well as job creation, through mergers and market penetration. Professor Peter Herriot of Birkbeck College, London, warns that Britain risks an exodus of skilled graduates to Europe ('designers to Dusseldorf, physicists to Freiburg, engineers to Essen'), a finding supported by the Institute of Manpower Studies at Sussex University in its report *The Graduate Labour Market in the 1990s*. Others caution that high salaries for, say, working in telecommunications in Frankfurt will be offset by high taxes and cultural dislocation. Headhunters Saxton Bampfylde, who recently surveyed managers responsible for 1992 in 130 large companies, say the successful Euro-executive will be the man or woman who knows the local culture well, rather than the 'Euro-yuppie' who stays in bland business hotels and is 'dressed out of the contents of a duty-free shop'.

The ripple effect of the single market

The single market stems from a complex of directives, regulations and other measures which together add up to a shift in the way the EC is organized—and in how we are governed. Whether we like it or not, 1992 is developing beyond the confines of the 1985 White Paper and taking on a life of its own. Almost any European-wide scheme, in fact, can now be related to the single market.

Broadcasting offers one example. Many governments and broadcasting authorities argue that harmonizing television standards and encouraging a 'European' culture in the media are not part of 1992. However, the White Paper refers to the need for 'a single Community-wide broadcasting area' on the grounds that the Treaty of Rome provides for 'a common market in services'. The Commission therefore drew up plans for common standards in advertising and the co-ordination of satellite technology and cable TV, arguing that television constitutes an economic service within the meaning of the Treaty, and that, because of the rapid development of satellite technology, there must be a framework to guide broadcasters and TV authorities in the integrated European market.

European policies directly affect products, from shoes (the British Footwear Manufacturers' Federation is appealing to the EC to act against a flood of foreign—i.e. non-EC—exports to the UK) to cigarettes. From 1 January 1993 cigarette packets must carry prominent, strongly worded health warnings. In 1991 the Commission debated proposals for banning tobacco advertising in newspapers and magazines and on hoardings, a measure which would mean revenue losses for the advertising industry amounting to £60 million a year, with similar losses for newspapers (especially colour supplements). Even horse racing and field sports are affected. Following a European Court case brought by Ladbrokes against Paris Mutuel, the French off-track betting organization, over its attempts to penetrate the UK betting market the Commission is considering EC-wide gambling legislation. If this is passed Britain might introduce a national lottery (it is the only EC state not to have one).

The air-liberalization package does not include the question of air-traffic control. Yet as Europe's skies become more congested, causing inconvenience and delays for air passengers (not least for those who have saved up for package tours), EC governments have begun to acknowledge that there should be a greater role for Eurocontrol, the under-used European air-traffic control centre at Maastricht in the Netherlands, even though Eurocontrol is not an EC body and has nothing to do with 1992.

Equally, there is no mention in the 1992 White Paper of defence. Yet it is increasingly assumed that, at some point, an integrated Europe will need some form of military integration—or at least military co-operation—to defend it. The Single European Act made provision for co-operation between EC states on 'the economic and political aspects of security'. It is a phrase that has given rise to varying interpretations, with the French and the Germans inclined to translate 'security' as 'defence' while the British prefer a far vaguer interpretation, implying only consultation on wider European security interests. But the Gulf War and the civil war in Yugoslavia provided further impetus towards a common defence policy, perhaps even the embryo of a European army following moves by France and Germany towards closer military co-operation.

There is growing recognition of the need to pool sovereignty in another area: environmental protection. Chlorofluorocarbons (CFCs), chemicals used in aerosols which harm the ozone layer, are to be phased out by the year 2000. Similarly, new standards have been set to cut noxious emissions from car exhausts (through catalytic converters) and power stations.

Education and the arts

No corner of life and commerce is likely to escape the long arm of Brussels. Even art dealers and auction houses, which might have thought themselves remote from arguments about harmonization and cross-border integration, face the prospect of a 1992 directive under which British dealers would have to impose Vat on works of art and antiques, thus risking (according to critics of the move) the loss of their current competitive edge and the transfer of international auction business to Geneva (Switzerland being outside the EC) and New York.

In education, traditionally regarded as a national prerogative, an International Baccalaureat (IB) could eventually challenge other certificates of higher education. The IB system, taught in 400 schools around the world, requires students to study three subjects in depth to the equivalent of A-level, but also to take three other subjects to a less exacting level, with a mix of science and humanities. Seventeen British schools and colleges teach the IB at present, with the examination board based at Bath University.

In higher education, the polytechnics have the edge in European business studies, with courses at Humberside College of Education, Kingston Polytechnic, Lancashire Polytechnic, Middlesex Polytechnic and Trent Polytechnic in Nottingham, which links up with the University of Paderborn in Germany and the Groupe Ecole Supérieure de Commerce in Toulouse. Such links are supported by the EC's Erasmus fund.

Dutch and French socialist MEPs have proposed a European history book in which national viewpoints on Waterloo, the Franco-Prussian war or the Second World War would be counterbalanced by other viewpoints and 'descriptions of events which occurred simultaneously in all member states, to stimulate an awareness of belonging to a single political entity'. Hugh McMahon, a former history teacher and Labour MEP for Strathclyde West, dismisses this as 'Euro-culture gone berserk': the EC cannot produce a 'sanitized version of the conflicts and wars which took place in Europe in previous centuries'.

There is, nonetheless, a detectable shift in arts syllabuses—and reading habits—towards European literature. Publishers at the Frankfurt Book Fair report a search for 'the big European novel rather than the big American novel'. One HarperCollins executive says that British publishers 'now spend more time at Frankfurt with the Europeans than with the Americans'. Publishers are buying European—rather than just UK— rights to American books to protect themselves against US editions being brought into the UK cheaply across unrestricted EC frontiers.

The advertising industry is also preparing for the single market, focusing on the concept of the 'European High Street'.

Eliminating the cost of twelve separate markets

The drive for integration, in other words, is as much political as economic. It stems not only from Euro-idealism (and not only from an impulse to complete the work of the EC's founders) but also from a fear that unless the EC works more closely together, not least in industry and technology, it will prove unable to compete effectively with other giant trading blocs, notably Japan/Asia and the United States.

The official Cecchini report on the benefits of the internal market —*The European Challenge 1992*—estimates that the integration of twelve national markets will save the EC £140 billion (about 5% of the Community's gross national product), will create millions of jobs and stimulate enough growth to 'put Europe on an upward trajectory of economic growth lasting into the next century'. This, the report declares, is 'a firm prospect, not a tantalizing chimera'.

The Cecchini report can be criticized for biasing the evidence in a way

its 'Brussels' will on EC citizens. The more the Commission tries to avoid this image, carefully pointing out that it is an executive body and that there is a constitutional balance to be observed between the Commission, the Council and the Parliament, the more power and influence seems to flow towards the Berlaymont, the Commission's star-shaped plate-glass headquarters in Brussels.

The European Commission

Despite its power and importance, the Commission is appointed, not elected. It is often described as the EC's executive branch or central bureaucracy. However, its function is more wide-ranging than this might suggest. It was established under Article 155 of the Treaty as the body which would originate draft legislation to put before the Council of Ministers and Assembly (Parliament), and which would then implement the resulting directives. However, Article 155 also gives the Commission the right to 'have its own power of decision and participate in the shaping of measures taken by the Council and the European Parliament'. The Commission can issue regulations of its own accord, without reference to the two legislative bodies—as it did, for example, after the Chernobyl nuclear accident, by imposing a *cordon sanitaire* around the EC against the importation of goods contaminated by radiation. However, the Commission also has the power 'to participate in the shaping of measures' which do pass through the Council and Parliament. It does this by sitting in on Council sessions, and by meeting at the Parliament building in Strasbourg once a month, when Euro MPs are in plenary session. Commissioners are therefore present—and active—at all three stages of the decision-making process: initiation of draft proposals, debate and implementation.

This is of particular importance where 1992 is concerned. Quite apart from powers given to it under the Single European Act, the Commission has been able to originate 1992 legislation; take part in, and even guide the modification process as 1992 directives pass through the Council and Parliament; and then implement the resulting laws. The key role in the first phase of the 1992 programme (1985–8) fell to Lord Cockfield, as Internal Market Commissioner: it now rests with Martin Bangemann of Germany, under the direction of President Delors. The Council and Parliament can overturn draft 1992 legislation if they are so minded, since they have the final say. However, in practice, the discussion of 1992 takes place within a framework defined by the Commission, and on the basis of proposals devised within the Berlaymont. This makes Delors and his 16 Commissioners potentially powerful figures. In the first Delors administration, for example, Peter Sutherland, the Irish Commissioner, matched Lord Cockfield's 1992 crusade with a forceful campaign of his own to exploit to the full the powers given to the Commission by the Treaty to intervene in mergers and takeovers if they distort competition.

The Commission is not, on the other hand, a 'foreign junta', as one peer memorably claimed in July 1988 during the debate in the House of Lords on the Rover–British Aerospace merger. Its national composition is carefully balanced, and Britain plays a full part in it—as in the Council of Ministers. In the present Community of Twelve there are 17 Commissioners—two each from Britain, France, Germany, Italy and Spain, and one each from Belgium, Denmark, Greece, Ireland, Luxembourg, the Netherlands and Portugal. The 17 Commission members are appointed by their national governments—in practice, their respective prime ministers, who discuss the appointments at the EC summit preceding the four-yearly change of staff at the Berlaymont. Heads of government naturally seek to appoint Commissioners who will represent the national interest. As a result of Maastricht, there are to be 12 Commissioners only.

By some unwritten law, however, Commissioners almost always 'go native'—the charge most often levelled at Lord Cockfield before his replacement by Leon Brittan—leading to perpetual tension between Brussels and the national capitals. The contradiction is built into the solemn oath Commissioners take on arriving in Brussels, which commits them 'to perform my duties in complete independence, in the general interest of the Communities'. Commissioners also vow 'in carrying out my duties neither to seek nor to take instructions from any Government or body'. The oath adds pointedly that all member states of the EC have undertaken to respect this principle and 'not to seek to influence Members of the Commission in the performance of their task'—a promise sometimes more honoured in the breach than the observance.

Each Commissioner is given one or more portfolios dealing with specific areas of policy (a list of the current Commission portfolios is given at the end of this book), with portfolios traditionally allotted by the Commission President over dinner at a chateau on the outskirts of Brussels, in a 'night of the long knives'. For Britain the most significant move in the Delors reshuffle of December 1988 was the allocation of the internal market portfolio, previously held by Lord Cockfield, to Martin Bangemann of Germany—albeit divested of responsibility for financial services and fiscal approximation. But the two British Commissioners were nevertheless given key portfolios. Leon Brittan took over from Peter Sutherland as Competition Commissioner, with responsibility for relations with the European Parliament and financial services, while Bruce Millan was put in charge of the Community's regional development funds. The controversial issue of fiscal approximation was given to the junior French Commissioner, Mme Christiane Scrivener, who is known to be sympathetic to the problems faced by Britain and Ireland over the proposed abolition of value added tax zero-rating. The powers of the European Commission President should not be exaggerated: he is not 'President of Europe', since power is shared with the other EC institutions, nor is he equivalent to a national prime minister, since Commission decisions are taken

Passage of Single Market Directives into EC Law

EUROPEAN COMMISSION
initiates legislation by
drafting directive.

COUNCIL OF MINISTERS
debates directive, either at
ministerial level or through
COREPER, the permanent
committee of ambassadors to
the EC.

EUROPEAN PARLIAMENT
amends directive. Single European Act gave MEPs limited power
of veto over 1992 legislation; Maastricht strengthened veto powers
in specified areas such as transport, the environment and
consumer protection.

EUROPEAN COMMISSION
further modifies the directive
in the light of Council/
Parliament deliberations.

COUNCIL OF MINISTERS
votes on the directives, using
qualified majority system in
some cases and unanimity in
others. Directive becomes EC
law.

EUROPEAN COURT OF JUSTICE
rules in cases where an EC
law is not observed by a
member state or causes
disputes between states and
the Commission.

NATIONAL GOVERNMENTS
enact the new EC law by
putting it to vote in national
parliaments.

collectively, usually by majority vote. However, the President adopts an increasingly high profile, and attends Western economic summits alongside other Western leaders on behalf of the EC as a whole.

Each Commissioner has a staff or cabinet. The Commission bureaucracy is not as large as is sometimes imagined: including its 23 Directorates General, which report to Commissioners, it has about 15,000 staff (including interpreters and translators), less than the administration of Edinburgh —although the Eurocrats' high tax-free salaries and perks help to create the popular image of a bloated bureaucracy. It is also regarded as one of the most open bureaucracies in the world. The Council has a staff of 2000 and the European Parliament 3200.

The Commission meets on Wednesdays to review draft legislation, take legal action against recalcitrant states through the European Court of Justice, issue regulations and so on. A regulation differs from a directive in that it applies in detail to all member states. A directive, by contrast, lays down the aim and principle of a measure but leaves it up to national parliaments to put the new law into national form. In addition, the Commission administers EC funds, such as the regional fund or the farm support budget, and negotiates trade agreements on behalf of the EC.

The Luxembourg presidency draft on political union put forward in the first half of 1991, and used as the basis of the Maastricht summit at the end of 1991, offended Delors by proposing that the European Parliament should have co-decision powers with the Council of Ministers (see below), with the Commission still able to initiate legislation but less empowered to amend it. Delors described this as an inexplicable attempt to 'enfeeble' one of the institutions enshrined in the Treaty of Rome and a violation of the principles of the EC's founding fathers.

At the end of 1991 the Commission announced that it was abandoning the Berlaymont, which had become unsuitable and was, in any case, a health hazard because of the asbestos used in its construction. The Commission continues to be in dispute with Belgium, the host nation, over the siting and funding of a new headquarters.

The Council of Ministers

The Council represents the governments of the Twelve, and thus acts as a counterweight to the Commission, whose main focus is EC-wide rather than national. On the other hand, the Council also has to bear in mind the wider European interest. This is especially true of the twice-yearly EC summit, or European Council, which takes fundamental decisions about the Community's future direction.

As noted earlier, the Council does not meet continuously but is an *ad hoc* body made up of national ministers with responsibility for the policy area under discussion—Foreign Affairs, Agriculture, Transport, Industry and so on. The supreme body, therefore (the summit), is made up of prime ministers, or in one case (France) the president (hence the formal reference to 'the heads of state and government' at European Councils). Summits were not formally provided for in the Treaty of Rome, and only began in 1975. The institution of the twice-yearly (formerly thrice-yearly) European Council is now laid down in the Single European Act, and therefore in the Treaty. There is a growing tendency for the summit to deal with complex 1992 issues which in theory should have been sorted out at a lower level but which have proved intractable.

Unlike the Commission, which has a President appointed for two years (usually renewed, making a four-year term), the Council is chaired by each member state in turn for a period of six months. This rotating chairmanship is referred to—rather confusingly—as the presidency of the Council of Ministers, in addition to which the European Parliament has its own President (Lord Plumb). The three EC Presidents sometimes hold joint meetings (for example, to sort out a dispute over the budget).

The President of the Council is the prime minister of whichever country holds the six-month rotating presidency. In the first half of 1989 this was Felipe Gonzalez of Spain, in the second half of 1989 President Mitterrand of France (because France follows España in the alphabet of the country concerned). In 1990 the Council Presidents were the leaders of Ireland and Italy, followed by Luxembourg and the Netherlands in 1991, and in 1992 Portugal and Britain (United Kingdom). It will therefore fall to Britain to preside over the celebrations on 31 December 1992, handing on the presidencies of the single market to Denmark and Belgium in 1993. Since the foreign ministers meet regularly to deal with day-to-day Council business (when they become known as the General Affairs Council, rather than the Foreign Affairs Council), in practice the foreign minister of the Presidency nation is in the chair most often, and is therefore also referred to as President of the Council.

If the function of the Commission is to draw up draft legislation, including the draft EC budget, the task of the Council, in its various ministerial forms, is to examine the draft measures in conjunction with the European Parliament and in due course to amend, accept or reject them. Measures are usually examined first—and comprehensively—by EC ambassadors in Brussels, the Committee of Permanent Representatives, known collectively by the French acronym COREPER. When COREPER agrees unanimously on a measure (usually an uncontroversial one) it passes through the full ministerial Council on the nod, appearing on the agenda as what is called in the jargon an 'A Point'. Otherwise a directive can only become EC law when it has been passed by the ministers of the Twelve in the Council, sometimes by unanimity, sometimes by majority vote. The question of majority voting (strictly speaking, qualified majority voting, based on a complex mathematical formula) is crucial to the 1992 process, since under the Single European Act internal market measures can be passed by majority vote.

The system of rotating Council presidencies is also relevant to the 1992

programme, for the simple reason that each EC nation has different attitudes and priorities. Under the German presidency in the first half of 1988,
for example, EC–Comecon *rapprochement* moved forward, and a large
number of single-market measures were approved. Greece, which took
over from Bonn for the second half of 1988, also pursued 1992 objectives,
despite fears that the abolition of borders would expose the relatively weak
Greek economy to cross-frontier competition. However, Council President
Andreas Papandreou, the Greek prime minister, put the 1992 stress on
social issues such as health and safety at work and (more controversially)
worker participation in industry, a trend opposed by Mrs Thatcher, notably at the Rhodes EC summit (European Council) in December 1988, just
before Greece handed over the presidency to Spain. Since Spain and
France, which inherited the rotating presidency in the second half of 1989
(after the EC summit in Madrid on monetary union), broadly share the
Greek outlook and also have left-wing administrations, social issues have
come to the fore alongside 1992 economic and political ones.

Like Commission meetings, sessions of the Council are held behind
closed doors, a practice which has increasingly led to the charge that EC
decision making is unacceptably secretive. Ministers retort that—unlike
Commissioners—they are elected in their home countries and are therefore accountable. Equally, there is a large Brussels press corps which is
regularly briefed by national spokesmen, both during and between Council meetings, and which reports what goes on behind the scenes through
contacts with officials. Nonetheless, concern is growing over what is
known in EC jargon as the 'democratic deficit' or lack of democratic control
over EC decision making, and there is pressure for the Council to open
at least some of its proceedings to the public, with a press gallery at the
Charlemagne building (the Council's headquarters, opposite the
Berlaymont) on the lines of the press galleries at Westminster and other
EC parliaments.

Ministers continue to argue that their deliberations are too sensitive to
be exposed to the public gaze, partly because Council debates involve a
great deal of bargaining between nations as ministers try to find a balance
between national interests and the wider interests of the EC as a whole.
Once back home, ministers sometimes find it convenient to blame an
unpopular measure on 'Brussels'—but, in the last analysis, 'Brussels'
means the Council, in which all twelve nations take an equal part.

For three months in the year (April, June and October) Council meetings are held not in Brussels but in Luxembourg. This practice is jealously
guarded by the Luxembourgers, who have built a large European Conference Centre in the Grand Duchy, but it is a constant source of irritation to
the large numbers of officials and journalists who have to make the 2½-hour
journey to Luxembourg from Brussels. Moving documents and staff
between the three EC centres (Brussels, Luxembourg and Strasbourg) is
also estimated to cost the EC taxpayer up to £100 million a year. There is

growing pressure to move the European Parliament from Strasbourg to Brussels as part of a campaign to centralize most EC functions, making Brussels the administrative and legislative centre for the single market and making good its claim to be 'the capital of Europe'.

Qualified majority voting

Since qualified majority voting in the Council is so central to 1992—and so strongly criticized by those who think that power is shifting to Brussels too far, too fast—it is perhaps worth looking at it in detail. Under the Single European Act, 1992 issues can be (and in practice are) decided by a system of voting under which each member state is given a number of votes more or less consonant with its size and importance in the EC. Thus Britain wields ten votes, together with Germany, France and Italy; Spain has eight; Belgium, Greece, Holland and Portugal have five each; both Denmark and Ireland have three; and tiny Luxembourg has only two. A qualified majority simply means 54 votes out of the total 76 from at least eight member states—meaning, in reality, that even two of the 'big boys' (for example, Britain and Germany) acting together cannot block a decision. It takes three of the larger countries (or two of them plus one or two smaller states) to muster enough votes to stop a 1992 decision going through. But qualified majority voting does not apply to fiscal issues, which remain subject to the national veto.

The question of majority voting is a sensitive one, since it strikes at the heart of the national veto—that is, the right of any member state to veto legislation it does not like. Originally, most EC laws had to be passed by unanimous vote, but in the 1960s pressure built up for a switch to majority voting. When this ran into difficulties (mainly because of French opposition) the Six (as they then were) agreed on an informal arrangement known as the Luxembourg Compromise. This said that majority voting would be gradually introduced, but that the right of national veto would be retained where 'very important interests of one or more partners are at stake'. In practice, this proved unworkable. The advent of qualified majority voting under the Single European Act seems to have ended the Luxembourg Compromise, at least for 1992 issues, although this will only really become clear in the course of time, as qualified majority voting is tested in practice (it is already being used increasingly). On non-1992 issues the right of veto is unaffected: on the other hand, the dividing line between 1992 issues and non-1992 issues is not always obvious. (For a discussion of whether the European Central Bank proposal can be vetoed, see Chapter 8.)

The Commission has come under fire for categorizing controversial proposals such as the European Company Statute as internal market legislation requiring only a majority vote. Similarly, the Commission has invoked Article 90 of the Treaty of Rome to bring in new directives liberalizing the telecommunications equipment market, a move contested by

France in the European Court of Justice. The Commission also drew criticism in 1989 for alleged corruption and excessive perks within its bureaucracy. Delors replied that such accusations amounted to a 'phoney war' to divert attention from key 1992 issues.

The European Parliament

It is sometimes supposed that Euro MPs are the decision makers in the EC, by analogy with Westminster. This is a misconception. The other widely held view of Euro MPs—that they enjoy a comfortable lifestyle with many perks—is less inaccurate, although MEPs can point to the arduous journeys they are obliged to make between their home constituencies and the Parliament's premises in Brussels and Strasbourg, or to conferences outside Europe (for example, for meetings with representatives of the ACP countries).

The Parliament has its origins in the European Assembly (initially the Assembly of the European Coal and Steel Community, before the EC proper was formed), to which national MPs were seconded. At first, the Assembly had 142 members; this was increased to 198 when Britain joined the EC in 1973 together with Denmark and Ireland, making an EC of Nine. However, the major change in the Parliament's fortunes came in 1979, when the first direct elections were held to a body of 410 seats, expanded to 434 seats for the next Euro elections in 1984, by which time Greece had joined the Community. The present Parliament has 518 seats, because of the entry of Spain and Portugal in 1986. After German reunification in October 1990 Bonn began to argue that Germany should have more than the 81 seats allotted to itself, the UK, France and Italy, but by the Maastricht summit this remained unresolved.

The last elections, in June 1989, saw victories for the Socialists and Greens and losses for the centre and right-wing parties which had dominated the previous Parliament. Voter turnout was 56% for the EC as a whole and 37% in the UK (higher than the 32% turnout of 1979 and 1984). The British Labour Party won 13 extra seats at the expense of the Conservatives, whose electoral campaign was described by Sir Leon Brittan as 'negative, damaging and confusing'. Even before the vote, the Spanish Partido Popular abandoned the Conservatives for the Christian Democrats.

The voting pattern throughout the EC was one of protest against ruling parties, with startling gains for the Greens in the UK and for the far right in France and Germany. However, because of the lack of a common electoral system, despite provision for one in the Treaty of Rome, the success of the Greens in the UK—with 2.3 million votes, or 15% of the vote, compared to the Conservatives' 34% and Labour's 40%—was not reflected in seats. Britain uses the first past the post system, whereas most other EC nations have some form of proportional representation (Ireland uses the single transferable vote). The Euro MPs, who sit in political groupings rather than national blocs, re-assembled in July 1989 with renewed confidence in their status as Europe's legislature. Lord Plumb (Conservative) was replaced as President by Enrique Barón Crespo, a Spanish Socialist, reflecting the new left-wing dominance of the chamber (260 seats, a narrow majority). On many 1992 issues, from the environment to workers' control, the Left and the Christian Democrats have informal understandings.

On the other hand, the Parliament did not become a true legislature even in 1979, and it took the Single European Act to give Euro MPs greater powers, especially with regard to 1992. Until this Act the Parliament was an almost exclusively advisory body in nearly all policy areas; Article 137 of the Treaty refers to its 'advisory and supervisory powers'. It offers 'opinions' which the Council can (and does) ignore, with one notable exception: the budget, where Euro MPs exercise joint control with the Council of Ministers in non-obligatory expenditure—that is, all spending except for farm support ('obligatory' in the sense that farm spending is a legal obligation laid down in the CAP).

Even here, however, the Parliament's powers are limited: farm spending, over which it has little or no control, still accounts for some two thirds of the budget, even after the Delors reforms, so that Euro MPs can only really influence one third of EC expenditure. They do so through a series of readings of the draft budget, which, after being drawn up by the Commission, goes back and forth between the Council and Parliament. However, the Parliament cannot increase expenditure beyond a 'maximum rate', which is set by the Council. This gives the Council the upper hand, and has in the past led to a wearisome annual tussle between the two institutions, often resulting in failure to adopt a budget at all and forcing the EC to resort to emergency monthly funding based on the previous year's budget (a system known as 'provisional twelfths') until a compromise is reached.

The Delors reforms, designed to prepare for 1992 by ridding the EC of budgetary wrangles, have greatly eased this problem, and annual budget crises no longer arise.

The Single European Act, moreover, gives the Parliament two further important roles in addition to its budgetary powers. Under the new 'co-operation' procedure (in effect, a second reading of 1992 legislation) the Council adopts a common position on a bill, taking into account the Parliament's opinion, and the Parliament then has three months to accept the proposal. If it does so, or takes no action, the proposal passes into law: but if MEPs propose amendments, or reject the bill, on its second reading by the Parliament, the Council can only pass its original version by unanimous vote. Otherwise it must accept Parliament's version, or drop the bill altogether. Second, a new 'assent' procedure gives the Parliament a final say in commercial agreements negotiated between EC and non-EC countries (and indeed in the admission of new member states to the Community).

In the European Parliament debates on the Single European Act after it was signed at the Luxembourg summit of December 1985 many Euro MPs argued vehemently that the Act should be rejected, on the grounds that the new powers it gave to Strasbourg were inadequate, even insulting. The majority view, however, was that the Act's powers could be used as a basis for Parliament's campaign to transform itself into a true EC legislature. Euro MPs have indeed made effective use of both the 1992 'second reading' and their power to accept or reject trade agreements (in the latter case, for example, by repeatedly holding up three trade protocols with Israel because of Israeli behaviour towards Palestinian Arabs). According to a study by James Elles, MEP, until the Single European Act the Commission took up wholly or in part about 85% of the Parliament's amendments to proposals—but the Council accepted far fewer.

Will the European Parliament ever become a true EC legislature? The weight of the EC's institutional structure, even as amended by the Single European Act, is probably against it. MEPs can put written questions to EC Commissioners and insist on a published answer (at an estimated administrative cost of £500–1000 per answer); ministers from the country which is in the EC chair must appear before Euro MPs to report on current EC issues and answer questions; and, in theory, Euro MPs can even dismiss the entire Commission—a power never so far used in practice. However, many Euro MPs themselves feel that the Parliament will not become the voice of the peoples of Europe until it has greater legislative powers and until its activities are centred in one place, preferably Brussels. At present, Euro MPs hold their plenary debates at their chamber in Strasbourg, in the Palace of Europe, and their committee and group meetings in Brussels, at the parliament building not far from the Commission and Council, while the Parliament's Secretariat is located in Luxembourg.

As part of the current rebuilding of the Brussels EC quarter to make a vast 'Euro City' for 1992 and after, a new debating chamber (described as a conference centre) is being built behind the Parliament's committee rooms. The Treaty of Rome, in fact, does not fix any seat for the Parliament, and in September 1988 the European Court overruled French objections to plans for holding plenary sessions in Brussels. A move by British MEPs in April 1990 to move the Parliament to Brussels was narrowly defeated.

In time, the pressures of the integrated market may force the Parliament to re-organize its work to resemble more closely that of a national parliament, with debates held continuously rather than for one week in four and increasing liaison between the European Parliament and national MPs. One estimate is that the Single European Act has increased the Parliament's workload by 30%. In Britain the House of Commons Select Committee on European Legislation sometimes scrutinizes EC laws only after they have been passed, because of the sheer volume. Options for increasing Westminster's scrutiny include a special question time on EC matters and allowing the Commons committee to see draft EC directives. (See also Chapter 10.)

In the summer of 1991 new arrangements were agreed between Strasbourg and Westminster, with British MPs allotted a special travel fund to enable them to visit EC institutions, and British Euro MPs given greater access to the Commons—reserved seats in the front two rows of the public gallery (MEPs previously had to queue with the public) and the right to reserve tables in Commons dining rooms (though for lunchtime only).

Strasbourg's powers were further tested in May 1990, when the European Court of Justice allowed the European Parliament to bring a law suit against the Council of Ministers for bypassing the Parliament when taking its decision to limit sales of food after the Chernobyl accident. The Court noted that the Council had used the Euratom Treaty as the basis for its action and not Article 100 of the Treaty of Rome, which would have required lengthy consultation with Strasbourg.

In July 1991, Euro MPs passed a resolution protesting that EC governments were still refusing to allow the Parliament to fill the 'democratic deficit'. In fact, of the 1,367 first reading amendments tabled by the Parliament from 1987 to 1990, 63% were accepted; and of the 357 amendments tabled on second readings, 55% were accepted. But the Parliament, in accordance with a recommendation by David Martin, MEP, wants the power to initiate legislation, coupled with 'co-decision taking' with the Council and Commission. Martin, the rapporteur on institutional reform, advocated a federal parliamentary republic of Europe, with the Council of Ministers as an upper Chamber (*European Union and the Democratic Deficit*, from the John Wheatley Centre). 'If the EC was a state and applied to join the Community it would be turned down on the grounds that it was not a democracy' he observed. Luxembourg, which held the EC presidency in the first half of 1991 and drew up the draft treaty revisions for Maastricht at the end of 1991, proposed co-decision making in specific areas: development aid, research, regional and social funds, and the environment.

In the event, Maastricht gave the Parliament powers amounting to co-decision making through a new 'negative assent procedure' laid down in article 189b of the political union treaty. Whereas Strasbourg had previously needed the backing of the Commission to get its amendments through the Council, it now has the right to negotiate directly with ministers on the changes it wants to see made, and to reject bills which fail to take account of those changes. The new powers cover laws on the single market, consumer protection, the free circulation of labour, the right of individuals and companies to establish themselves in any EC country, vocational training and health, as well as framework research and environment programmes. In addition, Maastricht required the assent of Strasbourg for structural funds, the rights of European citizenship and the harmonisation of electoral systems. The Commission and the Parliament are to run concurrently, and the Commission is reduced from 17 members to 12.

Maastricht did not, however, give Strasbourg a direct role in the new

common foreign policy arrangements. Some MEPs welcomed the aug-
mented powers: Enrique Baron Crespo, the outgoing President of the
European Parliament, said Maastricht had at least acknowledged that the
problem of the 'democratic deficit' was central to the EC and its future.
But Egon Klepsch, his successor, said the Maastricht concessions were
inadequate and 'Parliament must continue to fight for the extension of
its rights'. Many MEPs deplored the decision to allow the UK to 'opt out'
of common social policy, arguing that the move would create a 'two-
speed Europe'.

The European Court of Justice

The 13 judges and six advocates-general of the European Court are nomi-
nated by member states and serve for a six-year term. They are required to
be persons of the highest legal qualification 'whose independence is
beyond doubt'. The Court, situated in Luxembourg, is the guardian of the
Treaty and the EC's supreme legal body. It is not to be confused (but often
is) with the European Court of Human Rights in Strasbourg, which is a
Council of Europe body. (Still less is the European Court to be confused
with the International Court of Justice in The Hague, as happened in one
quality newspaper.)

EC law takes precedence over national law. Thus one function of the
European Court is to give preliminary rulings on cases referred to it by
national courts when a point of EC law is at issue. The national court then
has to apply the ruling. However, cases can also be brought directly to the
Court by individuals, companies or governments. In many cases it is the
Commission which brings cases against both companies and member
states for infringement of EC rules—including 1992 legislation. The first
stage involves a written complaint and defence: there is then an oral hearing, in which both sides present their cases to the judges; in the third stage,
the advocate-general gives an opinion; and finally, the judges deliver a verdict, arrived at by majority vote. The verdict usually (though not
invariably) follows the advocate-general's opinion, as it did, for example,
in rulings in 1988 against Britain over Vat exemptions.

The Court, like the Commission, is not an alien body but draws its
members from all twelve states. Until recently, its President was a senior
British judge. However, as 1992 approaches, its workload is becoming
intolerable (it has only 500 employees), and in July 1988 the Council of Ministers agreed to the setting up of a lower-level EC Court of First Instance to
sift cases before they reach the European Court proper. The new lower-
level court should reduce the time taken to produce judgments in Luxembourg (currently anywhere between eighteen months and three years).
However, there is no prospect of the Court's workload decreasing. On the
contrary, as more and more 1992 directives are passed, an increasing
number of test cases will be brought as the limits of single market legislation are probed—and as those who failed to stop 1992 laws passing

through the Commission, Council and Parliament use the European Court as a last resort.

At the opening of the Court of First Instance in 1989, the presiding judge said that its workload highlighted the dual function of the ECJ. It has not only to decide matters of law but also to intervene in disputes over fact—customs classifications, agricultural regulations and the like. He also complained that the Court was overloaded with Commission cases brought under Article 169 against member states for their failure to implement EC directives. The UK has a good record in this regard; Italy and Greece are the worst offenders.

The Economic and Social Committee

This is an advisory body which brings together trades unionists, industrialists and other sectors of EC opinion to provide a sounding-board for ideas and to exchange news on current EC policies and proposals.

3 REVISING THE TREATY OF ROME

From the Single European Act to economic and political union

The Single European Act entered the world with a bang—literally. As European leaders gathered for the EC summit in Luxembourg in December 1985 a small bomb was thrown from a passing car onto the roadside near the Euro-Conference Centre on the Kirchberg. No motive was ever discovered: there had been a number of isolated, small-scale bombings in the Grand Duchy during the previous year, for no apparent reason, and this was assumed to be another such attack. Mrs Thatcher, who had survived the Grand Hotel bomb at Brighton the previous year, remarked calmly that bombs always caused anxiety but that the EC leaders had continued their deliberations unchecked.

Nonetheless the incident was perhaps symbolic, for the Single European Act, largely misunderstood or underestimated at the time, was itself a time-bomb. It was the culmination of 30 years of EC post-war history, and had given rise to a 'volcanic' display of opposition from Mrs Thatcher only six months before, at the Milan EC summit in June 1985, at the end of Italy's Presidency. The Act marked the first real attempt to bring the original Treaty of Rome up to date and shape the EC of the future. To understand its explosive content, it is necessary to go back to the Treaty of Rome itself and the beginnings of the Community.

The origins of European union

The idea of a European-wide system of government can be traced to medieval times, when the concept was one of a united Christendom. Scholars such as Aquinas or Erasmus thought of themselves as European, and moved freely from one university to another. In the seventeenth century William Penn, the Quaker, even proposed a European Parliament. In practice, however, European unification for the most part meant unification by force, through empires, from Charlemagne to Napoleon and Hitler. The rise of the nation-states in the eighteenth and nineteenth centuries, moreover, militated against the concept of unification, with notions of pan-European identity replaced by a balance of power between states, as at the Congress of Vienna in 1814–15. The First World War destroyed the old order but left Europe in a confused and disorganized state, prey to Fascist and Communist dictators.

It was the Second World War and its aftermath which produced a desire for union based on a determination to pool resources and make Europe into a peaceful force on the world stage. Hitler, it has been said, was the unwitting catalyst for democratic European unification. The apparently eternal problem posed by German power would be solved by bringing Germany (or at least West Germany) into a closely enmeshed, democratic Europe. The post-war enterprise had its roots in the 1948 Benelux Union between Belgium, the Netherlands and Luxembourg, and grew over a period of six years into the EC of Six, with Benelux joined by France, Italy and West Germany. This post-war process of integration was given added impetus by the two emerging superpowers—from the United States in the form of Marshall Aid and American support for European reconstruction and from the Soviet Union (less benevolently) in the form of an armed menace to Western Europe which had the effect of pushing the Europeans closer together for common protection. Britain, despite Churchill's rhetoric about the need for a United Europe, remained aloof.

In the early post-war years the impetus towards European union was simple and direct. As early as 1948 there was a defence dimension to the process in the form of the Treaty of Brussels establishing the Western European Union (WEU), which included Britain. In the 1950s the WEU became moribund, partly because of the formation of NATO, and attempts to form a European Defence Community (EDC) also foundered in 1954—because of a French veto. Instead, the emphasis was on economic union as a first step. However, it was always understood that the eventual aim was a union which had political and even defence implications as well as economic ones.

Monnet and the Franco-German axis

The main driving force came (as much of the 1992 impetus was later to come) from a Frenchman: Jean Monnet. Originally from a family cognac firm (and its pre-war salesman in Britain), Monnet helped to co-ordinate the economies of the Allies against Hitler, and became a passionate advocate of Anglo-French integration after the war. However, the fulcrum of European union was, in the end, Franco-German, with Britain still standing on one side. The French fear was that after two world wars, and centuries of Franco-German conflict before that, Germany would once again dominate Europe, through its possession of key coal and iron industries in the Saarland, a border region like Alsace, which had often caused bitter rivalry in the past. Together with Robert Schuman, the French Foreign Minister, who came from Alsace and who was also an ardent proponent of European integration, Monnet put forward a plan—which bore Schuman's name—for a European Coal and Steel Community (ECSC) to oversee the industries in a common supranational interest. This duly came about in August 1952, under Monnet's chairmanship, with the Benelux nations and Italy joining France and West Germany.

Three years later the same Six, under the influence of Monnet's Action Committee for a United States of Europe, began work on the Treaty of Rome, founding a European Economic Community with much wider powers than the ECSC. The 1955 meeting of the Foreign Ministers of the Six at Messina, in Italy, on the legal basis for a Common Market led two years later to the signing of the completed Treaty in Rome, on 25 March 1957. Euratom, the European Atomic Energy Community, was also established in Rome on the same day as the EEC. In 1967 the three 'Communities'—the ECSC, Euratom and the EEC itself—were merged. It is therefore technically correct to refer to the 'European Communities' —but in practice the EEC was the one that mattered. (The phrase 'European Economic Community' has since been almost universally shortened to 'European Community' as integration has proceeded and the Community's political character has developed.)

Largely due to continuing Franco-German *rapprochement*, helped by the personal relationship between de Gaulle and Adenauer, the EC made rapid progress towards its first goal: the removal of internal tariffs and quotas. As in the later case of 1992, the founding fathers laid down a target date for this customs union: 31 December 1969, 12 years after the signing of the Treaty. In the event, the removal of internal tariffs was completed over a year early, in July 1968, accompanied by the erection of a common external tariff to protect the new common market. The EC also fulfilled the Treaty's provision for a Common Agricultural Policy involving farm subsidies—a measure which was intended to support Europe's farmers and ensure food supplies but which was to consume a growing proportion of the EC's limited budget.

An ever-closer union

It swiftly became apparent, however, that the drive for integration went beyond a customs union and farm support. The subsequent history of the EC is a history of lurches towards the original goals of the Treaty preamble: 'To lay the foundations of an ever-closer union among the peoples of Europe . . . to ensure economic and social progress by common action to eliminate the barriers which divide Europe'. One early effort to fulfil this goal by creating a political as well as economic union was the Fouchet Plan (Marks I and II) of 1961, which proposed a joint foreign policy. However, this, like many other such plans, foundered on the objection—put forward most vehemently by de Gaulle—that foreign policy was a national prerogative not a supranational one. Similar objections ended the 1970 Werner Plan for Economic and Monetary Union by 1980; once again, governments declared that handing over control of monetary questions to the EC would be an unacceptable surrender of national sovereignty. The plan for European Union developed in 1976 by Leo Tindemans, then Belgian Prime Minister (and now Belgian Foreign Minister), also failed—not surprisingly, perhaps, since the Tindemans

Plan not only combined the two earlier failed Plans for a joint foreign policy and monetary union but added schemes for common regional and social policies, a common industrial policy and a programme for a Citizens' Europe.

Yet Euro-Plans have a way of lingering on EC shelves rather than disappearing. There is now a social and regional policy, co-ordination of foreign policy ('political co-operation') and a plan for a Citizens' Europe, while monetary union is obstinately back on the agenda. It became clear as early as 1959, when both Greece and Turkey applied for associate membership status, that the EC had a centripetal pull which would lead to its further expansion. The key development was Britain's decision—under Harold Macmillan's premiership—to apply for full membership, beginning in 1961 (barely a year, paradoxically, after Britain had been instrumental in setting up the rival EFTA, the European Free Trade Association). The British application was vetoed by de Gaulle—the first French 'non'—in 1963, on the grounds that Britain's ties were transatlantic rather than European. It was renewed by Harold Wilson in 1966, and again vetoed by de Gaulle. However, de Gaulle's nationalism and Gallic disdain were at odds with Community philosophy. He clashed frequently not only with Britain but also with leading statesmen such as Dr Walter Hallstein, the West German President of the European Commission, who favoured a switch to majority voting in the Council of Ministers.

Enlargement: Britain joins the Community

In 1969 de Gaulle resigned, and a year later he died. With Pompidou and Brandt leading France and West Germany, respectively, the British application was again renewed under the premiership of the pro-European Edward Heath, amid tough bargaining over the accession terms. Denmark, Ireland and Norway (which had submitted and withdrawn applications in accordance with Britain's applications and rejections) also applied. Britain, Denmark and Ireland finally became EC members in 1973, bringing the total from Six to Nine. All three ratified the decision in popular referendums—in the British case in 1975, after the new Wilson government had renegotiated entry terms to ensure a British budget rebate. A Norwegian referendum on EC membership in 1972, by contrast, produced a narrow majority against, with the result that Norway stayed out—although the 1992 process has brought renewed signs of interest in Oslo in full membership.

In 1975, the year of the British EC referendum, Greece put in its membership application, followed by Spain and Portugal two years later. Greece duly entered the Community in 1981, bringing the membership from Nine to Ten, and the entry of Spain and Portugal in 1986 completed the enlargement process for the foreseeable future, producing a Community of Twelve and providing further pressure for economic and institutional reforms as part of the 1992 process.

However, the development of the Community has been far from easy, and more a matter of 'two steps forward, one step back' than of smooth progress towards the dream of Monnet and Schuman. In the 1970s the CAP began to become unmanageable as the subsidies system for both production and storage gave rise to surpluses—the beginnings of the notorious food mountains. On the plus side, moves towards a common foreign policy took on new life, with the agreed Davignon Plan of 1970 on regular contact between EC foreign ministers in 'political co-operation', or POCO for short. Enlargement to Nine and then Ten failed to produce the expected economic benefits, partly because of the global oil crisis of 1973 and partly because of the lack of a coherent plan for EC growth. On the other hand, in 1974–5 the Regional Development Fund was set up to close the gap between prosperous and less-prosperous regions of the EC, and it was agreed that the European Parliament should be directly elected. In 1979, through the joint efforts of Helmut Schmidt, the West German Chancellor, Valéry Giscard d'Estaing, the French President, and Roy Jenkins, President of the European Commission, the European Monetary System (EMS) was founded, with an exchange rate mechanism designed to limit currency fluctuations by linking member currencies to a newly devised European Currency Unit—the ECU.

The 1980s thus found the EC advancing unevenly towards the vision of the founding fathers, facing institutional and budgetary problems inherited from the 1950s and 1960s, and suffering—after the de Gaulle–Adenauer and Giscard d'Estaing–Schmidt years—from lack of overall direction, guidance and leadership. Of the major EC statesmen, Mitterrand and Kohl lacked strong personal rapport and did not, on the whole, lend new dynamism to the Franco-German axis, the traditional motor of EC progress. Mrs Thatcher, continuing the British tradition of standing aloof (indeed, reinforcing it) did not appear to regard the European cause with any enthusiasm, to put it mildly. If anything, her instincts lay in another direction—the Anglo-American transatlantic relationship so feared in earlier times by de Gaulle. Mrs Thatcher's rapport was with President Reagan of the United States rather than with her Continental counterparts.

The early 1980s were dominated not by visions of the future but by Mrs Thatcher's determined—and justified—campaign to persuade Britain's EC partners that Britain's contribution to EC coffers was unacceptably high (Harold Wilson's renegotiated terms not having been fulfilled). With the help of President Mitterrand, the campaign eventually led at the Fontainebleau summit of 1984 to a compromise involving a rebate to Britain of 66% of the difference between its Vat contributions to EC funds and its share of EC benefits—in other words, the difference between what Britain put into the EC and what it got out of it (less than France or West Germany, which gained more in farm support). The Fontainebleau settlement also involved an increase in the limit on overall

Vat contributions to the budget from 1% to 1.4%, with further rises to be discussed at a later stage.

All this had the merit of focusing attention on the chronic budgetary crisis and on the fact that the EC's 'own resources' were being outstripped by the cost of running a Community of Twelve. Reform was needed, but the shrill tone of Mrs Thatcher's campaign (and resulting anti-Common Market feeling in Britain) did not augur well for the reform effort. In the absence of convincing leadership from London, Paris or Bonn, much would depend on the new European Commission, led at the beginning of 1985 by a quiet, dapper Frenchman: Jacques Delors.

The Delors reform package

At the beginning of 1985 Delors made a tour of European capitals to introduce himself and to sound out opinion on four ways of moving the EC closer to the founders' goals:

1 Revival of the idea of a defence union;
2 Revival of the idea of monetary union;
3 Reform of the ECs institutional structure of Council, Commission and Parliament; or
4 Completion of the internal market through the complete dismantling of obstacles to trade (in other words, further development of the customs union).

In the end, the 1992 concept has come to embrace all four, either formally or informally, but in 1985 it was the proposal for completing the market which most appealed to EC leaders (Mrs Thatcher included), because it implied deregulation and freer competition. The difficulties began when Delors went on to argue that completing the internal market involved a mass of new legislation and that the Treaty of Rome would have to be amended—the birth of the Single European Act.

The practical basis of the Delors concept was simple: moves to harmonize EC standards and practices since the completion of the customs union in 1968 had come up against the obstacle of national protectionism. No state wanted to give up long-cherished practices in the wider interest. Therefore some supranational way would have to be found of persuading them to 'harmonize' or (as a first step, referred to as 'the new approach') mutually to recognize each other's standards. This became known in EC jargon as the 'Cassis de Dijon' ruling, after a celebrated case at the European Court of Justice in 1979. This arose when a West German firm found that it was prevented from importing Cassis de Dijon because it allegedly did not conform to exacting West German standards for liqueurs. The Court ruled that Bonn could only prevent the import of a French drink if it could prove that the liquid was harmful to health or contravened tax or consumer protection laws—which cassis (the basis of a popular aperitif called kir) did not.

In formulating their new plan for the internal market Delors and the Commission seized on the 'Cassis Principle' that, for goods to move around the integrated market unhindered, they need only conform to commonly agreed standards. Lord Cockfield, the Internal Market Commissioner, devised 300 measures to eliminate the technical, physical and fiscal barriers to intra-Community trade. In addition, the Commission took up earlier, unsuccessful ideas for institutional reform, monetary union and a common foreign policy. The last in this long line of failed visions was the Draft Treaty of European Union, devised by Altiero Spinelli, a veteran Italian Communist Euro MP, and adopted by the European Parliament.

The Milan summit: partial failure

The 1992 process which resulted is a diluted version of what union visionaries like Spinelli had wanted. On the other hand, the Single European Act goes further than sceptics had wished. When the EC Milan summit convened in June 1985 to take a first look at what was to become the Single European Act, Mrs Thatcher was highly suspicious of anything which went beyond the opening up of internal frontiers to facilitate movement and trade. Britain led the way in proposing a common foreign policy, going so far as to suggest a joint EC approach at the United Nations—which does not appear in the Single European Act as eventually agreed. However, Mrs Thatcher set her face firmly against changes to the Treaty of Rome, and—with the backing of Denmark—said that she saw no need for a special inter-governmental conference to agree such changes. Increased use of majority voting, the Prime Minister declared, could be covered by a 'gentleman's agreement' along the lines of the Luxembourg Compromise, with the national veto retained. Talk of European union was 'airy-fairy'.

The Milan summit was marked by bad feeling, caused by British anger over a Franco-German draft declaration on European Union which drew heavily on British proposals, and then went beyond them. However, at the end of the summit Mrs Thatcher was outvoted over the setting up of the Inter-Governmental Conference (IGC). President Mitterrand remarked tartly that the summit had sorted out 'those who favour a strong, united Europe from those who are hanging back'. The Milan summit communiqué (or rather, the Presidency's conclusions, since not all points were accepted unanimously) was the first mention of 1992 as a target date. It confirmed 'the need to improve the operation of the Community in order to give concrete form to the objectives it has set itself, in particular as regards the completion of the internal market by 1992 and measures to promote a technological Europe'. It also noted the need to improve decision-making procedures, partly by revising the powers of the Commission and the Parliament. The key section concluded:

> The summit discussed in detail the convening of a conference to work out the following with a view to achieving concrete progress on European Union: a treaty on a common foreign and security policy on the basis of Franco-German and United Kingdom drafts: and amendments to the Treaty of Rome . . . The required majority has been obtained for the convening of such a conference.

Amid the row over amending the Treaty it almost went unnoticed that the Milan summit had instructed the Council of Ministers 'to initiate a precise programme of action, based on the White Paper . . . with a view to achieving completely and effectively the conditions for a single market in the Community by 1992 at the latest, in accordance with stages fixed in relationship to previously determined priorities and a binding timetable'. The Milan meeting, in other words, was not as disastrous for EC unity as it appeared at the time. The only question was whether, when the EC leaders re-assembled in Luxembourg at the end of the six-month Luxembourg presidency, Mrs Thatcher would still be as adamantly opposed to Treaty changes.

The Luxembourg summit: Mrs Thatcher signs the Act

The Luxembourg summit began more auspiciously. The IGC Mrs Thatcher had so fiercely opposed at Milan took the modest form of a series of Foreign Ministers' meetings in autumn 1985. By the time the Luxembourg meeting convened, many of the basic issues had been agreed. The leaders were anxious to avoid a further display of disunity, and began by agreeing that Mrs Thatcher was right to put the 1992 emphasis on deregulation. Completion of the internal market would be designed to give a great impetus to the European economy, with special help for small and medium-sized enterprises. There was also initial agreement on giving the European Parliament a second reading of internal market legislation. However, France and Italy, with support from the Benelux nations, still wanted to turn the proposed Treaty amendments into an Act of European Union, creating a 'European space'—a phrase dismissed by the British as imprecise. They also wanted an expanded EC secretariat with power to co-ordinate EC foreign policy.

For Britain, again with support from Denmark, the priority was to make the existing EC institutions and mechanisms function more efficiently (for example, by revising the CAP) and to ensure that the move towards a frontier-free Europe did not imperil Britain's control as an island over drugs, immigration and plant and animal health. The summit eventually produced a compromise, but the tension between these two visions of 1992 has resurfaced in various guises ever since.

There was alarm on the second day of the summit when Denmark and Italy both threatened to walk out—the Danes because for them the draft agreement on 1992 went too far and the Italians because it did not go far enough. In a vivid if gory image, a distraught Delors protested that the changes insisted on by Britain amounted to a 'Texas chainsaw massacre'. However, in the end, late at night, the Single European Act was born, and the history of the EC had taken a major step. 'We decided to sit it out until we had a clear and decisive position,' a tired Mrs Thatcher told reporters after she had reversed her earlier opposition to Treaty changes—provided that they met British concerns. She still regarded amending the Treaty as unnecessary, 'but if they wanted it to be this way, so be it'.

Main points of the Single European Act

The Act laid down eight basic points:

1 1992. 'The Community shall adopt measures with the aim of progressively establishing the internal market over a period expiring on December 31 1992 . . . The internal market shall comprise an area without internal frontiers in which the free movement of goods, persons, services and capital is ensured in accordance with the provisions of this Treaty.' States could apply for exemptions, and the Act included a 'General Declaration' as follows: 'Nothing in these provisions shall affect the right of member states to take such measures as they consider necessary for the purpose of controlling immigration from Third World countries, and to combat terrorism, crime, the traffic in drugs and illicit trading in works of art and antiques'. On the other hand, the EC leaders agreed to avoid such continued national controls by introducing 'common measures' on police co-operation, visas, extradition and immigration. The Act also empowered states to take fellow states to the European Court if exemptions were 'improperly used' to restrict trade.

2 Practical steps to reduce the administrative and legal constraints on small and medium-sized businesses, with a Commission task force to oversee this deregulatory process.

3 In a concession by both Britain and West Germany, which had the strongest doubts about monetary union, the Act's preamble referred specifically to monetary union as an EC goal, to be 'progressively realized'. However, monetary union was not among the 1992 priorities laid down by the Act as legally binding, and Mrs Thatcher argued that the wording went no further than that of the Paris summit in 1972.

4 Disparities between richer and poorer regions of the EC were to be reduced (the policy known as 'cohesion') through the more efficient use of the structural funds or regional and social funds. To avoid a 'two-speed Europe', states would use their economic policies to promote 'harmonious development in the EC' and overcome 'the backwardness of the least favoured regions'. On Britain's insistence, this embraced 'declining industrial regions' in the north as well as rural areas in the south. The Act authorized the Commission to recommend 'amendments' to the structural funds —and at the Brussels summit of February 1988, the leaders agreed to Delors' proposals for the funds to be doubled by 1992.

5 The European Parliament was given a new 'co-operation' procedure, enabling it to amend legislation through a second reading and in some cases—notably commercial agreements—to have the final say. On most issues, if the Parliament rejected a bill on its second reading the Council could still have the last word by passing the measure unanimously.

6 Technological research to be encouraged within an agreed framework. Britain held up the resulting five-year (1987–91) research framework programme—eventually reduced to £4 billion (5.3 billion ECUs)—on the grounds that the technology projects involved had not been properly approved and there was too much research duplication among the EC nations. However, the programme—including information technology (ESPRIT), advanced telecommunications research (RACE) and industrial technology (BRITE)—eventually went ahead, albeit with a smaller budget than the 7.7 billion ECUs the Commission had wanted.

7 The environment. The EC was to take action to improve the environment, contribute towards the protection of human health and ensure 'a prudent and rational utilization of natural resources' on the principle 'that environmental damage should be rectified at source and that the polluter should pay'. Denmark's objections that its own standards were higher than those of the EC were met by a clause stating that the Act need not prevent member states taking 'more stringent measures' than the EC norm.

8 A separate Title provided for 'European co-operation in the sphere of foreign policy'—as distinct from external or trade policy, which is handled by the Commission, although it also impinges on foreign policy. The leaders undertook to formulate and implement a European foreign policy by consulting one another

'so as to ensure that their combined influence is exercised as effectively as possible through co-ordination, the convergence of their positions and the implementation of joint action', with Foreign Ministers meeting at least four times a year on political co-operation issues. Most controversial was paragraph 6a: 'The High contracting Parties consider that closer co-operation on questions of European security would contribute in an essential way to the development of a European identity . . . They are ready to co-ordinate their positions more closely on the political and economic aspects of security'. This should not conflict with the competence of either NATO or the WEU, the new Article said. A new foreign policy secretariat would be set up in Brussels (and duly was) but with purely administrative functions.

Ratification of the Act

The day after the Luxembourg summit, Delors declared that the EC could now undertake 'the adventure of progress towards union'. In fact, every EC summit since December 1985 had grappled in one form or another with the consequences of the Single European Act and of its inbuilt contradictions. Nonetheless, the Act is in force, and the arguments are about interpretation, not about repealing it—which is impossible. In the course of 1987 the Act was ratified by every national parliament, including Westminster, where the Lords almost staged a rebellion but in the end consented. Every ratification debate revolved around the degree to which the Single European Act involved a partial surrender of national sovereignty to the EC. In the case of two countries—Denmark and Ireland—it took popular referendums to resolve the question of the Act's constitutionality—in Denmark in March 1986 (56.2% in favour) and in Ireland in May 1987 (70.2% in favour).

The Act was passed, the Treaty was altered and with it the nature of the EC, even if some of the 1992 goals—such as monetary union—were put off to the distant future and others—such as foreign and defence policy co-ordination—were diluted or left ambiguous. The heart of the matter was the commitment to a single European market by 31 December 1992, and the agreement that the EC had the right to lay down policy throughout the Community in areas from taxation to tourism.

Further treaty revision: the Maastricht agenda

The Madrid summit of June 1989 gave Delors the go-ahead to develop a three-stage plan for economic and monetary union, with phase one beginning on 1 July 1990. But by the time of the Dublin summit a year later, at the end of the Irish presidency, pressure was building not only for economic and monetary union but for political union and institutional reform in the shape of further revisions to the Treaty of Rome. As with the Single European Act, preparatory moves took the form of an IGC—or, since two treaty revisions were proposed, two IGCs, one on monetary union and another on political union. The need for the latter was agreed in principle at the extra Dublin summit of April 1990, on a Franco-German initiative, to 'strengthen the democratic legitimacy of the union' and to ensure that the EC could 'respond efficiently and effectively to the demands of the new situation' created by events in East and Central Europe.

At Dublin in April and again in June Mrs Thatcher, perhaps surprisingly, raised no objections to the summoning of the IGCs, with their progress to be reviewed at the Rome summit in December 1990. In fact Mrs Thatcher praised the first report on political union, produced by EC foreign ministers for the June 1990 summit, on the grounds that it 'respected the separate identities of member states, reaffirmed that the Council of Ministers was the main decision-making body, and underlined the principle of subsidiarity'—meaning that EC institutions should only decide what could not be better handled at a lower level.

In October 1990, however, the Italian presidency, which had taken over from Ireland, called an extra EC summit, ostensibly to discuss aid to the Soviet Union, on the grounds that the December summit would be taken up with the IGCs. In fact, the October summit unexpectedly set the timetable for phase two of the Delors plan (the European Bank, beginning 1 January 1994) and phase three (the single currency, to start in 1997). Mrs Thatcher angrily denounced this outcome as 'putting the cart before the horse'. But the following month her role in shaping British policy came to an abrupt end when she was forced to resign as Prime Minister, with John Major succeeding her.

Luxembourg, which inherited the presidency in the first half of 1991, pressed ahead with draft treaties on monetary and political union to be adopted at the Maastricht summit at the end of the ensuing Dutch presidency in December 1991. In some respects the drafts were acceptable to the UK. On the social dimension, the Luxembourg summit of June 1991 agreed that social legislation had to be in accordance with national practices and traditions and would not affect national social security schemes, for example. Equally, Luxembourg defined the conditions for the introduction of a single currency. This would occur when EC economies had converged by achieving similar levels of inflation, interest rates and public spending. There would be co-ordination of police and immigration services; EC citizens would have the right to vote in any member state; and the Commission would be reduced from 17 members to 12 (one for each state).

However, Major made clear that the provisions in the Luxembourg draft for 'co-decision making' by the European Parliament (see Chapter 2) were unacceptable, as was majority voting on some foreign policy issues and above all the draft's reference to the EC's federal goal, or

'vocation'. 'Federalism' became an objectionable 'F word' in the British
lexicon. 'We will insist on its removal before we sign any treaty at the
end of December,' Major declared. The 'F word' was quietly dropped. In
September Major disagreed with Mitterrand over the pace of integration,
with Major insisting that the EC should be broadened to include the new
democracies of Eastern Europe and Mitterrand placing the stress on the
integration of the existing Twelve.

The Dutch presidency, to the alarm and annoyance not only of Britain
but also—in varying degrees—of France, Portugal, Ireland and Denmark, revised the Luxembourg text in an even more federalist direction.
It firmly reinstated the word 'federal', made foreign policy and police
and immigration affairs a matter of common policy agreed by majority
vote, rather than co-operation between states, and increased the powers
of the European Parliament further. After a stormy session of EC foreign
ministers in the Netherlands at the end of September the Dutch text was
withdrawn and the Luxembourg text reinstated as the basis for discussions at Maastricht. However, the impetus towards further treaty
revision in the direction of a federal union remained strong.

The Maastricht summit

The outcome at Maastricht in December 1991 was seen as a disappointment by some arch-federalists, not least because Britain successfully
manoeuvred to 'opt-out' of two key provisions: the introduction of a
single European currency by 1999, and the application of Community
legislation to social policies, on which the other eleven agreed to sign a
separate protocol. On the other hand, the treaty on economic and monetary union provides for Britain to 'opt in' to the single currency, subject
to Parliamentary approval, provided (as seems likely) Britain satisfies
agreed criteria for economic convergence within the EC. Similarly, the
overall thrust of Maastricht was toward closer union.

The Maastricht treaty on political union established a 'European
Union'. In the final wording, the phrase 'ever closer union' (already in
the Treaty of Rome) replaced the contentious draft phrase 'Union with a
federal goal'. The aims of the Union were defined as the promotion of
economic and social progress through the creation of an area without
internal frontiers, and through economic and monetary union 'including,
finally, a single currency'; the assertion of a European identity on the
international scene through a common foreign and security policy, 'to
include the eventual framing of a common defence policy'; the protection
of citizens' rights through 'the introduction of a citizenship of the Union';
and close co-operation on home and judicial affairs, with co-operation
across frontiers on asylum, immigration, drugs and terrorism, and a
common visa policy to be agreed by unanimity in the Council until 1996,
and by majority vote thereafter. Significantly, the Council has the power
to introduce common visa requirements in the event of 'an emergency

situation in a third country posing the threat of an inflow to the Community of nationals from that country'.

The Union is to have 'due regard to the national identity of its member states', however, and must also respect the European Convention on Human Rights, which results from 'the constitutional traditions common to the member states as general principles of Community law'. Article 3b enshrined subsidiarity in treaty form for the first time, declaring that the EC shall take action 'only if and insofar as the objectives of the proposed action cannot be sufficiently achieved by the member states and can therefore, by reason of scale or the effects of the proposed action, be better achieved by the Community . . . Any action by the Community shall not go beyond what is necessary to achieve the objectives of the Treaty'.

The political union treaty also re-defined the functions of the EC, adding the following to the wording of the Treaty of Rome and the Single European Act: measures concerning the entry and movement of persons in the internal market; economic and social cohesion; the environment; research and technological development; energy; consumer protection and tourism; the establishment and development of 'trans-European networks'; and for the first time the extension of EC competence into health ('the attainment of a high level of health protection') and education ('education and training of high quality and the flowering of the cultures of member states . . . as well as improvement in the knowledge and dissemination of the culture and history of the European peoples.'). The EC is to 'respect the responsibility of the member states for the content of teaching, the organization of education systems and their cultural and linguistic diversity' but will issue non-binding recommendations (adopted by the Council on a majority vote) to foster a 'European dimension in education' and encourage teacher and student exchanges. Health and education thus remain outside EC competence for the most part, but are brought into the EC orbit through co-ordination and co-operation.

The concept of European citizenship was also new ('every person holding the nationality of a member state shall be a citizen of the Union . . . every Union citizen shall have the right to move and reside freely within the territory of the member states'), with detailed arrangements to be worked out by the end of 1994 giving citizens 'resident in member states of which they are not nationals' the right to vote and stand as candidates in municipal and European elections.

On institutions, the Maastricht treaty gave the European Parliament extra powers of veto and amendment, and authorised it to scrutinise EC 'maladministration' and EC finances. The Commission was reduced from 17 to 12, with a term of office of five rather than four years as of 1 January 1995. The president of the Commission is to be appointed by EC leaders 'by common accord, after consulting the European parliament'. A new advisory body, the Committee of the Regions, was set up, with representatives from EC regions and local authorities appointed to it for a four-year term.

Finally, in a separate protocol, the eleven states other than Britain adopted common measures on social policy, with the treaty authorising them to 'have recourse to the institutions, procedures and mechanisms of the European Community' for this purpose. It remains to be seen what this means in practice. The protocol commits the eleven signatories to 'the promotion of employment, improved living and working conditions, proper social protection, dialogue between management and labour, and the development of human resources with a view to lasting high employment', with action to be taken by qualified majority voting. Unanimous voting is required for measures affecting social security, worker-management contractual negotiations, and conditions of work for third-country nationals living in the EC. John Major commented that all this represented unacceptable interference in national affairs, and would have 'handed over the government of this country to trades unions abroad' had he agreed to allow the social dimension to remain in the treaty proper. The Commission, however, has made clear that it still hopes to secure the agreement of all Twelve to a range of social policies by using existing powers to legislate on health and safety issues.

The Maastricht treaty is subject to review in 1996, when a further Inter-Governmental conference is to meet. The treaty states that 'any European State may apply to become a member of the Union', and it may well be that by 1996 the pressure for enlargement will have become so great that further treaty changes will be necessary to accommodate the needs of a wider EC.

4 STANDARDIZING INDUSTRY

Harmonization from pharmaceuticals to exhaust emissions

Imagine the frustration, delay, and unnecessary increase in costs faced by a British truck-manufacturing company trying to export its latest lightweight model to Italy, which has the vehicle's brakes dispatched to Turin to be inspected and approved by a recognized auto components inspector before receiving the licence needed to ship over the finished product for distribution and sale. There is no guarantee that the vehicle's brakes will be approved, even if they meet local technical standards, especially if the national government is determined to protect its domestic truck-manufacturing industry from external competition. Such obstacles have become all too familiar to EC manufacturers trying to export their products, whether cars, telephones or pharmaceuticals, to other EC member states, and have helped make a mockery of the European Commission's goal of creating a common market.

Conflicting product technical standards are by no means the only informal trade barrier likely to be encountered by companies seeking to develop markets in other EC countries. Because of the increased concern over industry's impact on the environment, some member states have been under great political pressure to introduce 'green' regulations on a wide range of industrial activities, processes and products, such as tighter controls on vehicle emissions. Although the political pressures that have given rise to such demands stem from a genuine concern over industry's impact on the environment, there are now widespread anxieties that a new hierarchy of 'green' standards could be used as a pretext for restricting the free circulation of goods around the EC. Consequently, the European Commission is engaged in drawing up new environmental standards for industry to provide increased protection for the environment without inhibiting trade.

However, the Commission's environmental initiatives go much further than simply ensuring that environmental concern is not distorted into creating new obstacles to commerce. Taken collectively, the proposed environmental protection package, which contains more proposals for legislation than any other aspect of the internal market programme, are aimed at nothing less than creating the conditions for a new 'ecological market economy'. Companies which have traditionally relied on 'end-of-pipe' solutions for the pollution created by their activities are now being asked to reassess completely their production processes, from the acquisition of raw materials to the delivery of the finished product. In consequence, businesses, governments and consumers are likely to face increases in costs expected to run into billions of pounds.

Proposals for a new energy tax alone, unveiled by Brussels in September 1991, are expected to raise £37 billion a year, as well as leading to significant reductions in carbon dioxide emissions. Because of fears that the so-called 'dark green' states—Germany, Denmark, and the Netherlands—would take unilateral action and thereby create distortions in the internal market, the Commission felt that it had no option but to come up with a proposal of its own. Under the Commission's scheme, a low-carbon tax would be introduced on coal, petrol and natural gas in January 1993 and progressively increased until the year 2000. Most of the tax would be likely to fall on the advanced economies in northern Europe, leaving the poorer south able to pursue its development goals without penalty.

Demolishing technical barriers

In June 1985 the European Commission published what has perhaps become its most widely known White Paper, *Completing The Internal Market*, which outlined an ambitious strategy and timetable for the task of removing the Community's internal barriers to trade and merging twelve disparate economies into one by 31 December 1992. It defined three separate categories of internal barriers to the free movement of capital, goods, labour and services. These were the fiscal, physical and technical barriers to trade, whose existence had been identified by the Delors Commission as being responsible for the 'economic balkanization' of the Community.

The White Paper argued forcibly for the complete and effective removal of all three categories of barrier. But it is the removal of the technical barriers to trade, the plethora of different technical standards for individual products drawn up by each member state (ostensibly for health, safety and environmental reasons) which holds out the prospect of creating a single industrial market of continental proportions, thereby enabling Europe to compete more effectively with its competitors in Japan and the United States.

Along with the creation of the Common Agricultural Policy, setting up a Common Market, as specified under Article 100 of the Treaty of Rome, was one of the fundamental objectives inspiring the foundation of the EC. However, despite a promising start, the Community soon lost its way. The first step towards the creation of the Common Market was the establishment of a common customs tariff, completed well ahead of schedule in 1968. It was followed ten years later by the adoption of the Sixth Vat Directive, which formed the basis of the Community's indirect taxation system and provided a common method for allocating revenues from national Vat receipts to the Community budget.

However, the impact of the two oil crises of the 1970s, and the unprecedented combination of inflation and recession that resulted, brought the promising progress of the Community's first 20 years to an abrupt halt. The impetus towards economic integration rapidly dissipated, and in many respects the Community began to move backwards. Member states, although required by the Treaty of Rome to dismantle all tariff barriers between them, showed a polite respect for the letter of the Treaty and systematically set about undermining its spirit by erecting a large network of non-tariff barriers, epitomized by divergent technical standards, in a forlorn endeavour to protect themselves from intra-EC competition.

The Community's preoccupation with the accession of new members during the 1970s and 1980s effectively ruled out any serious attempt to rectify this deteriorating situation. In this context, the Commission's efforts to harmonize every technical standard on a product-by-product basis were reminiscent of the labour of Sisyphus. In the mid-1980s the European Commission and the Council of Ministers launched a long-overdue resuscitation package for the ideals expressed by the founders of the EC.

A new approach to technical harmonization

Following recognition by the Council of Ministers that, in the field of technical standards and regulations, the goals of all national legislation were more or less identical, the European Commission was granted a licence to abandon its traditional one-dimensional approach to technical harmonization in favour of a new multi-dimensional strategy based on selective harmonization and mutual recognition.

The traditional approach, which required years of tortuous negotiations to arrive at a common position for a single product standard, was inherently bureaucratic, extremely unpopular and very time consuming. In many cases it had proved to be completely futile. By the time the new product standard had emerged from the bureaucrat's briefcase and onto the shopfloor it had often been made redundant by the rapid pace of technological development. The whole legislative process was rather like moving a mountain to bring forth a mouse, and it had brought into disrepute the Community's laudable efforts to create common industrial standards.

The most systematic expression of the new approach to the harmonization of technical standards was given by Lord Cockfield in the Internal Market White Paper. In this he called for a distinction in all internal market legislation to be made between 'what is essential to harmonize, and what may be left to mutual recognition of national standards'. In future, the traditional approach of legislative technical harmonization will be restricted to those areas where it is vital to create a uniform Continental market. Companies previously limited to national markets for products manufactured under national product standards will benefit from the economies of scale that the single internal market will create.

In 1985 the Commission acknowledged that exclusive reliance on Article 100 of the Treaty, which required a unanimous vote by the Council of Ministers to secure passage of all technical harmonization legislation, would be likely to present the same sort of difficulties experienced in the past. It therefore announced its intention to pursue legislative harmonization under Articles 30–36, which prohibited national governments from adopting policies which constituted an 'arbitrary discrimination or a disguised restriction on trade between member states'.

However, by the time the Single European Act had been ratified in 1987 the Commission's ability to secure legislative approval of technical harmonization measures by the Council of Ministers had been immeasurably strengthened. Article 100a of the amended Treaty introduced the principle of qualified majority voting for all measures 'which have as their object the establishment and functioning of the internal market'. The built-in institutional unanimity had been bypassed, allowing the Commission to press ahead with the task of laying the foundations of a single internal market. Henceforth, all legislative technical harmonization measures will be confined to establishing minimum health and safety requirements, conformity with which will guarantee manufacturers the right of access to the markets of other member states. In addition, legislative technical harmonization will be complemented by the systematic implementation of the principle of mutual recognition of non-essential national product standards. On the assumption that all such regulations are designed to lay down minimum health and safety standards, it follows that all governments have basically the same objectives in mind.

Following a series of seminal judgments by the European Court of Justice, notably the 1979 Cassis de Dijon ruling, which specified that Community law demands the mutual acceptance of goods from one member state by other member states, the Internal Market White Paper laid down that in future:

> The general principle should be approved that, if a product is lawfully manufactured and marketed in one member state, there is no reason why it should not move freely throughout the Community. The objectives of national legislation in this respect are essentially identical. Although they may take different forms, they amount to the same thing.

As a result, member states must now accept products from other member states which are manufactured to a different design but which nonetheless perform the same as those manufactured to national technical standards. This principle (which may in retrospect seem to be nothing more than common sense) is in fact little short of a revolution, given the historical context of Community attempts to harmonize technical standards. Moreover, working on the principle that it is better to privatize as much harmonization as possible, the task of establishing European-wide product standards has now been taken out of the hands of the bureaucrats and allocated to the new European standards institutes such as the European Committee for Standardization (CEN), the European Committee for Electrotechnical Standardization (CENELEC) and the European Telecommunications Standards Institute (ETSI). Most of the new European standards-setting procedure was completed in April 1990, with the creation of the European Organization of Testing and Certification (EOTC), a move widely acknowledged as a landmark on the long road towards the establishment of mutual recognition in testing and certification procedures throughout the Community.

Each organization, composed of industry experts and representatives of consumer bodies, has been authorized by the Commission to build on legislative technical harmonization by developing common industrial product standards applicable throughout the EC. Initially, Britain's participation in the new standard-setting organizations was extremely poor, and many of the key positions were allocated to Germany and France. At a meeting of 300 senior business executives in Glasgow in October 1988, Lynda Chalker, Minister of State at the Foreign Office, expressed the Government's concern that Britain was being overshadowed by its Continental rivals, and warned that: 'The common standards which get adopted in Europe are bound to bear the character of the countries which put the most effort into their creation'. Similarly, product testing and certification procedures, which are used by national regulatory authorities to ensure that imported goods actually comply with national technical standards and regulations before being granted authorization for sale in the national market, are now also subject to the principle of mutual recognition. However, with the appointment of Dr Ivan Dunstan, the director general of the British Standards Institute, as the president of CEN in 1990 and the appointment of Gordon Gaddes as head of CENELEC Britain had managed to make up some lost ground.

The old system of national product testing and certification procedures (which meant, for example, that before a British-made vehicle could be sold on the Italian market its brakes would have to be sent to Italian inspectors for testing before going back to Britain for installation and eventual shipment back to Italy) is finally on its way out. Member states who continue to protect their national markets from Community competition by taking refuge in Article 36 of the Treaty, granting them the right to restrict imports because they do not conform to their 'essential requirements', will no longer have grounds for doing so. If the new approach is successful, the different essential requirements of member states will be replaced by harmonized Community essential requirements.

In order that member states do not sabotage this strategy by continuing to lay down national product standards independent of the work of the new European standards institutes they are now obliged to notify the Commission in advance of their intention to introduce any new regulations and technical standards that could have an impact on other member states. Under a Directive on Mutual Information Procedures, which came into effect in January 1985, the Commission also has the power to prevent member states from implementing any new technical regulations until it has established whether they create any new barriers to intra-Community trade. To date, over 30 such technical standards have been blocked by Brussels.

According to Commission statistics, about 60% of the total number of complaints received from member states concerning other member states who fail to honour the provisions of the Treaty relate to the Common Market provisions of Articles 30–36. Because of its limited resources, the Commission has only been able to resolve less than half of these infractions, which has acted as a significant brake on progress towards the creation of a genuine internal market. However, under the new multidimensional strategy for harmonizing technical standards, Commission officials are confident that the combined impact of legislative technical harmonization, the principle of mutual recognition of non-essential national technical standards, the work of the new standardization organizations and the recently implemented mutual information procedures will produce a considerable improvement in the record of member states adhering to Community regulations. A new directive tightening up existing legislation on cross-frontier public procurement procedures (and another extending these procedures to the hitherto-excluded sectors of telecommunications, water, transport and energy) will give the Commission's strategy an additional impetus. Once adopted, these directives will require all public works and supply contracts to incorporate Community technical standards.

The new approach should also be strengthened as a result of the establishment in September 1988 of Eurocert, a Brussels-based organization, composed of national inspection and certification bodies from Britain, Belgium, France, Luxembourg, Portugal, Spain, Sweden and Switzerland, which is designed to ensure that product certificates issued by one member state will be recognized and accepted without difficulty by all other member states. The success of this initiative will depend on mutual confidence between the various national inspection and certification bodies, each of which will be required to have a stringent internal quality-assurance system, subject to regular audits by other members of Eurocert.

Yet for all its improvements over the traditional approach to technical harmonization, the new strategy is not without its problems. Where differing technical standards are not essential to cross-frontier trade, few difficulties should present themselves. However, in those cases where technical differences are essential (and they are many) the picture is considerably less optimistic. No amount of mutual recognition will, for example, enable a three-pin electrical plug to fit into a two-pin socket. Mutual recognition will not by itself establish the kind of European-wide industrial standards needed to create the economies of scale that would be offered by Community-wide industrial standards. It will be many years, perhaps decades, before the new technical standards authorities have completed the task of harmonizing essential technical standards.

In December 1990, after the European Commission had reviewed the progress made by the new standard-setting organizations, it was evident that their impact, although far from negligible, had been considerably more modest than anticipated. Admittedly, the number of European standards had grown from 56 in 1983 to 870 by 1990, including new standards for toys, pressure vessels, construction products, personal protective equipment, gas appliances and medical devices. But with the Commission calling for the introduction of more than 1,000 new standards by 1993, it was clear that the standard-setting process would have to be accelerated.

In its Green Paper on standardization the Commission recommended a further reorganization of the standardization machinery to create what it called a new European Standardization System (ESS), designed to give added impetus to the laborious task of standard setting. The Commission called for the new structure to be made up of a European Standards Council, composed of representatives from industry, consumers associations, trade unions, the presidents of CEN, CENELEC, ETSI, and Commission officials. The new body would be responsible for all aspects of policy making. In addition, a smaller European Standardization Board, made up of Technical officials, would be responsible for the management and co-ordination of the ESS. These bodies would oversee the standard-setting process, while at the same time bringing home to governments and industry the importance of creating European-wide technical and industrial standards at the rate needed to improve the Community's competitive position with America and Japan.

Furthermore, because European standards do not exist in their own right, the Green Paper called for the national standard-setting organizations to be made subordinate to the new Community organizations. The standards created by CEN, CENELEC and ETSI have no formal or legal status until they are transposed into the national standards arrangements of each of the Twelve. The Commission wants to see this replaced by the primacy of the European Standardization System. Finally, the Green Paper opposed the expansion of the technical bodies, such as CEN, CENELEC and ETSI, to allow technical officials from the new East European democracies access to the standardization process, although it did not object to granting them associate member status. The proposed reforms, however, could only come into being with the approval of the Council of Ministers, which has yet to respond to the Commission's initiative. Consequently, hopes for speeding up the standard-setting process are likely to remain in abeyance until well after 1993.

The cost of divergent technical standards

Less than a year after the Community's new harmonization procedures were fully in place the Commission published a report outlining its estimates of the total cost of all fiscal, physical and technical barriers to trade within the EC. The report, *The European Challenge 1992: The Benefits of a Single Market*, was the first to attempt to quantify how much European companies were losing as a result of border controls, protectionist public procurement policies and divergent national product standards.

The report was compiled under the chairmanship of Paolo Cecchini, a special adviser to the Commission, and was based on a survey of 11,000 business executives, conducted by 15 companies of consultants, academics, economists and Commission personnel. The central conclusion of this unprecedented two-year study was that effective implementation of the White Paper Internal Market programme would save European industry about £130 billion, the equivalent of some 5% of the Community's gross domestic product. The precision of the report's estimates has been the subject of a heated dispute, but few have denied that they are pointing in the right direction.

In addition to demonstrating the cost of maintaining twelve separate markets the report also highlighted the opportunities for economic growth, job creation, reduced costs, improved productivity, increased competition, greater professional and business mobility and enhanced consumer choice that were there for the taking. 'Now we have the hard evidence, the confirmation of what those who are engaged in the building of Europe have always known: that the failure to achieve a single market has been costing European industry millions in unnecessary costs and opportunities,' Lord Cockfield said in his foreword. However, even more revealing than the overall estimated costs of market fragmentation was the report's examination of the costs of market fragmentation in specific areas, such as border and administrative red tape, public procurement and divergent technical standards in particular.

According to the Cecchini survey, divergent national technical standards were the second most important obstacle to the creation of the internal market after administrative formalities and border controls. The operation of some 100,000 different technical specifications across European industry meant that European companies were compelled to operate in a technical Tower of Babel, which was losing them billions of pounds because of duplicated product development, lost economies of

on to Rome, and who needed to keep in constant touch with head-quarters, would need three mobile telephones to do so.

During negotiations on technical standards for the second generation of mobile cellular telephones most European countries favoured the use of a narrow transmission band, while France and Germany proposed the adoption of the wide band. After months of difficult negotiations, France and Germany finally capitulated. The breakthrough was widely acknowledged to be unprecedented. However, the difficulty in arriving at common technical standards for the next generation of mobile cellular telephones showed the enormity of the task facing ETSI. Despite this success, even the most optimistic observers expect the standardization process to be slow and patchy, effectively ruling out the prospect of large-scale standardization in the telecommunications sector by 1992.

Technical standards as barriers to foreign trade

Shortly after the new technical standards organizations were in place, they were subject to many criticisms from abroad. American politicians in particular were concerned that one of the consequences of the new organizations would be European technical standards which would exclude US products from the European domestic market. Richard Mosbacher, President Bush's outspoken Commerce Secretary, accused the Commission of engaging in an ingenious form of protectionism through the standards-setting organizations. These fears were also expressed in a constant stream of US newspaper reports, which were given added credence by the House of Representatives Foreign Affairs Committee in its report on standards published in June 1988.

However, in a letter published in the *Financial Times* the same month, Roy MacDowell, the former President of the International Electrotechnical Commission (IEC), a Geneva-based organization responsible for drawing up worldwide electrotechnical standards, challenged this 'pessimistic US view'. MacDowell pointed out that most electrotechnical standards in Community countries were 'already based on standards written by the International Electrotechnical Commission'.

Furthermore, he pointed out that the IEC was a world organization whose standards are formulated by experts from all member countries—including the United States. America was therefore 'already in a position to participate directly in European harmonization through the international forum provided by the IEC'. Moreover, the Commission has given an undertaking to the world trade body, the General Agreement on Tariffs and Trade, to adopt existing world standards as the new European ones.

MacDowell added that an agreement also exists between the IEC and its sister Community organization, CENELEC, 'under the terms of which information on European standardization and harmonization activities is transmitted to non-European countries via the IEC headquarters in

Geneva'. As a result, the 'principles of openness and transparency' demanded by Secretary Mosbacher were already in operation.

The pharmaceuticals sector

As in the telecommunications sector, the creation of a single market for the European pharmaceuticals industry, worth some £20 billion a year, faces complex problems. So far, the Commission's attempts to reconcile the need for strict control on the quality, safety and efficacy of new drugs with industry's desire for more efficient drug-registration and sales-authorization procedures have not convinced industry officials or national authorities that the objective of creating an internal market for the pharmaceuticals sector will be realized by 1992. Under the present system a pharmaceuticals company wishing to introduce a new product into a particular market must submit it to the appropriate national registration authority, which is responsible for establishing whether the drug is safe and actually does what the manufacturers claim of it. However, because each member state has its own registration procedure, acquiring twelve separate approvals to market a new pharmaceutical product (each of which can take in excess of two years), this is a laborious and expensive process which takes up the time allowed for drug patent protection.

Furthermore, the major purchasers of pharmaceuticals in the EC are the state-owned health authorities, which exercise considerable influence on the price at which drugs are sold. The great variation in national public health authority pricing policies (which invariably discriminate in favour of domestic drug manufacturers) also have a direct influence on company profits. Removal of such barriers would save the European pharmaceuticals sector an estimated 1% of the industry's annual costs. The pharmaceuticals companies maintain that, on average, it takes ten years to develop a new drug at a cost of £50 million, and unless the Community is able to introduce uniform registration, market-authorization and pricing procedures they are sceptical of their ability to compete effectively with their foreign rivals in the race to produce the next generation of high-technology drugs which require increasingly heavy investment in research and development—the return on which is never guaranteed. However, in the wake of the Thalidomide tragedy in the 1960s most European governments introduced complex and time-consuming drug-testing procedures (for example, Britain's 1968 Medicines Act) to reassure public opinion about the safety of the drugs they were consuming. Such anxieties have since been heightened by the appalling side-effects of the anti-arthritic drug, Opren.

As part of its attempts to facilitate the free circulation of medicines the Commission has proposed the creation of a Central European Medicines Agency (similar to the US Food and Drug Administration) to be responsible for testing all new biotechnology products. This would have the merit of streamlining national drug registration and authorization procedures, while permitting any new biotechnology-derived drugs to go on sale throughout the Community once they had been given the European seal of approval. Some industry officials have, however, already expressed fears that a European drug-licensing authority could become too bureaucratic. In addition, the Commission has also proposed that national testing agencies be retained for the licensing of the more traditional new products, supported by the principle of mutual recognition of member states' registration and marketing requirements where possible, and arbitration by the central agency in the event of unresolvable national disputes where necessary. But while this element of the proposal has been designed to avoid the dangers of excessive bureaucracy, it seems almost calculated to arouse national anxieties over whether other member states' testing procedures are as effective as their own.

As far as other aspects of the programme are concerned, the Commission has already produced a draft directive on price controls which would require the national public health authorities to make their pricing systems more open, thereby giving pharmaceuticals companies more certainty about the price at which their products will eventually be sold. A major breakthrough came in December 1986 with the adoption of directives setting out market-authorization procedures for high-technology medicines. This was followed in December 1991 by an agreement to extend drug patents by five years, thereby boosting pharmaceutical companies' profits and providing added incentives for new research. The Commission is still consulting the pharmaceuticals industry and the national regulatory bodies about their preference for a new EC drug regulatory system. The issue remains sensitive.

The construction sector

Contrary to popular perceptions, the European construction products industry is a major influence in cross-frontier trade. In 1985 the Community market for construction products was valued at around £70 billion, but the prospects for substantial future growth are tarnished by the enormous variations in customer specifications for building materials such as bricks, glass, plaster, concrete, aggregates, timber and steel. The cost of market fragmentation has been put at some £55 million a year, while their removal could generate £1 billion in extra business.

In Britain, the construction and construction products industry is already a highly competitive sector, where profit margins are tight. Consequently, British companies are more likely to find new business in Europe than Continental companies are likely to find in Britain. Leading British construction and construction product companies, notably Trafalgar House, Wimpey, Laing and Tarmac, have already established their presence in Continental Europe with a view to exploiting the potential offered by the creation of the internal market. Nonetheless, the British construction industry appears to be lagging behind some of its European rivals, particularly in France, where overall preparations for a European construction industry without frontiers appear to be considerably more advanced.

Unlike most industries, construction is both a service and a product. Prospective clients have an understandable preference for using construction companies with whom they are familiar and in whom they have confidence. This puts a high premium on having a physical presence in a given market and acquiring familiarity with the local environment. Such efforts would be to little avail if a construction company, having established itself in a particular market, was effectively prohibited from operating in it because the technical specifications of the construction products being used were unacceptable to the regulatory authority of the host country. However, the experience of one French company, which had to fight for five years to obtain the technical certification to sell its steel girders in Germany, demonstrated that such obstacles are all too frequent.

As in other major industrial sectors, technical specifications and product certification procedures are used to keep competition in the construction sector from other member states to an absolute minimum. The Cecchini report even claimed that the 'so called inherent divergencies in customer requirements may be largely a case of national tastes determined by national regulations'.

The Internal Market White Paper, in accordance with the harmonization and mutual recognition procedures outlined above, proposes a basic framework of European technical standards for construction products, in accordance with mutually accepted criteria of stability, safety and health. The standards organization (CEN) is currently drawing up a European code of technical standards for the construction industry, and although it is clear that the new standards will not be ready by 1992, the Commission has agreed to accept and enforce the mutual recognition of current national standards in the interim.

The foodstuffs sector

A similar approach has been used in the foodstuffs sector. Here the Commission's strategy involves the adoption of a series of general framework directives, governing the areas of additives, flavouring, labelling, packaging, public inspection and irradiation. These directives will establish the broad principles to which national food laws must adhere, leaving the details to be worked out largely by the Commission and the European Food Industry Association (CIAA) in a series of more specific foodstuffs directives.

The strategy is designed to capitalize on a succession of rulings by the European Court of Justice, notably the 1987 one against Greece and West Germany for prohibiting imports of beer that did not conform to national 'beer purity' laws and the 1988 ruling against Italy for prohibiting imports of pasta made from soft rather than hard wheat. The judgments have established that if a food product is legally manufactured and sold in one member state it can be manufactured and sold in all.

The new approach, as in so many other areas, represents a significant departure from the past. The old system of food standards harmonization focused on the specific composition of foodstuffs (known as recipe law) on a case-by-case basis. Attempts to lay down recipe law for particular foodstuffs gave rise to the popular misconception that Brussels' bureaucrats were trying to do away with the British sausage. Indeed, the BBC television series *Yes Minister* even had them trying to rename the British banger an 'emulsified high-fat offal tube'. The fact that British pork sausages can contain as little as 65% meat, defined as animal flesh, fat, skin, rind, gristle and sinew, while German sausages must contain 100% meat, defined as animal flesh only, seemed less important than the apparent assault on the traditional sausage as a symbol of Britain's national sovereignty. In any event, recipe law proved completely unworkable. In the field of additives alone there are an estimated 40,000 applications, making regulation of each a practical impossibility. On the principle that it is better to delegate as much harmonization to the private sector as possible, the CIAA, composed of the various trade bodies of the European foodstuffs industry, is now responsible for compiling compositional standards. As much research on foodstuff additives has already been carried out there is no need for the CIAA to start from the beginning, and the Commission has restricted its legislative activity to the protection of public health, consumer information, fair trading and public inspection. This change of direction represents a modest victory for Britain, which has persistently argued for the abolition of recipe law.

There is agreement on the immediate horizon on a host of quality and packaging regulations for the food and drink industry, including common procedures for verifying the quality of food imported from other member states (particularly important in the wake of growing public concern over salmonella and listeria poisoning), along with common rules on irradiated food and the labelling of health foods. The internal market for foodstuffs, excluding labelling, is therefore all but complete.

In March 1990 the Council of Ministers reached agreement on a new nutrition-labelling directive, which requires manufacturers and processors to specify the nutritional content of packaged foodstuffs where nutritional claims are being made for the product in question. The objective of the legislation is to provide consumers with an accurate picture of what is in a given foodstuff, and prevent manufacturers from providing only a partial account. As a result, manufacturers will no longer be able to say, for example, that crisps are high in fibre and ignore the fact that they are also high in fat and salt.

The implications of the successful creation of an internal market for the European foodstuffs industry (which now looks more optimistic than at any time since the White Paper was launched) are far-reaching. Small manufacturers, unless they are able to develop small national niche markets on a European scale, can expect much competition from their European counterparts. Many family food concerns, which owe their existence to the fragmentation of the European market and who are unable to form cross-border alliances, are likely to fail. Larger companies, who will benefit from the economies of scale that the abolition of trade barriers will produce, should find themselves facing the prospect of new markets emerging throughout the Community.

With a large European market now on the horizon it seems almost inevitable that foodstuffs manufacturers, processors and distributors will follow the trilingual labelling precedent set by the French manufacturer of Benedicta Mayonnaise, whose jars of salad dressing are already available in local supermarkets with a single French, British and Dutch label —assuming, of course, that the Commission keeps labelling requirements to a minimum. In the restructuring that is likely to follow the opening up of national markets some smaller companies may fall by the wayside, but consumers will benefit from lower prices brought about by increased competition and a significant expansion of the variety of food products available for consumption.

Concern remains, however, that the failure to specify what kind of products, and in what quantity, should go into particular foodstuffs, may force manufacturers to substitute cheaper ingredients in an effort to fend off competition from unscrupulous rivals. After all, how many consumers will have the time to read the various lists of ingredients used in competing products of, for example, apple pies, cream cheese or smoked ham? In an effort to prevent such substitution Commission officials have been under pressure to extend the Appellation d'Origine Contrôlée stamp used to prevent the fraudulent sale of wine to traditional and gourmet foodstuffs, although there appears little prospect of this happening at present.

Other sectors

The White Paper envisages applying the same strategy to every sector fragmented by divergent national technical standards, whether in the car, civil engineering or chemical industries. The same approach has also been applied to sectors outside manufacturing, including public procurement, air, sea and road transport, veterinary and plant controls, the free movement of workers and professionals, capital movements and financial services.

The White Paper singles out the liberalization of financial services, such as insurance policies, mortgages, consumer credit and unit trusts, as a potentially major source of economic growth and job creation. The Commission's proposals for deregulation are based on the co-ordination of national rules governing the authorization of companies wishing to operate in the financial services sector. The proposed Community regulatory system is to be based on the principle of 'home country control'. Supervisory responsibilities will lie with the appropriate authorities in the member state in which the company is based, regardless of which member state the company is operating in. Ironically, in most countries it is the governments of the member states who are pressing hard for deregulation, often in the face of bitter resistance from financial service institutions, such as those in Germany, who are very comfortable in their protected national markets and do not relish the prospect of competition from across the border.

Business and the environment

The environmental awareness that gathered pace during the 1980s assisted by a series of regional environmental disasters such as Bhopal, Chernobyl and the accidental dumping of 30 million tonnes of chemicals into the Rhine, the more global consequences of acid rain, the depletion of the ozone layer and the greenhouse effect have given environmental issues a political urgency that was unimaginable ten years earlier. After more than two centuries of unrestrained industrial activity, increased public anxiety about quality-of-life issues such as air purity and drinking water has forced politicians into counting the cost of the wholesale pollution of the land, sea and atmosphere. Although the new European environmental protection programme is in its formative stages, it is already clear that the clean-up effort will cost governments, businesses and consumers billions of pounds. The Clean Air Act, which was passed in 1990 by the US Congress, for example, is estimated to cost American industry $25 billion a year. The European Commission's new environmental protection programme is expected to dwarf that figure.

While environmental considerations were not seen to play a prominent role in the early stages of the internal market programme, they rapidly moved towards the centre of the political stage. Under Carlo Ripa di Meana, the Italian Environment Commissioner, there are now more proposals for legislation in the environmental arena than any other single sector of Community activity. An early indication of the newly found commitment to the environment came during the gathering of EC heads of state in their Dublin summit meeting in June 1990. Issuing a declaration on the environment, the Council said: 'The natural environment which forms the life support system for our planet is gravely at risk . . . the continuation of life could no longer be assured were recent trends to proceed unchallenged.' The declaration was widely seen as the first official attempt to reconcile the objective of increased economic growth contained in the internal market programme with the ostensibly antagonistic goal of sustainable economic development.

Prior to the Dublin declaration, the Community's commitment to protecting the environment, while far from negligible (witness the decision to reduce sulphur emissions from power stations by 60% from 1980 levels by the year 2003) fell far short of what many in the scientific community felt was required. The original Treaty of Rome makes no reference to the environment, and the Community's first environmental action programme did not begin until 1972. It was, however, the Single European Act which gave the Commission the legislative authority to take the initiative under Article 130, which stipulates that 'action by the Community . . . shall be based on the principles that preventive action should be taken, that environmental damage should as a priority be rectified at source, and that the polluter should pay'. Shortly after the Act was ratified, Jacques Delors, the President of the European Commission, remarked dryly: 'This victory went unnoticed in 1985–86.'

These three principles—preventive action, damage rectified at source, and the polluter pays—are in the process of transforming the face of European agriculture, industry and the consumption habits of tens of millions of its citizens. Between 1972 and 1991 some 100 separate pieces of environmental legislation were enacted, and the Commission is currently engaged in drawing up its fifth and most ambitious environmental action programme. This includes the unprecedented use of economic and fiscal instruments, such as taxes on carbon consumption, to lay the foundations of what is becoming known as the 'ecological market economy'. In short, the externalities of modern economic and industrial processes, such as the consumption of finite resources, waste, pollution and environmental destruction, will increasingly be factored into individual product costs.

British businesses received a taste of the new environmental regulatory regime following the introduction of the 1990 Environmental Protection Act. The legislation introduced two new pollution control systems, the first, enforced by HM Inspectorate of Pollution, imposing stringent controls on the land, sea and air emissions of some 5,000 industrial processes; and the second, enforced by local authorities, regulating the air emissions of some 27,000 less harmful industrial processes. Many British businesses are clearly struggling to cope with the new environmental regulations, which often involve large-scale structural change and substantial additional costs for large and small businesses alike. Unlike traditional end-of-pipe environmental remedies, the new regulations frequently entail a complete reassessment of production processes, from purchase of raw materials to the sale of finished products. Moreover, more exacting legislation is expected in the years ahead, and, as Michael Heseltine, the Environment Secretary, warned in May 1991, companies which fail to comply with the new environmental standards and take advantage of the opportunities presented by what he called the 'green renaissance' could face corporate catastrophe.

In one sense, because of the increase in popular support for environmental protection initiatives, the task of incorporating environmental considerations into all other sectors of Community activity is easier in the early 1990s than it was in the middle of the 1980s. Indeed, in a veiled comment on the former reluctance of some member states to support such initiatives, notably Britain and France, one recent Commission publication noted that: 'The last couple of years have been marked by a distinct jockeying for position on the diplomatic front with hitherto reluctant member states keen to be seen taking the lead on new initiatives'. That transformation is due, in large part, to the series of international conferences, such as the Vienna Convention on the Ozone Layer, the Montreal Protocol on Chlorofluorocarbons (CFCs) and the Basle Convention on the Movement of Hazardous Waste, which put environmental questions firmly on the international diplomatic agenda along with the great questions of war and peace. Now that national governments are eager to impress their domestic electorates with their commitment to environmental protection, the days when governments could deal with environmental issues under the heading 'globalony' have long since passed.

In another sense, however, it has become much more complex. One of the greatest problems faced by the Commission is preventing unilateral environmental protection initiatives by the 'dark green' countries such as Denmark and Germany from being opposed by 'light green' ones such as Spain and Portugal on the grounds that such measures constitute a new form of non-tariff barrier. New German laws, for example, will make it mandatory for the European packaging industry to collect and recycle virtually every box, can, bottle, tube and container sold in the Federal Republic. They have caused consternation among other member states. At the same time, the Commission is under constant pressure not to dilute its legislative programme to the lowest common denominator in an attempt to preserve some form of face saving by artificial green consensus.

Although the Commission's fifth environmental action programme is being finalized, the broad principles of the initiative, along with the principal areas of concern, are clear. In the five categories of concern—energy efficiency, waste management, air pollution, water purity and transport —almost 100 separate directives have been implemented or planned. In the energy conservation sector alone, some 14 legislative proposals are in the pipeline and designed to reduce energy consumption as the single most effective means of stabilizing carbon dioxide emissions—one of the principal causes of the greenhouse effect—at 1990 levels by the year 2000. The measures range from labelling the energy consumption of household appliances such as refrigerators, washing machines, tumble driers, ovens and lighting equipment (enabling consumers to make informed choices about the energy consumption of household implements) to the introduction of taxes on energy or carbon, known as a pollution added tax (PAT).

In the field of waste management, more than 20 directives have been implemented or are under consideration. Solving Europe's waste problem is one of the most formidable tasks facing the Community. According to Commission estimates, member states generate some two billion tonnes of waste a year, 150 million tonnes of which comes from industry and about 30 million tonnes of which is hazardous. Much of the remainder comes from household refuse and agriculture. With 60% of household waste dumped in landfill sites, 33% incinerated and 7% composted, there is already great pressure on existing disposal outlets. In many member states the infrastructure for disposing of and treating human waste is inadequate or even non-existent. In Italy, for example, 48% of the 1,580 sewage treatment plants no longer function, while in Spain, 80% of municipalities are without any treatment works. Moreover, contemporary intensive farming techniques have created a situation in some countries, such as the Netherlands, where the volume of animal slurry now far exceeds the soil's ability to absorb it.

Waste management directives have been drawn up to cover the entire spectrum of waste products, from the disposal of batteries to the removal and treatment of sewage, and the regulation of landfill sites to control of emissions from incinerators. The directives will introduce severe penalties for uncontrolled disposals, incentives for recycling and the use of cleaner technologies, and stringent regulations on the shipment of toxic and hazardous goods across frontiers. The Community's regional development funds will be used to help lay the sewers, build the waste-water treatment and incineration facilities needed to bring the poorer regions up to the same level of the more affluent regions, and help make the Community self-sufficient in the modern technologies of waste management.

No less than 24 directives have been adopted or are under discussion in the field of air pollution, including the total phasing out of ozone-depleting CFCs and halons by 1997, and a series of anti-pollution restrictions on emissions from cars, lorries and combustion plants. Few issues have, however, generated more column inches than the Commission's decision in 1989 to haul Britain in front of the European Court of Justice for its failure to comply with the directive on the purity of drinking water, one of the first pieces of legislation targeted against water pollution. The fact that France and Belgium were already before the court for similar offences, and that Germany and Luxembourg soon followed, failed to receive similar prominence in the British press. The drinking-water directive is one of 12 measures aimed at cleaning up Europe's rivers, lakes, beaches and seas. In an attempt to bring about a wholesale improvement in the aquatic environment, it would prohibit the discharge of untreated sewage and impose restrictions on agricultural production to prevent fertilizer nitrates seeping into the water table.

With traffic volumes forecast to increase considerably in the Community during the next decade, threatening to neutralize the reductions in carbon dioxide emissions obtained from imposing restrictions on other areas of economic activity, the transport policies of member states can be expected to come under increasing scrutiny from the Commission. Altogether, some 14 directives have been adopted or proposed. They are designed to encourage more environmentally benign forms of transport, particularly rail, and to reduce the consumption of oil and the production of carbon dioxide by harmonizing taxes on petrol, diesel and other fuels. In addition, initiatives such as the 1988 Environmental Impacts Assessment Directive, aimed at integrating ecological awareness into the planning stages of all agricultural, industrial, transport and regional development projects in the member states, could make it much harder for governments to destroy large tracts of countryside for new motorway and trunk road schemes. In October 1991, for example, Ripa di Meana, the Environment Commissioner, initiated legal proceedings against Britain for allegedly failing to comply with the directive on seven key construction projects, including the extension of the M3 through Twyford Down in Hampshire and the proposed East London River Crossing, which threatens the last ancient woodland in London.

However, while few could deny that Brussels has set about cultivating a new awareness of environmental issues, sceptics have been quick to point out the fundamental contradictions between the Commission's determination to accelerate economic growth and its environmental initiatives. Quite simply, the internal market will create more pollution —not less—and there is a widespread fear that, apart from a few nods in the right direction, little of substance will change. A report on 1992 and the environment compiled by Commission officials in 1991 noted that: 'Electricity generation and transport are major sources of air pollution, together accounting for around 60% of sulphur dioxide and 80% of nitrogen oxides.' It also pointed out that: 'Notwithstanding the favourable impacts which can be expected to result from the implementation of existing environmental policies, the growth impact of the Internal Market is likely to cause atmospheric emissions of sulphur dioxide and nitrogens of oxide to increase respectively by 8% to 9% and 12% to 14% by 2010'. The report proved so controversial that the Commission refused to endorse it.

Two recent developments, however, promise to strengthen the Commission's legislative programme for protecting the environment. The first involves a proposal to extend the qualified majority voting procedure to environmental initiatives. This received approval from the Council of Ministers and was incorporated into the treaty reforms agreed by EC heads of state at the summit meeting in Maastricht in December 1991. Unanimity will, however, be retained on all environmental issues dealing with taxation (such as the proposed carbon tax), town and country planning, land use, water and energy. The second involves the creation of a European Environmental Agency (EEA). There have been arguments over whether the EEA's role should be confined to the collection of scientific data or extended to embrace the enforcement and monitoring powers granted to atomic energy inspectors under the Euratom Treaty. The Commission is eager to follow the precedent set by Euratom, although the Council of Ministers remains adamantly opposed. The debate over inspection powers, however, is likely to remain somewhat academic until a location for the agency has been decided, and this is not expected to happen before the member states resolve their long-running dispute over the seat of other EC institutions. Unfortunately, the Maastricht summit highlighted yet again the Community's apparent inability to come to grips with this issue. Despite mounting pressure to agree on a location for the new agency, the French government insisted that Strasbourg must first be formally acknowledged as the home of the European Parliament.

Checklist of changes

- The traditional case-by-case approach to the harmonization of different product technical standards has been replaced by legislative harmonization where necessary and mutual recognition where possible.
- All essential technical harmonization measures will be brought into force by majority voting.
- These legislative measures will stipulate an obligatory minimum of health and safety standards, conformity with which will guarantee manufacturers the right of access to the markets of other member states.
- Legislative technical harmonization will be complemented by systematic implementation of the principle of mutual recognition for non-essential product standards, reinforced by the 1979 Cassis de Dijon ruling.
- The task of establishing European-wide technical standards has been allocated to the new European standards-setting organizations such as CEN, CENELEC and ETSI.
- The traditional system of national product testing and certification procedures will also be subject to mutual recognition.
- Under the directive governing mutual information procedures, the European Commission has the power to prevent member states from implementing any new technical standard likely to create additional barriers to trade.
- The White Paper programme calls for the introduction of cross-frontier competition in the supply of terminal equipment by 1990, the end of national monopolies in the provision of value-added services by the end of 1989 and some degree of tariff price harmonization by 1992.
- National drug registration and authorization procedures will be

streamlined with the introduction of either a central drug-licensing authority or mandatory Community-wide testing procedures, along with mutual recognition of member states' registration and marketing requirements.

- National public health authorities will be required to introduce more open drug pricing policies.
- Essential technical standards will be laid down for all other sectors, including the construction, car, civil engineering, and chemical industries. The same approach has also been adopted for sectors outside manufacturing, notably financial services and foodstuffs.
- Nearly 100 directives are expected, covering a wide range of environmental issues in the fields of energy conservation, waste management, air and water pollution, transport and the transport and treatment of toxic and hazardous substances.

5 TERRORISM, CRIME AND ILLEGAL IMMIGRATION
Internal frontiers and external borders

Complementing the European Community's attempt to demolish internal barriers to the free movement of goods, people, capital and labour is a parallel effort to strengthen its external frontier. Once internal restrictions are removed, many of the functions carried out by trade, security, customs and immigration officials will have to be transferred from individual internal frontiers to the Community's external border. The early years of the internal market programme were marked by a preoccupation with whether the new external barrier would result in greater protectionist pressures towards increased competition from non-Community countries. Attention has since shifted, however, to the more sensitive questions about whether the Community's defences against terrorism, crime and illegal immigration, are sufficiently effective or excessively stringent.

The IRA bomb which blew up the Visitors' Gallery at the London Stock Exchange in July 1990 and the car bomb which killed Ian Gow, the Conservative MP for Eastbourne, ten days later, were disturbing reminders of the apparent ability of terrorist gangs to operate throughout the Community with impunity. Record increases in the volume of drugs seized at Britain's ports and airports were seen as a testimony to the alarming growth of the international drug-trafficking trade. Finally, the increase in the number of residence applications from immigrants and refugees provoked bitter debates in many national parliaments over the effectiveness of existing immigration and asylum policies. Should the EC relax these policies or was Europe full up?

The promise of free movement

One of the main benefits of 1992 is the promise it holds out of free movement—the fulfilment of the dream expressed in 1951 by Ernest Bevin, Foreign Secretary in the Attlee government after the war, that one day he would be 'able to take a ticket at Victoria Station and go anywhere I damn well please'. Conversely, one of the main fears about 1992—expressed most forcefully in Britain but not only in Britain—is that it will create 'an internal market' for terrorism, crime and illegal immigration. In her forceful speech at the College of Europe in Bruges in September 1988 Mrs Thatcher supported 1992 in so far as it opened up markets, widened consumer choice and encouraged enterprise, but declared it to be a 'matter of plain common sense' that frontier controls could not be totally abolished if citizens were to be protected.

This demand for the retention of frontier controls contradicts the undertakings contained in Article 8a of the Single European Act, which defines the internal market specifically as an 'area without internal frontiers'. Andreas Papandreou, Greek Prime Minister and the then President of the Council of Ministers, accused Thatcher of 'putting in question, unilaterally, an Act which binds the Twelve by validated international treaty'. The Act does have a loophole, in the form of a General Declaration allowing states to 'take such steps as they consider necessary' to prevent drug smuggling, terrorism and illegal immigration. However, the Declaration is subordinate to the overall aim of abolition of frontiers, and EC leaders agreed to avoid national controls by laying down 'common measures' on visas, immigration and extradition while also intensifying police co-operation throughout the EC.

Under the 1992 process, in other words, as agreed in negotiations for the Single European Act, the apprehension of criminals and terrorists is provided for through the strengthening of external frontiers, European-wide police and intelligence co-operation, and common visa and immigration policies on the grounds that most arrests do not, in any case, take place at air- or seaports or border crossings. Where they do, the criminals have often in reality been tracked for miles through police co-operation (for example, from Spain or Italy to a Channel port) and the frontier is simply a convenient location for a police or customs operation.

As the impact of the Thatcher speech in Bruges demonstrated, the abolition of frontiers arouses fears of threats ranging from gunmen to rabies, and raises directly the issue of national sovereignty. It may be a mistake, however, to conclude that a majority of people therefore oppose the abolition of borders, provided that measures against crime are adequate. No aspect of the internal market programme has captured the imagination of European public opinion as much as the proposal to abolish the Community's internal frontiers and replace them with a single external one. In an age marked by ever-increasing amounts of intra-Community tourism and travel the prospect of being able to move from Britain to France, Germany, Greece or Spain without obligatory travel documents, inspection at internal frontiers and time-consuming delays is perhaps the single most tangible benefit of the Community's economic integration process. In a survey published in May 1991 by Euro-Barometer, the EC's public opinion research organization, most people in the Community believed that by the year 2000 they will be able to travel freely and work anywhere in an enlarged EC, be paid in a single currency and be defended by a common EC military force.

There can be little doubt that the Commission has been emboldened in its determination to press ahead with the abolition of internal frontiers by the decision of the so-called Schengen Group—the Benelux countries, Germany and France—to introduce their own border-free zone by 1990 —regardless of progress among the Twelve. The Schengen Agreement was finally signed in June 1990, although it will not go into effect until ratified by all five national parliaments, probably in the middle of 1992. The Commission clearly regards the Schengen initiative as the laboratory for its own proposals for a frontier-free Europe, and is confident that its anticipated success will help to force the more reluctant member states into following the Schengen example.

In February 1989, for example, Martin Bangemann, the Commissioner responsible for the internal market, announced the Commission's intention to press ahead with the introduction of common policies governing extradition, the right of asylum and the granting of visas. Bangemann's extraordinary claim that the entire edifice could be in place within six months seemed reckless in the extreme, but he also used the occasion to hint that the Commission might be prepared to accept the introduction of spot checks at frontier posts to replace systematic border controls, which observers in Brussels interpreted as an attempt to win Britain over to the controversial scheme.

Moving from one member state to another as one moves from Kent to Essex or Yorkshire to Lincolnshire is also a major attraction for European companies trading across national frontiers. Industry has been compelled to shoulder an immense burden as a consequence of the delays, red tape, form filling, and transport and handling charges associated with the maintenance of frontier formalities. The European Commission argues forcibly that the complete removal of these physical barriers to trade will not only reduce costs and stimulate competition but will also encourage many smaller firms (who have traditionally been inhibited from expanding beyond national borders because of the costs involved) to seek new markets throughout the Community.

The Commission's proposals have met much criticism. The fear that any attempt to abolish internal frontier controls to facilitate free movement for business executives, labour and tourists will have the potentially disastrous side-effect of laying the foundations of an internal market for terrorists, drug traffickers, criminals and dangerous diseases such as rabies has been most commonly expressed in Britain, Ireland, Denmark and Greece. Moreover, the difficulties posed by the pressures for increased immigration along the Community's external borders, particularly the anticipated rise in immigration from Eastern Europe following the collapse of the Communist dictatorships, will also have to be dealt with. Some observers fear that increased immigration from the East could lead to the displacement of existing migrant communities inside the Community, leading to a different kind of Fortress Europe, one in which European peoples are given preferential access to jobs and houses.

During a debate in the European Parliament in December 1985, shortly after publication of the Internal Market White Paper, the basic arguments of the anti- and pro-abolitionists were stated in terms that have been repeated in much the same form ever since.

Bob Cryer, the Labour MEP for Sheffield, challenged Lord Cockfield by saying: 'Would the Commissioner accept, with his well-known enthusiasm for the removal of all frontiers, that neither he nor anybody else has produced any solution to the question which keeps being raised . . . how one can control increased drug smuggling, how one can control rabies and how one can control the spread of plant diseases if customs supervision and frontiers are entirely removed as he wishes?' In his customary sardonic manner, Lord Cockfield replied: 'It was made clear in the White Paper that there were a number of problems, particularly in the field of terrorism and drug trafficking, which would require careful consideration before the full White Paper proposals are implemented.' The Commissioner then went on to give Cryer a lesson in how to work from first principles.

> If, for example, you were considering how to deal with the drug problem and assumed that you had no frontiers to start with, would you end up by saying that the right solution to the drug problem was the creation of national frontiers? I very much doubt whether you would. In fact most of the drug seizures are not made at national frontiers at all, nor are they made as a result of routine checks on every single person who goes from one country to another. I agree that these are very important problems, they need to be studied, and they need to be studied with an open mind.

The Commission's proposals, in fact, offer the basis for a fundamental transformation in the way the Community organizes its defences against terrorists, drug traffickers, criminals and plant and animal diseases. However, Britain is still looking for a 'balance of advantage' between free movement and control of crime.

The case for the abolition of internal frontier controls

Despite the abolition of customs duties and quantitative restrictions imposed on intra-Community trade by individual member states that followed the completion of the single external tariff in 1968, customs posts have remained a feature of national frontiers, even though they have been largely deprived of the function that gave them their name. Because there are no longer intra-Community customs duties on goods and services at internal frontiers, customs posts no longer really exist within the EC, even if the signs suggest otherwise. What are still often referred to as customs posts are in fact frontier control posts; they are only customs posts for goods entering member states from outside the

Community. Duty on alcohol and tobacco, for example, are excise, not custom duties.

The White Paper describes internal frontier controls as the most visible example of the continued division of the European Community into twelve national segments. Concomitantly, their removal would be the clearest sign of the integration of the member states into a genuine single market. The need to remove these internal frontier controls does not arise simply out of any idealistic or aesthetic sentiment. Rather, it stems from the practical necessity of stimulating economic growth by removing all physical barriers to trade as part of the Commission's overall strategy of making European industry more competitive in world markets.

According to Cecchini's report, the cost of these frontier controls is intolerably high, from both the perspective of the companies who have to go through them and the governments who have to administer them. The report estimates that some 25% of company profits are taken up by frontier control-related costs and delays, the equivalent of 2% of the value of each trans-frontier consignment of goods, which works out at roughly £6 billion every year. Frontier controls were identified by business executives as the single greatest obstacle to the expansion of intra-Community trade and a crippling burden on the smaller companies. Moreover, they cost Community governments an estimated £670 million a year in taxpayers' money to administer. The report also estimated that their removal could be worth around £10.5 billion in new trading opportunities, the equivalent of about 3% of the present value of intra-Community trade.

The Commission clearly shares the concerns of member states regarding the growth of terrorism, drug trafficking and major crime, and the role played by internal frontier controls in attempting to control these problems. However, the White Paper insists that:

> Frontier controls are by no means the only or most effective measures in this regard. If the objective of abolishing all internal frontier controls is to be met, alternative means of protection will need to be found or, where they exist, strengthened.

It accepts that many of the proposed changes will present difficulties for member states, and time will be needed for the necessary adjustments to be made. But it is quite adamant that such difficulties 'should not be allowed permanently to frustrate the achievement of the greater progress . . .'.

The White Paper then goes on to list all the internal areas in which common policies need to be developed, such as indirect taxation, plant and veterinary controls, the movement of individuals and the collection of trade statistics. Focusing on the movement of individuals, it points out that most of the Commission's initiatives (notably the introduction of the European passport) 'have been aimed at making checks at internal frontiers more flexible as they cannot be abolished altogether until, in line with the concerns expressed by the European Council, adequate safeguards are introduced against terrorism and drugs'. Meanwhile, the Commission envisages the gradual introduction of separate channels for Community citizens at sea- and airports, just as we already have for British nationals re-entering Britain at Gatwick or Heathrow, and the abolition of systematic controls over departures to other member states. Metal detectors at airports would remain in place, and member states would retain the right to re-introduce systematic frontier controls in the event of an emergency.

Crime and detection across frontiers

Turning to the external areas in which common policies need to be developed, the White Paper outlines a programme for the approximation of national legislation governing public security, illegal immigration, the possession of firearms, and visa and extradition policy, all of which will be enforced at the Community's external border. By 1992 the Commission hopes to arrive at the situation in which individuals can travel freely from one member state to another without having to undergo systematic checks on entry.

What lies behind the Commission's proposals, in addition to the attempt to reduce the costs borne by companies involved in intra-Community trade and the irritations endured by Community citizens travelling from one member state to another, is a recognition that terrorism, gun running, drug trafficking and major crime have long ceased to be national problems. As challenges to the fabric of both political and civil society everywhere in the Community, logic and reason would suggest that they are best dealt with on a Community-wide basis.

Furthermore, there is only a limited benefit to be obtained from effective frontier controls around Britain if British armed forces personnel on the Continent remain vulnerable to terrorist attacks. The continued fragmentation of member state policies in these areas works to the advantage of the terrorist, the drug trafficker and the major criminal. What the Community needs is a strict external frontier to act as the first line of defence against these organizations and individuals in the first place, backed up internally by increased co-operation between national law-enforcement and intelligence organizations. Such co-operation is already responsible for the great majority of terrorist apprehensions and confiscations of drug consignments, long before they get to internal frontier controls.

Addressing a London audience in November 1986, Lord Cockfield emphasized this point:

The way to deal with these problems is not simply to retreat behind

national frontiers, to man the barricades against our fellow European
citizens . . . There is no *a priori* reason to suppose that reinforcing
the internal frontiers of the Community as we know them today
is likely to prove the most effective way of dealing with these
problems. And in so far as—inevitably—it obstructs the
objective of creating a Europe without frontiers, it carries a heavy
cost to trade, to industry, and ultimately to all our citizens . . . There
are no customs officers on Hadrian's Wall, or immigration officials
manning Offa's Dyke. That is what our ambition is to create.

Police and intelligence co-operation: the Trevi Group

The attempt to improve co-ordination between national police forces pre-
dates the White Paper by a decade. Although the Treaty of Rome does
not provide for measures designed to combat terrorism, drug trafficking
and major crime, the Council of Ministers, meeting in Trevi, Italy, in
December 1975, recognized the growing necessity of improving co-
operation between the interior and justice departments of member states.
Ministers agreed to set up three groups to deal with terrorism, drug
trafficking and crime, which were supplemented with a fourth in October
1986 dealing with illegal immigration. Strictly speaking, the initiative,
known as the Trevi Group or Trevi Process, exists quite independently
of Community institutions, although for convenience it is often referred
to as if it were a normal function of the Council of Ministers.

Despite a promising start, Interior and Justice Ministers did not meet
again for almost ten years. However, as soon as Middle East conflicts
began to spill over into the streets of European capitals the Community
was forced to react. Since 1986, Interior and Justice Ministers, senior
police and intelligence officers, and forensic scientists have been meeting
in secret with increasing frequency to exchange information and ideas on
how to stem the rising tide of international crime. These exchanges have
been instrumental in breaking down traditional professional and national
rivalries and laying the basis of trust and mutual respect, without which
any attempt to increase cross-frontier co-operation would simply foun-
der. At the same time, increasing concern is being expressed by civil
liberties organizations about the activities of the Trevi Group, which are
not subject to traditional parliamentary controls.

Following a series of bombing outrages in Paris in 1986 by the so-called
Solidarity Committee for Arab Prisoners, who were attempting to intimidate the French authorities into releasing three Arab terrorists, an emergency Trevi Group meeting was held in London at the request of Paris
in September 1986, with Douglas Hurd, then Home Secretary, acting as
President of the Council of Ministers. The meeting produced an agreement to improve the flow of intelligence and information, develop a
co-ordinated response between member states, identify and close the
loopholes through which terrorists gain entry into the Community and

tackle the political problems which create terrorist violence in the first place.

At the end of the meeting Hurd described terrorists as being increasingly members of organizations which operate across national frontiers, who have access to substantial sums of money, arms, equipment, technical knowledge and training, which was forcing governments and their counter-terrorist agencies to organize themselves on a Community-wide basis. 'These new measures will help us to target terrorists' movements, supplies of money, arms and equipment, so that we can harry and disrupt them,' and would be followed up with further practical measures, the minister said.

In October 1986 Community Interior and Justice Ministers met to discuss the security implications of the Commission's proposals to abolish internal frontiers by 1992, in which the Commission was represented by Lord Cockfield. They agreed to launch a concerted assault against terrorists, drug traffickers, criminals and, for the first time, illegal immigrants, while simultaneously pledging themselves to the goal of free movement around the Community for all law-abiding citizens. The ministers agreed to consider the possibility of harmonizing member state visa and right of asylum policies, increase co-operation against the abuse of passports and exchange information gathered at spot checks on internal frontiers. Hurd publicly stated that the objectives of allowing free movement of Community nationals, while restricting criminals, were not irreconcilable. However, he then went on to insist that Britain would continue to conduct a full examination of every passport, reflecting Britain's actual but as yet unstated conviction that they were indeed irreconcilable.

Aspirations for closer and more effective action between member states appeared to receive a setback towards the end of the month, when Sir Geoffrey Howe, the then Foreign Secretary, demanded a united Community response against Syria, following evidence indicating Syrian complicity in the attempted bombing in April of an El Al airliner at Heathrow by Nezar Hindawi. The request was initially greeted with a mixture of caution, scepticism and outright hostility. After much agonizing, the Community, with the exception of Greece, agreed to a ban on all new arms sales and high-level visits to Syria, a review of Syrian embassy and consular staffs, and tighter security for the national carrier, Syrianair. Although Sir Geoffrey put a brave face on the agreement, he had clearly wanted much tougher action—much earlier.

The subject was also high on the agenda at the EC summit meeting in London that December. The meeting produced a communiqué committing member states to three principles: no concessions to terrorists or their sponsors, solidarity in preventing terrorism and bringing the perpetrators to justice and (in a veiled reference to the delay in reacting to the Hindawi affair) a concerted response to terrorist attacks. It was also revealed that the Trevi Group had produced a secret document listing those countries and organizations responsible for recent terrorist outrages and who continued to pose a serious threat to public security in the Community. Again, however, Greece refused to sign—a position that was modified substantially after the terrorist attack on the *City of Poros* cruiser in July 1988, which resulted in the death of 11 passengers.

Although the member states were moving in the direction of increased co-operation the increase in kidnappings in Beirut had placed an enormous strain on the Community's declared commitment to adopt a united front in the face of terrorist threats. During 1987, France and Germany, both of whom held known terrorists believed to be responsible for a variety of hijackings and assassinations, were under pressure to release them in exchange for their own nationals held hostage in Beirut. Throughout 1987–8 there were repeated reports that the United States, Germany and France had made significant diplomatic and financial concessions to secure the release of their hostages from Lebanon. Nonetheless, despite the temptation to waver from the principles outlined in the December communiqué it was becoming clearer that the only effective response to terrorism, whether internal or external, was a collective one.

At a meeting of Community Justice Ministers in Brussels in July 1987 member states took another step forward by agreeing to streamline extradition procedures, allowing nationals sentenced in one member state to opt to serve their sentence in their state of origin, and laying down that an individual could not be prosecuted more than once for the same offence anywhere in the Community. During the summit meeting between the leading industrialized countries in Venice in June 1987 an agreement to prohibit flights from any country failing to prosecute or extradite terrorists involved in offences involving aircraft was signed, adding considerably to the sanctions available against state-sponsored terrorism. During the EC summit meeting in Hannover in June 1988 Chancellor Helmut Kohl of Germany even went so far as to suggest the creation of a European police agency modelled on the American Federal Bureau of Investigation. The idea was not warmly received, but while it may still be premature to think along these lines it is likely to attract more serious consideration in the years ahead.

Indeed, at a meeting of EC justice and interior ministers in Dublin in June 1990 the Twelve agreed to set up a European Central Drugs Intelligence Unit (ECDIU), with the specific tasks of co-ordinating information and establishing a special training unit for drug-enforcement officers. If successful, the ECDIU could prove to be the model for further experiments in cross-border co-operation, which could conceivably develop into the European FBI or Europol suggested by Herr Kohl.

The next major breakthrough was made following a series of IRA attacks on British armed forces personnel in Germany and the Netherlands in 1988. Community Interior Ministers meeting in Munich in July 1988 agreed to further increases in exchanges of information and forensic evidence, a study on the security implications of 1992 and, perhaps most important of all, to launch an examination into possible Community-wide legislation to examine the bank accounts of terrorist organizations and seize their financial assets.

During its periodic review of the Prevention of Terrorism Act Britain had decided to introduce a new provision granting the government the power to inspect bank accounts (and confiscate their contents) where there was a suspicion that the money could be used to finance terrorist activities. However, Hurd was fully aware that there was little point in Britain acting in isolation. The legislation would be useless if terrorist organizations could move their accounts around Community banks. It was clearly apparent (although no government minister has yet conceded the point) that Britain could no longer take refuge in its island status from terrorists, drug traffickers or criminals.

However, the days when criminals can hide their ill-gotten gains in Continental retreats such as the Costa Brava may now be numbered. The success of the 1986 Drug Trafficking Offences Act, and the 1988 Criminal Justice Act (both of which gave British courts powers to confiscate the proceeds from drug trafficking and other forms of major crime), has encouraged the Home Office to try to persuade its Community partners to adopt similar laws.

Admittedly, France and Germany retain grave reservations over such a development, but progress has been particularly promising with Spain. Although still a long way off, the Home Office's ultimate objective is to facilitate the introduction of a fully harmonized system of judicial seizure for the proceeds of major crime—effectively preventing criminals from laundering money through Continental banks, and enabling the Community to establish a policy of 'no hiding place' for criminal fortunes. In December 1990, Leon Brittan, the Competition Commissioner, took the first step in this direction with the announcement that EC finance ministers had agreed to introduce a anti-laundering directive designed to reduce profits from drug trafficking and criminal activities. The measure, which came into effect in June 1991, will require anyone from January 1993 depositing more than £10,500 in a bank to identify themselves and the source of the money, thereby enabling the authorities to track the ebb and flow of proceeds from the international drugs trade.

In his recent book, *Terrorism, Drugs and Crime in Europe after 1992*, Richard Clutterbuck, a seasoned observer of European security issues, suggests that the dangers presented by the abolition of Europe's internal frontiers could be negated by using information technology to hamper the activities of terrorists, drug traffickers and major criminals. Such technologies, which include techniques to prevent impersonation by the digital recording of fingerprints, voice and vein patterns, linking Europe's national police computers and detecting explosives by vapour sniffing and neutron bombardment, are now all readily available. The difficulty facing Europe after 1992, he warns, will be how to protect lives and property, without unwarranted erosions of civil liberties.

The case against the abolition of frontiers

Nevertheless, the fact that terrorists such as Germany's Red Army Faction, or RAF (heirs to the notorious Baader–Meinhof Gang), the IRA and the Italian Red Brigades remain active gives cause for concern. The terrorists, too, are preparing for 1992, as was shown by the attempted murder in September 1988 of Hans Tietmeyer, a senior Bonn official, by the RAF with the active help of the Red Brigades, as part of a co-ordinated terrorist effort to disrupt an IMF ministerial meeting in Berlin. Similarly, the murder of Herr Alfred Herrhausen, the chief executive of Deutsche Bank, who was blown up in his bullet-proof Mercedes in November 1989, was yet another reminder that the RAF was still active. Partly because of such incidents, Britain's police forces, backed up by many of their Continental colleagues, have grave reservations about the proposed abolition of frontier controls.

During the annual meeting of the International Union of Police Federations (IUPF) in August 1988, which represents over 500,000 officers, a resolution was passed against abolishing frontier controls by a majority of one. However, most of Europe's police forces appeared to think that abolition was inevitable. But what irritated them more than anything was the failure of EC governments to consult them over the implications of abolition. This is a shortcoming which member states ought to rectify as soon as possible. Peter Tanner, the Secretary of the British Police Federation and President of the IUPF, also warned that if internal borders were to be abolished there would need to be rapid progress on establishing common procedures for extradition, criminal justice and the right of hot pursuit across borders, all of which the Commission hopes to have in place before the 1992 deadline expires.

The surprise announcement in November 1988 by the Belgian Cabinet to overturn the recommendation by the Belgian judiciary to extradite Patrick Ryan, the former Roman Catholic priest wanted by Scotland Yard in connection with four offences of conspiracy to commit murder and illegal possession of explosives, caused exasperation in Downing Street and overshadowed the forthcoming EC summit meeting in Rhodes. The rejection of the extradition request, originally made on 9 September, almost three months after Ryan had been detained by the Belgian authorities for entering the country with a false passport, was prompted by the Government's fear of possible IRA retaliation if Ryan, then on hunger strike in St Gilles prison in Brussels, died on Belgian soil. This was the first time that Belgium had denied an extradition request from a NATO partner for over 20 years, and it took the issue of increased co-operation against terrorism to the top of the Community's agenda.

During an otherwise low-key summit meeting at Rhodes in

December, Mrs Thatcher had some frank exchanges with her Belgian and Irish counterparts over the Ryan affair. However, the controversy at least resulted in a new initiative to tackle the problems of controlling terrorists, drug traffickers and criminals, in an internal market without frontiers. The twelve heads of government agreed to appoint a special official to take charge of intergovernmental negotiations on controlling terrorism, drug trafficking and illegal immigration, in advance of a Trevi Group meeting in December in Athens on the problems presented by inter-national crime and the abolition of internal frontiers. Similarly, the decision by a Dutch court to acquit four suspected IRA terrorists of the murders of two Australian tourists in Roermond in 1990 provoked out-rage from the Home Secretary, Kenneth Baker, who protested strongly about the decision during the Trevi Group meeting in the autumn of 1991.

Although the Commission is engaged in an attempt to wipe out a whole range of plant and animal diseases across Europe, British public opinion has tended to focus on the danger of rabies. These anxieties are not difficult to understand. *La rage* is a killer, and Britain has been free of the disease for over 60 years. However, there is much truth in the observation that Britain's island status, far from easing popular anxieties over the spread of rabies, has actually heightened them. In reality, the threat posed by rabies is marginal. In over 40 years of quarantine controls Britain has never found one animal with rabies. According to statistics collected by the International Organization of Epizootics, there were 19,000 cases of rabies recorded in the whole of continental Europe for 1985. Of this total, 14,000 were foxes, 3,000 were other wild animals and 200 were domestic animals. There was one recorded case of rabies among the human population—and that was in Finland.

Rabies is overwhelmingly confined to wild animals, most of which are foxes. Even so, the Commission is taking no chances. Officials have been monitoring closely a series of field tests with an oral vaccine for wild animals. If the tests prove successful the Commission is expected to launch a Community-wide rabies-eradication programme, which holds out the promise of eliminating the disease completely. Moreover, the Home Office has made it clear that Britain will retain its quarantine con-trols at sea- and airports. The Home Office has also been closely involved with the Eurotunnel contractors on devising ways to prevent animals from crawling along the floor of the tunnel. In short, Britain's defences against rabies will be as effective as ever. Equally as important, Europe's defences against rabies will be strengthened by the internal market pro-gramme.

Partly because there is still some time to elapse before the Com-munity's external frontier is in place, Britain has shown a deep ambiva-lence towards the Commission's proposal to abolish all internal frontier controls by 1992, and is clearly leaning in the direction of keeping them intact. Reflecting on the Commission's proposals in October 1986, the Home Secretary said:

> A lot depends on the way we can strengthen our external frontiers. The more effective we are in keeping drugs, terrorists and major criminals out of the Community in the first place, the easier it will be to relax our internal controls.

Even so, the minister warned that 'it was not around the corner'.

Now 1992 is just around the corner, and the British position has hardened considerably. At the June 1988 meeting of the Trevi Group in Munich Hurd insisted that:

> Frontier controls do provide an effective means of dealing with these problems. They are not 100 per cent effective but they are more effective than internal arrangements.

Hurd seemed to be suggesting that Britain had its own ideas about European integration—a sort of internal market *avec frontières*. Addressing the annual conference of the Association of Chief Police Officers in Eastbourne a month before, the minister declared: 'We owe it to ourselves, and to our fellow citizens, to continue to do all we can to see that the terrorist, the drug trafficker or criminal, is not the unintended beneficiary of changes designed for the development of the Community, and the benefit of law-abiding Community citizens'. As a result of such anxieties, particularly after Britain's anger over the refusal of Belgium to extradite a suspected IRA terrorist, the Trevi Group, meeting in Athens in December 1988, agreed to examine the possibility of introducing a common extradition policy.

Controlling crime in the single market

These statements raise two fundamental questions about the proposed abolition of internal frontier controls. First, are these so-called internal arrangements—increased police co-operation, the creation of common policies on extradition, confiscation of terrorists' assets, immigration and the right of hot pursuit across national borders—more effective than internal frontier controls? British ministers think not, but at the same time acknowledge that without parallel legislation in other member states Britain's attempt to control terrorism and drug trafficking will be to little avail.

Moreover, while there are isolated examples of the efficacy of internal frontier controls, such as the chance apprehension of two IRA gunmen by a West German border guard in September 1988, the great majority of terrorists, drug traffickers and criminals are merely arrested at frontier control points, having been identified as a result of co-operation between

Community intelligence agencies long before. Furthermore, the most difficult internal frontier to monitor in the entire Community is the border between Ulster and the Irish Republic—which has no frontier controls.

Second, a major fear is that if Britain decides to keep its internal frontier controls there will be no changes benefiting law-abiding Community citizens. Movement in and out of Britain will remain more or less as time consuming and costly as it is at present. The Commission insists that one either has internal frontier controls or one does not—there is no half-way house—and it is disingenuous to suggest that we can have both.

At the kernel of the dispute over the abolition of frontier controls lies one of the many historic differences between Britain and its European neighbours. Continental Europeans have tended to rely more on individual identity cards than frontier controls for the apprehension of criminals—an idea which has never been particularly popular in Britain. However, at an address given at the Crime in Europe Conference in York in September 1988 David Faulkner, a deputy Under-Secretary of State at the Home Office, suggested that Britain might be forced to re-evaluate its traditional hostility to the introduction of a national identity card as a result of growing pressures for greater freedom of movement around the Community. At the Rhodes summit in December 1988 Mrs Thatcher raised the idea of EC identity cards without either endorsing or rejecting it.

This, coupled with intensive police and intelligence co-operation under Trevi arrangements and common EC policies on immigration and extradition, may point the way forward and allow the Single European Act's commitment to 'an area without internal frontiers' to be fulfilled. The alternative—the retention of national controls by Britain in isolation from the other Eleven—could lead to action against Britain in the European Court after 1992, which was not what the framers of the Act had in mind and is not what other members of the EC wish to see happen.

However, Britain is confident that the Single European Act does allow member states to retain internal frontiers. It has also challenged Lord Cockfield's claim that the great majority of drug seizures are made as a result of increased co-operation between national police forces.

A report released in Brussels in March 1989, based on statistics collected by the Home Office, showed that 36% of the volume of drugs seized in 1986 came from or via another EC country. That figure rose to 41% in 1987, and provisional data for 1988 shows an increase to 44%. While acknowledging that 'investigators depend on frontier staff to intercept intelligence targets', it nonetheless insisted that 'seizures made "cold" or according to "profiles" of likely smuggling types, depend on officers being at the frontier to observe, select, question and examine'.

Erecting the external frontier

EC interior ministers had begun work on erecting Europe's new external frontier long before September 1989, when the first images of thousands of Trabants spluttering from East to West Germany via Hungary and Austria flashed across television screens around the world. The exodus from the East did, however, have the effect of focusing the attention of governments on the urgency of tackling the problems presented by potentially large movements of people—the scale of which has not been seen since the nineteenth-century migrations from Europe to America—and efforts to complete the task before the 1992 deadline began in earnest. Simultaneously, human rights and refugee groups began to air misgivings about the new frontier controls, fearing that the Community was being panicked into taking excessively restrictive measures which would remove an essential avenue of escape for asylum seekers.

Under the 1951 refugee convention, a refugee is defined as someone who does not want to return to their country of origin because 'of a well-founded fear of being persecuted for reasons of race, religion, nationality, membership of a particular social group or political opinion'. The convention was drawn up at the height of the Cold War, when strict Communist border controls kept the flow of refugees from the Soviet Union and the East European satellites to a trickle, and when the lucky few who were able to cross the Iron Curtain were welcomed with open arms. Because these political refugees were so few in number, the Western tradition of granting asylum was never put under strain.

The migrations to Europe from Africa and Asia which occurred during the 1950s and 1960s were quite different. Although many of the new immigrants were fleeing political persecution, most came in search of a better life, often at the invitation of the host governments. But because of the large numbers of people involved, West European governments began to tighten their immigration controls during the mid-1970s, signalling the end of large-scale immigration to Western Europe. As the scope for immigration declined, the number of applications for asylum began to increase. By the mid-1980s, Community countries saw themselves confronted by the difficult and sensitive task of distinguishing between political refugees and economic migrants.

After years of simmering on the back burner, the issue was propelled to the top of the political agenda during the Luxembourg summit in June 1991, when John Major issued a call for urgent action to control what he described as the rising tide of economic migrants seeking a better life in the EC. 'We must not remain open to all comers, simply because Paris, Rome and London seem more attractive than Bombay and Algiers,' he said. Moreover, 'If we fail in our control efforts, we risk fuelling the far right, something we saw in the UK in the mid-1970s, and have since kept in check,' he added.

The Prime Minister's speech was not well received by Britain's immigrant community. In a front page article in the *Caribbean Times*, headlined 'Fortress Europe: Major Plans Iron Curtain II'', the Prime Minister was accused of making 'an extraordinary and highly offensive attack on the presence and contribution of visible minority people in Britain and throughout the European Community'. In fact, the attack was more imagined than real, but the incident served to highlight the difficulty the Community faces in erecting the external frontier without alienating existing immigrant communities.

As the negotiations on the external frontier went into a higher gear, a number of EC countries decided to embark on unilateral action. In July, after a series of suburban riots involving Arab minorities, Edith Cresson, the French Prime Minister, announced new controls on illegal immigration, and predicted that up to one million people could be deported. Following an increase in migrations from Yugoslavia, Romania, Turkey, Iran, Afghanistan, Poland and North Africa, Bonn also announced a tightening up of immigration laws. In addition, throughout the summer of 1991, television viewers witnessed the tragic spectacle of the thousands of destitute Albanian boat people arriving in Italian ports, most of whom were promptly sent back to their homeland.

With Britain receiving 1,000 applications for asylum each week, ten times more than in 1988, Kenneth Baker, the Home Secretary, announced a package of measures designed to reduce the number of people seeking asylum in the UK. The package included the withdrawal of legal aid for immigration and asylum cases, a doubling of the £1,000 fine imposed on airline and shipping companies under the Carriers Liability Act for allowing passengers to enter Britain without the proper documents, and the withdrawal of oral hearings in asylum and immigration cases the government regards as unfounded.

The announcement provoked an angry response from Britain's refugee and immigration organizations. The Asylum Rights Campaign, a steering group made up of a wide range of bodies, including Amnesty International, the Immigration Law Practitioners' Association, and the Refugee Council, denounced the measures for denying 'the victims of persecution and injustice the possibility of seeking and obtaining asylum'. On 3 July an editorial in *The Times* went further, insisting:

> Asylum is an honourable British tradition not to be abandoned even under the present pressure. Mr Baker should prefer the risk of admitting an 'economic refugee' by mistake to that of sending back to persecution, torture or death a single real refugee entitled to asylum.

In a letter to *The Times* in October, Louis Blom-Cooper, QC, the former chairman of the Press Council, described the Baker reforms as 'deeply worrying', and accused the government of 'not fully implementing the [1951] convention'. Responding to the allegation, Peter Lloyd, the immigration minister, insisted that: 'The threat to the institution of asylum does not come from the government but from the growing number of people who abuse it by making specious asylum applications in order to circumvent the normal immigration controls'.

Nonetheless, Baker's measures were seen by critics as a particularly blunt instrument for distinguishing between political refugees and economic migrants. The withdrawal of legal aid cut off access to Britain for the less affluent in both groups. In addition, the reliance on the Carriers Liability Act, which has resulted in fines exceeding £30 million since it came into effect in 1987, ignored the difficulties faced by genuine applicants attempting to obtain authentic travel documents from the very authorities responsible for persecuting them, and effectively made the airline and shipping companies the reluctant front-line arbiters of Britain's asylum and immigration law. Observers also predicted that the Community's new external frontier would incorporate many of the elements of the Baker package.

The need to erect an external frontier stems from the Internal Market White Paper's objective of abolishing internal frontiers. If Community citizens are to be able to travel freely within the EC, then member states' conflicting rules and regulations on the rights of asylum and entry have to be harmonized so that non-EC nationals are subject to the same set of checks. Hitherto, negotiations have focused on two new instruments, a convention on asylum and a convention on crossing external frontiers or a common visa policy. The convention on asylum, also known as the Dublin Convention, grants applicants the right to seek asylum in one member state only. In an effort to prevent what is known as 'refugees in orbit', rejection by one country means rejection by all. What remains to be agreed, however, are the common criteria by which applicants can be granted asylum status.

After assuming the Community presidency in July 1991 the Netherlands made the harmonization of asylum and visa regulations a priority. However, given the secret nature of these negotiations, few details about their content have been released. With predictions of a possible exodus from Eastern Europe of between two and four million migrants, combined with further large-scale migrations from Africa and Asia, refugee organizations fear that the Community is being stampeded into a panic reaction. Their greatest concern is that ministers will adopt policies similar to those in Britain. But predictions that EC governments will undermine the 1951 convention seem somewhat alarmist. Moreover, there are indications that the Commission is moving towards the recognition that the only effective way to restrain migratory pressures is to provide incentives for potential immigrants to remain in their country of origin by accepting more of their exports and providing increased Community aid and development funds.

In the run-up to the EC summit in Maastricht, Britain was in support of proposals to harmonize Community visa, asylum, and immigration procedures as part of the wider attempt to create the conditions that will allow free movement of people from 1993. But it remained adamant that the harmonization of conditions of entry should remain the responsibility of national governments working together through the Trevi Group of justice and interior ministers, rather than being transferred to Brussels. In the event, the Maastricht treaty acknowledged that immigration policy should remain the preserve of inter-governmental co-operation. The Commission was, however, given the power to define a common visa policy, which must be approved by Council on the basis of unanimity, unless faced by an emergency (such as a sudden influx from a particular country), in which case visa policy could be decided by majority voting. While the Maastricht compromise removed the delicate issue of immigration from the EC agenda, few observers expect it to remain that way for long. Elections in Austria, Switzerland, Belgium, France, Germany, and Italy have seen fresh gains for many of Europe's expanding right wing parties, much of which has been attributed to increased hostility towards immigrants, high unemployment, poor housing, and alienation from established political institutions. The Maastricht treaty could even exacerbate the difficulty by providing ammunition for right wing radicals to exploit growing fears about the effects of opening borders and pooling national sovereignty, particularly in France and Germany.

Checklist of changes

- The European Commission hopes to oversee the complete abolition of all internal frontier controls (the so-called physical barriers to trade) by the end of 1992.
- The abolition of internal frontiers will result in significant cost reductions for companies involved in cross-frontier trade, and will also make travel and tourism for the ordinary citizen considerably easier.
- The manpower and resources freed from internal frontier controls can then be redirected towards defending the Community from terrorists, drug traffickers and other criminals at the Community's external frontiers.
- The approximation of member states' fiscal taxation arrangements will eliminate the need to collect value added tax at internal frontiers.

- There will be increased co-operation between national police and intelligence forces in the fight against terrorists and criminals.
- Common Community initiatives on immigration, visa, extradition and right of asylum policies, the possession of firearms, confiscation of terrorists' and criminal assets, and the right of hot pursuit across national borders may also be introduced.
- Common programmes for the elimination of animal and plant diseases, possibly including rabies, will also be implemented.

6 PUBLIC WORKS AND PRIVATE TENDERS
Public purchasing across frontiers

As the barriers to free trade within the Community started to fall towards the end of the 1980s it became evident that many small, medium and even large businesses felt inundated by the directives designed to open up the European market for public contracts supplying equipment and services to local government, nationalized companies and other state organizations. Those companies that were quick to grasp the significance of the Commission's initiative rapidly assembled internal market management teams, fostered closer relations with Commission officials and started to test the uncharted waters of the new era of competition. Many more, however, appeared content to let things drift. In May 1991, Sir John Cuckney, the chairman of Investors in Industry, the venture capital group, warned that an alarming number of small and medium-sized British enterprises were in danger of losing out to their Continental rivals as the public procurement market started to open up. Observers attributed much of Britain's commercial complacency to a deep-rooted scepticism towards 'things Continental', and an equally embedded inertia towards change.

Although the principle of free trade is the cornerstone of the Treaty of Rome, the past 30 years have demonstrated that public procurement is the last area in which anyone would ever find it in operation. According to the provisions of Articles 30–36, member states are obliged to remove all quantitative restrictions (or any other measures having an equivalent effect) that obstruct the free movement of goods within the Community. Similarly, Articles 59–66 make it incumbent on member states to remove all obstacles in the way of the free flow of services across national frontiers. However, like so many other commitments entered into by national governments, these particular provisions were signed with the best intentions and promptly filed away.

The public purchasing programmes of central and local government (which includes their agencies and enterprises) have persistently reflected the defensive and parochial outlook displayed by the once-famous group of secretaries from Croydon who launched the 'I'm backing Britain' campaign in the 1960s. Both were motivated by the intensely patriotic (if somewhat economically misguided) conviction that buying national was the answer to Britain's economic difficulties.

During the past 30 years the growth of cross-border trade in goods and services in the private sector has been impressive. By comparison, the volume of such trade in the public sector has been comparatively static. There is a marked contrast between the demand by national governments for the private sector to adjust to the laws of supply and demand, on the one hand, and the way in which the public sector has been allowed to seek refuge behind national barriers, on the other. This raises charges of double standards.

The national bias of public purchasing bodies in favour of domestic manufacturers and suppliers covers three broad categories of goods and services:

1 All basic supply goods, ranging from office equipment to commercial vehicles and school and hospital supplies;
2 Public works such as roads, buildings, bridges and other civil engineering projects;
3 The so-called 'big-ticket items', which include sophisticated telecommunications and scientific facilities and power-generating and defence equipment.

The justifications used by member states to support biased national public procurement policies have depended on social considerations, economic necessity and outright national pride. At its most basic, governments have argued that domestic political exigencies have forced them to place public procurement contracts locally in order to reduce unemployment in declining industries or to support emerging industries in the early stages of development. More compelling, perhaps, has been the insistence that major industries such as telecommunications, aerospace and defence (which have massive research and development costs and where governments are frequently the only significant purchaser) would face collapse without government help. The implications of such a collapse, it is claimed, go far beyond considerations of social policy and regional development and into the realm of national security. All too often, however, economic necessity, social policy and strategic considerations have contained more than a hint of national pride. Governments have repeatedly asked themselves how an advanced industrialized country can be worthy of the name if it cannot support its own steel, car or defence industries.

However, it has become increasingly evident that the inescapable problem with a world view that stops at national boundaries will lead to long-term economic annihilation. Public procurement programmes that discriminate in favour of national champions reinforce the market fragmentation of the European economy, and cost the member states billions of pounds a year in unnecessary premiums to local firms. Market fragmentation denies companies the economies of scale they need to survive without government help, and leaves them vulnerable to competition from their larger external rivals. In the short term, discrimination in favour of local producers and suppliers may be a palliative for economically declining regions and companies unable or unwilling to survive without government assistance. However, in the long term it cannot generate the kind of competitive environment that companies need to survive in the increasingly competitive international economy.

The cost of national public procurement policies

According to the survey on the costs of European market fragmentation conducted on behalf of the European Commission by Cecchini in 1987, the value of all public purchasing contracts in 1986 was in excess of £355 billion, or £20 billion more than the value of all intra-Community trade during the same year. The sum of £355 billion is equivalent to 15% of the combined gross domestic product of all twelve member states, and therefore constitutes one of the most important single categories of European economic activity.

The Cecchini survey acknowledged that a sizeable portion of this sum was allocated to the purchase of goods and services that were inherently non-competitive, non-tradable or required in such small volumes that few manufacturers or suppliers outside the country in question would be prepared to compete against their domestic rivals. However, the survey insisted that, even making allowances for this factor, the estimated value of member states' annual public purchasing contracts were in the region of £230 billion. Of this total, less than 2% went to bidders outside national boundaries, which was costing the Community an estimated additional £14.5 billion a year. The assumptions and projections lying behind these figures have been the subject of a bitter dispute. The authors of the Cecchini study, in their enthusiasm to demonstrate the costs of discriminatory public purchasing policies, have been accused of considerably overstating their case.

It would be foolhardy, however, to accept the claim advanced by member states that the cost of national bias in public procurement programmes is negligible. No government likes to be accused, especially by bureaucrats in Brussels, of squandering public money. However, according to a report on the internal market published by Britain's independent Royal Institute of International Affairs in 1987, the costs of national discrimination in public purchasing was estimated at about £14 billion a year, thereby vindicating the Commission's estimates. It is therefore evident that national governments pay far more than they should for their purchases of works, goods and services, and in so doing finance inefficient and uncompetitive producers. An examination of some of the key sectors of the European economy would illustrate this point.

The European telecommunications market has become the classic example of the absurdity of protecting national markets from external competition by favouring national producers through biased public purchasing programmes. The Community market for telephone exchange systems is worth about £5 billion a year. However, the market is divided between eleven national producers, who are now installing no less than seven different exchange systems, five of which have been developed by European companies, most of whom are state owned.

If public procurement was opened to cross-border competition telephone exchange manufacturers would have a major incentive to link up, rationalize the number of exchange systems on offer and thereby reduce development costs, which would, in turn, be reflected in cheaper prices. In anticipation of 1992, a number of telecommunications companies have already begun to restructure their operations. The acquisition of AT&T's European interests by the French telecommunications company Alcatel, the purchase of the French company CGCT by the Swedish giant Ericsson and the link-up between the telecommunications divisions of GEC and Plessey represent the first wave of mergers in the European telecommunications industry.

Such distortions are also evident in other industrial sectors. The European locomotive industry, for example, is valued at about £70 million a year. There are no less than 16 locomotive manufacturers (compared to two in the United States) competing in an industry that has a 50% overcapacity and is characterized by little intra-EC trade. Boilermaking presents a similar picture. The market is worth an estimated £1.5 billion a year. There are 12 EC manufacturers (compared to six in the United States), and it is characterized by a phenomenal 80% overcapacity with negligible intra-EC trade. The same is true of turbine generator manufacturers. There are ten European manufacturers (compared to two in the United States) chasing orders in a European market that is valued at about £1.5 billion a year, and which has 40% overcapacity. Indeed, it would be difficult to identify a handful of industries that do not rely on the industrial equivalent of social security for their survival.

However, there is more to the cost of discriminatory public purchasing than simple market fragmentation. According to the European Commission, 'protectionist support, often portrayed as a shot in the arm for industry, is in fact a striking example of governments' shooting themselves, and their competitive ideals, in the foot'. Even more alarming is the report's prediction that 'unless restrictions on public purchasing are swept away, far from strategic industries being protected, whole areas of industry which have high multiplier effects on other sectors of manufacturing could cease to be viable'.

Opening up public procurement: round one

Because the member states had failed to honour the free-trade provisions of Articles 30–36 and 59–66 of the Treaty (and had shown no indications of ever doing so of their own volition) the need for additional legislation was abundantly evident. During the 1970s two directives were issued in an effort to remedy this situation, the 1971 Directive on Public Works and the 1977 Directive on Public Supplies.

The directives replaced divergent national procedures for issuing public procurement contracts with a Community-wide procedure governing all public works contracts over £670,000 and all public supply contracts over £134,000. Consequently, all public authorities responsible for awarding contracts falling above these thresholds were required to ensure that their invitations to tender were brought to the attention of companies and suppliers anywhere in the Community. This could be achieved comparatively easily by publication of tendering opportunities in the supplement to the *Official Journal of the European Communities*. The directives also made it illegal to split up tenders so that individually they fell beneath the two thresholds.

Under the new directives the contract-awarding bodies were explicitly prohibited from discriminating against non-national contractors or suppliers under the provisions of Articles 30–36. These articles prohibit all quotas on imports and exports between member states or any measure, whether by law, regulation or administrative practice, which has an equivalent effect. There are two exceptions to this requirement. First, member states are permitted to restrict trade on grounds of public morality, public policy, public health or public security. Second, they are permitted to restrict trade where the product in question fails to meet the member state's essential technical standards. However, any member state attempting to abuse these two let-out clauses could find itself before the European Court of Justice.

In an attempt to encourage public bodies to think in commercial rather than patriotic terms the two directives set out a series of objective criteria for evaluating competing tenders, and made it incumbent on the public bodies to award contracts to those companies who had submitted the lowest-priced or most economically advantageous offers. Where a contractor or supplier had evidence or suspected that it had been discriminated against by the awarding body it was empowered to register a complaint with the Director General for the Internal Market. The Commission could then conduct an investigation into the award procedure. If the investigation confirmed that discrimination had taken place, a formal letter could be sent to the member state asking it to answer the infringement allegation. If the member state failed to answer by the specified date, or if the answer was unsatisfactory, the case could be passed on to the European Court of Justice.

Although regarded as a major step forward in the cause of intra-Community free trade, the significance of the two new directives was soon demonstrated to be rather more apparent than real. In order to secure acceptance by the Council of Ministers the teeth of the original intention to open up public procurement to cross-border competition had been drawn out—one by one.

Under the terms of the two directives, a contract-awarding body had the choice of two basic types of tendering procedure which effectively enabled the authority to preserve its traditional national biases intact. The first is the open procedure, which requires offers to tender to be made available to all potential bidders. The second is the restricted procedure, in which only the contractor or supplier invited to tender may do so. Moreover, all construction and supply contracts awarded by the public authorities responsible for air, land and sea transport; the production and distribution of drinking water; the exploration, development and distribution of coal, oil, electricity and gas; and the development and maintenance of the telecommunications industry were excluded from the scope of the two directives. By the time they came into force, less than 20% of Community public procurement contracts were affected by them.

If this minimalist attempt to promote competition in public procurement became too onerous, the contract-awarding bodies were soon to demonstrate their ingenuity in finding new ways of evading the new works and supply directives in the limited areas in which they applied. Member states' failure to respect their commitments has varied from mild abuse of tendering procedures to outright violation and evasion. The two directives have still not been properly incorporated into national law in a number of member states, and failure to publish advance notification of contracts in the *Official Journal* has been widespread.

Most awarding authorities have insisted that contractors and suppliers adhere to national technical specifications, even in those areas where Community technical standards have been established. Tenders have been systematically divided up into separate contracts in order to fall below the thresholds at which publication in the *Official Journal* is mandatory. Use of the open tenders procedure has been kept to a minimum, while the conditions under which restricted procedures are permitted have been interpreted broadly. Some member states have not even bothered with such subtleties, preferring instead to ignore the conditions under which restricted procedures can be used while systematically eliminating tenders from other member states.

The Commission's powers of enforcement were no match for the ability of member states to ignore the two directives. It proved to be extremely difficult for construction or supply companies to produce evidence demonstrating that they had been discriminated against illegally. On the rare occasions such evidence was found, a company faced up to a two-year wait before the European Court of Justice could hear the case, by which time a construction project was invariably completed and a supply contract long consumed. There was, however, one lesson to come out of the public works and supply directives that was to prove invaluable in the future: how not to make the same mistake twice.

The White Paper and public procurement

Recognizing the political sensitivity surrounding the issue of national bias in public purchasing, the Internal Market White Paper announced the Commission's intention to establish the Advisory Committee on the Opening Up of Public Procurement. This was to be staffed by representatives from the Commission, the member states and the public bodies with responsibilities for awarding contracts. By examining the reasons why the public works and public supply directives had failed to prove effective, and by developing a closer understanding of the needs of the public purchasing bodies, the Advisory Committee set about drafting a strategy for the Commission's second assault on a practice it had denounced as 'economic incest'.

The White Paper gave an outline of the kinds of areas the Commission had identified as those in need of urgent attention. These included closing the loopholes in the existing public works and supply directives, tightening procedures for advance publication of tendering opportunities, providing construction and supply companies with effective means of redress where public purchasing procedures have been breached and, most sensitive of all, extending the contract-awarding procedures to the four excluded sectors.

In the eighteen months that followed the publication of the White Paper the atmosphere of foreboding concerning the prospects for opening up public procurement gradually gave way to cautious grounds for optimism. In three consecutive summit meetings (in The Hague in June 1986, London in December 1986 and Brussels in February 1987) an unprecedented consensus had emerged singling out progress on public procurement as one of the priority areas of the internal market programme.

Member states had finally taken the first tentative steps towards overcoming their traditional reluctance to submit their cherished public sectors to the laws of supply and demand. It was a long-overdue acknowledgement that, in the context of continued government retrenchment and persistent restraint on public spending, the contract-awarding bodies had to abandon their misguided patriotism and pay more attention to commercial considerations when awarding public purchasing contracts.

Opening up public procurement: round two

Reflecting the priorities laid out in the White Paper, and acting on the recommendations formulated by the Advisory Committee on Opening Up Public Procurement, the Commission first concentrated on the existing public works and supply directives. A new Public Supplies Directive was proposed in March 1988, amending the 1977 Public Supplies Directive, and became effective in January 1989.

The type of supply contracts covered by the new directive, ranging from office equipment to employees' clothing, was clearly defined, and the rules for calculating their value for the purposes of applying the £134,000 threshold at which it had to be published in the *Official Journal* (or *Tenders Electronic Daily*, the Community's online database) were made more explicit. The open tenders procedure was made the rule, and any attempt by a contract-awarding body to use the restricted tenders procedure had to be justified to the Commission. Procurement authorities are now also required to give advance notice of their annual purchasing requirements in an attempt to enable supply companies to prepare for potential contracts in advance. All public bodies, from the House of Lords down to the local High Street library, are now required to open all supply contracts over the designated threshold to cross-border competition.

A proposal to amend the 1971 Public Works Directive has proved somewhat more difficult to draft, but the broad outline of the Commission's intentions has already been made known. The existing £670,000 threshold at which all public works contracts have to be published in the *Official Journal* has been made obsolete by the rising costs of construction work over the past 15 years, and is to be replaced by a new £3.35 million threshold. Contracts for public works whose value exceeds the new higher ceiling will have to be advertised in the *Official Journal*. Both categories of contract will, however, remain subject to all other Community rules governing tendering procedures.

The Commission also intends to extend the scope of the existing directive on public works by introducing a wider definition of contract-awarding bodies subject to its provisions, including the non-governmental agencies financed from public funds. As in the case of public supply contracts, the availability of restricted procedures is to be sharply curtailed and the open procedure is to become the norm. In order to ensure that the contract-awarding bodies have adhered to the new tendering procedures they will be required to explain on request why they have decided to reject a particular bid and submit a report to the Commission on each award decision. In future, recognition of Community technical standards will be mandatory.

Following the emerging consensus on the need to ensure greater compliance with Community regulations governing public procurement, in July 1987 the Commission submitted to Council a draft directive on proposals to improve the means of redress available to companies who have been illegally discriminated against by public purchasing authorities. Because of the nature of public procurement (and the inordinate amount of time it takes the European Court of Justice to pass judgment on infractions of Community law) the Commission has focused its efforts on prevention rather than cure. Once a building has been completed it would be difficult, even for bureaucrats in Brussels, to demand that it be demolished because the awarding body had discriminated in favour of a national construction company.

The proposed prevention strategy contains three separate but interlocking elements. First, the Commission would be empowered to suspend for three months any contract award if the awarding authority failed to make adequate provision for cross-border competition. The awarding authority would then be required to make good its breach of Community tendering procedures by issuing a new call to tender complying with the provisions of the public purchasing directives. If an awarding body persisted in its error it would be incumbent on the government of the member states to compel the awarding body to respect Community law. Second, should this prove unsuccessful, the company would then be able to challenge national tendering procedures through the national courts without having to register a complaint with the Commission first. Violations of public purchasing directives are likely to be met with large fines. Finally, if all else fails, the Commission reserves the right to take the member state to the European Court of Justice under the provisions of Article 169 of the Treaty. The Commission has indicated that borderline cases will be overlooked, and that it will only act where there is evidence of a clear and blatant infringement of the rules. Council is expected to endorse the Commission's proposals for effective redress before the 1992 deadline is reached.

Acceptance of the proposed directive on compliance with Community tendering procedures has been described by the Commission as vital in order 'to increase the credibility of the Community's efforts to break down the psychological reluctance of traders, industrialists, and more particularly, small and medium-sized enterprises, to bid across frontiers for public works contracts'. In June 1988 the Commission unveiled its wide-ranging proposals to incorporate the four excluded sectors (telecommunications, energy, transport and water), which have so far remained immune from cross-border competition, into the Community's system for awarding construction and supply contracts, thereby fulfilling a priority commitment in its goal of completing the internal market by 1992.

Before making its proposals the Commission took into account the extensive analysis of the four excluded sectors conducted by the Advisory Committee on Opening Up Public Procurement. This examination demonstrated that biased patterns of public procurement could not simply be attributed to the public status of the organizations operating in the four sectors. Similar difficulties could be expected even if all four sectors were in private hands. Far more important was the actual structure of the sector itself, whether electricity, gas, coal or oil in the energy sector; the seaports, airports and rail networks and municipal mass transport systems in the transport sector; the purification and distribution functions of the water sector; and the development and supply of telecommunications equipment in the communications sector. The Advisory Committee found that all four sectors were inherently monopolistic, consequently insulated from competition and characterized by a highly developed propensity to 'buy national'.

The main reason for the excluded sectors being left out of the scope of the 1970s directives on public purchasing was that the pattern of ownership throughout the Community varied considerably from private to public or a mixture of the two, and the Commission faced great difficulty in trying to find some regulatory formula that adequately catered for the different forms of ownership. The new directive ignores this question, and focuses instead on the more important area of state influence. Any organization in the four excluded sectors (whether publicly or privately owned) that is subject to official or unofficial pressures to place public procurement contracts with local firms will be subject to the new directive. The intention is not to force these organizations to buy foreign, but to ensure that they are free to exercise their commercial judgement, independently of nationalistic public purchasing pressures.

Because the organizations operating in the excluded sectors are more sensitive to industrial and commercial considerations than the public and administrative bodies covered by the existing directives on public purchasing, the new directive provides a considerably more flexible tendering procedure. The organizations can choose between requesting tenders on a contract-by-contract basis or periodically calling for expressions of interest from would-be contractors or suppliers. They can also avail themselves of the option to maintain a pool of contractors and suppliers, on condition that the terms of entrance to the pool are made public and that foreign companies have the same rights of access as national companies. A new system (known as a negotiated procedure) has been introduced in which an awarding body can enter into talks with prospective contractors or suppliers, but only where the response from open or restricted procedures has been unsatisfactory, or where issues of national security or defence are at stake. As with previous directives, Community technical standards must be used wherever possible. The telecommunications sector was the subject of a separate directive in 1989, and electricity in 1990.

The excluded sectors directive will cover all supply contracts valued at £134,000 and above, which the Commission estimates is enough to buy 4.5 miles of fibre-optic cable, two buses or a small crane, and all works contracts valued at £3.3 million and above, enough to pay for 6.5 miles of standard or 1.5 miles of high-speed railway line or the dredging of a major port. Access to the Community's public purchasing market by organizations from outside the EC can be excluded where more than 50% of the value of the contract is provided by companies outside the twelve member states.

The directive opening up procurement in the excluded sectors to cross-border competition was finally agreed by Community industry ministers in February 1990. Although welcomed as a milestone in the creation of the single market, in so far as it discriminated in favour of Community suppliers the breakthrough was also denounced by foreign critics as protectionist. But the so-called 'Buy-Europe' clause in the directive, enabling purchasers to ignore non-Community bids up to 3% cheaper than Community tenders, was defended by trade officials on the grounds that it was temporary and would be removed if the GATT talks succeeded in abolishing such restrictions worldwide.

Completing the Commission's internal market programme in the field of public purchasing is a new directive covering the flourishing market for telecommunications, known as Open Network Provision. In December 1988, the Commission announced its intention to launch an ambitious and highly controversial plan to compel member states to open up their national telecommunications services industries to free competition throughout the Community by 1991.

The plan, which was implemented under the competition provisions of Article 90 of the Treaty of Rome, makes it incumbent on member states to relinquish their monopoly rights over the burgeoning telecommunications services sector. Only voice telephony and telex services will remain outside the scope of the directive. In a separate but related move, the Commission also submitted to the Council of Ministers a draft directive calling for the introduction of harmonized technical standards, in an effort to open up the telecommunications networks to all equipment manufacturers, and thus bring an end to the arbitrary power of the private and state-owned phone companies to decide who has access to the network.

But the telecommunications services plan, which would open up the vast majority of the Community's £44 billion telecommunications services industry to free competition, was confronted with bitter opposition from a variety of member states, principally Germany, France and Italy, all of whom continue to exercise a virtually exclusive monopoly over their telecommunications services sector. The plan also faced opposition from Britain, on procedural grounds (despite the UK government's commitment to the objectives of the proposal), because it was convinced that the Commission was overstepping the limit of its powers by refusing to adhere to the normal procedure of drawing up a draft directive for approval by the Council of Ministers.

The plan was originally scheduled for finalization in March 1989, and would have eliminated all telecommunications services monopolies by January 1991. However, it proved so controversial that the Commission was forced to consider a one-year extension of the liberalization timetable in order to defuse some of the angry reactions its ambitious proposals had generated.

The Commission was taken to the European Court of Justice by France, following its decision in June 1991 to issue its own directive forcing member states to open up the Community's terminal equipment market to cross-border competition. But the Commission, backed by the powerful commercial telecommunications companies, expressed confidence that the Court of Justice would uphold its authority to liberalize the telecommunications sector under the powers granted to it by the EC's founding treaty—as it already had done in the field of competition policy and the liberalization of the air transport industry.

The Commission also remained confident that it would emerge victorious in the battle over the proposed liberalization of telecommunications services. As one official said: 'Eventually, the member states will have to reconcile themselves to the fact that they are signatories to the Treaty of Rome'. Yet there is no disguising the growing anxiety among the governments of member states over the Commission's determination to ride roughshod over national sensibilities—using every power at its disposal, and forcing them to adhere to the Community's timetable for the completion of the internal market by 1992. The Commission hopes to implement a new directive by 1992 covering the liberalization of telecommunications services, which will include everything from electronic mail to data processing and teleshopping.

Reviewing the progress in opening up the Community's public purchasing markets in the sixth annual report on the internal market, published in July 1991, the Commission noted that 'work is proceeding satisfactorily'. The directive enlarging public procurement in transport, telecommunications, water and energy services has been adopted, while the Public Works and Public Supplies Directives came into force in January 1989 and July 1990, respectively. In order to ensure that the directives were being transposed into national law correctly, new monitoring procedures were also put in motion. Checks are now made on all contracts awarded in connection with programmes supported by the Community's structural funds, and infringements can be met with the freezing of structural fund payments. The report noted, however, that: 'Most difficulties are caused by ignorance of the directives.' Consequently, 'information campaigns are being conducted, and training courses organized for administrators at national and regional levels'.

Checklist of changes

- The loopholes in the 1971 directive on public works and the 1977 directive on public supplies will be closed and procedures for advance publication of tendering opportunities will be tightened up.
- Public bodies will be required to open all supply contracts worth more than £134,000 and all public works contracts worth more than £3.3 million to cross-border competition.
- In order to make sure that the contract-awarding bodies adhere to the new procedures they will be required to explain why they have rejected particular bids.
- There will be a wider definition of contract-awarding bodies, recognition of Community technical standards will become

mandatory, and all works contracts above £3.3 million will have to be advertised in the *Official Journal*.

- The means of redress for companies who have been illegally discriminated against by the public purchasing authorities will also be improved, and substantial fines are likely to be imposed on anyone violating the Community's public purchasing directives.
- The four excluded sectors (telecommunications, energy, transport and water) will also be incorporated into the Community's systems of awarding construction and supply contracts.

7 PROFESSIONAL MOBILITY

Living and working in the new Europe

As a result of legislation governing professional and worker mobility, EC nationals are entitled to take up employment or set up a business anywhere in the Community. Much of the impenetrable bureaucracy that used to confront people attempting to work abroad has been dismantled, thereby giving professionals, workers and even the unemployed unprecedented opportunities to pursue employment prospects outside their country of origin. Although Community nationals are still required to obtain residence permits, the need to obtain work permits has been abolished. Nevertheless, much work remains before the Commission's goal of creating a genuinely free market for labour is complete. Even before the advent of 1992, some member states (notably France) have been erecting new barriers to labour mobility in an effort to protect their own domestic labour markets.

The attempt to create a single European market would be fatally flawed without a single market for labour. Along with capital, goods and services, the free movement of labour, whether unskilled, skilled or professional, is one of the vital factors of production necessary for the efficient functioning of the Community's economy. Indeed, in many respects the internal market programme would simply not work without the abolition of national labour markets and the freedom for labour to move around the Community in search of more attractive conditions of employment and new opportunities to exploit.

The need to eliminate the barriers preventing the free movement of labour is particularly acute in the case of the service sector, which has recorded impressive rates of growth in recent years and will continue to do so only in an atmosphere of free competition. However, the benefits to be obtained from increased competition between goods, capital and services apply with equal force to every aspect of the labour market. The free movement of labour also constitutes one of the central elements of the European Commission's determination to create a 'Citizens' Europe', in which such freedoms are enshrined in Community law.

The Treaty of Rome already provides the legal basis for Community citizens to establish themselves in any member state and to be treated equally with the citizens of the host state. Article 52 lays down that 'restrictions on the freedom of establishment of nationals of a member state in the territory of another member state shall be abolished by progressive stages . . . such progressive abolition shall also apply to restrictions on the setting up of agencies, branches or subsidiaries by nationals of any member state established in the territory of any member state'. It also specifies that 'freedom of establishment shall include the right to take up and pursue activities as self-employed persons, and to set up and manage undertakings', while Article 57, as amended by the Single European Act, made it incumbent on the Council of Ministers to issue directives facilitating the mutual recognition of 'diplomas, certificates and other evidence of formal qualifications', enabling individuals who qualify in one member state to practise without hindrance in any other.

In an effort to allay the anxieties of member states about the employment of other Community nationals in certain sensitive sectors, principally those of national defence and security, the objective of creating the conditions for the free movement of labour cannot be allowed to prejudice the right of member states to regulate those sectors vital to 'public policy, public security and public health'. However, member states are explicitly prohibited under Article 53 from introducing any new restrictions on the right of Community nationals to establish themselves and take up their professions in any member state of their choosing.

As a result of two landmark rulings by the European Court of Justice in 1974, the right of Community citizens to work in any member state, without discrimination, was further reinforced. However, despite the theoretical right of establishment, a complex web of national regulations governing skills and professions in most member states has proved to be virtually impenetrable for non-nationals, unless they have been prepared to take their professional or vocational examinations all over again. Free movement has effectively been circumscribed by the various national regulations governing access to everything, from plumbing and carpentry to medicine and corporate law. Having qualified in a given field in one member state, the ability to work or practise elsewhere in the Community was frequently barred because of national differences in training periods and qualifications, or because member states simply refused to recognize equivalent qualifications obtained in other member states in order to protect their professional and labour markets from intra-Community competition.

Previous attempts to create a free market for labour

Because most of the barriers to the free circulation of labour arise out of different national educational traditions, reinforced by the fact that professions and skills are essentially nationally based, the European Commission had previously tried to eliminate the differences in member states' level and length of training requirements on a case-by-case basis. The negotiations co-ordinating professional qualifications were both difficult and protracted, but, by 1985, significant progress had been made. Some eight directives had been issued by the Council of Ministers, harmonizing national requirements to take up and practise a variety of professions in any member state. These included directives for doctors (1975), nurses (1977), dentists (1978), veterinary surgeons (1978), midwives (1980), architects (1985), pharmacists (1985) and general practitioners (1986), which was to become the last of the sectoral directives designed to facilitate increased professional mobility.

At the time, the directive governing training for GPs was seen as the dawning of the age of the Euro-doctor. The measure was basically a consolidation and updating of the 1975 directive on essential medical qualifications for GPs, based largely on the British model. British GPs are already required to undergo six years' basic training, followed by three years' practical experience in the National Health Service before becoming fully qualified. By 1990, all other member states also required two years' practical experience in addition to the basic training requirements. Yet while the measure established uniform Community training requirements for GPs, very few have so far availed themselves of their freedom to work in any member state. According to Commission estimates, there are some 600,000 doctors practising in the Community, only 2,000 of whom work in member states other than the one in which they qualified. Language, as in so many other areas, remains the single greatest obstacle to professional mobility in the internal market.

Although the negotiations which led to the implementation of the eight professional mobility directives have helped to build links between related professions in the twelve member states, they were nonetheless a laborious and time-consuming process. The negotiations for the directive governing architects took 17 years to complete, thus acquiring the dubious distinction of becoming one of the longest discussions over a single piece of legislation in the Community's history. Nor was this an isolated phenomenon. The negotiations for the directive for pharmacists came a close second, having taken 16 years to complete, while the proposal for the free movement of lawyers has been on the negotiating table for over a decade with no sign of a breakthrough. With some 80 or so professions still to go, the Commission will be fortunate to have completed the task of creating an internal market for professionals this side of 2092.

Along with many other of the Commission's 1992 initiatives in the internal market programme, the prospects for rapid progress were enhanced immeasurably by abandoning the traditional approach of case-by-case harmonization in favour of a mutual recognition. During the EC summit meeting at Fontainebleau in June 1984 member states gave their approval to a scheme designed to build on the existing legal foundations for the freedom of establishment by introducing the principle of a general system of mutual recognition for all higher education qualifications. With its mandate in hand, the Commission promptly set about drawing up radical new proposals for creation of an internal market for labour and the professions.

The Internal Market White Paper made a sweeping assault on the remaining barriers to the free movement of labour. It declared that:

The Commission considers it crucial that the obstacles which still exist within the Community to free movement for the self-employed and employees be removed by 1992. It considers that Community citizens should be free to engage in their professions throughout the Community, if they so wish, without the obligation to adhere to formalities which, in the final analysis, could serve to discourage such movement.

It also pointed out that, as far as employees were concerned, free movement was now virtually complete, and a succession of rulings by the European Court of Justice had already severely curtailed the right of the public authorities in the various member states to reserve positions for their own nationals. However, certain problems still remained to be solved—for example, obstacles preventing the free movement and residence of Community migrant workers, particularly those living on the frontier of one member state and employed in another. Proposals to remove both the cumbersome administrative procedures governing the acquisition of residence permits in different member states and the taxation of frontier-migrant workers were put forward as potential solutions, and are still awaiting approval by the Council of Ministers.

In addition, the White Paper announced a two-stage programme designed to bring about the essential comparability of different member state vocational training qualifications. The first part of the programme called for the prompt approximation of vocational proficiency certificates among member states, while the second stage involved the introduction of a European vocational training card by 1990, serving as proof in all member states that the holder has been awarded with a universally recognized vocational training qualification.

In May 1987, and after much acrimonious debate between the Twelve, the Council of Ministers endorsed a multimillion pound Commission proposal to increase student exchanges between Community universities. Known as Erasmus, the programme (originally budgeted at £125 million and subsequently trimmed to £60 million) enables an estimated 5% of students in higher education to spend part of their courses in another Community country. Britain receives about £12 million, much of which is spent in the form of a travel allowance of about £1,500 for some 25,000 British students. The programme is to run for three years.

The Commission also declared its intention to propose legislation facilitating the mutual recognition of apprenticeship courses, as well as measures to ensure that freedom of movement is not restricted to only those gainfully employed. One of the most important initiatives in this respect is the 1987 programme to increase co-operation between further educational establishments, designed to promote increased mobility of students around the Community and act as an encouragement for the acquisition of language skills. However, while much of this work remains to be completed, member states have been able to agree on a general system for the mutual recognition of higher education degrees, which has been described as the single most important step towards the creation of a free market for people and services.

Mutual recognition of professional diplomas

In July 1985 the Commission put forward its proposal to create the basic conditions for the free movement of citizens who wish to take up a profession subject to regulation in another member state, and in which access is conditional on holding a specific degree of higher education. It was the first example of the Commission's attempts to create a 'Citizens' Europe', and is based on the principle that what was good for one member state was also good for all others. The proposal does not cover those professions already subject to sectoral directives, such as doctors, dentists and architects, but applies to everyone else, including surveyors, accountants, lawyers, physiotherapists, opticians and psychologists.

Initially, the Commission's proposals were greeted with some reservation by member states, notably Britain and France. Commission officials argued that the general recognition directive would only work on the basis of mutual trust and co-operation between member states. However, it was one thing to say that professionals from one member state would practise according to the requirements of other member states, and quite another to suggest that differences between member states in training and professional practice could be easily overcome on the basis of mutual trust and co-operation, combined with a probationary period of practical experience.

The legal profession, as represented by the Consultative Committee of European Bars, insisted that some mechanism (for example, an aptitude test to determine whether a lawyer from one member state was competent to practise in another) had to be incorporated into the proposal. The Commission objected to such modifications on the grounds that the professions were merely trying to preserve their closed-shop privileges, and that if it granted special concessions for lawyers, every other profession would soon be seeking preferential treatment, thereby undermining the whole purpose of the directive. Besides, one Commission official said indignantly: 'When it comes to the point, is a German lawyer really likely to seek to defend a client in a British court without knowing British law and being able to speak the language?'

At a meeting of the Council of Ministers in Luxembourg in June 1988 ministers agreed a compromise, allowing member states the freedom to decide whether to require non-national professionals to undergo a period of probation or sit an aptitude test before practising in their respective territories. Much to the irritation of the Commission, particularly Lord Cockfield, the compromise also made aptitude tests obligatory for all professions involved in legal work, provided that they were not another examination of 'the entire corpus of knowledge'. After a reading by the European Parliament, the directive was formally approved by the Council of Ministers at the end of 1988 and came into force in 1990.

The directive is predicated on four guiding principles. First, it is general in character, and will be applied to all regulated professions for which a three-year university degree is required. Second, mutual recognition is based on confidence and trust between member states, thereby avoiding the need to harmonize the different education and training schemes for the different professions among all member states. Third, the directive states that recognition is given to the 'finished product', defined as a fully qualified professional who has completed any training required in addition to obtaining a university degree. Foreign nationals can also use the same professional titles as domestic nationals. Finally, where important differences exist between the same profession among different member states, national authorities have the right to examine the competence of individual professionals by means of an aptitude test or a period of probation at their discretion.

The directive also makes special provision for the chartered bodies of Great Britain and the Republic of Ireland. These bodies, which regulate professional standards, are unique to Britain and Ireland. However, while membership of a chartered body is not based on the same level of higher education required in other EC member states in order to practise a particular profession, for the purposes of the directive there is no difference between them. Members of chartered bodies now have access to their sister professions in the Community, and, by the same token, their sister professions also have access to membership of the chartered bodies.

The agreement was described by Francis Maude, the junior trade minister, as 'an essential element in a genuine single market, leading to lower prices for services, and increased opportunities abroad'. It also gives European professionals greater freedom to move around the Community's internal market than is enjoyed by their American counterparts in their domestic market. However, proposals to extend similar rights of mobility to students, pensioners and the unemployed found considerably less sympathy from Britain, supported by Denmark, and remain effectively deadlocked. The Commission has, however, made clear its determination to prevent the new mobility freedoms from being restricted only to those gainfully employed, and will no doubt try again later.

In theory, the agreement on a 'general system for the recognition of higher education diplomas awarded on completion of professional education and training of at least three years' duration' provides an estimated 10 million Community professionals with the freedom to live and work in any member state of their choosing. As an instrument for the promotion of professional mobility, the initiative has been described by the Commission as being 'better than a passport'. However, the Commission is clearly unhappy about the incorporation of aptitude tests into the directive, and has declared its determination to monitor the situation closely in order to prevent the professions from erecting new barriers.

Any attempt by member states to preserve their national markets for professional services against foreign competition could provoke intervention from Brussels. One case of particular interest is the plan by the French legal profession to prohibit second-country lawyers from practising law in France from January 1992 unless they first join the French legal profession. Although the new law does not apply to non-French law firms already practising in France, there are fears that the measure could be used to exclude new entrants from gaining access to the profession. If such fears are borne out, the Commission will be forced to take action.

Proposals for a supplementary directive, known as the 'second general system for the recognition of professional education and training', have been under discussion since October 1988. The measures are designed to ensure mutual recognition for secondary levels of education and training, such as the ordinary national diploma, although they are still awaiting approval by the Council of Ministers. However, the proposed European Community Certificate of Experience, enabling, for example, hairdressers, retailers and hotel and catering staff to rely on the experience obtained in their country of origin when they apply for vacancies in other member states, has been endorsed by Council.

UK professions affected by the Mutual Recognition Directive

1 Institute of Chartered Accountants in England and Wales
2 Institute of Chartered Accountants of Scotland
3 Institute of Chartered Accountants in Ireland
4 Chartered Association of Certified Accountants
5 Chartered Institute of Loss Adjusters
6 Chartered Institute of Management Accountants
7 Institute of Chartered Secretaries and Administrators
8 Chartered Insurance Institute
9 Institute of Actuaries
10 Faculty of Actuaries
11 Chartered Institute of Bankers
12 Institute of Bankers in Scotland
13 Royal Institution of Chartered Surveyors
14 Royal Town Planning Institute
15 Chartered Society of Physiotherapists
16 Royal Society of Chemistry
17 British Psychological Society
18 Library Association
19 Institute of Chartered Foresters
20 Chartered Institute of Building

21 Engineering Council
22 Institute of Energy
23 Institution of Structural
    Engineers
24 Institution of Civil Engineers
25 Institution of Mining
    Engineers
26 Institution of Mining and
    Metallurgy
27 Institution of Electrical
    Engineers
28 Institution of Gas
    Engineers
29 Institution of Mechanical
    Engineers
30 Institution of Chemical
    Engineers
31 Institution of Production
    Engineers
32 Institution of Marine
    Engineers
33 Royal Institution of Naval
    Architects
34 Royal Aeronautical Society
35 Institute of Metals
36 Chartered Institution of
    Building Services Engineers
37 Institute of Measurement and
    Control
38 British Computer Society

The language barrier

Although welcoming the internal market programme as a much-needed stimulus for European industry, many critics have argued that, no matter how many technical, physical and fiscal barriers to trade are dismantled between now and 1992, the linguistic one will remain intact, effectively condemning the Community to permanent fragmentation. Even if all the directives are implemented by the deadline, language will remain the greatest single barrier preventing the creation of a genuine internal market. Linguistic differences are an unfortunate but brutal fact of life, and they will always be with us. They may be of minimal significance where member states have a long tradition of close economic ties, such as the historic relationship between Britain and Holland, but where no such relationship exists, any attempt to break new ground will be difficult —if not impossible—without the requisite linguistic skills.

At the institutional level the Community functions effectively only because it spends large sums of money on interpreters and translators, who account for about one in three of all Community employees. There are nine official languages in the Community: English, French, German, Italian, Spanish, Greek, Danish, Dutch and Portuguese, with Irish as an unofficial working language. Without the services of legions of interpreters and translators, the Community's modest bureaucratic machine, under strain at the best of times, would come to a precipitate halt. Few companies can afford to spend similar sums on interpreters and translators, so what hope is there for the internal market—especially for countries like Britain and France, which have a poor reputation for acquiring foreign-language skills?

According to a survey of 1,500 British companies conducted by Newcastle-upon-Tyne Polytechnic in 1988, the language barrier is far more significant than most British companies appreciate. This showed that a severe shortage of staff speaking European languages was costing British industry millions of pounds every year in lost contracts. Moreover, it found that while English has become the leading language in diplomacy, science and technology, it has been steadily losing ground to European languages in the fields of commerce and industry.

Perhaps even more alarming was the fact that this trend had been observed since Britain joined the Community in 1973, but a disturbing proportion of British companies had failed to take appropriate action, preferring instead to 'muddle through' by inundating foreign consulates with untranslated and (for the most part) 'unintelligible' trade literature. The survey discovered a direct correlation between export performance and linguistic competence, and found that Britain's trade deficit in manufactured goods, particularly in the car, textile, iron, steel, resins and plastics sectors, could be reversed if a more balanced trade relationship could be established with just three countries, Germany, Italy and Japan. Emphasizing the importance of language skills, the report noted that: 'It is not fortuitous that West Germany, Italy and Japan came respectively second, fourth and sixth in the rank order of foreign languages most lacking in British companies.'

Warning British firms that there was little doubt that the survival of manufacturing industry in Britain will come to depend on exports to non-English speaking countries, the authors stressed that: 'The key European languages—German, French, Spanish and Italian—are likely to play an increasingly important role in UK–EC trade if Britain is not only to maintain its market share, but also to increase it'. However, the omens are not favourable. In the decade between 1973 and 1983 the volume of manufactured goods imported into Britain from the Community rose by 300%, while Britain could manage only a modest 66% in the other direction. 'Other countries,' the report said, 'have mastered our language and market, but we have not reciprocated to the same extent. This deficiency, moreover, seems to apply to firms all over Britain'.

The survey also found that, in spite of a marginal increase in company awareness of the importance of language competence since the 1980s, there remained a marked reluctance for companies to employ individuals as much for their linguistic as for their technical skills. Many companies had been deterred from recruiting linguists because of the poor cost-effectiveness of employing a specialist if the frequency of foreign-language use was low. However, the consequences of underestimating the utility of linguists were inescapable. 'British companies are losing valuable trading opportunities for the lack of the right skills in the right languages, and many without realizing it,' the report concluded.

It is clear that it will be the linguists who will manage European industry and commerce in the 1990s. There is already a considerable premium in Europe for people with linguistic skills, and as the competition between European companies (as well as US and Japanese ones located inside the Community) intensifies, they are likely to become a scarce and extremely valuable resource—commanding ever-increasing financial rewards.

However, British students appear to be on course for allowing their Continental counterparts to take the largest share of the anticipated growth in the language market. David Smith, chairman of the 1988 Headmasters' Conference, a forum representing Britain's leading independent schools, warned his colleagues that many of Britain's schools and colleges were simply not prepared to cope with the challenge presented by 1992—particularly as far as foreign languages were concerned. Such predictions appear to be borne out by the statistical evidence. Despite the growing involvement of Japanese companies throughout the European (and especially the British) economy, British universities produce barely 50 Japanese-language graduates a year, while the number of university applications to study other foreign languages is declining steadily.

Although there is good cause to be concerned about the number of linguists produced by the education system, the problem is by no means confined to Britain. However, an attempt by the Commission to promote language teaching through the Lingua programme rapidly turned into an example of how Brussels, in its enthusiasm to promote the European ideal, has a marked tendency to overreach itself. The programme was an attempt to enforce the teaching of two languages at schools throughout Europe, as well as establish a new pupil exchange scheme.

In May 1989, Britain bitterly opposed the project, primarily on the grounds that the Commission had no powers under the Treaty of Rome to legislate in the field of secondary education. Downing Street also felt that the £160 million programme was 'poor value for money'. Domestic commentators felt that to have allowed the plan to be implemented, even for such laudable reasons, would have been to set a precedent that could have had serious repercussions for secondary education in the future.

Eventually, a compromise was reached in which the revised £130 million Lingua programme excluded all reference to secondary schools, and concentrated instead on promoting language teaching in post-secondary fields such as teacher exchanges, vocational training and language instruction for trainees in management, tourism and business studies.

Improving linguistic skills throughout the Community will not by itself be sufficient to encourage widespread mobility of labour and reduce existing disparities in the supply and demand for labour and skills. According to one survey produced by the City University Business School in 1990, demographic changes, combined with a demand for new skills, are likely to produce acute labour shortages in a wide range of sectors towards the end of the decade. Because of declining birth rates, the Community's labour force will begin contracting by 250,000 people a year from 1995 and by one million a year from the turn of the century.

With a decline in the number of young people entering the labour force, employers will find it difficult to make up numbers. Two obvious sources of supply—workers in the over-40 age group and women returning to work after having families—have frequently left school early, suffered protracted periods of unemployment and have had little or no retraining since they originally entered the labour market. Consequently, without the appropriate retraining programmes needed to equip workers with the skills required to fill the new jobs created by industrial change, employers could find themselves in the difficult position of being unable to recruit from surplus pockets of labour because of the lack of industrial and linguistic skills. Moreover, few governments have begun to tackle this issue on the scale many predict will be necessary if a crisis in the labour market is to be avoided by the end of the 1990s.

Checklist of changes

- Introduction of the general system of mutual recognition for all higher education qualifications will enable professionals to practise anywhere in the Community.
- Member states will be entitled to require an aptitude test or a period of probation for all professionals involved in legal work before allowing professionals from other Community countries to practise on their own territory.
- The eight sectoral directives governing professional mobility, passed prior to the White Paper programme, are not affected by the general directive on the mutual recognition of professional qualifications.
- The European Commission intends to introduce a two-stage programme designed to make member states' vocational training qualifications comparable, along with a European vocational training card serving as proof that the holder has been awarded a universally recognizable vocational training qualification.
- Student exchanges between Community universities and higher education colleges will be increased.
- Proposals for a directive governing the mutual recognition of apprenticeships will also be implemented.
- Legislation designed to remove the cumbersome administrative procedures governing the acquisition of residence permits in different member states and the taxation of frontier migrant workers will also be forthcoming.

8 ECONOMIC AND MONETARY UNION: 1
Cross-frontier banking and financial services

Plans for a single currency and a European Bank are part of a broad drive for economic and monetary union, which includes the liberalization of financial services across frontiers. Britain has, by and large, approved of the second but not of the first.

The desire for economic and monetary union derives ultimately from the Treaty of Rome. More recently, additional impetus has also come from the Treaty revisions debated between the Rome summit of December 1990 and the Maastricht summit of December 1991 (see Chapter 9). These, in turn, stem from the report on monetary union ordered by the EC summit at Hannover in 1988 and drawn up by a committee of experts headed by Delors. Key elements in the overall scheme for monetary union include:

1 A directive permitting banking across frontiers on the basis of a single licence, with associated directives on securities trading and other fiscal services;
2 The agreement fully to liberalize capital movements throughout the EC, which came into effect on 1 July 1990;
3 Britain's decision to commit the pound sterling to the Exchange Rate Mechanism (ERM) of the European Monetary System (EMS) in October 1990;
4 Economic convergence, with the Twelve reaching similar targets on inflation rates, interest rates, currency stability and budget deficits;
5 The Delors plan, which envisages a three-phase programme for economic and monetary union culminating in the creation of a European Bank ('Eurofed') to control the money supply in a united EC.

Much of the argument before and since Maastricht has been about the timing of the Delors programme—for example, whether the introduction of a single currency should precede or follow the setting up of a European Bank. But there are also fundamental points of principle at stake. Britain in particular has been reluctant to concede that a single currency is inevitable. Indeed, John Major repeatedly vowed in the run-up to the Maastricht summit that it would never be 'imposed' on the UK, though not least given his need to appease the pro-European faction of the Conservative party, he also made clear that it would be equally wrong to reject the possibility out of hand. Like all EC economic blueprints, the single-currency plan has powerful political overtones, with obvious implications for national sovereignty. Germany, too, has doubts about the pace of economic and monetary union following German re-unification. As the costs of German monetary union have risen, the guardians of the deutschmark at the Bundesbank have become less enthusiastic to agree a rigid timetable for EC currencies to unite. Equally, Germany saw concessions at Maastricht on political union as part of its price for allowing monetary union to proceed.

The Delors three-stage plan

The Delors Committee report, to which the heads of central banks and other financial experts contributed, was published in April 1989. At the Madrid summit in June 1989, EC leaders agreed that the first phase of the plan would amount to 'increased economic and monetary co-ordination' among the Twelve, beginning at the same time as capital movement liberalization in mid-1990. More controversially, and in the face of opposition from Mrs Thatcher, they also agreed to prepare 'completely and adequately' an IGC on stages two and three—understood by France, Germany and other countries to include the evolution of a federal banking structure, as recommended by the Delors report, and possibly a single currency. The Strasbourg summit of December 1989 acknowledged that this would require treaty revision; the Rome summit of October 1990 mapped out a timetable for monetary union and the Rome summit of December 1990 agreed that draft treaty amendments on economic and monetary union would be discussed at the Maastricht summit of December 1991.

Part of the debate at Madrid in 1989 revolved around the question of whether acceptance of phase one of the Delors plan necessarily entailed acceptance in principle of phases two and three. Britain, for example, has never accepted that this is the case. Nonetheless paragraph 39 of the Delors report stated: 'A decision to enter upon the first stage should be a decision to embark on the entire process'. The *Financial Times* commented that if Mrs Thatcher believed Britain could go along with phase one in the hope that the rest of the scheme would never come to fruition, she was mistaken: 'It should be burnt into the consciousness of the British Prime Minister that she may slow down an evolution on which all other members of the EC are resolved; she may influence its form; but she will not stop it'. John Major and his Chancellor of the Exchequer, Norman Lamont, take a subtly different line from Mrs Thatcher; they accept that the rest of the EC may proceed with a European Bank and a single currency, but argue that Britain retains the option to join in or not, as it deems fit.

The three proposed stages of the Delors plan were:

1 Greater economic convergence from 1 July 1990, with all currencies inside the EMS; central bank governors able to make proposals to the Council of Ministers; creation of a European Reserve Fund;
2 More collective decision making, though with national governments retaining ultimate control of fiscal and monetary policy; non-binding rules for national budget deficits; fewer exchange rate realignments; and the establishment of a federal European banking system through a European System of Central Banks (ESCB);
3 Fixed exchange rates; binding deficit constraints; ESCB (the Eurofed) to acquire far-reaching powers over national reserves and fiscal policy; finally, the replacement of national currencies by a single European currency.

Phase one—the least controversial—has been largely achieved. The Spanish peseta joined the EMS on 19 June 1989. At Madrid Mrs Thatcher, who had always insisted that the pound would only join the EMS fully 'when the time is ripe' (a phrase taken by many to mean 'never'), agreed to a list of specific conditions: the pound would join when UK inflation was down to the EC average; when France and Italy had emulated Britain in getting rid of exchange controls; when the internal market had been completed; when a free market in financial services had been achieved; and when competition policy had been strengthened.

Sceptics saw this as a delaying tactic: that is, Mrs Thatcher had joined the bandwagon with the aim of slowing it down. The then Chancellor of the Exchequer, Nigel Lawson, on the other hand, had long pressed for ERM entry, as had Sir Geoffrey Howe. Tensions came to a head within the Cabinet shortly after Madrid, with Sir Geoffrey Howe replaced (briefly) as Foreign Secretary by John Major. Then in October Lawson resigned over the issue, the immediate cause of his departure being Mrs Thatcher's refusal to sack her economic adviser, Sir Alan Walters, a noted opponent of British entry to the ERM. Major became Chancellor in place of Lawson, with Douglas Hurd moving to the Foreign Office from the Home Office.

However, the European monetary question remained an explosive one. In a bid to resolve the single-currency problem Major proposed a 'hard ECU', or parallel currency, as a halfway measure, and in October 1990 finally persuaded Mrs Thatcher that the time was 'ripe' at last for the pound to enter the ERM (see Chapter 9). The introduction of a more pro-European British 'style' since Major took over from Thatcher in November 1990 has helped to reduce tensions within the EC over monetary policy. As the run-up to Maastricht showed, key differences remain between Britain and the other eleven. But away from the public rows over the ECU and the Eurofed, quiet progress has been made in harmonizing other financial services, with Britain and the City of London playing a leading role.

Freedom of capital movements

The official EC Cecchini report on the anticipated benefits of 1992 suggests that deregulation and the absence of artificial barriers will have a major impact on financial services—banks, insurance and securities. To reverse the formula, freedom in financial services could provide the impetus for much of the 1992 programme as capital moves about the integrated market and banks compete across borders to offer services. EC officials estimate the 1992 saving to the financial services sector as between £14 and £15 billion. The four areas targeted for immediate 1992 integration are capital movements, insurance, banking and securities.

All 25 financial service proposals in the 1985 White Paper have been tabled. A number of directives have been in force for some time, such as the 1985 law liberalizing the marketing of mutual funds and unit trusts. However, British unit trust companies complain that they are still excluded from mutual trust markets in Europe, where distribution networks have been largely built up by banks and advertising is restricted. Other areas are even more complex, from motor insurance to 'own initiative' life insurance and group pension schemes. However, the governing principle of 'home country control' is firmly established, meaning that 'the home country supervising financial institutions should be responsible for the authorization of financial operators and the application of key prudential rules to those operators throughout the Community' (Geoffrey Fitchew, Director General of DG XV).

The liberalization of capital movements is already bringing closer an unrestricted market in financial services. The basis for this lies in Article 67 of the Treaty of Rome, which provides for member states to 'abolish all restrictions on the movement of capital belonging to persons resident in the Community'. Some loosening up of capital flows did take place after EC directives were passed in the 1960s, but it took the 1992 impetus to provide the final push. Britain, with its traditional strengths in the field, is likely to benefit more than most other EC countries from free capital flows, a prospect welcomed in the City and Whitehall. Britain abolished exchange controls as early as 1979, though this was more a consequence of the new Thatcher government's political philosophy than the result of developments within the EC.

The Cecchini report anticipates 'substantial economic gains' from the integration of financial markets, because of the pivotal role such services play in acting as the catalyst for European economies in general. The report calculates that the integration in 1992 of banking and credit insurance, brokerage and securities will save the Community 'in the order of 22 billion ECU'—about £15 billion. In the eight countries where financial integration is to take place—Britain, France, Germany, the Benelux nations, Denmark and Italy (Spain, Ireland, Greece and Portugal are excluded until after 1992, the latter two until 1995), the report found 'notably wide margins' in prices charged at present for mortgages, motor insurance and consumer credit. The 'competitive pressures of integration' will level these differentials out, to the benefit of the consumer, Cecchini suggests.

The first part of the Commission's two-stage plan for free capital flows across frontiers began in February 1987, with the liberalization of cross-border transactions in unit trusts, unlisted securities and long-term trade credits. The second phase, agreed in June 1988, completed the process by providing for full liberalization beginning in July 1990. There were some worries about the possible impact on the EMS, but in fact currencies have remained stable since July 1990. Though some countries maintained higher interest rates to restrain domestic demand, there was no excessive flow of funds from weaker economies, such as Italy's to stronger ones, such as Germany's, partly because domestic borrowers still find it troublesome to borrow abroad.

In banking, there is already a degree of free competition. In practice, however, as Cecchini noted: 'It appears difficult for many banks to compete successfully in other Community countries because new establishment involves considerable costs not borne by existing domestic banking networks'. The Second Banking Directive, tabled in January 1988 and adopted by the Council on 19 June 1989, deals with these hidden barriers —including restrictions on foreign involvement in local banks, prevalent in southern Europe—and lays the basis for a single licensing system, while seeking to allay US fears and to tighten up on possible abuses (see below).

Insurance in the single market

Similar restrictions are to be swept away in insurance and securities trading. There has been widespread irritation over barriers put up by insurance firms in Germany, where non-German insurance companies must have a permanent local establishment, pay penalizing tax rates which the Commission regards as discriminatory. The principle was tested in the European Court in 1986, when German insurers complained that they had been fined for obtaining for clients low-cost industrial and marine insurance in Britain. Due to these test cases, and qualified majority voting, a directive on cross-border competition in non-life insurance for commercial customers is already on the statute books.

In their study on Europe's domestic market, Jacques Pelkmans and Alan Winters write that 'insurance probably offers more scope for British gains from the European Domestic Market than does banking'. The 1986 ruling by the European Court freed co-insurance from restrictions, and set out once and for all the right of establishment for insurance companies in other EC states. As in other areas, barriers to cross-border trade in insurance were supposed to disappear in accordance with earlier directives, notably the 1978 directive on co-insurance. In practice it has taken the 1992 process to crack—or start to crack—a particularly tough nut.

The non-life directive, passed in June 1988, came into force in July 1990. It permits cross-frontier trade by larger companies, defined as those with a minimum turnover of 24 million ECUs (£16 million) or over 500 employees. It covers transport risks—marine and aviation, general liability, property and fire. Because national governments derive substantial income from life insurance tax, and because tax on insurance still differs from country to country, the directive concedes that tax can still be collected by the state within which the risk is insured. Sir Leon Brittan, the Commissioner for Competition Policy, observed that the existence of twelve separate markets for non-life insurance had 'cramped competition, pushed up prices and reduced consumer choice'.

Agreement on common insurance policies throughout Europe is still a long way off, but there are likely to be a growing number of cross-border mergers in insurance, as the recent acquisition of Equity and Life by the French Compagnie du Midi illustrates. Eagle Star has complained that French insurance companies, many of which are state-subsidized, are underpricing to win UK business. The business could just as well flow the other way: British companies such as Royal Insurance are actively expanding their Continental operations.

However, life insurance remains problematical. The Commission tabled its third directive on life assurance in draft form in February 1991. To meet objections from the insurance brokers, the draft proposes that customers would still be protected under the laws of their country of residence or nationality, regardless of where they bought the policy. Policy holders, moreover, would have a 30-day period during which to reconsider. John Redwood, the Trade Minister, said in June 1991 that Britain would use its EC presidency in the second half of 1992 to speed up adoption of the Commission draft directive. UK companies stand to do well, because they offer greater returns than their Continental counterparts. There are fewer restrictions on UK investment portfolios. A survey by Bacon and Woodrow, Actuaries, on behalf of the Association of British Insurers, shows that rates of return from 'with profits' insurance over 15 years averaged 8.2% in the UK compared to 6% in Germany and even less in other EC countries. This makes UK endowment policies attractive to other Europeans, whereas British buyers are unlikely to rush to take out European insurance (except for British citizens securing mortgages to buy property elsewhere in the EC and wishing to hold an accompanying endowment policy in the same local currency).

The main problem remains the German government's reluctance to allow foreign insurance companies into its protected market. Even in commercial insurance, which Germany has (in theory) agreed to open up to competition, rigid German regulations on premiums amount to a form of protectionism. There is, in addition, a German government monopoly on fire and property insurance, and special rules for health insurance. On the other hand, such restrictions may be undermined by cross-frontier banking, which is well advanced, as banks are permitted to offer a range of services across frontiers (insurance included).

Securities and stockbroking

The same applies to restrictions on stockbroking. The Commission's directives on cross-border dealings in securities and equities have been repeatedly held up. In the UK, the Securities and Investments Board and the Securities Association have lobbied hard in Brussels against directives which, they believe, will place tightly regulated British firms at a disadvantage to less-regulated Continental competitors. They also dislike the idea of an EC trading mentality, under which non-EC firms will be excluded where possible. The Commission issued proposals in this field at the end of 1988. The hope in Brussels is that by 1993 (if not 1992) the differing EC country regulations governing securities trading will be brought into line (see also the section on the Second Banking Directive, page 138). A harmonization directive on brokerage and investment houses is also under consideration in Brussels on the assumption that cross-border speculation will increase. A new draft 'recognition of particulars' directive would require any stock exchange in any EC country to accept a company for trading if its listing particulars had already been accepted by a stock exchange in another EC state. Under the directive, companies would have to have three years' trading experience to be listed. This presents few problems for countries like France, where similar regulations already apply, but creates difficulties for the London Stock Exchange, where the unlisted securities market requires a three-year track record but listed companies must have at least five years' trading experience.

However, resistance to cross-border securities trading comes mainly from the southern EC states—the so-called 'Club Med' of Spain, Italy and France—who want to protect their stock exchanges from competition for as long as possible. Given modern electronic technology traders could go ahead and deal across borders—directive or no directive—but protectionist-minded governments would almost certainly retaliate by requiring foreign investors to incorporate locally or set up local subsidiaries.

In May 1991 Andrew Hugh Smith, chairman of the International Stock Exchange in London, deplored the lack of progress on a single-licence trading system for securities. John Redwood, the Trade Minister, warned that if the directive was not passed the likely beneficiaries would be 'offshore centres' outside the EC such as Zurich. 'There is no economic law which states that the EC will always maintain a major financial services industry,' he said. 'Modern technology allows people to shift business around the world rapidly.'

Mortgages across frontiers

In theory, banks and finance houses across the EC will compete with each other after 1992 in offering home loans. The extent to which this happens will depend on how far home loan practices are harmonized. At present, they differ widely, as does home ownership, which is high in Britain and Spain (64% owner occupation) and in Ireland (74%) but low in Germany (37%) and the Netherlands (44%), where rented accommodation is the norm. The Commission has therefore not sought to table a mortgage finance directive, but instead is incorporating the mutual recognition of home loan standards into the Second Banking Directive.

French, Danish and Dutch finance houses have already set up subsidiaries in the UK to offer mortgages to home buyers. However, this is not seen as a real threat by any of the major building societies. They, in turn, are making modest forays into the Continental housing market: Abbey National has a Spanish subsidiary, Abbeycorp (with Swiss involvement) and the Midland Bank's French subsidiary is making inroads into the French mortgage business. Building society managers expect to see more cross-border activity of this kind in 1992. However, an EC-wide regulated home loan market is some way off, especially since countries like Germany operate strict rules for home loans through tightly regulated finance institutions, with home buyers obliged to prove that they have saved a high proportion of the value of the house. Some UK finance houses already offer ECU mortgages, based on the ECU basket of European currencies.

Export Credit Guarantees

Another intriguing question is whether the practice of using state agencies such as the Export Credits Guarantee Department (ECGD) to support trading ventures will continue to make sense either for intra-European trade or for EC-based trade with the rest of the world. It is possible that, as the financial barriers come down, credit insurance will increasingly pass to private rather than government institutions, or a combination of the two, along the lines of existing German private insurance companies, which reinsure with the government.

Export finance not only underwrites the export risk, it also insures the exporter against bankruptcy by foreign customers. However, in theory, a Dutch or French insurer could undercut the ECGD by offering British exporters the same service for exports to Holland or France, on the same terms as the ECGD but with the advantage of local knowledge. Moreover, the concept of 'national exports' will become increasingly outdated in the single market, and the concept of 'European' exports to non-EC countries will come to the fore.

This could lead in the long run to the development of a pan-European export credit agency. A step in this direction was taken in July 1991, when the Dutch group Nederlandsche Credietverzekering Maatschappij NV was given ECGD short-term business in the face of competition from other EC insurance groups, notably Assicurazioni Generali of Italy. There was disquiet in the House of Commons over the fact that the winning bid was not British. But the government replied that the Dutch company chosen had offered cash to help revitalize the ECGD, with the aim of helping British exporters by offering insurance against unusual risks such as buyer insolvency or even political upheaval.

Capital transfers and insider trading

The June 1988 directive on completing capital movements liberalization by July 1990 is a textbook example of the passage of a 1992 directive from draft proposal to law in the face of twelve differing national standpoints. Britain's initial objection was that the free flow of capital across frontiers should not be regarded as a step towards the harmonization of indirect taxes, over which the UK retains its veto. But others also had reservations.

France in particular, under the socialist government of Michel Rocard, expressed strong doubts, arguing that if EC citizens were able to move capital around the Community freely this could only encourage fraud and tax evasion. This objection was met by an undertaking from the Commission that it would report on ways of strengthening cross-border tax inspection to prevent abuses. France, unlike Britain, has no pay-as-you-earn (PAYE) tax system, and French tax officials rely on their right to obtain information from banks—a further reason for French objections to the directive. The City of London is bound to benefit from liberalization as EC capital flows to a proven financial centre, with market capitalization totalling $500 billion. Only Germany comes close, with $160 billion, while financial markets in France and Italy have $100 billion each. However, anxieties about fraud persist in London as well as in Paris. A further misgiving in London is that EC investors may regard the City as over-regulated under the 1986 Financial Services Act—drawn up by the government without thought of the implications of 1992.

Fears that the removal of restrictions on bank account movements within the EC could benefit tax dodgers and other villains rather than *bona fide* business executives and bank customers have been partly met by the new directive on insider dealing agreed by finance ministers in Luxembourg in June 1989 at the same time as the Second Banking Directive. The Commission's original proposals were adapted to meet the demands of the British Bankers Association and City institutions, to the point where they closely resemble UK legislation by laying down a narrow definition of insider trading, embracing both 'primary' and 'secondary' insiders who misuse information about a company they work for or are 'closely associated with', while allowing normal stock market activities to go ahead unhindered. The directive requires EC countries to co-operate across frontiers in tracking down illegal stock exchange activity. All states are obliged to bring their national laws into line with the directive by 1 June 1992, causing problems for Belgium, Italy, Ireland and Germany, which have little or no insider trading legislation.

Another proposal—for taxing bank interest and investment income at source—has had a less favourable reception. Such a withholding tax, proposed variously at 10% or 15%, would apply to National Savings and building society accounts, and would help—for example—to allay French fears of a diversion of savings to tax-free Luxembourg. However, when in July 1989 Pierre Beregevoy, the French Finance Minister, chaired a discussion on reducing tax evasion in an era of free capital flows, Mme Christiane Scrivener, the Commissioner for Fiscal Affairs, stressed co-operation against fraud rather than a withholding tax, a clear admission that the tax was unpopular. Britain described it as 'misguided', since it would add to business costs and raise interest rates. Germany announced in July 1989 it was abolishing its own unpopular 10% withholding tax and said it would seek 'a more viable tax on investment earnings' with its EC partners.

The Second Banking Directive: solvency ratios and reciprocity

The Second Banking Directive, adopted in June 1989, is a powerful force propelling the European banking world towards a financial revolution. Under the directive, due to come into force on 1 January 1993, any High Street bank in an EC member country will be able to operate throughout the Community on the basis of a single licence issued in its country of origin—not in the 'host' country. In other words, the directive accepts the principle that it is enough for banks to be properly authorized and supervised in their home country for them to be able to deal in deposits and loans of both cash and securities in any of the other states. The directive alters a situation in which banks can only open subsidiaries in another country, and then subject to local controls. Host countries retain the right to control bank liquidity for reasons of monetary policy.

Under the directive, Lloyds or National Westminster, for example, will be able to operate on the Continent without local authorization—and equally, Crédit Lyonnais or the Dresdner Bank can operate in Britain, competing with British banks in offering a range of services. British banks claim to be ready for the fray: Barclays, for example, says it has 3,200 offices 'from Munich to Murcia, Paris to Piraeus' with Barclays de Zoete Wedd particularly strong in France, Spain and the Netherlands (*1992: What Does the Future Hold for Your Business?*, Barclays Corporate Marketing Department). The Bank of England suggested in a survey in June 1989 (*The Single European Market: Survey of the UK Financial Services Industry*) that France, Italy and Spain offer the best markets for UK bank expansion.

Only post-1992 practice will show how far this can develop: for example, national home loan regulations will still differ widely. German home buyers have to prove they have saved one-third of the proposed mortgage. Banks licensed to operate throughout the EC must have a minimum working capital of £3.5 million and provide Brussels with information on their larger shareholders. Solvency ratios have proved a sticking point: under the Basle agreement of July 1988, reflected in an EC draft directive, the Group of Ten agreed that a bank's funds must constitute at least 8% of its risk-weighted assets. Both Germany and Denmark object that mortgage lending, which plays a large role in their banking objectives, is given too high a risk weighting both in the Basle agreement on solvency ratios and in the subsequent EC directive. (UK discount houses are exempted because of their 'special nature'.)

Ordinary bank customers will be more concerned with the standardization of cashpoint bank cards, beginning in Belgium, Germany, Denmark and—surprisingly—Portugal and Spain, with banks in those countries negotiating joint agreements on customer access to computerized networks. Such Euro-networks or even bank mergers will become a common feature. In the wake of the BCCI collapse in July 1991, the Commission proposed making countries in which banks are registered responsible for compensating depositors in other countries if one of their banks fails —a scheme designed to avoid 'brass plate' banks which avoid proper supervision.

Non-EC banks will have access to the EC, but the EC will retaliate by withholding approval for non-EC banking operations if EC banks are not given comparable treatment in third countries. This softens earlier proposals under which automatic penalties would have been imposed on non-EC banks from countries which created difficulties for European banks. According to Willy de Clercq, the then External Affairs Commissioner, speaking in Austria in August 1988:

> Our view is that Community credit institutions should have equal access to the financial markets of non-European countries. The Commission will check on a case-by-case basis whether similar institutions from all member states are given the same treatment in the non-Community country concerned.

However, in September 1988, Lord Young, the then Trade and Industry Secretary, told a meeting of the Italian Chamber of Commerce in London that the reciprocity proposal would erect a wall of protectionism round Europe and threaten London's position as a key financial centre open to all comers. His view is supported by the Bank of England, which opposed interference by Brussels which might, for example, prevent a US bank from opening in London because an undercapitalized Portuguese bank had been barred from the United States.

This had given rise to anxiety in the United States, where the federal banking authorities maintain that reciprocity would require radical changes in US interstate banking law. To meet this, the directive was reformulated to provide for 'case-by-case' negotiations with countries where commercial and investment banking are legally separate. It remains unclear, however, just how the EC's 1992 banking plans will overlap with the international supervisory regulations being drafted by the Bank for International Settlements (BIS) in Basle, although the BIS is involved in EC deliberations.

Remaining details to be cleared up involve how national laws requiring banks to disclose information for tax purposes will be retained. Governments retain their powers to control national instruments of fiscal policy such as interest rates—though this may also be eroded if the co-ordination of interest rates becomes a consequence of economic integration and EMS management in 1992 conditions. For Britain, a further problem arises in the field of securities, listed by the directive as one of the 'core activities' of banking, along with deposits, loans, credit, portfolio management and leasing.

The City is in a strong position, however, with a daily foreign exchange turnover of $90 billion, compared to $50 billion in New York and Tokyo. It attracts business because of its skills and its liberal regulatory system, both assets for 1992. This could put British banks in a strong position as cross-border banking strategies emerge: the cross-shareholding link-up between the Royal Bank of Scotland and Banco Santander of Spain—plus its German and Belgian subsidiaries—announced in October 1988 is just one example, though the first to involve a UK bank. The RBS and Santander are negotiating with a third partner, Crédit Commercial de France (CCF). Other link-ups include a deal between Amro Bank in the Netherlands and the Société Générale of Belgium; the purchase by the Deutsche Bank of Banca d'America e d'Italia; a joint venture between Belgium's Générale de Banque and the Amsterdam–Rotterdam Bank; and the acquisition by Crédit Lyonnais of a controlling interest in Credito Bergamasco of Italy. In July 1989 Hypotheken und Wechsel Bank of Bavaria took a 50% stake in Foreign and Colonial Management, the British fund management group, which said it was 'positioning itself firmly on the 1992 express'. In November 1989 Morgan Grenfell announced it had agreed to a $1.5 billion takeover bid by Deutsche Bank, a move said by the German bank to reflect 'the pre-eminence of London in Europe in corporate finance and asset management'. In 1991 the Dresdner Bank and the Banque Nationale de Paris exchanged 10% shares with a view to collaborating in international markets.

The attraction of such deals lies in increased capital assets and market access, but they also usually involve the harmonization of computerized cash-card services and point-of-sale systems, the most obvious benefit to customers. Consumer credit is a likely growth area, with further expansion by systems such as Eurocard and Visa. The European Council for Payment Systems, which groups 40 banks, is working on compatibility for all electronic card systems. In April 1990 larger banks and credit card companies issued a voluntary code of practice to forestall a Commission regulation on the subject. But the Commission believes that the code puts too much onus on the cardholder, who is obliged to 'take the necessary measures immediately to become aware of the circumstances of the theft or loss, and demonstrate that he took such measures'.

Checklist of changes

- All restrictions on movement of capital belonging to EC residents have been abolished
- Cross border competition in non life insurance for commercial clients is in effect.
- Cross border competition in life insurance should eventually be allowed.
- Restrictions preventing other EC nationals from trading in securities or acting as brokers are to be lifted.
- Any High Street bank will be able to operate throughout the Community on the basis of a single licence under the Second Banking Directive.
- A single licencing system for securities is proposed.
- Compatible credit/cash card technology to be more widespread.

9 ECONOMIC AND MONETARY UNION: 2
The European Bank and a single currency

Whatever the arguments over national sovereignty, many traders, customers and business executives support closer monetary integration on the grounds that changing money around the EC means sizeable financial losses, while transferring money from bank to bank within the Community is a haphazard and costly business. The European Consumers Bureau (BEUC) has concluded that, at the moment, banks do not listen to clients' instructions when making money transfers: fail to make clear the cost of a transaction in advance: and charge both sender and payee even where the remitter has agreed to bear the costs. As for *bureaux de change*, BEUC concluded that travellers making a round-trip of EC capitals would lose almost half their spending money just by paying handling charges—and by losing on official exchange rates. In 1990 Sir Leon Brittan, the Commissioner for Competition Policy, tabled proposals to eliminate currency handling charges, arguing—in the face of fierce opposition from High Street banks and agencies such as Thomas Cook—that in the run-up to a single currency, exchanging pounds for francs or marks need not be any different from exchanging English pounds for Scottish pounds—a cost-free transaction.

In Britain, however, the question of whether pounds, marks and francs should be replaced by the ECU, with money supply controlled by a European Bank, is seen not only as an issue of fiscal harmony but also as a matter of national sovereignty, with the pound sterling as a symbol of independence and national monetary control. Similar tensions lay behind much of the debate in 1989–90 over whether the pound should join the EMS, as provided for in phase one of the Delors plan.

Pressure for Britain to join the EMS became powerful after the 1989 Madrid summit, with Pierre Beregevoy, the French Finance Minister, observing that 'a common monetary policy cannot work effectively as long as Great Britain remains outside the EMS exchange mechanism'. Both Nigel Lawson and Sir Geoffrey Howe agreed, and Howe predicted that the pound would be inside the ERM by the time of the next UK election, in 1992. He was right—although the intense manoeuvring over whether and when the pound should join was part of the bruising Cabinet debate over Europe which led to his resignation, that of Lawson and, ultimately, Mrs Thatcher's too.

Opposition to ERM entry stemmed partly from the belief, expressed among others by Tim Congdon, economic adviser to Gerrard and National, that between 1987 and 1988, when sterling was informally pegged to the German mark, the effect on credit growth and inflationary pressures had been 'disastrous'. The EC nations, Congdon wrote in *The Times* on the eve of the Madrid summit, suffered from 'deep-seated financial incompatibility'. This was a view shared by Sir Alan Walters, Mrs Thatcher's economic adviser, who famously called the EMS 'half-baked'. Opponents of ERM entry argued that the merits of the EMS in keeping down inflation had been exaggerated; that sterling had a global as well as European role; and that once inside the EMS, sterling would be dominated by the mark, the most powerful European currency.

EMS: arguments for and against

The EMS dates from 1979, and was designed as a way of stabilizing currency fluctuations after the collapse of the post-war Bretton Woods fixed exchange-rate system, and the partial failure of the European 'Snake', which allowed fluctuations within agreed limits. Unlike the Snake, the EMS is a system for full currency management, under which currencies participating in the ERM have fixed rates against the European Currency Unit (ECU). The ECU in turn is based on the 'basket' of currencies participating in the EMS. Until October 1990 sterling was part of the ECU 'basket', but not of the ERM itself. When it joined it did so—like the Italian lira and the Spanish peseta—within the 'broad band' of 6%, that is, it could fluctuate in value up to 6% above or below its value at entry, giving a total potential fluctuation of 12%. (The 'narrower' band permits maximum variations of no more than 3% either way.)

The ERM currencies have their ECU rate realigned at sessions of EC finance ministers called for the purpose. Between realignment meetings the central banks intervene in foreign-exchange markets to support a member currency when it reaches its 'floor', drawing on a reserve called the European Monetary Co-operation Fund, based on members' gold and currency reserves. As the British debate continued, supporters of the EMS pointed to its stability since 1979 and to the steady reduction in inflation differentials. Many British executives argued that planning would be much simpler if the pound were part of a stable currency system. Delors marked the tenth anniversary of the EMS in March 1989 by saying it had 'given the rest of the world a concrete example of the Community's capacity to act together and create an island of stability in an ocean of monetary turbulence'.

Sceptics pointed out that France and Germany were—and are—often in conflict over monetary policy, despite their membership of the EMS and the existence of a Franco–German Finance Council, set up in March 1988. French officials express open anger when the Bundesbank raises its interest rates and sets off a European chain reaction without consulting its French counterpart. Indeed, French enthusiasm for a common currency and European Bank stems in part from the French desire to curb the dominant German currency and economy.

However, bankers and businessmen continued to urge ERM entry for the pound, and a Commons select committee report entitled *Financial Services and the Single European Market* said Britain should join the EMS 'as soon as possible' to enable the City to be 'the financial gateway to Europe' in 1992.

On 8 October 1990 John Major, who succeeded Lawson as Chancellor, announced full UK membership of the ERM, together with a 1% cut in bank base rates. The pound entered the ERM at a rate of 2.95 DM. Major said entry would reinforce firm monetary policy and help bring down inflation. Mrs Thatcher, a less convincing convert, declared that the conditions she had outlined at Madrid (see Chapter 8) had been met: 'The real thing that made this decision possible was the uncontestable signs that the economy is working in the way we intended it to in reducing inflationary pressures'. Lawson, not to be outdone, said in the Commons that the 'real tragedy' was that the pound had not joined the EMS five years earlier.

The move produced a euphoric surge in sterling on foreign exchange markets, and Beregevoy called it 'good news for Europe'. A year later, on the anniversary of the move, *The Economist* reported that it had been 'a great success', and ran a photograph of Lawson captioned 'Proved right', with another of Sir Alan Walters captioned 'Proved wrong'. Interest rates had fallen from 15% on the eve of entry to 10%, and inflation had fallen from nearly 11% to 4%—although a price had been paid in high unemployment. Analysts agreed that the timing of entry had not been particularly propitious, with German unification pushing German interest rates higher, a recession looming and UK wage inflation ahead of its EC partners—but any moment chosen would have had its drawbacks.

The ECU: a future single currency?

When sterling joined the ERM Major was careful to stress that this did not mean that Britain also agreed in principle to a single European currency. Indeed during his term as Chancellor, Major pioneered the concept of a 'hard ECU' in a bid to head off the single-currency idea. Delors was sceptical about sterling's entry into the ERM, telling EC foreign ministers in Venice that 'only the future will tell us whether this was a pretext for slowing down the process of integration'.

The 'hard ECU', as outlined by Major in June 1990, was intended as a 'parallel currency' alongside national currencies. Under the scheme, which received backing from Carlos Solchaga, the Spanish Finance Minister, a European Monetary Fund would be established (replacing the plan for a more ambitious European Bank), with powers to issue 'hard ECUS' and set ECU interest rates. Sir Leon Brittan took up the idea as an interim measure, observing that since British shoppers would be disconcerted to find their familiar pounds and pence replaced, 'our notes and coins could have a sterling value on one side and the ECU equivalent on the other'. Major, using language very different from that of Mrs Thatcher, conceded that the hard ECU could develop into a single currency if that was what peoples and governments wanted.

However, at the Rome summit of December 1990, which set out the timetable for proposed treaty revisions to be discussed at Maastricht a year later, Delors denounced the Major plan as a device for avoiding the single currency itself. As late as May 1991, on the other hand, Norman Lamont, Major's successor as Chancellor, was insisting that because a single currency was 'a long way down the road' and 'a leap in the dark with high risks', the hard ECU or parallel currency was still a valid initiative. *The Times* agreed, noting in an editorial that the hard ECU was no longer an 'unappealingly premature baby' and had some support from Spain, France and Italy as an evolutionary concept.

So far, the ECU remains largely a notional currency, used as a unit of account for EMS realignments and EC internal calculations. But it is increasingly also used as a unit of payment and reserve currency, and both travellers cheques and Eurobonds can be ECU-dominated. One EC country—Belgium—has even issued ECU coins bearing a portrait of the sixteenth-century Emperor Charles V. The coins—5 and 50 ECU pieces, minted in silver and gold, respectively—are intended primarily as collectors' items. In theory they are legal tender, but no restaurant or shop will take them, as we discovered when trying to pay with ECUs. Nonetheless, the issue is intended by Belgium as a gesture in the direction of a future common currency.

A clearing house for ECU transactions was set up in October 1986 by a consortium of seven European banks, including Lloyds and the Crédit Lyonnais. One Luxembourg bank has even issued Visa credit cards in ECUs. At present, less than 1% of business transactions in the EC are invoiced in ECUs, though this would change if it became a parallel currency. The European Parliament's Economic and Monetary Affairs Committee has urged use of the ECU for paying workers in EC border areas —for example, a Dutchman working in Germany might hold a bank account in ECUs and convert them to marks or guilders as required. One British firm, APV Baker, reported in 1991 being paid 71 million ECUs by the Soviet Union for food-processing equipment—but converted the ECUs into sterling. As the firm's finance manager observed, 'If you could feel a 50 ECU note, some of the resistance to using it [the ECU] might disappear'.

The ECU, meanwhile, remains little known in Britain, except to the money markets. When we offered Belgian-issued ECUs to London shopkeepers and bus drivers as an experiment while preparing *The Times Guide to 1992*, comments varied from 'What bright spark thought that one up?' (a bus driver) and 'We'd have to change all the tills and retrain the staff—try Harrods, they might take them' (a DIY store supervisor) to 'It might be useful if you did a lot of travelling, but people are already getting angry about Brussels having a say in what goes on over here' (a policeman in Trafalgar Square). 'I'm very British—it just wouldn't seem like England if we had a European currency. Why can't they all change over to our money?' was a typical reaction (in this case, a newspaper seller outside a London Underground station). There was no greater familiarity with the ECU when we tried again in 1991. Some object on the grounds that the ECU also happens to be the name of a medieval French coin.

In August 1988 the Treasury took the unusual step of issuing bills denominated in ECUs—the first such bills to be internationally tradeable. The aim was to diversify Britain's reserves while, at the same time, encouraging the development of an ECU market in London. Commission officials were quick to warn, however, that the issuing of ECU-denominated bills could not be a substitute for other moves towards monetary union—a warning they repeated over Major's 'hard ECU' plan.

The EC summit in Rome in October 1990 laid down a timetable for EMU, with phase two—the European Bank—set for 1994, and phase three—the single currency—set for 1997 (see Introduction). In May 1991 Delors announced a compromise formula under which the UK could sign a treaty at Maastricht allowing for a single currency, with the proviso that the UK Parliament could decide whether or not to join at a later date —an 'opt-out' clause. Before the EC summit in Luxembourg in June 1991, Major and Chancellor Kohl of Germany agreed that the summit would not rush into plans for a single currency and a European Bank, but would 'take stock'. Because of the cost of German monetary union following unification, Kohl's enthusiasm for a single currency has dimmed. 'No-one is ready to give up the stable deutschmark for an unstable currency— that is just stating the obvious' he remarked. Hans Tietmeyer, vice-president of the Bundesbank, said in Frankfurt in June 1991 that Germany needed a strong independent mark 'for several years ahead' because of the 'difficult situation' created by German unity.

However, in September 1991, when EC finance ministers met at Apel-doorn in the Netherlands under the Dutch EC presidency, Wim Kok, the Dutch Finance Minister, sought to force the pace by presenting a draft agreement under which any six EC members who met agreed economic criteria could go it alone on a single currency, leaving the others to join later. Lamont accepted this 'inner core' concept, noting that Britain would almost certainly qualify for the inner group if it chose—but emphasized that Britain might well choose to stay out. The Dutch came under fire for proposing, in effect, a 'two-speed EMU', but replied that what was proposed was a 'one-speed EMU' with countries like Britain or some of the southern EC nations granted 'temporary exemptions' if they so wished. This still implied, however—to Lamont's dissatisfaction—that countries which opted not to use the single currency would inevitably 'opt in' at some future date.

Theo Waigel, the German Finance Minister, said that Germany could accept the Dutch conditions for economic convergence before introduction of a single currency, with EC states having to converge on inflation, interest rates and currency stability, but argued that the 'core group' which met these conditions should consist of seven or eight countries rather than six. EC finance ministers could decide which countries qualified for a single currency, and EC leaders would confirm this at a summit. Under the Apeldoorn plan, however, plans for a European Bank would be delayed: instead of the Bank being established in 1994, with a single currency introduced later, a European Monetary Institute (suggested by Major as part of his 'hard ECU' scheme) would co-ordinate monetary policies throughout the Twelve, reporting by 1996 on whether convergence was sufficient to allow for a single currency, and transforming itself into the European Bank once this had been achieved.

In October 1991 EC finance ministers meeting in Luxembourg discussed a Dutch proposal that 'clear, strict and comparable' yardsticks for measuring budgetary convergence should be written into the Treaty of Rome amendments, including the power to fine an EC government which overspent. Germany backed a Dutch suggestion that an EC economy would be judged to have entered the 'danger zone' if it had a ratio of national debt to GDP of over 60%, and if its annual budget deficit amounted to more than 3% of GDP and/or exceeded capital investment. Greece and Italy opposed such rigid formulas, while Britain argued that economic performance should be measured over a period of years, not annually.

In the run-up to the Maastricht summit Major and Lamont vowed that they would never allow the EC to 'impose' a single currency on the UK. At the Conservative Party conference in October 1991 Lamont declared, to loud applause, that although Britain's future lay in Europe:

> I will not allow a single currency to be imposed on this country.
> Unlike the Labour Party, we do not want laws to be made and taxes to be raised in Brussels for which the British people have not voted.

Frankfurt versus London: the European Central Bank

The communiqué issued at the Hannover summit of 1988 which commissioned the Delors report did not include the words 'European Central Bank'. This was at Mrs Thatcher's insistence. She said she did not expect to see a European Central Bank in her lifetime and added flatly: 'I do not share the vision of a United States of Europe and a single currency'. On the eve of the summit Mrs Thatcher had remarked that a European Bank could only come about when Parliament was abolished and there was a European government instead.

However, a number of leaders had made it clear at Hannover that they regarded a European Bank or 'Eurofed' as an integral part of monetary union. The communiqué at Hannover recalled the objective of the 'progressive realization of economic and monetary union' affirmed in the Single European Act. The Delors committee set up by Hannover contained eleven EC central bank governors, including Robin Leigh-Pemberton (Governor of the Bank of England). The committee also drew on experts such as Alexandre Lamfalussy (general manager of the Bank for International Settlements), Niels Thygesen (a Danish economics professor), Miguel Boyer (a former Spanish finance minister) and Frans Andriessen (former Dutch Finance Minister and EC Agriculture Commissioner in the first Delors Commission, now External Relations Commissioner).

'We have a structure and a date' President Mitterrand of France declared after Hannover. 'If there is to be monetary union there must be a central body to manage it. What remains to be settled is its relationship to the existing central banks.' The options considered by Delors included:

1 The replacement of national central banks by a Bank of Europe;
2 Less radically, a European Bank, or federal reserve, controlled by the existing central banks;
3 Least radical of all, increased co-ordination among central banks.

Any of these options could be accompanied by the issuing of ECU's as a European currency to be used in parallel with national currencies—for example, for commercial transactions to pay travel bills. Under the Luxembourg and Dutch EC presidencies in 1991, however, a debate arose over whether the European Bank should take the form in the first instance of a 'European Monetary Institute', whose function would be to manage economic convergence—including co-ordination of the member states' medium-term economic strategies—and to preside over the gradual introduction of the ECU as a parallel currency before transforming itself into a fully fledged 'Eurofed'.

The Delors concept of an ESCB (European System of Central Banks) resembles option 2. However, even a central bank 'system' would entail new central banking institutions. There are fears in the City that, whatever form it takes, a future Euro Bank will be located in Frankfurt—unless Britain takes steps to ensure that, like the new European Bank for Reconstruction and Development (EBRD) to aid Eastern Europe, it comes to London or is shared with Frankfurt. British banking officials argue that a European federal reserve bank in Frankfurt would become the operational centre of official foreign exchange and money market intervention in the Community, thus threatening London's pre-eminence as a financial centre.

A further difficulty arises over the question of who would control the 'Eurofed'—the bankers themselves, on the model of the powerful and independent Bundesbank, or governments, through EC finance ministers? In November 1990, EC central bank governors drew up draft statutes for a future European Bank. These required central bank governors under the new system to be independent not only in relation to the Bank but also within their own national systems. Leigh-Pemberton placed a UK 'reserve' on these terms, arguing that Bundesbank-style independence would require changes not only in Britain (where the Bank of England is under Treasury control and directly linked to government instruments of monetary control) but also in France, where a similar system obtains.

The Rome summit of October 1990 envisaged January 1994 as the starting date for the European Bank, but with a three-year 'transitional period' to 1997 before it assumed full monetary responsibilities. The objective of the Euro Bank, under the draft statutes, would be to maintain price stability—a narrower remit than that of the Bundesbank, which is required, in addition, to promote employment and achieve balanced growth. In November 1990 Norman Lamont, in one of his first statements as Chancellor under the new Prime Minister, John Major, declared the Delors plan 'unworkable', noting that economic convergence was a long way off when inflation in the EC ranged between 2.5% and 22%, interest rates from 8.5% to 19% and budget balances from a 1% surplus to a 17% deficit.

In April 1991 the central bank governors, meeting at Basle for a session of the Bank for International Settlements, considered how profits from the European Bank or a European federal reserve might be distributed among the EC central banks, settling on GDP and population as the main criteria. But no decision was taken on whether the central bankers themselves or EC finance ministers should control Euro Bank interventions in foreign exchange markets. In the same month, London and Frankfurt both put in formal bids to house any future European Bank, as did Paris, Luxembourg and Amsterdam.

Single currency: the opt-out clause

In October 1991 the Dutch Presidency released the draft version of its proposed treaty on economic and monetary union, giving the UK parliament and indeed all other parliaments in the EC the right to say yes or no to a single currency by opting out within six months of a decision by other EC states to go ahead. Any country whose parliament 'does not feel able to approve of the irrevocable fixing of its currency' would be granted exemption from full EMU. In addition the Dutch proposed a non-binding declaration of intent on a single currency, alongside the treaty, in which states would declare it was their 'strongest intention to participate in EMU without exemptions'.

However Norman Tebbit, speaking for many anti-federalist Conservative backbenchers, warned that even a treaty which left options open still amounted to a long-term commitment to abolish the pound. As such, it should be rejected. Douglas Hurd agreed, saying: 'We are not going to commit Britain to joining a system called stage three, with a single bank and single currency. We are not going to make that commitment'. He added: 'We will not reach agreement at Maastricht on the final shape of Europe. That will probably be for our children. What we will have to try to decide is whether there is enough common ground for a further worthwhile step forward. I think there is'. Another EC summit on the issue after Maastricht was possible but not desirable, because 'it would be much better to deal with this in an orderly way during the Dutch Presidency and get on with the next stages in the Community,' such as enlargement and farm reform.

However, Wim Kok, the Dutch finance minister, said that any country which opted out of stage three would have little or no say in such matters as the make up and powers of the European Central Bank. Delors and the Commission expressed concern about the opt-out clause, pointing out that if Germany as well as the UK took advantage of it, economic and monetary union would be postponed indefinitely.

At the end of October, Downing Street dismissed the concept of a non-binding declaration as 'irrelevant', but left open the question of whether Major would sign the formal Dutch draft treaty, including the opt-out clause. Major told the Commons that Britain belonged 'in the mainstream of Europe . . . We cannot dictate what our children will make of the Community, but we must leave them in a position where they can effectively influence the shape of Europe'. He added that on EMU,

> it would be irresponsible for any government to ask the people to decide now that we should adopt at a future date a single European currency which will have far-reaching implications for the conduct of monetary and economic policy. A move to a single currency which was not backed up by convergence between the economies of the member states of the Community would be a recipe for economic disaster . . . I am not prepared to commit our country now to a single currency. We must be able to judge nearer the time— Parliament must judge nearer the time—whether a single currency is in the interests of Britain.

The Maastricht summit

At Maastricht Major stuck to the 'opt-out' clause, observing that the conditions laid down for economic convergence were in any case such that it was 'highly uncertain' when a single currency would be introduced. The final wording of the EMU treaty, however, defined the 'irrevocable fixing of exchange rates leading to the introduction of a single currency, the ECU' as an EC goal, and the German press was quick to record—with pangs of regret and doubt—the 'end of the Deutschmark'. The second stage of EMU—economic and monetary convergence—was set for 1 January 1994, and stage three—the European Central Bank—for 1997. The general impression left was that a single currency was all but inevitable, and Britain had not so much 'opted out' as reserved the right to 'opt in' at a future date.

The Maastricht treaty called for a single monetary policy to maintain price stability, sound public finances and 'a sustainable balance of payments', all in accordance with the open market and free competition. To co-ordinate national economic policies, the Council of Ministers is required—by majority vote—to adopt 'broad guidelines' for economic co-ordination. The summit agreed a vague formula for bringing recalcitrant EC members into line: if any country's national economic policies prove inconsistent with the guidelines, thus jeopardizing EMU, the council will make the 'necessary recommendations' for action against the EC state concerned.

To govern monetary policy the treaty duly established a European System of Central Banks (ESCB) made up of a European Central Bank (ECB) and the central banks of the member states. The tasks of the ESCB are given as the implementation of EC monetary policy; the conduct of foreign exchange operations; and the management of member states' foreign reserves. The European Bank President and other senior officials are to be appointed by EC leaders for a limited term of eight years and will run the Bank, together with the governors of national central banks, in a Governing Council. The bank is defined as independent—on the model of the Bundesbank—and is expressly forbidden to take instructions either from EC institutions or from member state governments.

The treaty prohibits 'excessive budget deficits', and obliges EC states to report their 'planned and actual deficits' regularly to the European Commission, which in turn is to monitor compliance with budgetary discipline. Maastricht gave the Council of Ministers teeth with which to enforce compliance through a graded scale of measures including fines 'of an appropriate size' and a requirement that the offending state shall make a suitable deposit with the EC 'until the excessive deficit has been corrected'.

The second stage of EMU is defined as beginning in January 1994, by which date all member states will have abolished restrictions on the movement of capital not only between states (as in stage one) but between member states and third countries. Similarly, by the same date they will have adopted—'if necessary'—multi-annual programmes to ensure 'lasting economic convergence' and have begun the process of central bank independence. At the same time, excessive budget deficits must also be avoided. 1994 also sees the setting up of a European Monetary Institute (EMI) to strengthen central bank co-operation, help co-ordinate monetary policies and oversee the development of the ECU. Above all, the EMI will prepare the way for stage three and the European Central Bank, setting up the 'regulatory, organisational and logistical framework' for the ESCB by 31 December 1996 'at the latest'.

The third and final stage of EMU, including the introduction of a single currency, should be fixed during 1997. But if no date has been fixed by the end of 1997, 'the third stage will start on 1 January 1999'. Thereafter the value of the ECU will be 'irrevocably fixed', and the ECU will become 'a currency in its own right'. By 1 July 1998, six months before the single currency comes into effect, the Council is to agree by majority vote, not unanimity, which member states qualify, according to agreed criteria: a rate of inflation close (within 1.5%) to that of the three best performing member states in terms of price stability; a consistent avoidance of excessive budget deficits, the guidelines being budget deficits of less than 3% of GDP and government debt below 60% of GDP; satisfactory performance within the EMS over a two-year period, with no devaluation against any other member state currency; and satisfactory long-term interest rates, that is, no more than 2% above the average in the three EC states with the lowest interest rates.

The opt-out clause, or protocol, for the UK reads: 'the UK shall not be obliged or committed to move to the third stage of economic and monetary union without a separate decision to do so by its government and Parliament . . . Unless the UK notifies the Council that it intends to move to the third stage, it shall be under no obligation to do so.' A Danish opt-out clause similarly allows an 'exemption' for Denmark should a Danish referendum on the single currency result in a no vote.

On the other hand, another protocol notes that all twelve states have confirmed 'the irreversible character' of the move toward a third stage simply by signing the EMU treaty: 'Therefore all member states shall, whether they fulfil the necessary conditions for the adoption of a single currency or not, respect the will of the Community to enter swiftly into the third stage of EMU, and therefore no member state shall prevent the third stage'. It seems likely that Britain will qualify for stage three, and so will be in a position to opt for the single currency if it wants to. John Banham, director general of the CBI, commented that Major had achieved what British business wanted: 'Agreement on economic and monetary union which leaves the way open for UK participation in a single European currency, with steps to secure the more even enforcement of Community legislation, but without an extension of Community powers that could threaten international competitiveness'.

Checklist of changes

- A Second stage of EMU to begin 1 January 1994, involving economic convergence, avoidance of budget deficits, and the establishment of a European Monetary Institute to strengthen central bank co-ordination.
- Third stage of EMU (introduction of single currency and European bank) to be fixed by 1997, and to start no later than 1999. ECU to be the common currency: countries eligible to join must meet agreed criteria involving rates of inflation, interest rates, budget deficits and performance within the ERM.
- UK 'not obliged' to join in single currency without a decision to this effect by UK government and parliament.

10 MERGERS AND ACQUISITIONS

European competition and industrial policy

In its annual report on competition policy in June 1991, the European Commission warned that the abolition of internal barriers to trade would fail to improve the competitivness of European industry unless companies, particularly those hiding behind walls of government protection, were forced to go out and compete with their rivals across the Community. Signalling his determination to extend the Commission's newly won powers of enforcement to every corner of commercial activity, Sir Leon Brittan, the Competition Commissioner, reminded governments and the captains of industry that: 'National champions in the Middle Ages generally fell off their horses under the weight of their own armour'. The illustration was designed to highlight the Commission's determination to eliminate unauthorized government subsidies to industry and to clamp down on illegal restrictive and monopolistic practices, rather than wait for protected and inefficient industries to fail in the face of foreign competition.

From the outset of the internal market programme, the European Commission's overriding objective has been to break down the fragmentation of the European economy into twelve separate and often conflicting components and create a single, unified market of 320 million producers and consumers. In essence, it is a strategy designed to benefit European business. The Commission believes that companies traditionally boxed into their national markets should be free to break out of their national confinement and link up with other European firms, whether through mergers, joint ventures or acquisitions.

Paradoxically, the Commission has two ostensibly irreconcilable goals:

1 To promote the restructuring of the European economy by allowing the various industrial sectors to consolidate their operations across national frontiers, shut down excess productive capacity, enhance economies of scale and reduce costs, thereby acquiring the kind of industrial strength needed to compete with American and Japanese companies on a more equal footing;
2 To prevent these newly restructured industries from engaging in the kind of practices that have earned big business a bad name the world over, such as illegal market-sharing arrangements, the abuse of dominant market positions to extract monopoly profits and

attempts to prevent new competitors entering given markets.

The internal market programme would be an exercise in futility if, at the very moment national barriers to trade were levelled, European companies immediately set about raising them by introducing a new set of commercial barriers to trade and engaging in ingenious forms of anti-competitive behaviour. The Commission was fully aware that there is a contradiction between allowing companies to co-operate with each other across national borders when the temptation to abuse such freedom is likely to prove irresistible. However, it proposed to reconcile the irreconcilable by introducing a comprehensive competition policy, granting it the power to appraise all large-scale mergers which have a Community dimension and decide whether the proposed merger should be allowed to go ahead, whether the terms of the merger should be altered in the interests of free competition or whether it should be prohibited outright.

Under the provisions of the Treaty of Rome, the European Commission already possesses considerable powers to monitor certain categories of business activity. Article 85 prohibits as incompatible with the common market 'all agreements between undertakings, decisions by associations of undertakings and concerted practices which may affect trade between member states which have as their objective or effect the prevention or distortion of competition within the common market'. In short, any agreement or conspiracy by companies, individually or collectively, to fix prices, limit production or divide up the market is illegal, and it can be broken up before or after the event has taken place, and the offending companies subject to heavy fines. However, the Commission also has the power to give its approval to any restrictive practice where such an agreement 'contributes to improving the production or distribution of goods or to promoting technical or economic progress', an increasingly controversial area known as industrial policy.

Similarly, Article 86 states that 'Any abuse by one or more undertakings of a dominant position within the common market or in a substantial part of it shall be prohibited as incompatible with the common market in so far as it may affect trade between member states'. Consequently, any business abusing its dominant position can find itself the subject of a Commission investigation, and, if found guilty, be compelled to stop and made to pay a substantial fine. Article 86 also applies to mergers that would create a dominant position likely to be abused, but here the Commission can only act after the event has taken place, a limitation regarded by successive Competition Commissioners as the Achilles' heel of the Community's competition policy.

In the separate but related field of government subsidies to industry, known as state aids, Article 92 grants the Commission the power to make a prior decision whether (and at what level) aid can be given. It can also compel companies who have received state aid without the Commission's approval to pay it back. The Commission can, however, give approval to government subsidies where they are designed to promote economic development in areas of economic decline, but only the Commission is empowered to decide what government subsidies fall within this criterion.

Collectively, the ability to police restrictive market agreements, dominant market positions, mergers that are likely to lead to dominant market positions and state aids is an impressive range of powers at the disposal of the Commission to regulate competition within the Community. However, the Commission felt that its inability to scrutinize mergers before they have taken place is an obvious deficiency in its powers of competition enforcement. The deficiency had become extremely acute as companies, in anticipation of the creation of the single internal market in 1992, have developed an appetite for US-style merger mania which has already led to a large increase in cross-frontier mergers and takeovers in an effort to strengthen their competitive positions. The Commission has been engaged since 1973 in a frequently acrimonious struggle with the Council of Ministers to fill this gap.

A comprehensive merger control policy

Few would dispute that until Peter Sutherland, the former Irish Commissioner for Competition Policy, joined the Commission in 1984 the attempt to obtain approval from the Council of Ministers for a directive on merger control had been given a low priority. No-one knew how the 38-year-old softly spoken Irishman would shape up to his new job. But for anyone prepared to look into his background, there was more than enough to indicate that here was a man who was going to upset the system.

Born the son of an insurance broker, he was educated at University College, Dublin, and the National University of Ireland, before becoming a barrister at the Irish, English and New York Bars. As the youngest-ever Attorney General in the government of Garret FitzGerald, he is credited with almost single-handedly persuading the Irish courts that IRA terrorists should no longer be able to evade extradition on the specious grounds that their actions were political and not criminal. Mr Sutherland was Ireland's fourth Commissioner since it joined the Community in 1973, and was to become universally acknowledged as one of the most rigorous Competition Commissioners Europe has ever had.

His success could be said to stem from a lifelong predilection for a good fight. During his university days he had a passion for rugby, and it is said that he fractured his nose no less than nine times, but refused to stop playing the game. He was to carry this enthusiasm for the scrum into adult life, and, in the course of his four-year term as Commissioner, forced many powerful corporate leaders and national politicians to leave the industrial playing field nursing their own bloody noses.

Presenting the Commission's sixteenth annual report on competition policy in July 1987, Sutherland gave notice to member states that he was determined to revive the stalled 1973 draft directive on mergers and takeovers. If they could not agree by the end of the year, at least in principle, to the necessity of augmenting the Commission's powers, he would use the full force of Articles 85 and 86 to try to fill the gap. Sutherland insisted that the new powers were needed to protect consumer interests, prevent mergers which distorted competition and provide companies with a predictable and effective Community-wide legal framework within which mergers and takeovers could be conducted.

Only Britain and France expressed reservations about the Commissioner's aspirations for new powers, and were confident that his threat to exploit existing legislation was little more than bluff. Then in November a decision by the European Court of Justice added considerable weight to Sutherland's warning. The Court approved an earlier decision by the Commission to allow the US company Philip Morris to take over a large minority stake in the UK-based company, Rothmans International, in the face of a legal challenge by British American Tobacco and R. J. Reynolds, on the grounds that the deal was against the interests of free competition.

However, in granting its seal of approval for the deal the Court also said that the Commission had a legal obligation to investigate any merger or acquisition that could lead to the creation or consolidation of a market dominance, and thereby violate the Community's competition code. It was a watershed decision. Hitherto, the Commission was under the impression that its powers under Article 85 were limited to investigations of price-fixing or market-sharing arrangements. However, the Court said that Article 85 could also be applied to mergers and acquisitions which might restrict competition (before the merger or acquisition went ahead), a decision which partially made up for the limitations of Article 86 governing mergers, which specifies that the Commission can act only after the deal has gone through. Now the Commission had the power to approve all mergers or acquisitions, except those between companies who do not have a dominant market position and whose combination would not lead to the creation of a dominant market position.

At an Internal Market Council the following month all member states except Britain and France (both of whom already have highly sophisticated merger control arrangements) granted their approval in principle to a comprehensive Community merger control policy. The Commission was then instructed to explore ways of overcoming the reservations expressed by London and Paris. A new, revised draft directive on mergers and acquisitions was tabled in March 1988, proposing that the Commission should have the power to regulate all mergers where the combined turnover of the companies involved exceeded £690 million, except where the company being taken over had an annual turnover of less than £33 million, or where 75% or more of the merged companies were in a single member state.

The proposal also called for a system of prior notification, powers to make dawn raids on company premises in search of incriminating evidence, fines of up to 10% of the combined company profits if the directive was violated and a commitment to speed up the bureaucratic process so that companies would be given a decision on whether the merger or acquisition could go ahead within a six-month period. 'Is it really acceptable,' asked Sutherland at a conference on 1992 in Paris the same month,

> that the same mergers between different companies in different member states should be subject to differing national laws, with the distinct possibility that conflicting decisions will be reached resulting from the fact that member states could apply different criteria? At least for important concentrations, which can have an impact on the internal market, the Community should be allowed to intervene.

Sutherland went on to warn that:

> Without a Community system of merger control, the door will remain open to the possibility that economic concentrations will be created in Europe which escape the existing rules. Clearly, such an outcome would contradict the very objectives that underpin the single market strategy—namely the creation of an environment for maximizing economic efficiency, competitiveness and technological progress.

Replying to Sutherland at the annual dinner of the Confederation of British Industry in May, Lord Young, the then Secretary of State for Trade and Industry, insisted that '1992 will not call for a sea change in mergers policy—just a further evolution of the approach we have taken for many years', effectively ruling out any British concessions on the Commission's demand for a comprehensive merger control policy. In Luxembourg the next month France decided to join its European neighbours and accept, in principle, the need for such a policy, leaving Britain the only member state to refuse to do so.

The junior trade minister, Francis Maude, denied that Britain was isolated on the issue of merger control. Did this mean that the rest of the Community was isolated from Britain? The minister could not be drawn into a reply, and took refuge in the statement: 'We are not prepared to say yes to the principle before we know the final form of the proposal'. In all fairness to the embattled minister, Britain may have been isolated on the question of the principle, but a number of member states had previously expressed grave reservations about the details. France had indicated that the £690 million threshold was too low, and Britain was not alone in its anxiety that the six-month period for decisions could jeopardize prospective mergers, even if the Commission could adhere to it.

However, no-one was prepared for the bombshell dropped by John Banham, the Director General of the Confederation of British Industry (CBI). In a June statement that brought him into direct conflict with government policy, Banham warned that:

> If counter-productive xenophobic arguments about hostile takeovers are to be avoided, it is essential that clear ground rules are set out and observed. The only pan-European agency able to ensure fair play in a free market is the European Commission.

Not content with pre-empting Lord Young, Banham went on to claim that one of the major reasons that British companies had not been able to link up sufficiently in preparation for 1992 was a fear of violating Britain's highly discretionary merger laws. According to Banham, not only were new EC controls necessary but the government's failure to accept the principle and get down to negotiating over the details was crippling the Department of Trade and Industry's campaign to prepare British business executives for the arrival of the internal market. Europe may have been open for business, Banham suggested, but Britain was not open for Europe.

Sutherland failed to get a merger control directive passed during his term of office, but he had managed to push the issue to the top of the European agenda. Moreover, he had won over eleven of the twelve member states to his point of view, leaving the British government isolated in Europe and cut off from its own business community. Despite this failure, he was nonetheless extremely effective in deploying the full weight of the Treaty of Rome against both companies and governments seeking an unfair competitive advantage over their rivals in the Community. It was left to Sir Leon Brittan, Sutherland's successor, to complete the negotiations on the new merger control regulation—which would probably have been impossible had it not been for the groundwork prepared by the softly spoken Irishman.

Sir Leon takes the helm

Sir Leon Brittan arrived in Brussels under the cloud of the Westland helicopter affair of 1986, which brought his meteoric political career to an abrupt halt and cast him into the domestic political wilderness. Born the youngest son of a Lithuanian doctor who had emigrated to London in 1927, he was educated at Haberdashers' Aske's School, before going up to Trinity College, Cambridge, to read English and Law, where he obtained a double first. After becoming a highly successful barrister specializing in libel actions, Sir Leon was elected to Parliament in 1974, and rose to Cabinet rank within seven years. During that time he had moved from the 'wet' wing of the Conservative Party, where he had been chairman of the left-of-centre Bow Group, to become one of Mrs Thatcher's right-hand men. From the outset of his political career, however, he had been an ardent and vocal supporter of Britain's membership of the European Community.

Prior to Westland, Sir Leon's political career had not been without incident. After being appointed minister of state at the Home Office in 1979, he became associated with the now-notorious government pamphlet, *Protect and Survive*, which urged householders to whitewash their windows for protection in the event of a nuclear war. Two years later, without any formal training in economics, he was appointed Chief Secretary to the Treasury, and was exposed to the accusation of being under the influence of his elder brother, Samuel Brittan, the noted economist for the *Financial Times*. Similarly, Sir Leon's elevation to the position of Home Secretary in 1983 coincided with Mrs Thatcher's 'short sharp shock' initiative, winning him the dubious accolade as the minister for 'Laura Norder'.

However, it was Sir Leon's conflict with the then Defence Secretary, Michael Heseltine, over whether the ailing Westland helicopter company should be bought out by American or European interests, and the revelations of dirty dealing in high places that followed, that led to his resignation as Trade and Industry Secretary in January 1986. His supporters insisted that he had been the scapegoat needed to assure Mrs Thatcher's political survival. But despite his loyalty, the promised recall to the front benches from the Prime Minister never materialized. In 1988 Mrs Thatcher offered him the position of successor to Lord Cockfield as Britain's senior Commissioner. After some hesitation, he accepted, becoming the Commissioner for Competition Policy in 1989.

Although some expected Sir Leon to become 'Mrs Thatcher's Commission poodle', the British members of the Brussels' press corps lost no time in placing wagers on how long it would take Sir Leon to 'go native', as his predecessor was widely reputed to have done. From the perspective of Mrs Thatcher, that transition must have occurred with uncomfortable speed. Although consistently opposing radical proposals for a federal Europe, Sir Leon rapidly set about extending competition policy into the energy sector. In addition, he frequently issued calls for Britain's full membership of the ERM, urged the government to participate fully in the negotiations on economic and political union, and never flinched from criticizing Mrs Thatcher's abrasive attacks on Community 'personalities and institutions'.

The enforcement of Articles 85 and 86

One of the most effective powers available to the Commission (powers denied to the Office of Fair Trading under British competition law) is the ability to make dawn raids on companies suspected of abusing a dominant position or engaging in a conspiracy to restrict free trade. In December 1985 the European Court of Justice found that Akzo, the Dutch chemicals multinational, had been abusing its dominant position by undercutting its prices in an attempt to force Engineering and Chemical Supplies Ltd, a small Gloucestershire-based firm, to withdraw from the organic peroxides market. The managing director of the company could obtain little protection under British law from the predatory pricing activities of a foreign rival. However, after receiving a complaint from the ESC, the Commission made a dawn raid on the Dutch company's premises and obtained all the incriminating evidence needed to secure a conviction. Akzo was fined £6.4 million, the ESC was still in business and the whole episode demonstrated how the Commission was able to come to the rescue of a small British firm (or indeed a small company anywhere in the Community) in the name of free competition.

In April 1986 15 international chemical companies (including the British firms ICI and Shell) were fined £38.75 million between them for engaging in an illegal price-fixing and market-sharing arrangement in polypropylene between 1977 and 1983, in violation of Article 85 governing conspiracies. However, in August the following year the Commission gave its approval for ICI and the Italian company Enichem to form the European Vinyls Corporation, a joint venture that planned to shut down 300,000 tonnes of excess capacity. Together, the two cases highlighted the Commission's dual approach towards business combinations. Agreements designed simply to fix prices will not be tolerated by Brussels, but agreements seeking to promote industrial restructuring are likely to get the Commission's blessing.

Although in December 1987 the Commission had given provisional approval of the conditions laid down by the Monopolies and Mergers Commission for British Airways' £250 million takeover of British Caledonian, it still had an obligation to make sure that the merger did not restrict the access of other carriers to routes shared by the two merged airlines as soon as the deal had gone ahead, under the authority granted it by Article 86. Once the Airlines of Britain Group (made up of British Midland Airways, Manx Airlines, Loganair and Eurocity Express) complained that the merger would lead to a restriction of trade the Commission launched its official investigation. The Community's powers to regulate the air transport industry had been severely circumscribed until the approval of a package of measures the same month, granting the Commission tough powers to monitor competition between the European airlines. The BA–BCal merger thus became a test case of the Commission's new authority to regulate the air transport industry.

By March 1988, when the Commission had announced its conditions on which the takeover would be authorized, it was abundantly clear that Sutherland was determined to carry out his threat to use the Treaty's competition powers to the full. British Airways was forced to surrender most of British Caledonian's European network to its smaller competitors, accept limitations on its use of landing and take-off slots at Gatwick Airport and comply with restrictions on extending its monopoly at Heathrow. Although these conditions were to remain in force for only four years, they were significantly more stringent than those demanded by the Monopolies and Mergers Commission. The deal was a major concession by Lord King, the company chairman, and another success for Commissioner Sutherland.

However, the significance of the affair went beyond the problems for the personalities involved. It emphasized the shortcomings of national merger regulation and highlighted yet again the case for impartial and effective merger control arrangements at Community level.

The attempt in 1988 by Nestlé, the Swiss foods group, to take over Rowntree, the British confectionery manufacturer, produced a nationalistic reaction almost identical to that which followed the attempt by the Italian entrepreneur, Carlo de Benedetti, to take over the Belgian conglomerate, Société Générale de Belgique. Both sides were motivated by the 'buy now or get bought later' ethic that has dominated Europe in the past few years. According to Gary Hamel of the London Business School, the large increase in cross-border mergers and acquisitions was the result of a realization by European companies that 'By 1992, all the good-looking girls on the dance floor will have partners'.

At the same time, the two bids were a reminder that—at least psychologically—many businesses (and most member states) had yet to understand the implications of the European single market. Both bids were characterized as an assault on the very fabric of the nation by some outside predator intent on stealing a national asset. In an article in *The Times* in May 1988 Kenneth Dixon, the chairman of Rowntree, portrayed Kit Kat, Polo, Smarties and After Eight as an integral part of Britain's heritage, similar in stature only to the Crown Jewels, the Union Jack and the Houses of Parliament. The distinction between the company's interest and the national interest was lost completely, and the two concepts were projected as being identical and inseparable. By arguing (mistakenly, as it transpired) that the bid should be stopped because Swiss law prevented Swiss companies from being taken over by foreign companies, Dixon had inadvertently implied that if British companies enjoyed the same rights in Switzerland that Swiss companies enjoyed in Britain, he would have no ground to stand on. Likewise, de Benedetti (known in the Italian press as 'Carlo-Grab-It-All') was presented in Belgium as a swashbuckling marauder in search of foreign plunder. Observers felt that unless Société Générale was able to fend off the attack, Belgium would find itself under Italian domination.

In both cases the acquiring companies were not as predatory as the victims made out. Nestlé had been in Britain for 120 years, and as the manufacturer of Branston Pickle, Findus Frozen Foods and Nescafé coffee, was as much a part of the English cultural heritage as any box of Quality Street. Furthermore, it is simply not true that Swiss law prohibits foreign firms from taking over domestic ones. As Helmut Maucher, Nestlé's managing director, pointed out in his reply to Dixon's article in *The Times* the following week, Swiss companies can provide in their articles of association a provision granting them the right to refuse to register a shareholder, thereby making it extremely difficult for them to be taken over. However, companies who do this pay a heavy price, as unregistered shares trade at a much lower price than freely transferable ones. Besides, similar mechanisms are available to British companies seeking to protect themselves from unwelcome takeover bids.

Despite the rather colourful language of the Italian press, neither could de Benedetti be described as an avaricious raider. His companies, which include a variety of computer, publishing, car component, food and financial service concerns, employ over 100,000 people in Europe. Like Nestlé, his bid for a foreign company was motivated by a determination to be prepared for 1992. In the end, de Benedetti lost, and Nestlé was cleared by the Monopolies and Mergers Commission to go ahead with its bid for Rowntree. The experience of the two besieged companies was a salutary lesson for every other sleepy European firm that thought 1992 would not affect them. Sutherland could not intervene in either case, as there was no prima facie evidence for an investigation under the conspiracy or market dominance provisions of the Treaty. However, the bids demonstrated beyond doubt that, despite the promise of a European single market by 1992, economic nationalism remains a powerful force to be reckoned with by any company seeking to acquire firms in other member states.

While the Commission was unable to act in the Nestlé or de Benedetti bids, a bizarre combination of circumstances enabled it to intervene in the attempt by GC&C Brands to take over the Irish Distillers Group (IDG) with a £169 million bid before the deal went ahead—an event unprecedented in the history of Community competition policy. GC&C Brands, the consortium created in May 1988 by Grand Metropolitan, Allied Lyons and Guinness for the specific purpose of acquiring and then dismembering IDG, could barely disguise its surprise when it learnt on 29 July that the Commission was investigating it for conspiracy under Article 85. IDG, the makers of Jameson, Powers, Paddy and Bushmills whiskies, had complained to the Commission that GC&C was attempting to deprive its shareholders of the possibility of more competitive individual bids by creating the consortium.

In these circumstances the Commission's ability to approve mergers was not restricted to Article 86. Article 85 also applied, reinforced by the decision of the European Court of Justice over the Philip Morris case in November 1987. Commission officials could not recall another example of a joint venture takeover, but were delighted at the opportunity to show their strength in a takeover bid before it took place. The Commission's performance was widely seen as a test case, demonstrating how quickly and effectively it would be able to deal with mergers should the proposed directive on merger control ever get approval by the Council of Ministers.

The Commission issued its decision on 17 August—a record 20 days after the complaint was made—forcing the break-up of the consortium but allowing its individual members to go ahead with new individual bids. To emphasize the point, Sutherland issued a statement saying that: 'The Commission's intervention in the IDG case shows that it can and will act quickly and effectively to ensure that collusive practices restricting competition do not take place'.

Anyone who expected Sutherland's successor to relax his tough line against violations of Community competition policy was in for a rude awakening. In December 1990, ICI of Britain and Solvay of Belgium were fined a staggering £36 million—one of the largest penalties ever imposed by Brussels—for operating a cartel in soda ash, a raw material used in glass making.

The enforcement of Article 92

The Internal Market White Paper provides member states with a reminder of the Commission's declared intention to restrict illegal state aids with a rigorous application of Article 92. 'As the Commission moves to complete the internal market it will be necessary to ensure that anticompetitive practices do not engender new forms of local protectionism which would only lead to a re-partitioning of the market.' It goes on to point out that there is a tendency among some member states

> to spend large amounts of public funds on state aids to
> uncompetitive industries and enterprises. Often, they not only
> distort competition but also in the long run undermine efforts to
> increase European competitiveness.

Any government thinking that they were somehow exceptional was soon to receive a rude awakening. Initially, Delors had wanted Sutherland to adopt a soft line on government subsidies, but the Competition Commissioner insisted on a strict interpretation of the Treaty, and eventually got his way.

The Commission had already cut back large amounts of state assistance from the Community's ailing steel and ship building sectors before it turned its attention to the car industry. In March 1986 Sutherland launched an inquiry into plans by the German motor group, Daimler-Benz, to build a £577 million car plant in Baden Württemberg. The local authorities had offered to pay for the preparation of the greenfield site and connect the plant to essential services. The Commission insisted that the offer constituted an illegal subsidy, and the offer was eventually withdrawn.

In December 1987 the British government was forced to trim £70 million from its £750 million aid package for the Rover Group as a condition of the sale of Leyland Trucks to DAF of the Netherlands. Three months later it was the turn of the French government to come under the Commission's scrutiny. It was given permission to give the state-owned company, Renault, a £1.9 billion subsidy, somewhat smaller than the government had initially sought, but only on the condition that its status was changed from a public to a private company subject to commercial law. It was also made clear that failure to carry out this commitment would be met by a demand that the subsidy be repaid. When Roger Fauroux, the French Industry Minister, announced in September 1988 that he had decided to keep Renault's public status intact, Sutherland made it abundantly clear that such action would give the Commission no option but to withdraw its consent for the proposed debt write-off. If France decided to go ahead with this write-off it would be summoned to the European Court of Justice.

The Commission is also currently investigating a £9.7 million subsidy from the Italian government to Alfa Romeo in 1985 and the sale of Alfa Romeo to Fiat in 1986. It considers that the price paid by Fiat was much lower than the value of Alfa Romeo, and thus involved an undisclosed illegal subsidy. Despite the evident reluctance of the Italian government to have its state aids subject to external scrutiny, the Commission has refused to back down.

By the time the British government had completed its plans for the privatization and sale of the Rover Group to British Aerospace in March 1988 for £150 million there should have been no doubt in anyone's mind that the deal could only go ahead after receiving the seal of approval from Brussels under Article 92—but there was. Professor Roland Smith, the former chairman of British Aerospace, told MPs in parliament that if the Commission stepped in and demanded changes in Rover's proposed £800 million debt write-off he would pull out. Such talk may have been designed to intimidate the Commission, but it was to little avail. When the deal finally went through in July, Smith was forced to accept a £253 million reduction in the government's proposed cash injection into Rover.

The Commission had saved the British taxpayer millions of pounds in excess subsidy, and, as far as it was aware, had fulfilled its obligations to make sure that the disposal of a major public company did not confer an unfair advantage on the new owner in relation to other European enterprises operating in the same sector. The National Audit Office, however, subsequently accused the government of under-valuing Rover's assets, prompting the Commission to demand an explanation. A formal investigation was launched, and evidence of illegal actions by government ministers was disclosed.

Under the provisions of Article 92, Sir Leon had no option but to demand in June 1990 that the British government recover £44.4 million of illegal state subsidies or 'sweeteners' paid to British Aerospace when it acquired Rover in 1988. But, like the report by the House of Commons Trade and Industry Committee (which was also to investigate the sordid affair), Sir Leon was unable to find any evidence to justify Opposition allegations that Rover's assets were considerably undervalued. The case did, however, highlight the difficulty of deciding what is a fair price for an industry, especially if, as was the case with Rover, the government had ruled out competitive bidding. The government accepted the Commission's decision, although British Aerospace announced its intention to challenge the Commission's verdict in the European Court of Justice. When the case came before the Court in October 1991, Commission lawyers accused Lord Young of trying to hide millions of pounds in illegal government aid to British Aerospace. The court was told that Lord Young advised the chairman of BAE in writing to 'keep things quiet' or risk alerting the European Commission. Contrary to popular perceptions, the Commission's action was motivated by a desire to ensure that the competition rules were enforced equitably, not to make life difficult for Britain.

In July 1989, for example, the Commission approved a £731 million aid package for Short Brothers, the ailing Ulster-based aerospace company. The greater part of the package was for writing off accumulated debts and anticipated future losses, in an effort to make the company more attractive for sale to a foreign buyer—a practice traditionally disapproved by Brussels. However, because of the vital role the company plays in the economy of Northern Ireland, accounting for 10% of manufacturing employment in the region, the Commission was moved to make an exception to the rules against subsidies. Justifying its action, the Commission insisted that 'the social and economic consequences of a closure would be far reaching, and would inevitably result in a loss of confidence amongst potential outside investors who are crucial to Northern Ireland's economic development'. A year later, however, the Commission announced that it was launching a formal investigation into allegations that the £700-million plant being built in Derbyshire by the Japanese car manufacturer, Toyota, had received a hidden subsidy in the form of undervalued land for the new plant.

In addition to following the precedent of fighting illegal state aids and restrictive practices set by his predecessor, such as the new investigation launched against the European steel industry in April 1991, Sir Leon also began to apply the Community's competition regulations to areas hitherto untouched by Community Competition law, notably the energy sector. Aware that only 5% of Community electricity was traded across borders, the Council of Ministers approved a Commission proposal for a new electricity and gas transit directive in 1990, thus enabling power utilities in one member state to be able to buy and sell electricity and gas in another.

The 1990 power transit directive was limited to cross-border trade. Sir Leon's aims, however, are far more ambitious. They amount to little more than the total restructuring of the European electricity and gas industries. The Commission's objective is to enable large industrial consumers to shop around the Community for the cheapest source of supply; to oblige national electricity grids and pipeline networks to act as carriers between producers and consumers; and to increase competition by allowing new producers to enter the market. In March 1991 Sir Leon fired his opening shot. Letters were sent to the national electricity utilities in ten member states, requesting information on their compliance with the Community's competition laws. Following the privatization of Britain's electricity industry, only France, Ireland, Portugal, Italy and Greece have publicly owned electricity industries. Nonetheless, it is clear that the Commission is convinced that most are engaged in some form of monopolistic trade.

The initiative provoked a bitter debate throughout the Community over the liberalization of EC energy markets, especially after the European Court of Justice aproved the Commission's use of Article 90 to open protected markets with or without the approval of the Council of Ministers. Defending his action, Sir Leon said that 'such monopolistic companies have to justify their existence if they want to remain in business'. Competition, he added, 'and the freedom to export and import are essential components of the policies needed to create an internal energy market'. The move against the electricity sector was widely seen as a rehearsal for the more formidable task of opening up the Community's gas market. Here, however, the Commission will have to act with greater caution if liberalization is to avoid creating conditions of uncertainty, thereby threatening investment in new infrastructure, as happened in the United States.

Comprehensive merger control endorsed

Capitalizing on the groundwork laid by his predecessor, Sir Leon Brittan began to break new ground in the quest for a comprehensive merger control regulation. In January 1989, Lord Young, the then Trade and Industry Secretary, indicated that for the first time Britain was prepared to endorse new Community powers to approve all large-scale mergers. After his meeting with the 17-member Commission, Lord Young said that while Britain retained reservations about the proposed merger control regulation, it nonetheless accepted the necessity of avoiding the problem of 'double jeopardy', where mergers had to be approved by both national and Community authorities. He suggested that it might be possible to reach an agreement whereby large mergers were approved by the Commission while smaller ones would be left to national bodies such as the Monopolies and Mergers Commission. Although he gave no indication of the turnover threshold that might initiate a Commission investigation, it was clear that the end of the Commission's 16-year campaign for new powers to regulate mergers was in sight.

In April Sir Leon unveiled a new proposal which would grant the Commission powers to approve in advance all mergers where the combined turnover of the merged companies exceeded 5 billion ECUs (£3.5 billion). The revised turnover threshold was transitional, effective until 1992, when it would fall to 2 billion ECUs (£1.4 billion). After further talks in Brussels in October, Britain, France and Germany agreed on the 5-billion ECU turnover threshold tabled earlier by Sir Leon. Agreement on the compromise proved elusive, however, because of the determination of Italy and a number of smaller member states to hold out for a 1-billion ECU threshold, largely because they had little or no effective merger control apparatus of their own, rendering them reliant on Brussels for the enforcement of competition policy.

The Council of Ministers finally accepted the Commission's case for comprehensive merger control in December 1989, and the Commission's new powers came into effect in September 1990. Under the new regulation, the Commission has the authority to monitor all mergers where combined global turnover exceeds 5 billion ECUs, although mergers between companies with more than two-thirds of Community turnover in one member state are exempt. Companies are required to provide the Commission with prior notification of an intention to merge, along with copious amounts of business information. Firms failing to meet these requirements face fines of up to £50,000. The Commission then has one month to decide if the proposed merger is subject to the regulation, and four months to reach a decision on whether to 'bless or block' the combination.

The Commission monitored its first business merger under the new regulation in November 1990, when it gave approval for the link-up between Renault and Volvo, as part of the wider effort to restructure the European car industry. The procedure was completed without incident or delay. By September 1991, when the new merger control regulation had reached its first anniversary, 53 mergers had been approved. But it was the decision to block the proposed Franco-Italian takeover of de Havilland, the ailing Canadian aircraft manufacturer, which marked the first real test of the Commission's new powers. The Franco-Italian bid, the first to be blocked under the new regulation, was disallowed on the grounds that it would have created a 'powerful and unassailable dominant position in the world market for turboprop aircraft'. Sir Leon insisted that the acquisition would have simply increased the market share of the bidders without bringing improvements in competitiveness. But the decision caused bitterness in Paris and Rome, provoking demands for a revision of the merger control regulation.

Early indications suggest that most companies have adjusted to the Commission's new powers, and approve of the clear demarcation between national and Community merger control law. Nevertheless, much disquiet exists over other aspects of Commission competition policy. Apprehension over the proposed 13th directive on company law announced in January 1991 on the regulation takeovers is acute in Britain. Following the exposure of the international fraud carried out by senior executives of BCCI in the summer of 1991, Sir Leon announced that the Commission was to consider prohibiting certain kinds of corporate structure in an effort to prevent financial institutions from abusing the new commercial freedoms created by the internal market. BCCI had been able to sidestep direct regulation because it was not classified as a bank under Community law. But any attempt to tighten up the banking laws could provoke protests from the Community's powerful financial institutions. Finally, the Commission's determination to extend its control on illegal state aids, highlighted in July 1991 by the demand that governments provide financial information about national enterprises, can be expected to meet fierce resistance from countries like France and Italy, which continue to have large public-sector manufacturing and industrial interests.

The European Company Statute

Since June 1988, when Jacques Delors announced his intention to revive a long-standing Commission proposal to table plans for a European Company Statute as part of his personal commitment to add a 'social dimension' to the internal market programme, EC governments, companies and trades unions have been preparing for what promises to be a major showdown over the controversial issue of workers' rights.

In essence, the proposed European Company Statute would act as an alternative for companies currently required to register their existence and activities under national law. By incorporating under the European Company Statute, companies involved in cross-frontier mergers would be freed of the present requirement to adopt the company law of either member state. In addition to simplifying the legal situation, the Commission declared that the European Company Statute will also allow companies with operating losses in one member state to offset them against profits in another.

However, the proposal has a sting in its tail. In exchange for the benefits offered by the European Company Statute, companies would be required to accept certain minimum standards of worker participation in the running of the industries in which they are employed. Incorporation under the proposed legislation would be optional, not mandatory. The proposal has already received much criticism from Britain, which regards it as 'irrelevant', bitter opposition from UNICE, the European Employers' Federation, which fears it could become a millstone around the neck of European companies, and considerable scepticism from the European Trade Union Confederation, which insists that the proposals do not go far enough.

The idea of a European Company Statute is by no means new. The original proposal was made in 1970, following an initiative by France, but it proved so controversial that it was eventually shelved in 1982—a fate which befell all other attempts to revive the idea thereafter. It has, however, been brought back to life by Delors, in the conviction that the internal market programme could be placed in jeopardy unless the Community's workers believe that there is something in it for them too.

In a consultative document on the company statute circulated in the summer of 1988 the Commission outlined three models for worker involvement in company decision-making structures, each with varying degrees of worker participation. Officials have insisted that the proposal represents 'a modern approach for employer–worker relations through-out the EC', and that if consultations between governments, industry and trades unions showed enough support for the move, the Commission will go ahead and draft the legislation.

During preliminary discussions in Luxembourg in October 1988 the Commission expressed fears that, once the internal barriers to trade had been demolished, companies located in the more affluent Northern regions of the Community might be tempted to move some of their operations South, to avail themselves of cheaper labour costs and less stringent worker-protection legislation.

However, the Commission's argument received a hostile reception from member states anxious about the consequences of imposing new burdens on recently deregulated business, and from those who feared that the European Company Statute could provide a loophole enabling companies to bypass their own more restrictive worker-protection legislation. Francis Maude, the junior trade minister, told his European colleagues that the government had already consulted British companies about the proposal, and most saw little or no need for company law to be harmonized throughout the EC.

In her forthright speech in Bruges the previous month, Mrs Thatcher warned that the Community 'certainly does not need new regulations which raise the cost of employment, and make Europe's labour market less flexible and less competitive with overseas supplies'. The Prime Minister went on to state that if Europe was to have a company statute it must contain the least possible regulation, and warned that Britain would fight any attempt to introduce 'collectivism and corporatism' at the European level.

The European social dimension

Alongside the Commission's attempt to secure approval for the Company Statute lies a related but separate effort to give the 1992 implulse a human face in the form of what has become known as the 'social dimension.' In essence, this is an attempt to ease the social consequences of market deregulation with improved protection for workers. After his speech to the TUC in Bournemouth in September 1988, Jacques Delors won over the anti-EC tendencies in the British trade union movement, thereby helping to create a clear division on social policy between Labour and the Conservatives. But the conversion of the British trade union movement to what the Conservatives dismissed as 'continental type socialism' led to even more bitter exchanges between the two parties. In the run-up to the Madrid summit in June 1989, Mrs Thatcher increased her assault on the social dimension by declaring: 'From the accounts that I have received about the social charter it's more like a socialist charter.' As a result when in 1989 the other eleven member states decided to implement the Social Charter, Britain decided to exclude itself.

Mrs Thatcher's departure from the European stage in November 1990 and replacement by John Major was accompanied by expectations in Brussels of a more measured approach by Britain towards Community social legislation. Initially, the omens appeared favourable. In January 1991, after accusing Britain of jeopardizing the internal market because of its opposition to the social charter, Vasso Papandreou, the Employment Commissioner, noticed what she called 'a change of style' following talks with Michael Howard, the Employment Secretary. During the talks, Howard had agreed to the social charter 'in so far as it generates employment', but he reiterated the British government's view that some of the proposals would 'add to business costs'.

In April the Commission recommended the creation of a formal employee consultation machinery for companies with workforces in more than one member state. The recommendation was a greatly watered-down version of the proposed Vredeling directive of 1980. It was, nonetheless, rejected, and was met by a counter-proposal from Howard for consultation procedures based on a voluntary approach. Howard's proposal was then dismissed by Norman Willis, the TUC General Secretary, as a 'smokescreen'. By now, many commentators felt that Britain and the Commission had become locked in a sterile debate on industrial relations more appropriate to the 1970s than the 1990s. An article in the *Financial Times* the same month, while sympathetic to the goal of improved worker–management relations, doubted that legislation was the correct way to bring it about, especially as Japanese management techniques, involving employees directly in working arrangements, were in the process of transforming British industry.

However, while Howard's opposition to worker-participation schemes appeared to generate little interest in Britain, his opposition to other elements of the social dimension proved more controversial. Opposition to Commission proposals in June to grant working women 14 weeks' paid maternity leave and impose a 48-hour ceiling on the working week provoked an outcry. The media were quick to point out that Britain has one of the poorest records for maternity provision in the Community, second only to Greece's. Howard insisted, however, that the Commission's proposals would cost employers millions of pounds a year in additional costs, while at the same time impairing the employment prospects of large numbers of people.

Although Britain's negotiating style had become more conciliatory since the fall of Mrs Thatcher, it was clear by the autumn of 1991 that the Conservative government could not reconcile itself to the Commission's vision of a new social dimension or social charter for Europe. Ministers no longer fought over every aspect of social policy, but they continued to object strongly to a dozen or so of the charter's 50-odd legislative proposals. By and large, proposals in the field of improved health and safety caused little difficulty. But where those proposals extended to social policy or industrial relations, Britain remained hostile. During the Maastricht summit in December, the impasse forced Britain's European partners to opt for an inter-governmental accord embracing the aspirations set out in the social charter, thereby avoiding a political showdown.

Checklist of changes

- Proposals to grant the European Commission new powers to monitor all large-scale cross-frontier mergers with a combined turnover of £3.5 billion have now been approved.
- The Commission will continue to exercise all its powers to appraise state aids to companies in both the private and public sectors in order to prevent governments engaging in anti-competitive practices.
- An optional European company statute, enabling companies involved in cross-frontier mergers to incorporate under European rather than national law, will also be introduced, along with measures designed to facilitate some degree of worker participation in company decision making.
- New health and safety standards governing working practices will be introduced. Measures to increase worker rights will also be implemented, but they will not apply to Britain.
- A series of measures aimed at providing European companies with a common framework for conducting their operations will be implemented, including a Community trade mark, a European patent law and legislation harmonizing variations in national audit and fiscal procedures.

11 OBJECTIONS TO THE SINGLE MARKET

Arguments against 1992 from Right and Left

The programme for the completion of the single market by 1992 is designed to benefit businesses, consumers and travellers, but it does not arouse universal enthusiasm. There are fears that free movement will help criminals and terrorists in Europe and (mostly on the centre and right of the political spectrum) that 1992 will entail a serious loss of national sovereignty and enmesh Britain in European-style socialism. John Major's new style on Europe has, to some extent, calmed Euro-fears on the Right. But many still believe that, as Mrs Thatcher put it at Bruges:

> It is ironic that just when those countries such as the Soviet Union which have tried to run everything from the centre are learning that success depends on dispersing power and decisions away from the centre, some in the Community seem to want to move in the opposite direction. We have not successfully rolled back the frontiers of the state in Britain only to see them re-imposed at a European level.

The Left, while on the whole approving of 1992 after initial hostility, fears that cross-border activity by multinationals will benefit big business rather than ordinary employees, and lead to the erosion of workers' rights and health and safety standards—the 'social dimension'. Many business executives, for their part, fear that their companies will suffer commercial losses, or even fail.

Most of the critics of 1992 accept that, in Mrs Thatcher's words, 'by getting rid of barriers, by making it possible for companies to operate on a Europe-wide scale, we can best compete with the United States, Japan and the other new economic powers emerging in Asia and elsewhere'. This is the Government's view of a Europe 'open for enterprise'. However, not all sectors of industry share this view. DRI Europe, an international forecasting group, claimed in a report issued in July 1988 that the advent of the single market would not bring benefits on the scale envisaged by the Commission, least of all in sectors struggling for survival, such as the car industry. Harmonization of technical standards for and taxes on cars would be slow and incomplete, the report said. The 1992 programme did not envisage a policy for dealing with import threats from outside the Community. There would be cross-border trade distortions if VAT rates on cars were not brought into line, and companies such as Fiat and Renault could suffer sales losses so heavy that the French and Italian governments might try to maintain special restrictions on imports to protect them. Some fear that cross-border mergers in fields from banking to manufacturing will create Euro-conglomerates which will overpower small and medium-sized enterprises (SMEs) unable to compete in terms of resources and capital, even though the Single European Act specifically acknowledged the need to help SMEs in 1992.

The loss of national sovereignty

Even if such gloom is exaggerated, the 1992 process has aroused a widespread feeling (often nurtured by the tabloid press in Britain but also expressed by politicians and commentators) that power is ineluctably slipping out of the hands of national authorities and into those of faceless Eurocrats in Brussels. Pro-European Conservatives like Sir Geoffrey Howe argue that sovereignty is a 'flexible, adaptable organic notion which evolves and adjusts with circumstances'. When Mrs Thatcher resigned, the *Sunday Times*, in an editorial headed 'A Reluctant Goodbye', declared that her determination to defend the British pound and parliament rested on 'misplaced chauvinism', adding: 'It lacks vision or encouragement for our entrepreneurs, who have to trade with Europe, or for the brightest and best of our young, whose careers will increasingly depend on Europe'.

However, some Tories still resent what they see as a transfer of power to Brussels symbolized by plan for a single currency. Sir Keith Joseph wrote in *The Times* on 26 September 1991 that the notion of 'one market, one currency . . . suggests what is false—that a single market can come only with a single currency—and suppresses what seems to be true— that one currency means one government'. In other words, a Europe with a single currency controlled by a European Bank would lead to a European supranational government. Mrs Thatcher continued to speak out in similar terms after her resignation, observing on a tour of the United States in August 1991 that 'Our parliament is 700 years old, and, if its powers are curtailed, then that means curtailing the powers of the British people'.

The Times noted in a leader in June 1991 that, in practice, national sovereignty was eroded by 'every treaty, every negotiation, every military alliance'. But, it added, there are

> thresholds of sovereignty, points at which national electorates lose control over certain economic and political activities . . . Modern nations are not archaic embarrassments to some new international consciousness. They are real expressions of democratic feeling; if suppressed or neglected they will fight back, as they are doing to the East.

Roger Scruton, defining Englishness for the BBC2 series *Think of England* maintained that the English people, 'the most eccentric of peoples', had

> cast away its quirky weights and measures, standardized its goods, forsworn its right to control its frontiers or determine who should dwell within them, subjected its historic common law to the half-baked reasoning of foreign judges, conferred on foreign bureaucrats unlimited right to trample on its national customs, deprived its sovereign of the power to govern and cancelled the centuries-old right of its Parliament to advise, correct and control her.

The case was perhaps best put by Brian Walden, the columnist, in the *Sunday Times* in July 1988, under the headline 'The line must be drawn at rule by Brussels'. After establishing his European credentials ('I admire Dutch tolerance, German cleanliness and efficiency, Italian family life and love of children, French worldliness and realism') Walden continued:

> But a nation is not a mere social arrangement that can be submerged into something better at the whim of planners and bureaucrats. The UK has not managed to solve its own nationality problems . . . Creating a single government for Western Europe is an infinitely more difficult operation than holding the UK together.

Comment of this kind has been encouraged by Delors' observation in June 1988 that an 'embryo' European government would emerge in the 1990s, and that 80% of economic and social legislation would be decided at the European level within ten years. The 1992 programme itself envisages no such development, since it is confined to the creation of the internal market. However, the critics have noticed that the process will not necessarily stop there. As Walden remarked:

> There is no point in subjecting Delors to an abusive tirade, because much of what he says is true. The creation of a single market is bound to mean that many decisions affecting our economic and social life will be taken in Brussels and Strasbourg. British politicians have been very slow to visualize what the new Europe will mean for national parliaments and national sovereignty . . . But I draw the line at a single European government.

The British people, Walden said, had not agreed to such a move when they voted in the 1975 EC referendum:

> and were specifically assured by several pro-Europeans, including me, that no such political arrangement was intended. We must

dig in our heels, before the EC is ruined by the haste and intemperance of political dreamers.

On a different level, the popular press has presented a picture of Britain surrendering sovereignty to Brussels. In August 1988 the *Star* newspaper carried a front-page headline reading '1992 Euro shocker', listing three points: 'Dearer clothes, food and power; our athletes to join Euro-team; Our troops to take orders in German'. 'Mrs Thatcher does not run Britain any more,' the report began:

> Nor does the Government. The Civil Service is powerless, and the highest courts in the land can be overruled. This is not the nightmare scenario of George Orwell's *1984*, it is the amazing reality of what life will be like in 1992. For that is the year when Britain will virtually disappear into a United States of Europe.

The *Today* newspaper brought this up to date in June 1991 with what it called 'Delors' Charter':

> Finger on our nuclear button in Belgium; taxes and VAT paid straight to Brussels; beer served in litres, yards become metres; British police become part of FBI-style force; our soldiers serve in European Army; compulsory Saturday schooling in German.

A favourite tabloid tactic is to add to such predictions some of the more eccentric proposals advanced by fringe elements in the EC, such as a small group of Euro MPs (who have little real power) obliging British motorists to drive on the right or to cut their lawns between midday and 2 pm on Sundays.

While such reporting has little serious aim (apart from the arousal of indignation) there is genuine political concern among some commentators that by signing the Single European Act EC leaders have gone too far, and have created a monster which may get out of control. The tone was set by the debates in the Commons and Lords in 1986 as the Single European Act passed through both Houses of Parliament. Writing in *The Times* in May 1986, Sir Edward du Cann, MP for Taunton and president of the Conservative European Reform Group, summed up the Act as follows:

> The directive powers of the Commission are to be massively enhanced, the national veto is to be reduced in scope, progress toward European political union is to be accelerated. Thus, whether British people approve or disapprove, the establishment of a European super-state is under way.

Sir Edward added: 'Almost overnight and largely unnoticed by our fellow citizens, Britain's right to decide many practical matters, even her own destiny, is being surrendered to the majority vote and the interests of other nations not all of whom share our parliamentary traditions'.

The House of Lords Select Committee appointed to scrutinize the Act concluded that 'in the long term the position of the UK Parliament will become weaker'. Two eminent QCs, Peter Horsfield and Leolin Price, in *The Times* the same month said that the Act involved profound constitutional changes and was a step towards European political union. In the House of Commons this view was most forcefully expressed by Teddy Taylor, Conservative MP for Southend, and a noted anti-Common Market campaigner. 'It would surely be in our national interests if the EC were to resolve its existing problems and implement its existing agreements before seeking further powers,' Taylor wrote to *The Times*:

> Is it wise to give even more power to the EC, which has so abysmally failed to resolve the crisis in its agricultural policy . . . ? More majority voting will simply mean more Euro laws being applied to the UK, which could well be wholly against our wishes or our interests. If this is not a major step towards federation, I wonder what is.

Paul Johnson, the columnist and historian, complained in *The Times* of public apathy as 'fundamental and irreversible changes' were pushed through, partly because of 'the sheer soporific effect of the leaden jargon with which the EC conceals its doings'. The Act was:

> a completely new treaty, which ought properly to have been placed on a level of significance equivalent to that of the original Treaty of Rome . . . When Britain joined the EC we had to accept that membership would involve some limitations to our national sovereignty. But the understanding was that these limitations were finite . . . and that any further limitations would be carefully negotiated by us from a position of strength within the EC.

As the Act passed over the final hurdle at Westminster, approval by the Lords, Lord Denning, former Master of the Rolls, warned that the aim of the Act was 'to transform Europe into a single nation with its own Parliament and its own legislation'. Westminster would become a 'subordinate body'.

For many, the EC is a 'fact of life', but one reluctantly accepted. British assertions of national sovereignty are greeted hypocritically on the Continent, right-wing critics say, since the French and other Europeans are adept at advancing their own national interests while claiming to be *communautaire*. According to Oliver Letwin, formerly a member of the Prime Minister's Policy Unit, fair competition and free movement of capital and labour within the EC under the 1992 programme are welcome, but have to be balanced against the fact that—as Enoch Powell once warned—Britain is losing its national autonomy:

> The idea that a majority group of French, West German, Italian, Belgian, Spanish, Portuguese and Irish ministers sitting behind closed doors in Brussels could pass what is effectively binding legislation on Britain, with our own parliament powerless to intervene, would have struck anyone as a crazy proposition until recently. But this crazy proposition is now a fact.

In September 1988, *The Spectator* declared, after the row over the sacking of Lord Cockfield, that 'there is nothing to be gained from isolation from the Continent, and much to be said for institutionalized co-operation between powers which are geographically and politically close and on the whole friendly'. But it added that it was lukewarm about the European idea:

> Will people really accept that their lives can be ordered by Brussels? Will they only be prepared to accept this if Brussels is controlled by a powerful European Parliament? If so, what will be left of our own Parliament?

The *Sunday Telegraph* editor, Peregrine Worsthorne, argued that much right-wing opinion on the Continent is all too ready to accept 'collectivist' views of 1992, because:

> Quite simply they are not conservative in the way Mrs Thatcher is conservative. They are for the most part Christian Democrat, with deep roots in Catholic social and economic doctrine, which is light years away from Mrs Thatcher's brand of free enterprise economic and social doctrine.

Strong centralizing traditions are common to Left and Right on the Continent, 'making Leon Blum, the great French socialist, at one with Bismarck, the great German reactionary'.

Professor Elie Kedourie of London University, a noted authority on nationalism, agreed that the problem goes wider than arguments over harmonization. Writing in *The Times* in September 1988, he made the point that:

> Whether through good luck or the wisdom of its political leaders, Britain has enjoyed for generations now a stable, constitutional mode of government in which the citizen has not had to fear for his freedom and where legality is the accepted norm and test for all

official action. This is far from having been the case on the
Continent where, since the French Revolution, a disagreeable,
visionary and destructive style of politics has been in the habit of
now and again erupting,

Spain, Greece, Italy and Germany all offer examples of instability and
extremism. 'What is to hold such a disparate union together?' Kedourie
asked. Writing in *The Independent*, Sir William Rees-Mogg, a former editor
of *The Times*, suggested that Delors was trying to impose a socialist view
of 1992, yet 'the European Commission has no remit to re-impose by
subterfuge what Britain has thrown off after disastrous experience'.
    Anti-Brussels feeling emerged during the European election in 1989,
following the Government's warning to Brussels not to 'interfere' beyond
its powers. *The Economist* commented that Mrs Thatcher's 'blind spot'
about Europe was lethal, and she was 'ignoring the fact that much of
what is happening in Western Europe is excellently Thatcherite and will
continue to be if only she has the sense to embrace it with a bit of
Continental warmth instead of treating it to unending English *froideur*'.
James Elles MEP wrote in *The Times* on 26 June 1989 that 'The objective
of the EC is not just simply to create an internal market. It is a means by
which its member states can move, step by step, towards closer European
integration, without actually specifying the destination'. But precisely
because of this, thirteen academics, led by Lord Harris of Highcross,
chairman of the Institute of Economic Affairs, in 1989 formed 'The Bruges
Group'—more properly, The Campaign for a Europe of Sovereign States
—to oppose European union in the spirit of Mrs Thatcher's Bruges
speech. (The group had been initiated earlier by an Oxford under-
graduate.) Edward Heath declared that 'any intelligent Conservative'
could support a sharing of sovereignty, adding: 'Of course, if you go to
a member of the British public and say, do you want your British pound
and British pint of beer taken away by a lot of nasty foreign Marxists he
will indignantly reply that no, he does not. But I believe the British
public reject such false popularism, such distortions of the truth for the
patronizing, self-serving hypocrisy that they are'. Jonathan Aitken MP
replied that Britain was in danger of surrendering its sovereignty 'almost
through sleepwalking'. Aitken said he was 'madly in favour of Europe',
with a European wife, children born in Europe and 'lots of European
friends'. But 'I am amazed at the willingness of some politicians to apparently throw out 900 years of constitutional history, headed by a sovereign
parliament, in favour of what is still a European Blancmange . . . The
Single European Act has been used by Delors and many others as a new
Meccano set for constitutional, financial and legal experiments, a good
many of which will turn out to be very damaging to this country' (*London
International*, Summer 1989).

Democratic accountability

Criticisms of this kind carry a great deal of force and express widespread concern about integration. On the other hand, the Act was extensively discussed in Britain and other EC countries (as the comments themselves show) and it was ratified democratically. There was no secret about what it contained. According to an opinion poll published in *The Mail on Sunday* in September 1988, after Mrs Thatcher's speech in Bruges, many Britons now accept a degree of integration with Europe and an erosion of sovereignty. The key question is how the resulting European institutions can be subjected to popular control. The Single European Act does provide for qualified majority voting in the Council of Ministers, and to this extent involves a loss of national sovereignty. On the other hand, joining the EC in the first place entailed some loss of sovereignty, and most supporters of European integration argue that by pooling sovereignty the EC becomes stronger and so more able to promote the interests of all its members. National governments, moreover, retain the right of veto in many vital areas, since the majority voting system applies to internal market matters only. However, there is a widespread perception that EC institutions must be more tightly controlled as European influence in our lives and work increases.

Some anti-EC feeling and comment reflects an unexpressed regret that Britain took the decision to join the Community in 1973. Others accept that EC accession was the right step, but regret that Mrs Thatcher subsequently put her name to the Single European Act, thus allowing the EC to take the process of integration a stage further. However, while such regrets are perfectly legitimate they can have no practical impact, since both the Accession Treaty and the Single European Act are accomplished facts, legally drawn up and ratified after long debate and negotiation. Britain, in the words of one senior EC diplomat, has 'passed the point of no return'.

The answer to fears of loss of control over our daily lives must therefore lie in increasing democratic control over the institutions of the EC, to ensure that EC developments meet British interests and concerns. This is the solution proposed, among others, by Bill Newton Dunn, Conservative MEP for Lincolnshire. The major omission in the 1992 programme, in Newton Dunn's view (which is widely shared by all parties in the European Parliament) is the lack of any provision for ensuring that, as integration proceeds, so democratic control over EC decision making is increased. Proposals are scrutinized at every stage as they pass through the decision-making procedures, particularly when they are approved by European Parliament committees. Nonetheless, in the final analysis decisions are made and proposals passed into law during deliberations of the Council of Ministers, which are confidential.

The argument for retaining confidentiality is that the Council of Ministers is not only a legislature but also a negotiating body, in which ministers win and concede points in a way likely to be impaired if the proceedings were made public. British Cabinet proceedings are not open to the press, the argument runs, so neither should those of the EC Council of Ministers be exposed to the public gaze. In any case, EC ministers all come from national parliaments and are therefore democratically accountable in their own countries.

However, the development of the 1992 process seems bound to lead to further demands for 'accountability', with at least partial media accession to Council meetings, instead of the present system under which Brussels-based correspondents are briefed by national spokesmen and have to find the whole picture (in so far as it can be found) by cultivating official contacts.

On 25 July 1989, as the newly elected European Parliament assembled for the session leading up to 1992, *The Times* noted that Conservative Euro MPs had for the first time been invited to hear the Prime Minister report to the 1922 Committee to increase MEP–MP liaison, but added:

> In practice, Westminster's machinery has been overwhelmed by the quantity and detail of European regulation. The European Parliament has remained weak. In the gap between lies the 'democratic deficit' . . . The approach to monitoring EC regulations taken so far by most Westminster MPs must rapidly change. The work of the select committee on European legislation and debates in the House are adequate only for considering general principles. EC matters need to cease being an alien subject and to be dispersed where they belong—an integral part of almost every aspect of national life considered by the House of Commons.

Attitudes on the Left

The demand for democratic accountability has also been taken up by the political left, and above all by the Labour Party, which, after a long period of hostility towards the EC, has given its support to the 1992 programme while at the same time seeking to ensure that the internal market not only benefits big business but also protects the rights of employees. Most of the Labour Party Group in the European Parliament, paradoxically, remains virulently anti-EC, but national Labour policy has altered.

The key event in the emergence of Labour's new policy was the decision at the beginning of 1988 by Neil Kinnock, the Party leader, to abandon Labour's previous commitment to withdrawing Britain from the EC if it won power. The intellectual ground for the change was prepared in a Fabian pamphlet written by David Martin, MEP, then leader of the Labour Group at Strasbourg, and published in February 1988, which argued that Labour should work with other socialist parties in Europe to 'bring common sense to the Common Market'. The aim, the pamphlet said, should be to increase social spending, redistribute resources as 1992 brought greater prosperity and protect the EC environment. In a preface Kinnock wrote: 'It is surely realistic to acknowledge that Britain's integration with the other European economies by 1990 will have proceeded so far that talk of economic withdrawal is both politically romantic and economically self-defeating'. The aim of socialism, Kinnock declared, was to 'prevent the hardship, exploitation and waste which can result from the operation of unregulated markets'. Labour's view of 1992, in other words, is diametrically opposed to that of the Right, which—in Kinnock's eyes—'puts profit before people'. He concluded that if the Left did not take part in 1992 there would be

> unimpeded movement to the complete economic and political domination of Western Europe by market power, with all of the effects on civil rights, environmental conditions, individual opportunities and collective provision which that implies.
> Leaving the European field to that is no more acceptable than leaving Britain to permanent Thatcherism.

On a visit to Brussels in February 1988 Kinnock followed this up by declaring flatly: 'The prospects for withdrawal in my view are nil'. In September 1988, in a speech to Labour Euro MPs in Glasgow, Kinnock urged all socialists to take part in 1992, remarking: 'If the single market was to mean nothing other than a big finance free-for-all, it would be a social, industrial and environmental catastrophe'. At the Labour Party Conference in Blackpool in October 1988 Kinnock took much the same line, accusing the Government of 'pathetically inadequate' preparations for 1992, and declaring that social justice had to be a central component of the single market if it was not to benefit rich regions and become 'expensive, ugly, a constant source of waste, and a constant source of tension between peoples'.

This appears to be accepted by a broad spectrum of left-wing opinion. In an article in the July–September 1988 issue of *The Political Quarterly* entitled 'Beyond One Nation Socialism: An Agenda for the European Left' Frances Morrell, former leader of the ILEA and a noted left-winger, argued that it was a mistake to examine the reasons for Labour's electoral decline, such as the loss of traditional working class support, in national rather than European terms:

> The shaping of Europe should not be abandoned to the Right. Labour, and indeed all Social Democratic Parties out of office, have a duty to oppose and to lead.

In July 1989 Glyn Ford, new leader of the Labour MEPs at Strasbourg, moved still further from Labour's anti-EC line, saying the Conservatives were 'hardly European' whereas 'we represent the party that is determined to work within the EC'. Kinnock supported this when visiting Strasbourg the same month, but, like Thatcher, was cautious on the pace of economic and monetary union.

In the run-up to the 1992 general election, Kinnock and the Labour Party faced a dilemma in opposing Major and the Conservatives. Though seeking to capitalize on the Tories' difficulties over Europe at the same time they could not afford to be seen as any more 'integrationist' than the government. Kinnock observed of schemes for federalism that 'any attempt to superimpose political union from the top is bound to end in tears'. Equally, monetary union could impose 'tortuous pressures on the British economy'. Kinnock endorsed the concept of a European Bank, but said that exchange rate interventions would have to be supervised by EC finance ministers. George Robertson, Labour spokesman on European affairs, warned that the market could not be left to tackle problems of education, environment or transport: 'At a European level, if you are going to have a single market, then you have to have control'. At the Labour Party conference in October 1991 Kinnock declared that a Labour government would put Britain in the 'first division' of Europe, remarking:

> People look at our society, and they look at our neighbours in the rest of the Community. They see the high standards of training, the quality of child care, the investment in public transport, and they ask: 'Why not here?'

The social dimension: a 1992 Workers' Charter?

Kinnock's lead has been followed by the trades union movement, whose espousal of 1992 was given great encouragement in September 1988, when Delors travelled to Bournemouth to appeal to the TUC to back the internal market. In doing so Delors—a French socialist—indirectly criticized the interpretation of 1992 advanced by Mrs Thatcher, and lent support to the Left's campaign for a 'social dimension'. 'It is impossible to build Europe only on deregulation,' he declared, to an ovation from the trades union delegates:

> 1992 is much more than the creation of an internal market abolishing barriers to the free movement of goods, services and investment. The internal market should be designed to benefit each and every citizen of the Community. It is therefore necessary to improve workers' living and working conditions, and to provide better protection for their health and safety at work.

He assured the TUC that he believed in 'social dialogue and collective bargaining' as pillars of a democratic society. These assertions won Delors

TUC backing and the affectionate sobriquet 'Frère Jacques' (Brother Jacques). He had ceased to be, in the eyes of the Left, a soulless and overpaid international bureaucrat and had become the champion of the workers as the single market approached.

The significance of the change of heart in the Labour Party and the TUC lies partly in its impact on British politics. However, given the Conservative Party's current dominance of British politics, in the long run the most important impact of left-wing thinking on 1992 will be in the European context, where socialist parties are stronger and where some are in power. At the TUC in September 1988, Ron Todd, of the Transport and General Workers Union, speaking for the TUC General Council, called on British trades unionists to link up with their European counterparts to ensure that 1992 was moulded in the right direction. Todd admitted that the TUC had once been 'sceptical about there being any benefits in the European dimension'. But he added:

> The only card game in town at the moment is in a town called Brussels, and it's the game of poker . . . We've got to learn the rules, and pretty fast.

The TUC agreed to set up links with Continental unions to explore the possibilities of Europe-wide collective bargaining with employers, and called on the European Commission to produce a 'European Workers' Charter' to protect employees in cross-border mergers and takeovers.

Such a charter has been considered by the European Commission, and is favoured, in one form or another, by several of the EC countries which at present have socialist administrations. As it happens, three of them—Greece, Spain and France—hold the presidency of the EC Council of Ministers consecutively. Felipe Gonzalez, the Spanish Prime Minister, who held the Presidency in the first half of 1989, is an enthusiastic proponent of the 'social dimension'. When Mrs Thatcher visited Madrid in September 1988 she expressed her opposition to new Europe-wide regulations on company law and worker participation in industry, remarking that the EC term 'social space' was imprecise:

> It is a new piece of jargon. I am never quite sure what it is. But if it means having a regulation on Community company law, then I would oppose that particular thing. I am a democrat and I am a meritocrat and I believe you get on by merit, not by giving particular privileges to one particular group.

Gonzalez, however, insisted that a social dimension to 1992 was indispensable, with employees' rights protected and with help for the socially and economically disadvantaged.

The social dimension figured prominently in the European election campaign, when Michael Meacher, the then Labour employment spokes-man, leaked details of a report by a group of EC lawyers showing that Britain lagged behind other EC countries in rights of workers to annual leave, minimum wages and working hours. Norman Fowler, then the Secretary of State for Employment, retorted that economic growth and job creation had brought down unemployment in Britain without the need for regulation or charters. At a meeting in Luxembourg of EC Labour and Employment Ministers in June 1989 he opposed the social charter, which, however, was backed by ten other states (Denmark abstained, saying it had to consult employers and trades unions at home). 'We are being asked to sign a blank cheque before anyone has defined what these rights would be and how much they would cost' Fowler declared. Britain also opposed the related proposal for a European Company Statute (see Chapter 9).

Proposals for a charter tabled in September 1988 by Manuel Marin of Spain, then Commissioner for Social Policy, were restricted to voluntary common measures for training schemes, common standards for social security benefits and common health and safety provisions, to which Britain has no objection. However, France and Germany have since appealed to Mrs Vasso Papandreou of Greece, the present Commissioner, to follow the proposed charter—adopted at the Strasbourg summit at the end of 1989—with binding legislation on social issues and workers' rights by the mid-1990s. Mrs Papandreou issued a revised version of the charter in September 1989. In a letter to *The Times* on 29 June 1989 Norman Willis, then the TUC General Secretary, said the social charter 'would not seek to impose one particular model of worker participation on all member states'. But Mrs Thatcher dismissed the charter as 'backdoor socialism'. Michel Rocard, the then French Prime Minister, memorably mixing his metaphors, accused her of having a view of Europe as 'a jungle, a house with its windows wide open to the winds, a plane without a pilot'. At the Madrid summit in June 1989 the issue was avoided but resurfaced under the French EC presidency in the second half of 1989, when Mitter-rand and Rocard actively pursued it in the run-up to the Strasbourg summit in December 1989.

In the course of 1990–91 other EC countries such as Germany and Ireland sided with Britain on the social dimension, arguing that some issues—such as working hours, minimum wages, the rights of part-time workers or pregnant women at the workplace—could not be decided by majority vote, as Mrs Papandreou wanted. On the other hand, Germany, with a strong Christian Democrat lobby against Sunday trading, pressed for a ban on Sunday working as an alleged 'health and safety' measure, a move denounced by Delors as nonsensical. Further workplace legislation, however, was passed by EC employment ministers on the eve of the Maastricht summit in December 1991, in the face of British objections.

The politicization of 1992

These developments show that the single market programme, initially seen as a technical one for harmonization and freer trade across frontiers, has rapidly acquired a party-political dimension as the reality of 1992 approaches. Anxieties on the Right about 'corporate socialism' and interference from Brussels at the expense of British cultural traditions and national sovereignty are matched by concern on the Left that the 1992 agenda has been set by conservative parties in power in Britain and Europe and by big business, which is able to influence both national governments and the European Commission.

The outcome of this debate is not clear, nor can we see how far the debate will shape 1992 and how much it will merely be a domestic political football to be kicked around for domestic political reasons. Speaking to German trades unionists and business executives in Cologne in September 1988, Delors responded to criticisms from the Right by attacking the 'verbal excesses of the advocates of deregulation', and called for a 'new Keynes or Beveridge' to lay down a comprehensive EC social and employment programme for 1992, together with a plan for the redistribution of wealth. 'We thought we had this debate behind us,' Delors said, 'There can be no Europe without a social dimension . . . Europe must never become an instrument to weaken the trades unions.' The debate is far from over, however, and seems likely to intensify as 1992 approaches.

An indication of how strong the 1992 backlash might become was given in a speech by Sir John Hoskyns, the outgoing Director-General of the Institute of Directors, to an audience of 3,000 business executives in February 1989. Describing the internal market programme as a 'complete fiasco', Sir John attacked the Community and its institutions for 'shifting objectives, bad organization, wrong people, poor motivation, inadequate methods, weak management, personal politics and pilfering on a heroic scale'.

In addition to alleging that 'there are signs that the Brussels machine is becoming corrupted both intellectually and financially', Sir John astonished his audience by calling on the Community to scrap its 1992 achievements and start all over again! No less striking was the co-ordinated and instantaneous government assault on Sir John's provocative views.

Sir Geoffrey Howe, the then Foreign Secretary, later told a Birmingham press conference that: 'It is, quite frankly, perverse and faint-hearted to claim that the single market has been blown off course, or risks being submerged in collectivism or bureaucracy.' These sentiments were also echoed by Lord Young, who accused Sir John of ignoring 'many of the facts', and expressed fears that 'Sir John has been reading too many scare stories in the press and not attending closely enough to what was really happening'.

12 ABOLISHING FISCAL FRONTIERS
The value added tax dispute

Although the European Commission's plans for harmonizing indirect taxation have been seen as a further example of unwarranted attempts by Brussels to extend its authority into areas traditionally regarded as the preserve of sovereign governments, the overhaul of the Community's indirect taxation regime is a logical and inevitable consequence of the agreement by member states to abolish their internal frontiers, as enshrined in the Single European Act. Apart from the objective of reducing the costs imposed on business and commerce of having to pass through border posts, which has been estimated at 1.5% of the value of intra-Community trade, the different rates of indirect taxation among member states and the need to ensure that value added tax (Vat) is remitted on exports and charged on imports is one of the main reasons frontier controls remain in existence. If frontier controls are to be abolished, then rates of indirect taxation must converge, and new mechanisms must be found for preventing fraud and ensuring that national governments are able to levy Vat on consumption.

Rejecting allegations that the harmonization of indirect taxation was little more than an attempt to augment its powers, the Commission insisted that:

> The prime objective is to abolish tax frontiers, in other words, to eliminate the need for checks at internal borders. The Commission's proposals are not therefore designed to achieve tax harmonization for the sake of harmonization . . . The aim is more modest. It is limited strictly to what is needed to remove tax frontiers.

The harmonization of indirect taxation, or more accurately, the approximation of Vat and the harmonization of excise duties is therefore regarded by the Commission as central to the 1992 process.

Nonetheless, for two reasons the tax-harmonization proposals have aroused fundamental passions and fierce opposition, particularly in Britain. Traditionally, taxation has been seen as the preserve of national governments, and therefore free from supranational control or interference. Moreover, the Commission's plans for the approximation of Vat, at least as originally tabled, would mean the end of Britain's cherished zero rating of basic goods such as food, fuel and childrens' clothing—a development any government would regard as politically sensitive, if not potentially explosive. In addition, the harmonization of excise duties, the specific indirect taxes levied on the consumption of certain products such as tobacco and alcohol, will have the effect of bringing down the costs to the consumer of cigarettes, beer and spirits. This has given rise to the charge that 'Brussels' is planning as part of 1992 to increase the prices of food and children's shoes (socially useful products) while reducing those of tobacco and alcohol (socially harmful ones).

Because indirect taxation is one area where the right of national veto has been retained, the proposals put forward by the Commission have to be approved by the Council of Ministers before passing into national law. After a seemingly endless series of negotiations between EC economic and finance ministers, the broad outlines of the new Community indirect taxation regime had emerged by December 1990. New proposals advanced in May 1989 by Mme Christiane Scrivener, the Commissioner for Fiscal Affairs, had already made significant concessions, allowing Britain to keep Vat zero rating on food, children's clothes and other basic items, and by the end of the year a consensus on how the new system of indirect taxation was to be implemented and operated had begun to take shape.

Confusion between new proposals and court rulings

The debate over Vat and 1992 in Britain has been marked by the confusion of two separate points: the 1985 White Paper's plans for the removal of fiscal barriers; and rulings by the European Court on exemptions granted to Britain in 1977, when the Sixth Vat Directive was passed. The first refers to future proposals arising from the Single European Act; the second to a directive which is already in existence. Both tend to be regarded as interference by Brussels in British tax affairs, although this overlooks the fact that Britain has already agreed to the principle of Vat harmonization by putting its name to the 1977 directive (during the last Labour Government).

The 1977 concession does not mean that Britain or any other state is obliged to comply with the White Paper's vision of the removal of all fiscal barriers. Indeed, the Commission's proposals have already undergone a process of modification to meet the objections not only of Britain but also of other countries where Vat rates are either higher or lower than the proposed Vat bands contained in the draft 1992 directive. The Commission can (and does) argue that Vat approximation has long been on the agenda in one form or another. On the other hand, its approach to the problem illustrates the delicacy of the issue, especially the approach adopted in the 1992 White Paper itself.

The White Paper section on fiscal barriers (Section Three) was one of the most controversial aspects of the original 1992 programme. The Commission was well aware of this, as the careful if sometimes argumentative language of the White Paper shows. Section Three was the only one to depart from the overall principle of 1992—that member states should accept common goals and work their way towards them through mutual recognition, with adjustments made afterwards as the realities of the single market developed. Instead, the White Paper made a direct attempt to force EC governments to approximate their indirect tax rates.

It begins by noting that the removal of frontier controls 'is bound to have inescapable implications for the member states as far as indirect taxes are concerned'. In 1968, at the time of the customs union, it was already apparent that 'the mere removal of tariffs' would not create a true common market, and that differences in turnover taxes 'were the source of serious distortion'. The Treaty of Rome itself, the White Paper said, had provided for Commission proposals on the approximation of indirect taxation 'when this was needed for the completion of the internal market' (Articles 99 and 100). This remains the basis of the Commission's drive for Vat approximation: that Vat differentials distort trade in a frontier-free Europe; and that harmonization—or approximation—is necessary for the completion of the single market. Both are distrusted by anti-Marketeers and by a number of EC governments.

Vat has always appealed to EC policymakers as an instrument of fiscal policy because of its relative simplicity—as a principle, that is, not in terms of its complex paperwork for both business executives and Vat inspectors. Now used in all twelve EC states, with Portugal the last to come into line in 1989, Vat is a tax levied at each stage of the process of production and marketing but collected by the government of the country at the point of sale. In practice, however, Vat rates vary considerably from one country to another. A system of limited allowances has been developed for the carrying of tax-free goods across EC borders, but this causes problems for countries like Denmark and Ireland, which have tried (illegally, according to the Commission, which is threatening to take them to the European Court) to restrict such allowances to *bona fide* travellers by imposing arbitrary definitions of what constitutes a traveller.

Steps towards harmonization of indirect taxes

The first major step towards harmonization came in 1967, at the time of the Six, when turnover taxes were replaced by Vat levied on a common basis through a series of Vat directives (the First Vat Directive, the Second Vat Directive, and so on). Three years later, in 1970, came the decision to give the EC its 'own resources'—a common EC fund as opposed to national budgets—by raising revenues based partly on farm levies but mainly on a proportion (up to 1%) of national Vat contributions. This system eventually proved inadequate, and under the Delors reforms of February 1988 has given way to a revised own resources system based partly on Vat and partly on a tax derived from a calculation of gross national product. This more fairly reflects each country's ability to contribute to the EC and, incidentally, creates difficulties for Italy because of the extent of the black economy, making the true Italian GNP almost unknowable. But even under the Delors package, Vat contributions remain a central part of the revenue system.

In 1977 the Sixth Vat Directive laid down the outlines of a common Vat base, yet so sensitive was the issue, and so great the resistance of national governments, that the directive contained a number of loopholes and exemptions, known in EC jargon as 'derogations'. On the other hand, the directive made it clear that such exemptions were only temporary, hence the subsequent cases in the European Court over whether exemptions granted to Britain on medical and social grounds were justified. At the same time, the EC decided to harmonize excise duties, beginning with cigarettes and tobacco, alcohol and hydrocarbon oils. By 1985 the White Paper was able to declare that 'the harmonization of indirect taxation has always been regarded as an essential and integral part of achieving a true common market'. Momentum had been lost between 1977 and 1985, it admitted, but this was due to 'the impact of recession on the economic policies of member states, and preoccupation with other problems'. Progress was now being resumed, 'and we must proceed vigorously if we are to achieve the target date of 1992'.

What are the technical arguments for Vat approximation? EC officials argue that if frontier controls are to be abolished so that people, goods and services can move about within the EC as if it were one country, this clearly affects those controls 'primarily designed to ensure that each member state can collect revenue in the form of indirect taxation'. Whether in the form of Vat or of excise duties, indirect taxes become part of the final price to the consumer. According to the White Paper:

> Different levels of taxation are reflected in different price levels. If the differences in level are substantial, the differences in final prices will also be substantial . . . We need to consider whether or not it would be practically possible, in the absence of frontier controls, for member states to charge significantly different levels of indirect taxation.

The Commission's own answer, unsurprisingly, is no, it would not. Under the Commission's draft Fourteenth Vat Directive—tabled in 1982 and eventually withdrawn in 1987, after much heated debate—EC states would all have had to shift to a system of 'postponed accounting' used in the Benelux states. Under this system, Vat accounting is done at inland tax offices rather than at frontiers. The Commission sought to meet member states' concerns by agreeing that 'some documentation' would still be needed at the border and governments would still have the right to check the movement of goods to prevent fraud. However, the Commission's basic principle remained that Vat incurred by a consumer should be deductible 'irrespective of the member state on which it has been charged'. Under a parallel proposal there would be a computerized central clearing house to ensure that Vat collected in the exporting state but deducted in the importing one was reimbursed to the importing state and not the exporting one. In the end, the Council of Ministers judged that the proposed clearing-house system was too unwieldy and too open to abuse. The Commission's position is that fraud and evasion could best be avoided if the current system of divergent Vat rates was replaced by a common one of approximated rates.

Similar arguments apply to the question of cross-border shopping. Because of the differences in Vat, and hence in prices, people in high-tax countries naturally cross where possible into neighbouring low-tax ones to reap the benefits. Cross-border shopping is particularly intense in Benelux, France and Germany; on the Danish–German border; and between Northern Ireland and the Irish Republic. It applies less to Britain, because of the natural obstacle of the Channel. But arguably, Continental housewives would find it worth making the crossing if British Vat zero rates for 'basic products' were retained after 1992 in an otherwise harmonized EC, and mail order businesses would also benefit. Mother-care—to take one example—would be able to compete with an unfair (and highly lucrative) advantage over Continental mail order firms with a similar speciality in children's clothing and supplies.

Modification of the Vat proposals

In practice, as the fate of the Fourteenth Vat Directive shows, the Commission has found its arguments for harmonization fiercely opposed, and has moved to a policy of 'approximation' instead. This is a concession, but its outlines were already visible in the 1985 White Paper. This conceded that while excise duties could and should be harmonized—which is still the Commission's policy—Vat approximation need only be 'sufficiently close that the operation of the common market is not affected through distortions of trade, diversion of trade or effects on competition'. Opponents of Vat harmonization often point to the example of the United States, where variations exist between the federal states without any noticeable effect on what might be called the single American market. The Commission took this argument and used it for its own purposes, holding up the American system as a model for an integrated Europe—adding, however, that cross-border tax variations must still be limited, with a proposed permitted divergence from the EC norm of plus or minus 2½%. Brussels also now acknowledges that Vat is only one element in the make-up of consumer prices, and that price is only one factor in consumer choice along with service, brand image and convenience: 'Retail markets are often tolerant of quite significant differences in prices'. A further problem admitted by EC officials is that Denmark and Ireland derive a larger proportion of their revenue from indirect taxation than most other EC states (16% to 17%, compared to around 10% in Britain Germany), so that major adjustments for approximation would give Copenhagen and Dublin budgetary problems.

Nonetheless, the Commission has remained determined to bring EC Vat rates broadly into line, whether under the banner of 'approximation' or 'harmonization'. It noted in the White Paper that Vat rates at present vary from zero (in Britain and Ireland) to a high point of 38% in Italy, with Denmark applying a standard rate of 22%.

In July 1987, after much internal discussion at the Berlaymont, Lord Cockfield, the Internal Market Commissioner, announced the Commission's 'approximation' proposals. Vat rates would be grouped into two broad bands: a standard rate of between 14% and 20% and a reduced one of between 4% and 9% on 'items of basic necessity'. The Commission, Lord Cockfield said, was ready to meet the 'particular difficulties' of Britain and Ireland over zero rating by considering temporary exemptions 'where these can be justified, for states for which the proposals could pose political, social or budgetary problems'.

The resulting reaction was, if anything, fiercer than that which greeted the Commission's earlier plans, largely because of the impact on zero rating. Not only would the abolition of zero rating affect lower income groups, the argument ran, it would also affect the economy as a whole, since nearly 30% of all consumer spending in Britain is accounted for by zero-rated goods—i.e. food, energy, children's clothes, water, newspapers, books and drugs. The then Paymaster General, Peter Brooke, declared: 'There is no question of our accepting anything that conflicts with the pledges the Prime Minister has given on our zero rates,' a reference to undertakings given during the 1987 election campaign. Shortly afterwards, Mrs Thatcher confirmed in the Commons that Britain would veto the Vat changes if they were put to the Council of Ministers. Nigel Lawson, the Chancellor of the Exchequer, repeatedly told fellow EC Finance Ministers that the Vat proposal was unnecessary and unacceptable. Lord Young of Graffham restated the British view in *The Times* in July 1988. The Government's rejection of the Vat proposal was 'absolutely final', he said, adding: 'We are not going to harmonize'. Differing Vat rates did not affect competition, he argued—and if distortions did arise, they would, in any case, be corrected after 1992 by market forces. The new Scrivener proposals are the result of the Commission's efforts to meet such objections. Although the issue of Vat rates remained unresolved, ministers had agreed on the means of collection, by maintaining the existing system of leaving Vat on goods and services in the country of consumption, despite Commission objections that this would entail retention of elaborate border controls.

The search for a compromise

The EC's influential Economic and Monetary Committee, composed of senior finance officials from the twelve governments, issued an interim report in April 1988. This sought to balance the opposing views on Vat, arguing that approximation along the lines advanced by Lord Cockfield can be combined with the 'market forces' line of reasoning. On the other hand, the Government's view has received support from leading experts, notably the Institute of Fiscal Studies, which in a report issued in February 1988 agreed that completion of the internal market did not require substantial changes to national Vat systems. The Institute suggested that instead of two broad Vat bands the EC should have common minimum Vat rates, or floors, allowing member states to set higher rates if they wished. It also took issue with the Commission's attempt to legislate for the good of the Community, declaring that if states with high tax rates suffered because of cross-border shopping they had only themselves to blame: 'It is not the business of the Commission to protect member states from the consequences of their own high indirect taxation policies'. It went on to argue that, as an island, Britain was less likely to be affected by cross-border shopping problems—an argument which may lose its force as cross-Channel traffic increases with the building of the Channel Tunnel.

A further compromise suggestion has come from the European Parliament. In July 1988 Alman Metten, a Dutch socialist MEP, proposed two broad Vat bands to replace those of the Commission, one ranging from zero to 6% or 9% and a higher rate of between 16% and 22%—in effect, taking account of the British–Irish zero rating problem and of Denmark's high standard rate of 22%. In October 1988 the European Parliament's committee on fiscal approximation approved this as an amendment to the Cockfield proposals. Ben Patterson, MEP for Kent West (who has himself proposed the retention of zero rating in a pamphlet entitled *Vat: The Zero Rate Issue*), welcomed the idea that zero rating should be a permanent part of the EC Vat system. On the other hand, critics of these compromise proposals argue that a system which tolerates variations of between zero and 22% can scarcely be called 'approximation' any more, let alone 'harmonization'.

The political and business climate in Britain remains suspicious of Vat harmonization, as is shown most vividly by reactions to the European Court's series of rulings on British exemptions under the 1977 directive. As noted earlier, the question of 1977 exemptions is, strictly speaking, separate from that of 1992 harmonization. Yet the two issues are, in a sense, linked aspects of the same basic drive towards harmonization— or approximation. In discussing the 1977 exemptions the White Paper made clear that they were (1) provisional only and (2) part of the wider process leading ultimately to harmonization: '. . .These derogations and social arrangements should ultimately be brought to an end . . . so that a common market permitting fair competition and resembling a real internal market may ultimately be achieved'. The 1977 directive itself stated that exemptions could be maintained until a date 'not later than that on which the charging of tax on imports and the remission of tax on exports in trade between the member states are abolished'. The date is not defined, but EC officials argue that it refers to the completion of the internal market—that is, 1992.

Rulings on the Sixth Vat Directive against Britain
The rulings arrived at by the European Court following cases brought against Britain by the Commission have certainly caused widespread concern in Britain. The rulings have come some ten years after the directive, but the wheels of EC justice grind slowly. In February 1988 the Court ruled that the Vat exemption granted in 1977 for the dispensing of spectacles and contact lenses could not be justified. Backbench Conservative MPs complained that an outside body was dictating to Parliament what taxes it could levy for the first time since the seventeenth-century ship tax. In June the Court caused another political row by ruling that the practice of either zero rating or exempting new commercial construction and certain services to industry (electricity, gas, protective clothing, sewerage, plus news services) was a further unjustified exemption (although it upheld the exemption for private domestic housing as well as for animal feedstuffs and livestock), leading to confusion in the media over whether Britain had 'won' or 'lost'. In the oral hearing in September 1987 the lawyer acting for Britain had argued that not all Vat exemptions in Britain were due to 'a funny Anglo-Saxon habit'.

Following the ruling on new construction, the standard British 15% Vat rate (increased to 17.5% in March 1991) applies to non-domestic construction, and the sale of land for commercial property development, from April 1989. The Court allowed the continued zero rating of private housing, as opposed to commercial building, because Britain was entitled to pursue—on social grounds—'a policy of home ownership for the whole population'. The Government softened the blow to commercial building and services by refunding or partially refunding the extra cost for health authorities and charities, but private schools, hospitals and charities still expressed dismay. (To qualify for a refund the institution in question must be registered for Vat purposes.) Teddy Taylor, MP, giving voice to backbench feelings, recalled in a letter to *The Times* in June 1988 that when the Commons debated the Sixth Vat Directive in November 1976, before its final adoption, the government of the day had repeatedly declared that the British right to retain zero rating was assured. The Court's ruling, Taylor said, was 'one more example of the wishes of the Euro-institutions to extend their powers and control at the expense of sovereign governments'. Responding to this and other charges that the Government had conceded sovereignty over taxation to the EC, Peter Lilley, then Economic Secretary to the Treasury, pointed out that the ruling arose from the 1977 directive, in which the exemptions were not time limited, and that Britain had no alternative but to comply. The European Court is the Court of last resort.

The Cockfield legacy: the logic of approximation

There is, in other words, a clear link—although one not stressed officially —between the various Vat directives which have so far introduced partial steps toward Vat harmonization and the full Cockfield vision, which is seen by the Commission as the logical consequence and fulfilment of earlier directives. The departure of Lord Cockfield and the advent of a new Commissioner for the period 1989–92 signals a change of tone, with Vat harmonization pursued in a less adversarial style. However, the basis of the policy remains the same. If Britain agreed to partial harmonization in 1977, the argument runs, why should it not agree to the end result?

To some extent, the Commission has the new EC law on its side. The Single European Act specifically provided for Vat harmonization as part of 1992. The full passage of Article 99 reads:

> The Council of Ministers shall, acting unanimously on a proposal from the Commission and after consulting the European Parliament, adopt provisions for the harmonization of legislation concerning turnover taxes, excise duties and other forms of indirect taxation to the extent that such harmonization is necessary to ensure the establishment and the functioning of the internal market within the time limit laid down.

The time limit referred to is 1992: the argument therefore revolves around the phrase 'to the extent that such harmonization is necessary to ensure the functioning of the internal market'. Senior British officials continue to argue that it is not necessary: senior Commission officials in Brussels maintain that it is. Britain is not alone in taking its stand. France has also expressed strong reservations about Vat harmonization, largely because the broad bands proposed by the Commission are too broad, and would leave French businesses vulnerable to lower Vat rates levied in neigh-bouring Germany. Both France and Germany fear that Vat harmonization will force national governments to reshape their fiscal policies because of single market considerations rather than because of priorities set by governments themselves. Martin Bangemann, the German Commissioner and former Economics Minister, is on record as stating that full fiscal harmonization can only come about after 1992, rather than before, since only after 1992 will the full effects of free competition in a frontier-free market become apparent.

Unravelling the deadlock on Vat

Meeting under the Greek presidency on the island of Crete in September 1988, Nigel Lawson, the then Chancellor of the Exchequer, announced a British plan under which there would be a gradual elimination of restrictions on cross-border shopping, a retention of differing rates of excise duty on alcohol and tobacco and a postponed accounting system for Vat to reduce frontier controls. Market forces, Lawson argued, would bring Vat rates into line after 1992. The proposal was given a cool reception, largely because it failed to make provision for the anxieties of other member states over increases in cross-border shopping. Consequently, most economic and finance ministers tended to prefer the Commission's proposals, while insisting that they be made more flexible.

Responding to the evident deadlock, Mme Scrivener did precisely that. In place of Cockfield's two-band Vat principle, at an EC finance ministers' meeting in May 1989, at S'Agaro in Spain, she presented a proposal to introduce a minimum standard Vat rate of 15%, a lower rate or rates for socially sensitive items, and the retention (at least for a transitional phase) of zero rating. In some respects, the proposal was a concession to Britain, although only a partial one, as the list of items to be granted zero-rated status was very limited indeed. The proposal included a gradual elimination of the restrictions on cross-border shopping and a case-by-case negotiation on the harmonization of excise duties. Madame Scrivener said that she had taken the 'market forces' argument into account, prompting Lawson to remark that a British dogmatist (Cockfield) had been replaced by a French pragmatist.

Although far from resolving the issue, the initiative nonetheless contributed to a more concilliatory atmosphere in the negotiations. During further talks in November and December the Commission's broad approach was endorsed by a majority of member states, and at the European Council in Strasbourg in December it was instructed to draw up proposals for the transition. The Commission's blueprint was announced in May 1990, and called for the abolition of all customs procedures governing the movement of goods between member states from January 1993. In effect, the notion of imports and exports within the Community was to become redundant, and the crossing of an internal frontier would no longer attract a tax obligation. Henceforth, people would be free to buy goods in any member state for consumption in any other. In an effort to prevent distortions arising out of different levels of indirect taxation, Vat on certain items (such as cars and mail-order goods) would be applied at the rate appropriate in the country of consumption.

Such transitional arrangements, however, would expire by December 1996. Excise duties were to be harmonized and co-operation between member states' tax administrations to prevent fraud (including exchanges of officials) would be increased. Finally, all frontier documents would be abolished, relieving traders of the legal obligation to complete and submit an estimated 60 million forms a year. The transitionary arrangements were welcomed by Europe's customs officials, and HM Customs and Excise announced that it was preparing to tighten controls on Vat fraudsters, hoping to exploit the internal market by moving 1,500 of their force of 7,000 officers into inland checkpoints in anticipation of a frontier-free Europe.

With the arrangements for implementing the new regime all but complete, attention then focused on the vexed question of Vat rates. Despite the substantial concessions granted to Britain, Norman Lamont, the new Chancellor, continued to insist that market forces must be allowed to determine Vat rates, implying that Britain would veto any attempt by the Commission to legislate on the issue. Britain's position was, however, unacceptable to France, Spain and the Netherlands, all of whom remained anxious about the prospect of an exodus of cross-border shoppers causing havoc to their revenues from Vat and adamant about the need for legislation to prevent member states from manipulating Vat rates.

Six years after the launch of the internal market White Paper, and 18 months before the 1992 deadline expired, final agreement was in sight. After three meetings of economic and finance ministers, held under the Luxembourg presidency in June 1991, the Twelve entered into a political agreement to charge a minimum standard rate of Vat of not less than 15% from January 1993 and binding rates of excise duty on mineral oils, tobacco and alcohol. The agreement requires Germany to increase its Vat rate from 14%, and Spain and Luxembourg to increase their rates from 12%. Member states would be able to choose between two lower rates of around 5% and 6%, while zero rating would be retained on a variety of products for a transitional period, subject to bi-annual reviews. All that remained was to overcome Britain's reluctance to have the entire package codified in law.

Although the original Cockfield twin-band proposals had been modified by the negotiations, the Commission's May 1990 blueprint had emerged from the process virtually intact. However, the Commission's attempt to end zero rating for exports and to charge Vat in the country of origin rather than in the country of destination proved too radical for the member states. Taxation in country of destination will, therefore, continue in the transitionary period from January 1993 to December 1996, although taxation in the country of origin remains the Commission's long-term goal.

Moreover, following the Council's decision in March 1991 to eliminate progressively the financial and quantity allowances for duty-free goods, there can be little doubt that the cherished perk of international travel is nearing the end of its days, even if the practice will not disappear as quickly as the Commission would like. According to Leon Gordon, an advisor to the Commission on indirect taxation: 'In an internal market, where the concept of export–import transactions within it has been made completely redundant, such sales will have no *raison-d'être*'. The point was reinforced by Brian Unwin, the chairman of HM Customs, who observed: 'In pure single-market logic, there can be no justification for continuing to grant tax allowances for crossing fiscal frontiers that no longer exist'. Nonetheless, in October 1991, Britain, Ireland, Greece, Spain and Portugal secured agreement that duty-free shopping must remain for a transitional period after 1993, was subsequently set to last until 1999.

At the back of Treasury minds, however, is the fear that the Commission will not stop at the harmonization of indirect taxes, and that Brussels will revive a forgotten 1975 proposal for co-ordinating direct taxes as well. The 1975 plan envisaged an EC-wide direct taxation band of between 45% and 55%, the logic being that if European economies are to be integrated the taxation of both companies and individuals becomes a Community concern. Before leaving office, Lord Cockfield said that plans for corporate taxes, including a common rate for company profits and dividends, were 'still in the formative stages'.

In addition, Mme Scrivener, complaining of the tendency for inter-company links to develop 'more between the US and Europe than between European countries', revived long-neglected EC proposals for avoiding double taxation of dividends paid by a subsidiary in one state to its parent company in another; deferring tax on company assets in cross-frontier mergers; giving Brussels the power to arbitrate between national tax authorities in disputes over transfer pricing practices involving multinationals; and fiscal consolidation of multinationals' profits and losses. The Commission finally abandoned its attempt to set a single rate of corporation tax in April 1990, although three directives removing the anomalies faced by companies operating in more than one country, as described above, were approved. Commission officials are still tempted by the introduction of a European-wide income tax. Though dismissed by Norman Lamont in June 1991 as 'eccentric', the idea seems destined to resurface in the years ahead.

Checklist of changes

- All member states have agreed to a minimum standard rate of Vat at 15% effective from January 1993.
- Mandatory rates of excise duties for mineral oils, alcohol and tobacco have been agreed, also effective from January 1993.
- Systematic checks at frontiers will be abolished as of January 1993, and all Vat fraud and other monitoring procedures will be conducted inland.
- Cross-border duty-free shopping will survive the abolition of internal frontiers in 1993, but only for a transitional (if protracted) period.
- New initiatives designed to harmonize direct taxation are also likely in the longer term.

13 A TRANSPORT POLICY FOR EUROPE

Trains, boats and planes in the single market

Charles de Gaulle's once-famous image of a *Europe des patries*—a continent riven by territorial boundaries, ideological tensions and a formidable array of water, mountain and land barriers—is slowly giving way to the vision of a Europe *sans frontières*. The cumulative effects of the internal market programme, the determination of the six members of the European Free Trade Association to participate in the process of integration it offers and the collapse of the East European and Soviet dictatorships is giving substance to the once-unimaginable idea of an economically, politically and geographically integrated Europe from the Atlantic to the Urals. But while the dramatic events which have unfolded in Eastern Europe and the Soviet Union have been dominating newspaper headlines, comparatively little attention has been paid to the more prosaic developments which are progressively eliminating the so-called 'missing links' in Europe's transport infrastructure.

Nonetheless, the historic natural barriers which have inhibited Europe's political and economic integration for decades, from the English Channel to the mountain ranges of the Alps and the Pyrenees, and the water masses of the Baltic Straits to the physical isolation of Greece (in the sense that it has no common border with any other EC country), are being overcome one by one. Viewed in isolation, each of these great physical barriers would appear to have little more than regional consequences, impairing the movement of goods and people between one neighbouring country and another. Taken collectively, however, they have acted as fetters on trade and commerce across the continent, while at the same time condemning the outer regions to bear the economic costs of geographical marginalization, known in Eurospeak as 'peripherality'.

The Channel Tunnel is perhaps the most well known of these great civil engineering projects. In an influential report published in 1990 by the Royal Institution of Chartered Surveyors (*Transport in the Nineties: The Shaping of Europe*) transport analyst Terence Bendixson described the Channel Tunnel as the single most expensive addition to Europe's transport infrastructure, and 'the first great infrastructure project to come out of the new Europe'. While the description may be tinged with hyperbole, the consequences are not. Completion of the Channel Tunnel will reinforce the historically dominant trading relationships within the so-called London–Frankfurt–Milan golden triangle at the very moment when northern Europe's economic pre-eminence is being challenged by the emergence of a European high-tech Sun Belt running along the Mediterranean from Barcelona to Trieste and by the lure of new economic opportunities in the east.

Attention is now being focused on the second of Europe's great physical barriers—the Alps. Because of the lack of additional capacity on the three main Alpine passes, the Simplon, the Gothard and the Brenner, which serve the flow of people and goods between Germany, Italy and Austria, ambitious proposals are being examined to excavate three new tunnels. Similarly, since the accession of Spain and Portugal, work has begun on taming the Pyrenees. Plans have already been developed for new and expanded road and rail tunnels, aimed at integrating the Iberian peninsula with the road and rail networks of the rest of continental Europe. Farther north, work has begun on the Scanlink project, a composite programme of road and rail bridges across the Baltic designed to link the Scandinavia peninsula with Denmark and mainland Europe. Funds from the European Investment Bank are also being used to upgrade the Autoput, Yugoslavia's equivalent of the M1, and the only road link between Greece and its European partners. Finally, Karel van Miert, the new Transport Commissioner, has drawn up ambitious plans for improving road and rail links between the EC and its eastern neighbours.

With the exception of the Channel Tunnel, however, most of these schemes are in their formative stages and face formidable financial and technical difficulties. With scant financial resources of its own to spend on transport infrastructure projects, the Commission's role in such schemes is, at best, marginal and, at worst, non-existent. There is little doubt that Brussels is eager to make a contribution towards the elimination of Europe's missing links, but the overriding priority remains the completion of the internal market in air, rail, road and sea transport before the 1992 deadline expires.

Honouring the Treaty of Rome

Before publication of the Internal Market White Paper the prospects for any significant progress towards the liberalization of the Community's heavily regulated air transport, road haulage, shipping and rail network systems—not to mention the creation of a genuine common transport policy—seemed negligible. Transport policy (or, more precisely, the lack of it) had become the single greatest failure of the EC. The architects of the European Community attached so much importance to transport as a means of promoting European economic integration that it was given its own chapter in the Treaty of Rome. Yet 30 years after the creation of the EC the highly prized goal of a coherent Community-wide transport policy still remained confined to the ever-receding horizon, with member states pursuing independent (and often conflicting) transport policies, united solely by their scant regard for the interests of the Community as a whole.

The failure of member states to deal effectively with the difficult issues involved in laying the foundations for a more efficient Community transport system has exacted a heavy toll. Community governments, businesses, employees and consumers have all had to bear the costs of fragmented, inefficient, poorly planned, unnecessarily expensive and environmentally insensitive transportation systems, while frequently being unaware or indifferent to the consequences of their actions. On the rare occasions that the *status quo* has been challenged, governments have all too often responded with the indignant defence that 'the traffic does flow'. So it may, at least most of the time, and especially if one is not trying to leave Heathrow in July or August, driving to work in the morning rush hour or bringing an articulated lorry through Italian frontier controls. However, as the Commission has been arguing for decades:

> If one takes a closer look it becomes apparent just how inefficient the conditions are. They make transport more expensive and in many cases slow down the integration of the Community.

Writing in *European Affairs* in autumn 1988 Stanley Clinton Davis, the then European Commissioner for Transport Policy, asked whether one could envisage a common policy for the free movement of products, services and citizens without a corresponding policy for the transport systems which carried them. Yet paradoxically:

> Road transport continued to be controlled by a complex system of licences effectively isolating each national market from its neighbours; civil aviation policy operated on a purely national basis designed to protect the national flag carrier against allcomers— sometimes offering better terms to American or Singaporean carriers than fellow Europeans—with a whole web of agreements between governments and airlines. Each member state had its own maritime policy, and the railway systems maintained the pattern of arm's length co-operation which had reached its peak in the nineteenth century.

Even before the internal market programme made a fresh attempt to create a common transport policy, a series of developments had emphasized to member states the growing urgency of abandoning shortsighted national protectionist policies and embarking on concerted action to solve the Community's increasingly acute transport problems. Following the example of deregulation of the US air transport industry (which resulted in considerable increases in efficiency, substantial decreases in air fares and a significant expansion of the number of passengers), its European counterpart began to face growing criticism—principally from consumer lobbies—demanding an end to the air transport cartel which had kept air travel prices at extortionate levels for the few who could afford to pay and far out of reach for most European citizens.

Almost simultaneously, the absurdity of member state road transport policies, which effectively cut the Community's road network into twelve incompatible segments, was highlighted by a series of expensive and time-consuming blockages at frontier crossings during the early part of the decade and discredited by the flourishing black market in cross-frontier permits needed to transport goods into other member states. Likewise, following the contraction of the European steel industry, the decline in consumption of coal and iron ore left Europe's merchant marine fleets in a state of chronic overcapacity. This problem was further exacerbated by the growing tendency of the centrally planned and developing countries to exclude Community fleets from their domestic trade. Member states were thus presented with little option other than to look to the European Commission to protect the interests of their shipping fleets in trade negotiations with the Community's trading partners around the world.

In 1984 the European Parliament initiated legal proceedings against the Council of Ministers in the European Court of Justice for its failure to carry out the provisions in the Treaty of Rome calling for the creation of a common transport policy. To the embarrassment of the governments of the member states, the Court found that the Council had been negligent in its duties, and ruled that its defence—namely, that it had proved too difficult to agree on a common policy—was completely unacceptable. The Council was now under a legal obligation to overcome such obstacles, a task greatly facilitated by the ratification of the Single European Act and the introduction of qualified majority voting.

In addition to symbolizing the end of Britain's physical isolation from Continental Europe, the decision to build the Channel Tunnel opens up the possibility of bringing new life to Europe's ailing rail networks. The construction of high-speed rail systems between Europe's capital cities would at last enable these networks to compete effectively with air travel in speed, cost and comfort, thereby offering a commercial opportunity for Europe's historically indebted rail transport systems and helping to relieve some of the pressures faced by the air transport sector in the process.

Finally, the growth of tourism in Europe over the past 20 years (particularly in Britain, where the advent of the package holiday has had a profound effect on popular attitudes to Continental Europe) has helped to break down many of the traditional prejudices held by the peoples of Europe against each other. In 1985 140 million Europeans took at least one holiday, and over 20% of this total went to another member state. Three out of every four Britons have now visited at least one Community country, suggesting that the old Victorian adage—'fog in the Channel, Continent cut off'—has long been obsolete. Furthermore, Europe's cultural diversity, natural wealth and rich historical heritage are likely to prove a powerful magnet for the continued expansion of tourism in the decades ahead.

These developments have helped to focus attention on the urgent reforms needed to develop the Community's transport system, which, after all, makes a greater contribution to Community GDP than agriculture and which provides employment for millions of workers either directly or through other key sectors heavily dependent on it, such as the car, aviation, shipbuilding, construction and steel industries. Consequently, although only half-way through the internal market programme, and with much remaining to be done, the Commission had already made a number of impressive breakthroughs which had eluded Community politicians for decades.

Railways and the Channel Tunnel

The subterranean rendezvous in December 1990 between Graham Fagg and Phillipe Cozette, the two construction workers chosen to chip away the last few feet of chalk separating the British and French tunnelling teams working under the English Channel, heralded the end of Britain's 8,000 years of physical isolation from Continental Europe. After successive financial crises and widespread scepticism over the project's viability, the two construction workers earned a place as a footnote in history by making the first dry-land crossing between the British Isles and the European mainland since the end of the Ice Age. The Channel Tunnel, which had been made possible by the 1987 agreement between Mrs Thatcher and President Mitterrand to grant approval for the construction of a privately financed fixed link under the Channel, had become a fact, and Britain was henceforth inextricably linked to Europe.

When Eurotunnel's new shuttle trains begin operations in June 1993 motorists and hauliers will be able to make fast, reliable and competitively priced journeys between the two Channel Tunnel terminals at Folkestone and Calais, both of which will be served by new and upgraded motorways linking them into the British and French national road systems. In addition, the Channel Tunnel will provide the railways with an unprecedented opportunity to challenge the dominance of air transport by offering international passenger services between London, Paris and Brussels. Plans to build a new network of high-speed railway lines linking the three cities are already well advanced, with the French link expected to be completed in 1993 and the Belgian one by 1996.

Britain's high-speed link between London and Folkestone is unlikely to be completed before 2005, following the government's decision to adopt an easterly rather than a southerly approach. British Rail is, however, spending £1.5 billion upgrading existing lines so that international services can begin as soon as the Channel Tunnel opens. When all the new high-speed lines are in operation, rail passengers will be able to travel between London and Paris in 2 hours 45 minutes, and between London and Brussels in 2 hours 15 minutes. Plans for through-services on the existing east- and west-coast main lines, linking Scotland and the regions with a variety of Continental destinations, have also been proposed.

British Rail's £1.5 billion package for the first phase of international services includes a new £120-million station at Waterloo, about £15 million of which will be spent on a new station frontier-control facility. Although much of the argument over whether Britain is entitled to retain frontier controls after 1992 appears to have dissipated following the government's assertion that nothing in the Single European Act prevents it from carrying out spot checks, it would seem that Community nationals disembarking at Waterloo will be required to pass through traditional frontier posts. Home Office officials maintain, however, that any immigration or security checks that are carried out will be kept to a minimum, and will possibly be 'even faster then those conducted at airports'.

The new London–Paris–Brussels service could be merely a sample of what is to come. In January 1989 the Community of European Railways, an organization of the twelve EC national rail companies, along with those of Austria and Switzerland, announced plans for a transcontinental high-speed rail network linking Europe's main urban areas by 2025. The proposals envisaged the construction or upgrading of some 20,000 miles of track, which would be capable of providing passengers with 190 mph rail services, thereby reducing many existing journey times by half. Rail planners presented the proposals as a means of reversing the ailing fortunes of Europe's railways by enabling them to compete with air transport, and predicted that the new high-speed system would act as a powerful catalyst for economic and regional integration in the twenty-first century, in much the same way as the construction of national rail networks had promoted an economic boom in the nineteenth.

The proposed high-speed rail network would help to relieve increasing air and road congestion which has been estimated to cost 3.1% of EC gross national product a year in wasted time and energy, and, at the same time, bring about substantial environmental benefits in the form of reduced pollution and damage to the countryside. However, the entire network is expected to cost somewhere in the region of £100 billion, and apart from the embryonic high-speed service between London, Paris and Brussels, there has been little indication that Europe's national rail networks are prepared to co-operate, much less to generate the resources to make the vision of Europe's transcontinental rail network a reality. Hitherto, the national rail organizations have been little more than state-controlled bureaucracies, burdened with decades of accumulated debt, with little or no incentive to operate on a commercial basis or to market their products through mergers or joint ventures across frontiers.

Although a number of national rail organizations have crossed the threshold into the age of high-speed trains, following the precedent set by Japan with the Shinkansen 'bullet train' between Tokyo and Osaka in 1964, such endeavours have not extended beyond state borders. For example, the French Train à Grande Vitesse network, launched in 1981 with a new service between Paris and Lyons, and the German InterCity Express, launched in 1991 between Hamburg and Munich, are incompatible. The new French trains cannot run on the German high-speed network because the power supply is different, while the new German trains cannot run on the French network because they are too heavy. In addition, while the track guages in most member states are the same, their loading gauges, which determine the height and width of locomotives and rolling stock that can be taken through tunnels, along platforms and past other lineside structures, vary considerably. Consequently, unless the existing infrastructure is demolished and rebuilt to common European standards, the national rail organizations face the prospect of remaining prisoners of their nineteenth-century origins.

The cost of such an undertaking would, however, be prohibitive. As a result, the only way out of the impasse is to ensure that any new lines are built with the European dimension in mind. The proposed high-speed service between London, Paris and Brussels, for example, is a case in point. The new fleet of Transmanche Supertrains which are being built for the international service will be designed to run three different power systems. Plans to build a new high-speed line between Madrid and Seville are being developed in the context of linking the new to the French high-speed network. In addition, it would not be impossible to design a new fleet of trains capable of running on both the French and the German high-speed networks, assuming that French and German pride towards preserving the integrity of their own national achievements can be overcome.

In January 1989 the European Commission produced a draft directive on railways designed to foster such cross-border co-operation. The proposal called for the abolition of existing state rail monopolies by separating ownership of railway infrastructure from the provision of services. It envisaged the creation of track authorities responsible for maintaining network infrastructure, thereby enabling state and private companies to compete with each other to provide services. Accumulated debts were to be progressively written off, and subsidies for loss-making but socially necessary services were to be strictly regulated. Admittedly, the proposal had shortcomings, not least in establishing an equitable way of deciding how to integrate the competing services offered by rival companies into a coherent timetable. For most member states, however, the idea of challenging established national rail monopolies was anathema.

Although by 1991 the Commission had made some progress towards the objectives of the Internal Market White Paper, the goal of creating a single market for transport remained distant. During a meeting of transport ministers in Luxembourg in June 1991, Malcolm Rifkind, Britain's new Transport Secretary, gave vent to his frustrations. 'I find it astonishing,' he said, 'that countries prepared to discuss a single currency and political union are incapable of implementing their commitment to the internal market by the end of next year.' He added: 'It is not enough simply to express aspirations, we have an obligation to create a single market by the end of next year.' Rifkind's outburst was in part prompted by the British government's evident frustration and embarrassment at having to deal with what it saw as a Community mesmerized by the high ground of political and economic union, while, at the same time, content to ignore the nuts and bolts of creating the single market.

Nonetheless, the following day, EC transport ministers took their first step towards creating a single market for railways by abolishing the monopoly of member states to provide rail services on their national networks, in the process laying the foundations of a trans-continental high-speed railway. Under the agreement, national rail monopolies are henceforth required to account separately for their infrastructure and operating costs, thus making it possible for new operators to be charged fairly for providing new services. In addition, joint ventures between companies of more than one member state have the right of access to the rail networks in other member states. As a result, for example, from January 1993 British Rail and Deutsche Bundesbahn will now be able to form a joint company to provide international passenger services between Britain and Germany, with an automatic right of transit through France.

Furthermore, plans to stimulate modern techniques of freight distribution have also been agreed. Commission proposals to create a network of 30 international freight routes, designed to promote the growth of combined transport—a technique for shifting freight from road to rail by enabling the bulk of the journey to be carried out by rail and final leg of the journey to be carried out by road—have been accepted by member states as a means of reducing traffic congestion on national motorway networks. From January 1993 any company providing combined transport services will have the automatic right of access to the rail network of other member states. Finally, transport ministers agreed to begin work on harmonizing standards for new rolling stock and lineside structures.

The air transport sector

Because governments exercise sovereignty over their own airspace in a way similar to that enjoyed over their physical territory, entry into a national airspace has to be authorized by its respective government. Few governments, however, are equipped to carry out this function, and so they allocate the task to their national carriers (most of which are state-owned), who are empowered to negotiate terms governing capacity, fares, landing and take-off rights with other national carriers—subject to approval of member state governments. Out of a desire for a comfortable life, and in an effort to guarantee themselves a stable income, national carriers have traditionally granted landing rights to one foreign carrier in return for reciprocal landing rights in its country of origin. The two airlines have then entered into negotiations about flight prices and schedules and confirmed the deal by dividing the income generated between them on a 50–50 basis.

This formula was duplicated with the national carriers of every other country, thereby creating a powerful cartel throughout the international air transport industry which ensured the least possible competition between national airlines. Air fares were thus determined by cosy mutual agreements which deprived any new airline wanting to compete on somebody else's route the right to gain access to the market. The result, especially after deregulation of the US air transport sector, was that a passenger seeking the cheapest flight from, for example, London to Madrid would have to go via New York. Just as the railway networks were the pride of states in the nineteenth century, so the national air carriers became the symbol of state virility in the twentieth, and governments were reluctant to sanction any liberalization that might jeopardize the viability of their own airlines.

Admittedly, charter airlines are now firmly established, but they have done little to promote price competition between scheduled airlines, who still cater almost exclusively for the business traveller. Confident that their position was unassailable, the Community's national carriers had little incentive to introduce any change. In 1974, however, the first breach in the air transport sector's protected market was made following a ruling by the European Court of Justice that civil aviation was not exempt from the competition provisions of the Treaty of Rome. This ruling was given added force in 1986 in a case brought by the French travel agency Nouvelles Frontières, in which the Court confirmed that the Community's competition rules applied to the skies.

A bilateral agreement between Britain and the Netherlands in 1984, which opened up the market for new carriers, resulted in the introduction of cheaper fares between London and Amsterdam, and a 10% increase in passengers almost overnight. Flag carriers were soon forced to follow suit, but the arrival of discount fares was invariably surrounded by innumerable restrictions in an attempt to limit their effect on flag carriers' standard prices. Discount fares were merely a small hole in the cartel's dyke, but they were, nonetheless, the first significant erosion of the industry's power to set prices independently of market forces.

The combination of the Court's rulings, the determination of the Commission to create an internal market for transport in the air as well as on the ground, the emergence of small independent carriers challenging the dominance of the established airlines and the relentless assault on the air transport cartel by European consumer groups had finally put the Community's air transport industry on the defensive. In an attempt to drive home its advantage, the Commission made a two-pronged assault on the air transport sector by trying to agree an air transport liberalization package in the Council of Ministers while simultaneously threatening legal action against the Community's national carriers under Article 85 of the Treaty, should the negotiations fail. Once the national carriers had backed down and had recognized the authority of the Commission to enforce the competition rules, attention turned to the discussions between member states over price fixing, capacity and revenue sharing, in anticipation of the long-awaited arrival of the age of cheap air fares for millions of European travellers.

However, despite the furore raised by the airline companies, the changes demanded by the Commission could hardly be described as revolutionary. The main elements of the package provided for the abolition of the clauses in their bilateral agreements which formed the corner-stone of the air transport cartel (the so-called 50–50 deals), guaranteeing flag carriers only 45% of capacity for a two-year period, falling to 40% in the third year. It also sought to establish freedom of entry for new carriers on major routes, and to open up services between major hub and regional airports, and the introduction of discounts of up to 45% on normal economy class fares subject to certain restrictions. The proposals were very different from the creation of a European air space and the dismantling of the principle of bilateralism upon which the air transport cartel rested.

Consumer organizations, sceptical that acceptance of the package would lead to any significant reform of the structure of the European air transport industry, warned of a possible sell-out, and demanded that the Commission avail itself of the power conferred on it by the Community's competition rules. The Brussels-based consumer organization, BEUC, a consortium of consumer groups drawn from all over the Community, warned that: 'Whilst the gradual spread of lower fares continues, the resistance to any real change by the majority of scheduled airlines has now become so apparent that a satisfactory outcome in the Transport Council, without Commission and Court action, is impossible'. BEUC insisted that only the unimpeded freedom of new airlines to compete with established operators would open up the air transport sector to the rigours of competition, and demanded the full application of the Treaty's competition rules in place of the proposed 'watered-down agreement' being tabled by the Commission.

As member states gathered in Luxembourg in June 1987 for a crucial transport ministers' meeting the Commission was confident that the air transport liberalization package would finally get their approval. It acknowledged that its proposals were modest, and that the airlines would need time to adjust to a new competitive environment, but maintained that acceptance of the package would be a major first step along the road to more substantive reform.

However, just as the member states were about to put their signatures to the historic agreement an unexpected diplomatic row between Britain and Spain over whether Gibraltar Airport should be included in the package delayed the deal for months. Because the majority voting provisions of the Single European Act did not come into effect until 1 July, Spain was able to exercise a veto over the package. Señor Jesus Ezquerra, the Spanish minister responsible for conducting the negotiations with Britain over the status of Gibraltar, maintained that the land on which Gibraltar Airport was built was not ceded to Britain under the 1713 Treaty of Utrecht.

Portraying Britain as a neocolonialist power refusing to give up the ill-gotten gains of centuries past, Ezquerra insisted that Madrid could not sign an agreement covering Gibraltar without enshrining its present status in Community law, and demanded that Gibraltar be excluded from the deal. British ministers, infuriated at Ezquerra's decision to introduce a long-running bilateral dispute into a Community context, emphasized that Madrid had already accepted Gibraltar's status when it ratified Spain's accession agreement, and, for good measure, discreetly drew attention to Spain's Moroccan enclaves, Ceuta and Melilla, to demonstrate that one former colonial power was at least as bad as the next. However, Ezquerra could not be appeased, the deadline expired and the Commission was forced to redraft its proposals and present them to the European Parliament and the Council of Ministers, as required under the new procedures of the Single European Act. Only the consumers' organizations, which regarded the package as a betrayal of consumer interests in any case, had a kind word for Ezquerra.

When the package came up again for approval in December 1987 Ezquerra failed to put in an appearance, and the deal finally went through. Its provisions were more or less identical to those on the table in June, covering air fares, capacity sharing and market access, and the application of the competition rules to the air transport sector. Only services between member states were subject to the deal, while the application of the competition rules was limited to scheduled airlines alone. The package was the first effective inroad into the power of member states to control their scheduled airlines and introduced competition into what Commissioner Sutherland had once described as 'the most uniquely anti-competitive cartel in Europe'.

As of 1 January 1988, a common bilateral procedure for the approval of discount and deep discount fares became effective throughout the Community and a timetable established for the phasing out of capacity-sharing arrangements between the major airlines. Under that timetable national carriers are entitled to only 40% of route capacity, and the Commission hopes that even this protection will be abolished by the 1992 deadline. Routes between most major hub and regional airports have been opened up, and procedures for applying Articles 85 and 86 to the air transport sector have also been established.

However, it is clear that the major airlines still regard the prospect of across-the-board lower fares as anathema. Despite the adverse effect of the lower fares charged by some of the smaller airlines on flag carrier profits, few have been forced to fundamentally overhaul their price structures. Indeed, most have done their utmost to resist reducing prices by trying to attract customers, especially business executives, with greater comfort and style. As Sir Colin Marshall, the chief executive of British Airways, said in an interview with *The Times* in October 1988: 'We are in business to make money. Low fares are available—at the back of the aircraft'. But greater competition in the post-1992 era could force many companies to trim their generous travel budgets, adding considerably to the downward pressure on prices.

As an indication of the Commission's determination to introduce greater competition in the air transport sector, the Belgian national carrier, Sabena, was fined £65,000 in November 1988 for refusing to give the Irish-owned air liner, Ryanair, access to its computer reservation system because the Dublin-based company was offering cut-price flights. The Commission's action followed a dawn raid on Sabena's headquarters the previous year, and was the first occasion on which the Community had exercised its new powers against an airline involved in anti-competitive behaviour.

As Community citizens were anxiously awaiting the arrival of the age of cheap air travel the Association of European Airlines (AEA), which represents 21 airlines responsible for approximately 90% of Europe's air traffic, began to issue a series of warnings about the shortcomings of the internal market programme. At its annual conference in Paris in April 1988 Karl-Heinz Neumeister, the Secretary General of the AEA, warned that the Commission's fiscal harmonization proposals would be a step backwards for the air transport industry. Once the internal market programme is completed, all intra-Community flights will be classified as domestic and therefore subject to Vat. However, Neumeister pointed out that the possibility of different rates within the lower 4% to 9% Vat band between member states would actually be a step away from a perfectly harmonized market, currently at 0%. Consequently, there was a need to maintain the zero rate or at least introduce a single rate throughout the Community.

Furthermore, Neumeister predicted that the abolition of internal frontier controls would require the expansion of the domestic sections of airports, while the introduction of new routes and more flights was likely to lead to a considerable expansion in demand, and yet few governments were planning to increase existing airport and runway handling capacity. Perhaps most important of all, the Secretary General drew attention to a major anomaly in the internal market programme which allowed member states to continue exercising sovereignty over their own air space (effectively fragmenting Europe's air space into twelve segments), a situation which was widely regarded as the major cause of the delays experienced by air travellers in the summer of 1988. In 1987 air traffic movements were already at levels forecast for 1991, and Neumeister predicted that the situation would only get worse until the member states overcame their traditional reluctance to relax control over their own air space:

> We would like to see an integrated European air traffic control system with co-ordinated plans, and at least working with the same standards. Perhaps we should give Eurocontrol the task it was originally designed to have: to co-ordinate and control the air traffic flows in Europe. Are we going to have the single market on the ground and still divide the skies?

In July 1988 the European Parliament accepted Neumeister's challenge by calling for the merging of Europe's air traffic control systems into a single Community network, under the authority of the Netherlands-based organization, Eurocontrol, which is already responsible for monitoring and predicting daily air traffic flows. Unfortunately, there was little to suggest that member states are prepared to accept the one remedy for freeing the Community's congested skies. Then in September, Paul Channon, then Secretary of State for Transport, gave the first indication that Britain was seriously considering the creation of a central unit responsible for flight planning in Europe. The issue was discussed by EC transport ministers meeting in Frankfurt in November, when the Commission formally proposed to member states that they create a single European air traffic control system based on Eurocontrol. By July the following year, when tens of thousands of tourists again faced lengthy delays at British airports, Community transport ministers agreed to a £40 million scheme setting up a centralized airflow management system based at Eurocontrol. However, while the new system will undoubtedly help to reduce departure delays, it is unlikely to be fully operational before 1992.

Meanwhile, the European Court of Justice had ruled the previous April that virtually all air fare price-fixing arrangements could be in violation of Community competition rules. Encouraged by a ruling which indicated that price-fixing arrangements on routes within member states (as well as those to non-Community destinations) were possibly illegal, the Commission announced three months later its intention to press ahead with phase two of the air-transport liberalization programme. In January 1990 Karel van Miert, the Transport Commissioner, proposed that member states should cede their right to negotiate air routes with the rest of the world to the Commission. If accepted, the proposal would give Commission officials the power to bargain with the government's of the world's carriers, such as those in America and Asia, granting routes and landing rights in the Community in exchange for reciprocal rights outside the Twelve.

Moreover, the Commission would also be able to exploit its collective negotiating position to open up competition inside the Community by using the attractive incentive of access to third-country airports to open the domestic markets of individual member states. The Commission is particularly keen on extending what are known as 'fifth freedom rights' —the right of an airline in one member state to pick up passengers in a second member state and deposit them in a third. As van Miert pointed out, the United States has 18 such routes in the Community, granting it fifth freedom rights, while Community carriers have no such privileges in the United States (not counting fifth freedom rights between the continental United States and Puerto Rico).

By the summer of 1990, however, most observers were becoming more sceptical of the Commission's ability to increase competition in air transport, and thus pave the way for the seemingly elusive era of cheap air fares. Indeed, the trend towards concentration, such as Air France's plans to take over its domestic rival UTA and Inter Air, and the proposed joint venture between BA, KLM and Sabena, were seen by many critics as a rearguard action by national governments to strengthen their national carriers by reducing competition.

Such enthusiasm for the liberalization of air transport was not shared by the industry, whose operators were becoming increasingly anxious about the potential growth of a Community bureaucracy governing the sector. These fears materialized in October 1990, when the Commission announced its proposals for rationing landing rights in Europe's congested airports. The objective was to ensure that smaller carriers were given fair access to the limited number of take-off and landing slots needed to run services, an objective described by one airline as like telling department stores that they had to hand over large areas of their floor space to smaller High Street rivals in the interests of fair competition. Nevertheless, in December 1990, the proposals were adopted. Under the new rules, surplus take-off and landing rights are to be put in a pool for distribution among carriers, half of which must go to new entrants, while proposals for cheaper fares can only be blocked by the so-called 'double disapproval' principle, which requires national governments at either end of the route to withhold their authorization.

Iraq's invasion of Kuwait in August 1990 and the subsequent Gulf War, increasing oil prices and collapse in demand for air travel were to cast an ominous shadow over the Commission's attempt to open up air transport. The crisis confronted airlines across the world with sudden and potentially huge losses, and many were to go out of business. In an effort to help European airlines to overcome the crisis, the Commission proposed a series of measures, including the temporary suspension of the competition laws to enable airlines to create joint ventures on loss-making routes, which were generally greeted with scorn by the industry. When British Airways announced its decision in the summer of 1991 to withdraw from air routes to the Republic of Ireland, a route which had been opened to competition from allcomers in 1985, many observers feared that the Commission's air-liberalization initiative was going to prove as disruptive to European air transport as the US government's earlier air-liberalization programme had been in North America. By May 1991 van Miert was openly saying that the third and final air-liberalization or 'open-skies' package was in trouble.

However, such pessimism turned out to be premature. In July 1991 van Miert tabled the Commission's final air-liberalization package, calling for the establishment of common criteria for licensing Community air carriers, open access to routes for all new carriers, recognition of the principle of double disapproval on fares and the introduction of cabotage —the right to pick up passengers and freight in a second member state destined for a third. Surprisingly, the AEA gave the open-skies proposal a cautious welcome, although the organization continued to have reservations about forcing existing carriers to cede their rights to surplus landing and take-off slots. The package would, in effect, give airlines the freedom to set fares themselves, subject to regulation by market forces, although approval from member states is unlikely to be forthcoming until well into 1992.

Road transport and coastal trade

One of the most pervasive barriers to free trade in the Community is the technically illegal system of bilateral licences governing the European road haulage industry. Road haulage companies obtain the right of access to the roads of other member states on the basis of a licence obtained from its national department of transport. These, in turn, are arranged through a series of annual bilateral negotiations between member states, which determine the number of licences that are to be made available. In 1986, for example, Germany granted 91,000 licences to Italian road haulage companies, while Italy granted 145,000 licences to German ones. But the system has long been denounced, principally by Britain, as iniquitous, inefficient and one which protects the interests of the larger member states at the expense of their smaller neighbours.

Road haulage, which accounts for about £322 billion of intra-Community trade, is by far the most important artery along which trade between member states flows, and it is long overdue for reform. However, the Commission's proposals to create an internal market for road haulage were regarded by Germany as a serious threat to its own heavily protected industry. The politically powerful German road haulage lobby, fearful that much of its road haulage trade would slip away to its more efficient Dutch and Belgian competitors, adamantly opposed any liberalization before progress had been made on harmonizing the industry's operating conditions, notably lorry and fuel taxes and drivers' terms of employment.

Under pressure of legal action from the Commission, and a persistent refusal by Britain to accept anything less than the complete implementation of the Commission's liberalization proposals, the Germans finally conceded at the Transport Council in Luxembourg in June 1988. The deal, which was widely seen as a major breakthrough for the internal market programme, committed member states to the complete abolition of quotas to Community and non-Community destinations by 1 January 1993, and required the Commission to specify the harmonization measures needed to ensure fair competition among road haulage companies by June 1991.

By the time the quota system is abolished, Community road haulage companies will be able to avail themselves of the freedom to make as many journeys as they like, anywhere in the Community. Far from increasing the number of articulated lorries on Europe's roads, the internal market in road haulage will automatically lead to a reduction of the number of empty lorries (estimated by the Commission to be around one in three), due to existing restrictions on trade conducted in other member states. In 1990, member states agreed to the progressive introduction of cabotage, which will enable, for example, a British road haulage company delivering a freight consignment from Manchester to Munich to be able to compete with local German firms for business between, say, Frankfurt and Hamburg. Despite attempts by British road hauliers to obtain government approval for an end to the derogation which imposes a 38-tonne limit on lorries on British roads by 1992 (thus bringing them into line with the 40-tonne ceiling enforced in other member states), Paul Channon managed to retain the derogation until 31 December 1998, on the grounds that the government's bridge-strengthening programme would not be completed until that date. Proposals to liberalize bus and coach transport have, however, been less successful. Attempts by one member state to introduce scheduled bus and coach services in other member states are still subject to prior government approval, which can often be refused if the proposed service competes with existing services.

Similarly, Britain has been less successful in convincing its partners of the need to abolish restrictions on Community ships trading along each other's coastlines. Britain, Ireland, Belgium and the Netherlands are the only countries that grant foreign vessels the unrestricted right to pick up and deliver loads between ports on their coastlines, known as coastal cabotage. Most of the Southern European states, fearful of increased competition, continue to reserve coastal trade for domestic shipping. If progress is not forthcoming Britain is likely to implement those provisions of the 1988 Merchant Shipping Act which grant it the power to demand reciprocal treatment. However, proposals to remove overcapacity in the inland waterways industry, caused largely by the decline of heavy industry, were adopted in 1990, enabling member states to scrap an estimated 1,600 surplus vessels—most of which were antiquated river barges—and thereby help the inland waterways to adjust to changing market circumstances. Similarly, following earlier attempts to halt the decline in Europe's merchant fleet, the Commission is now also seeking approval for a new Community shipping register and Community flag.

Finally, in 1989 van Miert was able to secure approval from member states to establish a new Community infrastructure fund. Although the sums involved are relatively small compared to other Community funding schemes, this is at least a beginning, and will no doubt expand as increasing demands are placed on it. The fund's first three-year action programme, which covers the period from 1990 to 1992, is designed to provide capital for high speed rail link projects, new Alpine and Pyrenean road and rail passes, the upgrading of the North Wales coastal road linking Ireland with the rest of the Community and improved road and rail links between the two formerly estranged halves of Europe.

Travel and tourism

Tourism now accounts for almost 5% of the Community's gross domestic product, is responsible for some 5.5 million jobs and is expanding constantly. An estimated 75% of Britons have visited at least one Community country, while the average Briton has visited 3.5 member states. The Community has spent millions of pounds developing a tourist infrastructure (holiday villages, pleasure harbours, ski-lifts and hotels) through the regional development funds and the European Investment Bank in an attempt to provide new employment opportunities and relieve some of the congestion in the more popular and overdeveloped resorts.

The Commission has also attempted to make life easier for tourists by introducing the Community passport, and producing brochures giving detailed information on existing border-crossing formalities, duty-free allowances and the availability of health care. Further publications listing places of interest such as museums and art galleries are in preparation, as are plans to produce a standardized classification of Community hotels (priced in ECUs) and a directive regulating the package holiday industry.

By 1992 millions of travellers and holidaymakers will be deprived of their duty-free allowances (now regarded as the legitimate booty of foreign travel) if the Commission's proposals on fiscal approximation are implemented. Yet the abolition of duty-frees is unlikely to be the unmitigated disaster predicted by the pro-duty-free lobby. Admittedly, Community-wide duty-free sales are estimated to be worth about £2 billion a year, and their demise, only as far as intra-Community travel is concerned, will have a significant impact on the revenues of short-haul ferries, charter airlines and regional airports.

However, everyone involved in the duty-free industry accepts that abolition is merely a question of time, and are already planning ways of compensating themselves for lost revenues. British ferry companies are planning to introduce a new generation of floating department stores for cross-Channel shoppers. Built from modified roll-on–roll-off ferries, the offshore superstores are likely to make extensive use of franchises, similar to those already in operation at most Community airports, to sell a wide selection of discount consumer products.

James Hannah, Sealink British Ferries' corporate communications director, is convinced that there are great opportunities for skilful marketing to a captive audience. Pointing to the success of franchising operations at airports, Hannah said that:

> Dublin Airport, for example, is now selling more black silk lingerie than many major High Street stores. It's quite a phenomenon. I suspect it's the only chance businessmen get to buy their wives a gift.

These sentiments are also shared by Graeme Dunlop, managing director of P&O European Ferries, who told *The Times* in an interview in June 1988:

> We are making our plans now on the assumption that the European internal market will be a reality in 1992. If we are going to survive, it's the only prudent course to take.

Indeed, in the face of the threat posed by the Channel Tunnel, the cross-Channel ferry companies have had to transform the way they do business. In 1988, James Elles, the Conservative MEP for Oxford and Buckinghamshire, was, with some justification, able to describe passing through the port of Dover as similar to going through an 'East European' border post. Elles demanded to know why the British ports were unable to introduce simplified frontier procedures, similar to the red and green channels used at major airports. By 1991, however, the ferry companies had been able to bring about significant reductions in the formalities and time taken to pass through Dover's port facilities.

Despite the generally optimistic prospects for the European tourist industry, greater mobility throughout the Community has brought with it the serious and growing problems of hooliganism and drunken rowdiness. These are by no means confined to British tourists, although the reputation is. During her visit to Spain in September 1988 Mrs Thatcher felt compelled to apologize to Felipe Gonzalez, the Spanish Prime Minister, for the behaviour of the small minority of British holidaymakers who have been responsible for disfiguring many Spanish resorts in recent years. Mrs Thatcher made it clear, however, that the Spanish authorities had her personal support in taking severe action against the trouble-makers. It may eventually be necessary to consider a Community initiative designed to temporarily deprive those Community nationals unable to behave responsibly in other member states of the right to travel in the internal market, perhaps through the issue of EC identity cards, withdrawable in the event of damage or nuisance to property or persons.

Checklist of changes

- The European Commission's determination to create an internal market for air transport will further erode the restrictive practices of the European air transport industry.
- There will be increased freedom of entry for independent air carriers on major European air routes.
- Services between major and regional airports will be progressively increased.
- National carriers seeking to restrict competition from the new independent carriers will find themselves subject to substantial fines imposed by the Commission for violating the Community's competition rules.
- The availability of discount fares can be expected to multiply as a result of increased competition from the new independent carriers.
- In an effort to ease the congestion in Europe's crowded skies, pressure for a single integrated European air traffic control system will result in the creation of a central unit responsible for flight planning in Europe.
- There will be an internal market for road haulage following the abolition of the system of national quotas for the road haulage industry.
- European road haulage companies will have complete freedom of destination within the Community.
- Coastal trade will also be opened up to free competition.
- Duty-free allowances for travellers will come to an end following the harmonization of member states' varying rates of indirect taxation.

14 SATELLITE BROADCASTING
Television technology in the 1990s

Towards the end of the 1980s Europe's audiovisual sector had clearly arrived at a cultural, technological and economic crossroads. The national film and television industries, which had flourished since the Second World War—largely, though by no means exclusively, within the confines of national boundaries—were suddenly confronted with the imminent arrival of a European-wide market for films and television and the broadcasting and reception equipment needed to transmit and receive them. As in so many areas of human endeavour, the rapid pace of technological development had, seemingly overnight, led to the internationalization of the entire audiovisual industry. By contrast, the legal and regulatory framework which governed the way in which the audiovisual sector operated in the individual member states continued to function along national lines. Unless the essentially national character of regulation was brought into line with the new international character of broadcasting, the long-term prospects of the Community's audiovisual sector were in danger.

The need for a new framework
Of all the internal market directives contained in the White Paper programme, few aroused as much passion as the European Commission's efforts to create a single market for satellite broadcasting without frontiers. Supporters of the Commission's unprecedented entry into the television broadcasting sector characterized the initiative (in imagery similar to that used in Hollywood's portrayal of the last days of General Custer) as Europe's heroic last stand against the twin assault of American cultural imperialism and Japanese technological dominance, and the only real hope of saving Europe's ailing cinema film and electronics industries from extinction.

This vision of the Community's predicament was not shared by everyone. Some member states, principally Britain, Denmark and Germany insisted that there was no compelling case for Community legislation in the field of satellite broadcasting and challenged the competence of the Commission to legislate on cultural matters. Many of the new English-language satellite companies endorsed the Commission's broad objectives, but were deeply opposed to the way in which it has set about putting them into practice. Finally, over the past few years there have been many prophets of doom, predicting that the age of satellite broadcasting will destroy civilization as we know it by submerging national values and culture in a tidal wave of smut, pornography, gratuitous violence, low-budget soap operas and game shows, manipulative advertising and, to cap it all, US-style television evangelists.

Passion aside, the Community was confronted by a series of wide-ranging changes in the audiovisual sector which it could do nothing to prevent. The rapid pace of technological change in the field of telecommunications had already conferred on satellite broadcasters the ability to ignore national boundaries and reach audiences of continental proportions. The so-called 'footprint' of satellite transmissions cannot be held up at national border controls for inspection by customs officers before being granted or refused permission to enter.

However, because of the great variation in national regulations governing television broadcasts, particularly on advertising, programming and public morality, the technical ability of the new satellite companies to reach large numbers of people was constrained by their legal obligation to respect the differing regulations of the various member states. Unless satellite broadcasters comply with national regulations, the cable companies who relay the satellite transmissions into our homes can be effectively prohibited from doing so. Even in the case of direct broadcasting by satellite (where viewers can pick up transmissions themselves after installing the necessary receiving equipment) the member states are capable of preventing transmissions which violate national law through the Community's legal system and, theoretically, by the use of sophisticated jamming techniques.

If the extraterrestrial technological advances were not to be stillborn as a result of divergent terrestrial regulations, twelve national systems had to be replaced by one set of common rules governing satellite broadcasting. Addressing the Independent Broadcasting Authority on the sensitive question of advertising regulations in April 1985, Dr Ivo Schwartz, the Commission official responsible for overseeing the Community's satellite broadcasting initiative, said:

> Given the reality of communication satellites and continental wide cable television, as well as the imminence of direct broadcasting by satellite, the Commission believes that it is essential to institute as quickly as possible a minimum of rules for European advertising within which the providers of commercially supported programmes may freely operate. Such limited approximation will make it possible that from then on, only the rules of the country of transmission shall apply to cross-border advertisements.

The same principle would also be applied to the European content of programming schedules, public morality and the protection of minors.

However, the Commission maintained that the audiovisual challenge faced by the Community goes far beyond the mere legal mechanics of creating a single unified market for satellite broadcasting. Europe is also confronted by a series of cultural, scientific, technical, industrial and commercial challenges, in which the United States and Japan clearly have the advantage. The Commission has forecast that somewhere in the region of 200 new satellite channels could be available by the 1990s. The very rapid growth in the number of broadcasting hours available is already beginning to generate an almost insatiable demand for new programming material, which European countries are unable to satisfy at competitive prices. Similarly, the expansion of satellite broadcasting has already begun to create new markets for transmission equipment and mass markets for receiving equipment. These new markets could provide a great stimulus to Europe's electronics industry, creating thousands of new jobs in the process. However, many EC and national officials feared that, unless the Community is able to respond to these challenges, the benefits of a single market for satellite broadcasting will be enjoyed only by film studios in Hollywood and consumer electronics companies in Tokyo.

Television without frontiers

The challenge to the Community's competence to legislate in the field of satellite broadcasting was effectively undermined following the adoption by all member states of the Internal Market White Paper, which made explicit reference to the need to create an internal market for cross-frontier television broadcasting. Furthermore, the Commission was able to point to its obligation under Article 3 of the Treaty of Rome, requiring it to approximate national laws 'to the extent required for the proper functioning of the common market', and Articles 59–62, which prohibit member states from exercising their supervisory powers to restrict trade in goods and services on a discriminatory basis. As 'services' include television broadcasting, these articles collectively confer on the Commission the authority to propose legislation regulating satellite broadcasting between member states.

They also provide the legal basis on which the satellite broadcasters themselves, even in defiance of the wishes of national governments, can demand access to audiences throughout the Community. However, member states retain the legal right to impose non-discriminatory restrictions on foreign and domestic broadcasters in the interests of public policy, security and health, or because of the need to protect copyright, until such times as the various national laws had been harmonized. As a result, by the time the satellite broadcasters had acquired the technical ability to reach European-wide audiences it was not only incumbent on the Commission to provide the necessary regulatory framework for them to do so but had also become a race against time to put this framework in place before or shortly after the satellite stations were operational. The urgency of this task was emphasized by the collapse of Europa-TV in November 1986. A group of networks from five member states had combined in an attempt to launch the first public broadcasting service as an alternative to the growing number of private, commercial stations. Using the latest technology for dubbing and subtitling, Europa-TV transmitted multilingual broadcasts to some 5 million homes in the Community. But after running up debts in excess of £25 million, the Netherlands pulled out, and the initiative came to a halt. According to the testimony given by a Commission official to the House of Lords Select Committee on the European Communities in 1987:

> Europa-TV faced formidable difficulties obtaining access to existing cable networks because of conflicting advertising regulations in West Germany, Belgium, Ireland, Denmark and even in its host country the Netherlands. It failed because it could not generate sufficient advertising revenues.

Following publication of the Commission's 1984 Green Paper on television without frontiers and extensive consultations with member states (including the various professions involved in the television industry), the Commission tabled a draft directive on satellite broadcasting in June 1986, later revised in March 1988. Behind the proposed legislation lay the conviction that the Community was more than merely an organization of states; it was also a union of peoples. The emergence of cross-frontier television broadcasting would reinforce the creation of the internal market by providing companies with access to a single market of 320 million consumers through satellite advertising. However, it also contained the rather visionary notion that new communications satellites would also provide the means by which the peoples of Europe would become more familiar with each other as a result of exposure to their different television cultures, thereby reinforcing (or, perhaps more realistically, at least making people aware in the first place) that they shared a common economic and cultural identity.

The directive is designed to enable satellite broadcasters to transmit programmes anywhere in the Community without restriction or interference from other member states provided that they meet certain minimum requirements governing the European content of programming, the organization of advertising breaks, copyright protection, public morality and the protection of minors. The directive also applied to ground-based broadcasters if their transmissions can be received in neighbouring member states. Lord Cockfield attached particular importance to the directive, regarding it as the 'flagship' of the entire internal market programme, and called for prompt action by the member states to implement the proposal which was already a year behind schedule. However, the draft legislation met with bitter opposition when ministers first discussed it in March 1988. From the outset, Britain had objected vigorously to any attempt to introduce programme quotas. Ministers made no secret of their conviction that the proposal was one of the most élitist and paternalistic documents ever produced by the Commission. It was denounced as an example of 'European cultural imperialism', and Britain felt that it had no alternative but to put all its hopes for a more liberal satellite broadcasting system on the rival convention being drawn up by the 21-member Council of Europe in Strasbourg.

Quotas, advertisements and copyright

Within three years of the March proposal being adopted, all satellite broadcasters would have been required to reserve at least 60% of their air time for feature films made in the Community or in association with members of EFTA and the Council of Europe. The proposal had nothing to do with abolishing barriers to the free movement of television across frontiers. In fact, it purposely sets out to achieve the exact opposite. Its overriding objective was to stimulate the European film industry by protecting it from foreign competition and providing it with a guaranteed part of the European market. The Commission maintained that such action is necessary because:

> Frequent warnings are heard about the dangers of the cultural domination of one country by another in motion pictures, although this is not a problem between member states. As for the production of television programmes within the Community, no individual member states are predominant. Statistics on the films broadcast on television in member states show that the proportion of films from other member states is regrettably small. However, most of the films shown come from a single non-member country, the US.

The main source of such warnings are the French and Italian film industries, who were already facing difficult times and feared that they would have to close if they were forced to compete with their American counterparts. Writing in the spring 1988 edition of *European Affairs*, Jack Lang, the National Secretary for Culture and Youth in the French Socialist Party, while paying tribute to the achievements of the American film industry attacked the view expressed by Britain that the new satellite broadcasting companies should be allowed to decide for themselves what proportion of their broadcast material came from within or outside the Community. Lang insisted that:

> At a time when Europe, the cradle of Western civilization, loses control over one of the main areas in which contemporary

culture is being made, the audiovisual, one can no longer react aesthetically to such liberal or ultra-liberal ideologies. Reality demands that concrete steps be taken as quickly as possible.

By which he meant quotas.

In defence of the proposal, Lord Cockfield maintained that the quota plan was not so much anti-American as pro-European. Commission officials, however, acknowledged that the 60% quota would present severe difficulties for specialized film channels, and indicated that a limited number of derogations or exemptions could be incorporated into the directive. However, such concessions did little to allay the anxieties of satellite and ground-based broadcasters, who feared that the Commission was asking them to drink a cup of hemlock in the name of the defence of European culture.

In 1987, for example, the BBC screened 709 feature films, of which 409 were made in the United States. Both Sky Channel, owned by Rupert Murdoch, and SuperChannel, owned by Richard Branson in association with an Italian company, are also heavily dependent on US feature films. The same applies to every other English-language satellite station planning to launch new stations, even the non-English-language ones showing dubbed or subtitled US films. Whatever the critics of the US film industry may say, American feature films are extremely popular all over Europe, and the attempt to restrict them to 40% of the European market would have deprived the new satellite stations of the large-scale audiences and advertising revenues needed to make them economically viable. After all, what one cannot see on television one can usually pick up in a High Street video shop.

The Commission argued that Britain's opposition to the quota plan was dogmatic, and points out that the Independent Broadcasting Authority (IBA) already accepts the principle of quotas by requiring 86% of all programmes on ITV and Channel 4 to come from Community sources. However, Britain insists that this is a regulation enforced by the IBA, and apart from specifying that a 'proper proportion' of all broadcast material should be Community sourced, broadcasters should be free from government or Commission interference to decide what that level should be. The problem faced by the Commission, however, is that it is not self-evident what a proper proportion means. Twelve member states would produce twelve different definitions, effectively creating a new barrier to satellite broadcasting across frontiers. At the same time, no amount of compulsory screening will make European-made films any more popular.

The Commission's proposed regulations on satellite advertising received a considerably less hostile reception from most member states. The directive established a maximum threshold of 15% a day or 18% an hour of total programming time which can be allocated to broadcast advertising. Any station transmitting above these thresholds can be prohibited by the member states. Governments retain the right to impose more stringent conditions on domestic broadcasters serving national audiences if they so wish. The directive no longer required broadcasters to group advertisements at the end of programmes, as specified in the 1986 version. Under the terms of the revised directive they were granted the option of broadcasting commercial breaks in concentrated blocks or periodic slots, provided that the 'integrity' of programmes was maintained and as long as programmes were not interrupted excessively. Advertisements must not fall below prevailing standards of decency or exploit the immaturity of minors.

Britain seemed to be quite content with the directive's provisions on broadcast advertising, in contrast to those incorporated into the Council of Europe's convention on satellite broadcasting. The government had originally agreed with the convention, primarily because of its opposition to the Community's proposed quotas and in the hope that it would prove to be a more liberal regulatory system. However, to the consternation of Downing Street, the Germans, urged on by domestic press barons who did not want to see their advertising revenues jeopardized by competition from the new satellite television stations, were able to insert into the draft convention a provision requiring satellite broadcasters to bunch commercial breaks in a 'block' at the end of programmes. Consternation turned to exasperation in the summer of 1988, when the Germans, without success, tried to have the same restrictions that were incorporated into the draft convention also applied to the draft directive.

Britain, as well as the other member states opposing this provision, was not obliged to sign or ratify the Council's convention. Yet too many refusals to sign would have undermined the entire purpose of the agreement, as individual member states would be forced to embark on bilateral negotiations with their European neighbours. Long before the convention was due to be ratified in November 1988 it was clear that the proposal was deadlocked.

Although ministers were unable to reach a consensus on the convention during their subsequent meeting in Stockholm, there was a considerable convergence of views between Britain and Germany on advertising breaks. Britain appeared ready to accept that 'serious' programmes should not be interrupted more than once every 45 minutes, while Germany seemed content with allowing more frequent advertising breaks for less serious programmes. Nevertheless, France still expressed grave reservations about allowing too much imported US broadcast material into the Community, and seemed to be determined to hold out for a quota of at least 50% of all programmes broadcast to be of Community origin. With agreement still out of reach, ratification was postponed until June 1989. The Commission, however, saw the impasse over the convention as an opportunity to rewrite their own draft directive and regain the initiative in the rivalry between the two organizations to create Europe's satellite broadcasting system for the twenty-first century.

In the summer of 1988 Commission officials let it be known that a plan to split the draft directive in two was being given serious consideration. The scheme would enable the Commission to deal separately with the issues of programme quotas and advertising regulations. If accepted, it would mean that the Commission could press ahead with issuing a directive on satellite broadcast advertising for an industry whose development was outstripping the ability of Community and national legislators to regulate it, while allowing the vexed issue of programme quotas to be given a reduced priority for EC cultural affairs ministers to sort out at their leisure. However, officials realized that the major obstacle in the way of the proposal would be the objections of France and Italy, who appeared to remain adamant over their demand for Community quotas.

Gradually, however, it began to occur to the French authorities that quotas and advertising restrictions could mean the end of the new satellite companies. If broadcasters could not transmit the kind of material likely to attract mass audiences, and if restrictive advertising regulations forced the advertisers to seek other outlets, then there would be no new satellite stations, and certainly no new money with which to stimulate the output of the ailing European film and audiovisual industry. In February 1989, EC trade ministers (taking their cue from the Rhodes summit meeting) managed to agree on a compromise on the controversial issue of quotas, allowing satellite broadcasters to transmit a 'majority' of European-made programmes 'where practical', thereby eliminating Britain's objection to the imposition of legally enforceable quotas. Unfortunately, the compromise began to unravel in June, due to last-minute reservations by Paris. The issue fell to France to resolve during its Presidency of the Council of Ministers.

In October, during a ministerial meeting in Luxembourg, the seemingly interminable wrangle of cross-frontier broadcasting regulations was finally laid to rest. On a majority vote, the ministers agreed to the 50% European programming restriction, and at the same time accepted that legal imposition of the quota was a 'political' measure, and thus legally unenforceable. Welcoming the agreement, Richard Dunn, chairman of the ITV Association said: 'ITV does not believe the directive will have a detrimental effect on our current practices in terms of advertising, programme content, and origin. We can certainly live with it'. The US, however, immediately expressed its hostility to the measure, and announced its intention to bring the issue before the disputes panel of the General Agreement on Tariffs and Trade.

The Commission believes that the existing system of copyright protection is also a potential barrier to the free movement of programmes across frontiers, and wants to replace it with one that allows satellite and cable companies to broadcast or retransmit any programme after two years, while ensuring adequate remuneration for copyright holders. The Commission argues that once a programme has been placed in the public domain in one member state, copyright regulations should not be used as a method of preventing it from circulating around the other member states. According to one Commission official: 'Once you have taken the fundamental decision to market your service, you cannot rely on national frontiers—in this case through intellectual property rights—to divide the market'.

The system would operate on the basis of voluntary contractual agreements between the copyright owners and broadcasters, sponsored by the individual member states. Broadcasters would have an automatic right to a licence on the copyright if terms could not be agreed within the two-year period. However, anyone broadcasting a programme before the two-year period had expired, or with the intention of depriving the copyright holders of their legitimate remuneration, would be liable to court action in the appropriate member state. The Commission acknowledges that without a system for providing authors, performers and copyright holders with equitable remuneration there would be a detrimental effect on the very industry responsible for generating the programmes needed to fill the new programme schedules. Consequently, copyright must be adapted to reflect the needs of the modern audiovisual age. Britain, however, has opposed the initiative on the grounds that copyright cannot be considered a barrier to trade.

As soon as the dust from the argument over quotas had begun to settle, a new dispute emerged over the Commission's attempts to regulate advertising. In August 1990 it was discovered that Brussels was drafting legislation restricting or prohibiting the advertising of alcohol, tobacco, certain foods, pharmaceuticals and children's toys throughout the Community. Britain's Advertising Association, the industry's trade body, warned that, if implemented in its draft form, the directive would cost the industry hundreds of millions of pounds a year in lost revenues. The plans also aroused great anxiety throughout the Community's television, press and magazine industries, all of whom would be faced by declining income from advertising if the Commission's plans were approved.

The row provoked a bitter debate on the role and influence of advertising, which is still generating more heat than light. On the one hand, it is evident that manufacturers of tobacco products, as with any other product, wish to be able to advertise across frontiers because they believe that such techniques will help to generate sales. This does not, of course, apply to the state-owned tobacco companies in France, Italy, Spain and Portugal, who support stringent restrictions on cross-frontier tobacco advertising because they do not want to see their protected market shares eroded by increased foreign competition. On the other hand, it is difficult to explain consumer choices by reference to advertising alone, as many other factors are involved. Until recently, for example, there were no cigarette advertisements in the Soviet Union or Eastern Europe, but sales have been increasing steadily for decades. Commission officials, along with members of the European Parliament, are still wrestling with the task of reconciling changing social attitudes towards tobacco and alcohol with the revenue-generating needs of the advertising industry. As yet, there is little indication that a compromise is at hand, although new restrictions on cross-border advertising seem inevitable.

Quantity versus quality

If the Commission's estimates are realized and there are some 200 new television stations by the 1990s what will they be broadcasting into our homes? Not enough new material is being produced to fill the existing satellite stations' schedules with new programmes, and many critics fear that an excessive proportion of what we get when the new stations are operational we will probably have seen already, and much of the remainder will be cheap imported soap operas, game shows and serials from the United States, which we will not want to watch in any case. Many fear that the age of satellite telecommunications will represent a giant step forwards for technology, matched only by a giant step backwards for culture.

Fearing the worst, the critics have predicted the end of the expensive quality programmes and the various wildlife documentaries, and because of the competition for advertising revenue, broadcasters will be compelled to fill their air time with popular and inexpensive off-the-shelf reruns. In short, satellite broadcasting will become little more than 'chewing gum for the eyes', and will probably turn us all into vegetables.

It is precisely this anxiety that has prompted the Commission to advocate the introduction of quotas in an effort to stimulate the European film and audiovisual products industry. Having created a single audiovisual market, the Commission wants to have sufficient European products to fill it with, and 'ensure that the new televisual media continue to reflect the Community's cultural diversity and richness, and that the large market does not simply operate to encourage a search for the audiovisual lowest common denominator'. However, there is no guarantee that the Commission's attempts to provide a stimulus for Europe's film and programme makers will prove successful. The French have never shown much of a liking for German serials, Holland is only going to have a a very limited interest in Portugal's news and Britain is unlikely to get too enthusiastic about Greek game shows. Even if some magic formula was found that overcame such national dispositions, it would be many years before there was sufficient material to satisfy the needs of the proliferating satellite television stations.

However, the experience of satellite broadcasting to date, while hardly a triumph, is far from being the unmitigated disaster the pessimists had predicted. Admittedly, the launch of SuperChannel was greeted with almost universally poor reviews, and the lack of late-night advertising forced it to reduce its transmissions from 24 to 20 hours a day. During the summer of 1988 most of its programme schedules were made up of old ITV–BBC reruns like *Some Mothers Do 'ave 'em*, *The Professionals* and *Spitting Image*. However, it has also shown some of the classics of television from the 1950s like *The Twilight Zone*, while its nightly 30-minute European news broadcast (since sadly abandoned) was thoroughly professional, with a breadth of outlook often lacking in British television news programmes.

Similarly, Sky offers a mixture of the high and lowbrow. In the summer of 1988, before it became generally available in Britain, Sky's schedules were filled with many childhood favourites like *Dr Who*, *Lost in Space* and *Fantasy Island*. It has bought in a number of old US programmes like *Hawk*, *Wanted Dead or Alive* and *Hogan's Heroes*, which put many of America's more recent offerings to shame. Sky has also broken new ground with its *Earth Watch* environmental programme and its current affairs programme *Roving Report*. Since linking up with the Arts Channel, viewers have also been able to see a broad selection of classical music, opera and jazz—albeit after midnight. Many adults have objected to what they regard as excessive amounts of music broadcast by satellite channels —a criticism not shared by the Community's teenagers.

The calibre of advertising, by any standard, is atrocious, and is in desperate need of improvement. Nothing much could be done for washing-powder advertisements, which seem unable to break out of the traditional formula in which a housewife compares a new version of the old brand-name to an unnamed rival and decides to go for the newly packaged old washing powder which, as a result of successive unexplained biological breakthroughs, is now washing clothes nuclear-white. Such advertisements are undoubtedly destined to remain appalling, no matter what language they are in. However, for Britain's advertising companies, who, in the words of one observer, have already managed to send the nation to work on an egg and succeeded in getting a respectable proportion of British holidaymakers onto the beach before the Germans, the European advertising market could provide new, interesting and potentially rewarding challenges.

Amid great publicity, Rupert Murdoch's satellite television service was formally launched in Britain in February 1989, with four new channels providing general entertainment, sport, films and a 24-hour news service. The joint venture between Murdoch (who owns *The Times*) and Alan Sugar, the chairman of the Amstrad consumer electronics company, had produced the satellite dishes viewers needed to receive the new channels for around £250, and Britain's satellite television revolution began in earnest. Sky's programmes included newly imported American serials such as the comedy *Wings*, the law drama *Equal Justice*, the mini-series *Lonesome Dove*, many of Hollywood's latest releases and a few British offerings such as *Sale of the Century*. Many critics attacked the new service for targeting the lower end of the market and for failing to produce any new programme ideas. Meanwhile, sales of satellite dishes continued to mount.

The launch of British Satellite Broadcasting (BSB) in April 1990, which provided five new channels of films, sport, light entertainment and current affairs, inaugurated a fierce commercial battle between the two rival satellite companies. BSB, which was owned by a consortium of media groups, including Pearson (owners of the *Financial Times*), Reed International, Granada and Chargeurs, attempted to pitch its product towards the upper end of the market. With both companies confronted by huge start-up costs, mounting operating losses and breakeven dates that were years away, they rapidly became bitter opponents in the struggle for control of the British satellite market. Along with multi-million pound promotion schemes, the two companies traded personal abuse and libel writs, leaving the existing terrestrial channels unscathed.

While observers were debating whether there was room for two satellite stations in Britain, the multi-billion-pound satellite war was brought to an abrupt end with the merger of the two companies in November 1990. Three weeks of secret negotiations led to the creation of a new company, British Sky Broadcasting (BSkyB), in which Sky and BSB shareholders each hold 50% of the combined assets and obligations. But while the merger eased the financial crisis facing the two fledgling satellite companies, it also created many political and legal difficulties.

Roy Hattersley, the shadow Home Secretary, condemned the merger, and threatened to break up large-scale media empires if Labour came to power by seeking an enquiry by the Monopolies and Mergers Commission into 'overlapping' television and newspaper ownership, 'with the intention of breaking up unacceptable concentrations of power'. Critics of the deal demanded to know how it was possible to allow Murdoch, who owns one-third of Britain's national newspaper market, to have a satellite monopoly as well. What was not widely appreciated, however, was that what was seen as a monopoly in Britain amounted to a miniscule share of the satellite television market in Europe, where the competition was widespread—and growing. Separately, the two companies would probably have bled each other to death. Together, they provide Britain with a presence in the new European satellite television industry, and have a prospect of mounting an effective challenge against the existing BBC–ITV duopoly. The European Commission could find no grounds to vet the merger. In a separate action in February 1991, however, Eurosport, the joint venture between Sky, the BBC and the European Broadcasting Union, was prohibited on the grounds that it was likely to 'restrict and distort competition within the Community'.

However, there were more substantive criticisms of the merger. Lord Thompson of Monifieth, a former chairman of the IBA (now the Independent Television Commission) and the Liberal Democrat spokesman on broadcasting, said that the Sky–BSB merger would be 'a setback for prospects of wide screen, high-definition television of the future, in which Britain is a leader'. Before the merger, BSB broadcasts (via the Marco Polo satellite) had been using a new set of technical standards, known as D-Mac, which provides a 35 mm picture quality and stereo sound (although few viewers were equipped with television sets able to receive it). By contrast, Sky broadcasts, via the Astra satellite, use the conventional transmission standards, known as Pal. But the merger required BSB to switch over to Astra, raising fears in some quarters that the new high-definition television technology would fail to receive the boost it needed to become commercially viable.

Under an agreement with the Independent Television Commission, BSkyB will continue to broadcast the merged programme output on the Marco Polo satellite until the end of 1992. The new company also undertook to supply owners of BSB 'squarials' with the Sky satellite dishes needed to receive the Astra signal. Immediately after the merger, Comet, the High Street electrical retail chain owned by Kingfisher, obtained a High Court writ against BSkyB for £6 million in damages for a breach of contract which left it holding obsolete stocks of BSB satellite dishes, although an out-of-court settlement was finally reached in October. In addition, Philips, the Dutch electronics multinational, issued a £100-million law suit because of the losses it expected to incur as one of the manufacturers of D-Mac technology.

However, as BSkyB began to deal with the political and legal implications of the merger the government was faced with a new problem presented by the emerging satellite broadcasting industry—pornography. The issue came to a head in June 1991, when David Henry, a Scottish businessman, announced plans for a new channel called 'After Twelve', which would provide viewers with 'the sort of material they might find in *Playboy* magazine'. The tabloids seized on the announcement, calling Henry: 'TV's Mr Porn—the man who is going to bring bonking onto British TV sets'. In fact, similar material has been available on a number of channels using the Astra satellite for some time. An article in the *Sunday Telegraph* pointed out that British viewers had long been able to watch 'adult movies' on Filmnet, a Belgian company broadcasting to Scandinavia, and *Tutti-Frutti*, an adult game show from Germany. Pointing out that 'The BBC shows "art films"—it does not show contestants whipping off their blouses on game shows', the article described such programmes as 'the first wave in the tide of pornography that many claimed would engulf British living rooms once satellite TV arrived'.

Harmless fun or degrading dirt? The 1989 broadcasting directive prohibits the transmission of pornographic programmes unless they have been approved by one member state. Clearly, however, definitions of pornography vary. What might be acceptable in one country could easily be seen as offensive in another. In fact, British viewers are not supposed to be able to receive Filmnet at all, but word of its availability created a flourishing black market in the pirate decoders needed to receive it. Kenneth Baker, the Home Secretary, and Jacques Delors, the President of the European Commission, promptly received strongly worded letters from Mary Whitehouse, the President of the National Listeners and Viewers' Association. But many critics of the directive characterized the government's response as similar to 'bolting the gates after the stable was empty'. Others pointed out that no-one was being compelled to watch such programmes, and insisted that what people do in their own home is their own affair.

The availability of pornography was not the only issue that generated public debate about the arrival of satellite broadcasting. Some observers suggested that the anticipated widespread appeal of satellite television was wholly misconceived. It was pointed out, for example, that viewers in the Netherlands had no less than 21 channels to choose from, yet the two main channels accounted for almost 90% of television audiences. In addition, the situation was similar in the United States, where cable stations had been in operation for many years. There was also a body of evidence that suggested that family television viewing times had been declining in the face of competition from videos, and that the new satellite stations were likely to find it extremely difficult to win these audiences back.

Writing in *The Independent* in July 1991, Steven Barnett, the Director of the Henley Centre's media group, argued that the predicted arrival of the age of satellite broadcasting in Britain was 'pie in the sky'. He dismissed the idea that Britain was on the threshold of a multi-channel television revolution, described the sale of satellite receiving equipment as proceeding at 'a crawl' and ridiculed forecasts that there would be 8 million satellite dishes on British homes by the mid-1990s as 'fallacious'. Responding to Barnett's article, John Clemens, the Chairman of Continental Research and a Fellow of the Institute of Practitioners in Advertising, accused the Henley Centre of misrepresenting the statistics. Clemens pointed out that satellite dish sales had grown from 63,000 to 1.5 million in two years. By contrast, video recorders (launched in 1977) took five years to reach 1.5 million sales, while colour televisions (begun in 1967) took four years to reach 1 million sales. By August, when the *Financial Times* published its monthly satellite sales monitor, 1.7 million homes had access to satellite television, while installations of satellite receiving equipment had increased by a staggering 80% in 12 months. At the time the monitor was published, one in every ten Britons lived in a home with multi-channel television. The age of satellite television, for better or worse, had already arrived in Britain.

High-definition television

Long before the arguments over programme quotas, advertising regulations and declining moral standards in broadcasting, the European Commission had embarked upon an initiative to avert what was described at the time as a potentially devastating technological challenge from Japan. In the face of increased competition from some of the newly industrialized countries in the Far East, a number of Japanese electronics companies took a decision in the early 1970s to abandon the market for traditional television sets to their more cost-efficient neighbours and to concentrate on developing a new generation of high-definition television (HDTV) sets that would offer the viewer 35-mm picture quality and stereo sound. In 1985 Japan submitted its own technical standard for HDTV (known as Muse) to the International Radio Consultative Committee (CCIR), the world broadcasting organization, as the first step towards making the Japanese standard the world standard.

For Europe's struggling electronics companies the implications of Japan's attempted demarche were profoundly disturbing. The proposed HDTV standard would significantly increase the number of lines that go to make up a television picture, and would establish the technical parameters for television sets in the same way that the VHS standard has set the technical parameters for video recorders. If Japan succeeded in getting its standard adopted, Japanese electronics companies would have pulled off one of the biggest commercial coups in the history of consumer electronics, forcing other electronics companies to produce their equipment to Japanese standards, thereby enabling Japanese companies to dominate the industry well into the next century. In addition, Europe's 140 million television sets would have been made obsolete overnight, as they would not be able to receive the new HDTV broadcasts.

At the CCIR's annual assembly in Dubrovnik in May 1986 the European electronics companies argued against Japan's all-or-nothing approach, and put forward the case for a more evolutionary approach that would be compatible with existing television receiver sets. Europe's leading consumer electronics equipment manufacturers joined forces under the Community's Eureka telecommunications research and development programme in a bid to perfect the new HDTV technology before the Japanese. In the same year, Council adopted a directive on common technical standards for direct broadcasting by satellite (known as the Mac-packet family of standards), requiring all new satellite broadcasting companies to use the D-Mac technology. The D-Mac standard was not a fully fledged HDTV standard but it is superior to the existing conventional Pal standard, and was widely regarded as a stepping-stone towards the ultimate goal of HDTV.

The 1986 directive, however, contained a fundamental flaw. It did not apply to Astra, which is classified as a telecommunications, not a broadcasting satellite, and is thus exempt from the directive's provisions. With the 1986 directive due to expire at the end of 1991, the Commission was presented with a second opportunity to help provide a boost to the new European technology, an initiative vigorously supported by Philips, the Dutch electronics firm, and Thompson, its counterpart in France, both of whom had invested heavily in HDTV. But Société Européene des Satellites, which owns the Astra satellite, to which there were some two million subscribers at the beginning of 1991, feared that the Commission was trying to phase out Pal in favour of the new transitionary standard. Moreover, after the debacle of BSB, one of the first satellite companies to use the new transitionary standard, some critics accused the Commission of promoting a 1960s-style industrial policy which would increase the cost of receiving equipment and depress growth in the new satellite market.

Under the draft directive tabled in June 1991 by Filippo Maria Pandolfi, the Commissioner for Research and Development and Telecommunications, all new satellite broadcasting companies are required to use the new D-Mac standards from January 1993, while manufacturers must incorporate D-Mac decoders in new television sets wider than 22 inches from the same date. In addition, the Commission offered some £350-million worth of incentives for research into equipment that would allow satellite companies to broadcast in both standards simultaneously, and gave assurances that companies broadcasting in Pal would not be forced to switch over to D-Mac.

However, the compromise satisfied no-one. John Redwood, Britain's Trade and Industry minister, accused the Commission of trying to compel broadcasters and consumers into accepting the new standards. French and Dutch ministers demanded assurances about when and how Pal was to be phased out, while the satellite companies, many of whom were prepared to broadcast in both standards, remained anxious that the Commission would try to force the new standards upon them. Moreover, a report published in August by the independent consultants, Coopers & Lybrand, suggested that the Commission's HDTV strategy would cost European taxpayers, broadcasters and consumers up to £15 billion over a ten-year period in upgraded equipment. In the absence of a workable agreement between manufacturers, satellite operators and broadcasters, the Commission appeared reluctant to press ahead with its proposals, raising the prospect of the 1986 directive lapsing without anything to replace it.

By December, however, agreement was in sight following Pandolphi's decision to relax the provisions of the proposed HDTV directive. Under the revised formula, all new satellite services are required to broadcast in D-Mac, as the transitionary stage to full HDTV technology, But existing broadcasters will be allowed to transmit in Pal indefinitely, with no obligation to broadcast simultaneously in both standards. Admittedly,

Pandolphi's concession falls short of the industrial strategy advocated by France, and the broadcasters and satellite companies have still to put their signature to a legally binding memorandum. But the prospects of their doing so have never looked more optimistic.

Checklist of changes

- There will be considerable expansion in the number of satellite television channels available to viewers.
- Satellite broadcasters will have the right to transmit television programmes anywhere in the Community, provided that they meet certain minimum requirements.
- Broadcasters will be obliged to reserve a specified quota of their air time for feature films made in the Community.
- Television advertisers will have the option of grouping commercials into blocks or slots, and will be required to abide by prevailing standards of decency.
- Satellite and cable companies are expected to have an automatic right to broadcast or retransmit any programme within two years of original transmission, as long as adequate remuneration for the programme copyright holder is provided.
- New regulations are expected on cross-frontier advertisements for alcohol, tobacco, certain foods, pharmaceuticals and children's toys.
- Viewers could benefit from a considerable improvement in television picture and sound quality if the implementation of high-definition technology is commercially successful.

15 REGIONAL DEVELOPMENT

Economic cohesion and the North–South divide

Complementing the European Commission's attempt to increase the competitiveness of European industry through the 1992 programme is a parallel effort to reduce the economic disparities that exist both between and within the Community's rich and poor regions. The objective, in brief, is to ensure that the integrated market develops cohesively. Hence the jargon words 'cohesion' or 'convergence' for the 1992 policy of avoiding a North–South divide or 'two-speed Europe' in which the Northern states (Britain, France, Germany, Denmark and the Benelux countries) enjoy most of the economic benefits of the single market while the Southern states (Greece, Spain, Portugal, parts of Italy and the Irish Republic) lag behind. The Commission provides economic assistance to the regions by means of grants from three distinct but related funds—the European Regional Development Fund (ERDF), the European Social Fund (ESF) and the guidance section of the European Agricultural Guidance and Guarantee Fund (EAGGF), which are collectively referred to as the structural funds.

Preventing the emergence of a North–South economic divide is, however, only one of the overall objectives of the structural funds. Partly on British insistence, the definition of economic cohesion has been broadened to include the redevelopment of declining or depressed rural and urban areas in Northern countries, such as parts of Scotland and the run-down industrial towns and derelict urban areas of Britain. To equip the Commission for the task of ensuring that the Community developed cohesively, the Council of Ministers, after much resistance from some of the Northern member states, agreed to double the money made available to the structural funds to some £9 billion by 1992. In addition, the administration of the funds has been overhauled to ensure a more co-ordinated and coherent approach to regional development by focusing on a programme rather than a project-based approach to aid distribution.

Applications for economic assistance from the structural funds, which must normally be made by government departments, local authorities and other publicly funded organizations, are required to satisfy at least one of five objectives or categories, defined by the Commission as:

Category **One**: To assist those regions whose development is lagging behind.

Category **Two**: To revitalize regions affected by serious industrial decline.

Category **Three**: To combat long-term unemployment.

Category **Four**: To integrate young people into the job market.

Category **Five**: To adjust agricultural structures and develop rural areas.

Generally, although there are exceptions, each of the three funds is restricted to certain areas. The ERDF covers Categories One and Two, the ESF Categories Three and Four and the EAGGF covers Category Five. Consequently, while all the UK qualifies for assistance under Categories Three and Four and parts of it qualify for support under Categories Three and Five, only Northern Ireland qualifies for help under Category One.

During a lunch for British Brussels' correspondents shortly after taking up his new post as the Commissioner for Regional Development, Bruce Millan, Labour's former Scottish Secretary, expressed surprise at the media attention given to Leon Brittan, the UK's senior commissioner. 'He may have got the top job but I've got all the money,' Millan said wryly. The Commissioner's sense of humour was to be sorely tested, however, in a long-running dispute with Whitehall over how money from the structural funds was to be used. From the outset, Brussels has insisted that support from the structural funds, unless otherwise agreed, must be provisional on co-financing from member states. According to the Commission's guidelines on EC loans and grants:

It is an important principle of Community aid that it supplements rather than replaces resources allocated at national level. In almost all cases Community aid must be additional to and matched by at least an equivalent amount of money from national resources.

British Treasury officials, however, disagree—and therein lies the origins of a dispute over what has come to be known in Eurospeak as 'additionality'.

Cohesion: reducing regional disparities

The aim of 1992 is to bring all areas of the EC up to a high standard of living and economic growth, largely by raising extra revenue and distributing it around the Community on the basis of priorities decided by successive EC summits and implemented in detail by the European Commission. Whether throwing money at the problem in this way will prove effective is a moot point: as with any aid programme, there is ample scope for abuse or misuse. Widespread fraud in the southern countries—especially Italy and Spain—where agricultural funds are concerned does not offer an encouraging example, and the Commission lacks the resources or the powers to carry out adequate inspections to ensure that funds are properly used. On the other hand, the regional and social funds already have a record of achievement, and British citizens are often unaware that motorway schemes, youth training programmes or urban regeneration projects have been funded wholly or partly by the EC.

The commitment to 'cohesion' pre-dates the 1992 programme but has been given added impetus by the single market. In its current form it stems not only from the original Cockfield 1992 programme but also from the Single European Act. The Commission has always been conscious of the North–South problem, and Delors has made 'cohesion' something of a personal crusade. The 1985 White Paper referred to the issue in its introduction in the following terms:

> The Commission is firmly convinced that the completion of the internal market will provide an indispensable base for increasing the prosperity of the Community as a whole. The Commission is, however, conscious that there may be risks that by increasing the possibilities for human, material and financial services to move without obstacle to the areas of greatest economic advantage, existing discrepancies between regions could be exacerbated and therefore the object of convergence jeopardized. This means full and imaginative use will need to be made of the resources available through the structural funds. The importance of the funds will therefore be enhanced.

Shorn of Eurospeak, this conveys the Commission's fundamental worry that money and resources will move towards the more prosperous north in the EC after 1992, with the southern states—and backward regions—unable to stand up to cross-border competition. This anxiety has also been strongly expressed by the southern countries themselves, not least by Greece—which held the presidency of the Council of Ministers in the second half of 1988—and Spain, which had the presidency in the second half of 1989. As a consequence, many 1992 directives (for example, the directive on the liberalization of financial services by July 1990) contain exemptions for the southern states, to allow them a 'breathing space'. Other exemptions originate from the accession terms negotiated by the southern countries. On the other hand, all these exemptions are provisional, and it is assumed that in due course (in the later 1990s, perhaps) the southern economies will be strong enough to co-exist with other European economies in a frontier-free commercial environment.

Increasing the structural funds

To achieve this, the EC 'structural' funds are being increased, so that the southern states and backward regions can benefit from greater investment and—with the aid of the regional and social funds—stage an economic recovery. The White Paper referred, rather coyly, to the importance of 'enhancing' the funds. What the Commission really wanted, however (and achieved at the important Brussels summit of February 1988), was to increase the funds substantially, and even to double them—a proposal resisted at first by Britain and other states but eventually agreed as part of the Delors reform package which followed the Single European Act and 'cleared the way' for 1992 legislation.

Even the Act avoids direct reference to a 'doubling' of the structural funds. The relevant section (Title Five) notes that

> In order to promote its overall harmonious development, the Community shall develop and pursue its actions leading to the strengthening of its economic and social cohesion . . . In particular, the Community shall aim at reducing disparities between the various regions and the backwardness of the least-favoured regions.

To achieve this, the EC states undertook to co-ordinate their economic policies in such a way as to avoid a North–South split, although it was not altogether clear what this meant in practice. More immediately, the EC was committed under the Act to making better use of the three 'structural funds': the European Agricultural Guidance and Guarantee Fund; the European Social Fund; and the European Regional Development Fund, as well as loans from the European Investment Bank. Article 130c outlined the purpose of the regional fund in particular: 'The European Regional Development Fund is intended to help redress the principal regional imbalances in the Community through participating in the development and structural adjustment of regions whose development is lagging behind, and in the conversion of declining industrial regions'.

So far so good: but the Act went on to authorize the Commission to submit 'a comprehensive proposal to the Council, the purpose of which will be to make such amendments to the structure and operational rules of the existing structural funds as are necessary to clarify and rationalize their tasks in order to contribute to the achievement of the objectives . . . and to increase their efficiency'. In practice, Delors and the Commission wanted nothing less than to double the funds so that 1992 could go ahead without major disruption and the further creation of regional imbalances.

The European Regional Development Fund

The structural funds had been operating for ten years before the 1992 process began. Yet oddly enough, the need to redress regional imbalances to prevent one part of the EC developing faster than another (or rather, to bring more backward regions up to the higher levels of development) was not foreseen in the Treaty of Rome, which has no separate clause on regional problems. The preamble refers to the need for the EC to 'ensure harmonious development by reducing the differences existing between the various regions', and in the 1960s there were plenty of examples of backwardness—in the low-subsistence agriculture of the Italian south, in depressed coalmining regions in Belgium and the Ruhr, and in central France. Some funds were channelled through the European Investment Bank (EIB).

However, the ERDF was only created in the mid-1970s, after the Six had grown to Nine with the addition of Britain, Ireland and Denmark in 1973. Britain, although not one of the underdeveloped regions on a par with the Southern states, did (and still does) have important areas of both rural and, above all, industrial decline, including Northern Ireland —which is still singled out as a high-priority area for regional aid under the 1992 programme, partly with the political aim of promoting harmony between the conflicting Ulster communities. Denmark had a poor region in Greenland—it subsequently left the EC after a local referendum; and the Republic of Ireland, for its part, had a low per capita income and added to the weight of what was to become the 'southern bloc' with the entry of Greece in 1981 and Spain and Portugal in 1986.

What had started as mainly a 'rich man's club' in 1957 had become a much more diversified Community by the 1970s and 1980s. It quickly became apparent after 1973 that the 'less favoured' EC regions were either backward rural areas with high unemployment levels and poor communications and transport, largely in the south, or—no less important to Britain, Germany, France and Belgium—regions which were formerly thriving centres of traditional industries, such as iron and steel, but which had increasingly fallen on hard times because of changes in global trading patterns and competition from outside Europe, with a consequent cost to Europe in unemployment, economic decline and social malaise.

However, the allocations made to member states under the regional fund, set up in 1975, were not universally regarded as fair or just. The practice was that member states propose projects—a new motorway, inner-city developments, irrigation schemes—and the Commission decides which projects are worthy of the most support. Both public authority and commercial projects can qualify. However, in the early days the Commission took the view that each country should have a part of the regional aid funds, even if Country A's depressed regions were far better off than those of Country B. In practice, it is true, most of the aid between 1975 and 1985 (one eighth of the EC budget) ended up in the regions which arguably needed it most: the Italian Mezzogiorno; Greece; Ireland; Britain (including Northern Ireland); and the French overseas departments, which also count as EC territories.

The allocations, however, needed adjustment, and at the time of the 1992 White Paper in 1985 the rules were changed to give each country a maximum percentage of the regional fund budget rather than a fixed annual quota. The maximum percentage of the ERDF budget allocated to Britain was 19.31% and the minimum guaranteed 14.48%. This compares favourably with the 9.96% upper limit allocated to France, the 3.40% given to Germany and even with the 10.64% allocated to Greece or the 14.20% for Portugal. Only Spain and Italy had higher allocations than Britain, with upper limits of 23.93% and 28.79%, respectively. Following the Brussels agreement of February 1988 the Commission proposed a new system under which it would reserve to itself 15% of the structural funds to ensure a fair redistribution of wealth, while issuing 'indicative allocations' for the remaining 75%. In practice, 'indicative allocations' have been equivalent to the old quotas, which remain informally in force.

The southern states also benefit from a separate fund known as the Integrated Mediterranean Programmes (rather amusingly abbreviated to IMP), which derive from the accession terms negotiated by Greece, Spain and Portugal and which benefit selected Mediterranean regions through a system of grants and loans (the French Mediterranean regions also receive IMP funds).

In addition, the European Social Fund—which, unlike the regional fund, was included in the terms of the Treaty of Rome—has the principal aim of encouraging job creation in areas of high unemployment, partly through retraining schemes. The Fund's importance has grown together with unemployment, so that it now accounts for almost the same proportion of the EC budget as the regional fund. The Government's Youth Training Scheme, for example, was established with help from the EC Social Fund—although again, not many people are aware of this. The Fund also helps to retrain employees unfamiliar with new technologies, migrant workers and women whose families have grown up and who return to full- or part-time employment only to find that techniques and work patterns have changed.

The February 1988 Brussels Agreement

The key question as 1992 approaches is whether the Commission and Council will succeed in further developing these funds to prevent a North–South division, or whether the less-advantaged regions will fall further behind as free competition benefits those economic sectors most prepared for it. The decision to double the structural funds by 1992 has certainly improved the chances of avoiding a 'two-speed' Europe. Taken in February 1988, it appears to have surprised even those—like Delors —who had sponsored the proposal. On the other hand, the increase in regional and social spending is directly related to the Delors package's overhaul of EC finances. Europe can only spend more on its regions because it is increasing the revenues coming into central EC funds while at the same time cutting back on farm spending under the Common Agricultural Policy, despite protests from EC farmers and farm ministers.

The decision, in other words, only came after the Northern countries, with Britain heading the campaign, had insisted that extra regional spending was a luxury the EC could only afford once other expenditure (above all, farm support) had been brought under control. The Commission, for its part, recognized that budgetary reform was needed if the 1992 programme—regional aid included—was to be based on a 'sound economic footing'.

The process of bringing EC spending under control to allow for greater regional aid, and the framework programme for technological research, dominated the last four years of the 1980s, just as the preceding four had been overshadowed by the question of the British budget rebate. The crisis really came in June 1987, at the Brussels summit marking the end of Belgium's EC presidency, when Mrs Thatcher demanded 'good house-keeping' in the EC before budgetary increases for 1992 could be contemplated. Chancellor Kohl of Germany declared Bonn's willingness to increase the regional and social funds by up to 50%, but Mrs Thatcher declared that the CAP had to be curbed first, and there was, in any case, room for improvement in the way the existing structural funds were administered. 'The EC is not a mechanism for redistributing wealth, it is a common enterprise for producing it' was her spokesman's terse comment.

The result was a 'Maggie versus the Rest' summit, in which Mrs Thatcher held out against a compromise package because it lacked budgetary rigour, arguing—correctly—that she was 'doing the Community a service'. At Brussels, Mrs Thatcher was mocked by Jacques Chirac, the former French Prime Minister, for taking a 'housewifely' view of the budget. A senior British diplomat at the EC subsequently compared Mrs Thatcher—rather more admiringly—to a nanny: 'She says to the others, if you don't eat your porridge up now you'll have to eat it cold tomorrow'. The alternative, Britain insisted, was EC bankruptcy as expenditure continued to exceed revenue.

On the eve of the next summit, in Copenhagen in December 1987, France and Germany suggested a compromise, allowing states to escape farm spending cuts 'in exceptional circumstances'. Sir Geoffrey Howe, the then Foreign Secretary, replied on Britain's behalf that there was no point in filling the proposed spending deal with loopholes 'like a motheaten sock'. The British solution lay in strict ceilings on farm output, known as 'stabilizers', coupled with a German-backed scheme for taking land out of production (set aside, and an altered revenue system, as devised by the Commission, to include a GNP tax), provided that there was no consequent alteration for the worse in the British budget rebate agreed in 1984. In the end, Copenhagen failed, but the debate was better tempered, and the leaders moved closer to agreement, with the summit vowing to take action when it reconvened in special session in Brussels in February 1988, under German chairmanship.

The extraordinary Brussels summit, when it met, was on the verge of breaking up several times, with French leaders taking a hard line against farm cuts because of the impending French presidential election and Mrs Thatcher still insisting that the regional funds could not be increased by more than 50% to 60%. Chancellor Kohl, after allowing the summit to drift, held separate talks with his fellow leaders—'confessionals' in EC jargon—to break the deadlock. In the final negotiation Chirac went one better (or worse) than his earlier 'housewife' epithet when, late at night on the second day, he shouted a crude French word (*couilles*) across the table at Mrs Thatcher after she had accused him of holding up the deal by going on interminably about non-arable products.

In the end, the February 1988 summit reached an historic deal. With last-minute concessions on all sides—not least from Mrs Thatcher—it finally reformed EC finances along the lines of the original Delors plan, thus not only allowing for a doubling of the structural funds by 1992 but also 'clearing the way for 1992' as a whole, in the Prime Minister's own words. The Brussels agreement included:

1 An overall increase in the EC budget from £31 billion in 1988, to £37 billion in 1992, with revenues based not only on Vat but also the GNP tax (the resulting mix producing revenue equivalent to 1.9% Vat);
2 Preservation of the British rebate, which Mrs Thatcher said had saved British taxpayers £3 billion over three years;
3 Legally binding limits on cereals and other crops, with the proportion of farm spending in the budget to decline from two thirds to 56% by 1992; and, above all,
4 A rise in the structural funds to £9.5 billion a year by 1992, or over a quarter of the budget, with most of the new aid going to Portugal, Ireland, Spain and Greece.

Britain and the structural funds

Since the Delors reforms, the argument has mainly been over the official definition of a 'less-developed region' and of a 'depressed industrial area', defined in the summit conclusions as an area with unemployment higher than the Community average. There is concern over the Commission's interpretation of this to mean that the very poorest EC regions should be developed first to help them to cope with 1992. The Commission pro-posed giving most of the new money to 'Category One' regions, in which per capita income must be below 75% of EC average (with only Northern Ireland among the British regions therefore qualifying for high-priority Category One). The Government objected in the Council that other British regions deserved special treatment—rural Wales, the Highlands and Islands of Scotland (which officials had hinted would be Category One), parts of Devon and Cornwall, and inner-city 'black spots' in London, Liverpool, Manchester and elsewhere.

In late 1988 a further difficulty arose over British objections to public spending being taken into account in the allocation of structural funds. The Commission, for its part, does not want to see member states using regional funds as an excuse to cut public spending.

British special pleading—accompanied by special pleading from other countries—has had some effect, partly because the logic of earlier regional grant awards supports the British case. The Highlands alone received £100 million over the first ten years of the ERDF, with EC cash supporting projects like the new Perth-to-Inverness trunk road. Neither Scotland nor Whitehall was keen to lose this support. The government aim was (and is) to maintain a situation in which Britain was a major recipient of structural funds, and especially ERDF cash. According to figures published by the Commission, in the first ten years of the ERDF Britain was near the top of the league of aid recipients, with over £3 billion in aid. The initial Commission list of regional aid recipients in March 1988 gave the whole of Greece, Ireland and Portugal as 'Category One' regions, together with regions of Spain and Italy, Corsica, the French overseas departments and Northern Ireland. However, Britain has since been given assurances that other of its regions—including both rural areas and those of industrial decline—will benefit substantially from the new funds, up to Britain's allotted ceiling, even if they are in Category Two rather than Category One. Under the new criteria, Category Two covers areas of industrial decline, defined as areas where there has been higher than average unemployment for more than three years, or where there has been an 'observable fall' in industrial employment.

In the spirit of 1992 Kent County Council has joined forces with the regional Council of the Pas de Calais (Nord) to apply to Brussels for £1 billion worth of aid over a ten-year period to help develop the infrastructure on both sides of the Channel for the Channel Tunnel. On the other hand, under the new criteria neither Kent nor the Pas de Calais qualifies as a high-priority depressed region in terms of regional aid—although both qualify for Social Fund cash.

In other words, the new approach to the expanded structural funds —concentrating resources on the most backward areas—still gives rise to concern in Britain. The government has put forward plans for including areas of 'high deprivation' such as Merseyside and Strathclyde in future EC aid allocations to Britain. Some areas (Cornwall is one example) have even launched their own campaigns to ensure they do not lose out in 1992. Cornwall received £125 million worth of aid from the ERDF between 1975 and 1985, but the decline of tin mining and other local industries has brought continuing high unemployment.

The government's anxieties about losing out because of the overhaul in the way the structural funds are managed was, however, over-shadowed by a more pressing argument over the way the funds were used. In July 1990 Millan announced that Scotland and Yorkshire were to receive an additional £44.3 million in regional aid for a variety of job creation, economic regeneration and transport improvement programmes. The announcement followed an unseemly row between Brussels and Whitehall over the vexed question of additionality, one that was to resurface the following year. By the summer of 1991, newspapers were reporting that Britain's depressed regions were being prevented from claiming hundreds of millions of pounds in structural fund aid because of the government's tight control of public spending. Although the Commission had agreed a total budget of £850 million in ERDF aid for Britain in the three years leading up to 1993, only £350 million had actually been handed over. As local councils were forced to stay within the spending ceilings imposed under the new Community Charge, or poll tax, many councils found themselves unable to raise the co-financing they needed to release Community funds. Consequently, some £500 million was held up in administrative limbo, jeopardizing numerous projects in the Black Country, Merseyside and West Cumbria.

Similarly, in July, Millan announced a total of ECU 1.87 billion in aid for other member states, while refusing to release £100 million designated for depressed coal-mining regions in Britain under Category Two because he was not convinced that the government would use the money in addition to—rather than as a substitute for—national funds. Disputes between Brussels and London over the principle of additionality also extended to the ESF, which is designed to provide assistance for the long-term unemployed and youth unemployment, with particular attention to women, migrant workers and the disabled. In September, *The Times* reported that a confidential study prepared on behalf of the Commission by Coopers & Lybrand, the firm of management consultants, had concluded that some £200 million in social fund grants should be paid direct to training and employment councils, local authorities and voluntary organizations because the government had taken the social fund money and used it to replace part of its own training budget which would have been paid for by the Treasury.

Britain does not benefit from the guidance section of EAGGF aid as much as it does from ERDF and ESF assistance. About 7.5% of the fund's guidance section—by far the smallest part of EAGGF—will go to Britain, mostly to rural areas in Scotland, Wales, Devon and Cornwall. The bulk of EAGGF is used (squandered some would say), on intervention and export subsidies to help stabilize the market. Guidance section cash is designed to help rural communities to diversify away from traditional forms of production to new ones of agricultural activity such as forestry, while, at the same time, preserving the fabric of rural society. However, this can be expected to change significantly under new proposals designed to bring about a radical overhaul of the CAP.

All previous attempts to reform the CAP (notably in 1973, 1978, 1986 and, most recently, in 1988) have met with little success. In January 1991

Ray MacSharry, the Agricultural Commissioner, forecast that the CAP would cost the EC £5.6 billion, thereby breaching the ceiling imposed on agricultural spending at the EC summit in February 1988. By the summer, both the Commission and the member states had begun to accept that the CAP's central problem of overproduction had to be tackled, although some member states, notably Britain, were opposed to the Commission's proposed remedy. Nonetheless, in addition to external pressures for reform, internal reform pressures were also mounting—not least because the policy of spending 80% of EAGGF cash on subsidizing the richest 20% of farmers (most of whom are located in the northern states) made a mockery of the goal of fostering economic cohesion and avoiding a North–South divide. The MacSharry reforms, which include penalties in place of incentives on overproduction, are likely to cost more in the short term. But once spending on agricultural production declines, substantial sums of money should be released for the three structural funds.

Helping the North to help the South

On balance, the doubling of structural funds by 1992 will benefit Britain as well as the southern countries. Whether it will succeed in achieving Delors' aim of averting a North–South split in the integrated European market remains to be seen. One often-overlooked aspect of the increase in structural funds is that British and other northern companies can benefit from aid granted to the southern countries by entering into joint ventures which have the approval of Brussels and which draw on regional fund allocations. This is a particularly attractive proposition to companies which specialize in development aid projects in underdeveloped economies but which have been adversely affected by problems in the Third World, such as indebtedness or the decline in oil revenues. EC officials argue that many southern countries in the EC will have to turn to northern companies for help in development, since the funds they are likely to receive under the social and regional fund reforms will exceed the capacity of local industry and commerce to meet the challenge (for example, in construction). It is already becoming clear, however, that to benefit from 1992 joint ventures in the south, British companies would do well to have close arrangements with local firms in Spain, Greece, Portugal or Southern Italy, and will probably gain the most benefit if they have a local subsidiary.

The DTI—which has a projects and export policy division dealing with 1992 joint ventures—has warned that other north European countries such as Germany or the Netherlands will not be slow to seize this 1992 opportunity. Will the tables eventually be turned, with southern EC companies which benefit from increased EC aid becoming strong enough to challenge northern European firms on their home ground under the rules of the single market? In the short run it is unlikely, but if the integrated market develops after 1992 to the benefit of the south, the north may find its present superiority under challenge, not least from countries like Spain, which have a policy of economic dynamism backed by a great desire to prove to the rest of the EC—and the world at large —that they are part of a modern European economy and culture. If skills, labour and plant—including high-tech industries—move south in the integrated market, Spain and Portugal, and perhaps southern Italy, could become the European equivalent of the American Sun Belt.

Not all scenarios are so optimistic. At Madrid in June 1989, Bruce Millan, the Commissioner for regional development, said structural funds reform was 'off to a good start' and 'going pretty well to schedule'. He outlined a possible stark alternative to southern enrichment, however, saying the Commission had serious doubts about 'further concentration of resources in major central conurbations' in rich northern areas because of pollution, traffic congestion and poor housing. The Commission, Millan said, wanted 'a more centrifugal view of Europe' in the 1990s because of the danger of a cycle of decline in less-developed and depressed industrial regions if economic expectations were not met and then fell. The rich areas, from southern England to northern Italy, would be unable to sustain the pressures of migration from a declining south, and the 'rich centre' would then itself fall into a cycle of overcrowding and decay. To avoid this, the regional funds needed yet more cash, and new technology and market economics must be exploited to show that peripheral regions could be just as competitive as central regions.

During a visit to London in June 1991, Millan was asked whether the Commission was mapping out policies for the structural funds in the period after 1993. Responding with some caution, the Commissioner said:

> I have always taken the view that we cannot talk about a real Community if you have the disparities that we have at the present time. Therefore, if we are moving towards closer political integration, as well as closer economic and monetary integration, that has to be accompanied by continued efforts to remove the disparities between member states.

Spain, Portugal, Greece and Ireland were insisting that additional help would be needed if they were to avoid being caught in the second tier of a two-speed Europe, the Commissioner added. Spain has even gone so far as to suggest the creation of a new 'cohesion fund' to act as a sort of wealth-redistribution mechanism. Indeed, the Spanish government has indicated that its support for closer economic and political union will depend to a considerable degree on even larger transfers of wealth from more developed northern countries to their less-developed southern neighbours. Partly in response to such anxieties, the Commission asked national governments in May 1991 to submit medium-term economic strategy or convergence plans to Brussels by the end of 1991, as a prerequisite to moving on to stage two of EMU.

Satisfying the economic aspirations of the Community's poorer regions will, however, be but one of the tasks facing the Commission in the years after 1992. Closer economic ties with the six members of the European Free Trade Organization (EFTA), together with the impending association agreements with Eastern European countries such as Poland, Czechoslovakia and Hungary, will undoubtedly entail new economic development responsibilities and even greater calls on the resources of the structural funds, which will have to be borne by the more prosperous members of the EC.

Checklist of changes

- The Community's structural funds have been doubled to £9 billion in an effort to ensure that the poorer regions also benefit from the single market programme's aim of increasing economic growth.
- The structural funds will be targeted towards assisting those regions whose economic development has lagged behind, revitalizing the regions experiencing industrial decline, reducing unemployment and developing rural areas.
- Most of the new funds will go to Category One regions, for which only Northern Ireland qualifies in the UK. The UK will, however, benefit considerably from assistance to declining industrial areas, anti-unemployment programmes and rural development schemes.
- Companies in the more developed countries will be able to benefit from the funds allocated to poorer ones by participating in urban and rural development projects.
- Financial resources allocated to the structural funds are likely to be increased again after 1992, in an effort to meet the demands for additional assistance to the Community's poorer regions and to help East European countries to make the adjustment to free market economies.

16 PROTECTIONISM AND TARIFFS

The risks of Fortress Europe

Efforts to regenerate the EC's original vision of creating a common market entailed a wide range of implications for the world beyond Europe's borders, although little attention was paid to this so-called external dimension when the Internal Market White Paper was published in 1985. But while the European Commission would undoubtedly have preferred to focus its limited negotiating resources on the internal aspects of the single market, a succession of events in the outside world was to deny it any such luxury. In addition to fending off allegations from around the world that the new drive for European integration was inherently protectionist, the Commission found itself on a collision course with the United States in the closing stages of the Uruguay Round of international trade talks over the EC's reluctance to undertake a wholesale reform of the Common Agricultural Policy. In December 1990 the Uruguay Round, which promised to do for the world what the single market promised for Europe, was on the verge of collapse and Europe was being singled out as the guilty party.

Moreover, the Commission's attempts to redefine the nature of the Community's relationship with the neighbouring European Free Trade Association (EFTA) was suddenly overtaken by the eagerness of some EFTA states to abandon their allies unilaterally and opt for full membership of the EC. Although the Community appeared initially to favour the deepening of existing institutional and economic bonds between member states over the creation of new ties with non-member status, the collapse of the East European dictatorships, followed by the end of Communism in the Soviet Union, confronted EC decision-makers with a radically different Europe to that with which they were familiar when the old Cold War certainties were still in place. Consequently, as well as facing the prospect of a wave of accession applications from EFTA, Commission officials suddenly realized that they could be facing a similar onslaught from the East. Finally, while Brussels was struggling to find ways of bringing the fledgling East European democracies into the Community's orbit, Third World countries began to express fears that their meagre amounts of aid and assistance would dry up as financial resources were increasingly diverted to provide support for Eastern Europe and the Soviet Union.

A Fortress Europe

Complete and effective implementation of the internal market programme will have a number of profound implications for the global economy and for the Community's world-wide trading partners. The gradual
removal of Europe's internal barriers to trade will create the single largest
advanced industrial market in the world. An integrated European economy could act as a major stimulus to world trade or it could become a
major obstacle in the path of such expansion. Decisions about who has
access to this market, and on what terms, will affect millions of people,
from the humble banana producers of the Caribbean to the giant trading
houses of the Far East, all of whom depend on a healthy and expanding
trading relationship with the European Community for their livelihoods.

The ink on the Internal Market White Paper was barely dry before
some observers had begun to complain. The European Commission
found itself accused of turning its back on the world by planning to
increase trade between the member states at the expense of business with
their traditional trading partners, and of scheming to restrict access to
the internal market to only those countries that granted the Community
reciprocal access to their own domestic markets in return.

From Australia to Latin America and Japan to the United States, many
were alarmed at the prospect that, as Europe's internal barriers began to
crumble, they would be replaced by a unified external one designed to
limit the benefits of the internal market to a new 'Fortress Europe'. Business executives began to express anxieties that, once the external barrier
was in place, the Community would have the power to dictate who
should be let in and who should be kept out.

These fears were increased by a series of articles in some of the world's
leading business publications predicting the worst. In May 1988 the
influential Hong Kong-based *Far Eastern Economic Review* ran as its cover
story an eight-page account of how Europe was preparing to steal the
initiative from the dynamic, newly industrialized countries of the Pacific
Rim, and bring the centre of gravity of international trade back to the
Old World. Warnings that 'the Fortress Europe of such simple protectionism as national quotas could give way to a complex citadel of Europrotec-
tionism, enshrined in Community-wide quotas, a generally stiffer trade
policy, and less liberal policies towards outside investment' almost
seemed calculated to confirm the international business community's
worst fears.

At the same time, the European edition of the *Wall Street Journal*—
published just as the controversial trade bill with protectionist clauses
was passing through the US Congress—predicted that the next frontier
of protectionism would be found emerging from the borders of Europe.
It insisted that the combination of the EC's historical record, especially
the Common Agricultural Policy, which it called 'a black hole of protec-

tionism', and the growing pressure from European car manufacturers, financial institutions and other industrial sectors for Community help in the face of external competition would turn the internal market programme into one of the most restrictive initiatives ever implemented by a regional trading group, precipitating a new and vicious round of trans-Atlantic trade wars.

Much influential US opinion concedes that the European Commission, along with the General Agreement on Tariffs and Trade (GATT), is one of the leading advocates of free trade in the international community yet remains convinced that, without any legislative power of its own, the Commission would soon fall victim of the protectionist instincts of member states. However, US attitudes to 1992 are by no means uniform. For the giant corporations like IBM and Caterpillar, who have regular access to the Commission, the internal market programme is seen as a great opportunity. For the small and medium-sized exporting companies, whose access to information about the Commission's activities is considerably more limited, the fear of being excluded from the internal market is very real. Such anxieties have undoubtedly been increased by political rhetoric and alarmist newspaper reports, such as that in the *Wall Street Journal*, which reminded its readers that 'Protectionism is as much a part of the European business climate as the three-hour lunch'.

A new strategy for external trade

Much of the blame for such visions can be attributed to the Commission. The Internal Market White Paper failed to address itself adequately to the vital issue of the external implications of the 1992 programme. The whole question was neatly averted with a passing reference to the necessity of replacing the separate national import policies with unspecified 'temporary measures'.

Under Article 115 of the Treaty of Rome, member states are granted the right to impose quantitative restrictions against each other on imports from third countries. They are also empowered to inspect intra-Community trade in order to establish the origin of a given import, and thereby prevent what is known as trade deflection, the ability of external exporters to gain access to the protected market of one member state via the unprotected market of another.

However, a central part of the internal market programme is the abolition of frontier controls, and as Article 115 relies on these to monitor intra-Community trade from third countries, it will have to be gradually phased out. The White Paper, however, gave no indication of how the Commission intended to deal with the problem posed by the different policies member states have adopted towards third-country imports. Will the restrictions on, for example, imports of cars adopted by one member state (whether through quotas, tariffs or voluntary export restraints) have to be adopted by every other member state? Will the member state in question have to abolish its national restriction and bring it into line with everybody else? Or will there be some sort of compromise between the two extremes? If so, what will be the level and nature of Community protectionism on 1 January 1993?

These were the kinds of questions being asked by the international business community when the Commission began to give the first indications of the strategy on external trade that it was in the process of evolving. In his various addresses, Willy de Clercq, then Commissioner for External Relations, began to make much use of the word 'reciprocity', indicating that external trade relations were to be based on the principle 'You scratch my back and I'll scratch yours'. On one occasion de Clercq said bluntly, 'If our partners want to take advantage of our integration, and profit from the dynamism it will create, they will have to co-operate with this effort and be determined to open up their markets on equivalent terms', effectively confirming the worst suspicions of business executives around the world. In a keynote speech in London in July 1988 de Clercq attempted to dispel some of the fears prompted by his earlier comments.

> The Community is already the world's largest trading partner. Our exports of manufactured goods represent 26% of those of the OECD countries, compared with 14% for the United States, and 17% for Japan. Our share of world exports of services is even greater. As a result, we have a vital interest in the maintenance of a worldwide liberal trading system.

Having reaffirmed the Community's commitment to an open trading system, de Clercq then went on to outline three principles that would guide the Commission's external trade policy in the run-up to 1992 in practice. In the first place, he acknowledged that the internal market programme would automatically lead to the reinforcement of the external identity of the EC as a result of the phasing out of Article 115. However, he insisted that the Community would adhere to its commitments under the current round of trade-liberalization talks being held in Geneva under the auspices of the GATT not to introduce any new protectionist barriers.

He also made it clear that as the GATT does not yet cover trade in services, the Community saw no reason why the benefits of internal liberalization 'should be extended unilaterally to third countries'. Asked what this meant in concrete terms, the Commissioner illustrated the point by saying that any American or Japanese bank already resident in one member state would not be allowed to expand into other member states, unless Community banks were granted the same privileges in return. Britain was especially unhappy about the use of reciprocity as a means of securing access to foreign markets, as this was likely to invite retaliation which could harm British interests, particularly in the financial services sector. In August 1988 Sir Nicholas Goodison, the former chairman of the London Stock Exchange, expressed Britain's fears by warning the Commission that any attempt to put a 'ring fence' around European financial markets would 'lull Europeans into a false sense of security'.

Finally, de Clercq confirmed that the wide divergence between the import arrangements of the 12 member states would have to be eliminated. In most cases, import restrictions could be abolished without difficulty. However, he insisted there were a number of 'hard-core cases' where abolition would cause considerable hardship in some member states, and that national protective measures would have to be replaced by 'appropriate measures at Community level' for a transitionary period.

Shortly thereafter, the Commission gave the first indication of its plans for one of these so-called hard-core cases. These call for the complete abolition of all the fiscal and technical regulations fragmenting the European car industry and a severe restriction on state subsidies. The Commission also proposed to replace the quantitative restraints imposed on Japanese car exports by Britain, France, Italy, Spain and Portugal by a Community-wide ceiling of one million units per annum until 1992, in order to give European manufacturers time to adjust to the new climate of international competition. The Commission maintained that this is the only way that member states could be cured of their addiction to quantitative restrictions in the car sector.

The proposal represented a compromise between the two extremes of outright abolition and permanent Community quotas outlined above, and was even seen by some as the model solution for all other divergent national import arrangements. But the question of what level of access to grant Japanese car exporters proved to be so politically sensitive between those favouring a high degree of protection and those in support of a more liberal import system that the Commission was forced to postpone repeatedly the publication of the Community's strategy towards Japanese car imports.

In December 1989, and in the face of repeated demands from European car producers, the Commission finally agreed that a transitionary period would be needed to protect EC car manufacturers after 1992, and that this should take the form of a voluntary export restraint (VER). The following February, Japan let it be known that it would accept VERs, much to the Commission's relief. Japan's Ministry of International Trade and Industry (MITI) urged Japanese car manufacturers not to increase sales to the Community, though made clear that such arrangements would no longer be acceptable at the turn of the century. When the details of the deal were published in August, Japanese officials were clearly unhappy about the length of the transitionary period, although relieved that Japanese car production in Britain and Spain (known as transplants) could circulate freely around the Community. France and

Italy, however, continued to insist that the Commission had given too much away.

In many respects, the conflict over Japanese car exports, and the level of protection demanded by some European producers after 1992, highlighted one of the central dilemmas faced by the internal market programme. While the Commission was eager to reduce the level of protection in order to increase the Community's long-term competitiveness, countries like France and Italy were deeply alarmed at the industrial restructuring and large-scale job losses that such a policy entailed. In July 1991 Raymond Levy, the chairman of Renault, warned that the European car industry would have to shed 'several hundred-thousand' jobs in order to fend off the competition from Japan, and few politicians could ignore the electoral consequences of job losses on such a scale. But the alternative to industrial restructuring was to maintain obsolete high-cost plants with large public subsidies. Hitherto, protectionism has rarely encouraged manufacturers to become more competitive, and considerable sums have been squandered in the process.

Despite his protestations to the contrary, in the eyes of many critics de Clercq's three principles collectively constitute a violation of the spirit of the GATT. That system, which has been struggling to overcome the increase in protectionism throughout the world, is based on the principles of non-discrimination and multilateralism. By contrast, the de Clercq system of international trade asserts its commitment to multilateralism where possible, but makes no attempt to hide its readiness to revert to discrimination and bilateralism where necessary. Admittedly, the GATT does not yet cover trade in services, but the willingness of the world's largest trading bloc to show its strength in a pursuit of its own self-interest does not bode well for the future of an international trading system, already under severe strain from the increasing temptation of nation states to resort to bilateral solutions to trade difficulties.

The main reason the Internal Market White Paper had not dealt effectively with the problems posed by the strengthening of the Community's external identity was that it was an entirely new area of Community competence, in which definitive policies are still in the process of being formulated. In September 1988, however, EC external relations policy underwent a major transformation following a ruling by the European Court of Justice, which conferred on the European Commission the right to take legal action and impose fines on non-Community companies that violated EC competition laws.

The decision was the first to grant the Community powers in the highly sensitive area of extra-territorial jurisdiction, and was seen by legal experts as one of the most important rulings by the Luxembourg-based court—effectively granting the Community global jurisdiction. The ruling followed an appeal by a group of wood-pulp producers from the United

States, Canada and Finland against punitive price-fixing fines levied on their exports to Community manufacturers in 1984.

The producers (most of whom are based outside the EC) initiated legal proceedings against the Commission on the grounds that it had no authority to interfere in the activities of companies operating outside the EC. In a preliminary ruling earlier in the year, the court said that the Commission did have the power to take action against non-EC companies engaged in price-fixing or market-sharing conspiracies if it believed that 'free competition within the Community would be affected'. The ruling was based on the highly controversial US 'effects doctrine', granting American authorities the power to regulate foreign companies whose activities outside the United States have a damaging impact on domestic ones.

However, in what legal experts interpreted as an attempt to avoid the potentially divisive issue of infringing the sovereignty of other nation states the final judgment made no reference to the so-called effects doctrine. Instead, the court based its decision on the consequences of external activities inside the Community, arguing that 'the decisive factor is the place where the agreement is implemented'. The court found that 'where wood pulp producers sell directly to the Community and engage in price competition in order to win orders from those customers, that constitutes competition within the common market'.

At the time, observers acknowledged that the distinction between price-fixing agreements and their place of implementation was little more than a legal fiction, but it did enable the court to avoid dealing with the effects doctrine. Morever, the implications of the decision were far-reaching, as the Commission can now exercise jurisdiction over the supply of all raw materials to the EC.

Europe and the Uruguay Round

When the eighth round of international trade-liberalization talks were inaugurated in Punta del Este, Uruguay, in 1986, few observers expected them to be completed by the time the four-year negotiating timetable expired. Indeed, given the nature, complexity and range of conflicts involved in global trade, most analysts were astonished that they had begun at all. Under the auspices of the GATT the so-called Uruguay Round was initiated by President Ronald Reagan in an effort to inhibit growing protectionist pressures in Congress, to extend the global trade rules to new areas such as services and to reverse what has become known as the 'new protectionism', the increasing tendency of countries to take refuge from foreign competition in an elaborate series of semi-permanent non-tariff barriers such as voluntary export restraints—a technique often referred to as 'managed trade'.

The GATT (a specialized agency of the UN, based in Geneva) had come into being in 1948 in an effort to prevent a repetition of the growth of protectionism in the 1920s and 1930s that had contributed to the Great Depression and to build up an international momentum in support of the principles of free trade. The GATT, the nearest the world has to a legal framework for international trade, is based on the two core principles of reciprocity and non-discrimination. In essence, the trade rules require that what you do for one country you must do for all others at the same time. Consequently, if country X decides to reduce its tariff barriers for a specific product for country Y, then that bilateral agreement must also be applied to every other country in the international trading system, a practice known as the most favoured nation (MFN) principle or multilateralism.

During the 1950s and 1960s much of the GATT's efforts were spent on eliminating export quotas. The so-called Kennedy Round of GATT negotiations launched in 1962, for example, was designed to prevent the introduction of the EC's new external tariff from provoking a global increase in protectionism. However, in the face of falling rates of economic growth, rising unemployment and intense domestic pressures to protect indigenous industries from foreign competition, the 1970s and 1980s witnessed an alarming increase in the growth of non-tariff barriers and a tendency to abandon the MFN principle in favour of bilateral trade accords. In addition to arresting these tendencies, the Uruguay Round also set itself the ambitious task of extending the GATT rules to trade in agriculture, textiles, services and intellectual property rights—all hitherto beyond the reach of the multilateral trading system. But if the developing economies were to make concessions granting the developed economies access to their potentially multi-billion pound markets in, for example, financial services, the developed economies would also have to make concessions—particularly in the field of agriculture, where the cost of global protection in the form of production and export subsidies was running in excess of £100 billion a year. It was evident from the outset, therefore, that powerful vested interests were at stake, and that the negotiations were going to be difficult at best and acrimonious at worst.

For most of the Uruguay Round's four-year negotiating period little was heard of the talks. But in October 1990 an apparently intractable conflict within the EC over agricultural reform propelled the issue into the headlines and cast a shadow over the prospects for the Uruguay talks and the future of the global multilateral trading regime itself. In the face of demands from the United States and the Cairns Group (an organization made up of 14 leading agricultural exporters, including Australia, New Zealand, Canada, Argentina, Brazil, Chile and Indonesia) for a 75% cut in domestic production subsidies and a 90% cut in export subsidies, the Community was torn between the advocates and the opponents of reform. Ray MacSharry, the new Commissioner for agriculture, had proposed a 30% cut in production subsidies, which was instantly rejected by Germany, France and Ireland. Moreover, the United States and the

Cairns Group refused to entertain MacSharry's 30% offer as a serious proposition and denounced the failure to address the question of export subsidies, leaving the Commission to face mounting domestic and international criticism.

By November, Arthur Dunkel, the chain-smoking multi-lingual director of the GATT, had alarmed everyone by alleging that the EC's intransigence was threatening the future of the world trading system. The EC finally overcame its internal deadlock in the same month, after no less than seven meetings between agricultural ministers, in which Germany, France and Ireland accepted the Commission's 30% cuts package. But the agreement did little to appease the Community's foreign critics. During a tour of EC capitals, Clayton Yeutter, the US agriculture secretary, warned of the 'high political price to be paid by the Community' if the talks failed. 'If the reform that is achievable is the amount encompassed in the EC proposal, then it simply isn't worth it. I'd rather simply forget the whole thing and go about protecting our interests in our own way,' he said defiantly.

As more than 100 GATT delegations arrived in Brussels for the Uruguay Round's 'final' set of talks in December, an estimated 30,000 farmers from all over the world demonstrated their opposition to the proposed subsidy reductions on the streets of Brussels. Police fired tear gas and used water cannon to disperse protesters who had burnt tyres and ripped up traffic lights. From their perspective at least, the outcome of the Brussels talks was a victory, albeit a hollow one. Because EC governments refused to sacrifice the interests of its 10 million farmers, the Uruguay Round, the largest and most ambitious negotiation ever undertaken by a group of sovereign states, was postponed indefinitely. The United States promptly announced its intention to impose 200% punitive levies on a range of EC agricultural exports. The Commission, deeply embarrassed at being held responsible for the collapse of the talks, tried to talk up its free trade credentials by emphasizing its support for liberalizing services, which the United States had originally opposed. Meanwhile, trade experts warned of the potentially catastrophic consequences if the multilateral trading system was replaced by a series of semi-autarkic trading blocs, and Arthur Dunkel was left to find a way of salvaging something from the wreckage.

While the EC continued to insist that 90% cuts in export subsidies and 75% cuts in production subsidies were unrealistic, the US administration's fast-track authority (the procedure by which Congress waived its right to amend the GATT treaty when it was finally ready to be submitted for approval) was due to expire in March 1991. Without this authority, Congress would tear the trade treaty to shreds, thereby undermining the prospects for ratification in other countries. But there was little point in obtaining an extension of the fast-track procedure if the trade talks remained deadlocked over agricultural reform. That impasse was overcome in February 1991, when Dunkel managed to talk the Community into accepting 'binding commitments' to reduce production and export subsidies and improve market access, which enabled President Bush to secure a two-year extension of his negotiating authority.

Nonetheless, transatlantic relations continued to deteriorate over the agriculture issue, with US and EC trade negotiators frequently unable to bring themselves to speak to each other. In a fit of exasperation in May, Dunkel hit out at both sides, saying that US–EC relations were 'bedevilled by accusations, self-righteousness, mutual misunderstanding and an inability to distinguish between special-interest pleading and the public good'. It is a sterile procedure, he insisted, 'for the main trading nations to throw figures backwards and forwards, as if merely winning the numbers argument somehow supplies an answer to the real challenges of the Uruguay Round'. Addressing his criticisms directly to Washington and Brussels, Dunkel added: 'Let us be in no doubt, the days of passing the buck all around the globe as a means of avoiding the crucial political challenges in trade policies are long gone'.

Despite pleas from the OECD in June and the leaders of the Group of Seven industrial nations in July to put completion of the GATT talks at the top of the international diplomatic agenda, farm subsidies remained the make-or-break issue. MacSharry's 30% cuts were adopted by the Commission in July. The scheme called for the deepest price cuts in agricultural support ever contemplated by the Commission, coupled with full compensation for small farmers, and scaled compensation for larger farmers taking land out of production. Although designed to end the 20% over-production of agricultural produce in the EC and abolish export subsidies, Britain, which had long campaigned against the more blatant absurdities of the CAP, found itself in the awkward position of opposing the reforms because they would cost more to implement and would discriminate against the larger, more efficient farms. Responding to the Commission's proposals, John Gummer, Britain's Agriculture Minister, said: 'We oppose them, we hate them, and we consider them dead'. In short, Britain feared that the reforms would 'maintain in perpetuity a peasant society'.

By November, the GATT talks passed another deadline, and still no resolution of the conflict between Washington and Brussels was in sight. Even more alarming was the growing feeling in the US that perhaps it was time to abandon the multilateral trading system and concentrate on building the North American Free Trade Agreement between the US, Canada and Mexico. A new deadline was set for December, and trade negotiators betrayed a rare hint of optimism after the US moderated its demands for cuts in agricultural subsidies and Germany showed the first signs of abandoning France in its opposition to reform. Dunkel drew up another compromise document, known as the 'final act', calling on both the US and the EC to make further concessions. But December passed without agreement, and with it, commentators feared, the last chance of a rapid breakthrough, especially as President Bush's fast-track mandate would run out in the spring. As 1992 progressed, America would become increasingly preoccupied with the US presidential election, while the EC concentrated on completing the internal market and choosing a new Commission. Few 'wanted the trade talks to collapse or to be postponed, but with Washington and Brussels increasingly focusing on internal matters, the omens were not good. A breakthrough was likely, however, only if the draft compromise was improved, thereby giving the US and Europe some face saving concessions.

The European Free Trade Association

Few countries outside the European Community have been forced to think harder about the external implications of the internal market programme than the six-member EFTA. Formed in 1960, following ratification of the Stockholm Convention the previous year, EFTA was basically a reaction to the creation of the EC three years before. The EC and EFTA reflected the two conflicting visions of Europe's future which were fighting for ideological ascendancy in the immediate post-war period. The first saw Europe moving in the direction of economic and political union, with supranational institutions in a federation of states, while the second had the more modest ambition of creating a loose commercial association, thereby enabling its members to preserve their traditional economic relations with other parts of the world.

Despite initial rivalry and suspicion, each survived to become the other's most important trading partner. Following the implementation of the 1972–3 free trade agreements between the two trading blocs, the volume of two-way trade flourished. In 1986, 25% of EC exports went to EFTA countries (more than the Community's exports to the United States or Japan) while 50% of EFTA exports went to the EC. Overall trade was valued at £120 billion. All seemed rosy—until the Commission published the internal market White Paper. Now, the Community's drive for economic integration by 1992 could mean the end of EFTA.

Composed of six small but highly industrialized countries—Austria, Finland, Iceland, Norway, Sweden and Switzerland—EFTA has been struggling to define its identity in relation to its larger and more powerful regional neighbour before the 1992 deadline expires. Will EFTA be allowed to preserve intact its privileged access to the Community's internal market? If so, will the member states be prepared to enact the same legislative programme of physical, technical and fiscal harmonization measures being implemented by the EC in order to be able to avail themselves of the Community's largesse? If not, will the organization break up as some or all of its members join in the headlong 'rush for Brussels'?

Prior to the publication of the White Paper, the two halves of Western

Europe had already been moving in the direction of increased economic co-operation. At the first ministerial meeting between the two groups in Luxembourg in April 1984 they announced their intention to create by the 1990s a 'European Economic Space', made up of all 18 nations. The most tangible expression of this rather vague rhetoric to date was the inclusion of EFTA in the Community's Single Administrative Document arrangement for simplifying the amount of documentation required for the cross-frontier transportation of goods, due to be phased out at the beginning of 1993.

At the first ministerial meeting between the two organizations since the announcement of the White Paper programme, held in Brussels in February 1988, the two groups reaffirmed their commitment towards the creation of a common economic space, later renamed the European Economic Area (EEA) so as not to imply a *'vacuum'*, and identified a number of areas for further co-operation, including common rules for technical standards, rules of origin and greater openness in the field of public procurement and state aids. However, by the time de Clercq met EFTA ministers in Tampere in June it was already clear that the Community was determined to impose strict limits on the extent to which EFTA could benefit from the creation of the internal market.

De Clercq, with a remarkable tendency for formulating principles in batches of three, enunciated another set of guidelines around which the Community's relations with EFTA would be organized:

1 Priority to internal market considerations over EFTA at all times;
2 The preservation of EC sovereignty to make decisions regardless of the extent of co-operation with EFTA; and
3 The maintenance of a balance of advantages and obligations between the two groups in any agreements made between them.

In addition, de Clercq told the EFTA nations that they must recognize 'that there is a difference between the European Economic Area [EEA] and the internal market, and only member states can expect to participate fully in the internal market'.

De Clercq's three principles may well have come as a shock to EFTA members, but the indications had been obvious for some time. Like most organizations, the Community's resources of time and manpower are limited, and any endeavour to incorporate EFTA into the internal market programme would divide the Community's attention from the primary task in hand. Equally, EFTA was free to mirror Community harmonization legislation if it so wished, but having done so it could not then expect to veto or influence any subsequent decision by the Community to alter or amend any part of the programme in any way it saw fit.

Finally, the Community insisted that it was entitled to benefit as much as EFTA from any closer association between the two trading blocs. This particular issue had already become the source of considerable friction within the Community. A number of the southern member states, anxious that they would not be able to compete with the more advanced economies of EFTA, had complained bitterly about the Commission's granting favours to rich non-member states instead of doing more to help the poorer member states. Spain, particularly, accused EFTA of seeking a free ride on the EC by wanting preferential access to the benefits of the internal market while remaining free of the financial burdens imposed on member states, such as the cost of the CAP. Indeed, this feeling is so strong that British Conservative MEPs openly refer to EFTA as EFRA—the European Free Ride Association.

Consideration has been given to the possibility of EFTA making financial contributions to regional development in the Community's poorer regions by way of compensation for the privileges of access to the internal market. Much of the controversy has since been taken out of this issue following the decision by the Council of Ministers during the February summit meeting in Brussels to double the structural funds to some £9 billion by 1993, most of which will go to the poorer member states.

The idea of paying a premium to the Community in exchange for certain privileges neatly encapsulates many of the dilemmas faced by EFTA nations in the run-up to 1992. Because of its determination to preserve its sovereignty over decision making the Community could not permit EFTA to say how the money was spent. However, ceding the power of decision making to Brussels represents a fundamental loss of sovereignty, far more serious than anything sustained by members of the Community—who at least play a part in the decision-making process. Such problems have already caused a debate in many EFTA member states (particularly Austria, which formally applied for membership in July 1989, and Norway, which is expected to follow suit in the near future) about the possibility of accession to the EC. However, while the Community could not possibly embark on yet another round of accession negotiations prior to 1992, it has accepted EFTA's initiative, announced after its summit meeting at Oslo in March 1989, to improve economic and institutional ties between the two blocs.

In November, Frans Andriessen, the new External Relations Commissioner, announced plans for a new round of EC–EFTA talks, designed to create a "common economic space" between all 18 countries, thereby extending the benefits of the single market to the Six without undermining the autonomy of existing EC institutions. The talks, which were initially expected to last for a year, began when foreign ministers from all 18 countries met to discuss the creation of new institutional relationships between the two organizations. The aim was to establish rules for allowing goods, capital, services and labour (collectively known as the four freedoms) to circulate freely around the combined market of some

380 million people without compromising the sovereignty of either organization. Because the Community's negotiating mandate prohibited the Commission from diluting the EC's decision-making autonomy, Brussels came up with the novel idea of creating special consultation bodies which would allow EFTA to 'shape but not make' Community decisions. But by the summer of 1990, serious disagreements had broken out between the two bodies, principally because of EFTA's desire to acquire some form of joint decision-making and its reluctance to be subjected to EC competition policy. The impasse raised the spectre of a collapse in the talks and a spate of unwanted accession applications. At the same time, a report published in August by the House of Commons Trade and Industry Committee called on the government to support the eventual entry of all EFTA countries into the Community, and dismissed the EEA negotiations as an 'unsatisfactory alternative'.

Although by May 1991 Commission officials had given a pledge to allow EFTA to follow its own trade policies towards the outside world after 1992, there was a widespread feeling that the EC–EFTA negotiations were about to collapse as EFTA members began to reconsider their earlier opposition to full EC membership. The EEA talks had been designed to forestall EFTA accession applications while the Community concentrated on completing the internal market. Now the EEA was being increasingly seen as a step towards full membership, and an unsatisfactory one at that. The EEA would not create a full customs union between the EC and EFTA, while EFTA states would only be allowed a say and not a vote in EC decisions. Understandably, Austria, Sweden, Switzerland and Norway, had begun to ask themselves what was the point—why not wait until the internal market was completed and apply for full membership?

Nonetheless, the EEA talks proved to be a constructive forum in the attempt to clarify a trio of issues which continued to cause friction between the two trading blocks, known as the 'cash, cod and trucks' disputes, which, in any case, would have to be settled before full EC membership could be agreed. Spain and Portugal were still arguing for additional economic assistance from EFTA in the form of soft loans and grants in exchange for access to the internal market, the Community wanted access to Nordic fishing grounds and Brussels was eager to negotiate transit rights for EC trucks traversing Austria and Switzerland. Although progress on these issues was slow, it no longer seemed beyond reach. Moreover, the vexed question of how to give EFTA a say in EC affairs without compromising the Community's decision-making authority was resolved in May, when the two agreed to create a new EEA panel, made up of five EC and two EFTA judges, who would be responsible for passing judgments on breaches of EEA rules. By now, however, the Commission's original goal of forestalling a wave of EFTA accessions seemed less important than laying the groundwork for further enlargement.

The final breakthrough came in October, after a marathon 16-hour negotiating session in Luxembourg, when foreign ministers from the two trading blocs signed the agreement creating the 18- (19, including Lichtenstein) nation European Economic Area, the largest internal market in the world, stretching from the Arctic to the Mediterranean. When the new agreement comes into effect in January 1993 it will bring into being an internal market of 380 million people, accounting for 40% of world trade. The breakthrough was reached after EFTA states made a series of key concessions. All EFTA members accepted demands from the EC's southern states for substantial economic assistance in the form of soft loans and grants; Switzerland and Austria conceded an increase in the number and weight of EC lorries crossing their frontiers; Norway granted increased access to its fishing grounds for British fishermen. In return for a commitment to adopt all EC single market legislation, EFTA countries were given unimpeded access to all aspects of the internal market. The agreement is expected to lead to a substantial increase in trade between the two organizations. Further, Britain's banks and insurance companies are expected to benefit substantially from the EEA, as they will now be granted access to EFTA's lucrative financial services sector. EFTA will not be able to participate in the EC's decision-making process until after accession (expected some time in the 1990s). Nonetheless, as far as trade in goods, services, capital and labour are concerned, 'they are in' as Frans Andreissen, the External Relations Commissioner, said.

The United States and the EC

Most American business executives, accustomed to thinking about the EC in terms of Eurosclerosis (a wasting disease attributable to endemic labour rigidities, rampant protectionism, an elemental fear of competition and, of course, the proverbial three-hour lunch) have been caught off-guard by the Community's version of *perestroika*. The initial reaction to the internal market programme was one of profound scepticism, but that has since given way to the conviction that the EC is in the process of erecting a giant industrial version of the CAP.

It took the US Administration over three years to make its first official response to the Community's internal market programme. That reaction finally came in August 1988, in an address given by Peter McPherson, a deputy secretary of the US Treasury Department, to the Institute of International Economics in Washington, DC. McPherson's speech betrayed a deep ambivalence towards the goals of the 1992 programme. On the one hand, he welcomed the Community's new initiative to the extent that it would help to promote economic growth in the EC, increase the demand for US exports and thereby help to reduce the US trade deficit, which had reached a staggering $170 billion in 1987. However, he gave a clear warning that the process of internal liberalization must not succumb to the temptation for greater external protection. If in abolishing the divergent import arrangements of individual member states the Commission opted for a common commercial policy that reflected the demands of its more protectionist members, McPherson left the Community in no doubt that the United States 'would respond'. Turning to the vexed issue of reciprocity, he insisted that any attempt to implement such a policy would provoke a serious deterioration in transatlantic trade relations.

The problem to be resolved lay in the conflicting approaches taken by each trading bloc to external trade. The Community's insistence on reciprocity appeared, on the surface, innocuous—if you grant us access to your market we will grant you access to ours. What could be more equitable? However, it failed to acknowledge that in countries like the United States there are stringent regulations governing interstate trade and commerce. US banks, for example, are not free to operate in any state they choose. The Community's demand for reciprocal treatment would mean revising federal and state banking laws to allow European banks greater privileges than those enjoyed by US ones. Hence the US Administration's insistence on the principle of national treatment, whereby foreign companies are governed by the same rules as domestic companies.

However, while warning the Community that 'the creation of a single market that reserves Europe for the Europeans would be bad for Europe, bad for the United States and bad for the multilateral economic system' McPherson had little to say on the Omnibus Trade Act, just then approved by the US Congress. This grants the President powers to employ sanctions against countries running chronic and persistent trade surpluses with the United States. The EC, for example, had a large $21 billion surplus with the US in 1987, and would seem to be a prime target for US retaliation.

The Trade Act is a clear indication that the United States has decided to take a more aggressive approach to reduce its trade deficits with its major trading partners. However, predictions that the move is the first step in a transatlantic trade war, possibly leading to the dissolution of the Atlantic Alliance, seem to be little more than an exercise in hyperbole. As one senior US official said:

> The US trade bill is nowhere near as onerous as it once was. Similarly, 1992 is not going to turn out to be Armageddon. Trade negotiators are sensible people who are not going to go around slashing each other's wrists. The international trading system is simply too important to sabotage.

Indeed, many Europeans have expressed fears that the large US and

Japanese companies will be the primary beneficiaries of the completion of the internal market. Many US corporations have been operating in Europe for decades (a few for considerably longer), and most are often more at home with the European way of doing things than companies from individual member states. De Clercq, however, has dismissed these fears as groundless, and insisted that:

> There is no *a priori* reason to suppose that the subsidiaries of American or Japanese companies operating in the Community will do better or worse than European-owned companies. Europe will be neither a fortress nor a sieve.

Europeans have yet to be convinced.

Nevertheless, the protectionist debate has continued unabated. By the summer of 1989, mutual recrimination between Washington and Brussels over the issue reached the level of a transatlantic propaganda war. Publication of the US National Trade Estimates Report in May, which singled out the Community for a host of restrictive practices, was matched two days later by the publication of a 41-page report by the Commission accusing the United States of more or less the same thing. However, as Commission officials were quick to point out, while the EC report merely described US protectionist practices, the US report triggered those provisions in the 1988 Trade Act which set in motion potential retaliatory action. But despite continued attempts by the Commission to convince foreign trading partners that the Community will not retreat behind a protectionist wall, many, particularly the United States and Japan, remain profoundly suspicious of Brussels' intentions.

An analysis of EC trade policy, published by the GATT in April 1991, threw light on how it was possible for the Community to be described as a supporter of free trade and protectionism at the same time. The report dismissed the Fortress Europe allegation, and pointed out that there had been no increase in the overall level of EC protection. Nevertheless, the GATT accused Brussels of targeting protection towards certain areas of industrial activity, notably car production, consumer electronics, and agriculture, in which the Community faced strong external competition. Highlighting the contrast between the EC's internal and external trade policies, the report said that Brussels had erected a 'complex hierarchy' of preferential trading agreements which had introduced a 'strong element of discrimination' into the multilateral trading system. The GATT was particularly critical of VERs (on the grounds that they could become permanent) and the extensive use of anti-dumping procedures, and called on the EC to match its internal integration with 'a parallel lifting of its external barriers, and closer adherence to the fundamental principles underlying the multilateral trading system'.

The Commission reacted strongly to the GATT report, and criticized it for being 'unbalanced'. Brussels insisted that temporary bilateral export restraints were permissible under GATT rules, pointed out that it was the largest importer of world food products (50% of which entered the EC duty free) and highlighted its record on imported textiles, which had increased 300% since 1976. The report did little to strengthen the EC's case in its periodic trade skirmishes with Washington. But while US anxieties over the potential threat of EC protectionism remained, the earlier paranoia had all but disappeared. The same could not, however, be said of Tokyo.

Japan and the EC

The US approval of the internal market programme (albeit with reservations) has been echoed by the Community's other major trading partner, Japan. During a major speech at the Mansion House in London in May 1988 Noboru Takeshita, the former Japanese Prime Minister, issued an unprecedented call for the strengthening of relations between Japan and the Community in an effort to remedy what he described as the 'weak link' in the US/EC/Japanese economic triangle. Displaying some of the growing concern in Tokyo over the protectionist tendencies inherent in the internal market programme, Takeshita also said that the Community had a responsibility to maintain an open stance towards the global economy as 1992 approaches.

Takeshita's concerns were more than academic. The EC has registered a series of bilateral trade deficits with Japan in recent years (which exceeded £14 billion in 1987), and the Commission has reacted by persuading the Japanese government to accelerate the opening up of its domestic market to Community imports and by inaugurating a severe restriction on imported components destined for Japanese manufacturing facilities located inside the Community.

Since the integration of the internal market programme the Commission has imposed a series of large anti-dumping duties on Japanese goods, including dot matrix printers, electronic typewriters, photocopiers and electric scales, produced by so-called 'screwdriver plants'. The Commission argues that its action is justified, because Japanese companies are trying to evade the Community's anti-dumping duties on imported finished products by building manufacturing facilities inside the EC and then supplying them with Japanese-made components at low prices.

The GATT rules allow countries to impose anti-dumping duties on products sold at below the cost of production where such action is causing hardship for domestic manufacturers, but the Japanese insist that the Commission has taken no account of the difficulties they face locating reliable Community component suppliers in the period immediately after a new manufacturing facility has been established in a member state. Moreover, the Japanese emphatically deny that they have been importing components at prices below those being charged in the Japanese market in an effort to secure an unfair advantage over Community producers, and appealed to GATT's anti-dumping panel to pass judgment on the legitimacy of the Community's action.

In March 1990, when the GATT finally delivered its judgment, the Commission was thrown into a state of confusion. The GATT disputes panel said that the so-called anti-circumvention duties were inconsistent with international trade, as the levies were not customs duties imposed at border posts but internal taxes, and therefore discriminatory. The decision effectively destroyed the EC's defences against what it regards as unfair competition from Japanese and Asian manufacturers. Brussels insisted that the GATT's anti-dumping procedures were ineffective without anti-circumvention levies, and accused the GATT of failing to address itself to the real problem posed by 'screwdriver plants'.

The issue is likely to remain highly sensitive and politically charged. A number of member states are making great endeavours to obtain Japanese investment to help reduce their levels of unemployment. Britain, particularly, has been competing with some of its Community partners to become Japan's gateway to Europe, and is distinctly unhappy about the way the Commission's anti-dumping policy has developed. Alternatively, many industrialists insist that Japanese 'screwdriver plants' are undermining the foundations of local industry, and are a major contributory factor to the very unemployment problem they purport to resolve.

In October 1988, for example, the French government made public its determination to impose restrictions on exports of the British-made Nissan Bluebird car in order to protect French car makers from Japanese competition. Initially (and unofficially) the Commission indicated that such action would be illegal under the free circulation of goods provisions of Article 30. Although, as a result of intense diplomatic pressure from France, the Commission was forced to 'rephrase' its assessment of the French plan, there seemed little doubt that once France appeared before the European Court of Justice it would be forced to back down. The row was, however, illustrative of the deep reluctance on the part of member states to subject their national industries to increased competition.

Yet if the logic of the internal market programme is to be applied systematically, European industrialists have little option but to adjust to the effects of competition from Japanese companies, or indeed any other foreign competitor. Assuming that Japanese companies are not increasing their penetration of European markets by unfair means, European producers must become equally competitive or accept that they lack any comparative advantage in particular manufacturing sectors, and divert their resources to those areas where they can compete more effectively. In the words of one leading economist, where the Community lacks comparative advantage, protection is costly.

At the end of the European Council meeting in Rhodes in December 1988 the EC issued a communiqué on 'Fortress Europe', in an effort to

convince the United States and Japan that they would not be discriminated against as a result of the abolition of internal barriers to trade. The
communiqué asserted that: 'The internal market will not close in on itself
. . . 1992 Europe will be a partner not a Fortress Europe'. Mrs Thatcher
had argued for a reference to the internal market programme serving as
a model for the rest of the world in the interests of free trade, thereby
thwarting attempts by Mitterrand and Gonzalez to give greater prominence to the concept of reciprocity. However, there could be little doubt
that the communiqué was as much a reminder to EC member states of
the Community's commitment to free trade as an attempt to appease
Europe's major trading partners.

Tensions between the free trade and protectionist wings of the Community, particularly over Japanese imports, continue to sour relations
between Brussels and Tokyo. In May 1991, Edith Cresson, the French
Prime Minister, made matters worse by launching a new tirade against
the Japanese, describing them as 'ants'. The outburst followed Cresson's
earlier calls for the EC to rally to the defence of Europe's car and electronics industries by providing itself with a new industrial policy. But
her attempts to bully the Commission into adopting a more protectionist
disposition towards Japan were to no avail, while her choice of words
did little to improve the tenor of EC–Japanese relations or contribute
towards a resolution of the complex trade tensions between them.

The Soviet Union, Eastern Europe and the EC

The Community's drive for economic integration, allied to EFTA's determination to ensure that it was not excluded from the benefits integration
would bring, have been complemented by the opening up of a new
chapter in relations between Brussels, Eastern Europe and the Soviet
Union. The process began in a modest way at a ceremony in Luxembourg
in June 1988, when the EC and the Soviet-led trading bloc, Comecon,
signed a declaration of 'mutual recognition', thus ending almost 30 years
of unremitting enmity between the two. Although described by Lord
Plumb, the former President of the European Parliament, as 'destined to
change the map of Europe', it was soon overshadowed by a series of
developments in Eastern Europe and the Soviet Union that really were
to open up the prospect of a Europe from the Atlantic to the Urals.

President Gorbachov's ascent to power in 1985 is widely acknowledged as the catalyst which liberated Eastern Europe from four decades
of Communist rule, thus paving the way for increased co-operation
between the two formerly estranged halves of Europe. But how this process was to be managed presented decision-makers in Brussels with a
host of new challenges. The rapid pace of the democratization process
in Eastern Europe (particularly the tearing down of the Berlin Wall in
November 1989) provoked an anguished debate over whether it was
possible to reconcile the Community's attempts to 'deepen' the relation-

ships between existing member states with the growing desire to 'broaden' its relationship with the new East European democracies.

At the beginning of 1990, while Comecon members were negotiating the demise of the state trading organizations, the EC started to focus its attention on the so-called second generation of trade agreements with Eastern European countries, designed to introduce real pricing, currency convertibility and recognition of private ownership, and to prevent a wave of premature accession applications. Discussions also began on how to provide the Soviet Union with the short- and long-term economic assistance needed to accelerate economic and political reforms. Both sets of negotiations were conducted against a background of sporadic demonstrations over price rises, which highlighted the vulnerability of former command economies and their fledgling democratic governments attempting to make the transition to a free-market system.

The creation of the European Bank for Reconstruction and Development, based in London, and an increase in funds for the European Investment Bank, based in Luxembourg, were a first step towards providing the urgent funds to finance long-term investment needs and short-term consumption aspirations. However, the funds available were a drop in the ocean compared to what many economists predicted would be needed to help the economies of Eastern Europe and the Soviet Union during the difficult transition from command to market economies. In addition, there was a clear reluctance on the part of some advanced economies to become involved with large-scale macro-economic adjustment programmes in the Soviet Union, which the United States and Britain in particular felt would be better left to the IMF and the World Bank (WB), after there had been more progress with economic reform.

Washington and London's opposition to Moscow's application for full membership of the IMF and WB in July 1991 was motivated not out of any residue of hostility towards the Soviet Union, as some critics maintained, but because of a fear that scarce financial resources would be squandered in supporting an obsolete economic system. Besides, full membership requires the disclosure of gold and foreign currency reserves and a wealth of statistical information about economic performance which, because of the breakdown of the old centrally planned economy, the Soviet Union was hardly in a position to provide. Nevertheless, after the abortive hard-line Communist coup in August 1991 there was a widespread feeling that something more should be done. Western businesses were clearly elated by the collapse of the coup but few felt secure enough to rush in with proposals for new joint ventures. Business conditions had deteriorated alarmingly before the coup, and many expected that it would be many years before any recovery would be in sight. Although East–West joint ventures had increased from 23 in 1987 to 3,000 by 1991, they still accounted for a miniscule portion of Soviet economic activity.

The attempted coup certainly provoked the European Commission into urging EC governments to embrace a more flexible attitude towards the new association agreements with Eastern European countries. Talks on the second-generation association agreements with Hungary, Poland and Czechoslovakia had become embroiled in a series of narrow disputes over accepting their coal, steel, textile and agricultural exports. In September, the Commission proposed an extension of the Community's relationship with the Eastern European democracies, including trade concessions to conclude the association talks with Hungary, Poland and Czechoslovakia, the extension of associate status to Romania and Bulgaria, and the opening of trade talks with Albania and the newly independent Baltic states. After much wrangling, the new association agreements with Czechoslovakia, Hungary and Poland were signed in December. But the difficulty in arriving at an agreement caused considerable resentment in Prague, Budapest and Warsaw over the apparent contradiction between the EC's enthusiastic support for political and economic reforms and its reluctance to back them up with increased access to its markets.

In addition, Frans Andreissen forecast that the wave of accession applications anticipated from EFTA and Eastern Europe would force the Community to convene yet another intergovernmental conference, probably some time in the mid-1990s, in order to overhaul the institutional structure of the EC before enlargement could take place. Otherwise, the Community would face the impossible task of trying to make decisions with up to 24 member states, 30 Commissioners and 1,200 MEPs. 'It is quite clear that the present institutional structure is not conceived for a Community of 24 members or more,' he said. Revolution in Eastern Europe had, therefore, brought the Community to the crossroads between deepening and widening, making it difficult to proceed with the former without at least taking into consideration the consequences of the latter. Meanwhile, John Major urged his Community partners to agree to full EC membership for the Eastern European countries and the Baltic Republics 'as soon as they are ready, politically and economically'. Admittedly, that might not be for many years, but the recommendation held out the prospect of slowing the more federalist impulses of some of the other EC member states.

The decision in October to grant the Soviet Union associate membership of the IMF may have fallen far short of Gorbachov's original request. But it did give the Soviet Union access to some of the world's top advisors on how free-market systems function, and opened the way for the transfer of thousands of Western technical advisors specializing in everything from banking systems to infrastructure projects. Gorbachov's pleas for large-scale direct aid (such as his request for £12 billion in economic assistance made at the end of the G7 summit meeting in London in July) met with less success—despite protests from Germany, France and Italy. The G7 countries were, however, forced to make some provision for helping the Soviet Union to overcome its shortage of foreign currency, which it needed to service its £34 billion external debt. Nevertheless, James Baker, the US Secretary of State, remained determined to adhere to the terms outlined in the G7 meeting, warning that:

> You're not going to see the Soviet Union succeed economically through the mechanism of free cheque writing on the part of others. There have to be fundamental free market reforms.

Money mountains were ruled out, but substantial amounts of short-term emergency aid had been pledged by the United States, Europe and Japan.

An increasing number of critics, however, were beginning to express fears that the approach of the Western industrial democracies was dangerously over cautious. In November, the UN Economic Commission warned that Eastern Europe, and the disintegrating Soviet Union, were spiralling downwards towards a 1930s-type economic depression. Unless far greater levels of economic assistance were forthcoming—at the least along the lines of the Marshall Plan after the Second World War—the East European and Soviet economies would continue to contract, popular support for economic and political reforms would evaporate and the new democratic impulses would be extinguished by a return to authoritarian government. Western attempts to respond effectively to this challenge are likely to become the dominant theme in international relations during the 1990s, the outcome of which will affect relations between east and west into the 21st century.

The Third World and the EC

Under the arrangement known as the Generalized System of Preferences, most developing countries are permitted to export specified amounts of their manufactured products to the EC with a partial or total reduction of customs duties. But the 69 members of the African, Caribbean and Pacific group of nations (or ACP states) are granted quantity-free access for their exports to the Community under the provisions of successive five-year trade accords known as the Lomé Conventions. In contrast to normal trade agreements between developed nations, the Lomé Conventions are not based on the principle of reciprocity, and are therefore regarded by the European Commission as one of the EC's most important mechanisms for promoting economic developments in the Third World.

The origins of the Lomé Conventions stem from an obligation felt by the former colonial powers who now make up the EC to assist their former dependencies. The Fourth Lomé Convention came into being in 1990, and, in contrast to its predecessors each of which ran for a period of five years, the current convention will last until the year 2000. The Lomé Conventions have been the focus of increasing criticism, not least from the recipient countries themselves, who have long regarded the conventions as a modest attempt to provide the ACP countries a guaranteed market for their exports, and so enable them to earn the hard currency needed to reduce the burdens imposed by heavy external debt (estimated to be in excess of $150 billion at the end of 1991). More recently, the conventions have come under heavy criticism from a variety of Western aid groups for failing in their primary objective of promoting economic development.

However, because of the internal market programme, and the necessity of creating a common commercial policy towards third country imports, the negotiations for the Fourth Lomé Convention created great anxiety among the ACP states. Many of these countries have benefited from preferential access to particular EC markets. The Windward Islands, Jamaica and Belize, for example, have been able to export bananas to Britain for decades under extremely favourable terms. Under the new harmonized external trade arrangements, preferential treatment on a national basis will be eliminated. But although the new convention stipulates that 'no ACP state shall be placed . . . in a less favourable position than in the past or present', Britain's Overseas Development Institute (ODI) forecasts a re-direction of trade away from traditional suppliers towards intra-EC trade. In a report published in October 1991 the ODI predicted that the most far-reaching effect on developing countries will be the progressive dismantling of traditional bilateral ties, in which exporters of certain products (notably bananas and fish) are likely to suffer. At the same time, however, exporters of coffee, tea and cocoa are likely to benefit because the harmonization of excise duties will lead to reductions in taxation levels.

The negotiations preceding the signing of Lomé Four (which provides some 12 billion ECUs in aid over the ten-year period) were accompanied by some awkward questions from non-governmental organizations specializing in aid and development. In addition to pointing out that the conventions have failed to improve per capita food production, aid agencies accused the Lomé treaties of confining ACP states to the export of a handful of primary commodities that have kept exports of finished products to the Community at roughly 3% to 4%. Moreover, while the ACP states have failed to diversify their production, nominal increases in aid have been eroded by inflation and population growth. In addition, although the general principles behind the aid programmes are 'progressive', they have been criticized for concentrating on prestige projects (such as building hydroelectric dams) at the expense of providing low-technology solutions which are more likely to improve the quality of life.

Most criticism is, however, reserved for EC food aid programmes, and their relationship with the CAP. Food aid accounts for roughly 33% of all EC development aid, which is spent on wheat, dairy products, rice, sugar and vegetable oil. While few would question the efficacy of emergency or disaster relief, aid agencies argue that the disposal of EC agricultural surpluses simply depresses domestic food prices, and takes away the incentives local farmers need for self-sufficiency. Moreover, the dominance of dairy products in EC food aid shipments (which are high in price but low in volume) have been singled out for reflecting the EC's need to dispose of its surpluses rather than meeting the requirements of food-deficit countries. Without a fundamental reform of the CAP, a re-evaluation of the objectives of EC development aid and a wholesale increase in the number of officials implementing Community aid pro-grammes, aid agencies remain doubtful of the Community's ability to promote genuine development in the Third World.

Checklist of changes

• The abolition of internal barriers to trade will be accompanied by a strengthening of the Community's external identity.
• National import quotas (such as those which currently exist for cars) will be phased out gradually and replaced with EC-wide quotas for a transitionary period.
• There will be increased economic co-operation between the EC and EFTA under the EEA arrangements, although many EFTA countries are likely to submit accession applications after 1993.
• There is likely to be an increase in the number of US and Japanese companies locating themselves in Europe in an attempt to capitalize on the benefits of European economic integration.
• The wave of accession applications from EFTA countries is likely to be followed by a second one of accession applications from East European states, principally from Hungary, Czechoslovakia and Poland.

17 COMMON FOREIGN AND DEFENCE POLICY

Towards a European army?

The question of a common European defence—largely theoretical until a few years ago—has been given added impetus by upheavals both inside and outside Europe requiring a cohesive European response. The Gulf War against Iraq in early 1991 brought British and French forces into a major Middle Eastern conflict alongside the United States, but, at the same time highlighted the fact that a common European approach to defence was still in the early stages. For Euro-sceptics (Mrs Thatcher among them) the Gulf conflict proved that a common European defence was a chimera. Others argued the reverse: that the Gulf War demonstrated how far moves towards a common defence policy needed to be speeded up. The Franco-German proposal for a joint army corps as the nucleus of a future European armed force put common European defence at the top of the agenda at the NATO summit in Rome in November 1991, with Britain criticizing the Franco-German move and arguing that nothing should be done to undermine the existing Atlantic Alliance.

Within Europe, the disintegration of Yugoslavia and its descent into civil war in the course of 1991 also underlined emphatically the urgent need for a common EC foreign and defence policy. Under the Dutch presidency in the second half of 1991, the EC intervened directly in Yugoslavia through diplomatic mediation, while also giving serious consideration for the first time to the formation of an EC peace-keeping (or even peace-making) force. The chosen instrument was the Western European Union (WEU), to which nine of the twelve EC nations belong, and which had, in any case, been gradually emerging as the EC's defence arm after years on the sidelines. In the event, given the reservations of Britain and others, the WEU confined itself to the sending of ceasefire monitors. But on several occasions in the summer and autumn of 1991 EC foreign and defence ministers (meeting as the WEU) drew up plans for a force of armed bodyguards to protect the 200 white-clad monitors, with further contingency plans for developing the bodyguards into a peace-keeping operation.

This is a striking development for the EC. Noel Malcolm, in *The Spectator*, saw such moves as the precursor of a European army, 'with jeeps and armoured cars decked out with little dark-blue and gold-star flags'. Hans Dietrich Genscher, the German Foreign Minister, spoke of a European Security Council, with a force of EC 'green berets' to match the 'blue berets' of UN peace-keeping operations.

A European army in fact remains a long way off. Nonetheless, even though three EC countries—Ireland, Denmark and Greece—are not part of the WEU, the WEU has, in effect, become the accepted defence forum of the Community. In the aftermath of the Gulf War and the beginning of conflict in Yugoslavia, in October 1991 Britain and Italy presented a joint paper to EC foreign ministers, accepting that closer political union embraces 'a stronger European defence identity'. Britain proposed a WEU 'European reaction force' for use anywhere in the world where 'the interests of WEU members or peace-keeping operations are threatened'.

Roots of a common European defence

As with other aspects of European unity, the trend towards a common defence can be traced to the Single European Act. This provided the germ for a common security policy. 'Security' is a wider and more political term than the purely military concerns of 'defence'—but the two concepts overlap, and, under pressure of events, the distinction has become blurred. At Maastricht, it was agreed that EC foreign and security policy would be dealt with though 'systematic co-operation' between states, rather than through EC institutional mechanisms. On the other hand, the Council of Ministers can agree—by unanimous vote—on the principles of joint action in foreign policy, with the actual implementation of that policy requiring only a majority vote. Some see this as the thin end of a wedge leading to a more integrated foreign and defence policy. Maastricht also agreed that the Western European Union would be 'developed as the defence component of the European Union', although the WEU is also to serve as the means of strengthening the European pillar of the Atlantic alliance, and WEU decisions 'shall not affect the obligations of certain member states to NATO'. The treaty foresees 'the eventual framing of a common defence policy, which might in time lead to common defence'. In January 1992 Delors noted that when that day came, the French nuclear deterrent (he did not mention the British) should be put at the disposal of the EC as a whole. This is unlikely, given national feeling in Britain and France over nuclear deterrence, and the complexities of joint control. A joint nuclear policy would follow anyway from common defence, with shared aims and military strategies. So far the EC seems to share common conventional defence aims, but has a varied approach to conflicts such as the Yugoslav civil war.

A European defence union was attempted (unsuccessfully) in the 1950s, foundering both because of the lack of political union to underpin it and of the complexities involved in combining the differing defence interests and technologies of the European states. There was also the difficulty of reconciling European defence with the functions of NATO. This problem remains, especially as France continues to press for a European defence distinct from NATO and the United States. But it is perhaps becoming less intractable as NATO redefines its role as the Western defence alliance in the wake of the collapse of Communism in Eastern Europe and the dissolution of the Warsaw Pact.

As defence priorities are re-examined, the prospect of sharing military costs through European co-operation in armaments design and manufacture has clear attractions. Even before the crises in Yugoslavia and the Gulf, this trend gained impetus when the Europeans found themselves not consulted by the United States at the time of the 1986 Reykjavik Reagan–Gorbachov summit. Europeans were shocked into taking the question of European defence interests more seriously, despite strong Danish and Irish reservations (because of their traditional neutrality) and a traditional EC reluctance to become involved in defence issues.

The process began as early as October 1987. When EC foreign ministers met for their semi-annual informal get together at the seaside resort of Nyborg in Denmark, one of the top items on the agenda was Gorbachov's speech at Murmansk, offering the West a pact on the partial demilitarization of seas in the Nordic area. The offer was considered and rejected, on the grounds that it merely reiterated a long-standing Soviet proposal, and would not materially add to Western security. What was worth noting, however, was that the EC was discussing an East–West defence and security issue. Between 1987 and the treaty-revising Maastricht summit on economic and political union in December 1991, arguments for a common defence gathered force. But it is still unclear whether the focus should be the EC Council of Ministers; the WEU; bilateral defence co-operation (with the Franco–German Defence Council as a model); or the 'European pillar' of NATO, with the Euro-Group of European defence ministers and officials acquiring an expanded role.

The Anglo–Italian EC paper on defence of October 1991 (disliked by France) suggested a combintion of the WEU and the 'European pillar', to bridge the EC–NATO gap. France, Germany and Spain issued a statement of their own in Paris the same month which made no mention of NATO;

> To come closer to European union, with a federal vocation, we recall that the implementation of a foreign and security policy is a necessary component of political union. Such a policy must include all questions relating to security and defence, with the aim in future of a common defence.

Of the Twelve, Ireland is neutral and a non-NATO member; Greece, although in NATO, has taken a maverick line more favourable to both the Soviet Union and the radical Arab states than that of other Western nations; while Denmark—also a NATO member—leans towards neutralism, and has a sizeable minority opposed to Denmark's membership of both the EC and NATO.

Common foreign policy

The question of formulating a defence or security policy is directly related to—indeed, grows out of—the EC's history of gradual, often crab-like moves towards a joint foreign policy, culminating in the growing importance of the EC foreign policy structure known as 'European political co-operation' (EPC, or somewhat inelegantly, POCO). Political co-operation meetings are usually held at foreign minister level, with the assistance of foreign ministry political directors responsible for POCO co-ordination. Discussion of security issues in this context is justified by the reference in the Single European Act to the need for 'closer co-operation on questions of European security' within the political co-operation framework.

The record of EC co-operation in foreign policy has been mixed. EC states remain divided over how they should proceed towards 'closer co-operation' in security, as well as over the difference between what is meant by 'security' and what is meant by 'defence'. The concept of a defence union to accompany economic and political union arouses fundamental issues of national sovereignty, since defence and foreign policy —like taxation—are normally considered the prerogative of national governments and therefore 'no-go' areas for the EC.

'Political co-operation' is a relatively recent invention, with its origins in the Davignon Report of 1970 rather than in the Treaty of Rome. Viscount Davignon of Belgium (later an EC Commissioner) was asked by The Hague EC summit of 1969 to put together a team of senior foreign ministry officials (he was himself in the Belgian foreign ministry at the time) to report on ways of increasing EC co-ordination in foreign policy. Despite objections on grounds of national sovereignty, the Davignon Report recommended the 'harmonization' of foreign policy views and— where possible—joint decisions on matters affecting the foreign policy interests of Europe as a whole. A number of countries (led by France) opposed the idea on the grounds that, whereas individual states had foreign policy interests, Europe as a whole did not. Nonetheless, the proposal was adopted, with provision for twice-yearly meetings of EC foreign ministers to discuss 'political co-operation' questions.

Subsequent events provide an object lesson in the way in which harmonization proposals tend to be agreed by the EC, with member states entering reservations which eventually become eroded or appear irrelevant. Initially, France made sure that a rigid distinction was drawn between 'political co-operation' meetings—held in the member state holding the Council of Ministers presidency—and normal EC Councils. At first, the distinction was strictly enforced: long-serving EC officials recall that foreign ministers used to hold their regular sessions in Brussels or Luxembourg and then depart, with their staffs, for the country holding the presidency in order to put their 'political co-operation' hats on. Eventually, however, this practice came to be regarded as wearisome and unnecessary, and the situation became blurred, making such elaborate arrangements seem quaint or redundant. French opposition declined after the death of de Gaulle, and it became common for foreign ministers to mix normal EC business with foreign policy (most often, by discussing foreign policy matters over lunch). More recently, East–West issues and matters related in one way or another to defence, security or the common fight against terrorism have come onto the agenda, thus completing the original Davignon vision. 'It is simply not realistic to expect EC foreign ministers, who may have just come from a United Nations meeting in New York, a Western economic summit or a NATO Council to confine themselves to the EC budget' one senior diplomat in Brussels argues, 'They are bound to carry on discussing issues of vital concern to the West and to Europe in particular—and increasingly that means defence issues.'

Under the Single European Act, a political co-operation secretariat was set up in Brussels to help the foreign ministry of the presidency country to co-ordinate foreign policy. The foreign minister of the presidency country speaks for the EC as a whole in the United Nations. In theory, at least, the Twelve work out a joint approach to international issues at the UN and vote together in the UN General Assembly; similarly the EC takes a common line on human rights and related issues at the Vienna European Security (CSCE) Conference. EC summits and foreign councils make declarations on global issues, from Afghanistan to the Middle East, and EC foreign ministers hold regular meetings with their counterparts from regional groupings (the Gulf, Central America, ASEAN, etc.). These declarations have sometimes been influential: the 1980 Venice summit declaration on the Middle East still reverberates in the region because of its implicit suggestion that the Palestine Liberation Organization (PLO) should take part in the peace process, provided it recognized the right of all states in the region (Israel included) to live within secure borders.

The EC has also taken limited sanctions against various states in an attempt to use its political and economic power for agreed European aims: for example against Libya and Syria over terrorism; against Iraq after its invasion of Kuwait in August 1990; and against South Africa over apartheid. Such sanctions have had mixed results (EC sanctions against Argentina in support of Britain during the 1982 Falklands War fell apart altogether).

Foreign policy, for the most part, still rests on perceived national interests. Splits in Europe over how to deal with Iran and the hostage crisis in Lebanon provided a case in point, with nations disagreeing on whether and how to deal with hostage-takers. Britain and France still have world roles and links which echo past glories and responsibilities;

Germany looks to the east; Spain, Italy and Greece all have special links with the Arab world and the Mediterranean; Denmark feels the attraction of the Nordic states and, more recently, the newly independent Baltic states, too. Danish ties with Scandinavia are formally acknowledged by the EC (for example, in allowing Denmark to maintain special trading and border arrangements with its Nordic neighbours).

NATO and the American presence in Europe

A common European defence, by contrast, was in the spotlight even before the end of the Cold War, because of a growing movement in the United States—not least in Congress—to oblige 'the Europeans' to shoulder more of the Western defence burden, 'roles, risks and responsibilities' in NATO jargon. In fact, the European members of NATO already contribute 90% of NATO's manpower in Europe and almost the same percentage of the Alliance's tanks, artillery and combat aircraft. Nonetheless, American demands for a larger European defence effort reflect a general rethinking in the Western Alliance, encapsulated by the Rome NATO summit of November 1991 and President Bush's offer the previous month of substantial unilateral cuts in the US nuclear arsenal, forcing the post-coup leadership in Moscow to match and even to exceed the proposals. The new East–West climate and the restructuring of NATO has led to the reorganization of NATO forces, with the emphasis on a British-led rapid reaction force able to intervene flexibly in conflicts. The decisive move away from Soviet Communism which followed the failed Moscow hardline coup of August 1991 confirms that the West need no longer assume a Soviet threat to Western Europe of the kind which has hitherto dominated NATO thinking.

On the other hand, Western strategic planners remain wary of instability in the former Soviet Union, and continue to regard a powerful independent Russian republic under Boris Yeltsin as a potential threat, especially since Yeltsin's Russia deliberately draws on the glories of the imperial Russian past for inspiration. There is thus no question of a total US withdrawal from Europe. But troop levels are being reduced under the Conventional Forces in Europe (CFE) agreement signed in September 1990, with the United States and the Soviet Union reducing forces in Central Europe to a ceiling of 195,000 each. As the US Presidential campaigns in 1988 and 1992 both show, it has become common in the United States to argue that, although the depth of American involvement in European defences was justified after the Second World War, the world has moved on in the past four decades. In 1988, the North Atlantic Assembly declared in its report *NATO in the 1990s* that a 'new transatlantic bargain' had to be struck. The European response has been to look for ways of meeting the American demand for fairer 'burden sharing' within NATO while, at the same time, exploring avenues towards a joint European defence—sometimes, paradoxically, to the alarm of the United

States, which wants Europe to pay more for its own defence but does not relish the thought of a European defence body emerging as a counter-weight or alternative to NATO itself.

Senior NATO and, indeed, EC officials (although this is less true of the French) remain anxious to preserve the transatlantic aspect of defence. Manfred Worner, the NATO Secretary General, noted in September 1990 —during the Gulf crisis—that while the EC must clearly 'take over greater responsibility for its defence', this did not mean 'decoupling' Europe from the United States. Similarly, Tom King, the Defence Secretary, observed when presenting the UK Defence White Paper in July 1991 on the 'peace dividend' resulting from the end of the Cold War:

> Building totally distinct West European entities, involving the eventual absorption of the WEU by the Twelve, would be disruptive of NATO. It would result in at least two classes of NATO European states and would erode the principle of equal security for all.

However, General John Galvin, the NATO Supreme Commander in Europe, upset the EC by suggesting in the *Washington Post* in October 1991 that US troops might have to stay in Europe, because 'the Euro-peans' had a long history of fighting each other that was not necessarily at an end.

The Western European Union

Efforts to develop an EC defence dimension have tended to focus on the Western European Union, which groups together Britain, France, Germany, Italy, the Benelux countries, Spain and Portugal, a total of nine out of the twelve EC states. The WEU was founded by the Treaty of Brussels in 1948 (the founding members were Britain, France, Belgium, the Netherlands and Luxembourg), and first expanded in 1954, when West Germany and Italy joined. The 1950s were not, however, a pro-pitious time for European defence efforts, as is shown by the fate of the proposed European Defence Community (EDC), which was set up in 1952 by France, West Germany, Italy and the Benelux states but which collapsed when the French National Assembly voted against ratification of the EDC Treaty two years later (West Germany joined the other Western nations in NATO shortly afterwards).

Unlike the abortive EDC, the WEU survived, with offices in both Paris and London, albeit in somewhat dormant form until it was revived in 1984 at foreign minister level. It has since been further strengthened under a triple impulse: the need to forge a closer European defence identity at a time when the superpowers are concluding far-reaching disarmament agreements directly affecting European interests: common European interests in areas outside Europe, notably the Gulf, with its vital oil supplies to Western Europe (less vital to the United States): and the fact that two European powers, Britain and France, have independent nuclear deterrents which could be used for European as well as national defence but are not yet included in the terms of reference of any wider international arms control process.

A key move in the development of the WEU came in March 1987, when Sir Geoffrey Howe, the then Foreign Secretary, in a speech to the Institute of International Relations in Brussels called for a European defence strategy, with the WEU headquarters moved from Paris and London to Brussels. This proposal, much resisted by the French, would bring the WEU institutions closer to NATO—and to the EC. In October 1987 at The Hague the WEU launched a 'Platform on European Security Interests', which recalled 'our commitment to build a European Union in accordance with the Single European Act, adding that the construction of an integrated Europe 'will remain incomplete as long as it does not include security and defence'. While partnership with the United States remained vital, 'we intend to develop a more cohesive European defence identity'. This declaration did much to revitalize the WEU. But it was the Gulf conflict of 1990–91 and the EC's efforts to resolve the Yugoslavian crisis in 1991 which brought the WEU out of the shadows and into the headlines.

The Gulf War and the EC

Iraq's invasion of Kuwait in August 1990 was the first major test of Europe's new cohesion in defence. During the crisis Mrs Thatcher, the then British Prime Minister, was scathing about EC disunity, as indeed she was later, observing in March 1991 in a speech in the United States that, once again, only America had proved capable of defending world freedom. 'Perhaps the most extraordinary suggestion yet to come out of Brussels,' she said, 'is that the disunity and half-heartedness of most European nations during the Gulf crisis demonstrates the need for a united European foreign and defence policy.' John Major, her successor, agreed. In January 1991, with the war at its height, he told the Commons there was 'a considerable disparity in the extent to which individual European countries have committed themselves . . . political union and a common foreign and security policy in Europe will have to go beyond statements and extend to action'. Only Britain and France, of the EC nations, sent troops on any scale, although Germany—after much debate —sent warplanes to Turkey and contributed financially to the war effort. There was particular anger in Britain over Belgium's reluctance to supply the UK with much-needed ammunition. France, too, was initially reluctant to become involved, and—without telling its EC partners—sought to avert war at the last moment with behind-the-scenes approaches to Baghdad through third parties at the UN.

The EC's initial emphasis was on economic sanctions rather than military action, with foreign ministers meeting in August 1990 to embargo purchases of Iraqi and Kuwaiti oil (the latter then under Iraqi control), freeze Iraqi assets in Europe, ban (rather belatedly) European arms sales to Iraq and suspend all trade with Baghdad. At the International Institute for Strategic Studies (IISS) in London in March 1991, after Iraq's surrender, Delors observed that the conflict had been a reminder of the need for a common European defence, not least because European interests— no longer directly threatened by Communism—were clearly at risk from other quarters such as the Middle East. The decision by Britain and France to send troops to guard Kurdish 'safe havens' in northern Iraq after the war was taken at an EC summit in Luxembourg in April 1991, at which John Major proposed the havens as a way of protecting Kurdish refugees fleeing persecution by Saddam Husain.

The Yugoslav civil war

The EC also faced a test of resolve in the subsequent crisis in Yugoslavia. The Gulf War involved a threat to European interests, not least because of European dependence on Middle Eastern oil supplies. But the Yugoslav civil war, caused by declarations of independence by Slovenia and Croatia, was the first serious shedding of blood on the European continent itself since the end of the Second World War. 'This is the hour of Europe, not the hour of the Americans,' Jacques Poos, the Luxembourg Foreign Minister, declared as the Yugoslav crisis began in the first half of 1991, during Luxembourg's EC presidency. Many doubted the wisdom of venturing into the morass of South Slav nationalisms dating back to the bitterness of the Serbian–Croatian conflicts of the Second World War and, even earlier, to the ethnic rivalries of the Austro–Hungarian Empire. But pressure grew for 'Europe' to solve a European conflict which threatened to spill across borders—to Italy or Hungary, for example. The EC withheld aid and low-rate credits to Belgrade (the capital of both Serbia and the Yugoslav federation) perceiving Greater Serbian nationalism to be one of the causes of the tragedy.

However, most EC states balked at German proposals for outright recognition of Croatia and Slovenia. France and the UK judged it wiser to preserve some form of Yugoslav federalism in the interests of future stability, while Spain feared that recognizing new states would encourage Spanish separatists such as the Basques. Instead, the EC established a Yugoslav peace conference in The Hague, chaired by Lord Carrington, sent several peace missions to Belgrade headed by Hans van den Broek, the Dutch Foreign Minister, negotiated a series of ceasefires, and sent monitors to supervise the fragile truces which followed.

The Dutch EC presidency in the second half of 1991 proposed an EC peacekeeping force of 25,000, but the WEU, at the end of September 1991, described this as 'long-term planning' for a 'worst-case scenario', and opted instead for a strengthened monitoring force. In October 1991 Lord Carrington and van den Broek persuaded Slobodan Milosevic, the

Serbian leader, to abandon his aim of a 'Greater Serbia' and acknowledge that internal borders could not be changed by force (a cardinal EC and CSCE principle), the eventual aim being 'self-determination' for Yugoslav republics, perhaps within a much looser form of federation. Douglas Hurd, the Foreign Secretary, declared that Yugoslavia could not be held together by force and 'those republics which decide for independence will get it'—eventually.

What is striking is that the Yugoslav crisis set a precedent for EC intervention in European disputes, even where they arise outside the EC itself. In Yugoslavia the EC, acting as the regional supra-national body, assumed a mediation role hitherto confined to the United Nations. But it was, in the end, the UN rather than the EC which arranged with both Serbs and Croats for a peacekeeping operation. Yugoslavia, moreover, threatened the very principle of common EC foreign policymaking just at the moment when it had been formulated at the Maastricht summit in December 1991. Chancellor Kohl pledged German recognition of Croatia and Slovenia 'by Christmas,' a move described by *The Times* as 'Germany's Balkan folly'. Lord Carrington warned it would prolong the war, and could encourage demands for recognition from other republics. Nonetheless EC foreign ministers, taking Bonn's lead, agreed to recognise the breakaway republics by 15 January 1992, provided they met agreed EC criteria for independence, including democratic rule, respect for human rights and the safety of ethnic minorities. A Yugoslav federal air force rocket attack on an EC helicopter on 7 January, in which four Italians and a Frenchman were killed, underlined the risks taken by EC monitors—including, for the first time, the risk of death and injury in a European rather than national cause. In early 1992 Cyrus Vance negotiated a ceasefire on behalf of the UN, and all parties—except hardline leaders of Serbian enclaves in Croatia—agreed to the deployment of a UN peacekeeping force of 10–15,000 men. The EC duly recognised Croatia and Slovenia as independent states, but Greece blocked proposals for recognising Macedonia.

Bilateral defence co-operation

NATO foreign ministers meeting in Copenhagen in June 1991 (and the Rome NATO summit of November in the same year) duly recognized the progress of the EC toward a common foreign and security policy, declaring that this would be reflected in the strengthening of the European pillar of NATO. At the same time, in addition to joint defence efforts, European defence policy is based on national conventional forces, plus the deterrent provided by the British and French nuclear forces (at present under national control, and, in the British case, assigned to NATO). Thinking of this kind has been encouraged by the development of limited forms of cross-border defence co-operation, notably Anglo-French and Franco-German. In his Brussels speech in 1987, Sir Geoffrey

Howe noted that France was moving tentatively away from the notion of a 'national sanctuary', protected by the *force de frappe*, towards the concept of a nuclear force for the protection of both Germany and France, and possibly of Western Europe as a whole.

Other bilateral moves include exploratory Anglo-French talks on nuclear co-operation—for example, joint targeting of the sovereign nuclear deterrents—and the formation of a joint Franco–German army corps at Strasbourg. This follows the creation of a Franco–German brigade—part of the 1988 Treaty renewing the 1963 Elysée Treaty—based at Boblingen, near Stuttgart, with 4,000 men plus light tanks and artillery. French and German forces have also held large-scale manoeuvres in Bavaria. The Atlantic Assembly's report *NATO in the 1990s* went further, and suggested building on the Franco–German example to form a European brigade drawn from the national armed forces of Europe. Such moves are clearly designed in part to coax France back into the orbit of Western defence structures, if not into the integrated military structure of NATO, which the French left in 1966. There are also moves towards Anglo–German bilateral co-operation within NATO, although such co-operation falls short of the Franco–German link and no Anglo–German brigade is envisaged at present.

Nation states remain reluctant to pool national resources in so sensitive an area as defence. There can be few more potent symbols of nationhood than a country's armed forces. The formation of a European brigade, let alone a European army, is as fraught with difficulty as the formation of a European police force to combat crime and terrorism in a border-free Europe. Defence expenditures vary widely from country to country, with the military budget amounting to 4.7% of GDP in Britain, 4.0% in France, 3.0% in Germany, 2.2% in Italy and 2.1% in Denmark. Britain, for its part, continues to place high value on its military co-operation with the United States. Anglo-French talks on British use of a French air-launched 'stand-off' nuclear missile to replace ageing British free-fall nuclear bombs have run into difficulties because the French ASMP rocket, used on Mirage fighters, has a range of 150 miles rather than the 300 miles Britain wants, and does not have radar-foiling 'Stealth' technology of the kind developed in America.

The impetus towards common defence

For all these difficulties, the impetus towards a common European defence is strong. David Greenwood, Director of Defence Studies at Aberdeen University, argued as long ago as 1988 that the transatlantic partnership was 'unhealthily unequal'. That American power and technology dominates NATO, for example, breeds 'European resentment', while the fact that the United States has what it sees as a disproportionate share of the burden of defending the West fosters 'American disenchantment'. Western Europe, Greenwood suggests, must develop not only a more assertive personality but more durable defence structures. He proposes three purposes for this: co-ordination of policy; co-operation in arms procurement; and collaboration in defence industry production.

The case for intra-European co-operation in arms procurement is particularly compelling, since 'no country in Western Europe can afford the price of self-sufficiency in weapons research, development and production'. NATO has a procurement agency in the form of the Independent European Programme Group (IEPG), and projects such as the Euro-Fighter testify to the growing importance of collaborative projects. But NATO officials want far more in the way of weapons harmonization, with a common defence research programme and a central register of defence requirements to match defence industry production and development.

François Heisbourg, director of the IISS also believes that constructing an effective 'European pillar' of NATO would be 'a logical corollary to ventures leading to the creation of a single unified European market after 1992', despite the differing national defence goals of Britain, France and Germany. The impetus towards European defence need not weaken the transatlantic alliance, which has so far survived tensions not only in defence matters but also in trade and finance, with US–European strains arising over protectionism and the dollar, and over regional conflicts.

The main problem lies within Europe, which is having to face up to the consequences of the collapse of Communism in the east, extensive nuclear and conventional disarmament, and the need to extend security structures to former Communist countries in Eastern Europe. Despite upheavals in Russia and Eastern Europe there is still insufficient common ground on defence between France and Britain, and between the two European nuclear powers and a reunified Germany.

A convincing collective European defence policy, like an effective joint European foreign policy, can only come about when Europe is fully integrated politically and economically, in accordance with the vision outlined at Maastricht. A European Defence Union, in other words, will be possible when the 1992 process is completed: it is very unlikely to precede it.

This need not, however, prevent the European nations from making preparatory moves now towards greater co-operation in arms procurement and other defence fields, thus laying the foundations for some form of closer defence integration to accompany other aspects of the 1992 phenomenon. In the end, in defence as in the political, economic and technological fields, Europe will progress as far and as fast towards union as its peoples and its politicians want. An integrated Europe of 320 million people not only has the potential to challenge the US and Asia in trading terms, it also contains within it the seeds of a powerful and technologically advanced defence bloc. As with a European Bank and single currency, whether the EC should have a European army will, in the end, be a political decision, and will partly depend on whether the EC widens its membership to the point where a joint defence force becomes too unwieldy to contemplate.

Checklist of changes

- Foreign policy co-operation to be increased.
- Defence and security policy to be co-ordinated more closely.
- Moves toward European defence to be based on Western European Union (WEU) within overall NATO framework.
- NATO to bring Eastern Europe closer to Western alliance through new East–West Co-operation Council.

18 TOWARDS A COMMUNITY OF THIRTY

The problem of EC enlargement

The 1992 programme, as originally conceived, did not anticipate the changes which were to take place in Eastern Europe in 1989, in Germany in 1990, and in the Soviet Union in 1991. Nor did it anticipate the list of applications for EC membership from countries as far apart as Malta and Sweden, and the creation of a European Economic Area through the October 1991 deal with EFTA, giving the seven EFTA nations and their 60 million people 'unimpeded access' to the single market and bringing them closer to EC membership. The EC has had to adjust its plans in the light of this redefinition of what is meant by a European 'community'. The paradox is that even a Community of Twelve is finding integration a complex and arduous task—yet the closer that integration looms, the more attractive it appears to those outside the 'magic circle', not least in Eastern Europe and EFTA, and even in the former Soviet Union.

In Western Europe, 1992 promises to make already successful economies even more prosperous. In Eastern Europe, by contrast, statues of Lenin have been toppled and symbols of the hammer and sickle thrown on the scrap-heap. In a manner and speed which would astonish the EC's founders, what began as an enterprise of Six, then Nine and now Twelve may come to embrace all or most of the Continent. In October 1991 Delors called on the EC to prepare for a Community of 24 or even 30 members, noting in the Paris-based magazine *Belvedere* that a 'new political and institutional programme' would be needed for this after Maastricht.

Delors's answer to the collapse of Eastern Europe and the growing demand from EFTA countries such as Sweden and Austria for EC membership has been to devise a system of 'concentric circles' with the Twelve at its core, EFTA countries in the second ring, and Eastern Europe in the outer ring. This presumes, however, that both the EFTA nations and the East Europeans will be satisfied with various forms of association with the EC. Already, with Soviet troops due to leave Poland altogether at the end of 1992 and Germany by 1994, the East Europeans are looking to the EC and NATO for some form of security umbrella to fill the vacuum left by the disintegration of the once-familiar post-war system of military blocs. The East European ethnic conflicts since the fall of Communism, especially in Yugoslavia, have reinforced this trend, with Jozsef Antall, the democratic Prime Minister of Hungary, calling for the nations of East and Central Europe to be in both the EC and NATO.

The future of Europe is 'a question now posed in the broadest terms since the end of the Second World War' *The Times* said in an editorial entitled 'Germany and Europe' in November 1989 as the Berlin Wall started to crumble. Since 1989 the 'other Europeans' have risen with remarkable speed and determination to throw off the Communist system imposed on them after the Second World War. Even in the Soviet Union —or the 'ex-Soviet Union'—Communism collapsed following the abortive and counter-productive coup of August 1991, when hardliners —including the then heads of the armed forces and the KGB—miscalculated disastrously in trying to overthrow President Gorbachov, introducing instead a new era of freedom built on the defiance of the coup by Boris Yeltsin and the Democrats who control the Russian Federation. The failed coup also gave the final push to persistent efforts by the Baltic Republic—often in the face of bloody suppression by Moscow—to regain their independence. Other republics, too, from the Ukraine to central Asia, have proclaimed independence, leaving Gorbachov with the task of trying to bring about some new form of political federation and economic union.

This has re-opened the question of what is meant by 'Europe', and of what is to be the link between the EC and its East European neighbours. The seismic shifts in European political geology have exposed differing attitudes on the part of key EC states. Britain, for example, urges a cautious approach to economic and monetary union within the EC as it tries to evaluate the new situation. France, by contrast, wants faster integration to ensure that Germany, united since October 1990, remains firmly anchored in the Community and is not tempted by virtue of its historical links with Eastern Europe to contemplate if its future, too, might not lie more in Eastern Europe.

After the thaw

Formally speaking, the end of the Cold War dates from the Malta summit between Bush and Gorbachov in December 1989, when Bush gave approval for German reunification provided Germany remained within NATO and the EC. Gorbachov at first resisted this, but in July 1990 agreed with Kohl that a united Germany could stay in NATO, provided that the combined German army was reduced from 600,000 to 370,000 and that no NATO troops were moved into former East Germany. Gorbachov agreed in turn to withdraw Soviet troops from East Germany over a period of three to four years. The end of the Cold War, and the collapse of both Comecon and the Warsaw Pact, were codefied in a new 'Charter for Europe' signed by leaders from East and West (and the neutral countries of Europe) at the Paris Conference on Security and Co-operation in Europe in November 1990.

The rush to German reunification became inevitable as thousands of young East Germans began to flee through the crumbling borders in the autumn of 1989, some pouring through the newly opened Hungarian border with Austria, others leaving by special train after taking refuge in West German embassies in Warsaw and Prague. Street protests against the East German regime took place in East Berlin and Leipzig, leading to the fall of Erich Honecker, the Communist leader who had once vowed that the Berlin Wall (the so-called 'Anti-Fascist Protection Barrier') would last 100 years. Overwhelming popular demand for change also engulfed detested Communist regimes across Eastern Europe, with the first non-Communist government in Eastern Europe since the Second World War taking office in Poland in August 1989. The term 'People's Republic' became redundant, and Communist parties reconstituted themselves as socialist parties, either suffering ignominious defeat in elections or forced into coalitions with parties of the centre and right. In the words of Gennady Gerasimov, then the Kremlin spokesman (and subsequently Soviet ambassador to Portugal), the 'Brezhnev doctrine' used to justify the 1968 invasion of Czechoslovakia to 'preserve socialism' had been supplanted by the 'Sinatra doctrine'—letting East Europeans 'do it their way'.

The EC Dublin summit of April 1990 welcomed the advent of democracy in Eastern Europe and the prospect of German reunification. Western fears of German resurgence surfaced in Britain in July 1990, however, when Nicholas Ridley, a government minister, told *The Spectator* that the European Monetary System was a 'German racket' designed to take over the whole of Europe. He also referred explicitly to Hitler and concentration camps, suggesting—in an apparent reflection of Mrs Thatcher's own thinking—that some aspects of 'the German character' might not have changed for the better. His resignation followed promptly.

However, in August 1990 the EC's conditions for German unity were worked out: special tariffs between the Soviet Union and former East Germany would continue for two years, and, because of the immense problems of absorbing antiquated East German industries and substandard goods, Germany would be given temporary exemptions from some EC directives. On pollution, factories in the eastern half of Germany have three years beyond the 1993 deadline to comply with EC directives limiting sulphur dioxide emissions. As part of his bid to reunify Germany despite the economic and fiscal costs involved, Kohl insisted that the almost valueless Ostmark should be exchanged one for one with the powerful deutschmark when German currency union was declared in the summer of 1990 (at a stroke delivering a death blow to what remained of eastern Germany's ramshackle economy). Political unification followed in October 1990, with elections throughout Germany in December, Kohl and the Christian Democratic Union (CDU) winning in both West and East.

In the year that followed, economic strains became evident as Treuhand, the government agency for privatizing and funding eastern German companies, struggled to unite a dynamic western economy and a moribund eastern one. At least for a time, Kohl, once feted in Leipzig and Dresden, became the target of abuse. Economic difficulties also gave rise to social pressures, including violence against foreign immigrants in eastern German states such as Saxony. In the Soviet Union, Gorbachov was criticized by hardliners for 'losing Germany' to the West—indeed, such charges became part of the move to oust him in August 1991. But when accused of 'losing' Eastern Europe, Gorbachov retorted:

> When you say this is a collapse of socialism, I counter—what kind of socialism? A variety of the Stalinist authoritarian and bureaucratic system which we ourselves have abandoned.

At his historic encounter with Pope John Paul II in the Vatican on the eve of the 1989 Malta summit Gorbachov spoke of the need to find 'solutions to common European problems' based on 'respect for peoples' national, state, spiritual and cultural identity'.

Nonetheless, the euphoria which greeted the exhilarating sight of young Germans from east and west sitting atop the once-feared Berlin Wall on 10 November 1989 and hacking away whole chunks of it has given way to more considered rethinking on Europe. Both the special EC summit in Paris eight days after the Berlin Wall was breached and the Strasbourg summit of December 1989 were dominated by the need to react to change in Eastern Europe, and by the desire to ensure that a united Germany did not either return to the militarism of the German past or—as a new German economic giant of 80 million people—upset the European economic and political balance, traditionally based on the Anglo–French–German triangle. The Strasbourg summit endorsed German reunification, provided it was 'peaceful, democratic and honoured existing treaties', and at the same time sought to bind Germany further into the EC by setting a date for the intergovernmental conference to discuss treaty revision and economic and monetary union: the Rome summit of December 1990. The summit also approved the creation of a new European Bank for Reconstruction and Development (EBRD) to assist East European economic recovery. This was founded amid much ceremony in London in April 1991. It is headed by Jacques Attali of France.

In 1992 the new democracies of Eastern Europe are still struggling to establish both mature political systems and stable banking and industrial systems. Poland, Hungary and Czechoslovakia have successfully conducted elections and begun to privatize industries and encourage Western investment. But other East European nations such as Romania are still undergoing periodic upheavals, and have less securely founded plural- ism. Indeed, the tradition of authoritarian rule, which pre-dates the Com- munist era, remains strong in Eastern Europe, especially in the Balkans. The descent of Yugoslavia into civil war has been of particular concern to the EC, leading to direct EC involvement (see Chapter 17). Forty per cent of Yugoslavia's exports go to the EC, which, apart from the disinte- gration of the federation, is worried by Yugoslavia's hyper-inflation and $17 billion foreign debt.

An obvious way for the EC to reinforce East European democracy lies in economic and financial investment. The EBRD draws capital of £7 billion from 41 countries, and numbers EC institutions among its share- holders. It offers a combination of investment in new infrastructure and private investment in East European economies. British companies have been in the forefront of investment in Eastern Europe, although Germany dominates the East European market, from banking and insurance to cars and supermarkets. Douglas Hurd told the Institute of Directors in February 1990 that investment in Eastern Europe was a question of 'get- ting in on the ground floor, at the start of something which is going to lead to an immense expansion of markets for goods and services'. On the other hand, much of the infrastructure, manufacturing and distribution systems in Eastern Europe remains backward, and it will be some time before work practices, professional attitudes and consumer expectations match those of the West. Foreign investors remain wary because of bureaucratic and time-consuming ways of doing business: direct invest- ment in Eastern Europe only amounted to $1 billion in 1991, with lending from state and private banks amounting to $13 billion—a lower figure than expected. General Electric, which bought Tungsram, the Hungarian light-bulb manufacturer in 1989, has had to prune both management and workforce to streamline the company. Like many East European firms, Tungsram operated as a subsidized social complex, with schools, sports facilities, kindergartens and holiday homes connected to the enterprise (*Economist Survey of Business in Eastern Europe*, September 1991).

The demand of East European countries such as Poland for access to West European markets, meanwhile, has exposed protectionist tenden- cies among the Twelve and has led to the charge that the EC, while wishing to encourage democracy in the East, is less willing to pay the economic price involved. This debate came to a head in September 1991, when the Commission proposed a reduction in import levies on agricultur- al products from Hungary, Poland and Czechoslovakia of 60% over three years. Coal quotas would be phased out over three years and textile quotas over five—proposals which aroused fears that Western Europe would be flooded with cheap East European fuel and clothing, in the process undermining Portuguese textile workers, French farmers, Ger- man miners and British fruit growers.

At a meeting in Paris in September 1991 John Major sought to persuade a reluctant President Mitterrand that Poland should be allowed to sell its beef within the EC. 'There is no point in giving countries aid and then denying them trade access,' Major said. East and West should be brought together in a common home numbering 400 million citizens: 'We must be prepared to widen our horizons and widen our membership'. France eventually agreed to Polish beef imports, provided French farmers were compensated. But the Polish beef argument was symptomatic of the gap between the ECs 'wideners' such as Major, who want to see the EC include Eastern Europe in some way, and the 'deepeners' such as Mitterrand, who believe that the EC in its present form must achieve full integration before expansion can be considered. As *The Times* observed in September 1991, while the EC had multiplied its moral, financial and political commitments to Eastern Europe, 'from the Baltics to Albania', after the abortive Moscow coup, and had provided substantial aid to help Eastern Europe make the difficult transition to the free market, at the same time it was maintaining protectionist barriers against East European exports. 'Europeans should remember their history . . . In the 1930s protectionism deepened the economic depression, which fed nationalist extremism and plunged the world into war.'

Towards a 'greater Europe'?

The EC dilemma over 'widening' and 'deepening' in relation to Eastern Europe also affects the aspirations of the many other European nations now lining up to submit membership applications. Sweden, which in 1990 was still declaring its neutrality to be incompatible with EC integration, a year later asked for membership, with pressure from Swedish industry sweeping most other considerations aside. Stockholm's pro-EC tilt was further confirmed when the Social Democrats lost to the Centre-Right in the September 1991 elections. The Commission gives its opinion on the Swedish application in the spring of 1992, and on Malta and Cyprus in the winter of the same year. (Turkey has already been told that its application is, for the time being, inappropriate.)

The Commission's view, however, remains that no applications can be seriously entertained until the current process of treaty revision and political and monetary integration is completed—the mid-1990s at the earliest. In July 1991 the Commission's opinion on Austria's application was that, although Austrian entry would involve few economic problems, Austrian neutrality remained an obstacle (in view of plans for a common defence policy) and that Austria could not be allowed in until the treaty revisions begun at Rome in December 1990 and continued at Maastricht in December 1991 had come to fruition.

With the EC thus still an exclusive club, some of the countries outside the magic circle (and some within) have begun to form regional associations. The Alpen–Adria association groups together with Croatia,

Slovenia, five of the Austrian Lander (states), three of Hungary's western regions, four of Italy's northern regions, and one German Land (Bavaria), with common problems relating to tourism, the environment, sport and energy on the agenda. The Pentagonale group brings together Italy, Austria, Czechoslovakia, Hungary and Yugoslavia, with Poland making the group a Hexagonale. A Black Sea Economic Co-operation agreement, still under discussion, would group Turkey, Bulgaria, Romania and the Soviet Union. Austria has also proposed a Danube association from Bavaria to Moldavia to promote trade and tourism along the Danube River.

The fear, however, is that without the powerful influence of the EC, with its democratic procedures and economic stability, East and Central Europe could fragment, with ethnic rivalries and feuds resurfacing after years of Communism, during which they were suppressed. Indeed, to some extent, this is already happening. There is also the danger that the darker side of nationalism will rear its head. On a visit to Poland at the time of the breaching of the Berlin Wall in 1989 Chancellor Kohl declared that the Germany of today was not the old one of dark excesses, but a Germany of democratic and Christian values, of which the EC integration process was a guarantee. 'We want European union, the United States of Europe,' Kohl declared firmly, 'The EC was, is, and will stay open for other democratic countries in Europe—Warsaw, Moscow, Prague, Budapest and Vienna are as much part of Europe as Brussels, London, Paris, Rome and, of course, Berlin.' The EC must 'approach with imagination and flexibility those Central and East European states which are embarking on deep reforms of their politics, economy and society'.

Yet Kohl's reference to 'dark excesses' strikes a chord, even causes a shiver in those parts of Europe whose present borders are the result of cruel and barbaric rule by Nazi and Stalinist totalitarianism. The democratization of Eastern Europe has raised not only the question of borders but also the even deeper question of whether the process of integration in Western Europe, founded on common democratic values, can be extended to the rest of Europe, perhaps even to Moscow, where such values have often had only shallow roots.

As Donald Cameron Watt, Professor of International History at the LSE, put it, freer travel across East–West borders opens up a vision of Europe as 'a total free-trade area', with 'its peoples living together in comparative amity, free from fear of war or violence, its security forces reduced to the minimum to combat civil war and international crime, the frontiers open, and the public, not excluding salesmen and investors, travelling freely'. Yet Europe was still obsessed with memories of '1870, 1914 and 1939'. As the Soviet empire crumbled, old national frictions were emerging: the Hungarian minority in Romania, the German minority in Silesia, the Albanians in Yugoslavia. Transnational management and planning were needed to tackle the legacy of Stalinist governments which had polluted and impoverished everything they touched. As Watt says:

Within French and Polish hearts, at levels much deeper than reason, talk of German reunification stirs images of the Gestapo . . . of the midnight knock on the door and the sealed train to the death camp. Pessimism sees ahead of us a Central Europe no longer dominated by the long shadows of 45,000 Soviet tanks or 1,400 Lance missiles, but still divided, disappointed and embittered with ancestral memories and hatreds.

Lord Callaghan, the former Labour Prime Minister, sounded a similar warning in the House of Lords: the Cold War, and Moscow's iron grip on Eastern Europe, had 'kept many of Europe's ancient antagonisms and feuds in the deep freeze'. The loosening of that grip could mean 'the Balkanization of Eastern Europe, for some of those countries do not have long experience of the conventions and constraints that a democratic system imposes'.

Behind the challenge for the EC in rethinking the single market, in other words, is the question of whether the process of integration started by Monnet and Schuman, and taken up by Delors, will prove equal to the weight of European history, a history in which rivalry and bloodshed have figured more often than co-operation, with a consequent cost in human pain and division.

If a 'greater Europe' is achieved, on the other hand, it would have a total GDP twice that of the United States by the early part of the next century, according to some forecasts. Delors told the German magazine *Der Spiegel* in October 1991 that economic and monetary union should lay the foundations of a European superpower of the future. Douglas Hurd, in June 1991, observed that the EC was trying to manage the 'enormous and welcome changes' which had broken the old mould before the new mould had had time to set. But he added: 'I do not see that the Europe of Twelve can shut the door of membership for any length of time against fully qualified European democracies which are anxious to join, whether they are in EFTA or in Central Europe'.

The key difference between the East European frictions of today and those of the past is that the EC now offers a model of prosperity and democracy at a time when the climate of world opinion is forcing authoritarian systems to give way to those based on human rights and the rule of law. The vision beckons of a Greater Europe embracing Poland, Hungary, Czechoslovakia, the Baltic states, and perhaps other parts of the former Soviet Union. As *The Independent* noted in June 1991, 'One of the paradoxes of today's turbulent new Europe is that the various small entities and nationalities struggling out from under the embrace of centralized power would like nothing better than to join the EC'. This, the paper said, suggested that people who had actually lived under centralized power, and hated it, did not share the Thatcherite view of the EC as a centralized superstate. On the other hand, they will have to wait outside the 'inner circle' of the EC until the 1992 process, and plans for economic and monetary union associated with it, have made clear what kind of European federation is likely to emerge for them to join in the 1990s.

EC—EFTA: the wider single market

In October 1991 the seven EFTA nations—Austria, Finland, Iceland, Liechtenstein, Norway, Sweden and Switzerland—finally agreed the terms of a pact with the 12 EC members, giving the EFTA countries access to the single market and creating the world's richest free-trade zone, a 'European Economic Area' (EEA) from the Arctic to the Aegean, to take effect at the same time as the EC single market on 31 December 1992. The EC and EFTA between them account for nearly 45% of world trade. Delors observed that the pact would provide a 'trial run' for EFTA countries such as Austria and Sweden which wanted full EC membership. Frans Andriessen, the Commissioner for External Affairs, also noted that the former communist countries of Eastern Europe might use the new trade zone as a stepping stone to EC membership.

Under the EEA accord, EFTA countries are obliged to incorporate EC single market legislation into their national statutes, including company law, consumer protection, social policy and environmental protection measures, to ensure harmonization. The complex documents laying down conditions for the EEA amount to 40 protocols and 20 annexes. The final obstacle to the pact was removed when Austria agreed that Greece could have an extra 2,000 permits for lorries crossing the Alps, provided it also agreed to transport more of its goods by rail rather than road, so as not to clog up the trans-Alpine routes. The EC countries have guaranteed access to Nordic fishing grounds, while EFTA will provide £1.7-billion worth of soft loans and grants to the poorer southern EC countries such as Portugal.

There are limits to the EEA. For example, only goods produced within the EEA can circulate freely, not goods imported from outside. Equally, common EC policies such as the CAP will not apply to the EFTA countries. However, the EFTA countries, including not only Austria and Sweden but Finland and Norway as well, have made it clear they will not in the long run be content with membership of a 'halfway house' to EC membership but would like to enjoy the benefits of full membership. The implications of such ambitions for future common policies in sensitive areas like defence and foreign policy are profound. Shortly after the EEA deal was announced Britain and Germany revealed they were planning joint diplomatic missions to independent Soviet republics as a first step toward pooling their foreign services in some parts of the world. Such initiatives in common foreign policy would become far more complex in an EC of 24 or more. As for Eastern Europe, EC officials want to see far greater evidence of moves toward economic and political stability before membership is countenanced, and NATO (at the Rome summit of November 1991) similarly offered 'consultative' or 'liaison' status to the East Europeans through a new 'Co-operation Council'. The likely end result, some years in the future, is an enlarged European structure, from economics to defence, in which an inner core of nations—the Twelve—continue to control the key decision-making institutions.

Checklist of changes

- New co-operation agreements with Central European countries to allow Poland, Hungary and Czechoslovakia greater access to EC markets.
- Formation of European Economic Area (EEA) by EC and EFTA creates world's largest single market.

CONCLUSION
Britain and the Reshaping of Europe

The Europe of today is the result of three years of political upheaval which amount to the biggest change in the region since the Second World War and the division of Europe that followed it. The changed Europe of 1992–93 has new underpinnings: a united Germany, achieved despite doubts not only in the former Soviet Union but also in France and Britain; the emergence of East European democracies from the ashes of Communism and the break-up of the Soviet Union; closer ties between EFTA and the EC; and—altered by these cataclysms, but not knocked off course by them—the development of a single market in Europe, giving rise to ambitious plans for economic, monetary and political union.

This Europe is the backdrop for a tug of war between the federalist view of EC integration as originally conceived for an EC of Twelve, and the desire of nation states to retain their individuality and traditions while pooling resources economically to gain the benefits of a single market. In the end, the tensions this engenders seem likely to lead to compromise: an enlarged Community in which the vision of a centralized European superstate—never seriously advanced in any case except by a few Euro-fanatics—fades into the background, while at the same time harmonization and the creation of cross-border political and monetary institutions make the wider Europe far more than a mere free-trade zone. Common policies on matters from defence to immigration and working practices to transport will be limited by practicalities and national differences. But they will exist, and with them the concept of a United States of Europe.

The post-Maastricht debate on Europe can be presented too much in terms of Britain versus the Rest. Germany has its doubts about the pace and nature of economic and monetary union, and the link between EMU and political union. France, for its part, is beginning to realize the implications of federalism, implications to which Britain has been alert for some time. After years in which France presented itself as more 'pro-European' than any other EC nation, the French woke up in the course of 1991 to the fact that they, too, had objections to 'interference from Brussels'. It took the decision by a British Commissioner—Sir Leon Brittan—to veto the purchase by Aerospatiale of the Canadian firm de Havilland on monopoly grounds to bring French concerns into focus. Angry French farmers' demonstrations against attempts to reform the CAP (and the import of British lamb) had a similar effect. As John Laughland pointed out in *The Spectator* (19 October 1991), there has never been a detailed debate on 1992 in France on the scale of the British debate.

British federalists who warn us that we might miss the [1992] train say that if France can accept federalism, so can we: but the truth is that the French media, parliament and public opinion have hardly given the matter a thought.

All EC nations have their views on the single market, all have hopes and fears. France, Spain and other countries are as concerned as Britain about the need to control drugs, terrorism and crime after 1992—and whether such controls should be for the EC or co-operation between governments. Germany is worried about the impact on previously highly protected sectors such as transport and insurance, and is keener than France on enlarging the Community to incorporate Eastern European countries. Most EC countries, moreover, have a far worse record than Britain when it comes to observance of EC law and the Treaty of Rome.

Even the stereotype of the insular Briton unable to speak European languages and secretly wanting to draw up the Channel drawbridge has its Continental counterpart. Anyone who has observed German tourists in Spain or Italy will note that the German capacity for speaking foreign languages is not much greater than our own. On many Continental trains, passport and customs checks are minimal already. Yet anyone taking a train from France to Italy, or from Italy to France, along the Riviera Coast, having to change at the border and pass through customs only to find that trains on either side of the border do not connect, will reflect that the French and Italians also have a long way to go before they regard one another as part of the same internal market. There is the danger that, contrary to the idealism of its founders, the EC will degenerate into xenophobia as nationalist feelings come to the fore in a belated backlash against 1992. Attacks on immigrants in France and Germany have been directed not only against Arabs and North Africans but also, in some cases, against southern Europeans. Anti-Semitism and xenophobia have resurfaced in France, Poland and Austria.

Nationalism and European identity

Nonetheless it is in Britain that awareness of the broader implications of the single market have been most acutely felt. When in October 1991 Carlo Ripa di Meana, the Italian EC environment commissioner, asked Britain in a personal letter to Major, to halt important road and rail projects so that the environmental effects could be studied, the reaction in Britain was vociferous. 'Fury over the Euro-Meddlers' ran the headline in *The Evening Standard*, reporting that backbench MPs thought Brussels had gone 'power mad' and should be 'curbed'. John Major described the Commissioner's action as 'astonishing', adding 'this is absolutely how the European Commission ought not to behave, and I have told them so'. Senior lawyers however, including Sir Gordon Slynn, the British judge at the European Court of Justice, pointed out that Ripa di Meana was fully within his rights in asking for the environmental impact to be assessed. 'It is as plain as a pikestaff', Sir Gordon told the Law Society annual conference in Brussels. 'You cannot say, "No surrender of sovereignty". It has gone, in a limited way. Pooling of sovereignty is a better expression'.

In her speech on Europe at Bruges, Mrs Thatcher poured scorn on the idea of an 'identikit European personality . . . To try to suppress nationhood would be highly damaging . . . Europe will be stronger precisely because it has France as France, Spain as Spain, Britain as Britain, each with its own customs, traditions and identity'. Yet Jacques Delors, at the opposite end of the Euro-spectrum, also acknowledges that national traditions will persist long after 1992. Perhaps as a Frenchman, he could hardly do otherwise: 'Naturally there is the question of national identity,' he told *Le Monde*. 'But in my concept of Europe the French will remain French, France will still be France. Quite simply, the French will also belong to a second country called Europe.

This is in line with Lord Cockfield's theory that the creation of a United Europe is analogous to the creation of the United Kingdom. Scots, Welsh and English owe fundamental loyalty to the United Kingdom, pay taxes to its government and are ready, if necessary, to don military uniform to defend it. Yet they do not cease at the same time to owe often intense regional loyalty to Scotland, Wales or England. There is no reason, in this view, why they should not in future owe a triple loyalty: to region, country and Europe as a whole. The trend in Eastern Europe and the ex-Soviet Union is towards local nationalism; equally, the Scottish National party advocates an independent Scotland within a barrier-free EC. The desire for national independence often goes hand in hand with a desire for membership of the wider Europe. The two are not necessarily incompatible.

It is in any case questionable to what extent the British are 'anti European'. Opinion polls conducted by Euro-Barometer, the EC's own polling organization, consistently show a majority of British respondents in favour of some form of European unification. A MORI poll published in *The Mail on Sunday* shortly after the Bruges speech produced similar results, with a majority of those questioned favouring unity up to and including a single currency, a result which suggests that anti-EC rhetoric is not necessarily a vote winner. As Christopher Huhne observes in his monograph on *The Forces Shaping British Attitudes Towards the EC* (Centre for European Policy Studies, Brussels, CEPS Paper No. 23, 1985), Britain is an island,

> but an island with a long tradition of trade and exchange with the continental mainland . . . the degree of foreign travel, the increasing willingness to learn other European languages and the opinion

poll evidence all suggest that the British people's attitudes would be unfairly characterized as isolationist.

Opinion polls in the run-up to Maastricht tended to reinforce this. For that matter, Mrs Thatcher as Prime Minister was not an isolationist. At Bruges she said:

> We British are as much heirs to the legacy of European culture as any other nation. Our links to the rest of Europe, the continent of Europe, have been the dominant factor in our history . . . And let me be quite clear: Britain does not dream of some cosy, isolated existence on the fringes of Europe. Our destiny is in Europe, as part of the Community.

Britain is inextricably enmeshed in the economic and political machinery of the EC, and plays a major role in it.

The appalling behaviour of British football hooligans on the Continent, and the drunken rampages of young British 'holidaymakers' in Spain, reflect a contemptuous and ignorant attitude towards fellow Europeans as well as personal inadequacy and social malaise at home. On the other hand, the modern generation of professional Britons is far less influenced by stereotypes of 'Continentals' than previous generations, and more likely to view Europe in terms of business and money-market opportunities. It's an approach that is relatively hard headed and unsentimental, and unimpressed by narrowly 'nationalist' values. To a degree, Mrs Thatcher's rhetoric masked the fact that she took a full and exhaustive part in EC decision making, often improving the end result by leavening wilder EC proposals with common sense and experience. John Major and Douglas Hurd played a similar role over Maastricht. As Hurd put it in a speech to the Atlantic Commission in The Hague, just before Maastricht, 'thoroughness and thoughtfulness should not be mistaken for reluctance and rejection'. Just as the internal market programme and the Single European Act both bear British hallmarks, not least in the emphasis they place on de-regulation, so, too, the treaties on monetary and political union are shaped by the British debate. This is hardly surprising. As Tom Hutchinson, a director of ICI and chairman of the CBE Europe Committee, points out, over 50% of British trade is with fellow Community states.

Britain, the EC and national sovereignty

Nonetheless, Britain is widely perceived as the country most resistant to European integration. The history of Britain's relationship with the EC —late application, rejection, accession, re-negotiation, budget rebate squabbles, objections to the single currency and to extra powers for the European Parliament—has produced a Europhobia in which Britain's natural reaction to EC proposals tends to be 'no' rather than 'yes but'. It's a position that derives from a number of geographical and political facts: that as an island race, the British do not feel culturally European; that by virtue of empire and historic links Britain has looked in the past as much, if not indeed more, to the US and to the Commonwealth as to its immediate European neighbours; that its role as the dominant world power of the nineteenth century has led Britain even today to play a global rather than purely European role in matters of defence; similarly, that sterling is a world currency as well as a European currency. In short, that in significant ways, Britain is *in* Europe but not *of* it.

There is, in consequence, a trend in British opinion which fears that, instead of 'willing and active co-operation between independent sovereign states', something more like a 'European super-state' will emerge. After resigning as Prime Minister Mrs Thatcher continued to warn against a federal superstate which would undermine NATO, exclude Eastern Europe and jeopardize the GATT negotiations. 'It is time to recognize even in Brussels that the age of empire is past', Mrs Thatcher declared in Chicago in June 1991. During the run-up to Maastricht Douglas Hurd used similar language, objecting to the use of the phrase 'a union with a federal goal' in the draft treaty. 'We do not intend to be committed to the implications which the phrase "federal goal" carries in the English language,' Hurd said. 'Federal has come to mean something tight and integrated in English.'

Though the Commission promotes symbols of European nationhood —the EC flag, the European anthem (Beethoven's 'Ode to Joy')—in reality the process of forming a European identity has barely begun. To suggest, as the Commission did in newspaper advertisements, that all Europeans should share in the glory of medals won by the Twelve at Olympic games, is counterproductive, since for many national feeling is expressed above all through sport—and will continue to be long after 1992.

Yet the single market and the Channel Tunnel will between them bring immense psychological changes in their wake, as the British adjust to having an umbilical cord tying them to the Continent. There is already a breed of businessmen who commute across the Channel, and British property developers—and house buyers—are moving into the Pas de Calais and the Boulogne area. This kind of cross-Channel fertilization will be commonplace.

Does this make inevitable something approaching a United States of Europe? Mrs Thatcher as Prime Minister thought not, and many still share her views. Others, by contrast, believe union of some kind is both inevitable and desirable. The case has been most forcefully put by Germany's Chancellor Kohl, who, as a Christian Democrat, is ideologi-aligned with the Conservative Party but nonetheless reflects German enthusiasm for European integration. In a speech in Brussels in October

1988, Kohl spelled it out graphically. Kohl said fiscal harmonization was indispensable in 1992. As for the fight against crime and terrorism, he called for a European police force along US lines, adding, 'I know this idea has far-reaching consequences, but the nature and size of the challenge we face leaves us no choice'. On defence, Kohl suggested the eventual creation of a European Army. Finally, the loss of sovereignty involved in 1992 was counter-balanced by a gain in pooled sovereignty. When President Mitterrand was presented, with Kohl, with the Charlemagne Prize at Aachen in November 1988, he defined the EC goal as 'one currency, one culture, one social area, one environment'.

'Socialist central control' and the European super-state

The process outlined by Kohl and Mitterrand and taken further in the inter-governmental conferences on monetary and political union in 1991 – 92 does not quite add up to a United States of Europe—but it is a step along the road. Part of the problem is that neither the phrase 'an ever-closer union' laid down in the Treaty of Rome preamble nor the goal of 'European Union' enshrined in the Stuttgart summit declaration of 1983 have ever been properly defined. This gives room for conflicting interpretations, including the Thatcherite 'nightmare' of a 'socialist' and 'collectivist' European superstate run from Brussels. At the Conservative Party Conference in Brighton in October 1988 the Prime Minister gave the formula a new twist: 'We haven't worked all these years to free Britain from the paralysis of socialism only to see it creep in through the back-door of central control and bureaucracy from Brussels'.

The choice, Thatcher said, was between two Europes: 'One based on the widest-possible freedom for enterprise, and one governed by socialist methods of centralized control and regulation'. The choice is not a real one, however. The 'social dimension' involves EC law in employer–employee relations, but few Continental leaders, whether of the left or right, would regard this as 'collectivist'. Most Continental systems rest on a political culture of consensus. For example, Kohl presides over a Centre–Right coalition which accepts worker participation in industry—*Mitbestimmung*—as much as the opposition Social Democrats do. The effect of the single market, German industrialists believe, will be to reduce over-protection of employees rather than the reverse. All EC leaders are committed to free enterprise capitalism, as is Delors, even though he is a French socialist by origin. Few EC countries have reacted with the same horror as Britain to EC social policies such as the maximum working week or the increase in maternity benefits for pregnant working women agreed in November 1991. Speakers at the CBI annual conference in November 1991 welcomed the single market but expressed concern about the additional business costs of the social charter, for example in overtime payments.

To some extent, generalized attacks on 'rule from Brussels' articulate a British aversion to the involvement of 'foreigners' in domestic British affairs. But to call European federalism 'socialist' is to confuse the issue. What such attacks really express perhaps is disagreement with the kind of federalism espoused by Christian Democrats such as Kohl and Wilfried Martens, the Belgian Prime Minister. Shortly after Bruges, Martens said elimination of trade barriers would make closer political unity inevitable, leading to 'some form of loosely constructed federal European government' responsible for economic affairs as well as for defence and foreign relations. Martens agreed with 'apprehension about an unbridled European bureaucracy' and 'centrally imposed over-regulation', but came to the opposite conclusion to that drawn by the Euro-sceptics. The answer lay in an all-European executive body 'answerable to a genuinely European and sovereign legislature'. National states would retain some powers to control crime and immigration, and, 'given Europe's history, steeped in diversity, a highly decentralized form of government is undoubtedly preferable'. But European government there would be.

The Commission, stung by the charge that the EC is controlled by 'appointed bureaucrats', has also joined the debate. To focus on the Commission, officials point out, is to ignore the Council of Ministers and the Parliament, which take decisions for the Twelve as a whole. The Commission's real aim is to enhance competition and enterprise, limit central regulation 'to the minimum level required for coherence', and give the regions a greater say in their own economic development. But many believe the Commission is too powerful, 'inserting itself into the nooks and crannies of everyday life' as Douglas Hurd put it during a clash with Delors at a pre-Maastricht meeting of EC foreign ministers.

Federalism: the end of the nation state?

Writing in *The Times* in October 1988, Peter Sutherland, the former Commissioner for Competition, called for 'a reasoned debate, avoiding emotional polemics' on how Europeans could deal with the loss of sovereignty flowing from 'our common commitment to the 1992 programme'. He continued,

> It is important to remember that with the ratification of the
> European treaties, concessions of sovereignty to autonomous
> European institutions have already occurred. An embryonic
> federal structure is in place, even if its powers are confined to
> certain areas . . . There is no vast bureaucracy in Brussels which
> seeks to impose itself on member states. It is inconsistent to criticize
> the institutions of the Community for being appointed rather than
> elected democratically and at the same time to ignore the claims
> of the European Parliament for powers which alone can develop
> control on a common European basis.

It's a view shared by Delors. Speaking to the Belgian newspaper *Le Soir*, he said, 'It is the Council and not the Commission which takes the real decisions. It is regrettable that attacks on the Brussels bureaucrats have become a scapegoat and a way of avoiding having to give concrete answers to what should be done to implement the Single European Act'.

But the problem of the 'democratic deficit' is not so easily solved. If transfer of sovereignty is inevitable, is the right answer to devolve further powers from Westminster, the Bundestag and the Assemblée Nationale, for example, to the European Parliament? The same Britons who supported European unification in the MORI post-Bruges opinion poll obviously thought not. 67% opposed giving greater power to Strasbourg, with only 25% in favour. Sheer volume of work, and the integration process, are pushing the European Parliament towards more frequent sessions—perhaps two weeks a month instead of one—and will almost certainly push it towards meeting in Brussels rather than Strasbourg. This is not the same, however, as the evolution of a European Government.

The idea of a European government in any case arouses horror in some quarters. In an article in *The Times* in response to Commissioner Sutherland, William Cash, Conservative MP for Stafford and a member of the Commons Select Committee on European Legislation, claimed European federalism was being introduced by stealth:

> The EC in principle has just about the right framework now. It will develop and must be reformed. The advantages it offers will help us to compete successfully with other continental giants. But political union on the same scale is unnecessary, and could provoke unwelcome hostility.

In November 1991 Nigel Lawson, who as Chancellor of the Exchequer had fought for British entry into the ERM, said in *The Evening Standard* that to go on from ERM membership to a single currency would risk breaching the principle that a government should be democratically elected and able to carry out the wishes of its people. If nations were denied their identity, the 'ugliest manifestations of nationalism' would come to the fore. 'Nothing could be better calculated to encourage the growth of M. Le Pen's Front National in France and its unpleasant counterparts elsewhere in the Community than the creation of full monetary and political union,' Mr Lawson wrote. Douglas Hurd also noted that to attempt common EC control of immigration was to try mistakenly to 'harmonize history' when asylum policy ought to be based on national backgrounds and conditions.

Yet according to Sir Leon Brittan, Britain's senior EC Commissioner:

> We have long since abandoned the idea that our sovereignty is absolute, neither to be shared nor diluted by one jot or tittle. We

joined the Community precisely because we decided we would be stronger as a country if some decisions were taken on a European basis . . . We would not now be contemplating the privatizing of a profitable British Steel Corporation if there had not been a powerful European steel regime able to bring about the necessary and painful changes required in the steel industry throughout Europe.

Some who are unhappy about the transfer of sovereignty fall back on a cautious 'step-by-step' approach. On the other hand, as Sir Nicholas Henderson, former British Ambassador in Bonn, Paris and Washington, and chairman of the Channel Tunnel Group, points out, 'a step-by-step approach is very reasonable, but it is also reasonable to believe that the steps must be leading somewhere'. He adds 'For many of the peoples of Europe the nation state has proved in this century to be not only inadequate to their needs, but disastrous. Without wishing to sacrifice national tradition or nationhood, they aspire to a new and wider identity'.

What is needed, in other words—especially in an era when there is likely to be further pooling of security and defence interests—is a redefinition of the nation state itself. In their study of *Options for British Foreign Policy in the 1990s* (Royal Institute for International Affairs) Christopher Tugendhat and William Wallace confront this head on:

There is now a structural contradiction not only between the logic of international industrial and economic integration and the national framework of popular loyalty, but also between the increasing integration of defence and security policies and the underlying rationale of the nation state. The force of this contradiction has not yet filtered through to the British electorate.

Defining Europe: the global context

One side-effect of Mrs Thatcher's approach was that it helped to bring home to British voters that the underpinning of the nation state—popular loyalty to the state within defined borders, management of common economic resources within the same borders, taxation to raise revenues, the maintenance of nationally defined police and armed forces—needs re-examining as some of these functions begin to take on a pan-European character. Traditionally, a nation defines itself by what its citizens have in common, or—though this is not quite the same thing—by the ways in which it differs from other nations. Ultimately, nation states are given internal coherence by their response to perceived external threats. In the past, such threats, whether commercial or military, have come to Britain from across the Channel, in centuries of commercial and military rivalries with France, Germany and other Continental countries.

To some extent, both the EC and NATO draw their *raison d'etre* from the need to ensure that the countries of Europe remain locked into intimate alliances which make cross-border European conflicts less likely, perhaps impossible. In the absence of an old-style Soviet threat, but with control of nuclear weapons causing new anxiety as the Soviet empire breaks up, the EC and NATO are still needed to provide internal security: hence the establishment at the Rome NATO summit of November 1991 of a 'North Atlantic Co-operation Council' to embrace East and Central Europe, the Soviet Union and the independent Baltic states as well as Western Europe and the US. Conversely, the perceived commercial threat—again to Europe as a whole—comes from the United States and Japan. Europe itself, meanwhile, grows more compact: the Channel Tunnel will reduce train journey time between London and Paris from 5½ hours to 3, between London and Brussels from 5 hours to 2½, and between London and Amsterdam from 10 hours to 5. Planned east–west motorways should also make trade and other contacts more coherent.

Certainly, the rest of the world has come more and more to look on Europe as a unit, and deals with it as such. The United States, Japan, and EFTA have been increasingly alarmed at the prospect of being shut out of 'Fortress Europe', with the EC building up barriers against the outside world while demolishing frontiers inside the Community. World competitors fear that in sectors such as cars and textiles EC quotas, replacing national ones, will be geared to the most protectionist EC states; that non-EC companies with subsidiaries in Europe will have to prove that their products have a 'minimum local content' and therefore count as European; and that the single market integration programme in services such as banking and insurance is premature when the GATT is still discussing an international liberalisation regime.

Yet increasingly, the Commission uses the term 'foreign' in official documents to mean 'non-EC'. The reaction of EFTA countries, many of which border directly on the EC, was first to draw closer to the EC and then, in a headlong rush, to apply for full membership. It remains to be seen how far the creation of a European Economic Area bringing EFTA into the single market will satisfy countries like Austria, Sweden and Norway. Non-EFTA countries know they will have to wait much longer: Turkey's application for membership, made in April 1987, has been put on ice by the EC until the mid-1990s at the earliest. On the other hand the EC made considerable efforts to bring Greece, Spain and Portugal— all of which had recent undemocratic records—into the Community, and it is increasingly difficult to argue that, say, the Scandinavian countries do not qualify. Denmark is already in the club; Sweden, though not a member, is unquestionably a powerful commercial force within the EC. As for Norway, it was only in 1988 that Mrs Gro Harlem Brundtland, the Norwegian Prime Minister, made it clear that Oslo had no desire to re-open the wounds of the 1972 referendum campaign, when Norway narrowly turned down membership. She even rebuked 'impatient voices in EFTA countries calling for a direct, bilateral approach to the issue of membership'. Now Oslo is as eager as Stockholm to join.

The United States remains suspicious that the single market spells protectionism, and views EC enlargement with mixed feelings. On the one hand any reinforcement of European democratic values in the aftermath of the collapse of Communism is welcomed; on the other, the Bush administration does not want to compete with a European leviathan. It already regards 'the Europeans' as more difficult to negotiate with in the GATT talks than the Japanese. As for defence, as Bush put it at Rome in November 1991, 'If you don't need us any longer, say so'. Every European leader including Chancellor Kohl, replied that while a united Europe was impossible without a united European defence, it was also impossible without an American presence.

Maastricht

Making industry and commerce more competitive on a European rather than national basis will also have painful consequences as well as benefits within Europe itself. This—together with belated resentment over the partial loss of political sovereignty—could lead to a popular backlash against integration. According to Sir John Harvey-Jones, former chairman of ICI, 'We are looking at a degree of attrition that we have not experienced at any time. In my judgment, at least half the European companies will disappear'. The EC has twelve major boiler-making companies, the United States only six: the EC has ten competing turbine manufacturers, the US only two. Something will have to give, and the consequences could be traumatic. Hence the Commission's concern over a 'social dimension' to soften the blow. Hence also the argument that the single market inevitably entails monetary union, which, in turn implies close co-ordination of economic and social policy, if not a supranational body to supervise such co-operation.

As Roy Denman, the former EC Director General for External Affairs, observes, it is ironic that as one kind of union is falling apart—the Soviet empire—another is taking shape in Western Europe. But the British horror of federation, Denman suggests, produces amusement across the Channel, 'Switzerland is a federation—but the citizens of Geneva and Unterwalden do not go to bed at night gibbering with terror at the prospect of a superstate in Berne'. Since the 1950 Coal and Steel Community, a European federation has been the long-term aim, in one form or another. As Denman observes,

> When businessmen can trade as easily between Hamburg and
> Lyons as they can between the states of the American union,
> they will not long put up with the expense and inconvenience of
> separate currencies. But a single currency means a single

economic policy, and that cannot be controlled by non-elected bureaucrats in Brussels. This means the start of a federal union, which means a common defence and foreign policy, which will probably happen in the next five to six years . . . Unfortunately the British attitude to the unification of Europe has been that of the Victorian mother who summons her nanny and instructs her to find out what the children are doing and tell them to stop it.

Conversely Sir Alan Walters, writing in *The Times* in October 1991, admitted he had been wrong to maintain that monetary union would prove a virtual impossibility 'because it would inevitably imply a centralization of power in Brussels which would be quite unthinkable to the peoples of Europe and particularly to the British'. The idea of a single currency had won far more support among businessmen and voters than he would have believed possible. He continued to insist, however, that, 'the economic union of Europe does not require a monetary union, and certainly not a single currency'. Furthermore, as economic union would be accompanied by political union, he repeated his warning that, 'the inevitable tensions and frictions between nations and groups in any conglomerate can be contained only if the central authorities practise light government . . . From the best intentions, I fear, a European leviathan will emerge to plague us all'.

Clearly the debate over Britain's role in a unified Europe is far from over. Indeed, as Maastricht showed, it has in some senses only just begun.

From Maastricht to Lisbon and Edinburgh

The Maastricht agreement, John Major said as the summit ended in December 1991 and Portugal prepared to take over the EC Presidency, was 'a good agreement for Europe and for the United Kingdom', one which 'safeguards and advances our national interests'. It was 'game, set and match for Britain'.

Was it? Major's skill in negotiation, and his non-strident tone, allowed an unusual deal to be struck in the early hours of the third and final day of the summit, with Britain opting out not only of plans for a single currency—which had been expected—but also out of the social chapter giving the EC competence in labour-management relations and working conditions. Major's style won him applause in his own party, and quelled the threat of a rebellion by arch-Conservative anti-federalist campaigners such as Norman Tebbit when the Commons voted on Maastricht shortly afterwards. On the other hand, the Maastricht treaties undoubtedly moved the EC as a whole—Britain included—farther down the road to a European Union. Similarly, while attention was focused on the social charter and the single currency, Britain gave significant ground in other areas such as common defence and the powers of the European Parliament. Maastricht also signalled a future European citizenship, and marked a shift toward a role for the EC in education and health.

Major's tennis metaphor, Ian Davidson wrote in *The Financial Times*, suggested he,

> did not seem to understand the difference between winning and losing . . . The Maastricht agreement must be considered, by any rational measure, one of the most important events in post-war European history. This is a treaty which will lead to a single currency in Europe in just over seven years, as well as to the gradual development of a common foreign and defence policy. If this programme is adhered to, the European Community will be well on the way to becoming a sort of federation.

What Maastricht highlighted, as Piet Dankert, a Dutch minister, pointed out, was the 'cultural difference' between Britain and most of its EC partners, above all Germany, for whom extension of EC powers is an article of faith. In the end it was the alliance built between Major and Kohl which made compromise possible. Yet as Germany increasingly dominates European policy, from Yugoslavia to interest rates, Britain seems likely to be pulled along in its wake, perhaps coming to accept a degree of European Union even in areas where Major stood his ground in December 1991.

The Maastricht deal on social policy, with the eleven forming their own 'European Social Community' to legislate on the labour market, was forged by Chancellor Kohl and Ruud Lubbers, the Dutch Prime Minister and summit host, who between them persuaded President Mitterrand that the best course was to let Britain opt out altogether. The CBI and leading British employers expressed relief. Michael Howard, the Employment Secretary, pointed out that foreign investors would regard Britain with favour because of lower labour costs and less rigid workplace rules. On the other hand, if the eleven go ahead with plans for works councils or harmonized legislation on part-time workers, trades union pressure on employers in the UK to match such measures will increase. British employers with Continental subsidiaries will in any case have to observe the new rules. Labour condemned the government for 'consigning Britain to the slow lane of a two-speed Europe', and vowed to impose tough social legislation on coming to power. Portugal continued to press during 1992 for EC legislation on maximum working hours, using majority voting rules under health and safety provisions, with Britain countering that such matters properly required a unanimous vote. The Maastricht compromise looks set to become a legal battleground, with critics arguing that Britain is infringing single market competition rules by maintaining labour laws which give it an unfair advantage over the other eleven.

On the single currency, too, the pressure will be on Britain to fall into line. It remains unclear how or indeed whether most EC states will meet the criteria laid down for economic convergence. Equally unclear at present is how the European Monetary Institute (EMI), the precursor of the European Bank, is to manage member states' foreign exchange reserves. But at Maastricht France and Italy between them secured German consent to an 'irreversible' move toward a European Bank and single currency, spelling the end of the all powerful Deutschmark, despite constant German worries—based on the relationship in German history between currency weakness and political instability—about currency stability. 'The end of the D-Mark' was the banner headline in the German mass circulation daily *Bild*.

It is true that Kohl failed to ensure the kind of political union treaty he had wanted as a *quid pro quo* for concessions on monetary union. But he won greater powers for the European Parliament, through the 'Negative Assent Procedure' giving Strasbourg the right to negotiate directly with the Council of Ministers the changes it wants to see made in EC laws—and the right to veto bills which fail to make such changes. Because of British sensitivities over the concession of sovereignty involved, this power is referred to in the treaty merely as 'the procedure laid down in article 189b'. But in plain terms it amounts to co-decision making for Strasbourg in key areas: the internal market, consumer protection, the free movement of labour, company establishment, treatment of foreigners, vocational training, public health, infrastructure projects, structural funds, international agreements, the rights of European citizens, and the harmonization of electoral systems for European elections (which could mean the introduction of PR into the UK).

On defence, too, Britain gave ground. The role of NATO is maintained, but the EC's common foreign and security policy is to 'include all questions related to the security of the European Union, including the eventual framing of a common defence policy, which might in time lead to common defence'. Tentative as the wording is, it is not altogether what Britain wanted. Nor did Britain particularly want the treaty to define the Western European Union as 'an integral part of the development of the European Union', which can request the WEU 'to elaborate and implement decisions and actions of the Union which have defence implications'. The foreign policy procedure requires unanimity on matters of principle, with majority voting only on the technicalities of implementing policy. Yet with the ink on the Maastricht treaties barely dry, at the end of December 1991, Germany succeeded in steamrolling the EC into recognition of Croatia and Slovenia by the middle of January 1992, this very much against the better judgement of Douglas Hurd, who observed wearily: 'It was a compromise, it always is.'

As the 'European Union' was being outlined at Maastricht, three of the former Soviet republics, led by Boris Yeltsin's Russia, were forming the new Commonwealth of Independent States at Minsk. By the end of

December, the Commonwealth had taken shape with the signing of a new treaty at Alma Ata and the resignation of Gorbachov and the formal dissolution of the Soviet Union. A new form of federation is being created in the East; but it looks for inspiration to the West. Poland, Hungary and Czechoslovakia all want EC membership following their new association agreements, signed just after Maastricht. While at the new NATO Co-operation Council at the end of 1991, Yeltsin astonished NATO officials by formally applying for Russian membership of the western alliance. History has been stood on its head.

As the European Union sketched at Maastricht and developed at Lisbon under Portugal's presidency in June 1992 takes shape, can Britain —itself chairing the EC in the second half of 1992—stand aside? Nicholas Ridley, writing disapprovingly of Maastricht in *The Times* (12 December 1991), described the thrust of EC policy as federal: 'The Community will enter upon stages two and three of the Delors plan for an economic and monetary union with a single currency and an independent central bank. This, inevitably, means the transfer of control of economic policies to the centre, and the end of the sovereignty of national parliaments over interest rates, exchange rates and budget deficits. It reduces them to the status of rate-capped county councils'. Ridley's fear is of a 'corporatist, regulated EC' whose protectionism makes a mockery of GATT, as opposed to 'a Europe open to all European states to join, with a free and open market both internally and externally, voluntarily co-operating on a range of subjects from immigration to foreign policy'. There is also an overriding fear—shared by many in the US—of Germany as the new European superpower.

Such views are rejected by Labour, the party which once wanted Britain out of the EC altogether. Rebutting Ridley's arguments, Gerald Kaufman, the shadow foreign secretary, declared in *The Times* (13 December 1991) that a Labour government would want to join the other eleven in common social policies, because

> in a single market with a single currency, working people in every kind of occupation require protection from the unbridled activities of commerce and industry . . . Community best practices will apply for all workers in countries which subscribe to the social charter, which simply provides an updated and Europe-wide extension of the kind of enlightened social protection pioneered by the Tory party's revered icon, Disraeli.

As for the ECU, Kaufman wrote, even investors wishing to profit from low labour costs would 'think twice before investing in a country outside the single currency area'.

Maastricht undoubtedly moved the agenda forward. Not so long ago the debate was over whether the pound should join the ERM; now, although arguments continue over interest rates and devaluation, the debate is over whether the pound should give way to a single European currency by 1999 at the latest. As *The Times* observed in an editorial after Maastricht, 'Where Britain's interests will lie by then it is impossible to say, which was precisely Mr Major's point.' Maastricht had been a 'job well done', but there were collective challenges beyond Maastricht such as the completion of the single market, the Uruguay round of GATT, and the problem of Eastern Europe. It was 'time for Europe to get down to real business'. Or, as *The Wall Street Journal Europe* put it, Maastricht did not create a United States of Europe, but it did amount to 'an economic and political transformation which will make it possible for the EC to embrace new members without crippling its decision-making structures . . . Maastricht has given the EC a road map for the next decade'.

The Portuguese Presidency in the first half of 1992 had budgetary reform and justice for the southern countries as well as the momentum of the single market at the top of its agenda. It falls to Britain, at the Edinburgh EC summit in December 1992, actually to usher in the single market. Germany and France have no monopoly on European credentials: it was Germany which broke ranks over Yugoslavia, and which used new ecological packaging laws to turn back goods, while France, as *The Times* observed at the beginning of 1992 'has given short shrift to the principle of collective industrial policy in its creation of a new nationalised electronics cartel'. To succeed, the single market needs the full co-operation of all Twelve—with Britain playing the role of 'good but sceptical European'.

Appendix 1 EUROPE'S TOP 20 COMPANIES

Company	*Country*	*Turnover (£ million)*	*Profits (£ million)*
Royal Dutch/Shell Group of Companies	UK/Netherlands	59,416	8,566
British Petroleum	UK	41,711	3,439
Daimler Benz	Germany	29,593	1,675
IRI	Italy	28,343	539
Fiat	Italy	25,489	2,607
Volkswagen	Germany	23,557	1,327
Unilever	UK	22,258	2,255
Siemens	Germany	21,535	1,470
Veba	Germany	18,895	1,046
Nestlé	Switzerland	18,773	1,974
Renault	France	18,696	1,042
ENI	Italy	18,211	2,390
Philips	Netherlands	17,107	555
Peugeot	France	16,391	1,782
BASF	Germany	16,137	1,141
Elf Aquitaine	France	16,053	1,080
Electricité de France	France	15,766	2,329
Hoechst	Germany	15,527	1,377
RWE	Germany	15,220	843
B.A.T. Industries	UK	15,027	1,347

Source: *The Times 1000.*

Appendix 2 EUROPE'S TOP 20 BANKS

Bank	*Country*	*Assets (£ billion)*
Crédit Agricole	France	150.5
Banque Nationale de Paris	France	143.6
Deutsche Bank	Germany	138.5
Barclays	UK	134.9
Crédit Lyonnais	France	130.7
National Westminster Bank	UK	121.1
ABN Amro Holding	Netherlands	120.6
Société Générale	France	109.0
Dresdner Bank	Germany	98.0
Union Bank of Switzerland	Switzerland	94.7
Paribas (Cie Financière de)	France	86.0
Swiss Bank Corporation	Switzerland	78.1
Suez (Cie de)	France	77.6
Commerzbank	Germany	74.7
Bayerische Vereinsbank	Germany	71.2
Istituto Bancario San Paulo di Torino	Italy	66.9
Midland Bank	UK	66.2
Rabobank	Netherlands	62.0
Crédit Suisse	Switzerland	60.9
Bayerische Hypotheken und Wechselbank	Germany	60.4

Source: *The Times 1000.*

Appendix 3 VAT RATES IN THE EC

Country	Lower	Standard	Higher	VAT as percentage of GDP
Belgium	1–6	19	25	7.67
Denmark	None	22	None	9.84
France	2.1–13	18.6	25	9.19
Germany	7	14	None	6.34
Greece	3–6	16	36	
Ireland	0–10	23	None	8.22
Italy	4–9	19	38	5.48
Luxembourg	3–6	12	None	6.04
Netherlands	6	18.5	None	6.83
Portugal	8	17	30	—
Spain	6	12	33	—
UK	0	17.5	None	5.22

Source: *Taxation in the Single Market.*

Appendix 4 EUROPEAN COMMISSION DIRECTORATES GENERAL

DG I	External Relations
DG II	Economic and Financial Affairs
DG III	Internal Market and Industry
DG IV	Competition
DG V	Employment, Social Affairs, Education
DG VI	Agriculture
DG VII	Transport
DG VIII	Development
DG IX	Personnel and Administration
DG X	Information and Culture
DG XI	Environment, Consumer Protection, Nuclear Safety
DG XII	Science and Research
DG XIII	Telecommunications, Information Industries, Innovation
DG XIV	Fisheries
DG XV	Financial Institutions and Company Law
DG XVI	Regional policy
DG XVII	Energy
DG XVIII	Credits and Investments
DG XIX	Budgets
DG XX	Financial Control
DG XXI	Customs Union and Indirect Taxation
DG XXII	Co-ordination of Structural Instruments
DG XXIII	Small and Medium Enterprises (SMEs)

Secretariat General
Spokesman's Service
Interpreting and Conference Service

Statistical Office
Official Publications
Source: European Commission.

Appendix 5 USEFUL 1992 CONTACTS AND ADDRESSES

Commission of the European Communities:
rue de la Loi 200
1049 Brussels
Belgium
Tel: 010 322 235 1111

EC UK Information Offices:
8 Storey's Gate
London SW1P 3AT
Tel: 071-222 8122

4 Cathedral Road
Cardiff CH1 9SG
Tel: 0222 371631

7 Alva Street
Edinburgh EH2 4PH
Tel: 031 225 2058

Windsor House
9–15 Bedford Street
Belfast
Tel: 0232 40708

European Business Information Centres:
Scottish Development
    Agency
Rosebery House
Haymarket Terrace
Edinburgh EH12 5EZ
Tel: 031 337 9595

Birmingham Chamber of
    Industry and Commerce
PO Box Harborne Road
Birmingham B15 3DH
Tel: 021 454 6171

Northern Development
    Company
Bank House
Carilo Square
Newcastle-upon-Tyne
Tel: 091 261 0026

Department of Employment
Small Firms and Tourism
    Division Limited
Ebury Bridge House
Ebury Bridge Road
London SW1W 8QD
Tel: 071-730 5874

European Documentation Centres in the UK:
The Library
University of Aberdeen
Meston Walk
Aberdeen AB9 2UB
Tel: 0224 4021

Library
Wye College
Wye
Ashford
Kent TN25 5AH
Tel: 0233 812401 × 242

University Library
University of Bath
Claverton Down
Bath BA2 7AY
Tel: 0225 826826 × 559

The Library
Government Publications
    Dept
Queens University
Belfast BT7 1LS
Tel: 0232 245133

William Kendrick Library
Birmingham Polytechnic
Birmingham B42 2SU
Tel: 021 356 6911

Main Library
University of Birmingham
PO Box 363
Birmingham B15 2TT
Tel: 021 414 3344 × 58

J B Priestley Library
University of Bradford
Richmond Road
Bradford BD7 1DP
Tel: 0274 733466

The Library
University of Sussex
Brighton BN1 9QL
Tel: 0273 678159

Law Library
University of Bristol
Queens Road
Bristol BS8 1RJ
Tel: 0272 24161

The Library
University of Cambridge
West Road
Cambridge CB3 9DR
Tel: 0223 61441

Arts and Social Studies
    Library
University College
PO Box 430
Cardiff CF1 3XT
Tel: 0222 874262

The Library
University of Essex
PO Box 24
Colchester CO4 3UA
Tel: 0206 862286

The Library
New University of Ulster
Coleraine BT52 1SA
Tel: 0265 4141

Lanchester Polytechnic
Priory Street
Coventry CV1 5FB
Tel: 0203 24166

University of Dundee
Perth Road
Dundee DD1 4HN
Tel: 0382 23181 × 4101

Official Publications Section
University Library
Stockton Road
Durham DH1 3LY
Tel: 091 374 3041

Centre of European Studies
University of Edinburgh
Old College
South Bridge
Edinburgh EH8 9LY
Tel: 031 667 1011

Centre for European Legal
    Studies
Exeter University
Law Faculty
Rennes Drive
Exeter EX4 4RJ
Tel: 0392 77911

The University Library
University of Glasgow
Hillhead Street
Glasgow G12 8QE
Tel: 041 339 8855 × 67

George Edwards Library
University of Surrey
Guilford GU2 5XH
Tel: 0483 571281

Brynmor Jones Library
University of Hull
Cottingham Road
Hull HU6 7RX
Tel: 0482 46311

The Library
University of Keele
Staffs
Tel: 0782 621111 × 300

Library Building
University of Kent
Canterbury
Kent CT2 7NU
Tel: 0227 66822

University of Lancaster
Library
Lancaster LA1 4YX
Tel: 0254 62501

The Library
Leeds Polytechnic
Calverly Street
Leeds LS1 3HE
Tel: 0532 462925

University of Leeds
20 Lyddon Terrace
Leeds LS7 9JT
Tel: 0532 31751

University Library
University of Leicester
University Road
Leicester LE1 7RH
Tel: 0533 522044

Liverpool and District
Science
and Industry Research
Council
Central Libraries
William Brown Street
Liverpool L3 8EW
Tel: 051 207 2147

EC Unit Room 61
Polytechnic of Central
London
309 Regent Street
London W1R 8AL
Tel: 071-580 2020

The Library
Queen Mary College
Mile End Road
London E1 4NS
Tel: 081-980 4811

The Library
Polytechnic of North London
Prince of Wales Road
London NW5
Tel: 071-359 0941

Reference Division
Department of Printed Books
Overseas Section
British Library
Great Russell Street
London WC1B 3DB
Tel: 071-323 7602

The Library
RIIA
10 St James Square
London SW1Y 4LE
Tel: 071-930 2233

European Depository Library
Central Reference Library
City of Westminster Library
St Martin's Street
London WC2 7HP
Tel: 071-798 2084

British Library of Political
and Economic Science
The Library
10 Portugal Street
London WC2A 2HD
Tel: 071-405 7686

The Library
Loughborough University
of Technology
Loughborough LE11 3TU
Tel: 0509 222344

John Rylands Library
University of Manchester
Oxford Road
Manchester M13 9PP
Tel: 061 273 3333

The Library
Newcastle Polytechnic
Ellison Place
Newcastle-upon-Tyne
NE1 8ST
Tel: 091 232 6002 × 4136

The Library
University of East Anglia
University Plain
Norwich NR4 7TJ
Tel: 0603 56161 × 2412

The Library
University of Nottingham
Nottingham NG7 2RD
Tel: 0602 506101 × 374

Bodelian Library
University of Oxford
Oxford OX1 3BG
Tel: 0865 277201

Frewen Library
Portsmouth Polytechnic
Cambridge Road
Portsmouth PO1 2ST
Tel: 0705 827681 × 401

The Library
University of Reading
Whiteknights
PO Box 223
Reading RG6 2AH
Tel: 0734 874331 × 131

The Library
University of Salford
Salford
Lancs
Tel: 061 736 5843

The Library
Sheffield City Polytechnic
Pond Street
Sheffield S1 1WB
Tel: 0742 20911 × 2494

Faculty of Law
University of Southampton
Southampton SO9 5NH
Tel: 0703 559122

The Library
University of Warwick
Coventry CV4 7A

British Library
Document Supply Centre
Boston Spa
Wetherby
LS23 7BQ
Tel: 0937 546045

Robert Scott Library
Polytechnic of
Wolverhampton
St Peters Square
Wolverhampton WV1 1RH

Source: European
Commission

**Private EC Consultancies
and Advisers:**
Allott & Lomax
Fairbairn House
Ashton Lane, Sale
Manchester M33 1WP
Tel: 061 962 1214

Advocacy Partnership
Limited
16 Regency Street
London SW1P 4DB
Tel: 071-630 1235

Ceres
Station House
Station Road, Wylam
Northumberland NE41 8HR
Tel: 0661 853982

CSM European Consultants
Limited
Eagle House
109 Jermyn Street
London SW1Y 6HB
Tel: 071-839 4544

CTA Economic Export
Analysts Limited
96 London Road
Reading RG1 5AU
Tel: 0734 66 8381

David Perchard Associates
23 Kingsbury Avenue
St Albans AL3 4TA
Tel: 0727 43227

European Strategy Council
18 Bolton Street
London W1Y 7PA
Tel: 071-493 0049

GJW Government Relations
64 Clapham Road
London SW9 0JJ
Tel: 071-582 3119

Galactic Trading Company
Limited
European Trade Index (1992)
38–40 Clareville Street
London SW7 5AW
Tel: 071-244 8697

Halcrow Fox & Associates
Vineyard House
44 Brook Green
London W6 7BY
Tel: 071-603 5783

Hambros Bank Limited
41 Bishopsgate
London EC2P 2AA
Tel: 071-588 2851

McAvoy Wreford Bayley
36 Grosvenor Gardens
London SW1W 0ED
Tel: 071-730 4500

Randall's Parliamentary
Service
7 Buckingham Gate
London SW1E 6JY
Tel: 071-828 2277

Sallingbury Casey Limited
25 Victoria Street
London SW1H 0EX
Tel: 071-799 1020

Spicers Centre for Europe
Information Division
4th Floor
Cavendish House
Albion Street
Leeds LS1 6AG
Tel: 0532 442629

SRI International
Menlo Park House
4 Addiscombe Road
Croydon CR0 5TT
Tel: 081-686 5555

Westminster and Whitehall
Consultants Limited
25 Victoria Street
London SW1H 0EX
Tel: 071-222 2025

Appendix 6 THE SECOND DELORS COMMISSION 1989–92

1 **Jacques Delors** (France) President of the European Commission
2 **Christiane Scrivener** (France) Fiscal Affairs and the Customs Union
3 **Martin Bangemann** (Germany) Internal market
4 **Peter Schmidhuber** (Germany) Budget
5 **Leon Brittan** (UK) Competition Policy and Financial Services
6 **Bruce Millan** (UK) Regional Development
7 **Abel Matutes** (Spain) Mediterranean Policy, Relations with Latin America, and North –South issues
8 **Manuel Marin** (Spain) Co-operation and Development (Lomé), and Fish.
9 **Carlo Ripa di Meana** (Italy) Environment, Nuclear Safety, and Civil Protection
10 **Filippo Maria Pandolphi** (Italy) Science, Research and Development, Telecommunications, and Joint Research Centres
11 **Frans Andriessen** (Netherlands) External Relations
12 **Henning Christopherson** (Denmark) Economic and Monetary Affairs, and Co-ordination of the Structural Funds
13 **Raymond MacSharry** (Ireland) Agriculture
14 **Antonio Cardoso** (Portugal) Personnel and Administration, Energy, and Small and Medium Enterprises
15 **Vasso Papandreau** (Greece) Employment, Industrial and Social Affairs, and Education
16 **Karel Van Miert** (Belgium) Transport, Credit and Investment, and Consumer Protection
17 **Jean Dodelinger** (Luxembourg) Audio Visual and Cultural Affairs, Information and Communication, and Citizens' Europe

Appendix 7 SELECT BIBLIOGRAPHY

The basic texts for 1992 remain the European Commission's White Paper *Completing the Internal Market*, June 1985; the Commission's Mid-Term Report on the Internal Market, December 1988; and the Treaties establishing the European Communities, incorporating the Single European Act and the Treaty of Rome, all issued by the Office for Official Publications of the European Communities, Luxembourg.

Other useful publications include:

Europe Without Frontiers—Completing the Internal Market, Commission of the European Communities, 1987.

The European Challenge 1992: The Benefits of a Single Market, by Paolo Cecchini and others, Wildwood House, 1988.

Pocket Guide to the European Community, by Dick Leonard, Basil Blackwell and The Economist Publications, 1988.

The EEC: A Guide to the Maze, by Stanley Budd, Melville Crawford Associates, Edinburgh, 1985.

The Economics of the Common Market, by Dennis Swann, Penguin, 1984.

Europe: More than a Continent, by Michael Butler (former UK Ambassador to the EC), Heinemann, 1986.

Making Sense of Europe, by Christopher Tugendhat (former Commissioner), Viking, 1986.

Europe's Domestic Market, by Jacques Pelkmans and Alan Winters, Chatham House Papers No. 43, Royal Institute of International Affairs, 1988.

The European Community. Past, Present and Future, edited by Loukas Tsoukalis, Blackwell, 1983.

The European Community: Progress or Decline? by Karl Kaiser, Royal Institute of International Affairs, 1983.

1992: Implications and Potential, by James Elles, Conservative MEP for Oxford and Buckinghamshire. The Bow Group, 1988.

VAT: The Zero Rate Issue, European Parliament discussion paper, by Ben Patterson, Conservative MEP for Kent West, 1988.

Common Standards for Enterprises: Document, Commission of the European Communities, Florence Nicolas, Office for Official Publications, Luxembourg, 1988.

Vacher's European Companion (quarterly), 29 Tufton Street, London SW1P 3QL.

Eurojargon: A Dictionary of EC Acronyms, Abbreviations and Sobriquets, by Anne Ramsay, Capital Planning Information, The Grey House, Broad Street, Stamford, Lincs PE9 1PR.

Europe 1992 Directory, published by Coventry Polytechnic Commercial Development Unit, Priory Street, Coventry CV1 5FB, in collaboration with the DTI Information Technology Unit.

Finance from Europe: A guide to loans and grants from the European Community, Commission of the European Communities, London.

Appendix 8 HIGHLIGHTS OF THE SINGLE EUROPEAN ACT

Article 8a
The Community shall adopt measures with the aim of progressively establishing the internal market over a period expiring on 31 December 1992, in accordance with the provisions of this Article and of Articles 8D, 8C, 28, 57(2), 59, 70(1), 83, 99, 100a and 100b and without prejudice to other provisions of this Treaty.

The internal market shall comprise an area without internal frontiers in which the free movement of goods, persons, services and capital is ensured in accordance with the provisions of this Treaty.
Article 8b
The Commission shall report to the Council before 31 December 1988 and again before 31 December 1990 on the progress made towards achieving the internal market within the time limit fixed in Article 8a.

The Council, acting by a qualified majority on a proposal from the Commission, shall determine the guidelines and conditions necessary to ensure balanced progress in all the sectors concerned.
Article 8c
When drawing up its proposals with a view to achieving the objectives set out in Article 8a, the Commission shall take into account the extent of the effort that certain economies showing differences in development will have to sustain during the period of establishment of the internal market and it may propose appropriate provisions.

If these provisions take the form of derogations, they must be of a temporary nature and must cause the least possible disturbance to the functioning of the common market.
Article 99
The Council shall, acting unanimously on a proposal from the Commission and after consulting the European Parliament, adopt provisions for the harmonization of legislation concerning turnover taxes, excise duties and other forms of indirect taxation to the extent that such harmonization is

necessary to ensure the establishment and the functioning of the internal market within the time limit laid down in Article 8a.

Article 100a
1 By way of derogation from Article 100 and save where otherwise provided in this Treaty, the following provisions shall apply for the achievement of the objectives set out in Article 8a. The Council shall, acting by a qualified majority on a proposal from the Commission in co-operation with the European Parliament and the Economic and Social Committee, adopt the measures for the approximation of the provisions laid down by law, regulation or administrative action in Member States which have as their object the establishment and functioning of the internal market.
2 Paragraph 1 shall not apply to fiscal provisions, to those relating to the free movement of persons nor to those relating to the rights and interests of employed persons.
3 The Commission, in its proposals laid down in paragraph 1 concerning health, safety, environment protection and consumer protection, will take as a base a high level of protection.
4 If, after the adoption of a harmonization measure by the Council acting by a qualified majority, a Member State deems it necessary to apply national provisions on grounds of major needs referred to in Article 36, or relating to protection of the environment or the working environment, it shall notify the Commission of these provisions.
  The Commission shall confirm the provisions involved after having verified that they are not a means of arbitrary discrimination or a disguised reaction on trade between Member States.
  By way of derogation from the procedure laid down in Articles 169 and 170, the Commission or any Member State may bring the matter directly before the Court of Justice if it considers that the Member State is making improper use of the powers provided for in this Article.
5 The harmonization measures referred to above shall, in appropriate cases, include a safeguard clause authorizing the Member States to take, for one or more of the non-economic reasons referred to in Article 36, provisional measures subject to a Community control procedure.

Article 100b
1 During 1992, the Commission shall, together with each Member State, draw up an inventory of national laws, regulations and administrative provisions which fall under Article 100a and which have not been harmonized pursuant to that Article.
  The Council, acting in accordance with the provisions of Article 100a, may decide that the provisions in force in a Member State must be recognized as being equivalent to those applied by another Member State.
2 The provisions of Article 100a(4) shall apply by analogy.
3 The Commission shall draw up the inventory referred to in the first subparagraph of paragraph 1 and shall submit appropriate proposals in good time to allow the Council to act before the end of 1992.

Article 148
1 Save as otherwise provided in this Treaty, the Council shall act by a qualified majority of its members.
2 Where the Council is required to act by a qualified majority, the votes of its members shall be weighted as follows:

Belgium	5	Ireland	3
Denmark	3	Italy	10
West Germany	10	Luxembourg	2
Greece	5	Netherlands	5
Spain	8	Portugal	5
France	10	United Kingdom	10

  For their adoption, acts of Council shall require at least:
—fifty-four votes in favour where this Treaty requires them to be adopted on a proposal from the Commission,
—fifty-four votes in favour, cast by at least eight members, in other cases.
3 Abstentions by members present in person or represented shall not prevent the adoption by the Council of acts which require unanimity.

Declaration on Article 8a of the EEC Treaty
The Conference wishes by means of the provisions in Article 8a to express its firm political will to take before 1 January 1993 the decisions necessary to complete the internal market defined in those provisions, and more particularly the decisions necessary to implement the Commission's programme described in the White Paper on the Internal Market.
  Setting the date of 31 December 1992 does not create an automatic legal effect.

Declaration on Articles 13 to 19 of the Single European Act
Nothing in these provisions shall affect the right of Member States to take such measures as they consider necessary for the purpose of controlling immigration from third countries, and to combat terrorism, crime, the traffic in drugs and illicit trading in works of art and antiques.

Appendix 9 GLOSSARY OF EC TERMS

ACP states
The 66 African, Caribbean and Pacific countries party to the Lomé Convention
ACPM
Advisory Committee on Programme Management
Additionality
Using EC funds to augment national funds
Agrimed
Mediterranean Agriculture
Aqua Europa
European Federation for Water Treatment
ASSILEC
Association of Dairy Industries of the EC
BCC
Business Co-operation Centre
BEUC
European Bureau of Consumer Councils
BRITE
Basic Research in Industrial Technologies for Europe
BTR
Basic Technological Research
CAOBISCO
Association of the Sugar Products Industries of the EC
CAP
Common Agricultural Policy
CARICOM
Caribbean Community and the Common Market
CCC
Consumer Consultative Committees
CCT/CET
Common Customs Tariff/ Common External Tariff
CEFIC
European Council of Chemical Industry Federations
CEN
European Committee for Standardization
CENELEC
European Committee for Electrotechnical Standardization
CEOP
European Committee of Workers' Co-operative Production Societies

CERN
European Nuclear Research Centre
CFP
Common Fisheries Policy
CICI
Confederation of Information Communication Industries
CID
Centre for Industrial Development
Cohesion
A term meaning reduction in disparities between regions
Comecon
Council for Mutual Economic Assistance
COMETT
Community in Education and Training for Technology
Comitextil
Co-ordination Committee for the Textile Industries of the EC
COPA
Committee for Agricultural Organizations in the EC
CORDI
Advisory Committee on Industrial Research and Development
COREPER
Committee of Permanent Representatives (i.e. EC ambassadors in Brussels)
Co-responsibility levy
A tax paid by farmers as a contribution towards the cost of storing farm surpluses
COST
Committee on European Co-operation in the field of Scientific and Technical Research
CPC
Community Patent Convention
CRM
Committee for Medical and Public Health Research
Democratic deficit
The need for greater democratic accountability of EC institutions as a result of European integration
DG
Directorate General

EAGF
European Agricultural Guidance and Guarantee Fund
ECB
European Central Bank
ECE
Economic Commission for Europe (UN)
ECSC
European Coal and Steel Community
ECU
European currency unit (mecu = million: becu = billion)
EFTA
European Free Trade Association
EIB
European Investment Bank
EMCF
European Monetary Co-operation Fund
EMI
European Monetary Institute
EMS
European Monetary System
EMU
Economic and Monetary Union
EP
European Parliament
EPC
European Political Co-operation
EPU
European Political Union
ERASMUS
EC programme to promote student mobility
ERDF
European Regional Development Fund
ERM
Exchange Rate Mechanism
ESA
European Space Agency
ESC
Economic and Social Committee
ESCB
European System of Central Banks
ESPRIT
European strategic programme for research and development in information technology

ETSI
European Telecommunications Standards Institute
ETUC
European Trades Union Confederation
EURATOM
European Atomic Energy Community
Eureka
European programme for high-technology research and development
Euro-Coop
European Community of Consumer Co-operatives
Eurofer
European Federation of the Iron and Steel Industry
EUROPMI
European Committee for Small and Medium-sized Industries
EUROSTAT
The Community's statistics office
EVCA
European Venture Capital Association
FAO
Food and Agricultural Organization (UN)
FAST
Forecasting and Assessment in Science and Technology
FIPACE
International Federation of Self-generating Industrial Users of Electricity
FIPMEC
International Federation of Small and Medium-sized Enterprises
GATT
General Agreement on Tariffs and Trade
GSP
General System of Preferences
IDN
Integrated Digital Network
IEA
International Energy Association (OECD)

IGADD
Intergovernmental Authority on Drought and Development
IGC
Intergovernmental Committee
IMF
International Monetary Fund
IMP
Integrated Mediterranean Programmes
IPM
Integrated Pest Management
ISDN
Integrated Services Digital Network
IT
Information Technologies
ITTTF
Information Technology and Telecommunications Task Force
JET
Joint European Torus
JRC
Joint Research Centre
LDCs
Least Developed Countries
MCA
Monetary Compensation Amount
MFA
Multi-Fibre Arrangement
MFTA
Medium-term Financial Assistance
MGQ
Maximum Guaranteed Quantity
MS
Member States of the EC
NCI
New Community Instruments (EIB)
NGO
Non-governmental Organization
OCTs
Overseas Countries and Territories
OECD
Organization for Economic Co-operation and Development

OJ
Official Journal of the EC
POCO
see **EPC**
QR
Quantitative Restrictions
RACE
Research and development in advanced communications technologies for Europe
SCAR
Standing Committee on Agricultural Research
SEA
Single European Act
Set aside
Taking land out of production
SMEs
Small and medium-sized businesses
STABEX
Stability in Export Revenue (Lomé Convention)
Stabilizer
A mechanism for controlling farm output
STMS
Short-term Monetary Support
Subsidiarity
Taking decisions at the lowest possible level
Sysmin
System for Safeguarding and Developing Mineral Production
Systran
Co-ordination of National Policies Relating to Machine or Machine Assisted Translation
UKREP
United Kingdom Permanent Representation to the EC (i.e. the British Embassy to the EC)
UNICE
Conference of Industries of the European Communities
Vat
Value Added Tax
WEU
Western European Union

Appendix 10 EC SUMMITS 1983–92

Stuttgart, June 1983 (West German presidency): Agreed budget needs reform, especially in view of coming enlargement, and Common Agricultural Policy must be brought into line with market realities.

Athens, December 1983 (Greek presidency): Stuttgart declaration reaffirmed.

Fontainebleau, June 1984 (French presidency): Principles of budgetary discipline agreed; British budget rebate agreed.

Dublin, December 1984 (Irish presidency): Laid down internal market without frontiers and the key to growth and jobs.

Milan, June 1985 (Italian presidency): Disagreement over Single European Act giving European Parliament more power and defining 1992 as date for completion of internal market.

Luxembourg, December 1985 (Luxembourg presidency): Single European Act finally agreed.

The Hague, June 1986 (Dutch presidency): Limited sanctions against South Africa. Budget reform deferred.

London, December 1986 (British presidency): Further progress on internal market and Community co-ordination against threat of terrorism.

Brussels, June 1987 (Belgian presidency): Disagreement (Thatcher veto) over proposed budget reform based on package put forward by Jacques Delors, the president of the European Commission. Britain said farm controls too weak.

Copenhagen, December 1987 (Danish presidency): Further refinement of Delors reforms, but still not enough to satisfy Britain. Agreement to hold extraordinary summit in Brussels in February 1988, to solve the crisis before the Hannover summit of June 1988 and the passing of the presidency to Greece.

Brussels, February 1988 (German presidency): Delors reforms agreed.

Hannover, June 1988 (German presidency): Delors Committee on Economic and Monetary Union set up. 1992 declared 'irreversible'. Delors confirmed as President of the European Commission for a second term.

Rhodes, December 1988 (Greek presidency): Presentation of European Commission's mid-term report on progress towards the completion of the internal market by 1992. 'Slippage' identified as cause of growing concern.

Madrid, June 1989 (Spanish presidency): Delors report on economic and monetary union debated. First stage adopted.

Paris, December 1989: special one-day summit, called after upheavals in Soviet bloc, agreed to link economic aid to Eastern Europe to political reform.

Strasbourg, December 1989 (French presidency): Endorses principle of German reunification, sets date for intergovernmental conference to reform the Treaty of Rome, and approves the creation of a European Development Bank and the European Social Charter.

Dublin, April 1990 (Irish presidency): Welcomes changes in Eastern Europe and impending reunification of Germany. Agrees need for further IGC on political as well as economic union.

Dublin, June 1990 (Irish presidency): Hears first report on treaty revisions. Thatcher raises no objections to report on political union.

Rome, October 1990 (Italian presidency): Called to discuss aid to the Soviet Union but sets timetable for economic and monetary union: European Bank to begin in 1994, single currency in 1997. Angry Thatcher condemns summit for 'putting the cart before the horse'.

Rome, December 1990 (Italian presidency): First appearance by John Major as Prime Minister, seen as more 'flexible' than Thatcher. Summit agrees to establish two IGCs on political and economic union to prepare draft treaty revisions to be put to summit one year later, at Maastricht. Discusses impact of Gulf crisis on Europe.

Luxembourg, April 1991 (Luxembourg presidency): Agrees Major initiative on 'safe havens' for Kurds in northern Iraq and EC aid for Kurdish refugees.

Luxembourg, June 1991 (Luxembourg presidency): Considers Luxembourg presidency texts for draft treaty amendments. Major objects to word 'federalism'. Economic convergence agreed as condition for single currency.

Maastricht, December 1991 (Dutch presidency): Debate on federalism, powers for European Parliament, common foreign and defence policy, co-operation on immigration and crime, timetable for European Bank and single currency comes to a head.

Lisbon, June 1992 (Portuguese presidency): Portugal in EC chair for first time since joining EC in 1986. Deals with consequences of Maastricht before handing over to UK, which is in chair for the run-up to 31 December 1992 and the single market.

Appendix 11 PERCENTAGE OF WORLD TRADE HELD BY PRINCIPAL TRADING NATIONS 1989

Country bloc	Imports	Exports
EC	16.2	15
US	15.6	12
Japan	7	9.1
USSR	3.8	3.6
Canada	3.8	3.8

Source of EC imports

EFTA	22.8
Japan	10.3
Latin America	5.8
ACP	4.4
USSR	3.4

Destination of EC exports

EFTA	25.9
US	18.8
Japan	5
Latin America	3.6
ACP	3.4
USSR	2.9

Source: *Europe—World Partner*, Commission of the European Communities.

Appendix 12 UK REGIONS ELIGIBLE FOR REGIONAL FUNDS

Category 1: Northern Ireland.
Category 2: *England*: Northumberland, Tyne and Wear, Durham, Cleveland, Humberside, South Yorkshire, West Yorkshire, Nottinghamshire, Greater Manchester, Lancashire, Merseyside, West Midlands, North Yorkshire, Lincolnshire, Derbyshire, Cheshire, Shropshire, Staffordshire, Warwickshire, Cumbria and Nottinghamshire. *Scotland*: Fife, Central, Strathclyde, Tayside, Lothian, Dumfries and Galloway. *Wales*: Gwent, Mid-Glamorgan, West Glamorgan and Clwyd.
Category 5: Devon, Cornwall, Plymouth, Bude, Bodmin, Liskeard, Newquay, Redruth, Cambourne, Falmouth, Helston, Penzance, St Ives, Scilly Isles, the Highlands and Islands and rural Wales.

The whole of the UK qualifies for assistance under categories 3 (to combat long-term unemployment) and 4 (to integrate young people into the job market).

Appendix 13 DECLARATION OF THE EUROPEAN COUNCIL
ON EUROPE AND THE WORLD (RHODES,
DECEMBER 1988)

1 Reaffirming its commitment to achieve concrete progress towards European Unity on the basis of the Single European Act,
—determined to strengthen and expand the role of the European Community and its Member States on the international political and economic stage, in co-operation with all other States and appropriate organizations,
—and aware that the completion of the internal market in 1992, which is already inspiring a new dynamism in the Community's economic life, will equally affect the Community's political and economic role in the world,
—the European Council reaffirms that the Single Market will be of benefit to Community and non-Community countries alike by ensuring continuing economic growth. The internal market will not close in on itself. 1992 Europe will be a partner and not a 'Fortress Europe'. The internal market will be a decisive factor contributing to greater liberalization in international trade on the basis of the GATT principles of reciprocal and mutually advantageous arrangements. The Community will continue to participate actively in the GATT Uruguay Round, committed as it is to strengthen the multilateral trading system. It will also continue to pursue, with the United States, Japan and the other OECD partners, policies designed to promote sustainable non-inflationary growth in the world economy.
2 The Community and its Member States will continue to work closely and co-operatively with the United States to maintain and deepen the solid and comprehensive transatlantic relationship. Closer political and economic relations with Japan and the other industrialized countries will also be developed. In particular, the Community wishes to strengthen and to expand relations with EFTA countries and all other European nations which share the same ideals and objectives. Open and constructive dialogue and co-operation will be actively pursued with other countries or regional groups of the Middle East, and the Mediterranean, Africa, the Caribbean, the Pacific, Asia and Latin America, with special emphasis on interregional co-operation.
3 The European Council emphasizes the need to improve social and economic conditions in less-developed countries and to promote structural adjustment, both through trade and aid. It also recognizes the importance of a continuing policy to tackle the problems of the highly indebted countries on a case-by-case basis. It looks forward to the successful conclusion of the negotiations for the renewal of the Convention between the European Community and its 66 African, Caribbean and Pacific partners during the coming year.
4 The European Community and its member states are determined to play an active role in the preservation of international peace and security and in the solution of regional conflicts, in conformity with the United Nations Charter. Europe cannot but actively demonstrate its solidarity to the great and spreading movement for democracy and full support for the principles of the Universal Declaration on Human Rights. The Twelve will endeavour to strengthen the effectiveness of the United Nations and to actively contribute to its peace-keeping role.
5 Against the background of improved East–West relations, the European Council welcomes the readiness of the European members of the CMEA to develop relations with the European Community and reaffirms its willingness to further economic relations and co-operation with them, taking into account each country's specific situation, in order to use the opportunities available in a mutually beneficial way.
   The European Council reaffirms its determination to act with renewed hope to overcome the division of our continent and to promote the Western values and principles which Member States have in common. To this effect, we will strive to achieve:
—Full respect for the provisions of the Helsinki Final Act and further progress in the CSCE process, including an early and successful conclusion of the Vienna follow-up meeting;
—The establishment of a secure and stable balance of conventional forces in Europe at a lower level, the strengthening of mutual confidence and military transparence and the conclusion of a global and verifiable ban on chemical weapons;
—Promotion of human rights and fundamental freedoms, free circulation of people and ideas and the establishment of more open societies; promotion of human and cultural exchanges between East and West;
—The development of political dialogue with our Eastern neighbours.
6 The European Community and the Twelve are determined to make full use of the provisions of the Single European Act in order to strengthen solidarity among them, co-ordination on the political and economic aspects of security, and consistency between the external policies of the European

Community and the policies agreed in the framework of the European Political Co-operation. They will strive to reach swift adoption of common positions and implementation of joint action.

7 The European Council invites all countries to embark with the European Community as world partner on an historic effort to leave to the next generation a Continent and a world more secure, more just and more free.

Appendix 14 DECLARATION ON ECONOMIC AND MONETARY UNION ADOPTED BY THE EUROPEAN COUNCIL (MADRID, JUNE 1989)

1 The European Council restated its determination to progressively achieve economic and monetary union as provided for in the Single European Act and confirmed at the European Council in Hannover. Economic and monetary union must be seen in the perspective of the completion of the internal market and in the context of economic and social cohesion.

2 The European Council considered that the report by the committee chaired by Jacques Delors, which defines a process designed to lead by stages to economic and monetary union, fulfilled the mandate given to it at Hannover. The European Council felt that its realization would have to take account of the parallelism between economic and monetary aspects and allow for the diversity of specific situations.

3 The European Council decided that the first stage of the realization of economic and monetary union would begin on 1 July 1990.

4 The European Council asked the competent bodies to carry out the preparatory work for the organization of an intergovernmental conference to lay down the subsequent stages: that conference would meet once the first stage had begun and would be preceded by full and adequate preparation.

Appendix 15 DECLARATION ON THE THREE STAGES TO ECONOMIC AND MONETARY UNION ADOPTED BY EUROPEAN COUNCIL WITH BRITAIN DISSENTING (ROME, OCTOBER 1990)

For the final phase of Economic and Monetary Union, 11 member states consider that the work on the amendment of the Treaty will be directed to the following points:

- For economic union, an open-market system that combines price stability with growth, employment and environmental protection and is dedicated to sound and sustainable financial and budgetary conditions and to economic and social cohesion; for monetary union, the creation of a new monetary institution comprising member states' central banks and a central organ exercising full responsibility for monetary policy. The monetary institution's prime task will be to maintain price stability. The institution as such, as well as the members of its council, will be independent of instructions. It will report to the institutions which are politically responsible.

With the achievement of the final phase of economic and monetary union, exchange rates will be irrevocably fixed. The Community will have a single currency—a strong and stable ECU.

The second phase will start on January 1 1994, after:
- The single market programme has been achieved;
- The treaty has been ratified, and, by its provisions;
- A process has been set in train designed to ensure the independence of members of the new monetary institution;
- The monetary financing of budget deficits has been prohibited and any responsibility on the part of the Community or its member states for one member states debt precluded;
- The greatest possible number of member state's have adhered to the ERM.

The European Council recalls that, in order to move on to the second phase, further satisfactory and lasting progress towards real and monetary convergence will have to be achieved, especially as regards price stability and the restoration of sound public finances.

At the start of the second phase, the new Community institution will be established. This will make it possible:

- To strengthen the co-ordination of monetary policies:
- To develop the instruments and procedures needed for single monetary policy;
- To oversee the developments of the ECU.

At the latest within three years of the start of the second phase, the Commission and Council of the monetary institution will report to the EcoFin and the General Affairs councils on the functioning of the second phase and on the progress made in real convergence in order to prepare the decision concerning the passage to the third phase.

The treaty may lay down transitional provisions for the successive stages of Economic and Monetary Union according to the circumstances of the different countries.

The United Kingdom is unable to accept the approach set out above.

But it agrees the overriding objective of monetary policy should be price stability; the Community's development should be based on an open-market system; that excessive budget deficits be avoided; and that there should be no monetary financing of deficits nor the assumption of responsibility on the part of the Community or its members states for one member's debts.

The UK, while ready to move beyond stage one through the creation of a new monetary institution and a common Community currency, believes that decisions on the substance of that move should precede decisions on its timing. But it would be ready to see the approach it advocates come into effect as soon as possible after ratification of the necessary treaty provision.

Appendix 16 SUMMARY OF THE MAASTRICHT SUMMIT

ECONOMIC AND MONETARY UNION

The key changes to the treaty at Maastricht are contained in article 109F, which defines the irreversible switch to a single currency for an as-yet unknown number of EC states. The important addition was the British opt-out protocol.

The second stage of European monetary union will start in 1994, with the creation of the European Monetary Institute (EMI), and all governments 'shall endeavour' to avoid excessive budget deficits. In 1996, the European Commission and the EMI will report on the fitness of each state for inclusion in the ECU zone. Stiff criteria include low inflation and stable exchange rates.

At the beginning of 1992, the criteria were met by only three of the 12 EC economies. In December 1996, an EC summit will see whether that number 'shall have reached seven. If it has, a majority vote will decide the start date for the 'third stage', a single currency. Otherwise, the European central bank will start work in the middle of 1998 and 'the third stage will start on January 1 1999'. No minimum number of states will be required.

The British protocol is attached to the treaty, with footnotes on the purchase of second homes in Denmark and the coinage of San Marino. Britain must say before December 1996 if it intends to merge its currency, but is 'under no obligation to do so'.

SOCIAL CHAPTER

The summit reached a solution whereby social policy was removed from the treaty on political union. Eleven of the 12 EC members adopted a special social policy of their own, including majority voting on 'working conditions'. This may raise more legal problems than the political log jam it was designed to break.

Two annexes were attached to the treaty at the last moment, and a six-clause chapter on social policy shrank to one sentence. Five draft pages expanding EC powers over employment and welfare law became: 'Present EC treaty provisions unchanged (c.f. Annex 111).' The annex has a protocol noting that 'eleven member states wish to make policies not applicable to Britain.' The text says: 'The United Kingdom shall not take part in the deliberations on and the adoption of the Commission proposals relating to fields covered by the above-mentioned agreement'.

FOREIGN AFFAIRS

Britain succeeded in limiting majority voting by requiring that a unanimous vote be required to agree the framework of a joint foreign policy. It agreed, however, that the implementation of policy could be by majority vote. The article describing the organisation of European defence was also a compromise. Both France and Germany, arguing for the foundations of a European defence run by the EC, and Britain and Italy, countering with demands that anything agreed should be complementary with NATO, gave ground. The wording implies that the EC will absorb the Western European Union, which will acquire greater status. The exact relationship between NATO, the WEU and the EC remains to be established.

EUROPEAN PARLIAMENT

The summit agreed a compromise under which the Council of Ministers will try to agree legislation with the 518-member Strasbourg assembly. If all else fails, for the first time, the parliament will be able to veto a measure in areas that fall under the new scheme, known as 'Article 189B procedure'.

This veto can apply to most new EC powers to be decided by qualified majority vote. These include: measures to complete the single market; consumer protection; free circulation of workers; 'rights of establishment' (of professionals and businesses); treatment of foreign nations, education; vocational training; research and development; programmes for environment policy; trans-European transport; telecommunications; health; and culture.

The parliament has won a veto over research and development, but Britain has retained a national veto on these.

IMMIGRATION

The treaty binds Community members into taking common action on asylum policy, immigration, and the fight against drugs and fraud; and co-operation between customs services, between home affairs and justice ministries in fighting crime, and between police in combating terrorism and international crime.

Britain made significant concessions in giving the Commission a say in this field, and in introducing qualified voting. On a common visa policy, the Commission will propose a list of countries whose citizens need visas to enter the EC, which the Council of Ministers must approve unanimously. But paragraph 2 of Article 100C says: 'In the event of an emergency situation in a third country posing a threat of a sudden inflow of nationals from that country into the Community, the Council may, acting by a qualified majority . . . for a period not exceeding six months, introduce a visa requirement for nationals from the country in question'.

COHESION

The question of 'cohesion'—the demand by poorer, southern countries, led by Spain, for greater transfer of money from the richer north—was removed from the main treaty.

It was included instead as a protocol that promises a 'thorough evaluation' of structural funds in the course of 1992 to see whether they are enough to support EC goals of social and economic cohesion. A general review is scheduled for 1993 under new EC budget procedure.

A new Cohesion Fund will be set up by the end of 1993 to provide money for the environment and trans-European networks (transport, telecommunications and energy). It will go to countries with a per capita GNP of less than 90% of the EC average. The protocol insists that these countries move towards economic convergence as specified in the EMU section of the treaty.

ENLARGEMENT

The summit issued a declaration reaffirming its readiness to open negotiations with any democratic European country applying for membership. The Twelve said talks could begin as soon as the EC terminated negotiations on its own budget and related issues in 1992. This means Sweden and Austria, whose applications are already on the table, may begin talks before 1993.

The final declaration omits reference by name to Sweden and Austria, which has been specifically mentioned in the original draft, so as not to be seen to discriminate against Turkey, Malta and Cyprus, which have also applied to join but whose accession the EC is in no hurry to consider. The declaration noted the consitutional role of the European Parliament in ratifying all accession and association agreements.

INDEX

(Entries in bold type indicate a chapter/section devoted to the subject entry. For names of Europe's top 20 companies and banks, see Appendices 1 and 2.)

About the authors

Richard Owen was *The Times* Brussels Correspondent from 1985 to 1988, reporting extensively on EC affairs from around Europe. Educated at Nottingham University, Stanford University, California, and the London School of Economics, where he received a PhD in Government and Politics, Owen joined the BBC in 1973 and transferred to *The Times* as a leader writer in 1980. He was Moscow Correspondent of *The Times* from 1982 to 1985, and Jerusalem Correspondent from 1988 to 1991. His previous books are *Letters From Moscow* (1985) and *Crisis in the Kremlin: Soviet Succession and the Rise of Gorbachov* (1986), both published by Gollancz. Since April 1991 Richard Owen has been deputy Foreign Editor of *The Times*.

Michael Dynes joined *The Times* in 1986 as a reporter, and has written extensively about the internal market from both London and Brussels. He was educated at the University of Kent at Canterbury, the University of Indiana and Linacre College, Oxford, where he received an MPhil in International Relations. Before joining *The Times* he worked on the Middle and Far East desks at an Oxford-based commercial consultancy. He is currently *The Times* Transport Correspondent.

BY THE SAME AUTHOR

Fiction
Help the Witch

Non-fiction
Notebook
Ring the Hill
21st-Century Yokel
Nice Jumper
Bring Me the Head of Sergio Garcia
Under the Paw
Talk to the Tail
The Good, The Bad and The Furry
Close Encounters of the Furred Kind

TOM COX
VILLAGER

unbound

First published in 2022

Unbound
Level 1, Devonshire House, One Mayfair Place, London W1J 8AJ
www.unbound.com

Text design by PDQ Digital Media Solutions Ltd.

A CIP record for this book is available from the British Library

ISBN 978-1-80018-134-2 (hardback)
ISBN 978-1-80018-135-9 (ebook)

Printed in Great Britain by CPI Group (UK)

1 3 5 7 9 8 6 4 2

For Ralph, my most psychedelic cat (2001–21)

'The Queen o' Faeries she caught me, in yon green hill to dwell'
'Tam Lin', *eighteenth-century ballad*

CONTENTS

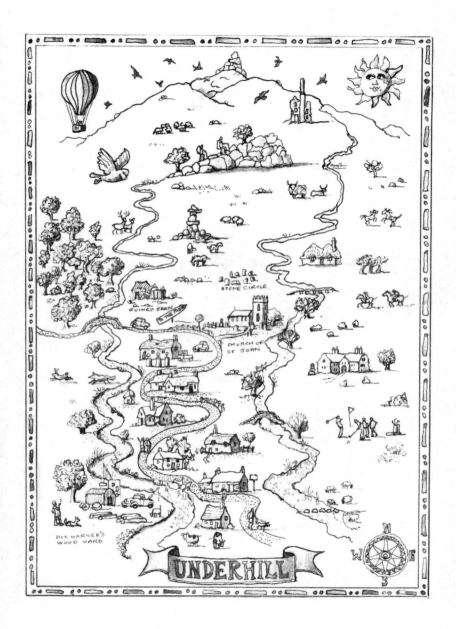

STONE CIRCLE

RUINED BARN

TO THE

CHURCH OF
ST JOHN

DICK WARNER'S
WOOD YARD

UNDERHILL

ME (NOW)

It's a heavy day, and it hangs all over me. I'm deep in it. I'm so far in it, I'm technically invisible, unless you're extremely near to me, and very few people are. I doubt that will change today, but tomorrow could be different. Days like this – the ones that stay heavy from beginning to end – are rare here. Yesterday, for example, started heavy, but became very light and boldly colourful, then was just a tiny bit heavy for the final part, in spurts and streaks. During the light, boldly colourful middle part everything radiated cleanliness, was so thoroughly fresh and laundered that you wondered where all the bad stuff it had washed away had disappeared to, what vast drain or waste tank the world could possibly possess that could have so efficiently put it out of sight and smelling distance. Small creatures woke up in the freshness, and were hungry, in a ferocious way. 'Hangry' I believe it is called nowadays by the young folk. A man walked through a dark corridor cut diagonally across a field of high late summer barley and got seriously messed up by horseflies, to such an extent that he increased his speed to a trot and then a run through the last third of the corridor, waving his arms like a crazy person who believes he is being attacked from both flanks by ghosts, until he reached a shady, thistle-dotted copse, which he decided, incorrectly, might offer some respite. The small mercy for him in all this was his confident belief that he had remained unobserved. The belief was misguided. I saw him and, I have to admit, I did have a good old cackle.

There's a painting which I very much admire. I think it's obvious that it's of, or very much inspired by, the village, but I doubt the person who now has it on their wall knows that, unless they have ever visited here, which I happen to know for a fact that they haven't. I doubt they even know the name of the artist, which was a faint scrawl in the bottom right-hand corner of the painting in the first place and became fainter when the second of the painting's four owners carelessly left it directly opposite a large south-facing picture window in a bungalow overlooking the Derbyshire spa town of Matlock Bath. The painter's name was Joyce Nicholas, and she lived here in Underhill between 1958, when she arrived in Devon from the north of England as a widow and retired teacher, and 1969, when her daughter Eva installed her in a retirement complex close to the stretch of coast known, jokingly by some and more seriously by others, as the English Riviera. She completed the painting in 1960 and, although she did sell one or two other similar expressionist works at that point via small local galleries and a short-lived bookshop owned by a friend, Joyce – always very hard on herself – decided it was not a success, and put it away in the loft. It did not leave her family until 1983 when, after his wife had fled from him and their legal union in a state of antimaterialist haste, Eva's daughter Jane's ex-husband Gerry gave it to the owner of a junk shop in Whitby, Yorkshire, free of charge. Gerry had hoped to receive a small sum for the painting but was hit with an uncharacteristic attack of guilt when, in examining a rug that Gerry was also hoping to rid himself of, the junk shop proprietor's hand came into contact with some still quite damp excrement that had come out of the arse of Gerry's bulldog The Fonz that morning, but which Gerry, in haste not dissimilar to Jane's upon leaving him, had not spotted. The proprietor stared off into the middle distance of a deep back room full of broken clocks, grumbled inaudible quarter words and exhaled spouts of air from both corners of his mouth, and stated he wasn't much interested in the painting. 'The bottom has dropped right out of the market for this stuff,' he said. 'I've got a ton of it in my garage at home and can't shift it for love nor money.' He was, however, playing it cool, having quickly marked the painting out as something a little out of the ordinary and Gerry as an easily manipulated man whose main goal was to exit the building as quickly as possible. The proprietor had been the first to see any merit in Joyce's landscape since a lodger who was living with Joyce, eight years after its creation. It now hangs above the stairway in a house in Edinburgh owned by two retired surgeons. Visitors remark on it more often than anything else in the house, apart from their cat, Villeneuve, who is white, fluffy and comically large.

I should probably pause to point out here, for those wondering, that I don't know everything. I have big gaps, moments of doubt and humility, just like everyone else, just like Joyce. But I do know a hell of a lot.

I love Joyce's use of colours in the painting. I suspect when she was mixing her palette she was thinking of a light day, or perhaps the light part of a day that had earlier been heavy, but certainly not an all-heavy day like today. The gradation of burnt umber to asparagus in the top left corner, then a suggestion of something darker, where the moor begins and stretches on for the next twenty miles or so. There's a hint of something black and jagged here, some shapes that remind me of rusty barbed wire. And beyond, above this kaleidoscopic hillscape that could just as easily be California as Britain's West Country, a swirling heaven or hell, a definite 'beyond place'. Below that, I think I can make out the familiar valley, the way it funnels down into the village and the lane that becomes the steep high street. There's no obvious sea or river in the painting but there is a suggestion that both are close. Houses? Joyce doesn't paint anything as literal as houses, but there are shapes that we could decide are buildings where people live. There's some interesting yellow and white blotching to the right, below that, which makes me believe Joyce was a big fan of the lichen you get on the rocks and older buildings – and even some of the newer ones – around here. The colours of the lichen are answered by the colour of the sun, in the top right-hand corner, or is it the moon... or is it some combination of both, some other unknown ethereal body representative of both day and night. Above this is what seems to me the most literal part of the painting of all: a patchwork quilt of what are surely farmers' fields. What makes it less literal is the fact the patchwork is *above* the sunmoon, and I wonder if this is Joyce's comment on the topsy-turvy nature of the region, the habit the hills have of disorientating you, the knack weather has here of frequently being below you, as well as, or even instead of, above you, or if Joyce was just feeling a bit like tearing down the walls and breaking the rules that day. I like this side to Joyce a lot, the hidden side that only the brushes and canvas saw, beneath the scrupulous account books, the perfectly plumped cushions, the always-mown-on-time grass. Joyce was a person with more layers than her family and neighbours realised, I think, and much wilder, toothier nightmares. In the middle top of the canvas, if you look into that greeny-black, celestial moorscape, you'll see what you might interpret as a wide, beatific, somewhat hirsute face. This is the part of the painting that possibly interests me the most.

I never did get any of the several art critic jobs I applied for.

Where does the moor start? That's a highly debatable question. Where does the true north start? Where do moths end and butterflies begin? Where is the border between 'sometimes fancies members of the opposite sex but doesn't actually want to touch their sexual organs' and 'is definitely gay'? Who decides what's soulful funk and what's funky soul? There's always some hard-bitten unimpressable bastard who'll tell you, when you're on the moor, that you're not on the proper moor, no matter how far into the moor you are. But let's not piss about. This – whether or not it's 'technically' on the moor, as the map defines it – is a moorland village. You know, very firmly, when you're in it, that you're not in London, or Kettering, or Ipswich. You're in Underhill. As you pass from the high ground down that funnel, so exquisitely depicted by Joyce, the air of the uplands remains in your nostrils, the trees have beards, the lanes have ferny green sideburns, and your hair is made of rain. *It's the bloody moor*, you pedantic bastards. I should know. I've been here long enough.

For many years, the first sign of life you'd see when you came down that funnel in Joyce's painting was an old blacksmith's cottage, but that fell into disrepair several decades ago, the more interesting parts of its structure gradually appropriated by passing opportunists in or around the building trade. The road bends sharply just at this point, with no warning, and once every couple of years you'll see a mangled, abandoned bike, formerly owned by someone who got carried away with the gradient and didn't quite judge the turn. The blacksmith's cottage was replaced during the 1970s by the Molesting Station. Despite society's disapproving eyes and the nature of its purpose being far less fashionable than it was during its outset, the Molesting Station isn't shy about telling you what it is. It even announces it publicly. 'MOLESTING STATION' it says in big letters, on the front of the building. OK, I'm not giving you all the facts here. It's actually a garage, owned by Phil Spring, who took it over when his father Brian Spring retired in 2013, and it in fact has 'MOT TESTING STATION' written outside. But as you approach from the north, the split trunk of a beech tree on the side of the road obscures the first 'T' and the roof of the second one, so it appears to say 'MOLESTING STATION'. I'm surprised more people don't comment on it. Whatever the case, the garage does good business, at competitive prices, and has a reputation for honesty. After Phil realised he overcharged Paul Pike recently for replacement brake pads and discs, when in fact his apprentice Alun had only replaced the discs, not the pads, he called Paul immediately and did a bank transfer for the difference plus a gesture of goodwill, which he suggested at ten pounds. 'Call it twelve?' said Paul. 'OK,' said Phil. I don't have a car for reasons that will in time become clear, but if I did I would definitely take it here, instead of one of those supergarages, where you not only pay for your repairs but for the flatscreen TV in the foyer and the machine next to it that pisses out bad coffee you drink purely because you're there and not sure what else to do with your hands, and the pointless little matching blazers of the employees milling all around you doing you're not sure what. Beyond the Molesting Station is what is, for now, the village's most northerly residential frontier: twenty-five hugely unimaginative terraces built in the 1990s, once going under the preposterous collective title of Otter's Holt, a name now blessedly forgotten, apart from, evidently, by me. I dislike these houses but I like all but two of the families who currently live in them, which softens the architectural anguish a little.

It's definitely not one of the most fashionable villages in the region, and it's not quite the least. One of the results of this 'middle of the table-ish' standing is that we have an Indian restaurant, House of Spice, and it is a good Indian restaurant. I have observed that the better-known villages and small towns nearby, where house prices are highest, either don't have Indian restaurants, or have Indian restaurants that make surprisingly substandard food. I don't personally take my meals in the village, so this is just hearsay, but it's widely recognised that House of Spice's onion bhajis – judged, at least, by the standards of other onion bhajis made in rural England – are in a class of their own when it comes to taste, shape and accompanying chutney. For a long time, House of Spice was also celebrated for the closing line of its menu, which thanked diners for their costume – a spelling error, rather than a genuine expression of gratitude to those visiting on Halloween or another occasion inviting fancy dress. It took a whole twenty-five months before the printing of a replacement menu, which merely thanked people for their custom, and the length of that gap can no doubt be attributed to the fondness that had grown for the menu in the locality and the resulting reluctance of anybody to point out its imperfections. The story about another misprint on the House of Spice's menu, offering a '15 per cent discocunt on orders over £20' is, however, apocryphal.

The moor has moods, and because the village is so close to it, it is subject to them. When the sky above the moor is storm-tossed and wretched, you'll hear more gossip and backbiting across the tables in the two cafés, especially the Green Warlock, where Jason and Celia, who are bored in their marriage, go on Fridays. When everything is heavy and damp, like today, you'll notice that people don't say thanks as much in the Co-op. Two almost-friends, who'd normally stop and chat on the street, will keep their eyes down and pretend they didn't see each other. It's something purely elemental, not personal, but it spreads. I don't feel great today, and my not-greatness influences those around me. I made a buddleia visibly ill at ease this morning. The tile warehouse, I think, looks particularly lugubrious and in need of a hug, but who is going to give it one? Colin on Weathervane Avenue just poured a pan of boiling water over some ants on his patio then instantly felt terrible about it, although he tried to transfer his anger with himself in his emotionally unavailable way, instructing his wife Mel, when she arrived home from the supermarket, to not spend quite so recklessly on fruit. There's a bad atmosphere in the dentist's waiting room. But if we are honest it's never had a great reputation as a dentist. It's doubtful anybody would go there at all, if they knew that on the exact spot where Jill on reception currently sits, in September 1723, a farmer and his two sons murdered a man from Minehead following a drunken quarrel that got out of hand. An orchard was planted in the same place a century later, but didn't take. It's the other side of town where most of the apples grow: partially russeted Nancekuke, Pengelly, King Byerd. Old, old apples. Apples of the insurrectionary underground. Apples which would upset the apples in your local supermarket with their foul mouths and lack of foundation and mascara. Many of their sweet culinary gifts will be wasted next week in the annual Apple Rolling Festival on Fore Street: a 'revived' festival thought by many local historians to date back to as early as the 1600s (it doesn't).

But it is not all folklore and bygone insular sword death. We have a post office! Jim Swardesley, the postmaster, is forty-five. He has his moods, like all of us. The dome of his head is entirely bald, but he says it's been that way since he was twenty-two. His theory is that it was the result of a rugby squad induction ritual in his university days, where he was required to shave his entire scalp with an old, rusty razor and no shaving foam, from which his follicles never recovered. Now a resident of the village for over a decade, Jim's arrival, with his young family, was part of the first wave of incomers to Underhill from more urban areas in the centre of the country: an influx that never fully took off as some expected and dreaded it would, and still happens in fits and starts, usually as a result of people finding that more fashionable villages nearby have become too expensive. Jim is now entrenched enough in local life to be slightly resistant to outsiders himself, if only for their repeated failure to queue for grocery products at the appropriate counter, despite his many handwritten signs encouraging them to. Two doors down from the post office is the granite cottage where Joyce painted her painting. The rusty wagon wheel that her predecessor dragged down the hill off the moor and into the garden is still there. Her deep red front door isn't, replaced long ago by some now off-white UPVC. It is good that she can't see this. There is a profusion of gravel that would be alien to her. The sports utility vehicle perched upon it would seem to her too big for any practical purpose, incongruous beside the building it belongs to.

Information comes back to me in isolated flurries, like cherry blossom on a strong breeze in spring, and then it's gone if I don't reach out and grab quickly, and grab well. You can never grab much. There's only so much you can know at one time, even if you're me; only so much room to store it. There's so much *to* know. It will never end, I suspect, even when it does. So much in all these lives, so many stories, even in this small place. And I try to keep abreast of the universe beyond it too, if I can. I'm broad and cosmopolitan, despite what many assume.

But I am remembering a little now, from the day she began to paint the painting. I was not feeling fully at my best that day. Some men and their dogs had raced across part of me and ripped an innocent animal into many pieces and the pieces were stuck to me. The rain would not come and wash the pieces off for a while. It was a few years into the era when I first felt new chemicals soaking into me, changing everything. Yet over there was a meadow: corncockle, poppies, yellow rattle. I'd rarely seen so many butterflies in my life. I was confused. I felt I could go either way, emotionally. One of my wicked episodes could easily have happened. They have to happen, sometimes. It's part of the balance. But in this instance I chose purity; namely, the quest to witness some of it. While I searched for the purity, a stallion and a mare began to mate on my back and I told them to piss off but then apologised, admitted that it was unfair of me, and assured them they were not the ultimate cause of my irritation.

She was in her kitchen, rescuing a moth from a spider's web. (It died two minutes later but it's the thought that counts.) Jazz was playing. That was not a surprise. The type of jazz, though, was. Definitely not grandma jazz, this. Not even 1950s hip grandma jazz. Modal. Louche. A little threatening. The back window was open, which, from where her easel was placed, gave her a good view of the tor and the rocks piled on top of it like a little crude stepstool to nowhere. The breeze was gently blowing in, flapping the net curtains, and a very old grey cat – a satchel of sharp bones, with some fur stuck to them in some places – snoozed on the table, next to a punnet of five strawberries that were on the turn. Joyce flailed a wrist, as if loosening up in preparation for an impressive bit of spin bowling, and in one final move, to achieve a state of ultimate looseness before she began, she lifted her blouse over her head and threw it flamboyantly to the floor. I got a bit shy then (I do!) before watching her go into her artistic trance. I'd never seen anybody paint my portrait before and I was very flattered. She had a glass of wine afterwards, and I can't remember the last time I've wanted to join anyone in that particular activity so much. You'd have to go right back to... Actually, I'm not even going to tell you. Blissful scene to watch, though, even if you couldn't be a part of it yourself. Oh, Joyce. How could you go from a day as carefree and wild as this to the retirement scene in Torquaydos, in less than a decade?

It was the following day when she had her misgivings and put the painting in the loft, with a little chunter to herself. She was being self-punishing, but perhaps she was only following the most sensible course of action. Ideally, we'd all put any art we created away for a while before we properly evaluated it. Two weeks? Probably not long enough. Let's call it two years. OK, ten. That will do it. Scratch that. Just to be sure, let's come back and discover our true worth as creators from the afterlife. 'Hi, I'm dead now. What? Yes, fully. I even have the papers to confirm it. Can you finally tell me my true star rating, out of ten?' Joyce, I think, were she able to pop south over the border between the dead and the living, then north over the other one, between England and Scotland, would be pleased at what she saw on the wall of Dr Micklewhite and Dr Micklewhite. But – and I'm not denigrating Joyce's talent for one second here – are enigma and the passing of the years to be given some credit for that? Is it maybe just possible that time itself has changed Joyce's painting? As if some spiritual lichen of its own has grown on and around it, deepening and enriching its texture? And, if so, what good does that do Joyce, now? What we need to do is get her trending online. Death: it's when we decide if everyone is good or bad, right, decide which of the two boxes to put them in, as well as the wooden one they're already in? Let's get her a Wikipedia page, get the conversation going. 'So sorry to hear Joyce Nicholas is no longer with us. I only met her once, for no more than nine seconds, but she was not stuck up at all, and even said hello to my dog.' 'I have always been a huge fan of Joyce, even when nobody was talking about her, and it was super uncool to like her.' 'Graham, can you remind me how much we paid for that picture above the spare bed?' '£300, I think. It was quite a long time ago.' 'Well, I've just found out from this newspaper article that it's worth £55,000 and by someone called Joyce Nicholas. She died in Devon in 1973.' Oh, Joyce, if only you'd have known your artistic worth, been raised in a different generation, and put yourself out there. You could be an influencer now. But you wouldn't have wanted that, you say? Why on earth not? Oh, because the very process itself was the important part of the matter for you? The feeling of being lost inside it, guided by invisible hands. The trance. The freedom. But what about the 'likes', what about the dopamine rush? How *old-fashioned* you are, Joyce. Don't you realise that even the dead have an Instagram account these days? Don't do yourself a disservice. Play the game. Everyone must.

I'm sorry; I've done something I said I wouldn't and permitted myself to get flustered. It's been one of those days. I think I spotted a couple of drones earlier, circling above the boulders. I have a pain in one of my toes and there's a very unwell, publicity-shy and sensitive ash tree I'm on intimate terms with and this morning someone plastered photos of it all over social media accompanied by the hashtag '#sadtree'. I think the toe pain comes from the fact that a pile of old compost bags and a hubcap are caught on a rock just past where the river emerges on the other side of town, almost but not quite, under the Victorian railway viaduct. It's bearable, not so painful, not even comparable to the time they found a dead owl down there, tangled up in a sky lantern. I should sleep. The forecast is better for tomorrow. I can see the bats powering over from their roosts. I heard that nineteen buzzards and a kestrel are flying up from Cornwall at dawn. But I will say this final thing, concerning the previous subject: Joyce isn't the only one. There are a lot of lofts and drawers and cupboards out there. Most of them have stacks of utterly worthless shit in them. But just a few of those lofts and cupboards and drawers contain a piece of art that's special and true and came from an honest, inspired place, didn't get shouted about at the time, and it's probably only going to get more special and true the longer it's left there. We're all getting older, and that has its pluses as well as its minuses. Over beyond the back wall of Joyce's old garden, the river isn't quite as diamond clear as it once was, and its dauntless song doesn't always quite succeed in drowning out the dual carriageway, but the lichen and moss on the rocks have become richer in texture. Quality lichen and moss isn't something you just cheat or shortcut or hack or hashtag your way to.

Here, in my big green hands, I hold some time. Consider it my gift to you. You will probably never receive a finer one.

I'm going to go now. A heavily pregnant ewe just did a very thick and powerful piss on my chin. But I'm OK. To be perfectly honest, I barely even felt it.

GROUND UNDER REPAIR
(1990)

The summer Mark and I found the man in the woods, Mark was sixteen and I was a year younger. We'd been playing a lot of golf that year and nobody much admired us for it. After our rounds and long practice sessions were complete, we'd walk home along the lane that led back to the village, carrying our clubs, and the inhabitants of passing vehicles would beep their horns and shout profanities at us. Considering it was a quiet lane where you'd only see about twenty cars per hour, it occurred with startlingly regularity. One time someone hurled a half-full Fanta can from a passenger window and it hit me in the eye and drenched the front of my polo shirt. When my mum saw the bruise, she refused to believe I had not been fighting. After that, Mark and I started taking a different route, over the corner of the tor and down through the woods by the river. Some of the paths weren't public but Mark worked out a shortcut and was fairly confident we wouldn't get into trouble.

The golf course had two personalities, and no smooth segue between them was in evidence. It threw visitors off balance, left them hot and gorse-scratched and irritated. Many who had begun the day in a positive frame of mind declined to visit the clubhouse for a drink afterwards, instead hurling their clubs into their car boot, not even bothering to change out of their spiked shoes, blowing out of the car park in a plume of exhaust smoke and a loud scrape of metal against speed bump, like people who'd stolen their own cars. For the first nine holes, everything was very polite and neatly mown, a sculpted suppression of nature that, were you blindfolded and dropped into it, would have been hard to distinguish from the one that characterises a thousand other golf courses. But after the ninth green players followed a steep tunnelled path through a small city of gorse and skyscraper ferns and emerged into a primal, unwashed otherplace that they had to trust, going by what the map on the back of the scorecard told them, was the tenth tee. Quarter-sheared, mad-eyed sheep and horned cattle roamed the fairways and tees indiscriminately. Jangly-nerved salesmen and insurance brokers backed off their putts as large dark winged shapes wheeled overhead, mocking them with shrieking beaked laughter. Balls struck sweetly from tees ricocheted off assorted hidden rocks into tussocky bogs, never to be seen again. These balls soared unpredictably owing to the dung caking their surface and sudden corridors of diabolical wind coming down off the moor. It was not uncommon to see visitors holding up play by attempting to herd sheep, cattle and ponies out of their playing line. Regulars were more nonchalant and casually floated their drives over the animals' heads, but even they were not exempt from pastoral strife. Believed to be assured of victory in the 1989 club championship as he strutted the mounds of the final fairway, Tom Bracewell threw away his advantage when a heifer sat on his ball and refused to move. A crowd soon gathered around the cow, the competitors who had been awaiting the result of the event in the clubhouse bar gradually filtering out to watch, until over a hundred of us stood staring at the animal. Christine Chagford, who before taking her job behind the bar at the club had spent a lot of time in close proximity to cattle, finally managed to sweet talk the cow into giving way and letting the group behind play through, but not before she'd planted a kiss on its forehead and posed for a photo which would later be framed and hung on the wall of the Men's Bar. Rattled, Bracewell racked up a triple bogey seven, putting him in a sudden death playoff with Christine's cousin Tony, which Bracewell subsequently lost. A year later, the general consensus was that he had still not recovered: a pallid, stooped figure, seen, if seen at all, staring forlornly at competition result boards and handicap tables in the back room of the clubhouse or down on the practice ground at sundown, scratching his chin and assessing the balls spread diversely in front of him, some or other mail order teaching contraption abandoned on the ground behind him.

Mark explained to me that he was on a mission, and that mission was to shag Christine before his seventeenth birthday. 'I'm working up to it and slowly getting her interested until one day she just won't be able to stop thinking about me,' he said. 'Is she not a bit old for you?' I asked. 'She's sort of thirty or something, right?' Mark waved the question away. 'Twenty-six. I'm tired of the girls our age. I don't want an immature idiot who writes the name of her favourite band on her pencil case then crosses it out next week when she changes her mind. I want a woman who knows who she is.' I was often dehydrated by the time Mark and I had completed eighteen holes, especially in what had been a very hot summer, and would have liked to have gone directly from the final green into the Men's Bar to order a pint of Coke with ice, but Mark always insisted that we followed protocol and visited the locker room to wash our hands and change into our soft shoes beforehand. I soon became aware that Mark, who was otherwise rarely guided by protocol, was driven by an ulterior motive on these occasions, which was to make sure his hair was adequately gelled before he saw Christine. 'How do I look?' he would ask me, after liberally applying the gel from one of the circular plastic tubs of it he worked his way through each week. 'Really good,' I would reply, more admiring Mark's hair as a whole than specifically its gelled state. So far, if the gel was having an impact on Christine, she was keeping her cards very close to her chest. To date, the only sentence she'd said to Mark, besides 'Thanks', 'What can I get you?', 'Pint or half' and 'With ice or without' had been 'Ooh, big shot!' – this being in response to the time Mark paid for two pints of Coke with a fifty-pound note, which he'd got purposely from the bank that weekend, after exchanging it for his birthday money and a month's wages from his paper round.

Mark's other goal for his seventeenth birthday was to learn to drive and, when he had done so, very quickly purchase a car and drive it to school where, by which point, he would be attending the sixth form. The comic genius of this plan, we recognised, was that everyone knew that the small council house where Mark lived with his granddad was only seventy yards from the school car park. It was, in fact, the closest house of all to the school.

School was in town, six miles away, and I went there too, but Mark spent a lot of time at our place, in the village, and when he didn't stay over in my mum and dad's spare room, his granddad was always on hand to collect him with uncanny punctuality and obedience. Mark's granddad's name was Leonard, but Mark never called him that, or 'Granddad'; what he called him was 'Old Boy'. 'Hey look! Here's Old Boy!' Mark would say, looking out of our living-room window and spotting Leonard waiting in his Datsun Cherry. Old Boy very rarely knocked on the door when he collected Mark, never seemed anything less than 100 per cent available, never stopped grinning, and always wore a brown tweed cap, which – along with the outmoded and modest nature of his transport – prompted me to think of him less as a grandfather and more as a particularly humble chauffeur. 'It's OK. I'll get Old Boy to take us,' Mark would say, if Mark and I had a plan for a trip where public transport was inconvenient, which, in Devon, on the brink of the nineties, was nearly all trips. When Mark and I went to Paignton, to play the slot machines, or to Exeter, to watch Iron Maiden in concert, Old Boy waited in the car, happily passing the time listening to the radio or reading a tattered paperback by Patrick O'Brian or CS Forester or another nautically inclined writer. 'How's tricks, Paulie, my boy?' Old Boy would sometimes ask me. 'Great!' I would answer. 'You just wait, you boys. It's all going to happen for you,' Old Boy would say. But apart from that, he largely just drove and grinned, with what struck me as the most relaxed of old faces. The Datsun was a car in which I never felt ill at ease, whose interior always smelt verdant and warm and earthy, like a greenhouse.

To my knowledge, Old Boy himself had no particular passion for golf, but it was well known that the clubs Mark used had come directly from Old Boy's loft: an assorted collection of irons and woods dating from the 1960s, the 1950s and, in the case of one tiny, hickory-shafted nine iron Mark was particularly fond of, 1912. My clubs were considered out of date by many, being second-hand and all at least four years old, but when I played alongside Mark they made me feel decadent and spoilt. 'You want to bin those sticks and get yourself some golf equipment, son,' Mike, the car salesman Mark played against in the 1988 club matchplay semi-final, had sneeringly told Mark, prior to Mark casually dispatching him by the handsome total of seven and eight, less than two hours later. New juniors at the club came and went, invariably carrying hi-tech weapons that glinted in the moorland sun. It didn't bother Mark a bit. A lanky bespectacled boy called Roger Glaister arrived, carrying a gold-shafted driver, hopping casually over the fence from a big house on the lane which his parents had recently purchased, a cigarette hanging from the corner of his mouth. He spat a lot, in a very idiosyncratic way where the spit forked out into the air through his front teeth. Soon, several other kids at the club were spitting this way too, but not Mark. In their one and only match against each other, the score was quite close for the first nine holes, Glaister taunting Mark all the way with under-the-breath remarks about charity shop clothes, but on the final nine – always his favourite – Mark turned up the heat. By the sixteenth tee, that gold shaft had become two smaller crooked gold shafts, languishing in a wooden dustbin 500 yards distant, Glaister's £50 Pringle shirt was damp from where his saliva had rebelled on him in a gust of wind, and his ankles were caked in cow dung. Mark beat him by eleven shots in the end. 'I enjoyed that,' he told Glaister, shaking his hand and taking a grudgingly proffered £20 note. 'We must do it again some time.'

We had both improved considerably in the two years we'd been playing together, coaxing one another on, but for Mark the process was different: calm, creative, unfussy. A bad round never seemed to bother him. For me, it was increasingly a case of three steps forward, two steps back, sometimes with one extra step back just after that. I'd noticed golf had been much easier when I knew far less about how to play it. At this point, when I had become much more than just somebody who hit a ball and tried to get it into a little hole in as few strokes as possible, my mind became fascinated with the margins for error, with the allure of the countless potential negative outcomes, as opposed to the one simple potential positive outcome. I watched the pros at Augusta and Lytham and St Andrews and Troon on my mum and dad's black-and-white TV, and, while there were a few inflamed exceptions – usually men from Spain or South America – the solidly successful ones often came across as robots in jumpers, pastel droids who might potentially sell you some insurance between shots. They did not appear to have exciting brains or, on the few occasions they did, they seemed to have the discipline to make those brains unexciting for the five or so hours they were on the course. They say golf is a game of the mind but that does not mean you actually require one to play it well. It could even be argued that possessing one is a distinct disadvantage. But Mark struck me as more akin to those rare pros who had a bit of swagger to them, who had plenty of intelligence but were able to somehow reduce it, control it, when they were over the ball. It had been me who'd first brought him up to the club, after I took a bag of balls down to the playing field in Underhill and found him already down there, with that prehistoric nine iron of his. I'd barely known him back then, only recognised him as a distant figure from breaktimes and the bus queue, but we'd instantly bonded, and I'd already been in awe of what he could do with just that one Edwardian club: fading it, drawing it, driving it low, more than 150 yards, into a strong breeze, then seconds later using it with great finesse for the featheriest of lobshots. I still had the authority at that point, though: it was me who told him how to grip the club properly, me who recommended his first pair of spiked shoes. I'd overcomplicated it for him, brought him into the universe of handicaps and etiquette and left-hand gloves and deconstructive video lessons and cruel bounces and lip outs and sucker-pin positions, when he could have just stayed happily thwacking balls all day, down behind the village. But, unlike me, he responded to the psychological torments of the game like a Buddha, appeared to sleepwalk through it all, even, shrugging, easy, that looseness in his swing that made him able to power his drives so effortlessly far being a greater looseness; a looseness of face, of eyes, of character, of mind.

That was what made Mark different to everyone else at the golf course: he just never appeared all that *bothered*. When I consider what would have been happening to him hormonally at this point in his life, this now strikes me as more remarkable still. Golf, so our schoolfriends told us, was a limp old man's game, a bollockless sport devoid of fireworks or passion, but every week we saw it transform men three times our age hailing from supposedly respectable echelons of society into swearing, club-hurling cavemen, grey hooligans spinning in enraged circles halfway up a hill. You'd no more try to strike up a conversation with these directors of sales and funerals, these commodity traders, these spiritually beige number-crunchers while they were on a bad run of putting than you'd try to stroke a hyena who hadn't eaten for a fortnight. One week, we bit into our sleeves to stifle our laughter as a retired headmaster greeted a triple bogey seven by taking off one of his shoes, marching several yards into the undergrowth and hurling the shoe into the roaring current of the river. The next, we bit harder still on the fabric as we witnessed an esteemed Plymouth solicitor lose the last of the twelve balls he'd started the day with, turn to a crowd of nearby sheep, and shout, 'MOTHERFUCK EVERY SINGLE ONE OF YOU.' We learned to play alongside those who made their living in outdoor professions if we could: the thatchers, the lumberyard proprietors, the deputy garden centre managers. They were a little less flappable. Still, like the others, many of them questioned why we spent so much time at the club, which was not in fact appreciably more time than the time any of them spent at the club. 'Don't you boys have homes to go to?' the grey hooligans in their pleated slacks would ask, in what, for me, was an early lesson in the fact that, when somebody attacks you out of the blue for something you're doing that isn't hurting anyone else, they're more than likely talking about a wrongness in their own lives. 'Yes, sir, you are correct: it is strange, us spending our free time playing a sport, in our mid-teens. What must our wives think? Don't we have livings to earn, mortgages to pay, kids to feed?' It was as if we were briefly on some upside-down planet, where adults, not children, were expected to misbehave, and indulged for it. Being together on this planet united Mark and me, fortified the walls of our City of Two. And that's really what we were. Other kids were often around, kids from more affluent families than ours, but they never stayed long, never challenged for competitions. In May, there was a proposal – thankfully quashed, in a rare moment of sanity – at a committee meeting to reduce the number of days junior members were permitted to play at the club. The proposal was talked about as if there were juniors everywhere, vast armies of them, running up the fairways every evening, farting on blackbirds and kicking over bins. But it was mostly just me and Mark. Then, after I broke my arm the following month, it was Mark, all alone, fending for himself amongst the grey yobs.

Up to this point, I'd not knowingly heard any genuinely offensive remarks directed towards Mark at the club. But, now he was winning more tournaments and shooting up in height, he was becoming more widely noticed, and I know his appearance would have been perceived as an extra threat by many of these men who nudged one another and muttered under their breath when they saw him take the prizes at their tournaments, this lanky mixed-race child from who knew where, with his untucked school shirt and hand-me-down equipment and that hair springing higher and higher above his head, towering above their combovers. Mark was good at saving the little money he earned from his paper round, and could no doubt have bought the standard kind of polo shirt most golfers wore, or even got his granddad or his mum to buy him one for his birthday or Christmas, but it would simply have never occurred to him as being important. Mark virtually never spoke to me about his parents. It had been close to a decade since he'd last lived with them. I knew from him only that his dad now resided in France. My parents, meanwhile, had told me that Mark's mum was currently 'living in Weston-super-Mare and having some difficulties'.

How did I break my arm? I think the official cause could be cited as 'having shit for brains'. My cousins were down from Walsall for the weekend, we'd taken a dozen cans of cheap lager up to the rocks on top of Underhill tor, and I was showing off. I took a run up and attempted to vault the gap between the two tallest rocks, the top ones on the bit that looks like stairs, and didn't quite make it. Truth is, I was lucky not to hurt myself a lot more severely, as it's pretty high there, and in the crevices between the clitter the granite sticks out like broken crowns in an old mouth. Even with my arm in its cast, I continued to follow Mark up to the practice ground once every few evenings. That's how pleasurable it was to watch him hit balls. That's what we *loved*: hitting balls. Not the shoes or the handicap system or the cut glass or the silverware or the single leather gloves or the wood panelling or the tee pegs or the gold shafts or the handshakes or the reserved parking spaces or the Eric Finch Foursome Matchplay Bowl or the Garden Room or the Men's Bar or the sixty-degree Tom Watson beryllium copper sand irons or the patriarchal badinage but the pure nirvana of metal cleanly strikingly rubber at high speed with minimum effort. I'd played tennis, and football, and squash, and badminton, and table tennis, but nothing quite compared, contact-wise. When you got it right, you felt like hitting golf balls – and here I mean hitting golf balls as a separate entity to the game of golf – was another preordained human need, like eating or breathing, something that was always meant to be here and always would be here. That was why Mark and I were here, at least four days out of seven, every week. That sensation, like sap rising up our arms, blossoming in our necks and shoulders, flowering in our brains like a million of the most vivid poppies all at once. I chased it in the way that later, in the mess of adult life, I'd chase the memory of my most transcendental orgasms. The elusive nature of the pure strike made it all the more appealing. It didn't actually happen that often, for me. But with Mark, it occurred in long, sustained bursts. He hit a sweet zone of rhythmical calm. He was a great player on the course, but on the practice ground, without the distractions of competition, he was an ethereal one, an alchemist, a Zen wizard. I could have watched him forever.

One night in late June, after he'd hit balls until we no longer could see where they landed, we took our usual route home over the jutting, unimpressed elbow of the tor. The last purple streaks of the sun toasted the hilltops and owls made lewd suggestions to one another down in the woods by the river. Mark, however, had not been the last man swinging. That honour went to the Irish Doctors, whose trolleys could be seen very slowly approaching the seventeenth tee in the mauve half-light. At the club, nicknames stuck like dog hair to merino wool. A wiry, anxious weekend player called Phil who'd once missed a crucial putt when he was distracted by the call of a skein of Canada geese overhead was thereafter known to all as 'Quack'. Carl Marchwell, who was infamous for telling all of his playing companions in great detail about his week and lacked the skill of self-editing, hadn't been called 'Carl' by anybody at the club for years; he was always 'Jackanory'. Ian Welcombe, who liked to bet big money on foursome matches but had never, to anybody's knowledge, actually won, was 'The Bank'. Jill, Ian's wife – one of the few female members of the club who actually seemed to enjoy the game – was not 'Jill' but 'Mrs Bank'. Recently I'd overheard people talking about somebody called 'Jam Jar' but I was yet to find out who that was. The Irish Doctors, however, were just the Irish Doctors. No nickname, collective or otherwise, could have been more definitive or catchy than their quintessential Irish Doctorness. There were six of them in all, although legend was that there had at one point been eight. Generally, playing in groups of more than four was severely frowned upon, but special, unspoken dispensation was given to the Irish Doctors, who always operated as a gang. This – and the fact that each of them was in his ninth decade – meant their pace of play was very slow and they spent a large amount of their round standing aside and letting other groups through. Mark and I liked the Irish Doctors, who were the jovial antithesis of the grey hooligans a generation or two beneath them, and we'd have both been happy to play alongside them, were it not for the fact that, not being Irish doctors ourselves, that would have been an affront to the natural rhythm of the earth, and would have made their progress even more excruciating. As was usually the case, today they would not hole their final putts before the light had totally vanished.

We passed through clouds of midges as we came down the back side of the tor and along the sunken track leading down to the river, watery rubble under our feet, the metal in Mark's bag pounding out a clanking beat several yards ahead of me. We always carried our bags on our shoulders, never resorted to a trolley and, as with many child golfers, the spinal damage it caused would be evident in my posture later in life. I heard a distant cry of 'Cracking shot, Seamus!' and a faint, delayed thud of a ball being propelled a modest distance forward by frail hands, then I rounded a sharp bend and all was silent, beside the chorus of the water. I found Mark sitting on the old packhorse bridge, rolling a cigarette, and joined him.

'Look at that,' said Mark, pointing to the liquid beneath our dangling feet, rushing clear over the black rocks and coppery pebbles. 'It's magic, that is. That's what it is. Think of all of what's up on the moor every day: all the dead sheep bones, all the pony shit, and peat, all our pollution, being sucked up into the clouds then rained down back into the streams. But it still comes down here every day, looking like that. You know what I do, the first thing I do, every time I've been away from Devon? I rush straight to the tap and fill a glass. It always tastes so good.'

'My dad said the water in London is full of women's pills and cocaine,' I said. 'So every time you have a drink out of the tap there, you're doing drugs and stopping yourself getting knocked up.'

'You know it's all bullshit, this? All wrong. Well, not this. Definitely not this. But that.' He gestured back up the sunken track, in the vague direction of the course.

'All what?'

'Just because there are cows and sheep and ponies there, just because they didn't get rid of some of the rocks. It doesn't mean it's real. If grass had a choice, it wouldn't do what it's doing up there. It was never meant to be like that.'

'But if it was never meant to be like that, maybe this footbridge wasn't meant to be like this, either?'

I had made a den close to here one time when I was little, a few hundred yards closer to the village, using an old mattress and a few other mouldy abandoned household bits and bobs I'd found. When I told my mum, she told me to avoid abandoned freezers because children climb into them then can't get the door open again and die.

'I dunno. There's natural and there's natural. You know the shit they pour onto that golf course. You know how many insects it kills? I'm just saying. I've been thinking about it a lot recently.'

'I've got to have a piss.'

I was always careful where I had a wee when I was outdoors. It was one of those ways in which golf made me an adolescent with a little more decorum than most. An older playing partner had told me it was very important to choose a surreptitious spot, in case any lady members were nearby, and my habit of doing that carried over into any pissing that I did in the fresh air, even beyond golfing parameters. I mention this because, had I not been so careful about picking my spot, I might not have pissed on the stranger's hand at all. I'd been pissing for several seconds before I heard him – or, as it seemed, the brambles and bracken in front of me – groan and as I did I leapt sideways, spraying urine on my left trouser leg and shoe in the process. 'Mark! Fucking hell!' I shouted, which in retrospect shows me just how much I looked up to my friend, viewed him as, in some way, my protector.

He rushed over and, careful not to touch the foliage that was still wet with my spray, parted the leaves and fronds to reveal a long male body, supine in the mulch below them. The body's eyes were closed and, when Mark asked the face on the end of the body if it was OK, it grunted, as if in dreamy reassurance. In a way the face seemed a bit like the faces of lads just a few years older than us but the paperiness of its complexion and the colour of the stubble on it made me perplexed about how old its owner was. A camera, quite an old one, hung around the man's neck by a strap. He did not look what I would have called healthy and seemed unable to open his eyes yet there was a sense that the reason he was not able to open them was that he was in a very delicious sort of sleep that he was reluctant to emerge from. Mark asked him some questions, including 'What is your name?', 'Where are you from?' and 'How did you end up here?', and when the stranger only answered with more oddly tranquil grunts and did not move, it was agreed that I would head into Underhill to get help. My arm, being still only half-healed, impeded my progress and it took me close to half an hour to reach the village.

My intention was to go home and call for an ambulance but part of me wondered if that would be time-wasting, as the man didn't actually seem hurt in any way, and on my way past the Co-op I bumped into Steve Clayton, who'd narrowly beat me in the club matchplay last year and used to be in the army. Steve obviously noticed that I looked flustered and asked me what was wrong and I told him about the man and he said he'd come back down the path with me. Steve was strong and I decided that with the help of Mark and both of Mark's working arms he could probably carry the man back to the village if it came to that. What had been confusing to me when I'd first met Steve was that, despite him being very muscly, Steve couldn't hit his golf ball very far at all, and the strongest part of his game was his putting. But since then I'd found out that obvious physical strength counted for nothing in golf. It was all about rhythm and timing and you often got blokes who looked like Tarzan or He-Man who barely hit the ball anywhere and people like Mark who only weighed nine and a half stone but could lamp it into the next county. Steve's massive arms were a moot point anyway, though, because when we arrived back at the spot where I'd done my wee neither Mark nor the stranger were anywhere to be seen. Now I was embarrassed and felt like Steve probably thought I was lying again, because last winter he'd asked me what kind of putter I'd used and it was a Wilson but I'd said it was a Spalding but only because I'd forgotten and when we played together he saw the putter and said, 'I thought you had a Spalding?' He was OK about being dragged out there, though; he just looked at me a bit queryingly, and said he had to get back to the shop and get some steaks for his missus to cook that night, and that it was dark and I should get home soon but that I should call him if anything else happened or I couldn't find Mark and he would call his mate John who worked for the police. I didn't walk back down the path with him because I felt like it might be weird and we might run out of things to talk about. Instead I went and stood by the packhorse bridge for a while, listening to the water and thinking about what Mark had said about it. I could hear a cuckoo up in the woods round the back of the tor, the first one of the year. My mum had said there had been loads when she was a kid. I walked back a different way, past a ruined barn above where my gran said they used to hold the old fayres, which always gave me the creeps, like something bad had happened there.

Something about the way Mark was, how thoroughly OK he always seemed to be, made me sure he'd be OK now, and I didn't feel like there was anything very scary or threatening about the man on the ground, but I was still a trolley of nerves for the couple of hours after I arrived home, doing my best to hide that from my mum and dad while also trying Mark's home number every ten minutes and getting no answer (Old Boy was clearly also out). Finally, just as I could hear the theme tune from the *News at Ten* coming from the telly downstairs, he picked up.

'What happened? Where did you go?' I asked, without even saying hello.

'Nothing. Well, some stuff. But nothing bad. He was OK. He got up after we left. We went back to his house. Well, it's not a house. It's a tent. In the woods. He's from California. We smoked some stuff he had. He plays guitar. He's cool. He has a bad head, he says, and it makes him sleep in weird places. But he's OK. It's OK. He coughed a lot, though. I was about to call you.'

'Steve Clayton might have told the police.'

'Steve Clayton? Why Steve Clayton? Doesn't matter. Don't tell me. It's fine. If they come round I'll just tell them it's OK, and he went on his way. I'm not telling them where his tent is, though, as I don't think it's supposed to be there. He's such a fucking sound bloke. He wants all the rivers to be clear and nobody to be able to own land.'

That was the summer Mark left school, which was one of the reasons that our friendship drifted a little after that. He chose to not come back for the sixth form and instead attend a further education college a few miles closer to the coast, which meant that much talked-up ambition of his to drive Old Boy's car all of seventy yards to attend classes was never realised. By September my arm had recovered sufficiently to begin golfing again and I called Mark a couple of times to see if he fancied a round but he was always busy. I got the impression he was making new friends at the college, people far more exciting than me, probably, who knew more about interesting leftfield music and films. I played some of my best golf that autumn and early winter but it all felt a little hollow with nobody to enjoy it with. 'You could be a pro, lad, if you put the work in,' some of the kinder adult members would tell me at the end of our rounds. But I was wise enough to know that there is a very big difference between being one of the best players at a provincial club in Devon and actually being able to make a career from the game. Also, I was beginning to get distracted by a new nagging feeling in my loins. That November on the Geography field trip to Bodmin, Martha Leigh Price, sitting in the coach seat behind me on the way back, leaned over and draped her arms over me and nothing was ever the same again. The following April I forgot to watch the US Masters tournament for the first time in three years. I started listening to The Smiths and, having seen Morrissey do it on an old TV clip, took to walking around with gladioli in the back pocket of my jeans, which failed to cause any of the stir I'd hoped it would with anyone, save for my mum, who – always obsessed with all matters olfactory – told me that Morrissey 'looked like a smelly person' and that at my age with my whole life in front of me I should be listening to music that felt less sorry for itself.

There was also quite a lot of bad feeling at the golf course around this time. In September, somebody had snuck onto the course at night and spray-painted the word 'WANKSHAFT' in huge letters over the fifteenth green. A month later, Fizz, the head greenkeeper, arrived at dawn to mow the first fairway and found the words 'GIVE IT BACK TO THE SHEEP BELLENDS' written in a decorous arc around the devilish pot bunkers situated in the customary landing area for tee shots. By the time a further two pieces of graffiti – 'WOKE UP WITH WOOD' on the third tee and 'GOLPHERS SUCK SAGGY BALLS' on the bank fronting the eleventh green – the story had made the early pages of both the *Western Morning News* and the *Plymouth Herald*, although no leads had been found pertaining to a suspect. It was one of two environmentally themed news stories featuring the area around the village at that time, the other covering around 300 battery hens from Cavendish's farm up near Wychcombe that had been set free on the high moor. The fact that I found the graffiti amusing highlighted the way that golf and I were slowly growing apart. The effort I'd put in to perfecting my chip shots the previous spring, this spring I rechannelled into trying to persuade Martha Leigh Price to kiss me. I had no luck; she'd never really been as effusive with her affection as that day coming back from Bodmin, and in May she confessed to me that nothing could happen between us until she'd found out if a guitarist called Ben Bishop in the sixth form had properly sorted out his feelings for her. This, however, didn't stop me regularly writing letters to her, brimful of innocent passion and hopes for our future, or using all the pocket money I had saved to get the bus to Exeter and buy perfume for her birthday, or walking down along the path through the woods to the river with her at least once a week. Passing the spot where Mark and I had found the American with Martha, I'd wonder about Mark, and the American, and where they both were now. Every so often on these walks Martha and I would also spot a stray chicken or two, enjoying their newfound freedom, in a confused-looking way.

'Do you always make sure you smell nice before you meet Martha?' my mum asked, one day when she found me moping about the house.

'Of course,' I replied.

'Well, it's her loss, then.'

Nowadays, periods of three or four years often feel like commonplace slips in time, as if you've decided to go onto the next song but put your finger too heavily on the button and actually skip three tracks ahead, although only realise a fair bit later that you have. 'Bloody hell! It's 2021, and 2017 isn't actually last year any more. How did that happen? Oh well. It's nothing new, just part of being a person over the age of thirty-two. This is just life now. Better get on with it.' How different to the final days of adolescence, when a three- or four-year period is like a whole country separating two other, bigger countries, one of which you're no longer interested in and the other seeming limitless in the promises its vast landscape contains. When I bumped into Mark in the garden of the Stonemason's Arms in the summer of 1993, it felt like the late twentieth-century peacetime equivalent of reuniting with a soldier who'd been part of a long war and irrevocably changed and emboldened by his experiences in it. He recognised me before I recognised him and I think the reason for that was not because he didn't look like him but because, for the half an hour that we'd been sitting two tables away from one another, I'd caught a hint of him in my eyeline and shied away from looking directly at him for fear of being dazzled by all that he was. He'd reached his full six foot two in height by this point, his hair was bigger than ever and his cheekbones had sharpened, his eyes deepened. He wore a silk scarf, a chunky belted cardigan and these dark green velvet trousers I can't even get close to doing justice to with words, which looked like they were glued to his legs in the softest, most complimentary way. It wasn't a look you'd have found in any fashion magazines in any era, but boy did it work on him. I was much more bashful in admitting my own appreciation of male beauty back then, it being only a couple of years past a time when most of my mates would have called me a poof or gayboy for making even the slightest suggestion that a bloke looked good, but, even so, I was stunned, and a yearning opened up in me. The off ramp from puberty had evidently been a very different adventure for Mark than it had for me. Why hadn't *I* got to spend it at a magic transformative castle of technicolour dreams too? It seemed a little unfair. Nonetheless, I think I succeeded in disguising my awe and envy and I pulled up a chair at the table where he and his friends were sitting so the pair of us could have a good catch-up. He was two years into university now, where he was studying Environmental Science, but was having reservations about going back for his final year. He talked about how he'd come to realise the drawbacks of institutionalised learning. I nodded, doing what I hoped was a decent job of pretending I knew what he was talking about. I was surprised to discover he was living closer to me than before, up at Runnaford Hollow, a small hippie and traveller community, down near Wychcombe on the back side of the tor. He said some of the guys up there were having a singaround later, as they did every Friday night, and that I should come up and join in. As we talked, I glanced back at the table where my friends were still sitting and couldn't help but be jarred by how different they were to Mark's crowd. I'd never thought of my pals – grunge and metal lads, mostly, misshapes and mild outcasts – as boring but by contrast the people Mark surrounded himself with looked like they had slipped through a rip in the space-time continuum. They were all tassels and belts and bangles and soft fabric and stroked shoulders and androgynous kisses. To my mind, they had nothing to do with 1993 and probably not a lot to do with the past or future, either. 'You remember Chris, don't you?' he said, gesturing towards a girl in a floral dress and floppy felt hat two seats to my left, and beneath the paisley I saw the face of Christine Chagford, Mark's old fantasy now turned reality. I asked her if she was still tending

bar up at the club, and she merely laughed and offered a hand –
the one not holding a roll-up cigarette – that looked like it had
never pulled a pint, a hand that seemed French in all the best ways.
By the time we all left for the Hollow, the ground was spinning
beneath me and I don't think it was solely because of the three
pints of Guinness I'd downed. I told my friends that I might catch
up with them later, but most of them appeared not to notice, since,
for a £20 reward, one of them was being challenged to drink some
vomit he had found in a pint glass on the wall behind him. I'm
ashamed to admit it, but I can't even remember his name now.

A bonfire was going strong in a clearing in the woods when
we arrived at Runnaford Hollow and a crowd of at least twenty
people were gathered around a girl sitting on a knoll of tree roots
with a guitar and dreadlocks who was singing a song I knew I
should know but didn't. A couple of wiry bearded dogs tussled
over a stick as their wiry bearded owners looked on. Looking at
the living conditions – caravans, tents, an electricity generator
but no running water – it was remarkable to me that Mark
looked as shiny as he did, but he later admitted to me that he
was only bedding down here three nights a week and having deep
luxurious baths back at home on the remaining evenings. He
fetched us a couple of mulled ciders and we sat on stools carved
from tree stumps, a few feet from the fire.

'So, you and Christine... it actually happened!' I said.

'Sort of,' he replied. 'It's cool. We hang out but she doesn't
want to be locked into anything. The way I think you'd put it is
she's not a one-man woman, and I respect that. She's taught me a
lot. All these people have. They're my brothers and sisters, really.
The ones I never had.'

'They seem very cool.' I looked across at a broad, bearded
man with a strikingly low and dense hairline, who carried a
shepherd's crook. 'I think I recognise that guy from the Green

Warlock café.' What I did not add was 'where I saw him getting ejected by the owner for trying to haggle over the price of a cup of tea and a doughnut.'

'Rory? Rory is exceptionally hip. A high priest of Extreme Dudeness, in multifarious ways. And of course you probably remember the American...' He pointed to a tall lean man in a flannel shirt, older than most of the people here, who, as if summoned by Mark's words, picked up a guitar and sauntered over to the knoll in the centre of the clearing, high-fiving the girl with the dreadlocks as he took her place on the organic stage. He hadn't changed much in three years, the main differences being that he was now vertical and had eyes that weren't closed. Much like on that day we found him in the woods, I felt like I was looking at a confusing hybrid of age and innocence. His hair was long and curtainlike, like mine and that of many of the other men who were here, but lightly streaked with grey. Looking at his face was like looking at a portrait of an eager teenager in which the paint had been smudged by a fat, rogue thumb.

'Isn't he fucking amazing?' Mark said, as the American began to play. It would not be truthful to say that I agreed. The music was confusing to me, spaghetti-like and intricate and not very angsty or anglicised, not very part of my small English life, the one whose cultural parameters I then kept far tighter than I arrogantly believed I did. Three of the four songs were instrumentals, which was frustrating to me because I was a stickler for lyrics in those days, and the one that did have words – his final number of the night – was far too blunt and folksy for my taste, a bit... old, more the kind of thing my uncle listened to. Yet I will also say this: an echo of that music has stayed in my head ever since, an echo that has blossomed and grown coloured petals, and I have countless times wished I could go back and hear it again in the flesh. I have experienced a similar phenomenon in other ways since, where I have realised with hindsight that the case was not that a piece of art was not good enough for me but that I was not yet good enough for the piece of art, but I don't think I have ever experienced it to quite this extent.

'This is pretty special because he doesn't get up and play much,' said Mark. 'He's a bit shy about it. He's a genius, though. He has his own method of tuning. Nobody has a clue how he does it.'

More people were arriving at the Hollow now. People of many ages, at least two genders, and many miraculous clothes. Sartorially, the crowd suggested a far more diverse and perplexing definition of 'alternative' than the one I'd become familiar with on nights out with my friends, which mostly resulted in everyone dressing in the same jeans and band t-shirts and Doc Marten boots. Smocks abounded; tunics and dungarees and felt hats and cut-off jeans and tweed and trenchcoats and waistcoats and flares and drainpipes. I noticed one girl in a long white blouse stood a little back from everything, watching, in the woods, as if nervous to join in, but by midnight most people were dancing and hugging, flutes and banjos and lutes and guitars were appearing everywhere and the wavy treeline encircling us began to feel more like a crinkle-crankle wall separating us from the world as it had been described to us by every cautious and boring person we had ever met. I did not see the girl in the long white blouse again, which was a shame as she had immediately interested me and I liked the way her hair reminded me of a holly wreath, and I had begun to worry about why she was alone. Christine – who I'd not realised was musical – played some songs, too, and they were good, in a folky, whispery way. The clear sky above me, with all its stars, was yet another element of the evening I did not appreciate enough, although I certainly did not *not* appreciate it, and I fell asleep under it, a reluctant virgin, two months off my nineteenth birthday, in the arms of a woman thirteen years my senior. I suppose to some there might have seemed something poetic about it if this had been the big one, the night I ended up losing it, but in retrospect to me there is a far greater poetry to the fact that it was not. Fran, she said her name was. A baker by profession, down from the other side of the moor. 'This is a weird request, but can I run my hands through your hair? I do so miss the feel of a young man's hair.' Yes, you can, Fran. In fact, please carry on. I am really ready for sleep now and this is helping me ease towards it. But oh, Fran. What would you think if you tried to do the same now, with the spotted stubble that remains there? Would you be surprised if you knew you'd triggered a lifetime of need for head rubs? Where are you now? And were you offended when your hand landed on my belt buckle and I moved it gently away? Did it make you feel like an interloper from full adulthood, a terrible raider of the young? And will you believe me if I said I did not intend to make you feel that way; I just felt it wasn't the right place, or the right time, despite all the bigger rightness of the occasion in so many other ways, plus the mulled cider was stronger than I'd realised and did not mix well with Guinness?

It wasn't yet fully light when I woke up to the sensation of Mark tugging at my sleeve. Christine was beside him, looking like anything but a former golf club employee who'd had less than three hours' sleep on a shared single bed in a caravan. 'Dude,' he said. He was talking like an American now, as well as hanging out with them. 'We're going on a dawn mission. You wanna come with?' Too bleary-eyed to know what I was being asked, but having nothing but an ordinary empty unemployed 1990s day ahead of me, I pulled myself off the ground and followed them through the trees, leaving Fran asleep clutching the ghost of my hair. The car that waited for us on the lane – a light blue Austin Maestro – was unfamiliar but the driver was not. 'How's tricks, Paulie, my boy?' Old Boy asked, placing a book about eighteenth-century Cornish shipwrecks back in the glove compartment as Christine and I got in the back seat. I told him, with total authenticity, that I was feeling pretty great, and the four of us started off for the coast. It was a journey of no more than three quarters of an hour and by the time Old Boy parked up again, beside a gate gap in the hook of a lane overlooking a pitted, zigzagging headland, part of which was home to a moderately venerated and exclusive links golf course, I was still in the dark as to the purpose of the adventure.

'We use environmentally friendly paint,' said Mark, heaving a tub out of the boot of the car. 'It's made from milk proteins, balsam and citrus. The metal can will be recycled. So this is a protest that doesn't hurt the earth. And even if we did use normal paint we'd not be doing a fraction of the damage that they're doing with their pesticides and poisons that they put on the turf every day. It won't take long. It's only about twelve minutes to the seventh green if we go over this field and we'll have the job done in no time. It's private land to get there, though, so keep an eye over your shoulder, because the farmers around here can be massive bastards. What's your favourite bit of swearing at the moment?'

'Pardon?'

'What's your favourite bit of swearing, right now? A word or phrase. Anything you like.'

The sky over the water was a friendly dark green and seemed like it was holding everything in a freeze frame for us, all apart from many dozen swifts who spun around us as we walked as if capitalising on this bonus pause before the uglier part of the day legally began.

'Big badger's arse!' I blurted out, before engaging my brain, and instantly felt disappointed in myself, knowing I could have done so much better.

'Perfect. Then that shall be today's message. You get one word. How about the arse? Chris and I will share the other two.

This is your big debut. It's like a dream come true. So won't you smile for the camera? I know you're going to love it.'

He sang the last bit, like it was already a song, and I grinned, pretending I knew it. I hoped there wouldn't actually be a camera.

*

It rained later that morning: light flicky rain out of a sunny sky, which we felt glad to sit in as it teased away the last of our hangovers. Old Boy, who didn't have a hangover, also appeared reasonably content to sit in it, just as he always appeared reasonably content about everything. Christine, under her floppy hat, still looked serene and impeccable, mysteriously free of environmental emulsion splashback. The four of us ate mostly in silence, perched on a wall above the shingle, staring out towards an arched rock that my dad had once told me was arched because a very strong whale had swum straight through the middle of it. I thought how beautiful the sun was as it glinted through the arch, and how magical the world we took for granted could be, the world already there that we placed all our paraphernalia and meaningless chaos on top of, and inextricably tied in with this realisation was the realisation for the first time since waking up that I was probably still wasted from last night.

'So it was you all along?' I asked Mark.

'Well, yeah. Me. Some friends. Christine, sometimes. But mostly me.'

'But why? I mean, I thought it was pretty funny. But why?'

'You really have to ask? You know what they called me up there, the way they spoke about me. I'd had enough.'

'No. Well, sort of. Yes. No. What? Who?'

'"Jam Jar". The members at the club. You didn't know that?'

'I didn't realise that was you. I always wondered who they were talking about and why they said that.'

'It's a reference to golliwogs, like you get on the Robertson's jam jars. The black-faced dolls. You know the ones. No, they didn't come straight out and call me "golliwog" or "wog" but you know what it means, you know what they're getting at: it's a degrading term for a non-white person. A belittling. A put-down. Thatcher said it, so why wouldn't they? And you know what? I actually accepted it for a while, just decided that shrugging it off was part of getting by, getting by around here, where there are so few black faces, just like my mate Rob who was the only black kid in his town and started calling himself "Chalky" just so he could get in there quickly before anyone else started doing the same thing. It could have been worse. And it was only a few of them. It was mostly just ignorance and repetition. But then I started thinking a bit more deeply about it, a bit more about what I was endorsing with my silence and acceptance.' I was struck by just how differently he now spoke, just how much more than me he was, just how much, again, his time at that magic castle had changed him.

'I'm sorry. I fucking wish I'd known. I don't go up there any more, if it's any consolation. Haven't in a long time.'

'Bunch of wankers,' interjected Christine, wanking off an invisible cock (small) with her hand.

'It wasn't all of them. Not even most. Some decent people play golf. We both know that. It happens everywhere, not just on golf courses. But it just so occurred that when I was having this revelation I was also having a revelation about golf itself, what it is, what it does to the environment. The amount of weedkiller that gets poured onto that course every month. The insects it kills. The waste it is of natural habitat for any number of creatures. All because some well-off people want to hit a ball around. A lot of them don't seem to even enjoy it. Do you know how many golf courses there are just in England? Over two thousand. Do you know how many acres of wasted wild space that is?'

'I see what you mean.'

'Have you read *Silent Spring* by Rachel Carson? Read it. Drop anything you are reading now and read it instead. It's your duty as a human being. She was dying of cancer when she wrote it but she cared so much about the planet she still went ahead and did it. She saw the future, and the destruction industrial farming was doing, the mindless greed of big businesses, and that was in 1962, and now it's more than thirty years later and people are STILL not seeing the future. We are breaking the fine threads that bind life to life and the results are going to be pissing catastrophic.' He was really gaining steam now and I was struggling to keep up, struggling to reshape him from what I had known him as; it wasn't all that long ago that our primary topic of conversation was the escape shots Seve Ballesteros played when he was stuck behind a tree. 'It all started getting bad in the Second World War. People experimented with new chemicals to make weapons and then we started using the same chemicals to blast tiny creatures to hell, just so we could grow even more wheat, expand the monoculture, make the countryside look even more uniform and dull. Look at the names they call these things. They make sure they're long and hard to remember, because if they are people are less likely to address what they actually are and the terrible harm they do. Golf. Agribusiness. It's all a part of the same giant disease. Waste and indulgence and humans acting like greedy, suppressive gods. What do you do with your plastic when you're done with it?'

'I put it in the bin in my kitchen.'

'Of course you do. That's what everyone does. But where do you think it's all going? Do you think it just vanishes? I'll tell you where it's going. Out there.' He pointed towards the waves, and the stone arch, and I pictured that apocryphal whale my dad had told me about, blasting through the stone then gobbling the container that had formerly held the takeaway sandwich I'd bought from the Newton Abbot branch of Boots on Monday. 'What are you doing a week on Sunday?'

'Nothing, I think.'

'Good. Fancy coming to the Quantocks? We're going to mess up one of the hunts up there. Stags, but probably foxes too. It'll be different to today. More risky. People get hurt sometimes. But there'll be more of us. The American will be there. Rory, too. I know some very excellent people. You'll be fine.'

'Er... OK.'

Unexpectedly, the light spaced-out drizzle had redoubled then retripled and become something more disparaging. In attempting to digest Mark's rant, I'd been slow at eating my chips, and now a deferred queasiness was rising in me, and I opted to leave the remainder of them for the gulls to pick at. Undaunted by the weather, a caterpillar of tourist-owned cars was moving down the hill towards the beach café car park. I realised we had lost Christine and Old Boy but neither were far away, Christine throwing a stick for a dog she had met on the beach, and Old Boy beatifically examining the half-sunken slimy hull of an old boat beneath the causeway. Mark turned for the car and whistled and both of them appeared swiftly beside us.

The fact that this was the last time I saw Mark in person is something that I quickly became disappointed about and is a fact that has become a little sadder and starker every year since. That Saturday afternoon I phoned him at home. He was out but I asked Old Boy to pass on my apologies: I had forgotten that I was supposed to go to my aunt and uncle's for Sunday lunch, I explained, and wouldn't be able to make it to the Quantocks. This was a lie, pure cowardice on my part. I loathed hunting as sport but in the end I could not picture myself in a crowd, trying to disrupt it. The prospect scared me. And I think if I was nineteen again, I'd make the same decision, but I do sometimes drift off into a little reverie about what difference it might have made if I'd acted more boldly and adventurously that weekend, and what other path it might have sent my life down. I got the impression it was a one-chance situation, from Mark's point of view, and sure enough I wasn't asked again to accompany him – wasn't asked to write profanities on a golf course, to help save wild animals being put through unnecessary suffering, or even to attend a party in some woodland with people who were a bit more exciting than the people I usually met. Did I call Mark again after that and invite him out to the pub? Maybe I did. Maybe I didn't. I couldn't say for sure. Let's say I did, for argument's sake. But, if I did, he was busy.

I did see Mark one further time but that was on a TV screen in 1996 during evening news coverage of the controversy over the Newbury bypass in Berkshire, when protesters camped out in the wild and, in an ultimately doomed attempt to prevent the destruction of 10,000 trees on the proposed route, chained themselves to trunks and branches ('I wouldn't like to be in the middle of that lot with a fully working nose,' said my mum, who was watching with me). Several celebrities marched to stop the road being built, including the children's television couple Maggie and Oliver Fox. During interviews with the Foxes and some of the other celebrities and protest organisers, I spotted what was unquestionably the left two thirds of Mark in the background, his aura and shine unmistakable, in clothes that he probably hadn't taken off for three weeks. Of course, in the years since then, I've attempted to look him up online, but been able to find very little of substance. Mark seems to have become one of those rare people who have ducked the gaze of the search engine, his soul too tricky and deep to be googleable. His name comes up on a stag beetle survey I found printed by Natural England in 2004 and a list of organisers for an early Climate Change march in Oregon in 2009, and I heard a rumour that – after Old Boy died, fifteen years ago – Mark had fallen in love and moved to the US west coast, but other than that I know nothing. Did he forge a new identity? Change his name? It's possible. Something in my gut makes me sure he is still alive.

Me? This isn't the place to go too deeply into my story. I was still toying with the idea of university back in 1993, but it never happened, and I've done a lot of different jobs you could probably think of since then, and a lot you couldn't. I no longer play golf: partly because I have long since lost the motivation, but partly because doing so would feel like a vote for a lot of what I am against politically. I painted houses. I delivered cakes. I half-completed a driving instructor training course. I acted as a dogsbody for a wealthy fleecer of the oppressed. I wanted to be a writer, and then a musician, and then an artist, but never really gave any of them a proper go. At a party on Millennium Eve I got talking to a girl called Rebecca who'd lived two roads from me for most of my childhood without either of us ever realising, and a year later we were married. We've had our hard times, like most couples I know, and even broke up for two whole years, when I was having a minor crisis about various small ways in which I'd decided I had spurned my life. In 2016 I was involved in quite a significant car crash, which I feel ecstatically lucky to have walked away from with a largely functioning body, and that year I sold the taxi I had been driving, Rebecca quit her job as deputy head of a coastal school with an insalubrious reputation and we opened a zero waste shop in the closest village to us, which we are never sure is going to survive for another year then does, just about, and hopefully will continue to do so. One Sunday every month we arrange a town litter pick, which has now got so popular that some of the regular attendees have started hosting their own subsidiary midweek litter pick. Life is... slightly fulfilling, fast, slow, small, comfortable, numb, scary. Rebecca and

I are very similar in many ways and very not-similar in others.
Rebecca likes whenever possible to see every event or incident
in the present, purely as an isolated event or incident, whereas I
cannot separate anything from the past and the queue of other
incidents that influence it. We have learned ways to surmount
this ideological disagreement, but it has taken time. We still live
within a twenty-minute car ride of Underhill and when I see
the tor as I drive by, I always think of Mark and wonder how
he is doing. I think of how brilliant he was at striking the ball,
where he could have taken that talent and the way he looked it
straight in the face and rejected it. And I think of me, a person
who has never been brilliant at anything, just a person who is
sort of OK at a lot of things. And then I wonder if Mark going
with that brilliance I witnessed in him, letting it play out to its
natural conclusion, would have truly made him happy, and find
myself wondering if being brilliant at something is perhaps a little
overrated, as a way to live.

Memory is a sly magpie, a seasoned frequenter of thrift fairs
and jumble sales, gradually sweeping the worthless tat aside to
reveal the hidden treasure behind it. Like a magpie, it needs to
be greeted and acknowledged once in a while, and like a magpie,
if you try to get really close to it, it usually won't let you. My own
has undoubtedly done some rearranging during its downtime
and I find that, amongst the nights of my youth that now seem
important, it's pushed that one with Mark up at the Hollow, by
the campfire, to the fore, and, within the night itself, it's probably
shone a light on parts of proceedings that didn't seem significant
at the time and snuffed out others that did. I come back to the
music a lot, the smell of the woodsmoke and the hot fermented
apples. I come back to Fran's hands in my hair. I come back
to Mark, who will never know what an etched part of me he
remains, and I come back to the girl in the long white blouse,

standing back from everyone in the pocket of the woods that holds her, the intentness of her gaze towards the American as he played. It seemed like such a small part of the night at the time, but I have never forgotten her face or her holly-wreath hair, and I wonder if one of the reasons I come back to it was something that Michael, my chiropractor, said to me during my treatment after my car crash.

Michael – a man who always looks haunted himself, as if his skin is trying to retreat from any room he is in and hide further behind his bones – and I were talking about a very picturesque walk on the west side of the moor, where you follow a path along an old broken pipe from the clay mine. He said one time he was walking up there with an old schoolfriend, and he saw two ghosts, although it was all quite mundane and not at all what he'd grown up to expect seeing ghosts to be, as an experience. It was twenty minutes or so before sundown, he said, and the ghosts wore headtorches and were in the clothes of miners from a century earlier and had walked straight past his friend and him into the very thick and spidery copse further up the hill, without saying hello. Nothing else happened but he and his friend had both been very sure they had experienced something just out of the normal pattern of things, something not quite correct. About this they were in total agreement. I wonder increasingly if that was the way with my sighting of the girl in the blouse alone in the trees, whose face, when it has appeared in my dreams, has made me want to burst into song and has, in some way I can't fully express, left me waking up steamrollered by a great and melancholic sense that my life has not peeled back the layers and found the magic that it should. It is probably all nonsense, of course. She was perhaps just a lonely girl, a quiet girl, a girl who had fallen out with someone, a girl who wanted some time alone, a girl who felt better on the perimeter of everything, a girl who just happened to have been wandering the woods and stumbled on a gathering that interested her. But sometimes when I am seeing that night in my mind's eye, I feel like I am seeing it as her, as a separate bystander, but one with a greater knowledge about what is really going on, in time's larger context: one who sees these people, some of whom are in the midst of the most thrilling twenty-four hours of their life, and sees their folly in not for a moment suspecting that it is the most thrilling twenty-four hours of their life, not seeing that this isn't the beginning of many, many other equally thrilling twenty-four-hour periods, for many years to come.

As her, the girl with the holly-wreath hair, I stand back in the dark part of the place and I listen to the music blossom and expand and I smell the fragrant burning rings of the trees. And then in my floaty blouse I float up and look down on the lights in the clearing, with another ultra perspective, the perspective of the person directing the film. And I see how everything is informed by everything, because there is no way it cannot be. And then I wake up, and choose not to trouble my wife with any of it.

DRIFTWOOD (1968)

He came out of the canyon with his guitar at dawn, queried by the distant howl of coyotes. He was wearing a stranger's shirt and had not been to sleep. The first truck he flagged down stopped and after one more ride, in a hoarse 1959 Buick LeSabre driven by a silent man who smelled of cigarettes and reminded him of his aunt in a way he couldn't quite pinpoint, he reached the airport. Everyone there looked almost but not quite as tired as him. The dehydrated fur all over his brain amplified a paranoia in him, made each of his small actions feel observed. On the plane a stewardess brought him a nest of dry chicken with some lettuce so papery and devoid of moisture it seemed like fake lettuce, lettuce made solely for photo shoots of lettuce. She asked him if he was travelling on some sort of business and a cough-laugh escaped his throat. What on earth kind of business looked like this? He'd told himself he had done enough of going where everyone said you should go, and wanted to try the alternative approach of going just somewhere, roll the dice across a map, but it was a little more pre-meditated than that. 'I'm going back where I come from,' he told her.

As the coach moved sluggishly through the last outposts of the city, it rained, just like it did in the songs. Rain-grey town, known for its sound. None of the flamboyant outfits he'd heard about were in evidence. All of his fellow passengers were wearing clothes mimicking the colour of the sky. As the rain cleared, he saw toy cars, made to measure for the toy road system around them, and the toy driveways of the toy houses beyond that where the toy cars secured their prescribed eight hours' sleep every night.

After a couple of hours, the bus passed over a ridge and the terrain became less populated, a light green moonscape. Big shaved-looking mounds that were more like dunes than hills. A place that looked like it hadn't quite yet decided on its long-term plans. It segued gently into light forest, little stone houses, something more polite, something that was finally like the England he'd been picturing when he set out, the England he remembered, although he didn't truly remember anything. He'd been four years old. Each of the only three people who connected him to this part of the world was at least 5,000 miles away. Yet many miles further on when the bus finally stopped and he got out, he realised a part of him had still been expecting a caretaker or guide to meet him at the station. A second, lost sister perhaps. A cousin. He discovered a new oneliness in the walk that followed, felt it in the centre of his ribcage.

Nearly all the streets in the city were steep, but they divided into two types: the grey ones that looked like they'd just been born from nothingness and the pastel ones that looked proud in a tired, touching way, like senior citizens still wearing their graduation gowns. He took a room on the top floor of a lanky old house that peered over the edge of a hill. He had his own sink in the corner of the room which he pissed into on lazier days because the bathroom was shared and the pipes clanged every time anyone turned on the hot tap, which hurt his head on the mornings after he'd drunk too much, which was quite a few of them. The previous occupant of the room had begun to paint a mural of a squashed face in two shades of orange on the wall next to a tall window where, until the beech trees across the road came into leaf, you could see a one-inch-high triangle of cobalt

sea. He figured the docks were the obvious place to find work
and it didn't take him long to do so. On Saturdays, he busked,
usually down by the coach station. It wasn't much of a music city,
but it was easy to score some weed down by the water at night,
an area of much dereliction, both architectural and human. Near
a warehouse with a tree growing out of it three women a few
years his senior who were high or drunk or both stopped him
and asked if he wanted to go to a club with them.

'You'll like it,' one said. 'There's music playing.'

'What kind of music?' he asked.

'Jazz, duuddde,' she said, in a mock version of his accent.

He followed them four streets further into the injured concrete
core of the city while they whispered conspiratorially and cackled
about people and places he didn't know, lagging back out of concern
they might smell the odour of oysters that always now clung to his
clothes, then finally allowing himself to blur back into the night
for good. They did not appear to notice and as it faded their hard
laughter mixed with the cries of gulls until he did not know which
was one and which was the other. The next day he bought a small
pot of liquorice-red house paint and finished the mural. The sea
smells were a constant social concern, even though he did little
socialising. Oyster, mussel, cockle, crab. He was convinced they
never went away, even after he washed. On the roadsides, in the
wet dust and weeds, yellow flowers with darker yellow centres
were appearing. Down on the containers, they never called him
Richard or Richie, only 'Pencil' or 'Flower'. 'Ere, Flower, you sure
you can 'andle this?' 'Don't give it to Pencil. It might 'urt 'is soft
'ands. Lovely 'ands, 'e got, like my missus. You seen 'em?' At night,
he dreamt he was on his back, with sealife cascading down on
him out of a metal chute. If not that, he dreamt of Alison, the girl
from Albany he'd met the previous summer, who, upon taking
the least amount of drink, would immediately want to jab and

prod everyone around her with no little violence, or jump on their backs. In the space of just one weekend, Alison, who at barely five foot was a whole sixteen inches shorter than him, had jumped on the back of Jim Morrison and the rhythm section of The Turtles. During the dreams, he was always crouched in a corner, watching helplessly as the jumping took place, knowing intervention was futile. In the apotheosis of the dreams, he crouched in the corner of a shipping container, his hands over his eyes, as haddock fell on his head and Alison leapt on the back of a giant dolphin who smiled nervously in the manner of someone who will pretend to have fun on the vague promise of sex. A fragile awareness was growing in him that his songwriting was coming on apace. In a temporarily clean new plaza in the main shopping district, he tried out two new numbers and took home the smallest amount of money in his guitar case to date.

When other, more rampant vegetation had swallowed the yellow flowers on the verges, he set out for the docks at the usual time, carrying all his possessions, but turned right, not his customary left, and soon reached the train station. One of the country's diminishing branch lines took him to a village by the coast, where he and nobody else disembarked. At a post office, he bought bread, scissors, knobbly fruit and – with only an intrigued suspicion of what it might be – Marmite. It wasn't just that the tunnelled lanes he walked along, with their floral specklings of pink and blue, merely seemed a simple, elemental contrast to the city he'd spent the last four months in; they appeared to have no topographical relationship to the small metropolis at all, to belong in a whole different country. He helped two men push a rust-caked pickup out of a ditch. Afterwards, they ran him a mile or two further down the road to their place and gave him a cold lager. They asked where he was going and, when he answered as honestly and specifically as he could, their only advice was to avoid Somerset because the people there weren't right. The garden was full of retired machinery, fading gently into the earth. The younger of the two men pointed at two wooden structures on the hill above them that he'd taken for some kind of hutches. 'Bees,' the younger man said, rolling his eyes, but did not elaborate. The sun broke through the clouds after he left, drying him out for the third time that day. At a payphone, he inserted a coin and dialled a number beginning with an international prefix, but when a woody male voice answered he hung up. Further on, in a steep valley where everything hid strategically from the wind he appropriated three cucumbers from a garden and planted a kiss on the nose of a sceptical bullock.

As a result of trial and error, he found a zigzagging path down a landslip which spat him out onto a deserted cove by way of a rusty ladder which bridged the final gap between undercliff and shingle. Huts of varying types were dotted here and there on the cliffside, with flags and tall, tropical-looking plants outside. For the next thirteen days he slept on the beach, although he had concluded, at one point, that he would probably expire before seeing his first morning there, having come out of his initial salty self-baptism with purple digits and teeth that didn't so much chatter as argue with themselves, then failed in his attempts to light a fire without the aid of matches. He had learned the cove's first stark lesson, which was that it was not Malibu or Venice Beach. But by the third day he had grown acclimatised to the water, and, aided by driftwood and the fruits of a nine-mile hike to and from the village store, lit fires, and worked on verses of a song that he felt like he'd reached up and plucked out of the bright waxing gibbous moon above him. It had totally slipped his mind that it was his birthday. He was twenty-two years old.

The sea on his nude skin made him feel virile, and he wished he had a companion to swim with, but also slightly didn't. The cliffs were red, redder than they looked further down the coast, and the sea tasted red too when he accidentally swallowed some of it. The cove was one that sucked in more flotsam than most. One morning he awoke to discover a small metal alarm clock twenty yards in front of his toes, on the tideline. The sea had a sense of humour but you'd probably be mistaken for taking that to mean it suffered fools gladly. Having finished both of the paperbacks in his rucksack, he began to collect driftwood, not having to use any huge amount of imagination to see faces in the knots and bends in it. He wedged it together to make animals, some real, some mythical. He forged further down the shore, looking for even more. One evening he ran back to his base camp with so much of it that he had to carry the biggest piece in his mouth. He realised he was grinning. 'I am a dog,' he thought.

'And what,' he wrote in his diary that evening, as a response to some points he'd put to himself a few days earlier, 'is the benefit when you do get there? Is there a perfect midpoint between feeling the cold indifference of the world and losing freedom and judgement through commercial success and the people surrounding you who will no longer tell you the truth about what you are doing? (Not that I speak as someone facing a choice between the two at this exact juncture in my life.) Everything went so hazy today I lost sight of where the water ended and the sky began. In the quiet, a gull skimmed the water – or was it sky – and the tiny distance between its beak and the surface never wavered, as if measured by some highly evolved internal calculator. You could believe for a moment that this was all there was in the world: this watersky vapour, stretching for eternity, and this bird. Exquisite. I would like to bottle it somehow. I think this, in the end, is the great challenge, once you can write the tunes (which, really, anybody can, with time and effort): the bottling of something else. Something that's not even yours but that's not another person's either. Something on loan from the earth.'

Closer to the weekend, people arrived and unlocked the doors of a couple of the huts on the cliffside. An old man, his face entirely ringed with coarse white hair, came down from one of the huts and swam naked, striding into the sea with all the confidence of someone reclaiming a swimming pool he had dug out with his own gnarled hands. Afterwards, the old man caught and cooked mackerel, the smell drifting down tantalisingly to where he sat scraping the last flecks of disillusioning Marmite from the jar. Later, he heard hammering from the old man's hut, metallic and dauntless. While he listened to the old man hammer, he hacked into his hair with the scissors and threw the clumps into the tide, wondering when and how and where they would biodegrade.

The sea of his new home beach had innumerable moods. Rusty anger. Muscular calm. Pungent clarity. Weedy broth. Blue fog. Stubborn debris trickster. When did one sea clock off from its shift and the other sea come in and take its place? You never witnessed that moment because that was not permitted because if you did that would unlock everything: the big secret to it all. He knew the sea was irascible, not to be trusted but, as its resident, he inevitably began to get his feet further under the table, as residents do. One day, doing front crawl seventy yards out, he realised that his intended movement, back towards shore, was going the opposite of to plan and, worse, that he was on an inexorable downward trajectory. It was all very befuddling, because nothing around him looked particularly vigorous or wretched, and, in his disorientation, he only got the chance to cry out twice before he was completely submerged, garbled protests in a futile language spoken by only one man. His next close-to-conscious realisation was that he was in Heaven and God was looking down on him. Because Heaven would always customise itself aptly to the manner in which you'd died, Heaven in this instance was made of shingle and raucous white birds, but God had a beard, as God always had, no matter what the cause of your death was.

'I thought you were a goner there, kiddo,' said God, who he now realised was not God at all, but the old man from the hut.

*

'You were in a riptide. The thing to do in a riptide is to swim parallel to the shore. You swam towards the shore, which is the worst thing you can do.'

They sat on old canvas chairs on the old man's creaking, salty veranda and ate mackerel and potatoes, which the man salted liberally, in accordance with their environment. 'How's your head now?' the old man asked.

'Sore,' he replied. He had hit the back of it on some rocks close to where he'd gone under, but in the end the impact had also saved his life since it was the sight of him bumping against the rocks that had alerted the old man to his plight, and allowed the old man to swim out quickly, and drag him clear, around the corner of the current, and back to shore.

'I used to do it for the county. Swim. I was pretty good, could have been better, if I'd put the effort in. I had the chance to go to the Olympics. Belgium. I was too busy falling in love. I rarely have cause to swim like that any more, but I've watched six people die in my life and I didn't much relish adding to that total.'

He slept on the floor of the old man's hut that night, on top of a blanket. The head of a nail, knocked slightly loose from a floorboard, poked into the back of his knee, but he still managed to locate sleep with little trouble. He was a person who lost consciousness quickly: on train seats, on beds, on floors, in deep, chilly water. In the morning, he felt the lump on the back of his skull. It was located on a part of his skull he'd never liked, but had had little regular cause to think about, until now. In the light, he took in more of the cabin. On the shelf on the bed he saw a gardening trowel, a thick wool blanket and a bottle of aftershave. Above the Calor gas stove hung two framed photographs: one of a black poodle, and one of a smiling, elfin lady in a thick herringbone coat. The old man came in with a towel around his neck. 'She's dead now,' said the old man, waving a hand towards the photographs. 'And so is she.'

They swam later that morning, and in the afternoon he slept and played guitar while the old man vanished up the landslip to he did not know where. He stretched out on the skin of the water and listened to the shingle moving beneath him. In the evening by the fire he spoke a little about home but mostly the old man talked about his life and he listened.

'I lost Eileen, she's the one in the photo, when I was sixty-one. I was entirely unprepared for it. I always took for granted that we'd have a bit longer than that. Look out there. Seal. See it? I was not always a good man in my youth. I had my... errant moments. But I, we, got past it. People will give up more easily now. But we didn't. We were OK. In the first year that I was alone, I kept coming back to an image, from years before. It was of Eileen, the first day I ever came here. Naked, in the water. Don't misunderstand me. I'm not talking about something erotic, although she was a beautiful woman. It wasn't that which kept bringing me back to it. It was her face, the freedom and happiness in it. It wasn't like her, to do that, permit herself to become naked in a place where she might be observed by strangers. I knew her to be a very cautious woman. She looked so different that day: like every muscle in her face had relaxed. That is a beautiful thing, to see a woman you love go naked into the sea for the first time. If you see it, don't go on in the blithe assumption you might see it again. Anyhow, not long after that, I came down with the dog and built the cabin. I was totally certain I needed to do it, for her. The dog and I brought the wood around on the boat. It took seventeen months, in total. I'm here half the year, if I can be. My name is Robert Belltower. You play guitar very well. Her ashes are up there. Have you thought of trying to secure a recording contract?'

'I had one. It wasn't for me.'

'Well, if it's not for you, don't do it,' said Robert Belltower. 'But make certain you're certain first.'

Above the path on the undercliff, huge, never-tamed buddleia nurtured vast dynasties of bees and bee mimics. The sweet smell of the buddleia dominated the evenings, along with the very nearly as sweet smell of Robert Belltower. Upon retiring on the fifth night, Robert Belltower announced he would be gone for a short while, possibly to Lyme Regis, or the old smugglers' village of Beer, he was not yet certain. Robert Belltower said he was welcome to use the cabin, so long as he didn't burn it down, and left the key to the padlock under the third rock behind the flag. The song he wrote the following day, which he gave the working title 'Sad Photograph of a Dog', felt like an attempt of sorts to finish a conversation. He deemed it an inferior song and, after further appraisal, decided he was certain he was certain.

Storms were spinning in from the west. They vanquished his fires, stirred and steepened the shingle, drenched his diary, conditioned the furze of his hair. He imagined giant clenched fists pulling the black clouds in on a rope with big concerted tugs and little pauses in between. In the strange aggressive sunblast that followed, he became aware of how long it was since he had been touched by anybody except Robert Belltower. He poured cold water on that thought and reconstituted it as the simpler desire to play a song for a gathering of twenty or more people and hear them clap and possibly whoop. He left the four of the driftwood animals that had not blown away outside the hut, so they defined a path of sorts to the front door. The undercliff seemed steeper, twistier than before, as he made his way up it, but he was aware of something more coiled and taut in his calves as they propelled him up the still-damp path, shimmying to one side every dozen or so steps to make way for jaywalking oil beetles. He stopped and peeled one of Robert Belltower's overripe bananas under a yew tree in a churchyard, ate it in three decisive bites. He threw the peel towards a gathering of wild rabbits then set out up a steep unmetalled road and through a latched gate weighted by an old rock. Cows looked up from their all-day meals, discussed the topic amongst themselves then made their way slowly, and then more quickly, towards him. The hillside shook under their hooves and he froze with his tanned arms spread wide, like some fibreglass cattle messiah, and the cows stopped in their tracks, looking up into his face, fascinated and confused, until, one by one, they returned to the more vital business of breakfast. His reverie was broken by a small, worrying question in his mind: Which rock had Robert Belltower said, and how far was it behind the flag?

He waved down the train at another small station, where there were no other passengers, and took it to a different city this time, less greyly rearranged by war, barely a city at all. He walked up a cobbled street to a cathedral and set up directly beneath a carving of a six-mouthed, six-nosed, five-eyed crowned head. All the office workers, even those of his age group, who bit into thin white sandwiches on the green in front of him had much shorter hair than him, even in his newly pollarded state. A woman holding a polythene bag overflowing with clothes stared sadly at him, then, after almost an hour, moved on, limping. Later, he realised a short man with a guitar was also staring at him, not as sadly, but intently, unwaveringly.

'You're in my spot, longshanks,' barked the man, before he had quite finished the song.

'Your spot?'

'Yes. This is where I go. Has been for a long time. Everyone knows.'

'I didn't realise they were reserved.'

'Well, this one is. Scram. Get lost.'

'Well, what if I'm not so down with that, man? There's a lot of space here. Enough for everyone.'

With that, the man transformed himself into a close approximation of a rhinoceros, bending and charging at his midriff with great speed, knocking all the wind from him. He fell back into the cathedral wall, the sore part of his head smacking against cold uneven stone. As he did, the rhinocerman kicked wildly at his guitar case, scattering coins onto grass and cobbles. He scrambled for his affairs and the lunchtime crowd on the green moved in, but nobody intervened or helped. As he flailed for coins and notes, he noticed the face of his watch, which his grandfather had given him, was cracked and the hands had stopped moving. All of the city's noise had become a single muffled high note and he waded in his stooped shock to the other shore of the cathedral green, dragging his possessions with him in a slapdash collection of arms.

He walked for a number of hours that he could not quantify. After leaving behind the last of the nervous almost-villages that the city had coughed out and passing over several successively higher wooded rims, he descended, stopped at a clapper bridge, drank from a small river and slumped in a cradle of moss beneath a tree and rested his eyes. The water level was low, revealing a quasi-wall that could have been built by a person, long long ago, but could equally have been built by nature and time; it was hard to tell. When he awoke again it was dark. When he awoke the next time, the sun was rising, illuminating rougher, higher land ahead of him: the three-buttocked crest of a hill. His head remained sore but his vision had cleared. A sign matted with thick gaudy lichen told him that he was one and one quarter miles from Owl's Gate, whatever that was. It was, factually speaking, very recently in his life that pretty much all of his goals featured people in some way, but now none did, and to him it was as if that had been the state of affairs for a long time. His goal now was to reach the middle, highest buttock of the three on that hill. Nothing was more important to him and nothing ever had been and nothing ever would be.

It took him longer than he thought. With its tough stalks and hard, half-raised root balls, the grass made him sway and stagger, like a drunk returning home from a regretful episode. Lambs scattered at his approach and clamped onto their mothers' teats for solace, as if in the belief that if they closed their eyes and sucked long enough when they opened their eyes the Bad Man would no longer be there to frighten them. When he reached the top, the sun had turned around to get a better look at him. To the south, he could not see the sea but he could see the light blue space where more land would have been if the sea hadn't been there. Everything was wild and bare and voluptuous in the other direction: buttocks upon buttocks, shadowed by buttocks, for as far as the eye could see. Yet down in the valleys everything was a darker green and there were more hiding places than you'd have ever imagined. A person could become this place, he suspected. On a sunken path with a leaf roof he passed remnant chunks of buildings that were barely distinguishable from the immeasurably older stones around them. An increasing dampness. Root and shale walls coated in bearded slime. As he crossed stepping stones in a brook, he was thinking about a summer day three years earlier when a photographer had taken him and the rest of the band deep into the canyon, down a dirt track, to a house that was falling down, and they'd goofed about, climbing on old refrigerators and sofas, then pulling themselves high into a magnolia tree in the backyard, all three of them, all looking down deep into the lens as if it was a future they wanted to undress and ravish, with Frank in the centre, and that had been the shot that was used. He'd ripped his military tunic jacket on the way down. Frank had been the one who noticed and told him.

The sunken path led him to a tiny lane, and another wooden sign told him to walk left, but the gate was padlocked and decorated with barbed wire. He climbed over it anyway, figuring there must have been some mistake, and he was soon in a meadow, high and sweet from months of reinventing itself. You couldn't stand still. It didn't work. Ask meadows. Below him in the valley he could see a village. He dipped below a neat line of beech, with foxgloves growing at their roots. An unseen horse coughed behind a hedge and two longer, thinner meadows later he saw buildings, barns, a house. He was regretting not drinking from the stream and was about to approach the house and ask for water when he saw a hole in its wall, which, because of the relative intactness of the rest of the building, conjured up the image of a small wrecking ball and an administrative error. He clambered through the hole, coughing away stone dust, and was momentarily dazzled by the darkness of the room. Dusty overalls were draped over a chair. A doorway led to a kitchen, with a sink containing dirty dishes and flies. On the counter was a half-full bottom of rum. He took a swig of the rum, which was warmer and thicker than rum he'd tasted before but not wholly unpleasant. He washed it down with a long blast of water from the tap and could not recall a time when water had tasted so good, so much like a drink that had been brewed and planned and fermented, rather than just like water. He found a small wooden door leading to an area of old stone sheds, which formed part of a high mossy wall that enclosed a rear garden on all sides. A huge wooden padlock hung on another door and an extra plank had been nailed across it. Up the stone staircase, the rooms were more bare, with no beds, but he found a bath and soap, and downstairs there were two large sofas. He found a ripped armchair and, discovering the back door to be locked, carried the armchair out through the hole and into the back garden. The grass was high and the air had a weight to it, as if for now it was holding everything in place.

'Ida Richards,' he wrote in his diary. 'She was my first. Her thirst grew in direct correlation with my uncertainty. I had wanted it so much, talked it up with my buddies, but when it came to it, I stalled, procrastinated. I hit upon new hobbies that would keep us out of her room. Eventually, she had to cajole, if not beg. She walked me through it, soft and kind. Afterwards, I was sore. Nobody had warned me about that. They'd told me that only happened to girls. Nobody was sweeter than Ida. We'd walk through the neighbourhood and she'd stop to kiss stranger's dogs softly on the forehead. Sometimes, while I read, she would sit on the bed, staring at me, playing with her nails, examining invisible objects in the wool of her sweater. She deserved better. I imagine that one day I will realise, on some even deeper level, that, by chance, at sixteen I met a rare kind of angel, but how can you know that at sixteen? When I finally ended it she didn't seem shocked. Her far greater disappointment always appeared to be that I never wrote a song for her, or about her. "But, Richie, why nnnnnot?" she would ask, sulking, shoving me, pouting in a joke-real way. "I thought I was special." I never told her the real reason, which was that I feared it would be a let-down. Not because of the lack of love or feeling, but because it could not be enough. The feeling is still the same. That nothing is enough. It is there every time I put down my guitar. Will it ever be gone?'

Two mornings later, dizzy with hunger, he hiked to the bottom of the valley, reaching a row of stone cottages with neat gardens with sunflowers and hollyhocks and runner beans and windows decorated with elegant watchful cats. Clouds followed him down, gave him their brief appraisal then moved out to sea. He crossed the river and reached a main road. Around the bend, three cars were at a standstill on the tarmac. Another car passed them in the opposite direction, very cautiously, taking a diversion up a muddy bank. A large black-and-white heifer sat on the white line in the centre of the road. Beside the cow stood a fretting, long-haired girl in a baggy sweater flecked with hay. 'She won't move,' said the girl. 'She's been here for over an hour now. She's from where I live, the farm. Over the ridge. I would get my dad to come and get her but I don't want to leave her.'

'How far away is the farm?' he asked.

'Less than a mile, really not far at all. I just need to get my dad, and she'll move.'

'I'll wait with her.'

'Are you sure? I don't know. Is that best?'

'It's fine.'

He crouched beside the cow, and put a hand gently on the animal's back, and began to talk softly into her ear. As the girl hurried away from them, a couple more cars appeared and stopped, and the people inside them got out to look and laugh at the cow, and he whispered to the cow about the people from the cars and who they probably were, and told the cow his full name and a little about what had brought him here, and told the cow a little bit about the world, and some of the ups and downs it might contain for the cow in the future, but in a reassuring, philosophical way, not in a hard, cynical way which might potentially have upset the cow and made it even more reluctant to face that future. By the time the girl had started back down the hill with her father and a rope, he and the cow had made it almost all the way up the lane to the farm.

'Well I'll be a dog's pudding,' said the girl's dad.

That night he ate with the girl and her family. They asked him where he was from and he told them California, first a part with lots of trees and fields and rivers, a little like here, but not as green, because he didn't think he'd ever seen anything as green as here; then the city, and then a part that was somewhere in between. They appeared to be greatly amused and delighted by his existence alone, the unlikeliness and potted story of him, and asked him what had brought him here specifically, rather than another part of the UK, and he said he'd always been told to go west, if in doubt, and he'd once briefly lived here, because of his father's job, a very long time ago, but he couldn't remember it at all, and this apparently caused them to be even more amused and delighted. They began, soon, to talk about somebody called Dick, who lived down by the river, sold logs and had formerly kept pet ferrets, and had once been found asleep in the back of a stranger's Land Rover, but only after the stranger had driven it many miles, and the girl's father began to tell some ruder stories about Dick, but the girl's mother told him to stop, as it wasn't polite, and there were children present. After dinner, the girl's little sister wrote an illustrated story in blue crayon on a sheet of paper and said it was for him. 'People had faces but it was a long time ago before there were cars or toast,' the girl's sister had written. 'A woman and a man and a bear built a house at the top of a tree but the tree fell down so they built another house in a better tree. One day another bear arrived as well. The tree still didn't fall down. It only fell down when the sun drowned in the sea and all trees stopped growing.' The girl's mother said she'd heard there was an attic room in the village to rent in Burrow Cottage and her father cut in and said he thought that had gone now and her mother said she wasn't actually sure if that was true, Grenville, but would try to find out for him tomorrow, and he could stay here tonight. Books were piled high and uneven on the window ledge of the room where he was to sleep. Their subjects were various but largely centred around hens and war but not both at the same time. As the girl, whose name was Maddie, made up his bed, he stole a look at her and thought about how her skin was different to skin he'd known before, something earthier, something sun but rain too. He remembered mirrors for the first time in a while and, finding one in the bathroom, saw something similar beginning in himself. He had altered, assimilated, was becoming the place. Tomorrow, he would look different again. He was not a photograph.

The village was called Underhill and Burrow Cottage was on a street that dug its nails into the edge of a steep slope that rose towards the north. Behind that was a far bigger hill, topped with rocks, underneath a sky that kept changing, over and over again, during his walk to the cottage, as if someone behind the sky kept closing and unclosing a heavy drape. He told the old lady who lived in the cottage that he would take her attic room for a month but wasn't sure beyond that and she said that was fine. He'd been lucky: a locum doctor had wanted the room but changed his mind at the last minute, although she admitted she'd been relieved, as he seemed to be what she called a miserable so-and-so. 'A very funereal, slightly cadaverous man. I wouldn't have liked to have him examine me at all. I'd have felt like he was measuring me up for my coffin. You're not a miserable so-and-so, are you?' the old lady asked.

'I have my bright days,' he said.

He had to stoop to avoid hitting his head on the beams but there was a single brass bed that he could stretch out to very nearly his full length on and a wicker chair and a hand basin and a shower but if he needed the toilet he'd have to go out into the backyard and use the outside one. She assured him it was very clean, although 'a bit cold on the bum in January'.

She gestured at a pile of canvases on the floor. 'If these are in your way, just move them to somewhere they're not. They're just my nonsense. I'll find another place for them eventually.' A couple of nights later, Maddie arrived in a small curvaceous car with wooden window frames and drove him to a pub in a town a few miles closer to the sea where anyone who desired it was permitted to stand up and play two songs. He remained sitting down but two Fridays later, when they went again, he took his guitar and got up and sang 'Mr Tambourine Man' and 'Clapper Bridge', a new song of his own whose chorus he had just about nailed down but whose verses were still a work in progress. This time, the crowd was scruffier, more bohemian. A group of long-hairs in the corner cheered loudly at the end of 'Mr Tambourine Man' and louder still at the end of 'Clapper Bridge' and called Maddie and him over. A drink and a half later a huge bearded man in a leather jacket entered the pub. 'CHICKPEA!' Maddie shouted, and the man enclosed her in a hug so enormous, she temporarily vanished. A girl to his left started talking about how she could predict the weather with her knees and asked him if he was at the college, too, or starting there soon. He said he didn't know of any college and asked her if she knew Monterey and she said she didn't and before he'd had the chance to explain why he'd even asked she'd begun talking to someone else. Afterwards, all eleven of them went back to a big white building with a central courtyard, where there were posters of bands, some of whom he'd met, although he didn't say so. Somebody put on 'Foxy Lady' at such a volume that the speakers kept crackling and cutting out and he strived to pay full attention while a girl told him the pitfalls of communism, and he began to wonder where Maddie had got to. 'You've not read Koestler,' the girl said. 'I can't believe you've not read Koestler!' He felt as stoned and as close to being home as he had since he got off the plane and fully expected, were he to return here the next morning, that the white building would have vanished and there would be only trees and other vegetation in its place. In between songs, someone squeezed a dog toy outside the window, and he wondered who would be both so baked out of their head and committed to take the time to do that between every one of well over a dozen songs, until he realised it was not a dog toy but the squeak of a female owl in a tree. 'Time to go, Cowboy,' said Maddie, grabbing his sleeve. Her hair was river wet and her eyes were tunnels of light.

'Howsabout you then, Bob Dylan?' she said, on the way home. 'The Quiet American. Full of surprises.' She drove even faster than earlier and the car squeaked against ferns and twigs, and bumped on rougher and rougher pebbles on the road until he realised it wasn't a road at all, merely a wider-than-average footpath, a bridleway, perhaps, but you'd be pushing it to call it even that. 'Shortcut,' she said. 'Trust me.'

And then days arrived when you wondered how much more moisture there was in the world. Days of incongruous chimney smoke, should-be-hot afternoons when clothes wouldn't dry and even though the rain wasn't *in* your house it was in your house, mornings when you looked up at the moor and realised it was the place where weather was made, the place where time ended, and that, beyond it, there was nothing comprehensible or civil, despite the lies that maps told you. He wrote his sister and wondered if she, always quietly perceptive to so much, would sense in the fourteen sentences on the page the changes in himself that he felt. He drank and read. He read and drank. He walked to a white pub in the rain and sat beneath an awning and polished off almost all of a paperback he'd borrowed from the old lady and realised when he got home that he'd left it there and the old lady told him off – 'Richard, I do notice that your mind often seems to be elsewhere' – but a few minutes later knocked on his door with a cup of tea. She noticed with surprise that he'd taken one of the canvases from the pile and balanced it facing out against the wall, on top of the tallboy. 'I hope you don't mind,' he said. 'I like it a lot.' Under the painting, perched on the room's one hard wooden chair with his guitar, he looked deep into the layers of swirling oil, layers suggesting destroyed sweetnesses. Within them, he thought he saw a face of green. He destroyed sweetnesses of his own, sang and strummed over them in big brushstrokes, left just tiny slivers of them showing, wished he had flutes and banjos and mandolins and pianos to work in the layers of gentle annihilation. The words were best when they came from somewhere exterior to him but connected to him by some invisible electric rod, somewhere very different to the place where you got words in a letter or a note or an essay you wrote at school or even a song you wrote expressly for somebody you knew who had the power to help it reach an audience, and when they did come from that exterior place they often frightened him and that was when it was best. When they didn't come like that any more, he knew that there was only one thing to do and that was to go back to the house with the hole in the wall, even though that frightened him too, in a different way. The rain drummed on the skylight in the old lady's attic room and through it the dark rocks on the tor showed through like an ominous growth on an X-ray of moist organs.

A garage a couple of miles away, near where the river levelled out and widened, had advertised for somebody to pump four star into people's cars and he went to see the owner about the position but the owner took one look at him and said it had been taken, which he accepted without protest, and also accepted to be a lie. He took the long, high route back. Below him, red berries had appeared on the hillside. He stood aside to let the kerfuffle of a hiking family pass. 'I stood in a hole and I think my foot is broken,' said one of two medium-sized children. 'Take your shoe off and rub it and it will be fine,' replied a red-cheeked mum. He hooked back west and saw a sign reading 'Job Vayckansie' next to a pair of large wooden gates. 'BEWARE OF THE DOGS (3)' said another sign to the right of that. 'DICK WARNER: SEASSONED LOGS' said another, above that. He'd not noticed the place behind the gate before but realised, upon entering it, he'd smelled its aroma drifting on the breeze many times. He walked along a track of rubble and bark past high log piles and knocked on the half-open door of a squat building with a corrugated iron roof. Getting no response, he peered into the kitchen behind it. The floor was covered in breadcrumbs and wood chippings, a pan of water boiled on a stove in one corner of the room and in the other a dog-eared poster had been pinned to the wall exhibiting a naked, full-breasted woman holding a bowsaw and winking. He stepped back outside and saw a small elderly canine limping towards him, on three legs. The animal flopped down at his feet and revealed a belly of patchy fur, which he tickled. He wandered between log piles behind the building and was turning to leave when a compact man wearing thick gauntlet gloves hurtled past him, seemingly out of the logs themselves, saying, 'Fuck fuck fuck fuck bastard.'

The man in the gloves entered the kitchen and emerged holding the pan of boiling water, whose contents he sloshed haphazardly onto the paving slabs around him. 'Ants,' the gloved man said, nodding his head at the ground, and also shaking it, as if to fully wake himself. 'Fell into a snooze. It happens. Come about the job?' 'Yeah, I...' he said. 'How are you with felling trees?' said the gloved man, whose age he could have put at anywhere between thirty-five and fifty-five. He confessed it was not something he'd had previous experience with, although he had used an axe plenty of times. 'Dunt matter,' said the gloved man. 'You won't be doing that. How you feel about clearing that lot?' He gestured towards a meadow: a vast unchecked space of brambles and gorse and poppy and waist-high grass and raging hypericum. 'No great rush. How does three weeks sound? Enough? Come when you can. Seen you in the village. Living at the Nicholas place aren't you. We can talk about money later. I've got tools coming out my arse so you won't need to bring any of them.' The gloved man was walking now, and he followed. After a few steps, the gloved man bent to pick up a small object from the woodchippings they were walking on, then hurled it far through the air, where it ricocheted off a silver birch into some undergrowth. 'Vole,' said the gloved man, shrugging and letting out an industrial fart.

Maddie came in the car to get him and he played guitar in town again. Wild angelica and maidenhair spleenwort grew against the walls of a small sunken network of alleys near the pub. A bearded man with a walking stick who appeared to be well into his eighth decade staggered up to the microphone and sang a folk song, unaccompanied, which he said he'd learned as a child growing up nearby, and introduced as 'Little Meg', although he said it was sometimes known by other titles. Afterwards the song lingered in his mind, especially something nebulous about its central subject. The next time, the old bearded man was there again, this time with his wife, and hand in hand they advanced slowly to the microphone and sang the song together. Everyone applauded, but before they did, the room was very silent for a beat. After last orders, he and Maddie walked down to the riverbank and he met a couple of new people from the college, and five or six people from it he'd met before, and willowy women in shawls and slight men in glasses talked animatedly at him and he nodded and Maddie sat with one arm around Chickpea and one arm around him but his mind was only a quarter there and the remaining portion was almost all trying to memorise the lyrics to the elderly couple's song. When he got home, he scribbled what he could recollect down in his diary and began working some chords around it. 'I feel like the year has turned over and I feel a turning in me too,' he also wrote in the diary, below that. 'Hooves and shouting outside. I can't see why from the window. Room is full of moths.' An encore of heat was hissing through the long grass outside, drying the glistening cobwebs. Between the long stalks and bracken, ticks were flexing their horrible legs. There had not been a better time to be a tick for a considerable period. After his shifts for Dick Warner, his gardening for a man without a garden, he picked the bloated, flailing bodies of the ticks out of his thighs, stomach and the soft unblemished underside of his arms. He learned to be careful when he mowed because sometimes there were beer and cider bottles in the grass. When the mower wasn't on, sounds drifted over from Warner's building, sometimes that of Warner's buzzsaw and sometimes the commanding bass and tenor sounds of Elise, an insuppressible, wide-faced woman who ran the greengrocers in Bovey Tracey and would drive over twice a week to bounce on top of Warner. He soon realised the trick with the ticks was to tease them out a little with tweezers then give them one big decisive tug.

He thought about his old life and it seemed less that he'd abandoned it and more that it was still happening, concurrently; that there was another him still out there, still doing all that he might have done. Nobody had recognised him since he got off the plane, just as he had expected them not to. Some days, he felt like he had been asked to write a book and said no and given the money back, and instead chosen to write another book, finish it and abandon it in a ravine at night. By now his sister had written him back. She said she'd heard from Frank that he was in England and that she was disappointed he'd not told her but that she had decided that he must have had his reasons and forgave him. (He had never told Frank but he guessed word quickly got around in the Canyon.) 'There's a lot happening here,' she wrote. 'In the house, and everywhere, too. I feel like so much has changed in such a short time. I have to tell you that Daddy is sick. I know he would like to see you. I haven't told him I'm writing this letter.' One day he had heard one of Frank's new songs on Maddie's car radio. He was surprised how little impact it had on him. He thought it was a very well organised song and was sure it would continue to do well for the rest of the year. The second time they heard it, Maddie sang along. 'You're my rabbit,' she shrieked. 'And you've got me on the... rrrrrun.' He said nothing. As if she'd somehow tapped into his thoughts, she said, 'There's a music studio at the college. I don't know if it's anything special. But I think Chickpea could get you some time in there, if you like?' He said maybe and that might be cool but he wasn't sure if he was quite there yet. 'Of course you're there, you silly sausage!' she said. 'You're more than there. The only reason you're not there is that you've gone past there and you need to reverse.' It struck him that there were two Maddies he was getting to know: Farm Maddie and Artistic Friends Maddie. Today she was somehow both. He had never been called a silly sausage before and he discovered it was not displeasing. The window had jammed the last time she'd opened it and now remained permanently in a three-quarters-open position. He dangled an arm out and let his fingers flick against the bracken as it whizzed by, enjoying the sting. Six old plastic bags full of apples were on the back seat, ripening in the sun. Several had come loose and fallen onto the composty area beneath the seats, and, while Maddie pulled over to let other cars pass on the narrow lanes, wasps flew in to investigate. There was a time and place to be an insect and that time was now and that place was here.

Frank had always been the one to announce, 'I've got something which I think is pretty special.' He, by contrast, would say, 'There's something I have been playing around with' or 'This might work, I guess.' It was, he had subsequently realised, the predominant reason why the writing ratio ended up 7/3 in favour of Frank. That, and Frank's tendency to deal directly in the politics of romance, whereas his habit was, at most, to weave around the topic. One of the advantages of breaking away on your own was you didn't write by committee and a song didn't get automatically consigned to the garbage just because you didn't bring it into the studio with its own ticker tape parade. 'Chickpea says he thinks you're very modest, and that you're an old soul,' Maddie said, after his second of three days in the music room, not really much of a studio at all, just a soft-walled black room with a reel-to-reel in the corner and Chickpea at the controls, damp and huge in the heat in the large established country of his beard and the leather jacket he never relinquished. Chickpea had left and he and Maddie were on the wide lawn behind the studio which spread out in the direction of a set of straggling medieval buildings. Opposite, two women in black leotards danced to silence and fenced with peacock feathers. Every few minutes, a girl would emerge from the medieval buildings and run screeching across the lawn to Maddie, hug her, and ask with great urgency if she'd heard about something desperately exciting that was happening the following week. Theatre, picnics, parties, music, art, other gatherings that were apparently a hybrid of all five. 'Sorry to interrupt!' the girls said afterwards, turning to him, appraising him with slow fascination, as if experiencing the pleased, lazy epiphany that he was not a tree. Almost all of them spoke very differently to the way Maddie did. Their voices were more precise and clean, more redolent of scrubbed residential streets and fussy gardens. It struck him as wild and impressive how effortlessly Maddie managed to be simultaneously of the college and very different to it. It struck him also as wild and impressive how effortlessly the college managed to be simultaneously of its geographical base and of a different planet: a place of geese, pottery and ballet, in equal measures. It was one of the most unlikely hillsides he'd ever stood on and he was here with this unlikely person all because of a cow. He noticed something unique in the curve of her chin in profile that he'd not noticed before. She had strong arms, arms that lifted many heavy objects, as different to her friends' arms as her voice was to their voices. Her language was full of wild plants that, enraptured by the music of their names, he was compelled to note down in his diary: bog asphodel and penny marshwort – or was it marsh pennywort – and purple loosestrife and bog pimpernel. She liked practical jokes and grapefruit. When she told him she came here once a week to teach people how to look after chickens he'd thought she was having him on. She wasn't. The previous weekend she had hidden his shoes in an oven. She would never find out, but she was the first girl he'd ever written a love song about.

After the third day of recording, which he grudgingly conceded was better, they ascended narrow lanes and crossed tiny humped bridges in the car, going higher and higher, parked, then walked to a stone circle. A scribble of rain had blown in through the gap in the window when they were in the car then gone and in its place there was more damp heat. She told him to place his palms against the stones in the circle and feel all the energy there.

'Ah, I'm so excited,' she said. 'My boyfriend is coming back next week.'

'Where is he right now?'

'Spain. He's been out there since May. He's in the army.'

He gazed back across the rocks, trying to pick out the car.

'I think most of it's probably trash,' he said. 'But I dunno. I guess I'll end up hanging on to the tape.'

But he was not a person entirely devoid of hubris. He had the complacency of many people who arrive in rural Britain from a country populated by bears, coyotes and mountain lions, and the sun massaged that complacency. He was still a newcomer to the moor and even oldcomers to it knew only a fraction of a fraction of what there was to know about it. One of the many things he didn't yet know about it was that, in late August, in days of heat after heavy rain, on the stretches where it was still most fully permitted to be itself, it breathed and growled as profoundly as it did in the height of the harshest winter. Terrain you'd visited always compacted its scale in your mind afterwards and he had begun to learn that but, even so, the route back to the ruined house was surprisingly arduous. The river told him he was going the right way but it seemed further than before and something had happened in the dripping folds of earth above the banks: an angry awakening, a last wet sucking of life into the lungs before autumn's dry death. Brown flies clung fiercely to his flesh. Huge tufts of grass shoved him from side to side, arguing over their custody of him. Blue and pink and yellow flowers spilled over the damp ground like ornate vomit. An old octopus of a tree reached down a rough tentacle and anointed his cheek with a bloody scratch. In his shoes, the soles of his feet sloshed about and blistered and began their transformation into a sore kind of paste. Every path became a whisper and then a lie. A stiff gate opened but led directly to a shrub of insanity. The song the old man and his wife had sung was in his head again and he hummed the song and then he barked it at the impassable bracken that stretched all the way up the valley walls and then he croaked it at the sky. An area of oxygen finally widened ahead but the ground beneath it drank his feet then low branches formed a roadblock and he crawled under them then lost most of his left leg in a peaty bubbling hole and had to use all his strength to retrieve it. He could not have been more wet if he was in the river itself up to his neck and the burnt moist state of him attracted more and more tiny winged life and he knew then that one day, once again, this would be the world. Not a car, not a sandwich, not an ambition, not sense, not a cow, not a horse, not love, not a song, not a girl. Just this sucking and gargling and burping thing beneath him. When the dizziness came, and the head pain, just before the light clicked off, it was a relief to submit, to just fall into the mouth of everything and not go on fighting any more. And then night fell smoothly in, and not thirteen yards away the river, which was not interested, continued to yell as it rushed over the rocks.

*

She was very good at keeping a straight face and she liked to take people on a journey. It was an addiction of hers but she viewed it as generally harmless. First there was usually the lie, which was thrilling in itself, but then there was the space of time after the lie, when the lie – and the imaginative invention that went with it – expanded, which was more thrilling still. It was like pulling an elastic band: if you pulled it back further you got more power, but you couldn't go too far or it would snap. She liked to take it quite far, because then when you punctured the lie the look on the face of the person who'd believed it was that much more delicious. But she'd quickly had her misgivings after she talked about the soldier in Spain. She'd misjudged it. It made her wonder about herself. It was a five- or ten-minute lie, she thought as she set out for the cottage, not a one-day lie, and definitely not a three-day lie, and it was different to many of her other lies because it played with something important. When she knocked on the door, the old woman answered and said he was not there and she had not seen him since yesterday. 'He does do his vanishing acts, Richard. He doesn't tell me where he goes. You can wait for him if you want, but I don't know when he'll be back. It's Madeleine, isn't it?' She resisted the other names that popped into her head on impulse – Jill and Rose and Sylvia and Thomasina – and the backstories she might invent for them, and instead replied that, yes, that was correct. 'If you could say that I called round, I'd appreciate that,' she said.

*

After he'd finished at the ruined house, he walked west for an entire morning, until he arrived at a pub. He ordered chips and sat on a bench outside and ate them, accompanied by a lone Muscovy duck. In a church foyer, farther up the lane the pub was on, he found a pile of free paperbacks, and put one in his rucksack. His feet ached and one of the soles had come loose from his left boot. On a bigger road, he waited for close to two hours, until a car pulling a caravan stopped for him. He sat in the back seat beside a child called Matthew with a bubble of snot in one nostril who stared at him the whole way, sucking a thumb. He got out within a mile of the village and went straight to Dick Warner's woodyard, but there was no sign of him. Outside the door to the kitchen was a trail of cold baked beans and many of the beans were stuck to the door itself. Within a swift breeze that whipped around the logs there was the aroma of wood and crow and something dead but briefly revived and not quite identifiable. When he finally reached the cottage Mrs Nicholas was out. He found some tape in a drawer and applied it to his shoe, threw his remaining possessions into his rucksack, and left the paperback and the remaining rent he owed on the kitchen table.

He started out west again and walked until he joined the next river, then followed it until it branched and widened to create a calm subsidiary pool, which he swam in. He examined the peeling skin on his feet, neither of which ever seemed to have dried out from the day he walked back to the ruined house. A new area of purple-black on one of his heels. He walked some more, until he came to another river, with a viaduct over it. He reached a quay and dark buildings, below a Tudor mansion with great sprawling gardens and a domed dovecote. Boats and parts of boats were everywhere and even a mile later, parts of boats could still be seen in numerous gardens. He crossed a stream and sat on an abandoned tractor tyre above one of the gardens, on the opposite side of a small valley and, having seen no sign of life in or near it, picked apples from its trees, and took lettuce and an artichoke head from its beds. The garden thinned and snaked on into woodland until it ended at a rusty gate, and next to the rusty gate was a small orange bus on bricks. He managed to force one of the windows of the bus open and that night slept inside the bus, stretched out along its ripped back bench. He woke up and felt like somebody had performed origami on his face in his sleep. He climbed a hill and took a small train to the grey city where he'd worked on the docks then he changed and took another train east, guessing at when he might be level with the point where the cliffs began to turn red and getting off at the first station after that. Cars pulling caravans were struggling up the tall hills that broke away from the coast in threes and fours, and he walked against the flow, flattening himself against nettles and brambles to let the vehicles pass. In many of the fields there were huge rocks and corvids could often be seen on the rocks, making their withering assessments of the day. The land was thrown audaciously together, had no order or mathematics to it. 'Dogs in field,' said a sign on a gate. 'Please keep your sheep on a lead.' He penetrated a long crevice between cliffs to the sea, which turned out to be further away than it looked, and corkscrewed down a gorse-lined path to a beach where he waited until the tide had gone out, then hooked around a jutting rock and walked east along the shingle while the sun fell softly into the salt. The tape had long since come off his shoe, the sole barely hanging on now, and its loud flapping cut through everything like an embarrassment.

Robert Belltower was not at his cabin but the key was where he had left it, under the third rock. Inside, the framed photos and the Calor gas stove and the chair had gone but the bed remained, and two of his driftwood structures were still outside. He emptied his rucksack on the floor and slept for eleven uninterrupted hours and dreamt for the first time in a while about fish. In the dream, gulls hovered and chuckled at the fish then he awoke and realised the chuckling gulls were outside. In the following night's dream the old man from the pub was by a campfire singing the folk song again, 'Little Meg', but when the old man spoke it was in his own young Californian voice. His beard was very long and he felt it to see where it ended and realised it was a vine and that it led into the hedgerows. As he felt along the beard into the hedgerows, the crowd around the campfire, who were young, and all in couples, pointed and laughed. When he woke up the song was very clearly in his head so that all he could do was pick up his guitar and sing it until it wasn't there any more. Afterwards, he walked up the undercliff, but something had changed in his foot, and he didn't get far. He swam, first under a setting sun that was like a lump of hot metal on the horizon, and then under a brighter moon, because when he swam the foot didn't hurt as much, and he hoped that perhaps the salt water would heal it in the way it had with cuts and bites he'd sustained. He went much further under and slept dreamlessly that night but was brought back to the surface by the realisation he was being hit by a rolled-up magazine, wielded by a woman he had never met.

'GET OUT GET OUT GET OUT!' she screamed at him.

He struggled for words, slurring his first attempt at them. 'It's OK! I'm his friend!' he managed to shout back at her, but she continued to hit him as he stumbled and clung to the walls.

'Who? Whose friend?' she asked.

'Him! The one who lives here! Robert!' he spluttered, stuttered, between blows.

'No you're not. He doesn't have any friends. He's dead! DEAD!'

And it was then, as the light faded again and he let himself fall into it, that he finally knew he was insane, and was a man who made friends with ghosts.

*

After he'd come to, and they'd got their stories straight, she offered him a ride. It had happened about a month ago, she said. His heart. It wasn't the first time he'd had problems with it. A fishing trawler had spotted the boat drifting about in the bay and called the coastguard. They reckoned he'd been in there for at least four days, his eyes looking at nothing but the wood they were pressed against. 'He was a fucking bastard,' she said. 'Or used to be.' She introduced herself as Helen. She reminded him a little of the Queen of England: something motionless about her hair. 'He promised my mum the earth. She believed everything he said. She was Swiss and they met while he was working out there. Doing something with roofs. I am not totally sure. I know the Belltowers were a very grand family, but that he escaped from it all and did his best to make himself one of the people. Roofs were one of the ways he did it. But there was still a natural arrogance there. My mum, I think, found it very attractive. It wasn't until later that she found out he was already married. By then, he'd vanished, and she had a couple of new things growing inside her. One was a permanent sense of mistrust. The other was me.'

'He saved my life,' he said.

'I can see how that could happen. He wasn't all bad. People aren't. With exceptions. He was tough and if he liked you he liked you. Years later, he came to find me. I didn't want to know. It took a long time for me to come round. I was working in Bishop's Waltham. A lot of people would have given up but he didn't. He didn't have any other children. Or none he knew about, anyhow. He rubbed a lot of people up the wrong way and it was only if they stood the rubbing up that they stuck around and found out who he was. I was all he had, at the end. Me, and the cabin. He loved it out there on the beach because it was away from the world and his wife. Not his own wife – I believe he was quite nice to her, in the end, and enjoyed being with her. The world's. It was something he always said. The world and his wife. From what I read in the newspapers they are currently in the process of getting divorced. Have you seen these donkeys here on the left? I just adore their noses. So anyway now it appears I have a cabin. Would you like a cabin? I am joking. I will probably keep it. I go up, clear some of it, then wonder what I'm doing, then come back, then wonder some more. Sugar! I've missed my turning because I'm talking so much. I am sorry about your head. Is it very bad?'

The road climbed into dense woodland and she parked on a sandy bulge just off the tarmac beside a sign with a picture of a bench on it. Through a gap in the trees, it was possible to glimpse the conurbation lit up in a hazy bowl at the bottom of the valley. 'I would take you further,' she said. 'But I don't drive in cities, as a rule.' He said it was cool, he could walk, and thanked her. 'Oh!' she said, looking at his boots. 'What size are you?' He told her he was an eleven and she opened the back door and handed him a pair of brown loafers. 'These were his,' she said. 'Nine and a half. It's not ideal, I know, but it's an improvement.'

A day later, in his window seat on the plane, he would find himself trying to pick out the exact hillside they'd been on, imagining the hole in the tree, somewhere down there, where he'd left his old boots, but it was no use: the altitude was too great by then. He could, however, still see the moor: a mass of fuzzy, raging green breaking up the politer patchwork around it. That was about an hour before he remembered the tape from the studio, saw it in his mind's eye still sitting on the low shelf beside the bed in the cabin where he'd left it, but by then he was in the middle of a larger letting-go. He wrote a note in his diary about a finch he had seen on the landslip writhing on the ground when they'd climbed back up to the car, the deep sadness he had felt about it, and a question – 'Does it get any easier?' – underneath it, then rustled once more in the bottom of his rucksack, which was just small enough to count as hand luggage. He was surprised to find a magazine in there. It was the one she'd hit him around the head with, an issue of *Homes & Gardens* from May. One of the main articles had the headline 'Buying Carpets.' He read it for a while but it failed to hold his attention.

STOPCOCK (2019)

JULY

Deep dark. Deeper than black, but not black. Red, and green, in a way. But so dark. Darker than any place I've lived. Nothing to corrupt it. Song of the stream behind the wall. Reka, my lodger, was out at work. Fumbling in my bag, I thought I had lost my key again, and would have to break in through the back window like last week, but the reason I could not find my key in my bag was because I was already holding my key. I have been walking until late on these long summer nights, making sure I have covered every footpath and small lane near the house. I usually get the timing wrong, and night is totally down when I arrive home. Bats are flitting about on top of the hill, gobbling up the day's less fortunate moths. At the bottom of the valley, young owls shout their complaints to the last rechargeable glow of the sun as it sinks behind the moor. A powerful, sinewy, medium-sized dog hurtled towards me down one particularly quiet lane – one of those that don't really lead anywhere and have a verdant central reservation of weeds – and I wondered when the dog's owner would appear, breathlessly bringing up the rear and calling the dog back, and just as I realised the dog was a hare, not a dog, the hare also appeared to realise I was a human, not a shadow or a ghost, both of which would probably seem more likely on this lane at this time of the evening, and made a sudden, impressive reroute, ninety degrees to its right, as if responding to some internal satnav, not losing a fraction of pace or finesse in the process.

When you walk a lot in the countryside, you get a crystallised realisation that most animals are united by one factor: their conditioning, over the course of thousands of years of hard, regrettable evidence, to be shit scared of humans.

Another thing I've been thinking about a lot recently is dead birds. Insects too, and rodents. Actually, dead things in general, in the wild. I mean, obviously we see quite a few of them, while we're out on walks, and even sometimes in our garden, but think how many are dying all the time, and just what a small percentage it is of those we do see. I mean, I know living wild things will swiftly move in to eat the dead wild things, and decomposition can happen very quickly, especially in summer, but there's still something to be learned from this, and it's probably that dead things often do their dying in secret places, known only to them.

Were there a fruit that grew in my garden throughout winter, I wonder if winters would seem a little less interminable. I watch the apples ripening on the tree out the back right now and it feels like I'm watching an hourglass containing the precious sand of summer. There's so much to do all the time, so much I want to do. Nobody told me I'd feel that way at fifty-eight. Fifty-nine! Fifty-nine, not fifty-eight. It's so easy to forget sometimes.

In Hungary, they don't say 'I don't want to play devil's advocate here'. They say 'I don't want to paint the Devil on the wall here'. I think I prefer their version. I learned it from Reka, who grew up there. I woke up to the sound of her coming home at around two last night. Her bar job means she's often home late, but this time I suspect she'd been on a date. Couldn't see the guy's face properly but he was her usual type: all shoulders, leather and hair. Motorbike. Reka has told me she has no interest in what she calls 'gamer boymen' of around her age, and her dates all tend to be around fifteen years older. Men with strong jawlines and engine oil in the folds of their hands. She is very matter of fact about it when one of them proves unsuitable, just as she is matter of fact about almost everything. She is an individual who makes a decision about what she wants and does not swerve from it, no matter whether or not it is expected of her. She decided she wanted to make a life in Britain, and, three years ago, came to Britain, alone. She saw the moor on a TV nature documentary, decided she wanted to live here, as long as it was within a couple of miles of a bus route to the city, and answered the ad I put up in the post office. She said she would learn to drive, and did so, within not very many weeks, and found a functional car for less than a thousand pounds. She is a good housemate, but has a habit of leaving full glasses of water at various points around the building. If she has been home for any period above three hours, I'll usually find at least four of them on tables, sideboards, sinks and the floor. When she leaves for work, they disappear, but she never comments on this, and I wonder if she thinks it happens by magic. Before I take them back to the kitchen to be emptied and washed, my cat, Rafael Perera, enjoys drinking from them. Reka was not a cat person when she moved in here, but has been converted, and Rafael Perera, who is named after a doctor who once saved my life, now sleeps on her bed as often as he sleeps on mine. She commented the other day that he was 'wide asleep' on there. I enjoyed this hugely and only reluctantly explained to her that it was a malapropism. Upon me then responding to her request to explain what a malapropism is, she told me that in Hungary malapropisms are referred to as 'golden spit'. I told her I would like to learn Hungarian but she replied that I should not bother, as it is 'crazy, a devil's language' and would take me at least twenty years of hard work to get the hang of.

Finding the right house is difficult. You have to be very on the ball, extremely assertive, and make sacrifices, because, if it's any good, you can guarantee several other people will want it too, just as hard as you do. In the case of me and this house, I thought I'd jumped through every hoop possible, acted as quickly as I could under the circumstances, but when I arrived here, in March, I discovered I'd been too late: some bees had secured the tenancy before me. As I unlocked my front door for the first time, I gazed up at the bees, who were congregating in a large group around my bedroom window and talking in low voices. I could see they were quite at home and had already moved all of their stuff in, whereas all I had was an air bed, a kettle and a car full of houseplants and crockery. But the bees and I soon worked it out. Since they are the kind of bees whose primary interest is in masonry, it turns out they only need a couple of feet of wall and the cornice and gutter attached to it and are quite happy to let me use the rest of the building. Occasionally, one will lose his way and end up in the kitchen or living room and get a bit dopey, as so many of us do when trapped indoors for long periods, and I will gently usher him back outside. The bees are very busy in the middle of the day, but tend to go to sleep at night and when it is raining. When the window cleaner arrived the other day, I asked him to omit the bee window from his schedule, as I didn't want them to get wet. This being the edge of the moor, the bees will already be well accustomed to moisture, but I reckon they wouldn't welcome any more of it from an unanticipated source.

The inside of the house was clean when I moved in but I decided to get a window cleaner in quickly, as the back windows were all very dirty, with yellow streaks: a hint of the lichen and moss that builds up in a damp place like this when it's unoccupied. This is also a small clue to the building's recent history, along with the newspapers in the old wood basket I found in the garage, all of which date from around half a decade ago. The house was unoccupied for four years before I arrived, and in that time the garden had become the lawless domain of insects and birds. I sense, once you peel back a couple of its layers, the house could tell you some stories, but I am sure the garden and its wall could tell you many more. There's the story of the fire remnants in the front yard, the wine glasses and melted plastic in the ashes, and, a layer deeper, the rusty items that were revealed when I began to chop back the brambles and expose more of the old garden wall: a rusty metal hook and mysterious, complex chain attached to it, a grass roller – quite possibly Edwardian, or even Victorian – with 'Millhouse Stores, Underhill' inscribed on it. What stories could you find deeper in the folds of this high, mildewy wall which surrounds the garden on all sides? What do the mossy steps – a little too grand for a building this small – know that nobody else still living does? As I peel the layers, it is my mission to tread lightly. I have thought a lot about what this garden might have looked like in 1991... in 1975... in 1948... in 1912, and further back, to however many years ago the wall was built. Two hundred? More? I don't intend to oppress my new garden, and, although I do want to bring a little more light and colour into it, I want to make it just as attractive a space for bees and blue tits and blackbirds as it has been for at least a couple of centuries. Because we're at the bottom of the valley, it's an amphitheatre for birds. Beyond the crab apple and magnolia and mulberry in the garden, there are the other, bigger trees which hang off the walls of this steep combe. The space gives the dawn chorus a different sound to any I've heard before, even on the edge of the moor, and I am not just referring to the bird who sings the question 'Have you eaten?' in the voice of a concerned New York matriarch every morning. Part of me is tempted to identify this bird but the bigger part of me, which prefers to leave the answer to my overactive imagination, is at present still winning.

Above me where I sit propped up in bed I can see two large spiders on the ceiling, their limbs entwined. I am careful not to vacuum or disturb the spiders when I clean. I have already severely diminished their habitat merely by moving here. For four years before that, they had the whole run of the place. Back then, I would sometimes drive past this house, with not the remotest suspicion that I would ever move to it, and wonder what kind of ghosts lived in it. It is red now but back then it was white, or rather you could still just about see the memory of the white it had once been. The dirt and damp and peeling paint looked like the place was enfolded in six or seven layers of giant cobweb. Spiders must have loved it even more than they do now. It is still damp, and time is revealing that – in the refurbishment works undertaken by my landlady before I took up the tenancy – some problems were merely painted over, rather than properly attended to. A few feet left of where the two romantic spiders are embracing, there's a deepening damp patch, on the side of the building past which the stream runs. The damp is slightly worse in Reka's bedroom, next door, and I am keeping an eye on that. She has more spiders in her room. They do not scare her and, through the wall, I sometimes hear her talking to them. It is one of the many times I am glad that she, and not a more squeamish and precious kind of twentysomething, ended up answering my ad. Looking up at these two spiders above me now puts me in mind of one time many years ago when Mike and I had been arguing for so long, and so exhaustingly, that finally I kind of flopped on him in defeat, and we awoke seven and a half hours later in the same embrace, embarrassed and surprised. It is the only time I can ever remember waking up in his arms, in our two decades together. Which seems sad, but if you're honest about it, how often do couples wake up in each other's arms? Besides, there are far sadder things to be sad about in that relationship.

Actually, now I look at them again, I think the spiders might be dead.

AUGUST

Eleven days of rain in succession. It is not the soothing kind of rain that makes you feel cosy and glad you are indoors. It sounds like war repurposed as moisture. It gives me no comfort at night. As I hear it toppling from the broken drain above my window and gathering in puddles on the back yard, there is a growing picture in my mind that every droplet of water from the moor is hurtling down the hill and congregating here at the low four-way intersection of tiny lanes where the house stands: four virtual waterslides, coming together as one. I took my eye off the garden for a week and now I fear it's escaped from me forever: a raging, dripping jungle. The damp patches on the bedroom walls are getting bigger. I had one of my funny spells coming up the stairs yesterday and reached for the wall for balance and the surface was so wet, my hand skidded across it, and I tumbled into a bookcase, bruising my hip. I messaged my landlady about the damp and she just said, 'I'll send my guy over.' That was four days ago and since then I have heard nothing. Her 'guy' is Nick, a cheerful, charming odd-jobber who loves a chat but never returns phone calls. The last time he came over to look at the damp, after a similarly wet period at the end of May, he recommended a mildew-removing spray and advised that I put the heating on more often. We were standing in the garden at the time, and I resisted the urge to show him the thermometer hanging in the greenhouse a few paces away, which showed the temperature as 27 degrees.

How do you get here, at my age? How do you get to a rented cottage, with no more worldly possessions to your name than a distressed Edwardian sideboard, a nice collection of trowels and just under seven grand in the building society? I will give you the short version. You move from your northern birthplace to university, and when, not long before graduation, your sophisticated floppy-haired lecturer asks you out for a drink, you shyly say yes, then wait while he disentangles himself from his first marriage, then move to a too-expensive house just outside Oxford with him, then put your own larger plans on hold to work part time as a suburban librarian and part time as his second mother, then seventeen years later when you realise he is doing the same thing with one of his students that he did with you when you were her age, and probably has done with several students in the interim, you walk away from it all, stubbornly asking for nothing, and then just when you are back on your feet, your lone known parent goes into a nursing home, and you realise that being ill and dying are both expensive; then the years pass, and you escape for a while, to another part of the world, with no thought of what you are doing afterwards, which is wonderful, but temporary, and then not long after that it is the present day, and you are a year shy of sixty. But is this all that terrible a place to be in? And what standards are we judging this by? The standards of another university graduate from my generation, who has spent four decades firming up their financial security, living like life is solely preparation for retirement? Or the standards of being fairly healthy, and still alive, and living in a place with clean air and owls, with a job you tolerate most days and like on some? If I ever get lugubrious and start looking backwards in a self-pitying fashion towards a point in my life where I could have... solidified my future, Reka gives me perspective. It is unlikely she will ever be in a position to purchase her own house, no matter how hard she works at her job, and how hard she saves, and she saves hard. Last week, she told me, her entire food bill came to £18.47. She lives mostly on lentils and reduced price veg she finds at the end of the day in Aldi or Tesco. She buys herself no treats, with the arguable exception of the bicycle she found on Gumtree for £50, owns only two bras, spends at least an hour of every day singing, and seems far less unhappy than any of the young – or old – people I meet on the reception of the community college where I work three days a week.

August: the most spiritually dark month that doesn't happen in winter. Everything is scruffy and angry and moist, waiting for September and October to come in to crisp it up and prettify it again. Chunks of crumbling wood in the lanes. A tree has come down on my route home from work so I'm having to go the long way around for now, which isn't such a great hardship as it gives me a better view of the tor, or at least it would, if it wasn't still raining for 70 per cent of each day. It feels like all this rain and wind is coppicing the countryside, knocking the excess wood off it. I detect a pinch of autumn in the air already and it is not too warm for a night-time fire. I gather kindling from up the lane. There's plenty. I avoid the stuff on the ground, favouring the bits caught high up in fences and branches, which is always drier. Today, in the middle of all the sogginess, we had three hours of brilliant sunshine, and I took advantage by doing some tidying in the garden and digging out a new bed. At least I have no trouble getting a spade in now. As I go down through the earth I feel like I am burrowing through tiers of history. Rabbit skulls, shards of pottery and thin old hand-forged nails turn up, and some bigger stuff, which I do my best to upcycle, such as a baffling rusty bracket, about two feet in length, with another baffling chain attached to it. I jammed this into one of the endless crevices in the wall and hung a bird feeder on it. Some primal instinct kicks in as I dig further and get more dirty and scratched up, some innate understanding of compost, something there in me from birth, always just waiting to be unleashed. Time stops being conventionally measured. Through the open window I heard

Reka talking on speakerphone to one of her sisters in Budapest, which – possibly in part because of all the extra letters in the Hungarian alphabet – always sounds more like seven people having a conversation than two. Later, I hear her singing. Folk songs from her home country. I have loaned her the old acoustic guitar I inherited from Mum. I called it a loan, but she can keep it, as I doubt it will be any use to me ever again.

More rain. The damp in Reka's room is worse. Some of the wall seems to be coming away. I offered to sleep downstairs in the living room and let her have my bed for a while. She waved the suggestion away, explaining that until she was sixteen she, her dad and her two sisters all slept in one room, in a tiny flat with no central heating. 'Summer is warm in Hungary but our winters, pffff, they make yours look like a beach holiday,' she said. She showed me a Dansette record player she found yesterday in a pile of electrical equipment at the tip. Remarkably, it works, albeit at a slightly slower speed than intended, and means she can play the nine 45s she brought with her from Hungary. These all formerly belonged to her dad, and were recorded by Hungarian acts in the late sixties and early seventies, with the exception of one by a British artist I'd never heard of called RJ McKendree: a distorted, fuzzy rock version of a folk song I've heard played in a couple of pubs here in Devon, quite a haunting tune. Reka tells me that, bizarrely, the record only came out in Hungary, and is worth over £400 now. She put it on and, despite the reduced power of the Dansette, bopped around the room to its nagging, oddly sexual beat. 'I don't know how they allowed this during communism!' she said, hurling herself onto the bed, and, for the first time, I was very aware that I wished to kiss her.

SEPTEMBER

What would we do without weather? Where would we be without the sideways rain of this morning and the sun that burned it off then made the remaining clouds curl above the tor like smoke from seven symmetrical bonfires, all smouldering at the same rate? How bland would the planet be? The fallen tree on the lane has still not been removed. I am enjoying driving the other route, along the ridge, and seeing the changes in the sky above the tor: the varying colours from day to day, and sometimes hour to hour, above those rocks at the summit that always remind me of piled pony poo. I pulled into a gate gap this morning on the opposite side of the valley and lingered a while to take it in and made myself ten minutes late for work. A queue of first years were already lined up at the desk, waiting for me to sign off their new library cards. Awkward, shy kids, vague about their own futures, who, when typing into their phones and laptops, find their bold and opinionated superhero alter egos. I am half-invisible to them, even the ones in their twenties and thirties. The young will always to some extent view ageing as a matter of taste, as if the fact you do not appear to be young any more is a decision you've made, like selecting a certain type of carpet or paint for your house. I remember back in spring, listening to a youth who was chatting with his friend about his discovery of old-school rap music, near reception while waiting for an appointment with the college counsellor. He mentioned Public Enemy. Not looking up from my screen, I offered the opinion that *It Takes a Nation of Millions to Hold Us Back*, from 1988, was their strongest album. Both boys went silent and turned in my direction with a look on their faces that suggested they'd just seen a goat driving a bus. But I feel for them, and their problems, and would not want to be young today, with all the added pressures of our new digital age. Reka is eight or nine years older than most of these kids but she seems at least a decade further from them than that, and from some less materialistic era. There is something generally, permeatingly vintage about her. Even her teddy bear – a rare reminder of how recent her childhood was – is ancient and tattered.

A week: that's how long it took the cabbage whites to decimate my kale. I leave them to it and don't begrudge them their meals. I grew far too much anyway and was beginning to tire of kale curries. After the caterpillars finished their business, they moved towards the house and appear to have earmarked it as an excellent place to pupate. I counted more than eighty chrysalises on the back wall and at least a dozen more have made it indoors. Today, I found an earwig in my lentil and tomato soup. Yesterday I watched an enormous spider stealthily lowering itself from the lampshade onto my pillow on a gossamer homemade rope. 'Hey! What are you doing?' I shouted, and it stopped, as if in embarrassment. The mason bees are turning up in the house more and more often, dopey or deceased. It's an insect's world here; Reka and I just live in it. I wonder if the introduction of sheep and cattle into the field across the lane is also contributing to the ever-larger number of flies in the house. Or perhaps a pigeon has got into the loft and died. I cannot check because the landlady, who lives in the Maldives, padlocked the hatch and did not leave a key.

When I arrived home today I noticed someone has cut the hedges quite brutally, without clearing up, and, as a result, one of the sheep had got a bit of blackthorn caught up its bottom. I climbed over the fence and tried to get close enough to the sheep to dislodge the blackthorn but it was too fast for me. After about five minutes of this, Reka arrived home and joined me, but being chased by two people caused even greater panic in the sheep and its companions, and several sheep all bumped into each other as we chased them. In the melee, the blackthorn branch was thankfully dislodged from the unfortunate sheep's bottom.

Flood in the kitchen this morning, after many days of suspicious smells. Water pouring through the ceiling from the bathroom. I put a bucket under it, switched the stopcock off and left a phone message for the landlady but after seven hours had received nothing back other than an email saying she would 'send my guy over', so I called an emergency drain company. Immediately, they identified the problem as backed-up water from a blocked septic tank, but I had been told by the landlady that there was no septic tank at the house. I managed to finally get her on the phone – the first time I'd actually heard her voice. She's very well spoken, called Flora, and I don't think I'm paranoid in thinking that as soon as she heard my accent, she identified me – in that way many privileged people do – as someone she could push around. She remained adamant that the drainage at the house had always 'worked solely on a soakaway' and, when I questioned this and pointed out that a soakaway always has to work in tandem with either a septic tank or reed bed and waste does not just 'vanish', she got very defensive and began to tell me how loved the house – which her parents once lived in – was and how many people had 'had a very wonderful time there'. She also said I had been rash in calling out the drain company and would have to pay the bill myself. 'So you reckon I'd have been more sensible to wait for however many days until your guy came out, sitting in a house without a working toilet or running water?' I asked, getting a bit pissed off now, and she put the phone down on me, but not before she'd announced, 'Nice speaking to you!' What followed, after the drain men's discovery of a totally blocked pipe, was a treasure

hunt, with the significant catch that unlike most treasure hunts
the reward at the end of it would not be treasure, but shit. Finally,
the drain experts uncovered a rusty grate deeply submerged
amongst many years of foliage. The chamber was full. Had been
for who knows how many aeons. That, combined with tree roots
growing into the waste pipe leading from the house, had been the
cause of the kitchen flood. The drain guys were bloody brilliant.
Not many people make it their life's ambition to work with drains
but what you find is that those who do end up in that area often
take a lot of pride in their work. They are rarely of an apathetic
or indifferent demeanour. The work of the drain men was more
like surgery than repair or maintenance, their camera tunnelling
deep into the house's stomach and telling them what was amiss. I
wasn't here afterwards, when the septic tank man came to empty
it, but the note he left, detailing the 'dangerous condition' of the
tank, is a small, dark, poetic masterpiece of some bygone English
I never knew existed. After reading it, it is hard not to picture a
man of ancient years and hawkish appearance who upon putting
an ear close to the ground can actually hear sludge speak to him.
One of the last of his breed. Perhaps *the* last. What had he seen,
in his time? I suspect this house, empty and in a state of disrepair
for a few years before my occupancy, and backed up with waste
of olden times, was child's play to him. Anyway, the overall result,
many hours later, is that the situation is fixed, temporarily, and
I am more than £700 out of pocket. Reka and I played Scrabble
later. She is getting better, very quickly, and I am sure will be
beating me within a month or two.

Over at Underhill churchyard today, whose kissing gate Jim
Boyland and I volunteered to rebuild a little while back. The
church is in an exposed spot and we were soaked and dried and
soaked again numerous times during the course of our work. It

was a very satisfying day, although Jim brought his dog with him, who is extremely boring. As the dog – a smallish one, of I don't know what breed, which never makes a noise and puts me in mind of a bereaved aunt from a drabber Britain – watched us with its sad eyes, Jim showed me how to hammer iron wedges into the grooves we'd made in the granite. As I hit the rock with the hammer, I noticed the sound it made change as I moved down the line. It made me think of the stories stone has to tell us, all the voices inside it. How many voices are inside the wall that surrounds my garden, and what could they tell me? I feel privileged to live within its shelter, like the humans and cats and dogs and horses who have gone before me, and am glad to be able to add a tiny new chapter to its story. I look into its crevices and grooves and clefts and observe its changing hues and I know where I am, who I am, and what I am doing: I am just passing through. Reka was cleaning the house when I got home. I told her she really didn't need to do that. She told me it is almost her time of the month and she feels very hyper and cleaning always helps. 'I was very lazy when I was young,' she explained. 'My grandma used to say to me, "If laziness hurt, you would be screaming."' As I write this I can hear the little stream across the lane raging, and rain tumbling off the roof, and I am a bit worried about the weather forecast for next week, and what it might do to this place, but maybe I am painting the devil on the wall here.

More rain. Coffee with James Boyland's wife, Edith, at the abbey tea rooms. She entered the building alone, without the dog, and as she did I noticed a relief in myself. Water pouring down the lanes. Hart's-tongue fern lapping at it from the verges. The last remnants of summer's ambition are fading. Someone has yet to take down the sign advertising the tug of war in Marybridge, which has caused much local amusement, due to the extra 'f' the sign's writer mistakenly added to 'of'. I took the car in for its MOT at Phil Spring's and was surprised that, with a couple of small improvements, it passed. I suppose it looks worse than it is. Typical Devon car: not bad on the right-hand side, dented and scratched to buggery on the left, with the wing mirror held on with tape. These lanes on the edge of the moor were not dug out with any cars in mind, and particularly not the huge fortified people-carriers of today. Curiously it's the individuals negotiating them in more modestly sized vehicles who often drive more apologetically. The countryside looks on, bemused at the way it's been outgrown, bludgeoned, smoothed over, suppressed, raped, waiting for the revenge it will surely enjoy when we are gone. I reverse into my drive in my smaller than medium car, only just squeezing through the small gap in the wall, imagining the Morris Minor or Triumph Dolemite it once more practically housed and the people who probably never conceived that anybody could possibly need anything grander. You can let yourself go into a gentle, cuckoo-soundtracked fantasy about life here in the unclaustrophobic 1950s but it's worth bearing in mind, as you do, that that's when we really started getting on the bad road we are on, environmentally speaking, and when some of the most irreversible damage was already being done.

Finishing touches to the kissing gate today. Jim – whose family have been associated with the church for centuries – and I posed next to our work, and Clive, Underhill's new vicar, snapped a couple of photos of us. Clive speaks very softly and has long slender fingers, which he often uses to gently tickle the palms of his own hands as he listens to you speak. I have heard that some in the village have not taken to him, finding his gentle and sensitive nature suspicious, but I like him. He does seem a little bored, though, and apparently the job leaves him a lot of time to work on his macrame skills. He offered to do some for me and I accepted, as I need a place for my spider plant to live. He and Jim also showed me what they call 'The Bird Lady': a very mysterious carving in the church that I suspect will linger in my mind for a long time. I took a long route back, just to glory in the beginning of the changing colours on the hillside, but my goal proved futile as the journey coincided with the fifth or sixth cloudburst of the day. As I came cautiously down Riddlefoot Lane, which is barely wider than an average car, a hooded figure in a red anorak pressed itself up against the foliage to let me pass, and as I pulled level, I recognised the figure as Reka. I opened the door and she got in. She could not have been wetter. 'Rain has been a big fuck today!' she said. When we arrived home I rushed into the living room to light a fire and Reka, having dispensed of most of her wet clothing, went straight upstairs to run a bath. Seconds later, I heard a shout of 'Jézus Krisztus!', dropped the log I was holding and ran in her direction, to find her standing in her room amidst a pile of stone and plaster, with water puddling all around her. She'd been so wet, it took me a couple of seconds to realise the water had mostly come from the wall and not her. I went to the airing cupboard and grabbed as many towels as I could carry, gave one to Reka to wrap around herself, and began spreading them on the floor, then left a voice message for Flora Prissypants. When I returned to the bedroom, Reka had found the dustpan and brush and was attempting to sweep some of the rubble into the corner. I told her to leave it, and that I would be sleeping downstairs this evening, she could have my room, and I would not hear any protests to the contrary. She finally went for her bath and while she did I put more towels down and, as I did, I froze. What appeared to be a tiny, dusty foot was sticking up out of the rubble. Tentatively I poked it, and was relieved to find it was merely an empty shoe: a very old one, designed for a tiny child. On further investigation, just to the left of it I discovered an arm sticking up from the mess, pulled it, and found myself holding a small doll: not a hard, plastic doll, of the type common over the last three quarters of a century, but one made out of fabric and stuffing, and missing an eye. 'Jézus Krisztus,' I muttered to myself, letting it fall from my hand, as you might an object you'd picked up and not realised was molten hot.

'It happens in Hungary, too,' said Reka. We were sitting in front of the fire, with Rafael Perera stretched out on the rug in front of us. Reka's face was the colour of a good pomegranate. She had chosen to dry her hair naturally and I could see that five or six drips still remained on her neck. 'My grandmother lives in the countryside near a place called Kaposhomok. You would not have heard of it. People haven't. She took down a wall in her cottage and found, how do you say it, when a shoe is harder?'

'A clog?' I asked.

'Yes, exactly this. A clog. It is sometimes a charm to ward off evil but also when one of someone's children has died young and they want to keep the spirit with them, in the building.'

When I asked Reka what had made her walk over near the tor, she told me she'd just needed time to think. 'Man trouble,' she said. 'I think people think they have too many options and that is one of the problems of the world of right now.'

I had already brought my duvet and pillow down and felt extremely relaxed, right there, with my lovely housemate and my cat, despite the troubling events of the day. I'd managed to soak up most of the moisture in the spare bedroom and fortunately none of it had come through the ceiling. I could not help but notice the way the firelight enhanced the extreme natural beauty of her face and, as I let my eyes close, I permitted myself to imagine what it might feel like if she reached out a hand, just six or seven inches from where it was now, and gently held the toes of my right foot.

OCTOBER

Flora Prissypants still refusing to pay me back for the drain company's bill. I am seeking legal advice. I am not feeling well. Last night I went to bed with a band of tingling, slightly burning pain stretching around from my navel to my lower back. I am sure it is nothing. There is usually something and usually it doesn't last long and becomes nothing. That's what it's like, having a body. Or at least having a body after a certain, not particularly old, age. Of course, before that there's a period that might convince you that having a body can mean going for long stretches of time where there's nothing much wrong at all, but that's in fact a very brief period, in the grand arrangement of life. 'You look tired,' said Kath, when she arrived to relieve me of my shift. 'Are you OK?' This means absolutely nothing, since approximately four times out of every nine she sees me, Kath, whom I jobshare with, says to me, 'You look tired. Are you OK?' In part to spite her, I took advantage of the beautiful late afternoon weather, nipped home to get my bathing suit, and drove to the beach, then let myself float on the water, watching skeins of geese fly above me towards France as the most golden of suns dropped its blessing on the hills. I did not feel tired, and was OK. Perhaps it was not the most sensible course of action, and I have started to feel a bit peculiar since then, but I have an enormous faith in the healing power of salt water and fear we might not get a day this perfect and unseasonably warm for a long time. I did text Reka and ask her if she wanted to join me but she said she had another date. I heard her come in, obviously not alone, at around twelve, then could hear her playing her guitar and singing – the melody seemed familiar, and I realised it was the Hungarian record she had shown me, the one by the American singer, albeit a much softer rendition of the song than his. The builders are coming soon to sort the wall and I shall be extremely glad to have my own bed again.

I have lived in the south west of the country for a long time now, long enough to consider it my home, but, as a transplanted northerner, one thing I do often miss about where I come from is people's unsugarcoated habit of, on the whole, but with some exceptions, saying what they actually mean. Today on the way to the car park after buying a cauliflower and some strawberries from the farm shop I bumped into Sheila from the arts college, and said hello. They're a bit weird there, all into their yoga, which is great by me, but it's never simple yoga, always got to be yoga with some extra element, yoga and darts, yoga done while wearing nothing but an anorak, or something like that. Toni, who works with Sheila, had asked me if I wanted to teach on their stonemasonry course a couple of months back and I hadn't been able to make it to any of the two dates Toni had proposed to chat about it, and – though I'm not bothered – I never heard anything more. Anyway, it transpires, from a couple of things Sheila said, that I had my chance, and because I wasn't able to jump at the opportunity, I've been replaced. I didn't fully realise this until after I'd left the farm shop, due to a habit Sheila has – just like quite a few people you meet connected with the art college – of making a piece of negative information sound like a positive one. 'It's a very exciting time up there!' she told me. 'There are a lot of ideas being floated around.' This after I'd gleaned from some other convoluted pseudo-enthusiastic things she'd said that the course would now not be co-taught by Grant Hope and me, but by Grant and Judith Sitwell, from Topsham, instead. 'You should talk to Toni,' she said. 'It's a very exciting time. I know she's aware of you.' Fuck that, I thought, but didn't say it; I just politely said goodbye and wished her a nice weekend – which makes me wonder, now I think about it: am I now also a person who doesn't say what she actually means?

I sometimes think about the small culture shocks I still feel living in this part of the country, after close to a decade, and wonder about the bigger ones Reka has had to deal with. She says she finds it hard to get used to the politeness of British people, finds it overdone, and was shocked at the levels of gossip when she first arrived in the UK. 'I hear so many conversations where people seem to be talking about a woman they know, in a disapproving way,' she told me. 'It's always "she" something, something she did, they are mentioning.' Ever since she told me this, I've become more aware of it myself – especially in the staff room and refectory at work. Today we talked about Christmas, which I plan to do approximately nothing for. Reka said Christmas is different in Hungary anyway, as it's the Baby Jesus, not Santa Claus, who brings the presents. 'But we also have Santa Claus Day, where we leave our shoes near the window.' She seems quieter at the moment. Maybe it is the distraction of the new man. He is called Greg and works at a garage in Exeter. I feel more ill, a bit like an animal with sharp teeth is eating my insides.

The builders didn't come to sort the wall but Nick, Flora's guy, did. I don't know how good a job he did but I have my suspicions it's of a temporary nature. Nobody came over to look at any of the other damp issues in the house. Before Nick arrived, Reka and I packed the shoe and the doll back inside the brickwork and covered them up. I am not superstitious, but I think some people who once lived in this house interred them in the wall for a reason, and I think it's best that we respect that. I don't know if Nick saw them when he repaired the wall. I certainly haven't mentioned any of it to Flora. I am still attempting to get the money back from her for the work by the drainage company. Still ill, and none of this is helping.

NOVEMBER

It turns out I have shingles. I remember at various points in my life people talking in a tone of great pity and sympathy about other people who had shingles but I don't think I'd ever properly considered what it was. Now I know. What happens is a furious stoat somehow gets inside one half of your body without you noticing and gradually begins to chew all your flesh and nerve endings. You never see the stoat, but after a while the scars from its interior work begin to show on the outside, then begin to blister. At night, it's a little different to that: you wake up at 2 a.m. feeling like you and the stoat have been involved in a fire at a biochemical factory. I've got quite a high pain threshold but, even so, I'm finding it all surprisingly nasty – particularly the bit where the stoat bought some hot chilli sauce as a dressing then ate my bellybutton from within. What is also startling is that shingles is actually a little bit of chickenpox that's been sitting dormant in your body, waiting patiently to come back and get you. My chickenpox was a bastard in 1977, when I was seventeen. Like me, they look less punk rock than they did back then, but they're still a bastard and have become more bitter and cynical with age. I will still walk, though. This afternoon, five miles. Everything is gold and green and brown down the deep lanes, with the one exception of the bright new red berries on the rowan. Every day, the sun thins a little more. Reka and I haven't played Scrabble for ages. We must. It's Scrabble weather. I heard Reka singing the song again, late at night, and then I thought I heard it again, at about 3 p.m., but it might have been just my half-dream state. I'm that kind of ill where songs spin in your head as you try to sleep. Hallucination, I suppose. Last night my pillow was a rock I tried to carve but a hand kept stopping me. I looked up and the hand belonged to Kath on reception. 'You look tired,' she said. 'Are you OK?'

Something nice happened today, then something not nice happened, and something else, also not nice. I was walking down the hill – staggering a bit, if I'm honest, holding my side, which is beginning to look like I've been in a fire – and I smelt that lovely smell you get when woodsmoke cuts through the cold misty late afternoon air at this time of year, then realised that the woodsmoke was coming from my own chimney. What a delight! I opened the gate and as I did a man – broad, bearded – charged past me, clutching his face, which had a line of blood running down it. It took a moment before I realised it was Reka's current boyfriend, Greg. He looked scared. I found Reka in the living room, tending the fire, and said hello, but she didn't seem to notice me at first.

'Is everything OK?' I asked.

'Everything is fine,' she said. The way she said it, there was something different, a bit slower, and she wasn't looking at me. It was as if something in the fire was very important, and I was a distraction.

'We have been experimenting,' she said, continuing to look at the flames.

I was really feeling like I needed a lie down so I opted not to press the matter further, and I heard her leave for work an hour or so later. The dishwasher needed to go on so I popped around the house, looking for half-full glasses of water. I found two in Reka's room and was just leaving when something on her bed caught my eye, sitting next to her ancient teddy bear. I couldn't quite believe my eyes! It was the doll from the wall. I'm sure it's the same one – all dusty and dirty with one of its eyes missing. After all, where else would you get a doll like that? I can only think she took it back out of the wall before Nick came to repair it. She'll be back soon but I won't ask her about it until tomorrow. Maybe I won't at all. I suppose it's her own business.

I love the rainy, sometimes sunny climate of the moor and its border villages: the pockets of weather that can vary so radically from valley to valley, the clouds that sink into vases of deep green land, do their work to help maintain that greenness then tumble on to their next appointment. I like walking in the rain here and I like seeing what it does to the plants in my garden. I like the way footpaths and streams are often interchangeable. Water was a very decisive factor in my decision to live here: the deafening rush of the stream, the taste of what came out of the tap, so immeasurably more flavoursome and soft and refreshing than what I used to drink in Oxford when I lived with Mike. 'Yep, that's it,' I thought, the first time I drank it. 'That's what's been missing.' You go and get some chips in a nearby town. You walk along the street in the town with your bag of rain and, strangely, you don't mind it, because you're very hungry after a long walk along the high shouting river, and there are some chips in there too right at the bottom of the bag, just a few, beneath all the rain, and they taste good, because everything tastes good after a long walk in the rain. Water is in your entire being here, altering it, influencing the taste of everything. I so often have rain and sea and river in my hair and damp pebbles in my shoes and cuts across my stomach and chest from when I scraped them against rocks when I leapt off other rocks into water. You feel it all even more after a summer that some other British people told you was dry and hot, not realising that the South West Peninsula is not really in Britain, and that weather is different here: cooler and damper in summer, warmer and damper in winter, rainier almost all of the time, especially recently. If you can't see the moor, it's raining. If you can see the moor, it means it's about to rain. Rain. Rain. Rain. Water. Water. Water. It's so much the theme of my life. I even used it to kill Mike. I didn't say? I killed Mike. I didn't. But I did. I told Reka I found the doll today. She said it was OK, that she knew I knew, and that we could all be friends: me, her and the doll.

Ah fuck. Rain. The song again. Such a nice tune. She has got really good at it. I'll explain it all better when I'm well.

DECEMBER

Oh so ill. I didn't kill Mike. Didn't stab him or shoot him or put arsenic in his favourite leek and potato soup or chop his nomadic penis and testicles off. Don't think that. But maybe I did kill him. It feels better now I write it. It was yonks ago now, and yonks after we broke up. I didn't find out until a couple of weeks after it happened, from Beth. She was all that was left by then, our only connection. She was the one who told me not to go out with him, then she ended up closer friends with him than she was with me. She thought I should know, in case I heard elsewhere. There was nothing about it in the newspapers but I might have found out online anyhow, she said. It was in Scotland. The top left bit. A boat. A storm. Him and his mates, fishing. Only one of the four of them survived. It didn't touch me for a while but I tracked it back and the dates matched up. That was the night: the night I wished him dead. But I don't really wish anyone dead. Resentment. They say it's like drinking poison then waiting for someone else to die. Only in this case it worked. I was angry: Mum was close to the end then, things were bad, I was in some other reality without hope, was thinking back to where it went wrong, held him responsible, but I didn't mean it. But that was the night I did it. Down in the cottage, the place before here, right in the village, sleeping in the loft room, with the view of the tor, and the pony poo on top. This rain is reminding me. That was the exact night he must have died. Maybe the exact moment. I worked it out. It was raining then too. Next day without any idea of what I'd done I walked up to the pool – the deep one. Seven miles there, seven miles back. I let myself jump. I hit the surface and let the momentum take me as far under as it needed to. I was under for barely any time at all but while I was I felt I was somewhere else: somewhere where nothing was anything any more. Somewhere darker than any night, any dream. I came up into the sunlight and the sunlight felt like something you could suddenly eat and I ate it, gulped it down without chewing it the prescribed seventy-two times, or even chewing it one time. I swam against the current, my front crawl just strong enough to defeat it and get back to the rocks on the bank. I didn't jump again. This rain is reminding me. It's so… everything. Maybe it wouldn't seem so fierce if the house was double glazed. There are eight reservoirs on the moor, all built between 1867 and 1972 as the expanding villages and towns below them demanded cleaner water. When the water is low, you see the remains of sunken farmsteads and clapper bridges and Bronze Age villages. When they made one, they drowned an entire farm. How could you do that? Did cows and sheep die? I hope cows and sheep didn't die. But more cows have died since then. Ever such a bloody lot of cows. Have I ever thought about that. Oh god, the water, the drips. Is the wall going to come down again? I know what's happening outside, all the rivers, filling up. They're all getting high. One is being a thug out back of the Co-op, hissing and swearing at the locals. Down under the bridge, near the dual carriageway, another is taking some drugs it found floating in a bag. All the water is coming, and this is the end point. It's rushing down the lane, right at me. The rain couldn't be louder if I was in a tent. The power in the house is going on and off every two minutes. I can hear Reka. The song. I didn't even know she was in. She's playing the song. The wind is up – I think it's coming through a gap in the wall – and it's harmonising with her. I remember now. I heard it up there, before. On the moor. There was the house that was high off the lane, with a door in the garden wall. I think I heard it once, behind the door. I don't know. It might have just been a dream. Everything's mixed up now and my stomach is burning. I want it to dry out. Everything is wet. It won't dry out. The walls won't dry out. My skin won't dry out. There's a folk tale from there, near that bit of the moor. The pixy – an ugly tiny man – comes to the nurse's house and asks her to deliver his wife's baby. They go on a horse, very fast, to his wife, who is very beautiful, and when the baby is born, he asks the nurse to put ointment on its eyes. When the pixies are not looking, she tries some of her ointment on one of her own eyes. Suddenly the pixy and his children are even uglier than before, but the wife is even more beautiful. The next week, at the market, she sees him stealing things, and asks how his wife and baby is. 'You can see me?' he asks. 'Yes,' she says, 'but only with this eye.' And he strikes her in the eye and blinds her with his sharp fingernails. I am lucky the shingles aren't in my eye. Edith Boyland and her boring dog told me her aunt Agnes got them on the left side of her face and lost her sight in that eye. But, Jézus Krisztus, it hurts, especially at night, and I don't know what is a dream. Last night I dreamt Reka stood over me with the doll and didn't say anything and I asked her to come and be beside me but she just stood, staring. When I am better, we can leave here, me and Reka. We will go somewhere dry. We will bring the bees, we can even bring the doll if she wants. But what if the bees can't come. What about the spiders. Will they be OK after we have gone. And what about the cows, everywhere. We can go and have our own cow, at least be nice to our own cow; selfish but that's all you can do, be nice to your own cow, because if you think about all the cows you go crazy. It will sit down when it's about to rain. That's what they do, they're always sitting down here. I like the noise of them when they move slowly and heavily through grass on a hot day. It's a lovely calming sound, unique to them, impossible to replicate by anything that isn't a cow. That will happen again. It will be spring again, and it will be dry again, this skin will be dry again, after the Baby Jesus has brought our presents and it is a new year and everything turns over. I just have to be patient. But right now, I admit it, Kath. I am tired, and I am not OK. Are you happy now, Kath? Can you finally shut the fuck up? The power is going on and off, every two minutes.

FEBRUARY

My name is John and I don't know why I'm writing this because nobody will probably ever see it or maybe they will but I reckon that will be long after my time. I'm the builder. One of them. Colin is the other one. We are the ones working on the house. Not that guy Nick. He's gone. We've been here two weeks now. The place was a right tip when we started and we had to shift a load of stuff to the real tip before we could even start knocking through and sanding down and working on the pargeting so we're only just getting started, but that's not my problem. The owner of the house doesn't even live in this country and she's paying. We'll be here another month, I reckon, but it would be two at the absolute minimum if she'd told us to go ahead and do all the stuff I said needed doing. I suppose she's going to sell the place and just wants it looking smart to the untrained eye so she can get shot of it. Like I said, that's all her business, not mine. I wouldn't want to live here myself, it's all a bit too wet and far away from everything. Anyway, it was a right mess and we found loads of stuff we didn't know what to do with and I didn't like throwing it away. I talked to the next-door neighbour and she said there were two women living here and one of them died – septicaemia, which I think is some kind of blood poisoning, but as you know now anyway if you've read this far she'd been ill in another way before that. There were old socks and this weird doll and loads of smashed plates and when we were shifting this mattress with a big dip in the middle and a spring coming out of it I found this diary under it and when Colin was over at the wholesalers getting emulsion I started reading it and then I just carried on because it was interesting and then I read it again. I didn't understand all of what it was talking about and why should I when it's just something someone has written for herself about her life, but it made me sad and it made want to read books, which I always want to but don't. Anyway, I haven't really got any more to say because it's all in here anyway, but I thought I should say something because I don't like thinking about what happened and the neighbour told me the woman didn't really have any family to speak of and she seemed nice in what she wrote and I feel like somebody needs to write or do something because if nobody did that's fucking awful and everything just isn't there any more. We're going to put the wall back up tomorrow and I'm going to put it in there, in a gap between the stones, before we make good. I'm not telling Colin. He wouldn't be interested anyhow.

ME (NOW)

Come, fertilise me, in your thousands, man and beast. Give me your sheep shit, your rotten berries, your own good piss. Do not be shy and hold it in for the public lavatories on Fore Street. Squat in my bushes, stand proud above my ravines, or shake your fluffy tail in my face – whatever is the most convenient method for you, I don't mind – and let it out. Do not industrially monostraddle me with your insane lust for profit. Rid me of this relentless chemical run-off. Farm me, by all means, but farm me with tact, kindness, sympathy. Farm me gently. Farm me slowly. Take it easy. Don't you know, that I have never been farmed like this before. At least not since some time in the mid-1800s, or during that short-lived organic project by that couple last decade, which sadly didn't come off due to funding issues.

A full moon bleached the sky white-blue last night. It shone in through the bedroom skylight on Jim Swardesley from the post office and he dreamt that he was a large bear, on all fours, running through an icy stream, with dripping bear legs, and one of the big bear grunts he did in the dream as he ran woke him up. He turned and pressed his 93.5 per cent erect penis into the bottom of Gillian, his wife. 'Mmmtired,' she mumbled, batting him away. 'Go to the workroom and calm yourself down.' Downstairs, the Swardesleys' son, Julian, sat on the back garden decking, smoking, unable to sleep, his mind rewired to a frenetic, fizzing, popping speed by the hundreds of messages he'd exchanged with girls on a dating app on his smartphone over the last week, all of which he knew would come to nothing, and all of which was some way to attempt redemption for the trip he'd made to Cardiff the previous week to meet someone from the same dating app, who had not only stood him up but subsequently vanished from the face of the online globe: a redemption that was ultimately less about his romantic life and more an attempt to convince himself that humans weren't ultimately cruel and heartless. Behind him, in the downstairs bedroom, his older sister Phoebe, who had passed through a similar phase in her life eighteen months ago and now used her phone in the most minimal way, slept soundly. In her dream, on the idyllic farm of her future, a group of demanding animals, including sheep, chickens, three goats and a needy open-mouthed frog, followed her around the edge of a pond, in whose unrealistically clear water she had just been washing three peasant blouses and her long blonde hair. She turned, startled for just a moment, at the gentle yet solid touch of a large slab of human skin on her bare shoulder, which she happily realised was the hand of her future husband, the co-owner of the farm, who also bore a striking resemblance to the square-jawed lead from her favourite American TV series. 'So tell me, dear wife,' he asked her, in his square-jawed American voice, his hair not moving a fraction in the afternoon breeze. 'Shall we ride Antonio and Bess to the beach this afternoon, or head to the mountain and meditate?'

I dreamt very vividly too, as if that white-blue light of the moon was shining down through my layers and illuminating my past, penetrating parts of my crust that no run-of-the-mill night, not even a run-of-the-mill full moon night, could normally penetrate. I was back right in the meat of a night not unlike this, a long long time ago. I thought I was old at the time, but I was not. This is how ageing works, again, and again, and again, until you die. OMG, can you believe I'm actually twenty-one? I'm so old! OMG, can you believe I'm actually forty? OMG, can you believe I'm actually 900? I'm so old! OMG, can you believe I'm actually 5,807? I'm so old! As I dreamt about the night, I refelt so much of the fear I felt on it, and was scared by the fear, but I also refelt how alive I felt, and I was more scared still by that. Men were killing each other on my flanks and my knee and my left knuckle and all six of my bums and my eyebrow and my clitoris and my bollocks – although not my bullocks, who had all fled to low ground – and the men had been killing each other for two days and even though it was the deepest part of the night they were still killing each other and the fierce light of the moon was making it easier for them to kill each other and it seemed, although at first some of them had been killing each other slightly reluctantly, more out of a sense of duty than anything, now those same men were taking more pleasure in killing each other. One group of men had originally ambushed and cornered another group of men near a thick, impenetrable stand of trees on my aorta. The group of men who had ambushed the other group of men had less refined accents than the other group of men, more odorous hair and beards, but that was not so noticeable as it initially had been, and no longer seemed to matter; they were all just men, with urine-splashed trousers and swollen bloody eyes and half-legs and three-quarter arms and strewn intestines and a lust for power disguised as a lust to stay alive and a lust for staying alive disguised as a lust for power and women at home they wished were holding and caressing them and nobody really knew who was who any more and what it was all for. I was terrified, watching these men. And now dreaming about that night I felt that terror again and I felt that aliveness and I felt what I felt in the weeks following it, when all the men had died or fled or dragged themselves off to expire elsewhere, when the liquid from their bodies seeped into me, which was a different kind of aliveness, and an amazing kind of rejuvenation and energy and, yes, virility. Startling, startling virility. And then I felt momentarily ashamed but then I thought: Why? I am not hurting anyone; I am not even pressing myself into someone and being told to go to a workroom and calm myself down. I was just feeling what I felt.

Look, I'm not the Cerne Abbas Giant, if that's what you think. You're way out geographically, for a start. I have never been chalked, I am barely in any guidebooks, and I am not a renowned site of pilgrimage and ritual, or at least have not been for so long that to even talk about that would involve talking in an entirely different language which, even if it was translated into twenty-first-century English, would make little sense. Also – and I don't mean this in a snide or judgemental way – some of us don't feel the need to show off graphically and publicly about what we've got and prefer instead to occupy a position of quiet confidence about it. Each to their own, though. I hear he's OK, the Giant. I certainly don't have any personal beef with him, and am not attempting to start a feud. There is enough aggro and unrest in the world as it is. Especially on a moonlit night such as the one that has just passed.

Because the moon scrubbed the sky so clear, it was actually pretty cold in the early hours. But now the sun has burned off a light mist, all the world's clouds are elsewhere, and we're getting the flipside: the most perfect blue afternoon, hot without being stifling, a five-days-a-year perfect day. From my vantage point I can see vividly all the way to the coast, fourteen miles away, and that does not happen often. I have just watched five young friends edge their way down a deep crevice in the cliffs. Max is the leader. He has no shoes and has been walking with no shoes for so long that his feet feel nothing of the burrs and thistles and rocks and gorse needles beneath them. Then come Jemima and Annie: surfing, kayaking almost-hippie girls who talk with that laidback drawl common to all the kids around here whose parents have money and moved over from the south east a couple of decades ago. Hollie and Joe, both twenty-two, bring up the rear. They get on well, in a not deeply emotional way with Hollie doing most of the talking, and are in the middle of a lengthy discussion whose theme was originally graphic novels but has moved on to cheese. Hollie is still annoyed with herself for a grammatical slip-up in a message she sent last night, in reply to a sequence of persistent, politely complimentary and slightly poetic missives from an anonymous male, in which she wrote, 'Hey, dude, I'm sorry but I have a boyfriend and I'm comfortable with the amount you are messaging me.' The reason she wrote 'comfortable', instead of 'uncomfortable' – the word she intended to write – was that she had just burned her hand on the door of her mum's wood burner. What she doesn't know is that the sender of the anonymous messages was Joe.

But now they are on the shingle, and there is not a hint of Internet or phone reception and that other universe in which those messages were exchanged feels even more like one totally separate to this, with very few of the same rules or beliefs or social guidelines. The Internet is still two full years away from arriving at the beach so everyone is being a person. Nine people are asleep and, of those, seven will remember this sleep, with the sound of the waves in the background, as their most delicious sleep of the summer. Near the cliffs, someone has left a packet of chalk sticks, and on the rocks somebody has chalked the message 'PHUCK "SOCIETY" MAKE YOUR OWN RULES'. Just left of that somebody else has chalked a naked male body from the shoulders down. The naked male body's penis is standing to attention. If we are talking purely in terms of how it relates to the body it is attached to, the penis is slightly bigger than the

Cerne Abbas Giant's. In front of it a woman called Sue is praising a Schnauzer for leaving a crab to just get on and exist as a crab. But it is not a beach day without problems. Three men have just arrived on jet skis, bludgeoning every pleasant noise the day had to offer, and are riding closer and closer to the people in the water. Jennifer Tomasovich, an occupational therapist from Lostwithiel, has been watching the jet skiers and has now marched down to the shore and is shouting at them and trying to wave them away from the beach but they can't hear her and, if they do see her hand gestures, it only seems to encourage them to continue to get closer and closer to the shore, buzzing in show-off circles on these machines that they have convinced themselves are their Cerne Abbas Giant-sized cocks (or maybe the cock of some other land form which is slightly bigger but doesn't feel the need to be outlined in chalk). David Ludgate, who retired from running the big corporate optician in Exeter last year, has strolled down with his son Sam to join Jennifer, whom neither of them has ever met, on the tideline. 'Go away!' he shouts at the jet ski pricks.

'Fuck off!' Sam adds. 'Nobody wants you here and nobody likes you.'

Now a bigger crowd is gathering, thirteen or fourteen people, most of whom have never previously met, all united by this common four-cylinder enemy. Three or four of them begin to throw pebbles in the direction of the jet skiers. The jet skiers stop, about twenty yards out from the shore, and switch off their engines.

'What's your problem?' says their leader. Bald, pointy-faced, fifty-fiveish, he – the people on the shore realise – is the father of the other two jet skiers. He has brought them with him on his jet ski replacement-penis journey, taught them from an early age how to use a jet ski as a replacement for their own penises, passed on all the jet ski penis-replacement wisdom he has learned to them, as they will in time to their own male children.

'Our problem is that what you're doing is DANGEROUS,' shouts Jennifer Tomasovich the occupational therapist. 'There are people swimming here. You are being massively antisocial.'

'Oh, get a life, *woman*,' shouts the self-appointed jet ski replacement-penis chieftain, whose name is Andrew Bannister and – even though it seems almost too depressingly predictable to be true – took early retirement last year from his job as a big city banker and still regularly snorts cocaine.

'You mean like your life?' shouts Jennifer Tomasovich the occupational therapist. 'Why would anyone with any sense want that? You're demonstrating right now that it's obviously totally fucking soulless and self-centred.' At this, chuckles and cheers ring out from the shore, and an energy that has been building around the strangers standing there solidifies into a powerful, vibrating bar: a warm, formidable thing. Even though the strangers have not locked hands or begun singing a song of purity and strength out to the ocean, it feels like they are doing both. It is too much for Andrew Bannister, who opens his mouth to tell them why his life is actually the best, searches down in his dry throat for the words, then further, right inside his drier heart, but cannot find those words anywhere. 'Come on! What even are the words?' his throat asks his heart but his heart says nothing. And while he falters, as if in response to this – almost as if the machine is part of his body after all, just as he believes – his jet ski falters too. It stalls, to the great entertainment of everyone on the beach watching.

Fin and Reuben, Andrew's sons, look nervously now to him for the strong guidance he has always given them, in terms of what to do when you are sitting on a replacement penis. But none comes. A pebble pings off Reuben's replacement penis.

'What a trio of prize tools!' shouts Sam Ludgate.

But it's OK! Andrew has got the engine going again! He presses the accelerator and does a victory lap of the water, followed by Fin and Reuben, getting even more dangerously close to the beach than before. Because as long as he tells himself that's what it is, it's real, in his head, victory. That mouthy woman and her hippie friends haven't won. He has. Because here he is showing them the way to live: that sitting on a beach reading a book, or doing your stupid yoga, or eating your stupid organic packed lunch, is for losers. Life is about making money and using it to find a penis that is more powerful than your own. And he is sure – even though his throat, and all the bits of his body it leads down to, are even drier now – everyone will know that, and be in no doubt of his victory, as he motors away to another cove, followed by those he has spawned, and passed on his wisdom and prowess to.

The calm that redescends after that is powerful. At the other end of the beach, Hollie resumes thwacking a tennis ball back and forth with Annie, and Joe resumes watching her, and wondering why she didn't like the poem his anonymous Internet self sent her. People slip back into their delicious salty sleeps. Swimmers swim in a less nervous way. Dogs are congratulated for further minor acts of restraint. There is a slight sense that Jennifer Tomasovich the occupational therapist has given the beach the therapy it needed.

But I am not satisfied.

You will have noticed I sided with the peace-loving fraternity in this situation. The 'hippies' as Andrew Bannister thought of them, even though that description would only truly fit a few of them. The people not forcing their lives on anyone else. I generally do take that side. I am on the side of the land (well, obviously), the side of freedom, the side of unpolluted sound of waves and spiteless laughter. But am I a hippie myself? No. I resist such simple boxes. But more than that, I am too angry. You cannot be me, and see all I have seen, feel all I have felt, and not be.

'Oh, so you're a nihilist then, are you?' is what you're thinking. And you'd be wrong there too. I am not a nihilist, a communist, a socialist, an anarchist, a libertarian, a liberal, a conservative, an anything. I am me, with all of what has made me, with all of what has soaked me, and with all of that you cannot be a label.

Let me tell you this: I happen to know something else about Andrew. Eight years ago, he was driving across my ribs in one of his other replacement metal penises – an SUV retailing at over £70,000 – and hit a young pony, while breaking the speed limit by a total of 34 mph. He very forcefully felt the impact of the pony, which broke the SUV's radiator grill and bumper and smashed its left headlight, and, though it was dark, saw the animal's descent over a ridge at the side of the road, to some rocks directly beneath, where the pony died, not quickly, but ninety-four full long minutes later, watched by three other ponies, who stood directly above it. But Alan decided to drive on, and to this day has still never told another soul about the incident. He was on his own in his SUV at the time, but even so, he still spoke aloud, directly after the impact, as if justifying himself to a friend. The words he spoke were, 'Ah sod it, it's just a bloody wild pony. Nobody even owns it.' He then drove over my hips, which nobody owns, and my knee, which nobody owns, to one of the houses which he bought with his wife, who nobody owns, where he was meeting his mistress, who nobody owns, where he would later take some cocaine, which was once owned by a man called Jake, who lived in London's Holland Park.

I know quite a bit more – but by no means everything – about what Andrew has done in his life, but this is the bit I take most personally.

So, no, when those pebbles were landing in the water near Andrew's jet ski, I was not just hoping he, trailed by Fin and Reuben, would piss off and leave the swimmers and sunbathers on the beach in peace. I was hoping that one of the pebbles would connect with his temple, and knock him into the water. Harsh? Maybe. But perhaps you are ascribing values to me that are not relevant to my kind. You have been lulled by my chatter and my jokes and the familiar names I call my constituent parts, lulled into forgetting that I am not a man or a woman or anything close. Also, I haven't done anything to hurt anyone (on this occasion); I am just feeling what I feel.

I desire love. I want to see it thrive. But I also want blood. I want it to seep into me and do its work. I want a balance redressed.

PAPPS WEDGE (2043)

'Get David Cavendish to sign that bloody document.' These had been Sally's words to Bob as he leaned in close to her over the bed in the hospital room that overlooked the half-empty skip and the three-quarter-empty car park, and then she had died.

It had been a lateish life romance: a second marriage for her, a third for him. Autumn, 2018. Shedding of old leaves and skin. They'd made their mistakes and out of them, sometimes it seemed almost directly, had come what they found in their union: a harmony but not like anything either of them had pictured earlier in life when focusing on the word 'harmony' and trying to pin down precisely what that would look like. A harmony made of old wood and notebooks and soup and a coffee grinder and shouting at robots on the phone and rejecting what nonsense they could and pianos and keeping out of each other's way for quite a bit of the week and car boot sales and a sheep and then two sheep when the first sheep got lonely and then three sheep just because they felt like it. He was forty-nine, she thirty-eight. He'd come to the book group that February, the first new arrival for a while, invited by Jane. It had been Sally's turn to choose that week, and she'd opted for *A Widow for One Year* by John Irving. She talked about what a warm, generous, funny and sympathetically human author Irving was. Bob sat in the corner on the most important-looking chair, frowning, filling his cheeks with wine and hogging the chilli-coated peanuts. 'He's bland and overlong,' he said. 'And why do his female characters always have big tits? It strikes me he's just writing out his sexual fantasies, getting off on his own inventions.' She thought Bob was a ghastly grump, a withered wirebeard, a molten meanmouth, a blown fuse of predictable cynicism. He didn't come again.

Seven months later, he crashed his car into hers at the half-blind junction outside the arts college where he went to talk about woodcraft one afternoon a week. Nobody was hurt and he admitted liability. He was so instantly attentive, so patently repentant and worried about the mistake he had made, that when he arrived at the driver's-side window after running across the road to her from his abandoned, fishtailed hatchback, she did not instantly equate his face with the jaded peanut hogger of the previous winter, even though the mouth and eyes seemed immediately familiar. He recognised her more quickly and they exchanged details for insurance purposes but it was not until the following week that she strolled out of the wallpaper of his days and became lifelike. That was in the garden centre. The nice one, with the mossy hanging baskets and the old man with the calculator. Not the big one, with all the weedkiller and all the screens that barked at you to buy stuff that would change your life as a gardener. He had his headphones on, was half-listening to a podcast about the building of early tanks and wondering why ferns were so expensive when you could just find them everywhere in the countryside around here anyway, when he realised a woman was staring at him, mouthing a word, over and over again. He removed the headphones. 'Car, car, CAR!' she said. And *now* he saw her. He saw empathy and rain and second-hand wool and an excellently cantilevered nose and forbearance and independence refusing to transmute into misdirected fury. He helped her transfer the Trachycarpus she'd purchased to the boot of her car but he got the angle wrong and one of the branches snapped. By way of apology, he bought her carrot cake at the tea room next door. Here she began to learn that what she'd met seven months earlier had been not so much a man as a set of trying recent events: a winter where he'd been assailed by a lost job and a lost parent, the last one he had. Things were slowly improving for him now. His time was divided between various endeavours involving wood. He had found the time to read four more John Irving books since February. He'd thoroughly enjoyed three of them.

Who even was that goblin who'd sat in the comfiest armchair in Jane's living room back at the beginning of the year? Bob's face had softened unrecognisably since then. She sometimes even forgot he had a beard and certainly forgot that beard looked like grey wire, even though it did. As they became Sally and Bob – always Sally and Bob to all who knew them, never Bob and Sally – she was the one who often had to step in to stop him trying to do too much for others, to stop his gentle surface being trampled on. Back then she was in the cottage in Underhill with the piano, and he was in the long house on the hill five miles away, behind the wall, with the town address even though it was outside the town, and outside the town's mains drainage network. He only rented a fifth of the long house, and a small courtyard adjoining it, which was a shame, because a colleague at the college had recently offered him a rescue turkey and he'd had to reluctantly say no due to space limitations. His house was an afterthought on the end of the long house, like something the long house had been meaning to say to support an argument but couldn't be bothered to properly articulate. Its windows never seemed quite right. Newts came in through the tiny lean-to in early spring, the side of the house which had, two centuries before, been the site of a large natural pond. The other four fifths of the building, and a couple of acres of adjoining land, belonged to Anita and Jac, a couple in their thirties. Bob never asked what Anita and Jac did for a living but he fed their pigs and chickens and cats while they were away, which was often, and took delivery of their online shopping packages, which were countless. When they were home, he listened uncomplainingly through the walls to their shouting matches, their reconciliatory humping, their unrelaxing Ibiza chillout albums, Jac bashing his drum kit in their conservatory and the piercing garden tantrums of Sorrel, their toddler.

Bob had only ever spoken to Jac in person once, which was not long after he'd first moved in, when Anita had invited him in for a coffee, and Jac had arrived home from work – whatever that was, something property-related, Bob tended to assume – and said, 'Anita, what is this strange *man* doing in my kitchen with you?' which was presented as a joke but also revealed itself, via its tone and Jac's face, to be very much not a joke too. Sally said she thought they were prize nobheads. She was vocally uninhibited during sex and they'd only done it twice when the first text message from Jac arrived on Bob's phone. 'Dear Bob,' it read. 'The walls are very thin here and I hope you know we can hear everything.' Bob did not reply and, for fear of embarrassing Sally, did not show her the message for a long time, nor Jac's second one, but did suggest sleeping in the spare room when Sally stayed over, for a change of environment, and because it could be argued that the mattress was more comfortable. The following week, Bob took delivery of the high-end drone Jac and Anita had ordered from the Internet and placidly took it over to their house when they returned from their latest international city break. The week after that, he transferred his half of the fee for the emptying of the septic tank shared by the two houses. Bob wasn't quite sure what went on with Jac's phone along the way but from what he could work out Jac must have had two different Bobs saved in the Contacts section of it and they had somehow got mixed up, without Jac yet cottoning onto this mistake, so by the time four more months had passed, and Bob was out of the house and into his new place, his thread of text messages from Jac read as follows:

Jac: 'The walls are very thin here and I hope you know we can hear everything.'

Jac: 'Bob. Please can you transfer your half of the fee to our account that you owe us for the clearing of the shared septic tank yesterday. Your share comes to £68.50.'

Bob: 'That should be in your account now, Jac. All the best. Bob.'

Jac: 'The walls are still very thin, Bob. Please can both of you be more considerate.'

Jac: 'Happy New Year, Bob. I hope life is treating you well. Please could I get eight bales of straw from you?'

Jac: 'Howdy, Boberino. We are in dire need of manure. Can you help? Take it easy, man. Jac.'

'Fucking hell,' said Sally, when Bob finally showed her the messages. 'Also why can't he spell his name with a "k" like a normal person?' They were in Bob's new kitchen. Water was all over them in every way except the way that would have made them wet: the kettle boiling, the cold tap running in an attempt to stop Bob's eyes stinging from the onions he'd just chopped, and a further, more captivating liquid story being told just outside the window. He lived by the river now, just under an hour's walk from Sally's, and he normally did walk, not drive there, arriving in mud-splashed trousers after cutting through woodland where fallen trees often blocked the path and the ground sucked thirstily at his legs. The front door to Sally's cottage led directly to the living room and if you had a bit of a belly, as Bob did, it was a squeeze to get yourself through the gap between the Kentia palm and the piano. The piano, a Bechstein which had once been her granddad's, wouldn't fit through the door so when she'd moved in it had meant getting permission to go through the

Dawsons' garden, four doors down, then using the ginnel that led behind all seven gardens on the cottage row. The removal men had not been pleased and she gave them a £50 tip, which had left her £371.23 overdrawn, rather than just £321.23 overdrawn. Sally rarely played the piano any more as tuning other ones all day could drive her what she called 'a bit doolally' and she had come to appreciate the opportunities for silence that home offered. Even though her business name, Sally the Piano Tuner, made matters fairly explicit, people still often expected her to be a man when she arrived at their house to tinker with their instruments, or much older than she was, or blind, or all three. 'So what do you do as well as this, for your actual job?' some of them asked. They found it strange, almost impossible, to believe that this is what she'd been doing for a full-time form of income since she left college. The job was not the quaint and refined Victorian existence she had imagined when she was younger. It could be territorial and shady. When she'd first moved to the area and tried to build up her clientele, rivals in the trade had badmouthed her temperament and stability as a tuner. One especially vindictive veteran had sent her a warning message by calling her out to a fake job at a fake address. As she attempted to solve the musical jigsaws in front of her at the houses of lonely men, she saw their desperate staring reflections in the polyester finish of the pianos. But there were still moments that made the job worthwhile. Old people, hearing her play dusty instruments that had not been touched for decades, burst into tears as they were sucked down tunnels into parts of their past that had been inaccessible to them for many years. The terminology of the trade never fully ceased to provide some level of amusement for her, although most of that was now her amusement at witnessing the reactions of others when they heard it. 'If you are lucky, I will show you my papps wedge,' she told Bob the first time she invited him over.

Now the legal matters relating to his father's death the previous winter had been finalised, Bob, with four or five dollops of luck and an immense amount of effort, had been able to buy the house by the river. To scrape the last bit of funds for his deposit, he had sold his furniture, his car and his record collection. Getting to the college to teach his class meant an hour's walk and a half an hour bus ride. For extra money, he took a job helping out at a woodyard, which was also not a short walk away, and felt like work more suited to someone two decades his junior, but he enjoyed its noises and smells, and it came with the advantage of free firewood. The first time Sally came over to the river house, they ate risotto beside the crackling logs, he squatting on the floor and she on a large cushion next to an ancient hi-fi unit. She heard a discrepancy in the toner arm of the deck and adjusted it. 'I think I might be becoming an interior decor commitmentphobe,' he told her. He said he liked the minimalism of the house, the sense of possibility the bare rooms offered, and enjoyed the way his three remaining LPs sounded in the empty rooms, but she saw him wince and hold his side as he got up to take the dishes to the kitchen. The next time she arrived, she brought a Lloyd Loom chair. 'But that was your mum's!' he said. 'You can't give me that.' She told him to call it an indefinite loan. On each of her next seven visits, she brought houseplants, so now it was a house of plants and a chair. He slept on a mattress and said he failed to see the point in bed frames, argued the case against them vehemently, even as he struggled visibly to pull himself upright. She worried about what he was doing to his back, carrying and splitting logs three days a week. She recommended a chiropractor – a haunted-looking man whose practice was based at the top of a haunted-looking building in the nearest big town – and, with some coaxing, he booked an appointment. In spring she filled the balcony with pot plants and Bob moaned that it ruined the view and diminished seating potential, but he nurtured each plant, inside and out, as if it were his own child, cooked every recipe she gave him, read every book she recommended, making notes as he went so he could give her feedback. He was the first man who'd ever listened to her.

The river house did not have a garden but when the water level was low Sally and Bob crossed the stones and sat on the opposite bank in the field belonging to the farmer David Cavendish, who didn't seem to have much use for it himself. It was a very steep field, which, when the mornings were misty and Bob looked out of his studio through the diagonal skylight, could give him the impression that roe deer were bounding through the sky. The hearing of the sky deer was so sensitive that even the sound of Bob reaching into a bag of chilli-coated peanuts, a hundred yards away, behind glass, would startle them, but soon they became more at ease with his presence. Formerly, a horse called Edna had lived in the field and chomped apples off the branches of the old tree at the field's centre. The tree was still there and it was not unknown for apples to cling to its branches until January. Edna had died way back in 2003 but Sally and Bob often speculated about her personality and the ensuing one of her ghost. Their conclusion that she was a very strict and disapproving horse became a running joke between them.

One day in summer 2019 a night of hot rain arrived, the river filled up with voices and Bob – unable to sleep – stood on the balcony naked for half an hour taking great pleasure in letting the full force of the saturated night hit him.

'Goodness!' said Sally. 'What on earth must Edna think of you now?'

The reason Sally and Bob knew about Edna was because they'd been told about her by Fleur, whose family the horse had once belonged to. Fleur was the one who'd sold the little river house to Bob. It was because of Sally's work as Fleur's piano tuner that Bob found out about the house being for sale and was able to buy it before Fleur decided to advertise it with an estate agent at a price Bob could not have afforded. Sally continued to tune Fleur's piano – even though she suspected Fleur didn't use the piano between each tuning, and asked her to tune it mainly because she enjoyed the company – and Fleur became a close friend of hers and Bob's, telling them stories about what life was like in the river house during the previous century, when Fleur's mum, Daphne, had lived there. Fleur called Daphne 'an indomitable woman' and 'Queen of the Combe'. The Cavendish family owned the field back then too, but allowed Daphne to keep Edna there. During this period, Daphne, who abhorred slothfulness, would ring a bell at half past six every morning to make sure everyone who lived in the other five cottages on the lane was awake. Fleur said that back then the combe was mostly home to alcoholics, that something about the way the light leaked grudgingly down into it sent people organically in that direction. When Daphne died, just a week after Edna, Fleur went to live in the river house for a few years but found that the noise of the water got inside her mind and began to play tricks on it, so she let it to tenants for several years before selling it to Bob. 'It can be a dastardly, opinionated beast,' she said. 'The river, I mean, not the house. The house does not force itself on anyone. It allows you to live the way you want to.'

Fleur had been correct. Bob lived in the house pretty much the way he wanted to, which was to say that after a while he lived with three chairs, fourteen houseplants and a table. There was never a time in any of the rooms when he couldn't hear the river, unless he had one of his three remaining LPs playing loud, and on spring nights when Sally stayed over and she and Bob sat up in bed, it often felt like having a conversation in a quiet annexe of a party, next door to a room where a bigger, noisier conversation was going on. Sally, especially, was attuned to every change in the current and flow, every small rise in the water level. In bed at night with the lights off, as they half-listened to the river's hot takes and counterpoints, she often had a lot to say and he'd keep pushing sleep away in order to hear it. When she finally dropped off, it was like a switch had been flicked – she described it that way herself, but said 'like a flick had been switched' because she had not fully woken up – and then, having pushed sleep away for so long and missed his chance for it, he'd be alone, stranded with his thoughts. He noticed she often slept with her arms folded, as if waiting for a dream to impress her. After a year, he knew everything about her except the trimmings. He knew that she had lupus but didn't like to tell people about it and enjoyed bananas when they had gone a bit bad and never stood on manholes and that her parents had both been music teachers and played in the West Newcastle Symphony Orchestra and that they had twanged door handles when she was little and asked her to identify the musical note they made. He knew about all her previous romantic partners, about Jake the narcissist web designer who now lived in Seattle, about Ben who cooked extraordinarily well but slept with her best friend when she was twenty-one and about Michael who had amazing hands and taught her to use his own unique non-standard tuning on the guitar but didn't like putting his cock inside anything or anyone. He knew where each of the four notable scars on her body came from and why and precisely which month in which year in which century they occurred. He knew that she did not believe in ghosts but was also adamant that one otherwise silent December day, when she could see the fog settling over the tor through the cottage window, she had heard her piano play two notes all on its own. He knew it all but it did not stop him loving every octave and quaver of her voice and eagerly awaiting what she had to say every time she opened her mouth.

By contrast, she sometimes felt she knew too little about him. His attitude was that his previous relationships had no place here in the present. They were like statues from previous centuries: they had been erected for old reasons, in a different cultural and political climate, and you wouldn't want to drag them to a new place and erect them for the same reasons now. She accepted his reasoning, even though it meant she had to guess at some of the shapes of who he was and what was behind them. She knew he was northern, like her, but his northernness was more of a rumour embedded deep in him: seven years living up in Southport, from birth. She knew he liked wood and worked with it but it was only when she asked him what the strange T-shaped object with the redundant rusty hinge in the window of the upstairs toilet was that she knew he made things for his own pleasure out of it, too: useful things, like lamp bases and mirrors and coat racks, but truly odd things too, things from another dimension. She knew the job he'd lost the winter he met her had been as a lecturer in Film, but it wasn't until they'd been together for close to two years that she discovered he also used to go into London to review movies for a magazine, one she used to buy.

'No way! I probably read your stuff!' she said.

'Oh dear,' he replied. 'I'm sorry you had to go through that.'

He talked about the jaded newspaper critics at the screenings in Soho who would sigh and say 'Oh, not another *film*' as if they were stacking corned beef on supermarket shelves rather than being employed to do something others gladly handed over their wages to do every weekend, and about the quite famous one who fell asleep on Bob's shoulder, and about the time Bob invited his music journalist friend Martin to a screening and Martin turned up late, still drunk from the night before, and, struggling to adjust his vision to the dark screening room, sat on the lap of a well-known radio presenter, spilling the presenter's yoghurt, or was it ice cream. There were usually sandwiches and crisps laid on by the PR companies before the screenings but the famous radio presenter always brought his own yoghurt or ice cream tub and noisily lapped up the contents before the film started.

'You don't mean Irish Martin who lives in Barnstaple? The one you said you never see any more because he's a recluse and just stays in his room meditating and chanting all day?'

'Yes. That Martin. He's not Irish, he just kind of... seems it. We met in London. He used to get me into gigs for free. He's... different now. He wrote some books. He hasn't been able to get most of them published, though.'

When Sally looked at the facts of Bob from a distance – the north-west childhood, the brief media career, the love of wood, the uncomplaining ability to be outdoors in all weathers, the grumpy resistance to change, the attentiveness to everything she taught him, the skill with his hands, the inability to detect when washed clothes were dry with those very same hands – it never seemed to quite make sense. But when he was in front of her, as Bob, real lumpy three-dimensional Bob, he made total sense. Nothing had ever made more sense to her. The following year – the first of the pandemic years – they decided she would move in to the river house with him. The national lockdowns gave them the extra nudge they needed. That, and the day a man who had asked her to tune an early 1900s Broadwood accidentally locked her in his house when he went out to work and Bob had to drive over and rescue her. Not that she needed a hero, but she looked at him a bit differently after that day, felt she was standing half a stride closer to him. In the car on the way home, she noticed a shard of glass was still sticking out of the t-shirted arm he'd used to smash the window. She carefully picked it out as he steered.

She said the living room with the piano had been full of clocks, all set to different times, and their chiming had made tuning almost impossible. 'Still,' she said. 'At least I got to work on a Broadwood. Those things are rare.' He said they used the wire from them to make planes in the First World War. 'Now how in god's name did you know that?' she asked. He told her he'd read it in one of her books one time when she was asleep.

She brought her piano with her to Bob's. The removal men managed to get it in through the doors of the small light room on the end of the house nearest the lane without anybody wanting to murder anyone with knives, and there it would have to stay, which meant the room couldn't be used for much else, but that was fine, because there were more places to sit, especially now she'd brought her furniture with her. Outside the world seemed to be ending. That's what people kept saying. In less than a year 'dystopian' had become such an overused word to have been rendered near-meaningless. Early hopes when the pandemic first hit that nature was 'healing' had turned on their head and it appeared that in fact the virus was on the side of greed and destruction after all, annihilating all that was small and true and firming up the grip megalomaniacs and madmen had on the planet, in an attempt to push us more quickly towards the abyss. Social fissures spread out in all sorts of unanticipated ways. Making snap judgements online about the lives and personalities of people you'd never met had already been a fashionable form of stupidity for quite some time, but now it became an international sport. Fear leaked while people weren't looking, crept through tiny gaps under doors and puddled. 'It's scary out there,' people said. 'Stay safe.' But much of the time it felt like the problem wasn't *out there* at all, it was *in there*, in the screens that everybody carried with them everywhere they went and nobody could stop looking at. Out there, David Cavendish had let twenty-four new sheep graze the field over the river. Out there, in the sky above the combe, there were marsh harriers and deer. When Sally and Bob stepped out onto the balcony and looked into the water, they did not see disposable masks and hand sanitiser bottles floating over the rocks. The air felt clear and quick and kept both of them looking six and a half years younger than they were. At night, during the hard pandemic winter, when everything accelerated, they did shiftwork spooning each other – four minutes each, then the changeover – and got no firsthand experience of the ache for physical affection that was pulsating in the chest of unattached people the world over, spreading like a pandemic within a pandemic. They existed in a little bubble of OK, and, as guilty as they felt about that, knowing the really calamitous state of everything, they protected the bubble fiercely, and would not have wished to be anywhere beyond it.

And now it was twenty-two years later and she was two years in the grave – or technically not in the grave at all, but in the earth, certainly, by now – and he was seventy-three and the world was not yet quite over. He had become the dropout he hadn't quite been able to commit to becoming when he was a young man or a middle-aged one. It was easier now to do it, and harder, because every bit of alleged progress in society always made everything easier and harder. When the visors came in, he refused to have one fitted, and that made it simpler than it ever had been to step outside of it all, with no half-measures. No rudimentary pay-as-you-go phone. No Gmail address he begrudgingly checked once a week. Nothing. He was in the minority as a result of his choice to live visorless, but he was not alone. It made him part of the Resistance and the Resistance made ways for themselves to exist on the cultural borders: they opened small shops, supported one another by sharing produce, lived in their own voluntarily insular way. The fact that the mortgage was now paid off made it more possible to live as part of this section of society, as did his choice to heat it solely with wood, to insure nothing in it and to plant a little veg in the field over the river every spring, to no longer travel abroad or drive. He was living in one of the easier places to be an outcast and it permitted him to not think much beyond the ensuing twenty-four hours in his immediate surroundings. There was no point. Everyone knew the state of play now, the chorus of denial of two decades ago had fizzled down to a low hum, and, while plenty was being done to stop the acceleration into the void, the two major obstacles standing in the way – corporate greed, and the illusory drive towards convenience – could not be circumnavigated. The planet as it had been known for the last few thousand years would end soon. It would end after Bob ended, but not long after. So in the meantime what you did was grab the good days with both hands.

In truth, he had become very unaware *what* was going on, in a wider sense. That was the choice he had made, in an era of infotainment tyranny. He rarely had any interaction with the people with visors, who remained plugged in. Vague bits of news drifted his way via encounters on footpaths and in the community shop and the free pub: the evacuation of west California, a few encouraging advances in sustainable building regulations, the closing of the French border, war across most of Eastern Europe, Shropshire drowning under deeper water every winter, a plan for the redistribution of wealth and second homes. But it was all a muddle, factoids spinning like dust in sunlight. It was a decade since the visors came in, thus a decade since he had switched on a machine to consult a news source. His news sources were the moor and the river, but they were reliable messengers, in their own way – perhaps no less reliable than anything else. During a long walk he passed the reservoir a couple of miles north of home and noticed a bridge in the clouds a few miles north west of that and realised they were rebuilding one of the old branch lines. When there was a storm now, it crackled with more electricity. Microwaves and multisockets and chargers in people's houses blew up, which made him even more glad to have none in his. Always prone to tempests, the river now had that bit more to say when it was incensed. He put his faith in the tiny seventeenth-century bridge behind the house. The water level had never risen high enough to overflow the mossy stonework but the December before last it had come close. The dog had still been alive back then, Jim, a Patterdale he and Sally had taken off Sally's cousin Beth when Beth moved to Ireland. Around 2 a.m., with a whimper and a nose forced into Bob's armpit, he had raised the alarm. The water had been steadily rising for hours, on a day of the most persistent rain imaginable which followed several days of other rain that by any normal standards would also have been classed as extremely persistent. Bob had never heard the water scream louder than just before he went to bed that night, as it raced past the living-room window, but by the point, four hours later, that Jim stood on the bed, nudging him awake, the noise had pinned the whole house in a headlock. It was not unusual for Jim to ask to be let out for a slash at this time but when Bob went downstairs and opened the back door, the little dog just looked up at him in terror. It was clear what Jim thought, which was that there was a huge monster outside, and he was not wrong. Bob could just hear a higher note within the water's experimental dirge and realised the piano was vibrating. He went out and stood on the balcony. The writhing white shapes beneath him looked like livid swimming ghosts: all the river's dead, raised in fury, on their way to the sea to seek the most terrible revenge. The water would have needed to rise another three feet to reach the balcony, but he had never felt more expendable. Within the white bar of howling sound, he could hear the grinding of the boulders on the river bed, as the current forced them against one another, again and again.

Since that night, he often wondered what would be the first to go: the bridge, the planet, or him. He decided that if the bridge did go, it probably meant the planet was going with it. And if the bridge went, it meant the house would almost certainly go too, and, since he went out increasingly rarely these days, it was highly likely he'd be in there at the time. He could think of many worse ways to die. It would also save him from the Alzheimer's that had taken his dad, which he increasingly worried was his fate.

Today, though, the river was a pussycat. It purred around the boulders beneath his feet. The water level was low enough for him to plot a route across the bendy line of stones to the field in summer shoes and barely get wet. The deep pool, up by the bridge, where he sometimes spied trout, was mild phosphorescent green. Through the hole where one of the planks of the balcony had rotted, he could see a leftover semicircle of peel from the orange he'd eaten yesterday, gyrating behind a rock, the current not strong enough to wash it away. How much citrus had he thrown in here over the years? And what of the rest? The ash from the fire, the rotten lettuce leaves, the nail and beard clippings, the curdling hummus, the avocado skins, the peanuts, the matted dog hair, the garlic skin that flew away on the breeze like the butterflies Jagger released into the crowd in Hyde Park in the year of Bob's birth? Of all the river's dark magic, its repeated vanishing acts were perhaps its most impressive. Again and again, that crystal-clear current renewing itself, making things that had existed not exist any more. This story had been going on a long time and it never stopped, still went on down below, even on the rare occasions the surface iced over. When he died, he would be part of this story, one of the water's innumerable voices, and nothing more. He had no children or grandchildren. His cousins

Rachel and Sheila up in Stroud stopped getting in touch around the time the visors came in: they had not joined the Resistance. Martin in Barnstaple, whom he'd only seen a couple of times a year anyway due to all the chanting and meditating, had met a Hungarian lady – a songwriter – and moved with her to a house on the great plains in her homeland. He'd written Bob a letter to say the place was disturbingly flat but the sex and music were excellent, but that had been over a year ago. There was Sam, the young ecologist from the village he sometimes walked with, who quizzed him for moorland knowledge, who would remember him for a while, he supposed. But Bob's stamp on the earth would soon fade, his sculptures remaining for a while in the houses of the people who'd bought them and then in other houses and then in dusty shops and then in other houses but with nobody who owned them having a clue about the person who made them. He would just be part of the river's story, just like Fleur – now five years dead herself – and everyone else who'd lived on its banks, including Edna, and Edna's tree, and that was fine, because life wasn't about what happened when you were no longer alive, it was about grabbing the good days with both hands, and probably always had been.

It seemed very likely that the tree, in fact, might even go before him, the bridge and the planet. It leaned at a twisted rheumatoid angle now, almost painful to look at, no longer yielding apples, thrashed and browbeaten by storms. It was an incongruous gothic leper on a frivolous spring day like today. Just below it, Bob could see something else incongruous: some new low wooden posts with string tied between them, stretching up the valley. He'd first spotted them about five days ago, although he'd not seen who had placed them there. They bothered him, bothered him probably more than anything else in his life that was currently bothering him, more than the pain that diagonally knifed from his left hip to the middle of his back more obnoxiously every morning when he got up, more than the fact that when Sam had come over for a cup of coffee last week to talk about some rare beetles he was researching Bob had entirely forgotten his name for two whole minutes.

Not for one day since Sally's death had Bob not thought about her final instruction to him. Leaning over the bed and putting an ear to her mouth in that wretched room which said nothing about the life she had lived, he had not been surprised that she had not said 'I love you', since she had not said that for a long time. But the vehemence and volume of the request, more of an order than a request, the 'bloody', the clarity of it, after weeks of no clarity at all, took him aback. It was a subject she'd not mentioned for years. He'd supposed she was thinking about his own welfare, wanting to know he'd be OK and have the best possible life without her, but more recently, when he thought about it and tried to coax himself into action, it was her interests he felt he was acting on, not his own. It was just a field; looking at the way it changed from season to season, growing produce in it, reading in it, seeing animals mooch about in it, all enhanced his day-to-day existence, but who cared who really owned it? That was his take on it a lot of the time. But then he remembered her face, the last time he ever saw it, tasted the texture of her words in his head. It was several months since he'd last been up to the Cavendish farm, which was barely a farm at all now, and spoken to the younger David Cavendish about the field. Nothing concrete had come of it, just as it hadn't the time before. These new posts and string, though, nudged him into action. He would head up there again; not this afternoon, maybe not tomorrow, but certainly the day after. He would be firmer and stronger this time, even though there were few prospects he relished less.

Bob had never been sensible or strategic or cautious with

money. He'd always known this fact about himself somewhere deep down but he knew it a whole lot more after she moved in. Although neither of their incomes had increased, a year after she came in on the mortgage, a year after they pooled their resources and she made some little adjustments to all the baggy parts of his administrative life, they suddenly felt better off. They had stopped seeing David Cavendish, or his sheep, in the field across the river by then. Bob knew how much she loved the field and, as a surprise, for her birthday the following year, he took out a loan and made David Cavendish an offer for the land, which, after some wrangling and vagueness, Cavendish agreed to sell for £68,000. Sally was furious at first when he told her, then a little happy, then furious again, when she found out that Bob had paid Cavendish for the field but not received any form of legally binding document as proof.

'So you just... shook hands on it?' she said. Her face had that heavy-lidded, burdened look it got sometimes. She'd just got back from a hammer recentring job and had been reaming flange bushings all afternoon. Tuning the piano they belonged to had then been made near impossible by three toddlers divebombing each other on a giant beanbag in the adjoining, doorless room in front of a blaring television. She had no idea if the piano was in tune when she left.

'Well, essentially, yeah,' he said. 'It's fine. I am sure he's not going to diddle me. It's different here on the moor. There's an ancient code of honour. If somebody fucked somebody over in that way, everyone would know about it.'

'You are insane, and you need to get in touch with a solicitor as soon as possible. Will you promise me you will do that?'

'I promise.'

'Next week?'

'Yes. Well, soon.'

'Next week.'

But next week had come and gone, then next month, then next year, and next decade, and he did not get in touch with a solicitor. The intention was there in his mind but also in his mind, every morning, was the question 'What exactly do you want to do with this, your one precious life?' and the answer to that question was never 'Paperwork and time-consuming back-and-forths with a member of the legal profession.' She continued to harangue him about his neglect of the matter for a short period but then she seemed to forget, and realising she'd forgotten was one of the outstanding reliefs of his recent life. He felt like a child who'd been forgiven for burning down a school. The field was effectively theirs anyway. They grew sweetcorn and carrots in it like it was theirs, sunbathed in it like it was theirs, grazed three Herdwicks – not for meat or wool but just for the sheer joy of letting them be Herdwicks – in it like it was theirs, erected a marquee in it for her fiftieth birthday like it was theirs. What difference did a piece of paper make? Every so often, Bob would bump into David Cavendish on the lane, and on approximately one in three of these occasions would ask him if he might be able to sort some official documentation, and Cavendish would promise to do so, but also somehow manage to convey that none of it really mattered, even the money itself didn't even matter, even though it was now safely in one of his three savings accounts; what mattered was the sun and the air and the birds and the day, on which latter point Bob was definitely in agreement about. Sally said he was a feckless man and a royal bullshitter. She said she had become better at spotting those as she got older, and happier to confront them. Cavendish's son, also called David, reared and shot pheasant, annihilated foxes for fun. Once on the lane when he almost drove into the side of her, she called him a cunt for it, and for his driving. Her argumentative streak – though rarely aimed at Bob – had grown in middle age. When she hit the menopause, her hair greyed and thinned, then stopped greying and got thicker, thicker than it had been since she was a teenager. She attributed this to her argumentative nature. She said it was her hair's way of disagreeing with what biology had planned for it. It became the first way that people recognised her, made her bigger and more impressive in the eyes of people they knew, made them even more Sally and Bob, even less Bob and Sally.

*

The river changed colour again over the next two days: heavy cool spring rain turned it the colour of beer, foamed up its margins. He sat out at dawn hoping to catch sight of otters. More had been spotted over the last few years, especially a mile or so upstream where the combe's steep walls of moss closed in and only allowed in secret sharp flashes of light. Two summers ago one of them had made off with a cod that Patrick and Mel at Russet Cottage had left exposed, marinating in honey and soy sauce on their kitchen table with the French windows open. He thought he saw one today but it was a false alarm: just a squirrel, skipping over the rocks, out of its element. He went inside and showered and put on his lone clean pair of trousers and ironed shirt. He resented himself slightly for doing it but decided it was wise not to add any element to his appearance that would put him at risk of being taken less seriously during the day's central task. Before he left for the Cavendish place, he mopped up the water droplets from the bathroom floor: an old habit, not quite yet dying its hard death. Sally had been an alarmingly splashy bather and in two years he had still not got used to living with a largely dry bathroom. He had never quite worked out what she did to make the floor and walls so wet. When her hair got bigger, it only made the explosion of water more exuberant.

Out on the lane, the hedgerows were settling into their high spring colour scheme of white, pink and blue: greater stitchwort, red campion and bluebells. Two decades ago the lanes had become quite dicey to walk along due to a combination of angry drivers living in a pandemic, population growth, urban exodus and people texting at the wheel. It all felt like it had been leading to a kind of breaking point. The work of the second and third pandemics and the rise of self-driving vehicles had altered that. In a climb of just over a mile, he saw nobody. He took a left at the top of the hill, past a half-demolished stone barn with a corrugated iron roof reddened with rust, then turned up the track leading to the farm and pressed the intercom. He found David Cavendish – the second David Cavendish, or rather the fifth, and second most recent, David Cavendish, if you were looking at the entire timeline – on the porch, in the middle of an animated conversation with an unknown, invisible entity. Cavendish acknowledged Bob with something not totally unlike a smile, using the small part of his face that wasn't absorbed in whatever was being fed to it through his visor. His head, though bald, looked smooth and youthful – certainly no older than his age, which Bob knew to be somewhere in his late thirties – but underneath it his body resembled eight or nine assorted pumpkins on the turn, stuffed into some cloth. Bob immediately felt mean for having this thought – after all, he'd let himself go a bit in middle age, too, before his exit from digital life – and it was up to individuals how they looked after their own bodies, and nobody else's business, but he had heard the rumours about what these visors were doing to people, about the so-called 'ultraworld' they lived in, where the virtual body they modified had superseded the physical one they still put food and drink into and walked around in and shitted and pissed out of. When they had to live fully in their physical body on the government-ordained Switch Off Day, they were antsy and frustrated. It was said that many of them could no longer properly taste food. He heard rumours of something called 'joyhacking': people coming to their senses, hundreds of miles from their home, disorientated, after strangers had recoded the electronic systems connected to their brains and ridden them around for a period of days, just for fun. But Bob didn't know if that was actually true, just as he didn't know if a lot was true these days.

He waited patiently, standing seven or eight yards clear of Cavendish and staring at a tractor and an old motorised go-kart, both seasoned with moss and half-sunk into the earth on the far corner of the farmyard. It was a long time since any agricultural work had happened here.

'Mr Turner,' said Cavendish, finally. 'What can I do for you on this perfect spring day?'

'David,' said Bob. 'How is life treating you? How is your dad?'

'Well, I have to be honest and say it is not looking good. I do not think there is very long left. It is a very sad thing to see for all of us.'

'I'm so sorry to hear that, David.'

'I imagine you are here to talk about what we talked about a little while back.'

'Well...'

'Did you know – and you will appreciate this, I'm sure, as a man who likes books – that the way the Crow Indian killed buffalo in the seventeenth century was rarely with arrows or tomahawks? What they did instead was drive them off cliffs, sometimes as many as 700 of them, far more than they could eat. They used songs. Can you believe that? Songs! At the time, the buffalo was the most common wild animal on the entire planet. Can you imagine it? Biting into some freshly cooked buffalo by a campfire? The taste sensation. Oh no, you are a lettuce muncher, aren't you. But still. Delicious, don't you think.'

'No, I did not know any of that, David.'

'I am a mine of facts these days. A mine, I tell you. It is driving Polly crazy. I won't shut up. It's ever since I opened up this new window on here,' Cavendish tapped his visor, 'that permits you to absorb an audiobook at six times the speed of the actual narration. It allows you to do so many other things at the same time. But don't think I don't envy you. I wish I had your life too, for sure. Living in the right here and now. Listening to the owls, without distraction. Firewriting on your coppiced hazel. See, the thing is, Bob, I spoke to Dad about the field a couple of times, and he couldn't remember anything about what you said. And now, well, you can't really talk to him at all. It's just isolated words and dribble. Sometimes he'll just say the word "anvil" or "lips" and a nurse will come in to mop up, and that will be it, for three days. Terribly sad for all of us. You know what he was like, Bob. He's a generous man. To his own detriment, it could be said, at times. He could sometimes offer people things he shouldn't. Maybe it was a flaw, but it's one of the things we all miss about him. Because what he is now, in that bed in that home... it seems terrible to say it, but it's not him. It's very heartbreaking for all of us to see.'

'I am sorry about that, David. It must be very difficult for you. But I do have a record of the payment on my bank statement: £68,000 transferred from my account to his.'

'If that's true, that's true. But who is to say what the money was for? Is there a record of that? Perhaps it was for something else you owed him. Maybe it was a gambling debt? Ha! We are all getting older and facts get misremembered. Isn't that the way with all of history? We think Indians killed buffalo with tomahawks but really they often didn't. They killed them with cliffs and songs. No, but seriously, we could talk about this, and that is fine, but I think the best way would be for you to contact the people you need to contact, and for them to contact some people in another office who act on my behalf, and that way we can move forward, or not.'

'I've noticed some posts in the field, and some string. Someone's painted numbers on the ground.'

'As I said, I think we could talk about this, and that is fine, but I think the best way would be for you to contact the people you need to contact, and for them to contact some people in another office who act on my behalf. I hope you have a nice afternoon in your house, Bob. That balcony must be a very nice place to sit and watch the world go by.'

On the way back down the track, as an act of defiance, Bob cut left through a gap in an attractive row of mossy-rooted beech, and across the Cavendish land, towards the river. As he did, he saw Cavendish's eight-year-old son, the freshest and most up to date of all the David Cavendishes, on a chair in the middle of one of the back fields, also talking animatedly into his visor, in much the same way his dad had, and with a smaller version of the same body. It gave Bob a vision of an entire alternate version of human history, measured entirely in David Cavendishes, all getting gradually more feckless and avoidant and lardy and technology-obsessed, until finally you reached the last David Cavendish of all, who was just a small shiny circuit box sellotaped to the top of a large blob of congealed out-of-date butter.

You could hook down from here, as a trespasser, to one of the most attractive and clandestine stretches of the river: a place of plaited lichen and abrupt rocky declivities and deep plunge pools where he and Sally had often swum in spring and summer. One of the advantages of Cavendish's fecklessness was that the fields down on this furthest section of the farm had reverted to meadows and now bled seamlessly into the wilder, beardier terrain beyond that was owned by only the water. Directly there, along this eastern bank of the river, was the route Sally had taken home on a day he'd never forget when he lost her up on the high moor. Half a mile further up the valley was an abandoned cottage, reachable down a steep track on the most resilient off-road vehicle but never boasting its own electricity and unoccupied for over fifty years, although it was said that a rich London banker now owned it and the land around it. It was marked on Bob's Ordnance Survey map as 'Megan's House'. The top branches of an alder tree now poked out of its roof. Every time he walked past it, he remembered Sally talking about the terrible things that had happened to pianos during the middle of the last century, when they were elbowed out of the hallowed place they had traditionally occupied in middle-class homes by televisions; the way people had burned them and nihilistically taken axes to them. All that craftsmanship gone, just like that. It made her want to weep, she said. He forgot now how they'd got onto the subject; maybe it was just because they'd been speculating about when Megan's House was last occupied and had decided it was probably around the time the first TVs started turning up in people's homes. Or maybe it wasn't that at all and was just the usual scattershot flow of conversation when they walked. Often, they'd follow the river all the way up to the bare, blasted moor at the top, and beyond. She was rarely without an observation and for every quirk of nature, every bit of wild growth he noticed, she noticed two more. Her mood seemed to rise with the moor itself. He'd always have a fold-away handsaw in his rucksack, in case he came across an old gate that had been thrown into a hedge. That's what the farmers and the National Park authorities did when they replaced them: left them to rot. He'd find about one a month on average, on their walks, during that period. If he was lucky, he'd find a latch still attached to it and, if he was super lucky, it would be one over a century old, darkened and bruised by the decades.

He decided not to turn right up the valley today, and instead fought his way over and under fallen trees above the river, until he joined the wall on the far boundary of the field, his field. The wall arced around and became part of the old bridge, then continued to arc until it met the house. It was, in effect, a continuation of the house, although it had been here centuries longer. Perhaps the stone of the house looked incongruously smart and new next to the wall at first but now weather and time had done their work on it, the two co-existed happily, like a granddad and great-granddad whose generational divide had been bridged by their longevity. He noticed some clumps of hair trapped in the crevices of the wall, just beyond the bridge; badger, he assumed, or perhaps an intrepid moorland pony who'd wandered down from higher ground. There were a thousand kingdoms in the stone and, in each kingdom, a hundred cities, full of microscopic gardens. Who was to say what was in there was not the world? Who was to say where the world began and ended at all? Why stop at the planet's biosphere? But, also, why go further than the end of the road? Who was to decide where anyone's going concern began and ended? He remembered that period when it was all getting bigger and bigger, directly before the visor implants were approved by the government, when everything had seemed too enormous, too connected. You could talk to precisely as many people as you wanted to about any subject you wanted and because of that there was never nobody not discussing or arguing about anything and there was never not anything to check and everything you did check just gave you more to check. The acceleration had been overwhelming, as if, just when you thought it was already going too fast, technology had hit black ice. It spun, unstoppably. It nibbled away at minds.

The future had arrived and it was not about outer space and fun, as he had been promised in his childhood, and Sally had been promised to a slightly lesser extent in hers; it was about gossip and meanness and the abolition of reasoned discourse. Addiction drove it and corporate greed drove the addiction. Neither Bob nor Sally had even been big users of social media but the space that opened out in their days when they disconnected, after the big changeover, left them gobsmacked. After the impulse to check gradually dissipated, because there *was* nothing to check any more, something else happened that they had not been expecting: they did not just regain their minds, they regained their bodies. They became more aware of their stomachs and hands and feet and sexual organs. They read a hundred pages of a book without moving from the place they sat. Their meals tasted better. Snow felt like snow again when it fell on their faces, like snow had felt when they were twelve. The universe became something you could roll around in the palm of your hand and feel the texture of again.

Sometimes they would go to towns and the city, or even to Underhill, and when they did they often saw people standing outside shops, standing in the road, standing in tram queues, screaming and ranting into their visors. Once such a thing would have been deemed deeply antisocial but everyone was used to it now. Sally and Bob kept their distance, because that was expected of them, as visorless people, and because they desired to. Each time they would think of these strangers 'You are arguing with a person you will never meet about something that will never be resolved and this is your one time on earth' and they would be glad, as hard as it had been, for the decision they'd made. And it *had* been hard: it made facts – facts about tomorrow's weather, or a song they liked, or the date a monarch died – suddenly, frighteningly elusive, until they remembered there was a whole other way to come across facts and it did not make life worse. A dazzling daily sense of hope and possibility seemed to have been blown out like a candle, until they realised what it had always been was a facsimile of hope and possibility, a fast-food version of want that you kept wanting even though you always felt ill afterwards. She'd not lived as long as she should have but he could reassure himself that at least she had not spent the last decade of her life in some suspended attention-deficit simulacrum of existing.

They were both Taureans: him early, her late, just a day from being a Gemini. He never forgot her birthday, even now, but he had forgotten his own again, for the second time in three years. It had been last Friday. He had realised he'd forgotten because the following day while loading the stove he'd found a parcel left under the log store. It was from Sam. Inside was a dark brown latch, with a beautiful weathered curve to its ring. Bob dated it as late 1930s, maybe earlier. 'To Bob,' said the card inside. 'Many gates still left to open! (Found up by the Trembling Hill Mine in January.) Love from Sam and Cami.' In the post, which always arrived in late afternoon nowadays, another package arrived. The postmark on it was Hungarian, which made Bob think it was probably from Martin.

The rain seemed to be holding off so he'd decided to walk down the far end of the combe to thank Sam for the present and to take him a ninety-year-old book he'd found for him featuring a collection of intricate illustrations of moths. Cami, off work from the hospital today, had opened the door and as ever an ache – a complicated ache, with a hole in its centre – had creaked open in him when he saw her smile. She had wished Bob happy birthday for yesterday and said Sam was out, surveying a type of newt that had unexpectedly returned to a lagoon down near Torcross, but that he was welcome to come in for a cup of tea anyway.

He'd thanked her but declined and said he'd stop by again at the weekend. Neither Sam nor Cami had ever been anything less than warm and accommodating to him, almost treating him like a second father at times, but he was also aware how magnetising he found their combined energy and how his loneliness made him more drawn to it. And because of that, when he was around them, or thinking of being around them, it was as if there was a little warden in his head, constantly checking he didn't overstep the mark. His admiration for the way they lived – surviving resolutely visorless in two poorly paid jobs, knowing they would never buy their own house, reading, knitting, planting, making, learning – was so deep, it was important not to be seduced into believing he was part of it.

The rain had begun again on his walk back and, because he had known the patch of sky above him for a quarter of a century now, and the patterns of all its varying moods, instinct told him they were in for a few more of those heavy days when all the moisture came down and hit them at speed, when the river filled up and made its presence so rowdily, overwhelmingly felt that everything else was put to one side and life became a matter of waiting it out until the water decided to calm again. At the second of the humpback bridges, three men in visors and fluorescent jackets had been watching a white van, driven by science, attempt to manoeuvre itself through the narrow gap between the stones. Each had looked like he wanted to offer the van some advice. The taller of the three men – fox-faced, sixtyish – had seemed familiar to Bob but he couldn't quite place him. That was nothing new these days, and the main worry that went with it – that the person would be someone who knew Bob well and would be offended by him not remembering them – was moot, since each of the men had ignored Bob, noticing him less than they would have if he was a minor gust of wind. He'd walked on, past an Edwardian post box in a cottage wall, repurposed as a plant pot. And, as he had, he'd remembered Sally talking about the story she had begun to write one day about an obsolete nineteenth-century post box where somebody posts a letter then gets a letter back from a person in that century, who becomes their penpal. She had got a third of the way through writing the story then abandoned it. She said she always had the ideas and the beginnings but lost interest in finding out how things ended. Her notebooks were a mirror of this, always two thirds blank, even the ones where she wrote down notes and reminders about her tuning jobs.

More and more, he found landscape and the landmarks within it sucking him back into past conversations, ghost feelings, old ambiences. It went beyond that, though. Even without the power of an evocative image as a trigger, he was able to spend whole hours – sometimes longer – swimming in a vanished event or afternoon. Perhaps this made him no more present and mindful than those who wore the visors but at least his mind was his own: nobody was dictating his memories to him and organising them into albums on a screen. Some of Jim's hair he'd found trapped beneath the piano lid while cleaning it a couple of weeks ago – the hair still turned up in the oddest places, even all these months after the dog's death – spun him off into an afternoon from two winters before, when he'd held Jim on his lap and gently cut knots of matted fur from his stomach, as Jim had lain there with a trusting look that broke his heart as it happened and rebroke it now as it rehappened. Maybe he misremembered much of what he lived through – timescales, sequences, the maths of it – but as he dipped into it via memory the feelings were refelt just as strongly, if not stronger.

He opened Martin's package, which turned out to be an album he had put out via his new label over in Hungary. 'I finally, fucking FINALLY, got this together!' said the note. 'Miss you, you hairy bastard. M. x' The record was called *Penny Marshwort: The Songs of RJ McKendree*. Martin had been obsessed for years with the work of McKendree, an American singer songwriter who'd blown across the edge of the moor in the late sixties and written a set of haunting folk songs that were coated in the place and the time but also in something otherworldly, something a little like shattered glass, something you couldn't quite piece together in your mind as you heard it. Martin, in a dogged fuck-the-naysayers Martin way, had been hugely instrumental in getting the late McKendree's work to a wider audience, even half-written a book on him many years ago, and now, with the singer's cult following growing, he'd managed to assemble an impressive group of neo-psychedelic songwriters and sensitive troubadours to pay tribute to his work. Amongst the covers of McKendree's songs was even a version of the title track by the reclusive former pop sensation Taylor Swift, released under the pseudonym 'Maddie Chagford'. Bob noticed that Martin's musician partner Reka was featured on the record too and wondered if that might turn out to be a bit of jarring nepotism on the part of Martin, but her rendition of 'Little Meg' – a traditional local folk song already made unrecognisable in McKendree's reworking of it, very different to the version Bob had heard Sally sing a couple of times – was utterly fantastic, and like nothing Bob had heard before: a half-chanted incantation that somehow managed to be simultaneously a brooding funk workout and sound like somebody inventing electricity in a moonlit recess in some rocks above a beach. Over the dirty dishes in the sink, as the record played, the identity of the fox-faced man on the bridge came to Bob. It had been Jac, his neighbour from the long house, all that time ago. But the fact meant little to Bob and he was mostly elsewhere in his mind. Something – he wasn't sure precisely what – had taken him back to a night in the summer of 1999, maybe a year or so before Martin had introduced him to McKendree's music. A club in Covent Garden, mostly full of tourists. Seventies-disco-themed. Martin, lit by booze and the city, trying to convince two Portuguese women that Bob had acted in porn. Bob, playing along, but wincing inside, feeling, at thirty, too old for it all, on the cusp of a form of cultural retirement. He'd lost his jumper – his favourite – at the end of the night. Forty-four years ago. The same gap separating his birth from the year Mussolini put Italy under a dictatorship. But from here, right now... an almost touchable time. Felt like the end of something, palpably. A deadened and toxic sensation in his oesophagus on the walk to the train station afterwards. A new resolve building out of that deadness. A Chinese restaurant. A wasted meal. Hard to eat when you're that particular kind of drunk. Martin had an extra job, as well as the writing, talent scouting for a record label. That was it: they'd been to see a band he'd been tipped off about. 'Rucksack full of wank,' he'd said, turning to Bob after three songs. 'The tedium compels me to go somewhere and dance.' 'Dance' being Martin's euphemism for fuck, but not always. Sometimes it meant fight, too. Always up for an argument with a stranger, Martin. A couple of times, chasing a woman, vanishing in the process, he'd left Bob stranded. Nowhere to stay. Five-hour gap until the morning train. Hash browns and a quarter kip on a cold metal bench. Bob forgave him. Always. Then one other night. A bit later. Martin on cocaine, wolf-eyed. Ripped Bob's favourite shirt off after finding out he was moving far away, to Devon. Bob forgave him less for that. But still forgave him.

In the forty-eight minutes the record had lasted, the river had redoubled its cry. The pounding bass of the rain was no match for it. The ambience was all treble. It was being retuned by cloudfall. Bob took Martin's note and put it in a drawer in his sideboard. Also in the drawer was the latch from Sam, a couple of other old notes and letters from friends, two eleven-year-old parking fines,

Sally's papps wedge, some pebbles and a sealed envelope with 'IN THE EVENT OF MY DEATH' written on it, containing a letter instructing the house and all the possessions within it to be given to Sam and Cami. He found a browning floret of broccoli behind the kettle and tossed it into the river, which devoured it. Wavelets lashed at the bridge then sprinted under the balcony. The water had been higher than this but rarely faster, and he could hear the granite grinding. Fleur had once said that it was a good job the boulders were under water because with the force that they rubbed against each other they could probably start a fire.

In late August the new dwellings began to go up: A-frames, oak. The chainsaws took down Edna's tree in minutes, making a mockery of all the years of its slow bittersweet decline. He'd been ready, having seen the sign on the lane at the top of the hill a few weeks earlier. 'BLACK DOG PARK: A Moorland Experience' the sign announced. Three acres of gorse bushes, tussocks, ferns, brambles – a bona fide galaxy of habitats for tiny creatures – were smoothed to a neat, levelled-off brownness. Men in hard hats with visors beneath the hard hats made offerings to the river of sandwich wrappers, drink cartons and urine. Jac sometimes milled amongst them, clipboarded, vulpine, pointy of face and hand. Bob considered taking him some of the manure he'd requested by text, with an apology that it was twenty-four years late. Maybe a couple of thousand tonnes of it. One evening at dusk after the men had all gone home, an actual fox, as if deeply offended to be so poorly imitated and misunderstood, wandered over, backed up and sprayed one of the half-completed lodges, and left. Fewer blue tits and dunnocks landed on Bob's feeders now. The pair of merganser ducks he'd been encouraging onto the balcony for most of the year had vanished. Bob looked at the solicitor's number he had written down in spring and did not use his still-functioning landline to call the solicitor's number he had written down in spring. He merely decided to further reduce what he had decided his world was. It now ended at the river's midpoint. Nothing else was his concern. There was enough to take care of here on the other side, anyway. He was still finding a lot of hair in the house. He began to wonder if after all some of it was his, not the dog's. He threw the hair in the river and the river made it vanish. The water level had been higher than usual for most of the summer and, because it was always higher in winter, he looked at the bridge and wondered if this winter would be the one when it finally happened.

On the occasions when they'd climbed the valley to the high moor, on the opposite bank, on the unofficial path, they'd learned a lot about all the secret places where the water gathered its voices and power. It was a long, vertiginous, weaving stretch of ground: almost three miles to the very top. All the way, the moss got thicker, the dripping sounds heavier. Often, by the time you reached the top and emerged from the woodland, you were on a murky cloud planet. Black shapes hovered in front of you, not making their identity known until the last moment. Ponies, sheep, gorse, rheumatic witchering half-trees that had been brought to the edge of death by weather, again and again, without being quite taken over the line. Vegetation up here got flayed by the bronchial output of the sky and only the strongest and wiriest of it survived. In the woodland, before they reached the top, the pair of them stroked the moss. It felt and smelt cleaner than any carpet. Sally said the tree trunks looked like they were wearing welly socks. He suggested that maybe this was why her hair grew so fast and big: it benefited from all this rain, like the moss. He was joking but maybe there was some truth in it. His own hadn't bounced back big and fierce like hers but its escape from his scalp had lost momentum since he moved here. They came back to the house with their clothes stuck to their bodies, their skin dripping, with many of the folds and creases they'd seen in the mirror first thing in the morning ironed out. But on the day he lost her up there it wasn't that kind of day. It was a frostier, stiller day – rare here – when the river was low and the moisture in the air was motionless. They decided to walk all the way up past the reservoir to Trembling Hill, to the abandoned silver and lead mine. By the time they got there the mist had fallen down, sweeping across the mine's deep black eye holes like a huge net curtain made heavy by years of cigarette smoke. They decided it was not wise to venture further and retraced their steps, past a pre-Bronze Age kistvaen that had been uncovered during the early part of the last century. Ancient trinkets and fancy evening wear buried deep in the peat. Visibility was reduced to almost nothing which meant he couldn't see the bit of the hill which always reminded him of a vast mouth that had had its teeth knocked out with a hammer, but he estimated that's where they were. The land began to tilt and the river, very faintly audible in the distance, was in the opposite direction to the one it should have been. His uncertainty made him press on more briskly, in an attempt to make the world make sense again, and it was his haste that caused him to lose her, although he didn't realise it for – what? – seven minutes, eight. He called out behind him into the mist, or was it really mist at all, no, and not fog either, but that other thing, quick and speckled and particular to the moor, that could not quite be categorised as either. Fist? Mog? Mog. The dreaded mog. The mog ate sound, swallowed it without needing to chew. Hearing no reply to his calls, the central worry of the last half an hour of his existence – that he had been upended into a visionless ghost universe with no way out by mythical beings – was entirely usurped by his guilt of what he had done in bringing her here. She'd not felt well that morning; the rash she often got across her face from the lupus had been worse than it had been for a while. He'd pushed her too hard. They should have gone the other way, over the back and up the lane and up the old sunken track – people said it was more sunken because of the medieval packhorses that pressed the earth down deeper and deeper – to look at a latch over there that Sam had told him about that had been made from two old horseshoes. It was the first time since the visors came in that he'd really ached for his old smartphone. Even though there'd never been a whiff of reception up here, he'd still ached for it.

She was only gone for two hours but it was the longest two hours he had lived since he was a child. Two hours of terror and weighing outcomes and decisions and possibilities. Two hours containing a novel's worth of small anxieties. He called and called for her then he listened hard for the river and found it and, even though it was not in the place it should have been, he followed it, tumbling and bumping back down the wild mossy valley as if pulled on a rope. Halfway down, he tripped on a tree root and landed on a gnarly outlying branch whose deep bloodwork on his left calf he would not notice until hours later. He could see only one thing and that was the telephone on the small table in the living room, and even though he couldn't factually see it, could see it only in his mind, he stared at nothing else until he had it in his hand. It was after he'd reached it, and called the moorland rescue team, and the police, and turned himself inside out wondering what else he could do, wondering if he should have stayed up top looking for her after all, that, in desperation, not in hope but in the pure inability to stay still, he began to march back up the valley and saw her walking towards him. Her hair glistened with crusts of frost and she looked dejected and sapped but she greeted him calmly. She told him she'd done just the same thing he had: listened to the river, then followed it. But why had it taken so much longer for her to get back? And was she OK? She said she was fine, it was fine, it had all been very simple.

She was here, and she was going to come into the house and lie down, and everything was going to be fine.

You didn't live on the moor and not know the stories about hikers being piskie-led on the high ground, disorientated in the sparkly mists, spun around, locked in place, tricked into thinking a place was another place. Tiny high-pitched laughter had been heard to ring out from deep in the cloud. Its melodies moved in circles, through the moisture. The little people – pixies, they were more modernly called, but he preferred piskies, the pre-twentieth-century version – came out from their hiding places and led you astray and the only way to reverse the spell was to turn out your pockets; he knew the drill so well but he'd forgotten and hadn't done it. It was just weather, nothing more, and the only reason it felt like dark magic was that weather itself was a form of dark magic, but he would never quite forget the stoned, tilted feeling he had up there that day, as if the landscape had spiked his drink. He knew it was just coincidence, that her health had been getting worse anyway for a long time, but it was after that day that the different period began for them. She had told him she loved him for the last time. She was withdrawn, more still, but not in a peaceful way. Her one remaining exuberance seemed to come out solely in the way she cleaned her body behind closed doors. It was as if the larger part of who she was had been cancelled. She worked less, which she'd said she'd wanted to do for a long time, but in the spaces that this opened up she didn't do any of the things she'd told him she would. One day he found her on the balcony with his craft knife, hacking into her hair, letting loose strands of it blow into the water below her. Next to her on the planks he saw singed grey tresses, candle wax. It was the first in a series of clandestine burnings, more often than not featuring small household objects, which culminated, a few months later, in him clearing out the fireplace one morning and finding the iron remnants of one of his sculptures in the cooling ashes.

'I am sorry, Bob,' she had said. She stared directly ahead into the ash and there was no meanness in her voice. 'But I didn't like that one.'

And then she got really ill, and was admitted to hospital. And he felt terrible that she was gone, and then he felt additionally terrible on top of that that he felt some relief about being able to be in the house without wondering where she was and where her mind was drifting to and what the next thing would be that she would set fire to. After the end, people talked to him like she'd been snatched from him but, although he never verbalised it, what he felt was that she'd been snatched from him a long time before that. Which was another thing that made that final instruction – that last burst of clarity and passion, when he almost saw who she used to be for a moment – so startling.

There had been a lull between the wooden posts first going in and the lodges beginning to go up, but now the construction work had begun, it was happening quickly. Within a fortnight, eight A-frames were up. Within a month, twenty. The foam on the edges of the river became different, tinged with pinks and blues. He did not see David Cavendish on the building site and did not expect to. Cavendish had not been interested in the field as a physical entity before and would probably be no more interested now, with the exception of the financial side of affairs relating to it. Bob wondered about his motivation, what could possibly come of this investment that would make the ultraworld the rich quasi-agriculturist lived inside more pleasurable and decadent. The pursuit of money for such people, past a certain point, seemed to be most of all a strident denial of mortality, and the more they were able to abrogate the nitty gritty of life via technology, the more emphatic that denial became. They used their wealth to protect themselves with bigger cars, to build more secure fences and walls to protect their three-dimensional living spaces, to build a digital wall around themselves to protect them from other parts of life. Finally, they seemed to want to use it to protect themselves against the banality of death, as if the cushion of power they had gained would secure a deluxe executive afterlife for them. But despite all science had achieved, and for all the money many had put into researching the idea, nobody had yet discovered how to live forever. In the end, the dust that would be David Cavendish would be no more exclusive or elite than the dust that had been Sally, the dust he had scattered on the hillside facing him two years ago. Dust that had immediately been washed into the river by the combe's heavy rains and, if some of it had remained on the grass and was now beneath the lodges, had surely now sunk deep into the earth.

The changes in building regulations and planning permission introduced by the government in the second and third decades of the century had been devastating for natural habitats on the edge of the moor. Underhill – and, to an extent, its surrounding hamlets – had expanded rapidly, but a lull followed: nobody had built anything new around here for several years. This perhaps made people in the valley a little complacent, slower to realise what was happening with the lodges and the impact they might have. Martina Whittaker had been over to tell him there was a residents' committee meeting scheduled to protest the development, to see if anything at all could be done at this late stage. He knew, because Sam had been over to invite him to the same meeting a day earlier. Bob said he would be there but when the night of the meeting arrived he found himself instead not at the meeting but on the balcony, a glass of whiskey in hand, watching the river. It was so full all the time now but tonight it was not angry. Its sound was more like the hushed chatter you get in an auditorium where people are waiting for an important announcement. Because the water level was now higher, more moss had begun to grow up the walls of the house, grey-green wiry wavy stuff. Autumn was happening and autumn never stayed long so you could more or less say it was winter and on winter's darkest days the combe let in so little light, it was like living down deep in the gap between two sofa cushions. Days soon became all beginning and end, a couple of bookends you convinced yourself was life. The sun found it difficult to get down in the gap between the cushions and kill the frost there. To maximise the last of the daylight before it all happened, he opened windows and doors all over the house. The through-draught stirred up more hair. There was ever such a lot. It showed him that maybe he hadn't really cleaned properly when he thought he had. Such a hairy place, the deep south west of the country. He thought of a film director, the only one he ever interviewed in his time writing for the magazine. Lived on a corner plot of land, a jutting elbow of salt soil, like a smaller replica of the far east elbow of the country where it was situated. Bald man. Immaculate house. No hair in it anywhere. But here, by contrast, you got hair on your walls, hair in your piano. One night in November there was a storm and Bob closed the windows. A long, sharp piece of concrete render fell from the roof, smashing outside the front door. If he'd been standing there, that would have been it for him, but he wasn't. The A-frames withstood the storm. Martina Navratilova – the lady who'd invited him to the meeting; he thought that was her surname but couldn't remember for sure – saw him when he was down the lane, looking for kindling. Her granddad had once punched a bull who charged at him. That's what Sally, who'd heard the story from Fleur, had once told him. Martina Navratilova said they'd all been disappointed not to see him at the meeting last week. Whittaker! That was it. Not Navratilova. That was someone else. He opened the gate leading to the field. He didn't like the latch on it: it was one of the ones with a coil, not yet bestowed with character by time. The wood made a nice sound but not the metal. He could see the highest of the lodges poking out over the hillside. It wasn't the most ugly set of buildings. You could convince yourself it was all quite rustic and pleasant if you blocked out all the beetles and dormice it had slaughtered. It was quiet now, no drills or hammers or diggers for several days. Some men in hard hats still wandered about with clipboards, not doing much. As, back at home, he pissed into the toilet with the blind up on the window facing the river, he saw one of the men looking straight at him from across the water. It might have been Jac but it was hard to tell due to the condensation on the glass. The man continued to stare and Bob continued to piss and then the man turned away and right then Bob knew Bob had won.

She used to say she wanted to run away.

'But you are away,' he'd say. 'Look where we live. We couldn't be much more away. Maybe if we lived in northern Canada or Finland or something, but not here.'

'Yes, I know, so why does it feel like that?'

There'd been a man, a customer, some bloody weirdo, who wouldn't leave her alone, kept wanting his piano tuned over and over again when the thing was totally fine, could not have sounded better, then when she told him she couldn't work for him any more, he contacted her via a fake identity on social media, tried to book her services again. It wasn't quite frightening enough to go to the police about but it had scared her. But it wasn't even that. It was a prevalent feeling at that particular time: a feeling that it was all in your face, everyone, everything, all the time, on your screens. They both had dreams about total strangers filing into their house, telling them what was wrong with the way they lived. It wasn't his fault and it wasn't hers; it wasn't most people's fault. People's brains – everyone's – were still pre-industrial village brains, brains built for the nineteenth century, and the eighteenth century, and a lot of the centuries prior to that, and could not be expected to cope with this overflowing rush of world, this full spate river of statement and opinion. But then after that they had felt like they *had* finally run away, for eight years, and maybe even for the two different years that came after. She, he knew, had felt more like she was in a place. And that made him more confident that sprinkling her remains over the thing – he forgot what it was called now, but it was green, and directly across the river from the house – was the right course of action. It had been a good time, that period. But he could not say if it was her best time. He could not even say if it was his best time, even though he told himself it was. A lot of it was guesswork, how you remembered your own life. He could not feel his body and mind as it had been on a day on a Tuesday afternoon in 1998 or a Thursday morning in 1982 or a Saturday evening in 2006. But sometimes when he went away from the present and swam about in snapshots of memory, he got close to it. Music helped. She told him about that once: how melodies worked, stimulating neuro-pathways that other things couldn't. In the orchestra she was in, they played old songs for people who had the illness. The big disease with the little name. No, that was a line from a song about something different. The little disease with the big name. No, not a little disease. A horrible thing, anyway, and music somehow penetrated it, took them back to something, revived something.

He wanted to play the piano. It shouldn't just sit there, gathering hair. The desire had come over him out of nowhere. Would it be too late to learn? Why had he never asked her to teach him? Was that neglectful of him? Could he have taken more of an interest? At least found out how it all worked? He opened the lid and wiped the hair off a couple of the keys and pulled some more out of the gap between them and hit the keys experimentally. He noticed starlings, more of a plume than a murmuration, out the window and as he did he felt this had all happened before: the opening of the piano, the slight cough caught in his throat, the birds, the bottle of Baby Bio on the window ledge. It was a kind of déjà vu he experienced now, but different to what déjà vu used to be. It always felt like he was experiencing the reality of a dream he'd dreamed and that he also knew what happened next but couldn't touch it. It was as vivid as when he got sucked into the past but it was different: it sucked him into the present, as imagined from the past. The moment always felt weighted equally with significance and banality until he lost it, like a small precious object dropped in a toilet bowl just as you'd pulled the chain.

The last person who'd played the piano had not been Sally but Fleur, not long before she died. In her seventies, she'd taken a younger lover – a town councillor of just forty-eight – and it had been the talk of the combe. Bob, now at a similar age, would do nothing of the sort. Firstly, how would that even happen? And secondly, it had not occurred to him as an ambition. He had met Fleur's younger man just once, a reedy human with a nervous chuckle who, even though he was of a roughly equal width and height to Fleur, gave the slight impression of living inside her coat. The encounter had been on the lane, around this time of year, and Fleur had talked about how late the bats were staying around now, and how much it worried her. Now they stayed around even later. December, sometimes. 'GO HOME, bats,' Fleur had said, to the bats.

Bob had never put a blind or curtain over the large skylight Fleur had installed in the bedroom, since it would have been too tricky, and waking up with the dawn light had never been much of a problem for him. But it could be confusing, on nights when the sky was clear and the moon was at its fullest. It could make you as confused as a bat who should be hibernating. Waking up to the bright white light, he had been known to head to the kitchen and put the kettle on, only to then look at the clock on the dining-room wall and realise it was somewhere around 2 a.m. So when he woke again tonight, with the moon full and the bedroom flooded with light, it was not initially perturbing to him. Two subsequent factors made him realise there was something extra at play: the glow was much more orange than usual, and the room was warm. Before he stepped out onto the balcony, before he'd even seen the deeper orange light, its spinning shapes, through the pane of the kitchen door, he knew what was happening, and with that came the knowledge that he'd always known it would happen, forever.

The fire was well under way, past the point of reversal or rescue. Five of the lower lodges had been brought to the ground and the flames were licking their way up the valley, deep into the bowels of the dwellings on the terraces above. The pure rage of it reminded him of the river when it was at its most unstoppable. It was not something that could be reasoned with. But standing on the balcony he did not worry for a second about it reaching him, or even about the smoke troubling his lungs. The river was at a brimming, tumultuous height – a height that defied the logic of the last few days' rain – and provided a protective barrier, a barrier even more inarguable than the conflagration. It splashed up high and wild against the walls of the house, splashed against him too. He realised, belatedly, that he was naked, but he was not afraid. He decided he could happily, very happily, let it take him: the river, the trees beyond, the valley, the moor, everything. He would be more than OK with that. He realised he was singing but he had no idea what the song was, only that he knew it. He grabbed his whiskey bottle from the kitchen sink and drank from it. The air smelled good and rich, like something being turned over and exposed, and he thought for a moment he could hear a siren in the distance, but then thought maybe he had imagined it, and he wasn't able to tell because his singing was so loud, and the river was loud too, and he had no wish for either to stop. On the right-hand side of the valley, where one of the higher A-frames – one of the taller, more high-specification lodges, which was to be rented at a greater price to the ones nearer the river – had fallen, the fire had also opened up a gap in the trees, but had not reached beyond that to the bigger trees where the valley began to get mossier, which would reject the advances of the fire with their immense moisture. The gap and all the light from the moon and the fire allowed him to see one particularly memorable, wide-armed oak and he thought about the time he had walked past it with Sally, which had been the same afternoon they'd walked past the abandoned house and she'd talked about people destroying the pianos in the fifties and sixties: thousands of them, kicked and smashed to fuck or set alight. It had actually been on this same walk that she'd told him about Martina Whittaker – yes, he had her surname now, and would not let it slip away – and her grandfather, who had punched the bull in the face when it charged him. There had been an old faded 'BULL IN FIELD' sign still up there at that point, which must have triggered the story. He recalled now also that he'd somehow got the details twisted: it was Martina's great-grandfather who had punched the bull in the face, not her grandfather. Standing there naked, illuminated by the flames, staring at the tree, he remembered everything Sally had told him; he did not forget a thing.

ME (NOW)

The village of Wychcombe is recorded as 'a manor call Wickcoomb' in the Domesday survey of 1086. By the thirteenth century, the parish could boast two churches: St Constantine's, situated precariously and impractically on a granite escarpment 730 feet above the main street and now no more than two ruined walls, and the still-standing St John's. By the 1500s, Wickcoomb had split into two settlements: Wychcombe and Underhill. After this point, Underhill expanded and Wychcombe stayed more or less the same size, coming to resemble, from above, a densely wooded forked tail attached to the posterior of the larger settlement. The 1921 census recorded the population of Underhill as 666, causing much merriment in the four alehouses the village then possessed, although by the census of 1961 that figure had dropped by 98: a reduction often assumed to be down to the human cost of the fight against Hitler but in fact down to the progress of agricultural machinery and the subsequent decrease in rural employment opportunities, resulting in an exodus of residents to urban areas. Many in the village would come to remember the war as the most fulfilling period of their lives. Most of the wealthier households by this point had a wireless, which had invariably been sold to them and repaired by a Mr Henry Salter of Plymouth, a small man who rarely paused for breath while imbibing liquor and telling his many embellished stories of life on the road and who, on his trips over to charge people's wet batteries, would often stay on for a few days and organise sing-arounds amongst his drinking companions. Always matriarchal, the village in this period became even more so. Social gatherings were organised by Land Army girls who had taken occupation of the outlying farms and Wychcombe Manor. The manor had until late in the previous century been the ancestral home of the Bambury family, who during the late 1700s kept fourteen parrots and England's last house jester: a man of barely four feet three inches in height whose routines included chewing the feathers off live sparrows to see if they would still fly (they didn't). These days the mainline train barrels over the viaduct past the luxury flats the manor has now been converted into, as passengers strive to stifle their irritation at the sound of one another's antisocial mastication and shrill offspring. Sometimes, a fox, hare or a deer will be visible from a window, but it is a rare commuter who will notice, since most are too deep inside the more compelling universe inside the screens they take with them everywhere. Few look up to admire the abandoned but still very attractive Wychcombe Junction station where some of those very foxes who run alongside the train have been known to sleep and breed.

The passenger railway arrived here in 1847, although it was predated by almost two decades by another, which took granite across my flanks, down to the coast, where it was shipped off and used to make bridges and walls. Before it fell under the infamous axe of British Railways chairman Dr Beeching in the 1960s, Wychcombe Junction – and its now defunct adjoining branch line – brought many a carless traveller to the moor. The station might also be considered partially responsible for an openness to outsiders not common to all villages in the area. Many who have visited Underhill have remarked upon a feeling of being 'protected' or 'watched over in a kind way'. It is thought that this can largely be put down to the presence of Underhill Tor, towering over the village at 1,350 feet, from whose summit it is said, on a clear day, both coasts of the south-west peninsula can be seen. Home to an acclaimed golf course and once believed to be the site of volcanic activity, the tor is not subject to the hype of some of the other more talked-about hills of the south west but is every bit the match for any of them in terms of history and natural beauty, and outdoes most of them in terms of height and girth, making, for example Glastonbury Tor, at just 518 feet, look kind of weedy by comparison. The tor is distinguished by the pile of rocks at its peak which have been variously likened to 'a step stool' (not totally inaccurate), 'a bumpy kind of nose' (maybe), 'some piled pony poo' (way off), and 'a small mystic staircase' (yes!). On its rear slopes is found some of the most beautiful ancient woodland in the country, hosting an abundance of wildlife, including roe deer, marsh fritillary butterflies, woodcock, bog asphodel, ring ouzel, cuckoo and kingfisher.

Look at me. I have fallen into my old trap of talking about myself again, haven't I?

You are all very fast nowadays. Nearly all of you, anyway (I strive to steer away from generalisation). I wonder where you believe you are going with it. It's an illusion, of course, most of the time: speed, and the efficiency and ease it promises. A new superfast train corridor smashes through ancient woodland, fucks over a couple of Elizabethan farmhouses, rapes and pillages the homesteads of hares, otters, stoats and badgers, but it's OK because Stewart will be home from the office a whole half an hour sooner, and be able to use the time to play computer games in his living room, rather than on the go. Your connections and your engines get slicker yet you feel more rushed, more pushed, and the days evaporate like never before. You fly at warp speed towards your destination, thirsty for it, never stopping to consider that destination is another word for death. You do not factor in what is missed until it is too late. The default position is that progress is pace. But when will this state of nirvana that it's all leading to occur, where each person will operate at peak speed and be perfectly happy and undelayed and no longer have to walk or use their mind? And will it all be worth it? Away from technology's grand illusion, everything moves at the same speed as ever. A grand old beech, poorly for some time, was felled on my shin yesterday. The 211 rings on its trunk tell the truth. Run your finger along them. They're smooth, consistent, redoubtable. The space between them didn't change just because somebody invented the microchip or the fax or the microwave oven.

It would be so much easier if there was one individual to blame for it, rather than collective human greed and self-delusion, if we could, say, pin it on Bill Gates or Steve Jobs or Dr Beeching or Tim Berners-Lee, but we are not in a superhero film, where a supervillain is mandatory; we are in the world, where supervillains are amorphous entities made of money and nepotism and spin and many many grasping hands. I will say this, though: Beeching trod on my toes once, during his brief destructive reign as British Railways chairman, and he was the smuggest of gits while he did it. He didn't even take the time to learn to pronounce Wychcombe properly before mooching around the station with his clipboard, condemning it – gave it the long 'y' at the beginning, like some nobhead. 'WHYchcoombe Junction, you say, over in Devon? Hmmrph. I suppose that is feasible, provided I am back in East Grinstead by supper.' Afterwards he submitted his findings to his boss, Ernest Marples, the Minister for Transport, who, it should be noted, was married to Baroness Ruth Alianore, a tarmac heiress who held a stake in the M1 and other new major roads. I rued a lost opportunity, so when Beeching returned eight years later, to officiate at the opening of a new heritage steam railway in the area (the chutzpah of the man!), I was ready. It was a windy day and the sharp, heavy tiles I succeeded in dislodging from the roof of the station as he walked past came within eight inches of doing their job, but ultimately – being six miles from here – it was outside my range.

No, I am not able to control weather. You could say I just have a stake in it, like Baroness Alianore and her early motorways.

Unlike a tree, I don't have rings, and they don't grow. I flourish, then I die back, then I flourish. The circle is not unbroken – at least not unless somebody builds a high-speed rail link through my core. But my contours do change. I have one more buttock than I once had. Over on my left knee, where St John's churchyard can be found, I'm lumpier than I once was. People look at the couple of hundred gravestones and they think that's it, that's history. They don't consider the others beneath the earth, all the centuries before that, all the bones piling up, changing the shape of the land. All the forgotten lives that felt like something more than this, something that mattered, when they were being lived. There was a period of about forty years, going from the last century, stretching into the very early part of this one, when the cemetery was kept very neat, over-mowed and over-strimmed. The shrieking of the beetles and butterflies as they died was a kind of tinnitus for me. Now mercifully the volunteers responsible for its upkeep lean towards a wilder aesthetic. The fact presents itself in stark beauty: wildflowers love dead people. On an early spring day like today, primroses, celandine and forget-me-nots are rife. It's a cheery technicolour place with a light mood but on an ink-washed afternoon in the darkest, wettest heights of winter walkers feel a shiver as they explore its corners. If the beheaded statue of John Maypoll, a six-year-old child who died of polio in 1913, or the three mysteriously nameless graves inscribed with nothing but 'Cholera, 1847' don't do it then the carvings inside the building itself generally will.

The oldest and crudest of these dates from the 1100s. Most frequently discussed is the Sheela-na-gig on the north wall, and what is variously referred to as 'The Bird Lady' and 'The Girls' on the font. These are described thus in the second issue of *Jack In The Green*, the pagan-inclined Devonshire history pamphlet, by the pamphlet's editor Simon Bridestow in May 1993:

'For me this is the most haunting of all the West Country's na-gigs, owing largely to the vastness of the exposed vulva and the angle at which the head is set back from the body, being redolent of both decapitation and extreme ecstasy. Such suggestion of ecstasy seems to support the argument that the na-gigs that appeared throughout Europe were not so much a warning against sin as a celebration of the power of the feminine. Not totally dissimilar in theme, and possibly carved at a very similar time, is the once-seen-never-forgotten Bird Lady carving on the font, in which a male figure adopts a supplicatory position below a female possessing some sort of club or staff and a wreath of hair, overlooked by birds and very similar apparent duplicates of herself. These duplicates have been called "sisters" and "ghosts". In 1988 while walking the north moor I met an old man called Graham who'd grown up in Underhill and told me that as a small child he'd heard the woman/ women on the font referred to as both "Sally Free and Easy" and "Old Meg" but had never known why.'

Other articles in the May 1993 issue of *Jack In The Green* include Jackie Tinsdale on Devon river sprites, Alan Bradford on the argument that some of the old carvings on the stones in the Trembling Hill stone circle are actually breasts, and Bangy Doddsworth's account of the time he was disorientated by piskies in the mist up on Combe Moor. Adverts included steer the attention of readers to a forthcoming gig by the partially reunited John McCandle's Dirt Band in Underhill village hall, the Whiddon Tracey Good Food Market and a family (in fact,

Simon Bridestow's) seeking accommodation on the high moor. Though barely remembered now, the magazine sold out of its 800-copy print run and was given pride of place in the post office by Jim Swardesley's predecessor, Jeff Bryant. When he took over, Swardesley continued the tradition of selling the work of local authors and, to this day, along with various walking guides, a visitor can, should they wish, while paying for their stamps, purchase such works as *Lunar Freedom*, the new collection by Kathy McGregor, better known as The Nude Poet. The cover features a tasteful shot of McGregor from behind, unclothed, sitting in the centre of the Trembling Hill stone circle, watching the sun rise over my head.

Looking down towards the post office now, I can see there is quite a queue outside. Swardesley, as ever, handles it coolly, cracking jokes, enquiring about the health of spouses and children and grandchildren and grandparents and parents, showing an uncanny recall for first names. 'SIT!' a woman yells at a Japanese Akita outside the door, sending a tremor through the waiting line. 'I think the whole village just sat down,' Swardesley wisecracks to Ruth Cole, who is waiting for a receipt for some handmade notebooks she just sent to Greece. Next up is Pat Gutteridge, who is here to collect her pension. Swardesley doesn't try her with a joke, as he knows from experience she's not one to stop for a chat. After this, in the stonewash jeans she is known for, she will purchase the two items she always purchases during her weekly shop, some vodka for herself and some sausages for the crows in her garden, plus some other provisions. She lives four miles from the village and always walks home, usually via Combe Woods. Last night a tree came down, entirely blocking the footpath, but today on both journeys she climbs the adjacent bank and vaults the trunk, in a manner reminiscent of a lanky nineteen-year-old boy. Next week, she will be seventy-one, an occasion she will celebrate alone by baking herself some cream cheese pound cake and watching a VHS of the film *The Full Monty*. People look at Pat and what they see is loneliness, countryness, a bony facade the world can't get past. But in her youth Pat engaged for several years in what those same people might describe as living. She resided in London, danced on tables, took cherubic musician boys home with her and told them what to do. Nobody would ever know now, apart from herself, but in a documentary about the touring life of the folk supergroup Equinox, she can be seen in a post-gig gathering in a hotel room, smoking and laughing, exuding Gaelic beatnik chic with her sharp cheekbones, black turtleneck and fringe. For an eighteen-month period, but no longer than that, people sometimes mistook her for the folk singer Anne Briggs. To her left in the hotel room sits the singer Donovan Leitch, whose advances, earlier in the night, Pat had batted away.

But Pat was quick-tempered in her youth, never one to stuff an opinion with feathers. Her fallouts were large, and often cataclysmic. When she lost a daughter to cancer and a partner to suicide, she – being an orphan – did not have a family to look to for support, and the friends she turned to instead let her down. The aggregate result of this, several years on, was her decision that the people she could truly rely on were crows. Crows, who never vanished during hard times, or stopped speaking to you when you gave them some unfiltered advice about their career. Crows, who would land on her arms and shoulders in the pub garden, always her arms and shoulders, never anyone else's. Crows, who ate every last bit of her sausages and never complained. They gathered around her waiting for worms as she turned the soil in her garden, which wasn't officially her garden, just a thirty square foot patch of ground between her back door and the dry stone wall where the moor in its harshest form began and which hadn't been claimed by anyone else and which some bastard could now prise from her cold dead hands if they wanted to take it away from her. People looked at her and thought, 'That's the kind of person who never cries.' But it wasn't true. Back in September of 2008, when she'd seen a crow nailed to a fence post outside the Cavendish farm, she bawled, sporadically, for most of the following day.

One day, when Pat was with her crows, turning the soil for her and for them, she found an axe. It's still only her and the crows who know about it, to this day. It's a quite remarkable axe, a little over ten inches long, apparently unused, and dating from 700 BC, although it might seem a little less remarkable if you knew just how many axes of a similar vintage were still buried on the moor. There are even a couple in the river around a mile further up the valley from Pat's, not far from the empty building the map calls Megan's House. I doubt they'll be found any time soon, as it's not a bit of the river people often have cause to get into. The ravine is too narrow and you couldn't get a boat down there. I could tell you properly about what is still buried here, down under the rivers, in the peat, in the soil beneath the reservoirs beneath the old farmland that they drowned to build them, and it would blow your mind into a million tiny pieces, which you'd never find again, and then those pieces would also sink into the earth, forever. So much is buried, so far down, and we live – even the more archaeologically inclined amongst us – only on the top one or two layers. Just as you can't any longer get to what Pat once was because it's buried under what Pat has become, with only the odd shard or two coming to the surface, you can't really reach the past of here, the past of me, and what I am made up of. But that does not mean it is not still there.

My thoughts didn't always take this form. I could have told you plenty of things but the language I spoke in was not the one I speak in now. 'Nope, sorry,' you would have said. 'That's just a noise.' But then the noise would have stayed with you, shaken you, loosened your bowels. You would have found great difficulty in not thinking about it, especially in the capacious hours just before dawn. But even then the noise was relatively comprehensible and well mannered by comparison to what it had been. Once, much further back, the noise came with fire and lava. Did it? I feel like I know it did, but it was so long ago, so all I can do is trust in the innateness of that feeling. And then the inevitable question follows: How did I go from that to this? How did I become so sapped, so self-conscious? How did I get this tediously well behaved?

It's your fault. You're seeping into me, in all your ways. You've been doing it for millennia, but you do it much more than ever now.

You keep photographing me. Why? Is it because you're worried you'll miss me when we are not together? I don't recall when the very first photo happened but the oldest known that remains intact can currently be found at the Devon Heritage Centre, at Chidleigh Babbots. It was taken in 1886 by Cecil Boyland, who, as a well-off rector, became the first resident in the village to own a camera. I am not the focal point of the image. That honour goes to the peat-cutting brothers Jude and Peter Mortimer, who can be seen outside their one-storey cottage, leaning proudly on their spades. A spectacularly large cockerel pecks away at grain to Peter's left. But I'm dominating the background, looking pretty damn fine, feeling myself in a major way, a slight monochrome suggestion of swirling mist above my rocks. It's probably the most mysterious and impressive I've looked on film, with the possible exception of a shot from 1977, where I'm looking down casually on a merganser duck taking flight above a clam bridge, captured by a lone, gangly figure, a regular visitor to the area, American. There was something about that day, too. A dank magic. I was in one of my moods, in the best and worst possible way. I think you can almost feel it in the photo, but not quite.

So, yes, there have been some good photographs of me. That is a stone fact and I have no quibble with it. But please can you stop taking them? Take a few, maybe, but not so insanely many. It's not helping anyone in the long run, least of all me. Why not paint me instead? Paint me like one of your French hills. Paint me like Joyce did. Not exactly like Joyce did, but as freely as Joyce did. Paint my trees in a way that reminds me of the time your Palaeolithic ancestors hunted wild pigs within them, swirl the colours and shapes in a way that hints at the still-discernible cellar holes where my old farmsteads have rotted back into the earth. Elevate me with your art, rather than devitalising me with your mimicry. Conjure your version of the fire-breathing cardinal enigma I once was.

It's getting dark now. Except that's not true because it never gets properly dark ever these days, even in the countryside. I can see the lights of the village twinkling in the bowl of land beneath my feet. It's one of the advantages of a hilly landscape, that view. It's extremely pretty when viewed from above. A fairytale scene. But later on, when people have gone to bed, some of those lights will stay on; there will always be some light somewhere, whereas in a true fairytale, the darkness, when it comes, is absolute. There are places where you still feel that dark up here, more than you will in 99.9 per cent of places in the rest of the United Kingdom. Some of the lonelier stretches of the river. Up by the kistvaen on Trembling Hill, half a mile past the silver and lead mine. But it's still not the same, not like the old dark. Imagine: you're in, let's say, 1544. You look at the carvings in your church from many centuries ago, a time that seems so unimaginable and unreachable, and you try to understand their meaning, and you can't read, so all you have to go on is what someone else in your village who also can't read told you. First came mass literacy, then came the light. We use the light and shine it on the literature. We read our pagan pamphlets and our books and our WikiLinks and attempt to comprehend the past, and often believe we do. But light, like speed, is often an illusion. We angle our light on our previous findings, which were also made in the time of light, and we make our theories and we think we understand. But that light is like a slim epilogue to history. No, not even an epilogue, nothing so large, more like a brief acknowledgements page at most. You just can't ignore the deep thick black that went before, just how long it lasted, just how dense and inexplicable it was, and all of what was buried within it.

I honestly can't tell you how dark it once was around here. I couldn't even begin to make you understand.

MESSAGE BOARD (2012)

Judith Sparrow: Has anyone spotted a horse rug on their travels? Purple, with red stripes. Last seen up near Hood Gate. Any information appreciated. My Thomas is getting cold.

Terence Black: Fantastic fish and chips tonight at the Stonemason's Arms. Just right. Mushy peas.

Diana Wilson: I had some last week. Overcooked.

Gary Oliver: Everyone keep their eye out there's a drone around in the night sky been seen looking for something worth pinching.

Gary Oliver: Don't suppose anybody has two concrete slabs they don't need any more?

Terence Black: Be vigilant about scam phone calls. A number has been calling me. International. Says I have been in a car crash nonsense I haven't.

Jennifer Cocker: Are Roger and Sheila OK? Haven't seen them for a while. They're very old and having trouble getting around now.

Sheila Winfarthing: We are fine. Thank you, Jennifer.

Jennifer Cocker: Someone should go round and check on them. I can't. I have the kids.

Sheila Winfarthing: I'm right here.

Gary Oliver: Anyone who has any engine oil they don't need please let me know. It shouldn't go to waste and can be used for heating my stone sheds.

Alan Rockwell: TALK ON OLD WOODCRAFT. WHAT HAVE WE LOST? UNDERHILL VILLAGE HALL. September 8th. 7 p.m. Alan Rockwell discusses woodland arts. SAMPLES FROM TALK: Sawn elm is often used for the partitions in cowsheds and other places where animals live, as it can cope with the kick of any beast. Cleft oak is often used for the rungs of ladders and can be trusted for its resilience. What does trimming a cleft with a froe mean? Find out. Snacks and non-alcoholic drinks. Entry £3.50.

Penelope Ralph: We have some oil you can have, Gary. But please can you return the drum afterwards.

Judith Sparrow: Congratulations to everyone on last week's cakes and plants at the Old Chapel. Over £300 raised for RNLI. A splendid effort for all concerned. Any village would be proud to raise half as much.

Diana Wilson: Well done but lemon drizzle cake was dry.

Mark Laggs: Heard a wheelie bin is on fire down near the Molesting Station. Think it belongs to the Cooks. They're not on here. I'm told they know.

Diana Wilson: So why did you write it on here?

Mark Laggs: Wanted people to know. In case it happens again. Could be kids. Only trying to help.

Judith Sparrow: Molesting Station??

Mark Laggs: The MOT Testing Station. Looks like it says Molesting Station. Because of the tree.

Judith Sparrow: You have an overactive imagination, I think, perhaps, Mark?

Jennifer Cocker: From a news report last year: 'RESURGENCE OF BURNING BIN CRAZE AMONGST TEENS. Wheelie bins are constructed from high density polyethylene, which when set alight releases carbon monoxide and dioxide. Such gases starve the brain of oxygen, and can be misinterpreted as a high, when in fact the burner of the bin is quickly and irrevocably destroying their own mind and body. Different coloured bins give off different fumes. Brown bins are believed to give off the most potent false high.' Useful?

Judith Sparrow: Does anyone have a horse rug for sale? Second-hand? Still haven't found the one belonging to my Thomas and the nights are drawing in.

Alan Rockwell: Thank you to all who came to the talk on old woodcraft last night. The total attendance was nine but I believe it was a case of quality over quantity.

Gary Oliver: There's a white goose on the grass at Riddle Bridge. If it belongs to anyone. It's OK it's just sitting there.

Megan Beaker: When I was a child my mother and father had many geese. As well as being eventually good for the pot, they provided a guard for the house and a deterrent when thieves were abroad. We did not lock our doors back then, of course.

Gary Oliver: Those were the days. My mate Rob in Stepsford never locked his door. Last August couple of junkies from Plymouth came up and cleaned him out. Left the whole house bare. Even took the family photos.

Mark Laggs: Old chair up for grabs if anyone wants it. Smells a bit of fags but not much. Will dump if no takers. Don't call on phone. No reception in the combe.

Diana Wilson: When you say 'dump', I do hope you mean at the Household Waste Recycling Centre.

Mark Laggs: FFS

Megan Beaker: I believe chairs do us more harm than good in the modern age. Squatting is excellent for the posture. We have forgotten this, as a race.

Penelope Ralph: Very true, Megan. Indigenous cultures know this.

Gary Oliver: Goose is still down at Riddle Bridge. Seems fine. Wonder if it sleeps there.

Megan Beaker: I named my favourite childhood goose Grunwald. When it came time to cook Grunwald, I was sad, but entirely accepting that this was the way of things. The fire was in the centre of the room which was what you would nowadays call 'open plan'. My sisters and I sat and watched the flames, with two oxen, who were also in the living room, as it was a very cold night. This was not long after my parents died.

Jennifer Cocker: Anyone getting cloudy water after issues the other day?

Sheila Winfarthing: And here I was thinking Roger and me were the oldest on here, Megan!

Mark Laggs: Keep it running and it will clear.

Penelope Ralph: Not strictly relevant because not quite geese but has anyone seen the door in the house up above Brent Moor, on the lane, which says 'DUCK' on it? I always think, 'That must be a really big duck who lives there.'

Diana Wilson: No.

Terence Black: Terrific steak last night (medium rare) at the Steam Packet in Wiliford.

Alan Rockwell: TALK ON THE HISTORY OF LETTERBOXES. HOW LONG WILL THEY REMAIN? UNDERHILL VILLAGE HALL. October 25th. 7 p.m. Alan Rockwell discusses the evolution of the posted letter in the UK. SAMPLES FROM TALK: Like Santa Claus, the first British post boxes were green, not red, but it was decided they were too camouflaged in their surroundings. The first red post boxes appeared in 1874 but it took another decade before all the green post boxes in the country had been repainted. The first British post box of all appeared in Wakefield in 1809. Snacks and non-alcoholic drinks. Entry £3.25.

Penelope Ralph: I have always admired the small Victorian post box in the wall down near Summersbridge. I recently found out that the reason it has a kind of soft brush in its mouth is to stop snails and slugs getting in and damaging the letters.

Gary Oliver: The way the world is going, some bastard will probably pinch it one day.

Diana Wilson: Post keeps getting later in the day all the time. Nearly 3 p.m. the other day. One day soon it will be so late it will be early again.

Alan Rockwell: In fact, Gary, you might find now is a relatively benign time, in terms of the theft of items in the custody of the post office. Attacks from robbers were so common in the late 1700s that the post office would advise customers sending money to cut all banknotes in half, send them at different times, and only send the second half after receipt of the first half had been acknowledged. I will also be covering this in the talk. Snacks and non-alcoholic drinks. Entry £3.25.

Judith Barrow: The post box in the wall of Linhay Farm also has a soft brush in its mouth. They put it in because some bees nested in there.

Alan Rockwell: The one beneath the Black Tree? Also Victoria-Regina, that one. I believe it's the oldest on the entire moor.

Diana Wilson: That tree has always been full of slugs and snails.

Megan Beaker: The Black Tree has always been what everyone in the village has called it. Nobody alive remembers a time when it wasn't there and wasn't black. A perplexing runt amongst its tall confident siblings, it never gets bigger, never dies, never withers. It is a tree of perpetual winter, a tree devoid of the relief of seasonal change. When people walk past it they often find their electronic devices misbehaving. Watches stop. Torches catch fire. Phones zap embarrassing photos to half-acquaintances, unbidden. It is said that many centuries ago a robber of the road – possibly one of the gang they called the Gribblins – was left to die in an iron cage attached to an earlier, blacker tree on the same spot, his last meal being three candles fed to him by a local resident, but that is just a story, teased and tickled by time. What is known for certain is that sheep have often been found dead on the boulder beneath the tree, rivulets of blood spilling from one eye. When lightning hit the tree during the early 1960s, a disgraced limping clergyman in his final half-decade of life, who'd settled here from up country, saw the entire trunk change to white and a face wag its wet tongue at him from the bark, but when he recounted the tale in the Stonemason's Arms later that evening, its authenticity was discredited because of his reputation, but also because he was quick with gin at the time and wearing an item of knitwear back to front.

Alan Rockwell: Thank you for this, Megan. Most edifying, and largely new to me. I have made a note in my journal.

Sheila Winfarthing: I remember that lightning strike well. 1962. Or maybe '63. I wasn't aware you were here as well back then, Megan.

Megan Beaker: I had already been here a long time by then.

Ted Wentworth: Sheep know 99 easy ways to die but are always searching hard for the 100th.

Gary Oliver: Stone sheds now toasty on these chillier nights. Thanks again to Penelope for the oil.

Mark Laggs: Ted some of your wall has come down up by Nettle Field. I saw a ewe on the road. Could be yours too?

Ted Wentworth: Thanks, I'll check. Could be Cavendish's.

Megan Beaker: A drystone wall should not have too much weight low down. The weight of the stones creates the adhesion that makes it trustworthy. Ventilation is important, especially in areas frequently subject to frost. The foundation of the wall is extremely important. Many walls are of double thickness. There is often a gap in the middle for what is called 'hearting': the placing of smaller stones, as a sort of filling. Even so, no mortar is used. This double thickness was echoed in many walls of actual dwellings on the moor, giving ample room for the interment of totemic objects and charms. Common plants that grow on drystone walls in the area include stonecrop, maidenhair spleenwort, wall rue, leafy dog lichen and – less often – the rare lanceolate spleenwort and parsley fern. Sheep – particularly the Blackface – will often seek out a weak spot in the walls, although a sheep that sees a hole in a wall will leave the wall well alone, for she senses it is in danger of collapsing on her.

Penelope Ralph: Whereabouts are you based, Megan? I don't believe we have met. Are you anywhere near Riddlefoot Lane?

Megan Beaker: Not far from there.

Gary Oliver: He's not on here so I'm posting for him but Steve Clayton's whippet Len had a seizure yesterday and ran off. Was seen by Cavendish's farm this morning at 7am but not since. Can everyone keep a look out.

Terence Black: Does anybody know if the Stonemason's Arms are still serving food in the afternoons? Can't seem to find it on their wwwbsite.

Jennifer Cocker: I spoke to Jim at the post office who saw a whippet running alongside the dual carriageway today. He said he stopped on the hard shoulder and ran after it to try and catch it and steer it away from the traffic but it ran off into Parker's Woods.

William Williams: I have some old sheet music here. Classical, but also some old broadsides and ballads. I keep holding onto it but it's just taking up space so if anyone would like to have a look and make me an offer, let me know.

Megan Beaker: The lyrics are mostly wrong.

Gary Oliver: Steve Clayton's whippet Len now been seen by Dimple Bridge, Fox Lane and Stumper's Cross. Nobody can get near him. Just runs in circles. The cancer has spread to his brain. Steve says best to just leave him now.

Jennifer Cocker: Oh, poor poor dog. Is there nothing that can be done?

Mark Laggs: Gary, do you still have that spare coving from last year?

Penelope Ralph: Funny story for everyone, going back to post boxes. I dropped Mike off at Modbury post office earlier where he was posting Sophie's birthday present and while I was waiting I drove around the block a few times to kill time. As I was coming back the last time I saw Mike coming out the door and, as he did, an Astra, exactly the same colour and model as ours, driven by an elderly lady, pulled up right outside the door, and Mike opened the passenger door and got in right next to her. She almost had a heart attack. I pulled up a moment later and we both apologised. She was shaken but we all laughed in the end.

Diana Wilson: Why did you go all the way to Modbury? It's miles away. There are at least nine post offices closer than that, all with reasonable opening times.

Mark Laggs: My mate Craig drove all the way from Devon to Robin Hood's Bay with a loaf of bread on his car roof. That was a Vauxhall Viva, though. They hadn't started making Astras yet.

Pete Micklewhite: Who does everyone use for logs and who is best (dry)?

Mark Laggs: I use Lloyd Warner down over the back side of the Tor but he's not the cheapest.

Diana Wilson: Surprising that Lloyd turned out the way he did. When you consider his father.

Jennifer Cocker: Can anyone hear the fireworks this evening? I have a lurcher and two cats, petrified, beside me. How can people be so inconsiderate?

Mark Laggs: Coming from the Rectory, I think. Sounds like war.

Diana Wilson: Call the police.

Judith Sparrow: Yes, I can hear my Thomas outside whimpering. He only neighs like that when he is very scared.

Pete Micklewhite: Thanks Mark. Lloyd is indeed a top lad. Bit different to his old man.

Alan Rockwell: TALK ON THE HISTORY OF VILLAGE NAMES. HOW DID WE GET TO WHERE WE ARE? UNDERHILL VILLAGE HALL. December 1st. 7 p.m. Alan Rockwell discusses the evolution of place names in the UK. SAMPLES FROM TALK: Did you know that Payhembury is called that because it was owned by a Saxon named Paega, and that Hembury once meant 'high fort'? Who was Totta and what was her ness (Totnes)? Who was Wineca and what was her leigh (Winkleigh)? Why is Underhill (Underhill) called Underhill? PLUS GUEST SPEAKER COLIN STAPLETON FROM BIDEFORD. Snacks and non-alcoholic drinks. Entry £2.75.

Diana Wilson: I'd have thought it was called Underhill because it's under a hill.

Megan Beaker: I know who Totta was. I met her and she was a supercilious prick.

Sheila Winfarthing: When was this, Megan?

Jennifer Cocker: So pleased to announce that our daughter Melanie has been selected to represent Britain at the Olympics in diving. This is the culmination of years of hard work and dedication for our Mel and we could not be more proud.

Mark Laggs: Well done Mel!

Megan Beaker: I used to dive, on frequent occasions. That was one of the reasons they selected me to take charge of our settlement, after my mum and dad died. I knew where the big sharp rocks in the river were and I knew how to pick my spot. I was able to stay under a long time, and I tickled trout out from under the granite. Within a year I could grab two at a time. Unatha and Joan (she wasn't called this but that's what you'd call her) were waiting for me above with my thick warm coat, which only I was allowed to wear. I was not alive much longer and believe my diving would have only improved, perhaps to Olympic standard, if that had been a thing. Later, when I had a different face and body but the same name, I remembered how, even though it was so many years later, and then again, and again. I never took the river for granted, as those who do rarely live to tell the tale. We said it had a voice. We called it Jack. But Jack's voice was many voices. It was the voice of my mum and my dad and my other mums and dads, and it is my voice too. I hear myself when I get close to it.

Penelope Ralph: Well, I don't know about anyone else, but I am enjoying Megan's stories a lot. Who was it who invited and confirmed you here on the message board, Megan? I don't think I have seen you around the village or the combe.

Megan Beaker: It was me. I did it. I invited me. I confirmed me.

Dave Busley: HAPPY DAVE'S GARDENING SERVICES. NO JOB TOO SMALL. COMPETITIVE RATES. CALL 01364 782435. INDOOR JOBS CONSIDERED ALSO. ALWAYS HAPPY TO HELP.

Rebecca Potts-Wellington: Bonfires are fine, but be considerate. Please check with your neighbours before lighting one. And DON'T do it on a windy day. Very antisocial. Naming no names.

Mark Laggs: There's a black lad running around Cavendish's top field. Not sure if anyone knows anything about him.

Penelope Ralph: Mark, this seems a bit racist. I don't see why it's cause for concern or that the colour of the skin of the running boy is relevant.

Mark Laggs: Typo! Black lab. Saw him on Squeezebelly Lane before that. Maybe was tied up outside Spar and broke his leash.

Mark Laggs: It's OK, he's Sue Pearson's. I just heard. She got him last week from Berry Pomeroy.

Anne Cherry: Free pair of Crocs. Size 6.

Jennifer Cocker: Has anyone seen Roger and Sheila recently? It might be worth going over to check on them.

Sheila Winfarthing: We are right here. Still walking and speaking in intelligible sentences without dribbling and making our own meals and everything. Some have described us as a miracle of modern science.

Anne Cherry: High-waisted jeans. Barely worn. Bought in Next sale, 2008/09. £7 ONO.

Megan Beaker: I lost my maidenhead around the back of the tor. It was the day of the fair. A French boy was responsible.

He wasn't the age of a boy and didn't think he was a boy but he was. There were lots of French on the moor, then. They had been in the prison, then were released, on the condition they stayed within the parish. At the fair there were heads on sticks, carved and painted black, and people threw rotten apples and onions at them and cheered. Mr Oldsworthy, Underhill's baker, played the fiddle. I could smell the nutty aroma that always lingered on Oldsworthy's dusty jacket as the French boy led me on past him by the hand and I knew the song from a long time ago and knew it was part of me. After that I could hear them start to play 'The Bonny Bunch of Roses'. Young dogs were wrestling, looping and twirling on the grass, out of breath. We went to the barn. It's still there. The cuckoo was crying from the tor top and as I looked into the stone in front of me and the French boy tried to find me and breathed hot breath into my ear I felt like I was the stone and I felt 15,000, not fifteen. The stone was full of stories and there would be more. But about this story I never told a soul. On the way home the words to the song were in my head: the roses one, not the one I felt was part of me. 'One morning in the month of June. While feather'd warbling songsters. Their charming notes did sweetly tune. I overheard a lady. Lamenting in sad grief and woe.' I stopped at a fallen tree and collected kindling, looking for the drier bits caught on branches above, like my father had told me. It had rained that morning but it was easy to forget that had ever happened.

Judith Sparrow: Terence Black, in case you are wondering, the Nissan Micra who you didn't thank when it made quite an elaborate manoeuvre down a farm track to let you pass the other day on the lane up to Hood Gate just beyond the sharp right-hand bend was driven by me.

Anne Cherry: Selection of old board (and other) games. Kerplunk, Downfall, Scrabble, Monopoly, Pictionary, more. All in excellent condition. £20 the lot. Individual prices considered if no takers.

Mark Laggs: When I was playing Downfall as a kid a bee once went in one of the holes on the turny bits, thinking it was a flower. I will always remember that.

Diana Wilson: Turny bits?

Megan Beaker: Someone said I once turned a man to stone. People retold the story, then embellished it. Even the unembellished version is untrue. I could not have done that if I wanted to (and I did want to, at times). But that doesn't mean the stones don't have a voice of their own.

Jennifer Cocker: Is Gary OK? I haven't seen him on here in a while.

Mark Laggs: He's been having a hectic time I reckon. Sorting the insurance and everything after his stone outbuildings burned down. I think he lost a lot of stuff.

Penelope Ralph: This year's Ball In The Hall will take place on June 22nd. Outdoor catering will be provided by Miranda's Kitchen. We are also very pleased to welcome Adverse Camber from Torquay, who will be enlivening proceedings with their mix of sea shanties, rock, ska and what the Plymouth Herald described as 'solid peninsula reggae pop' in a glowing 7/10 review. Tickets will be £10 and must be purchased in advance from the Stonemason's Arms or the community shop.

Mark Laggs: In case anybody is going up by Riddle Bridge, the road is closed. Massive fuck off elm has come down.

Judith Sparrow: Brilliant news! Thomas's horse rug has been found. Angela Paley from Wentworth Country Cheeses discovered it caught in a tree, a full half a mile from Hood Gate, and handed it in to Jim Swardesley at the post office. Jim called me and I went in and picked it up yesterday. Amazingly, it is only slightly torn. Of course, I'd got my Thomas a new rug in the meantime, because he can't go cold, so now he has two. He's an exceedingly happy horse!

~~Megan Beaker: Do you all sometimes hear me sing to you in your sleep? Do you notice how it intensifies when you are feverish and sick, how it becomes everything? Do you ever realise, as my song scores your dreams, that it has been the soundtrack to so many dreams in the past, too, but you never remember it when you wake up and are back in your surface world, which you laugh and shrug and joke your way through and pretend is the real story?~~

REPORT OF DEBRIS (2014)

I need a slash. I think I'll do it here. Gap in the tree curtain. Well-trodden. Ah sweet Mabel in heaven it stinks. Should have chosen a country lane instead. How many people have wazzed in this layby? Must be millions. Billions. Ye olde travellers on the trunk road into the west, unable to wait until the next rest facility. Services: twenty-one miles and twelve miles. Always try to get your horse to last out until the furthest one. Invariably a mistake. God, what's this ground made of. Weeds growing from pure urine. Don't think I'll kick off my new foraging career here. Let's leave that a while, shall we. Plastic bag caught in a tree. Nothing beautiful about that, whatever that emo kid in the film reckons. I was a big emo fan as a kid too. Rod Hull. Brilliant. Convinced it was a real bird until I was at least eleven. OK, here will do. Crisp wrappers. Plus-size drinks cartons. Do you want to get large for an extra 20p? Sorry, I mean go large. Litter bastards, slurping their McDiabetes after their day out to a renowned World Heritage Site. Tiffany, look here, isn't this remarkable, these larger blue stones were somehow transported all the way from the mountains in west Wales 4,000 years before cars or trucks or trains had been invented, although there is a conflicting theory that they are erratics which drifted in on Ice Age glaciers from their original resting place. No, Tiffany, leave it where you threw it. There isn't time. We have to be at Aunt Jackie's at six, and what's the point when there's loads of other crap there already and I'm sure there'll be a little man to come and pick it up before long.

That's better. Give it a shake for luck. Why is it they never do that in the films? Always goes back in the pants so quickly. Barely even a movement. No thespian concession to zipping up. Zero evidence of stains or droplets. Always a plot device piss, too, never just a piss. Is this a plot device piss too? 'If he hadn't have stopped, he would never have met that druid, and his life would never have turned around.' Doubt it. Who needs turning around anyway? It just means it's going to be that much more exhausting the next time, when you get turned back around the other way again. Could do with a drink. Just one. Three hours until the pubs open. The pubs where I'm going anyway. The Coach & Horses on Greek Street will be open by now. Johnny Slazenger and Steve Rizlas two pints of Fosters down, boasting about how they crushed another innocent with their knowledge of New York Dolls trivia. Pete Shapiro with another indie girlfriend, flicking peanuts into her cleavage ravine at last orders. Had a quiet word with the twat last time. Wanted to take her home myself and treat her good in good ways and bad in good ways but didn't; just walked her to the Tube station, asked her if she was OK, told her not to date music journalists and find a nice lad instead, a scientist or botanist or oil rig worker. Sign on a lamppost: 'LOVE CONQUERS ALL'. Arrow added between the 'CONQUER' and the 'ALL', leading to a 'FUCK'. Walked back into the pub and it looked like a battlefield, smelled like a yeast illness, oozed the spotty defeat of an old armpit. I put the Pogues on the jukebox and leapt around a bit while everyone else died in corners. Won't be doing that again. Not after last night. All gone now. You'll never work in this town again. Or mosh boisterously again in this town to snaggle-toothed Gaelic punk rock.

Going 60 now. Feels like 80 in this. Pleasant Jesus, are those poppies over there? Is that even real, or some fake carpet someone put down for a laugh to wind me up? There's a rattle that's bothering me. Hope this thing is going to make it the last ninety miles. Bought it from a granny in Enfield. 1989 vintage. One lady owner. Lady owner made me a cup of tea. Strong like I like it. Never seen a builder drink it stronger. Six digestive biscuits. Forced me to take the three I didn't eat home with me. Think the shady old crone might have turned the clock back, popped in a 1980 Lada engine. If it doesn't get me past Yeovil I'll sell it for parts and hitch the rest of the way. Better than the Renault 4 I used to have. Got nicked. Thieves changed their mind and abandoned it after 200 yards. Feck, I need MUSIC, but I've got no cassettes – who has, now, apart from hipsters and the dead? – so I'll carry on amusing myself by watching the place names zip by. Tintinhull? What sodding kind of name is that? I'm picturing North Sea poverty meets intrepid French reporting but sensing that's not what I'd find. Maybe that's it, that's why I became a journalist: reading all those Tintin books when I was ten. Never got the dog, though, did I, and it's all over now, isn't it, probably. Too late. Sorry, Snowy. Try an owner with a longer temper. You don't go decking Richard Peck in the most popular pub for north London journalists at 7 p.m. on a Friday and expect to walk out of it as an employable metropolitan freelancer. Don't regret it, though. Twat lied then tried to screw me out of a month's pay then when I sold his feature – *my* feature – to *The Times* he said he'd make sure I never got work from anyone he knew ever again. Too much silence about this shit, too much fear about what not being silent about it might cost you. Too many people in that world not from money being pushed around by people from money and not paid by people from money because the people from money don't understand the importance of being paid and the terror of not being paid. Too many people not from money complying and not sending the people from money sprawling across a lager-stained parquet floor, scrabbling for their glasses which they probably only wear as an affectation.

OK. Motorway now. Getting closer. Traffic slowing down. REPORT OF DEBRIS in orange computer letters. It's OK. Twenty-five miles left. This will be better. New start. Can feel the country air clearing up my eczema already just from those three minutes in it. Give me a week and I'll be a fully qualified country squire. Lazy afternoons of picnics and croquet and mild alcoholism. Looking forward to the pubs too. Saddlers and farriers and wheelwrights, sitting about, telling you about how they made their girth straps and shoe nails and spokes. You get the hippies down here, too, lots of them. Nothing hectic about anything. Very little aggro. A more meditative life. Finally get down to writing my bestselling memoir *Mindful Fighting* in which I explain how to stay totally in the present while lamping somebody at closing time.

Shouldn't get too excited. Room above a garage. Not exactly going to be Daphne du Maurier, am I. Saw her on an old documentary, saying her house wasn't too big just for her. Only 938 rooms. Quite modest, really, darling. Not as if it's the kind of place one *rattles* around in. Different bit of the wild west but the same in some ways. More trees, less coast, fewer ghosts of children who died in arsenic mines. I'll go down there too soon, though, Kernow. Loved both counties as a kid. Climbing trees. Any I could get into. As high as I could go. OK, off the main road now. Thank god. Left in such a rush forgot to do my road tax and was freaking out every time I saw the police. Always pulling me over, they are, perhaps sensing insurrection, despite my responsible adherence to the speed limit.

Giant rocks in the woods. Hobbitland. Came to a party near here in '99 with Jen. Big farmhouse where capitalist hippies sold their homebrew. Tiny men everywhere. Me towering over them. Tiny men and willowy women. 'You get taller when you're drunk,' said Jen. Correct, probably, as she is about everything. Best break-up ever. Still love her to bits, even though her family are poshos. Still looking after me even now, getting me out of tight spots. What are these things beside the road? Sheds? Look more like portals, bit charred-looking. Step in and everything spins and smokes and you fear incineration but actually just end up in 1968. Fine by me. It's where I'm planning on going soon anyway. Is this a road? I think it is, just about. Ah! Polytunnels. This'll be it. Jen said to come in the back way. So as not to embarrass him in front of his customers? I asked. No, because the main gate will be locked by that point, you prat, she said. Ooooh look at this, not what I had in mind when she said garage. I was thinking of the ones in Hackney. Don't get this there. Stone, pretty big, little old wonky steps going up to the living quarters. Daisies, multicoloured ones, growing out of them. I can deal with this. The place is just an afterthought for her cousin Titus, one of many annexes. Done pretty well for himself. Two years younger than me, Jen says. Not as if he started with nothing, though. Wonder what the main house is like. I'm fucking well early. Two hours. Saw a pub a couple of miles back up the lane. Sounds like a plan.

*

Wednesday. Titus has been over, brought three cucumbers. I tried to be polite about them, thanked him, even though if you ask me they taste of all the most disappointing parts of British life. He walked over to the window, turned this big Indian jug around, possessive like, stamping his authority on the space. I don't care which way around the Indian jug goes. It's not my Indian jug. Asked me how I was settling in. Great, I said, not totally fibbing. Refrained from complaining to him about the way if you're cooking a pizza in the oven you need to shove it right to the back then turn it around halfway through and even then it will probably burn on the edges and be frozen solid in the middle. He told me to put a rod down the septic tank if it gave me any problems. 'We are a tad feral around here, I'm afraid,' he said. He's all right, Titus is. Voice oozes everything he's from. Not super posh, laid-back Devon posh, as if the act of talking itself is a little tiring, as if words are a chair he's constantly pushing the reclining lever on. Heard that sound a lot here already. Reminders of my ingrained peasanthood everywhere. Bit alone but made some friends at the pub already. Maurice, a thatcher. Almost broke my fingers with his handshake. Saw Bob yesterday. First time in six years. Good to be close to him again. Grumpier than he used to be. Looks even more like a terrier. 'Mind out for newts,' he said, as I walked in. 'What?' I said. 'They're breeding out the back,' he said. 'They seem to still think there's a pond here.' Some people really own a room when they walk into it; Bob used to really rent a corner of that same room. Different now. Sense a new unwillingness in him to please. Listened to some records, a blast of stoner rock, proto-metal, some of our old touchstones. Didn't smoke. Drank tea. First time I've known him to be single. A good thing, too. Loved himself a loud, bossy lady, Bob did. Don't know if he still does. Always going straight from relationship to relationship with no time to take his clutter to the charity shop in between. Never the healthiest state of affairs. Big barrier to meeting someone on equal terms for him. Wouldn't have told him, though. Say something like that to Bob and he wouldn't express offence; he'd just go a bit silent then you wouldn't see him for an epoch. Hard to believe he ever lived in or near a city. Kind of bloke who whispers to sick trees and makes them well again. Told him I was trying to learn the names of the flowers. 'You?' he said, disbelieving. 'Have this,' he said, handing me a book. 'I've got two.' 'What's this one on the cover?' I said. 'Snake's head fritillary,' he said. 'The ones next to it are marsh marigold.' Took the book and wandered around a bit afterwards in the sun, steep steps, a water spout two inches above the pavement, 'NOT DRINKING WATER'. Good job they told me that because I was just about to get down on my back and clamp my lips around it. Ginnels and jitties behind cottages, covered in daisies. Not daisies. Fleabane. Just learned it. Ugly name for a nice plant. Pictured this place, 1968. Thought about its ghosts. RJ. Was this one a street he walked along? And did the Countenance Divine shine forth upon these clouded hills?

'I see your car's got Devon rash already,' Titus asked later, when I saw him by the polytunnel, stirring an organic nettle and comfrey-based fertiliser.

'You what?' I said.

'Devon rash. It's when the left side of your car gets scratched up from all the time you spend pulling over into hedges and banks to let other people pass.'

'Ah,' I said. 'Yeah. It's a good job people don't drive here like they drive in Manchester or London. I'd be dead by now.'

'Did you know?' he added, as if we'd been talking about it for a while. 'Apple used to just mean "fruit". It didn't mean "apple" until relatively recently – a few hundred years ago or so.'

Every day's a school day here.

Excerpt from rough draft of Wallflower Child: The Ballad of RJ McKendree

You don't realise you're part of history when you're in it. If you live in a time in history where you walk down from your village to defecate alongside your compatriots in a communal mire, you are not squatting there wishing 1596 would hurry up and arrive and Sir John Harington would outline an idea for the first flush toilet. By a similar measure, if you live in 1967, and are renting a house for an affordable price in a beautiful part of the world, near dozens of other artists who you rub up against every week and spark off, you probably do not think 'Hey, I am in the sixties when everything was better!' There is no awareness in you that everything will not always be this way, that you are part of a blessed generation, sprinkled with stardust, and in a few decades' time artists will auction several of their internal organs for the freedom you have.

But that stardust is only part of the story: the story of the Woodstock Generation that has been told a thousand times. We know magic filled the air. We know that it was a rare time when artistic bravery intersected with popular appeal and – frequently – vast ensuing wealth. But there are different stories still to be told of the same era. In a way, there were quite simply too many great records made in the sixties and seventies. The foyer got too crowded, and not everyone had room to move around and do their thing. Some less assertive souls, perhaps feeling that they could not breathe, decided to leave. What it means is that many records made during that era are only now getting the respect and love that they are due. Some of them are yet to receive it. This is a book about one of those records and about the man who made it. But it is a little more than that too. It is also an adventure in itself, a road trip, after which nothing in my own life was ever quite the same again.

'What it's probably hard to get your head around for people now is that we were not worried about money back then. We were just a little British folk band really yet we were playing huge venues, touring Australia and Germany, we all had big detached houses, and most of us had paid off the mortgage before very long. Of course, a lot of what we earned got squandered on beer. You'd go to Dick and Sheila's house and wait while they got ready to go to the pub – Dick and Mick always had to live within a mile's walk of a pub, it was part of their rules – and, as we were leaving, Dick would grab a wad of pound notes from a gap in one of the walls or a cranny behind one of the beams, which was also later where he kept his weed because after some of the other folk bands got busted, he started getting paranoid. Of course, Oliver and I had money coming in from *The Gribblins* and *Mingle the Tingle* by then. But we hadn't, a few years earlier. When Oliver had first started making them in his shed. It all happened very quickly, the change. Four years, something like that. But everything changed quickly back then.'

I'm sitting in a farmhouse kitchen. The room is full of ceramics and they're great ceramics – full of abstract slashes and curves and runes in bold primary colours – and I'm trying to stay calm but it's not because of the greatness of the ceramics that I'm trying to stay calm. It's because the kitchen belongs to Maggie Fox, *the* Maggie Fox, who is sitting right there in front of me on an Ercol chair talking to me. Maggie Fox, whom I watched present *Blackbird* when I was a kid. Talking to me about Equinox, my favourite folk-jazz band of all time, and about the costumes she made for *The Gribblins* and *Mingle the Tingle* and – later, slightly less successfully – *Brock of the Wood*, and about her ex-husband Oliver. And I'm also trying to stay calm because all of this interests me, all of this is a book in itself, and every story leads to another story, and every one is enthralling, but it's not even the real reason I'm here, and I want to talk to Maggie about the real reason I'm here, but I also don't want her to stop talking about the other stuff, but I also don't want to keep her all day.

Maggie is one of the all-time unsung, or certainly only partly sung, heroes of the children's-television acid-folk music crossover and a Renaissance woman of the first order. In the late sixties, with her husband Oliver, in a stone shed at the bottom of the garden of the old weaver's cottage they shared, she co-created the Gribblins: the tiny enchanting green creatures who disorientated humans – invariably rich, affluent ones – with their eerie flute music and dancing then stole their possessions and carried them back to their mossy lair to examine and hypothesise about them. While Oliver made the sets, using moss he had gathered from nearby woodland, and storyboarded the episodes, Maggie designed and made costumes for them of a mindboggling intricacy, tiny felt hats and gloves and the phosphorescent chainmail armour that covered their bodies – all of which, in the shadow of her better-known husband, she has never in my opinion received enough credit for. Not satisfied with the success of that, and her brief turn as co-presenter of *Blackbird*, singing slightly-too-eerie songs for children, she later took up an invitation to join the folk supergroup Equinox as singer and flautist for the final two of their five albums, replacing their original vocalist Bonnie Gosling.

Having emailed the address on her out-of-date-looking website and received nothing back, I had thought the easiest way to track Maggie down would be via the publishers of her now-hard-to-source children's book *Josephine Bigfish* or the company responsible for the 2003 DVD reissues of *The Gribblins* and *Brock of the Wood* (*Mingle the Tingle* is still to be rereleased due to contractual issues). Nothing came of either so I opted for the more direct route, driving down to the Cornish estuary village of Trewars, hanging out in a craft shop which sold some of her pottery, then skilfully and subtly managing to get the owner of the shop to let slip where the creator of the ceramics I was admiring lived. An hour later, here we were, in her kitchen, and I got no sense that my presence was unwelcome.

'You're on the moor, you say, or close to it?' she continues, handing me the second cup of tea of the afternoon. 'I miss being up there. Of course, I have little to complain about here, in terms of surroundings. But looking back I think the moor was a kind of seventh member of Equinox. Equinox, it was really me, Dick, Mick, Julian, Norman, Gill and the moor. All but two of us lived on or very near it. It's where a lot of the secret something we had came from, even though by that time the band were breaking up. Norman had already recorded his *Let Norman Steal Your Thyme* solo LP and Dick and Mick were thinking about new ventures. So it was very exciting and very fraught at the same time. And it was the same with Oliver and me with the moor. When he first had the idea for the Gribblins – which of course comes partly from some real robbers who lived on the moor in the sixteenth century – we'd be doing all these walks up there and he'd be fizzing with inspiration, asking me, "What type of monster do you think would live in this tree?" or running off to climb into an abandoned shed and root around. Then he read about tardigrades, these microscopic creatures who live in moss and can withstand boiling and freezing temperatures and sleep through an apocalypse, and that was where the idea for the Water Bears came from, who as you'll probably remember were the nemeses of the Gribblins in the show. We'd walk through the woodland, over the moss, "the Goddess Carpet" they call it, and Oliver would collect the moss for the sets. Probably not a very ecologically correct thing to do, actually. It was like being married to a big kid. Later he got a bit too involved in the world he was creating at times. He once told me he was convinced that one of them was alive and spoke to him. Meg, the smallest one. Not that there was much difference in size in any of them. They were all different, though, if you looked closely. I hesitate to say a girl because the Gribblins ultimately had no gender. They were before their time in that way, I suppose. I should hasten to add, however, that Oliver was high a lot at this point, as so many of us were.'

She got up and swept an intrepid ginger cat off the kitchen work surface.

'Dad, get down from there. We call her Dad because as soon as I got her, she went straight to get settled on my dad's old favourite armchair and Hannah, that's my daughter, started saying she looked like him and always seems to watch *Question Time* very intently, like my dad used to. But I digress. You wanted to ask about *Wallflower*. I think I have the copy that Dick gave me somewhere in the loft. Isn't it amazing the way the value of these things change, and it comes round again and people get interested? If I am being honest I haven't played it for several years now. I know I thought it was very special at the time. I am sure I still would. This is all – what? – forty years ago now, so you'll have to forgive me if I don't get all of this right. A lot of it was about Dick and Mick and their friendship which was sort of bowing and creaking under the strain of various internal dynamics. As I said, the band was already disintegrating by the time I joined, halfway through the recording of "Mountebank". Then before we started the last record Dick came in and said he had this song, "Mrs Nicholas", by this American guy, which was strange, because Dick could be very anti-American back then, and he wanted us to cover it, but even though we did and it went well, Mick was always very resistant to the idea, just, I think, because it was very specifically Dick's thing.

'The background to this, which I think you can't ignore, is that not long before that, Mick had slept with Sheila, and Sheila hadn't really enjoyed it, and had gone running straight back into Dick's arms. Of course, Dick hadn't precisely been any kind of saint before that, and viewed her infidelity as licence to be even less of one, which was not hard for him, what with the amount of time he was spending hanging around the art college at Chidleigh Babbots after he'd been doing some guest lecturing in the music department there. I don't know if it was there, maybe not, but he ended up cheating on Sheila with this girl called Sue Piduck, who, as soon as we found out about her, we all started calling "Superduck" in an attempt to cheer Sheila up. It didn't last long between Dick and Superduck but afterwards she wouldn't leave him alone and kept saying she had this tape with this incredible music on it and nobody knew who made it, and that Dick needed to hear it, that it would be an actual crime if he didn't, and she just would not shut up about it and finally, after about two months, Dick – realising it was genuinely about this tape, and not about the fact that Superduck wanted anything more from him – goes around to her house and listens to it, and it turns out she's not lying: it's an amazing record. The next day she brings it over to Dick's house, and we're all there, including Sheila, which meant there was a tension in the room, and nobody really seemed that mellow, but all of us – except Mick – totally got it that this record was not anything ordinary: utterly haunted, with this slight eastern edge to it, and with this amazing tuning that was even more advanced than the people of the time we thought were really advanced, musician's musicians; Davy Graham and Suni McGrath and Nic Jones and the like. I felt like I was listening to something that had been made centuries ago, not four years ago. "Mrs Nicholas" was the one Dick had earmarked and wanted us to cover and we did play it at a few live shows but we never recorded it, mostly due to Mick's resistance. I don't even remember it being the best song. But I'm skipping ahead. The thing was, there was this big chap from the college there at Mick's house, a biker type bloke, a sound recordist from the college who Dick was knocking around with and who everyone called Chickpea, and about two minutes into the first track, he says, "Fuck me backwards. I recorded this album!" And then he tells us that it was by this

American guy called Richie McKendree but that he didn't have a clue what had happened to him since but he knew this girl called Maddie who might, but it turned out she didn't either, only that he'd gone back to California years ago and nobody had heard from him since.

'Of course, things being things, and Dick being Dick, it took absolutely ages for it all to get sorted. The friend of Superduck's who'd had the tapes was in some kind of debt at the time and wanted a lot of money for them, even though she'd just found them in a beach hut belonging to her dad. Then Chickpea wades in and says they're as much his as anyone else's. Meantime Equinox are breaking up and Dick's trying to get Selkie started as a label and also trying to track down this McKendree guy to clear it all up. By the time Dick finally finds him, McKendree's working in a camera shop somewhere in Oklahoma and living above his mum's garage and has given up music altogether, and when Dick manages to get the record out it's December 1976 and a different kind of music is in vogue. Even Dick himself had lost a bit of interest in the more… mystical and bucolic aesthetic by then. He'd started writing those very raw and political songs about trade unions and whatnot, which – don't get me wrong – I always liked a lot, but they're not quite sprinkled with the same magic, are they? Selkie only lasted about three years in total as a label. Hardly any copies of *Wallflower* were pressed and even fewer were sold. I hear it's going for – what – £400 on the Internet now? Astonishing. Did you know Dick also managed to get McKendree over here, a couple of years later, here in Devon?'

I know it's a cliché, but I actually choke on a throatful of tea as she says it. 'Haggli fzz!' I say.

'Pardon?' says Maggie.

'Holy fuck!' I say. 'I didn't. Pardon my French. That's… I had no idea.'

'Yep. The Empire in Exeter. Long since shut down. It was a small disaster, really. Dick, who was piling the pounds on by this point, headlining, wearing these jeans that were far too tight, and with this really harsh crew cut Sheila had just given him. The venue had booked a totally inappropriate third support, this skiffle band from Budleigh Salterton called Cliffy Coggles and His Donkeys, who were all well into their forties. And then in the middle there's McKendree, playing the whole gig sitting on a stool with his back to the audience, and not saying a word, not even a thanks, between songs. He only played about four, I think. I was introduced to him afterwards, but he didn't say much, seemed like someone who'd recently had some bad news, but also like this lost little boy. I reckon there were no more than thirty people in the crowd, and three of those were me and Oliver and Angus Boon from Nannie Slagg, who now I come to think of it had a go at a McKendree song too. And then there was this really embarrassing moment backstage when this German couple turn up with a pen and an autograph book and Dick's getting poised to sign it for them and McKendree just looks like he wants to find the nearest manhole and hide under it and it turns out that it's actually Oliver's and my autographs the couple want. Dick was not pleased, I don't think. A complicated man with a very tangible ego. So many good points, though. He had put up all the money himself to fly McKendree over, at a time when money was less easy for him. Say what you like about him, he was always generous to a fault. Hard to believe he had only a decade left on the planet at that point.'

'Wait. Hold on. Did you say Nannie Slagg? The metal band who turned into Blacksmith?'

'Yes, although they were far less metal at first. More progressive. A filthy band, both in looks and sound. I believe they covered "Bog Asphodel" at their live shows, circa 1972. That would have been because of Dick. An almost unrecognisable version of the song, though. When Nannie Slagg became Blacksmith and got properly famous – a totally different kind of fame to Equinox's – Angus envied the freedom Dick had as a lone wolf, envied his new... anonymity, and he'd often hide from it all at Dick and Sheila's place. You'd walk in and he and Dick would be eating jam butties, sometimes ten of them in one go, all on doorslab bread and layered with Sheila's homemade butter. Both being Scottish, they didn't call them jam butties, though; they called them "jeely pieces"'.

Aye, get me, the walker. Walking. Bloody miles. Even got the jacket. Right country squire, I am. Map and mint cake and everything. And boots. The Converse All Stars weren't really working out up here. Bit bleak today. Think I can see November coming over the hill, December behind it, carrying its bad news in a sack. Not bleak like home but bleak. What's home? Where you lived until you were eighteen, I suppose. Doesn't seem like home in my mind any more, though, and then other times it does. Our house, tiny, end of the row, no garden but you went up the ginnel at the end and then past the tyre stack and the back of the garage and these old barns, all this crumpled corrugated iron, and then you were right there, at the bottom of the hill, and the strips of rusty metal and Coke cans would peter out and you climbed the top and up there you felt safe from everything and you looked down and all the shit wasn't visible any more; everything seemed much greener. And then the woodland, behind that: a little forest in the sky where there was a pond and the tadpoles made the water look black in April and I found a lost ginger cat then carried it back down to town in my coat and then just as I got to Gallagher Street I saw a picture on a lamppost of the exact same lost ginger cat that was in my coat with 'LOST CAT' written next to it and I took the cat straight to the address on the poster. Everyone hates the advertising industry until they lose a cat. Except the woman in the house didn't seem that massively over the moon about getting the cat back and the cat didn't seem that massively over the moon about being back and kind of gave me this look as I left, like it was much sadder than when I found it or when it was in my coat. But maybe the woman was glad and was just being the way people were around there, which was not that happy about anything. Which is different to the way people are around here, which sometimes seems a bit too happy about everything. And that's sort of the way the countryside in this place doesn't quite look like the countryside near this place: it's still all big but here it seems a bit happier. I remember the last time my dad came back, about three months before he left for the last time and about a year after he'd left the first time. He had this big plywood board, which he started attaching papier mâché to and making all these humps and bumps, and then when the papier mâché was dry he started painting it green, and brown, and grey, and then you realised that the green bits were hills, and the grey bits were roads and the brown bits were mud, and I got home one day and he'd put a load of plastic farm animals on it, plus a couple of dinosaurs, and left my toy cars there – the ones I had already and a couple of new ones he'd secretly got me in Stockport the weekend before – for me to brum all over it, which I did, for weeks afterwards, until after he'd gone for the last time, and it was all the fun I needed, even more fun than when my mum took the rugs up to clean and I scrunched them up and brummed my car through the folds. He never talked much about what he was making, my dad, he just went ahead and made it, mostly in secret. I wouldn't have been surprised if he had a secret shed somewhere, like Oliver Fox, where he was making his own Gribblins or something like that. And that was a lot of the problem, and why my mum didn't trust him, because he was so quiet and secretive about everything, but maybe it was her lack of trust that pushed him towards what he did, and that made him go off with Sandra Tunnard, and then go off with her again, after he'd changed his mind about it for a bit and tried to live with my mum again. And maybe my mum was right when she told me he was a bastard, and maybe he still is one if he is still around, but the point is I have never really had the chance to find out firsthand. Ah shut up, Martin. Tell it to your therapist. Not that you'll ever have one. Admission of defeat, isn't it, therapy? Not down here: they've all got one, even the trust fund techno hippies with the smooth life and no demons. Might as well be California, what with that and the coastline. Another sign of the north in me: that stubbornness. I'll sort myself out, thanks. Keep your couch. But anyway that was all about five years before I found the lost cat, and about two years before I found my dad's records in a box in the loft, and got on the road to wasting my life writing about rock bands instead of doing a worthwhile job that might help somebody. And what I remember now about that model village my dad made me, as well as the new impact of the realisation that he took the time to make something like that, just for me, is that the hills looked more like the hills down here than the hills up there: they had less space between them, like someone had really enjoyed squeezing them together and making all the angles between them and thinking about how they related to each other and making little secret places in all the folds where nobody could see you getting up to your secretive business.

Excerpt from rough draft of Wallflower Child: The Ballad of RJ McKendree

I was one of the lucky ones: I found my copy of *Wallflower* in a box marked 'Country/Folk/Misc' in the Heart Foundation shop in Sheffield in 1998, a time before the Internet had turned record pricing into a less exciting democracy. It cost me £5.49. I suppose you could say that I, on that day, was another person who didn't realise he was part of history. I was just a person taking a chance on a record that looked interesting. I might not have even picked it up if I had not been intrigued by the cover, which featured an abstract painting: a swirly heliocentric sort of hillscape, with dotted suggestions of houses, and with, I later realised, what could be argued to be just a suggestion of a face in it. On the inner sleeve the painting was credited to 'RJ McKendree, based on an original work by Joyce Nicholas'.

I loved *Wallflower* instantly, but it wasn't until much later that I developed my deeper relationship with it. I was recovering from a bad time in my life at that point. I had lost my job, been drinking far too much. I picked fights with men who deserved it and men who didn't. Stood in to defend the honour of women in trouble and women not in trouble, gradually lost my power to perceive which was one and which was the other. Went home with cauliflower ears and a carrot nose. Woke up with a crying liver and a clicking hip. I took off deep into the West Country, an outsider there, just as McKendree had been when he'd first arrived there, more than forty years earlier. I lived above a garage, just as McKendree had. I had no certainty of my future, drifted, just as McKendree had. I learned wildflower names, just as he had. Opened my eyes to their magic and the poetry of the dead, who had dreamt the names of the plants into existence. Greater spearwort. Reedmace. Purple loosestrife. Creeping bugle. Toadflax. Agrimony. Lady's bedstraw. All the while the record seemed to be growing each time I listened to it, as if someone had snuck in and, in fact, changed it while I had been partially neglecting it. I decided its grooves had actual ghosts within them yet they were not ghosts I wanted to run away from. I played McKendree's version of the traditional Devon folk ballad 'Little Meg' and his choral, semi-chanted 'Sad Painting of a Dog' sixteen, seventeen times a day. Then, later, as I explored my new terrain, met people connected – however tangentially – with the McKendree myth, the record stayed with me and waltzed me through the landscape. I found it extremely difficult to find out what happened in McKendree's life between late 1968 and the late seventies when he made the first of what turned out to be several return trips to Devon. It seemed like the most mysterious of many mysterious periods of his life. I knew his father passed away in 1969, and by 1975 he, his sister and his mum had moved from California to Oklahoma, where he was living in his mum's annexe and working part time in a used camera store. It appeared to be a time when he had abandoned music altogether. But then my research led me to an unexpected discovery that thrilled me to my marrow: in 1972, McKendree had reconnected with his old co-songwriter from Stoneman's Cavalry, Frank Bull, and recorded a one-off single, an almost unrecognisable electric version of 'Little Meg'. But even this turned out to be another rotten rung on the ladder separating McKendree from fame. Bull disowned the result, the pair clashed during its recording, and, following its conclusion, never spoke again. Meanwhile the label who were set to release it, Hemlock Jukebox, folded, yet in a surreal twist, owing to the determination and Eastern European background of one of the label's evacuees, the single was still pressed, but only for a Hungarian market. After many fruitless eBay searches I managed to track down a copy in Klagenfurt, Austria, for which

I was pleased to only pay £35. It's a truly mind-bending work, three minutes of echoey, raw-as-you-like fuzz where psychedelic furry FX pedal funk meets something frightening and primal, apparently roaring out of the mouth of a cave beyond the edge of time. Yet it is also... a duet. Bull's vocals have to me never sounded like this on any other recording, resembling, as the defunct Hungarian music magazine *Bounce!* so accurately put it in one of the single's few reviews, 'the voice of a man unsuccessfully attempting to dislodge a locust he's found stuck between his teeth'.

The more I learned about McKendree, the more I learned he was not merely an eerily, almost celestially gifted musician. He painted, he took uniquely atmospheric photographs. In his later years, he was an ahead-of-the-curve campaigner against climate change and ecological ruination. In some ways, perhaps part of the problem for McKendree, and part of the reason he has still not been reappraised in the way a Nick Drake or even a Judee Sill has, is that his story doesn't follow a traditional rock tragedy narrative. He did not die in his twenties and was not a suicide. He failed at all points to be a major abuser of drugs. He part-vanished rather than totally vanished, only part gave up making music. There was nothing emphatic about his path. But his story is as laden with tragedy as any other in popular music that I can think of. His music was lost, found, lost again. The one true love he'd ever found, the only woman he'd ever wanted to truly be with, rather than just float noncommittally around, had her life cruelly snatched from her in a freak agricultural accident, just as it seemed feasible the two of them might finally be united. He himself died in a manner that was no less freakish, suffering a fatal stroke while on a bed in his chiropractor's clinic, on the final morning of the twentieth century.

Full track listing for *Wallflower* (recorded 1968, released 1976):
Penny Marshwort
Mrs Nicholas
Little Meg
Bog Asphodel
Cow of the Road
Sea Cabbage
Villager
Clapper Bridge
Gods of Mist, and Stone
Sad Portrait of a Dog
Marsh Pennywort

Notes, from 2,300th listen:
Whose is the laughter you can just faintly hear at the end of 'Marsh Pennywort'?

How much better would this have sounded if it was pressed on heavy late sixties vinyl, rather than this flimsy Ted Heath-era frisbee I hold in my hand?

Let's say this record actually came out just after it was made, in 1968 and 1969. Let's say it found an audience, lots of cool people were whispering about it. Let's say I was my age, or younger, at that time. Would I have listened to this record? Or would I have been suspicious of it for being too popular with cool people, and possibly denied myself the chance to enjoy it until a few years later, when it had become less cool? Ergo: been the same kind of stubborn cultural edgeperson I am now. But, even if it had been given the right of birth in the era it was made, would *Wallflower* have found any kind of large audience of cool people? Is it not a little bit frail, too much of an elusive whisper, too much of a record – even in its actual sound – that you have to search for, and eventually find?

Question: What are they, the layers that you can put into a piece of music, that makes it improve with age? Are they things you can see and feel? Where do you find them? Are they in the grooves? Grooves of vinyl. The transference of sound to them. People tell me how it works but I still don't get it. It's the ultimate modern witchcraft.

Usable transcript from interview with Angus Boon:
'Equinox were round tae bend, away wi' tae fairies. Something mental always happened when we played wae them. Which we did a bit, in our very early days, and which might sound tae you like a weird pairing, if ye didn't properly ken us, but wasn't, in that stage of Nannie Slagg's musical evolution. And there's this one gig in Todmorden, ye listenin', and we've played our last song and we get backstage and Equinox are there, all ready to go on and then Mick says tae the rest of the band, "Hold on, where's the rug?" They had this Moroccan rug which they all had to sit on while they played and they couldnae play without it and Julian, the wee milksop who played the lute and yae could knock over with a feather, he'd been entrusted with its safety on this occasion, and he'd left it in their hotel room in Halifax. By the time he'd driven there and back they were an hour late going on and a rumour was going round that it was because the band were baked, but it wasn't; it was because they needed their RUG. There was a second rug, too, after the first one wore out. And there's a story about Mick getting pished and nailing the first rug down on top of Dick so he was totally trapped underneath, but I don't know if that's apocryphal now, laddie.

'The Exeter solo gig? Aye, I mind it well. Fecking class performance by Dick. As always. He was so obsessive about his craft, the laddie had made himself immune from ever being anything less than brilliant. Not many people there, though.

People paint it like it was all about the punks, like outside the venue streets were thronged with laddies and lassies wearing safety pins and gobbing on pedestrians. That's a load of pish and twaddle. It was just a little lean time, a general lack of interest for what Dick – and I – was doing. I remember McKendree was wandering around, looking like a lost lamb; ye can guarantee nae member of the audience who saw him would have kenned the long streak of piss was one of the star acts of the night. When Dick had finally persuaded him to come over he'd asked specifically if he could stay somewhere on the moor, which meant Dick couldnae get more than a couple of drinks, and had tae drive him to and from the venue, and Dick was ragin' about that, because if he couldnae get drunk it always ripped his knitting. McKendree looked like he was about tae start bawling and I asked him what was wrong, kenning that maybe the two of them had fallen out. He told me he'd been walking up near Underhill Tor that afternoon and been trying to photograph a pair of these merganser ducks, which were pretty rare, even then, and in trying too hard to get a close-up he'd managed to scare the female, which like all the females looked very fragile and had a right braw shagged crest on the back of her head – kind of like some of the lassies Dick picked up at gigs, come tae think of it, heh – and by doing that he'd sent her flying off 300 yards up the river, and sent the male the same distance in the other direction, and now he couldnae stop thinking about it and said he was feeling like a terrible person. I told him to stop being such a wee nancy.

'Before Dick moved down here, after when we first decided to leave Glasgow, the two of us were staying in a house in Kensal Green for a while, only a mile or so from all the bohemian stuff going on in Notting Hill Gate. You wouldnae have called it a *fashionable* place, but we did some of the fashionable stuff of the time. A wee lassie Dick knew back in Kilsyth hitchhiked all the way down after him and turned up on our doorstep one day wae some sugar cubes. Lassies would do crazy stuff like that, where Dick was concerned. I didn't even ken the stuff was acid. That was how fecking naive I was. Anyway we took it and I ended up in the bath just bawling, "When's this fecking shite gonnae start *working*?" Neither of us were really intae it but I do reckon it broke down some walls for Dick; he started getting a bit further taeward the peripheries after that, exploring death more in his songs. And then he bought his first rug, from the market on Portobello. So we were intae it all and weren't. A lot of the minted hippie laddies didn't really see eye-to-eye wi' me. I talked too much, whereas for them it was all about not saying much and just saying stuff like "cool" and "far out" and making yersen look mysterious. But that was another world; we didn't live there. We were often up late at night and a bunch of car thieves lived next door, and you'd see them in an alley in the back spray-painting a Rover P5 at three in the morning. But anyway, Dick was never much of a lover of yer pop music, but I do remember at the time he would just nae stop listening to this tune "Thirteenth Snake Woman" by Stoneman's Cavalry, which was just a B-side to this tune called "Right On" that had been a wee hit in the States. So after he got the tapes from Superduck and found out that McKendree actually had been in the band and had a co-writing credit on that song, he flipped right out. I'm sure the laddie would have got the record out anyway but that was the icing on the cake.

'Aye, Morag! That was the name of the lassie who brought us the acid. I've remembered it now. Have yae seen the photo on the back sleeve of the *Doubling Cube* LP that Mick and Dick did just before they got Equinox together? The one where they're playing backgammon? You can just see this bored-looking lassie sitting on the couch behind them, staring out the window, looking like death. That's her. She was aff her fecking heid. Followed Terry Reid everywhere on tour, after she'd had her business with Mick. Wouldn't leave the poor lad Terry alone. Cut off a big chunk of his hair one time when he was asleep and kept it in a box.'

Sodding hell, is that my problem? Is that what I've been doing all these years, interviewing all these fading emperors of sixties and seventies rock, convincing me they're just my uncle for an hour when actually I'm looking for a full-time father figure? Thank you for the chat, Carlos Santana, and just as an extra could you come back to the flat and do me some overcooked chips in the deep fat fryer and tuck me up under my Spiderman duvet? Also, how are you with papier mâché? Why do I ask? Oh no reason. Just wondered. Actually did once pencil in a casual drink with Rick Wakeman after our Q and A but he never called. Christian. Into his cars. Probably wouldn't have worked out for the two of us anyway. Another one today, Angus Boon, but nobody's paying me for that. Nobody does now. Listened to his stuff on the way over. The early work, Nannie Slagg; a folk band, really, once you remove the layers of noise sludge. Actually did some half-decent tunes right at the start. All burrs and incense and runny battery-farm eggs on pappy white bread. Then the well-known stuff. Blacksmith. Three albums, gradually getting more shit and famous with each one. Stadium rock for the hygiene-deficient. A band who looked more like their own roadies than their own roadies did. Not my thing at all. Solo LP after that: weird record, not quite right. Got to give him kudos for the title though: *Unmetalled Road*. Him standing next to a footpath sign on the cover, in a tight vest, looking sullen. Not quite carrying it off: the vest, or the shift in genre. Traditional Scottish folk songs and synthesisers. An uneasy mix. Still got his mullet now from not long after that. 1984: year of delusional concepts of hair progress in middle-age rock. Imagine he'll stay committed to it until the end now. Younger wife, Carol. His fifth. One more for the full Henry VIII. Carol kept coming in to the living room and asking if we had enough fudge brownies. We said we were OK. At least thirteen of them on the table at all times. Clues to the epic recent narrative of Angus's stomach. Buzzing a bit from the stories he told. Liked him a lot. Showed me a photo of him and Dick McKnight of Equinox walking through the docks in Greenock. Double denim. Possible absence of underwear. Couple of useful lads to have on your side in a brawl. Talked on with him. Gave me more leads in my detective story. Kills me that it might never get read. Tried to sell a book a while ago. Nobody was arsed. 'Thank you for sending us this. We thought it was excellent and really has something special and a unique voice and I particularly like the bit where you wrote your name on the title page in capital letters but we think what would really improve the structure is if you could kindly fuck the fuck off and never contact us again.' Why would this one be any different? 'We would actually love to publish this biography of a dead person very few people care about, written by someone who can no longer get work in the national media.' Not happening. £118.73 left in the bank now. Rent due with Titus in a week. Trying not to worry. Bob will help me out, I reckon. Clearing my head. Walking along the coast. Atlantic. Different to the south. Right big growling bastard. Sharper teeth, more root canals. Almost fell down a hole in the cliff. Salty spume blowing up at me through it. You'd think they'd tell you, put a sign saying 'HOLE' in front of it or something. Hut on the cliff edge. 'I LOVE ANNIE' scratched into the wood. We all want to be Annie. Wind spun me down some steps. Helicopter above, coast guard, following for a while, probably thinking 'What's this cunt doing out here?' Hair getting a bit long, a bit Angus, at the back. Wind blew it all the way round and it blinded me and I fell over a tough wiry wee shite cunt of shrub. Talking like a Scottish person too now. Happens, if you spend enough time with them. Shrubs have to be hard bastards up here, to survive all the blowing. Looked like one myself. Redhead cliffweed, also known by its Latin name Gingerus Twaticus. Everyone used to rub it when I was young, scruff it up. Always rough enough for it to hurt a bit but you weren't allowed to complain. What passed for affection, round our way. Last thing the old man did before he left. Rubbed his knuckles into it. Nobody does that round here. They give you a hug, even if you don't know them, make to shake your hand like they're about to do origami with it. Do what the hell you want with your fingers, pal, but I'm not game; I'm keeping my palm right here, in the archetypal loading position, like a human man.

Excerpt from rough draft of Wallflower Child: The Ballad of RJ McKendree

It's hard to imagine what impact Devon must have made on McKendree as a baby, if any, but one might assume that his decision to head there in 1968 was sparked by some seed of a memory, some kind of peeling back of the layers and searching for the child inside himself. His father was in the US air force, which meant he moved the family around a lot during McKendree's early childhood, until they settled in the town of Watsonville in California. From that point until the dissolution of Stoneman's Cavalry in 1967, Richard John McKendree's story was not markedly different to that of a lot of music-crazed kids growing up in sixties America: he gets into the Beatles, he grows his hair to the disapproval of his parents, he and Frank, his friend from school, begin to write songs in Frank's mum and dad's garage. Out with his bandmates, he smokes weed and drinks whiskey, but remains in fear of his father at home, shakes his mother's and sister's hands every night before going to bed. Stoneman's Cavalry get a record deal, have a minor hit, implode. He makes it known that he would henceforth prefer to be known not as Richard or Richie but RJ and drifts around the steep dusty edges of LA, almost gets convinced to become a born-again Christian by Bryan MacLean from Love, is rumoured to be briefly considered as a replacement when David Crosby leaves the Byrds, always seems trapped on the edge of everything, unable to quite reach the centre of any scene and become part of it, as if behind some kind of force field, possibly self-made. He doesn't appear in any memoir or biography or review of the time, besides very briefly in the cobbled-together, long out of print and somewhat trashy-looking 1970 paperback *LA and the Happening Scene*. Here, the young full-time dental hygienist and sometime singer Linda Perhacs, whose own lone solo album *Parallelograms* would also take decades to be recognised for its true mystical brilliance, remembers McKendree attending a gig at the Whiskey a Go Go in the company of his mother, presumably some time in 1969, not long after his return from Devon, and recalls noticing that they 'have each other's looming awkwardness and small ears'. It took a long time for me to track down Frank Bull, who never gigged or recorded again after his ill-fated reunion with McKendree to record what became the Hungarian-only 'Little Meg' single, and now is an abstract artist living – going on the evidence of his website – in an extremely long one-storey wooden house in Colorado. He told me he was reluctant to talk about that time, having been advised by his guru to place it in a locked box in the past, but after numerous requests from me did reply to a couple of questions in a fashion not a lot less abstract than his art, calling McKendree 'my original old lady' and 'the source of my river'. He claimed to have never heard the *Wallflower* album and to have no interest in doing so but was sure that 'my other self, on a parallel plane to this one, really digs it'.

One afternoon about a week after I've been to see Angus, my phone rings, and it's him, although I don't know at first because I haven't saved his number because rock stars you've interviewed aren't going to be your friend.

'I had one more thought, laddie, regarding your wee book,' he says. 'The boy who produced the album, Chickpea. The great big slab of beef. He might be able to tell you a bit more about your man McKendree. If ye can get any sense out of him. He still lives down here, up in the hills behind Dawlish. Shite thing is I don't have his number…'

'Damn.'

'I can tell you where his caravan is, though.'

*

Nobody talked about 'acid folk' in the seventies so nobody called the *Wallflower* LP that when it was released. 'Acid folk' is what it has been described as more recently by record collectors but I am not sure if that is truly accurate. Genres are just restrictive boxes that were made to contain something naturally slippery, and, often, the more slippery something is, the better it is. To me *Wallflower* is as bucolic as it is acid, as eastern as it is western, as jazz as it is folk, as elemental as it is mystic, as spectral as it is real. It sounds possessed to me, by a landscape, possibly by a woman, or maybe two. All of this is very hard to get a grip on for the listener, and it's perhaps in this slipperiness where another part of the mystique lies.

Songs such as 'Penny Marshwort', 'Marsh Pennywort' (a more hazy, whispery reprise of the earlier song but also something more than that), 'Mrs Nicholas' and the reworking of the little-known traditional Devonshire folk ballad 'Little Meg' all give the impression of a state of hypnosis induced by female characters, potentially even the same female characters. Once the listener learns of the close friendship McKendree struck up with Maddie Chagford, the daughter of a farmer living on the edge of the moor, it's tempting to speculate to just what extent she was his muse. Chagford died in 1974, aged just twenty-five, in a heart-breaking tractor crash on the farm, so by the time McKendree returned to the West Country for the deferred attempt to promote his album, he was too late to consolidate anything that might have sparked between them, and perhaps it is this, rather than the manner of his death, that is the biggest tragedy of all. Maddie was not his last romance, if a romance was what it was, but he never married and for the remainder of his life certainly never had a live-in girlfriend or sustained a relationship for longer than seven months.

'There is one other thing I just remembered,' says Maggie. 'I can't believe I forgot. I do worry about myself sometimes. Well, so the thing is, we did see McKendree one more time. Or at least I thought it could have been him, and Oliver was sure it was. It was at the march to protest the bypass. 1996, or 1995, was that? You'd probably know as well as I do. He was a few rows behind us but then we lost sight of him. I remember he was with this very beautiful black boy wearing a silk scarf. It can't have been all that long before he died.'

What is this hair on me? Tiny hairs, all over my t-shirt. Get off me, hairs. These things are ferocious. I think it's the sofa. Whose sofa is it? Seems familiar, but it's not mine, not Titus's. That's where the hairs are coming from, the sofa. But where did they come from before that? God, there are SO MANY of them. I just can't put it together. My brain is too dried out, too big for my skull. It's a wonder it's still inside there. If you took it out and tried to fit it back in you'd never manage it. Why do I continue to be this stupid when my brain is this big? Fuck this fucktangular life. OK, kitchen. Water. Tastes good. I need salt. Who decided to make taps so loud and why do they hate me? What did I ever do to deserve this? Who lives here and why am I alone here? Painting of a cow on the wall. Seedlings. Why won't my left eye open? I think an enemy might have Copydexed it shut. Scent of lily and coffee. Pot is warm. Guitar. Spider plant. Oxygen Steve who did the listings page at *Melody Maker* had one. Used to go to his house with Adam from Engine Room PR before gigs. Hated that plant, Adam did. Don't know why. Used to piss in the soil when Oxygen Steve was out of the room. Johnny Slazenger came over one time and joined in. PRs. Can't trust any of them. Nice table, this. I notice tables more nowadays, me. Coins on it. £1.56. Enough to buy some eggs from an honesty box outside a farm. RSPCA newsletter next to the coins. Dark bottle of hair product. Miss Delicious Sea Spray, 'for that "just out of the waves" look'. But does it also contain fish piss, mystery and the souls of the dead? If not, I'm not into it. Open laptop. Some bread! Is there anything to spread on it, I wonder. Ooh yeah. Watch out technology 'cause I'm using honey. Why is nobody else here? Not a man's house. 91 per cent sure of that. Sex? No. Didn't happen. Can feel my loins telling me that. Neglected of late. Must do something about it. Clean the pipes. 'A freelancer's lie down', the journos used to call it in London. But not here. Of course not here. Anyone could walk in. Well, not anyone, but the owner. Ah, I think it's coming back. A woman, her dog, limitless source of tiny hair. Cold flannel on my face. Such big sad eyes, looking down at me, eyes that seemed to stretch in their corners and reach out to try to tell their tale. French dress sense, a bit, sort of. Mid-forties? OK, that is enough of standing up. Tactical vomit might be in order. Finger down the throat. Puke's sweet release. Steps outside, an excited canine whimper, key unlocking a door. Does that paper bag have poppadoms in? Ooh, one left. Nice and rubbery, just like I like them. Which kind person did this for me? Ah, I think I remember: it was me. Top bloke, my past self. Like him a lot. Sometimes.

Excerpt from rough draft of Wallflower Child: The Ballad of RJ McKendree

When I arrive at Chickpea's, it's the smell that hits me, before anything else, before I get around the corner and see the rotting half Ford Escorts and three-quarter Mitsubishis, the motorbike wheels, the strange rusting gurney, the chimney pots, the tiny pink child's bike sinking into the weeds on the high bank, the pile of defeated smoking something behind the corrugated iron shed, the lone disconsolate horse with the fluffy feet tied to a stake, the caravan with the pen of barking dogs outside and the other caravan that looks like it's been subject to its own internal hurricane and the other caravan behind that with more penned and caged dogs outside. It's the smell of the last day of every music festival I've ever attended but as if that smell has then had oil poured on it and been grilled for a year. Dogs yell at me from all sides from behind fences and awful walls and wire mesh, and two more tousled black ones trot down the lane to meet me. I knock on the door of the red caravan, the one I have been told about, the one with the car engine on its roof, but there is no answer. An old unconnected sink looks up at me from the dirt, asking for help. The two black dogs follow me around the back, eager-tailed. 'And this is the place where we keep our old tyres and cookers,' the dogs seem to say, proudly. Half a Renault van offers 'OODLE GROOMING SERVICES, OTHER CANINES CONSIDERED'. I see nobody. I want to leave, just as I have since I first smelled the smell. The relief upon doing so is so immense, the relief makes having been there almost worthwhile. I proceed down the lane, out of this rust and asbestos apocalypse, out of this inexplicable steel village run by dogs. The smell departs and butterflies cartwheel alongside me, into the sun.

*

Devon retained its mysterious hold on McKendree and perhaps it was all about that first journey he made there, from California, and some kind of attempt to recreate it, and the inspiration that flowed through him as a songwriter for that one summer, which led to the recording of the songs on *Wallflower*. He returned in 1978, for his gig with Dick McKnight, and then again in the late eighties, and twice in the mid and late nineties, sleeping in tents and on friends' sofas, and at a travellers' commune in the foothills of the moor. Ever since his early twenties, McKendree had suffered from upper back problems and blackouts, and it seemed that his one-in-a-million death, on the morning of 31 December 1999, was a final sort of culmination of these. A haemorrhage during treatment for spine issues is not a rock-and-roll death but McKendree's was not a rock-and-roll life in much of an archetypal sense. It is perhaps fitting that it ended in Devon, the place where he'd made the defining artistic statement of his life. There is also a certain poetry to the fact that he never got to see the twenty-first century: a lost artist who was not made for an era where art didn't get lost any more, when music became so much more accessible, cheapened by choice, when archive footage was there for free, to be picked over, shared, and shared and shared, then shared again.

It is a little difficult to remember just how hard it was to access music itself in the seventies, eighties and the first part of the nineties, let alone to access a publicity-shy, commercially moribund creator of that music. No Facebook, Twitter, Instagram, YouTube, Spotify, Discogs, eBay. Prior to the arrival of the Internet, it was hard enough to track down your own estranged father, let alone a psychedelic primitivist's folk music from California whose last recorded output had come out three years before your birth, and even then only in Hungary. This book could not have been written then, I suspect. This dearth of digital network, of all the invisible wires that now loop and cobweb together and connect everything and make the world seem so small yet so much more intimidatingly massive and complex, was no doubt another reason why McKendree continued to go largely unrecognised as the paisley acid genius he was, but what it gave him was the luxury of living a life under the radar, the ability to stay modest and quiet and unexpected. The more I learned about McKendree from the few people I talked to who met him and were still alive, the more I suspect that living some other way would have been deeply uncomfortable for him.

Eye cleaned up now. Sat very patient while she did it, didn't even whimper. Still won't open but feeling better for a woman's touch. Walking now, me and her and the dog. Couldn't believe it when she told me her full name. But by that time I'd seen the painting – not the cow, the other one – and something in me knew, even though I hadn't even known she existed. All too convenient, really. Thought I was in my own fantasy. Film of my life. Maybe I am. Maybe I'm dead. If I am, being dead is OK. Some great ladies here in the afterlife. She takes me up the back of the tor, round past the house that looks like it has ghosts inside, the one where you watch and wait for the terrible face that will press itself against the depraved smudgy glass. Water is rushing down the lanes and beside them. A river, and then another dry something that used to be a river. 'They reclaimed the land in the fifties,' she says. 'Filled it in. But you still get the mist down there, looking for the river like it should still be there.' Poor mist. Like a lost soul looking for a dead lover. Like a singer looking for an old muse. Shut up. Don't think about that. Sheep carcass. Meat almost gone off the bones. Dog won't leave it alone. 'Come here, Sherlock, stop frolicking in former animals!' Viaduct. The hill and its stepladder of rocks. 'Used to be a volcano, once,' she says. '1976, I think it was.' Funny, she is. Effortlessly. Some of the lads at the paper used to say women couldn't do humour well. Fucking bullshit. She's not wearing make-up but her eyes seem smudged, somehow. Entrancing. Wish I'd properly decked that guy last night; caught me unawares before I'd got a chance. Didn't even know I'd cut in on him at the bar. Tracksuit bastard. 'What's your problem? Go over there and sit with Sad Susan while you wait your turn.' Well, here I am with Sad Susan. That's the main thing. Cows in this field. Coming towards us. Lary buggers. 'Nothing to be scared of,' she says. 'They're all lovely. Just stand your ground.' Ah, we're going past that bit of barn. Always freaks me out, that place. 'There's a rumour that someone photographed it and when the photo was developed the whole building was there, just as it would have been when it was built in the 1700s,' she says. 'Nobody has ever seen the photograph, though, conveniently.' Muddy. Her legs don't half motor, for a little person. Big puddles. I help her over; her hand is clammy and small. And then she lands, kind of in my sleeve, and stays there and holds on to me. There's so much I want to ask her. But all I say is 'Are you cold?' and we don't move for what feels like the next fortnight.

Excerpt from rough draft of Wallflower Child: The Ballad of RJ McKendree

> By 1989, RJ McKendree was a middle-aged man, albeit an oddly youthful-looking one, with few of the trappings of middle-aged life. He lived in his mother's house in the suburbs of Tulsa, which he'd inherited upon her death four years earlier. He socialised with few people besides his sister, who lived just two streets away. For income, he continued to work in a camera shop in the centre of town. His music had reached the pinnacle of its obscurity. Dick McKnight had died of heart failure a year earlier, Selkie Records had long since folded and *Wallflower* was remembered only by – at the very most – those still alive who were involved in its release or had bought one of the small number of copies of it that had been pressed. McKendree was sometimes known to busk in downtown Tulsa (note to self: FIND SOURCE/TULSA RESIDENT AND VERIFY THIS) but had largely abandoned playing music in any committed sense, yet it was at this point that he decided to buy a plane ticket, pack a few clothes and his guitar, and visit Devon for a third time. What was his impetus? We will possibly never know. Was he still searching for the ghost of Maddie? Had he finally realised, after all these years, that the UK's deep south west was the place where he most fitted in, or at least the place where he felt least like an outsider?

Not bad, this cucumber. Eating them all the time now. Bite into the fuckers like a Twix, just while idly doing my stuff. Had a word with Titus and he's agreed to defer rent payments for a couple of months. He's a good guy, the cucumber baron. Course he is. Related to Jen. Badge of quality. Teach me to write posh people off, that will. Veg paradise, this. Am allowed as much as I like. Sometimes find a box outside my door. Tasty rejects. Carrots the world wrote off as ugly without stopping to look into their pure soul. Soil-caked muscular dystrophy broccoli. Outsider sweetcorn. Rebel cabbage. Nobbled geek courgettes. Could almost stop going to the shop altogether if I cut out carbs and personal hygiene and accepted extreme dust as a part of domestic life. Got the stuff Chris asked for today. That bread she likes, with the olives in it. Why do they put a little plastic window in the packaging? Food doesn't look out and see what's going on in the street. It's not your nan. Newspaper. Don't know why. Thought Chris might like one. Good stories today. An aromatherapist in Paignton has been sentenced for terrorising her neighbour by repeatedly banging bin lids. 'The jury heard that Karen Birchall, who practises aromatherapy under the name "Mitzy Moon", started banging the bin at 3 a.m., asking her retired neighbour Denise Sutcliffe, "How are your nerves now?"' Bastard in front of me didn't put the divider down on the checkout. Sure sign of a wanker. Shit. Forgot candles, the scented ones. Will she hate me? Is this married life, suddenly? We only met two Fridays ago. Used her card to pay today. Waiting for a new one of my own. Lost mine in a peat bog, Sunday afternoon. Walked up by the cemetery, the burned-out church. Good names on the tombs. Meredith Bunce. Elsie Welsey. John Peter Trumbletits. OK, made that last one up. Stuck for a name for your novel? Go to a cemetery. Grave of a small child. First World War. Scary statue, head missing. Forget-me-nots. Wildflowers love dead people. Me? I'm coming back as a primrose in the next world. Walked up, up, up the hill that goes to the clouds. Past two old cottages. Thick stone walls built to withstand Satan's bronchitis. Sign above a door: 'DUCK'. The duck who lives there must be fucking massive. Sign above another door: 'REBUILDED 1847'. Great but more importantly can you tell me when was it builded? Higher, the old mine with the stone eye windows. Place where it looks like it all ends. Buttock hills. Wire grass. Ground like a mouth, sucking at you, not happy with just your feet, wants your knees too. Lose your whole leg around here if you don't watch it, or at least a good part of it. Why do you only have one foot, shin and ankle? Ah, I left the others up on Trembling Hill. It seemed easier in the long run than bringing them back. The earth owns them now. Moss everywhere. Trees all in their sartorial stoner-rock phase. Vincent Price's voice in my head, narrating my journey. What a mid-Atlantic accent would be if the mid-Atlantic contained a pagan island with its own thriving population of wolves. Thought I might meet one of Oliver Fox's Gribblins, go on an adventure, join the tribe, biggest member, only redhead, the new leader, a simpler life. Another hangover vanquished by the moor. Passed my Stepping Stone Proficiency Test, all the levels, breezed the Beginner and the Intermediary but then almost came unstuck at Holy Shit These Slippy Bastards Aren't Even Above The Water. Fucking bench up here at the top carved out of stone. What pre-industrial maverick did that? Garden furniture essentials. All the rage in the 1680s. Sat down on the granite, looked in my wallet to check how many stamps I had on my loyalty card for Toploaded Burrito in Camden. Don't know why. Not going back there any time soon. Just wanted to check. See what I was missing out on. Saw my debit card was missing. Panic! Remembered I'd stored it in my phone case pocket instead. Relief! Looked in my phone case pocket. Wasn't there either. Panic! Had my phone out to take a photo of some bog asphodel half a mile back. Must have dropped it. Walked back. Got on my hands and knees and ferreted around, trying not to sink. Wasn't there. Couple of hikers passed, binoculars, matching red anoraks. Twitcher types. Them: 'Oh dear, what have you lost?' Me: 'My bank card.' Everyday occurrence here on the moor, sort codes seeping into the peat. Gave up after twenty minutes. Three youths coming the other way. Duke of Edinburgh award types. Wholesome. 'Can you do us a favour? Can you call my number if you happen to spot a black HSBC card down there in the bog?' 'Sure. I'll just save it on my phone. What's your name? Don't worry. I'll just put it down as Bank Card Guy on the Moor.' No call. Trudged back to Chris's. Creaky hips. Blister bigger than the toe it was attached to. No money for beer. Can't take myself anywhere. Hope you know what you're getting yourself into, Chris.

Excerpt from rough draft of Wallflower Child: The Ballad of RJ McKendree

This book is not about me. There are enough examples of the rock biography where the ego of the author is permitted to take over, and he becomes as much the focus of events, if not more than, his intended subject, and I do not want to be another. But it is impossible not to tell the next chapter in my McKendree pilgrimage without detailing my own very personal role in it, since without that, and what I was going through at the time, the remarkable coincidence that took me deeper into the McKendree story would not have happened.

As I have briefly mentioned before, when I began to research McKendree I was going through a difficult period in my life. I would drink to excess, be quick with my fists in bar rooms and clubs and bus queues, spend mornings wallowing in regret about what I'd said or done, then look for a quick way to make it better, which, by mid-afternoon, I would have concluded could only involve a visit to the nearest pub. After a fruitful and exciting initial couple of months on McKendree's trail, when I'd found out just how many bit players in his story were still alive and well in the south west, I'd hit a bit of a wall. I had used almost all of my savings, the moorland sky – as it can sometimes – had done nothing but empty itself on the boggy ground for two weeks without let-up, and I found myself in the corner of the Stags Bar in the Church House in Wychcombe, staring morosely into my stout and wondering how it had all come to this. The precise ins and outs of what happened next need not be detailed here. Let it suffice to say two angry men got into a petty quarrel over their position at the bar, then one of them – believing he was acting chivalrously towards a member of the opposite gender who had recently entered the premises – slightly misjudged the size of the other man and ended up coming off slightly worse in the resulting melee, and was taken into the care of the person he believed he'd been defending, back at her house, before slipping into a semi-comatose state.

The following morning, while I slept, my new guardian angel walked her dog, a lurcher called Sherlock, and bought eggs and coffee from the Co-op. As I stumbled around the top floor of her cottage, my bruised pride was not slow in coming back to me, but the events of the previous night were revealing themselves in a staggering, painful way, one by one: my tussle, the kind and patient face of my benefactor, the late night Indian takeaway I'd insisted on then left half-eaten, the laugh we'd had at the bit on the menu where it said 'Thank you for your costume' and the way the laughter had hurt my bruised face. It was several minutes before I descended the stairs and set my astonished eyes on the painting in her stairway, by which time Christine – for now I remembered that was her name – was opening the front door on her return.

'This,' I said. 'It's the painting from one of my favourite albums. I can't believe it. It's… it's very… it's, well, fucking hell it's the reason I'm here, in Devon.'

'Ah, you saw that?' she said, elegantly easing off a boot. 'It's not an original. It's not even an original copy. Just a copy of a copy. I have been thinking of taking it down, to be honest.'

'Yes! The original is by Joyce Nicholas. It says on the LP sleeve. I looked it up online. It's worth a fortune now. But do you know it, *Wallflower*? The record.'

Seeing her properly in the sunlight that was streaming through the window above the front door, I remembered her many kindnesses from the previous night. I noticed now that she was older than me, maybe by several years, older than I'd first thought. Her face made me think of a mosaic: a very beautiful thing made entirely from shattered things. The elegant way she held the lead attached to the dog and hung her hat on the coat rail seemed to accentuate an ambience of Frenchness about her.

'Poor Sherlock, I think he has a gorse needle in his foot. I do know it, yes. I knew the man who made it, for a while. I also knew the person who helped to get it made. But that was a very long time ago.'

'Dick McKnight, from Equinox? No, what I am I talking about, he just released it. Chickpea? You're kidding. You knew Chickpea?'

'No, her name was Maddie. She was my sister.'

The two of us, under the trees. Feet in the river. Her: calm, Zen. Me: screaming like a little girl. Dragonflies around our heads. Trees greened up to the max, furred branches. Burrows in the moss. Holes leading to the underplanet. Total *Alice in Wonderland* shit. 'Just concentrate on breathing properly and it won't hurt.' All right for her to say. Doubt the water temperature would make much difference to her. Her feet are already like blocks of ice. Let her warm them on me every night, except nothing changes. 'Bad circulation,' she says. 'Runs in the family. My dad had it. Sister too.'

Sister.

Trying not to cry or shout but sweet Mabel in heaven it's cold. Find myself imagining him here, under the moss. The video he never made, the pop star he never was. 'He used to come up here,' she says, as if reading my thoughts. 'He walked a lot. It was probably part of why there was never any meat on him, even in his forties and fifties. He never wore proper shoes for it, always just some old trainers. They always had holes in them and bits of moss sticking out of them. He didn't have nice feet. He told me once about this house he used to go to, up over there, about a mile. Some rich Aussie bought it in the nineties and the barns are Airbnbs now. But it used to be abandoned. When they knocked some of the walls down there was a story in the local paper of someone finding a doll in one of them. It's not uncommon, around here, dolls in walls. Shoes, too. They say they were put there to help ward off evil. Although I saw the picture of that doll in the paper and it didn't look nice. Didn't look like it wanted to help. Anyway, Richie said he went to the house and sometimes it felt like voices were speaking to him through the stone. A woman. He said she watched him sometimes. I was a bit mean about it at the time. Thought it was nonsense, acid casualty talk, even though I later realised he wasn't one of those. He said a lot of weird stuff. It was before I'd really listened to the record, to be honest. I was twenty-nine, more dismissive, more beholden to irony. But now I think about him saying that and I'm not sure. Do you think music can be haunted?'

'Definitely,' I say. Got more to say on this subject, and I start, but then I stop. My role here is listener. Cold starting to get more bearable. Acclimatising. Zen feet of a Buddhist master. Give it a week and I will be able to walk on hot coals too.

'I met him in 1993 at the old commune, sort of a commune I suppose, anyway, up at Runnaford Hollow. But I'd actually met him before. I didn't remember that. Why would I? I was only a little kid, five. But when he started talking I knew, and he knew who I was straight away. It was a weird time, that summer, kind of like another little 1960s, and him being there probably made it more like that. He was older than everyone else but he still didn't seem like other people I knew who were his age. There were some quite odd people up there too, people with quite a bit of darkness in their life. We all knew he'd made a record but he was very silent about a lot of stuff. Everyone always stopped everything they were doing and listened when he played, though. We started hanging out for a while. I'd been going out with this guy Mark, younger than me, nothing serious, and we'd been doing a lot of animal liberation stuff. But then we broke into this farm where there were loads of geese and opened the gates but some geese went straight onto the road and got hit by cars and I didn't even know why we'd broken into the farm, which didn't seem terrible for animals in any way; that made me withdraw from all that, and start to hang out more with Richie. We even recorded a few songs, in the same room where he'd recorded *Wallflower*. Very lo-fi, definitely not what was in vogue with UK bands at the time, more like American stuff. Eric's Trip, Sebadoh. Chickpea still has the mastertapes. I've never asked him for them back. I decided they were a mess. Richie wasn't fond of them, either.'

'I went to his place, Chickpea's, to find him. There was nobody there. Just all these dogs.'

'I wouldn't go within 500 yards of that place. It stinks to high heaven. That's if he's living in the same spot. He might have moved on. I heard that he is pretty ill. He's been a very fucked-up guy for a long time. Did you know he robbed a post office and went to prison for a while? Someone told me they went into his caravan and it was just plastered wall-to-wall with eighties porn, with one great big poster of Princess Diana in the middle of it all. I don't know if that's actually true. Anyway, I have a cassette. So you can hear the songs if you like.'

'You are kidding?'

'No. The only catch is you'll need to find a cassette player. I don't have one.'

'So you and Richie. Did you...'

'Yes. No. Sort of. It didn't work, at all. He seemed like quite an asexual person. And there was the fact of Maddie too. It made it odder still. Maybe me getting close to him was a way to try to bring her back, a bit. After that, we sort of drifted. I know he stayed in Devon for a while, though. I would pass him in the car sometimes, walking along a lane, and wave from the car, but that was about it.'

'And him and Maddie...'

'There's no way of telling. I was ten when she died. She wouldn't have said anything to me and maybe I wouldn't have remembered if she had. My assumption is that maybe they didn't. He wouldn't have told me something like that, but I do know that when they met he'd been under the impression that she had a boyfriend. I don't remember her having boyfriends, not since school. She was very much a law unto herself, different from me and Mum and Dad. You can even see that in the way she died. We had two tractors, a new one and an old one, and Dad had told her not to take the old one with the iffy brakes to the far field, which was really steep, but she didn't listen. She was more arty than the rest of us, she read Russian novels and listened to what my dad called "drug music". Everyone loved her. Everyone. I couldn't have been more different, really. I was one of the boys, not many female friends. I ended up working at the golf club, drank pints, watched football. People found me a bit stroppy, I think. But then I changed, became a lot more like her. Started going up to Exeter and Bristol, hitting all the charity shops, where you could get some total bargains back then, and buying clothes like the ones she used to wear. Gabardine skirts. Felt hats. I became much quieter. This sounds really crazy but I even used her name as my own sometimes, answered the phone as her. It was this deferred way of processing grief, I think. And then after that, I kind of became me, whatever that is. That would have been not long after Richie died, I suppose. And that was when I repainted the painting.'

'I really can't wait to hear these songs.'

She doesn't seem to hear me say it, just hears the other question in my mind, the one that I was too afraid to ask.

'And you know what the most ridiculous thing was? It wasn't even the brakes that did it. It was just the slope. We were all supposed to go to the May fair that day, at Riddlefoot Meadow. They always had it on the last day of the month. I remember that, because she was a Gemini, and so was he, actually. She had a migraine, and said she didn't want to go. She must have felt better. She was always trying to move some stuff. It was some walkers who raised the alarm but it was too late by that point. It's hard to say how much too late.'

Are my feet purple? Think they are. Fish nibbling at them. Wouldn't even feel it if they were. Exfoliation. People pay good money for this. And bad money. Wondering about that house on the hill. Can just see an old woman down the valley, calling a horse, ringing a bell. Water is mellow, tinkly. River has a song but you have to get in really close to hear it.

Excerpt from rough draft of Wallflower Child: The Ballad of RJ McKendree

'She said love don't come for free and she pushed me into the trees.' – RJ McKendree, 'Marsh Pennywort'

McKendree might not have recorded during his thirties and early forties but in early middle-age he retained what many musicians of his generation did not, something he might not have maintained had he become rich and famous: a curiosity about new music. As a forty-something, his listening remained as diverse as ever, including Indian ragas, Zambian funk, fuzz-laden Polish psychedelia on the cusp of progressive rock, but also took in some of the most interesting low-budget American bands of the time: Pavement, Swell, The Amps, Guided By Voices, The Grifters. The sessions that McKendree recorded in 1993 with Christine Chagford yielded just four songs: 'Sister Blue', 'Rent My Head', 'Gribblins' and 'The Twice River'. The recording sessions took place in the same room where the songs for *Wallflower* had been recorded two and a half decades earlier, with the same engineer, Chickpea. The songs – all duets between Chagford and McKendree, with the exception of 'Sister Blue', which features Chagford's lone, gossamer vocal under a lagoon of tape hiss – are an unusual mixture of sunshine pop sweetness and Sonic Youth-like pre-grunge feedback and have a lo-fi quality that makes them sound like they're coming from a stairwell three rooms distant. The two vocalists, meanwhile, sound connected and not connected, awkwardly spliced together somehow, yet all the more charming from that, and exempt from the 'empty biscuit barrel' sound that blighted so many of the bigger budget records of the nineties and makes them sound so horribly dated now. The sessions themselves were fragmented and chaotic, with Chickpea – who was suffering from what was later discovered to be the first of three bouts of bowel cancer – swigging from a bottle of Jack Daniel's, leaving his post at the mixing desk every few minutes to use the nearest water closet, or just not turning up at all on the afternoon that had been arranged. The songs remain, to this day, unreleased.

'Have you heard the term "impostor syndrome"?' Chagford says to me. 'I wonder if most people – apart from the really arrogant and privileged – have it. I think maybe I have it more than most. I have this recurring dream where somebody comes and tells me I'm not allowed to go on living the way I am because there's a qualification missing from my past, and I have to go back and sort everything. I think it comes from this feeling in my life that I've never really stuck at something and completed it. I quit my bartending job and sort of ran away from it. I left school as soon as I possibly could. I chose not to stay on at the farm after it became too much for Mum and Dad to manage. Even the eco-terrorism stuff: I was never fully there with it. And those recordings were the same. It was another unfinished thing. But around that time I had another recurring dream, a proper nightmare, really. It was about Maddie. I didn't dream actually doing it but in the dream I always knew that we'd been arguing and I'd pushed her off something high into some water and in the dream she kept coming back as this doll, I don't know, maybe the really old doll Richie had told me about that he'd found in the wall, but maybe not, because I don't really know what that doll looked like, but what would happen is that as the doll Maddie would sing and tell everyone about what I'd done to her. And then this ultra-weird thing happened which was that at the Newbury bypass protest march a few years later I met Maggie and Oliver Fox, you know, who'd done *The Gribblin*s for TV, which I absolutely loved as a kid, with all that moss and everything, and the Water Bears always having a go at them, which I loved maybe even more. I was there with Mark, because we were still friends, although there was nothing else between us by this point, and he was really involved with the whole thing, getting arrested and chaining himself to trees, but I was really only a daytripper there, so it was just another example of how I am a bit half-arsed about everything, and at the end of the day I ended up getting a lift back down here to Devon with the Foxes, who were really lovely people, just as lovely as you'd imagine, and they invited me in to their house, which was this massive barn, which I remember had all these ladders and mannequins everywhere, and a swimming pool outside with frogs and leaves in it, and above the fireplace I noticed there was one of the actual Gribblins, just sitting there. And then after that, every time I had the dream where Maddie was the doll, she would be this Gribblin. So essentially the dream became about my sister, coming back as a seventies TV character, and singing a song to everyone about how I'd murdered her.'

Hot air balloon! Me! Who'd have thunk it? Up here. Me, who used to refuse to walk over the high bridge over the motorway and go a mile further along to the underpass instead. Is that turbulence? Do you get turbulence in balloons? No room for a black box recorder here. Not with four of us in the basket: me, Chris, Titus and Jen, who is down for the weekend. One of Titus's toys, this. Seems to be in control. Took lessons years ago. His dad. Professional. Did it for Virgin. Flew with Branson. Hung out with him and Mike Oldfield and Oldfield's kettle drums. Oldfield shy, still looking like a boy at thirty-two. Avoiding going over the field of cows now. You can't do that, Titus says, because the cows think the sound of the burning propane is the aggressive roar of a giant skybeast and freak out. Going south, down the river. Cottages on their own. Mystery homes, invisible to the land eye. Secrets of the sky. How on earth do you get to these places by car? Chris's hand in mine. Think Jen is cool about me and her. Seems it. Two of them talked about millinery. Jen is taking a course. Chris did one last year. Compared hats. Seemed to hit it off. Almost left them to get off with each other. Chris, eating a nobbly orange. Sailing the peel away on the wind. Likes the big ones. Not me. I'm more of a satsuma boy. I watch her. Lines blurring. What am I? Lover or biographer? Can I be both? Titus taking us lower, following the curve of the river. Don't think he's going to crash land. Got some champagne with him. Expensive stuff. If you end up on private land you have to give the bottle to the owners. Tradition. 'Every landing is a crash landing if you're in a balloon, really,' he says. Reassuring. That confidence, rife, even up here. Nothing touching him. Bending with the wind, fragrant, easing through it all like he's made of flowers. Could I make myself like that? Is being like that within my capability, with where I'm from, who I'm from? Anyway, doesn't matter. Not much matters up here. Not the book, because who will read it. Not the rent, because it's not due for another month, and besides Titus said I could earn some money by doing some picking if I like. Harvest soon. Reddening land below. Looks like a map: a map of what I'm writing. But who will ever see it? Who cares? And that doesn't matter either right now, because I've got Chris. Hand back in mine now, sticky from the orange. Does this work, two broken people together? Are we jigsaw pieces, or just shards? Shut up, Martin. Stay out of the future. Stay here. It's good up here. She's good. Life's good. Cucumber's good. Look at it all below you. Is that the spooky barn we walked past? It is. Is that the building where 'Sister Blue' was recorded? It is. Is that the sheep you cuddled last week? It is. Is that your estranged father? No. It is a Jersey cow. Is that the pub where you decked the esteemed newspaper editor Richard Peck? No, it's not. That's a million miles away, in another universe. We can do this, Chris. We can do it here, I think. Look, it's the mist. I can't believe it. The one you said still looked for the river, even though the river was filled in years ago. It's the actual, famous mist. Well, not famous, more like cult mist, really. Famous in a quiet way, underappreciated. That poor, sad mist. Never stops searching. And then it goes. But then there's more mist, and I suppose even though it's not the same mist, it is the same mist, and everything starts over again, and, even though it's different mist, made of different particles, I suppose it never forgets. It will always be here, trying to find the answer to its question.

BILLYWITCH (1932)

My name is William Millhouse. I am not a remarkable or interesting man, but these are my memories. It is late in the day now, and I have decided to set them down, not because I believe them to be a record of a great or interesting life but because if I don't, being survived by no living relative, I will take them with me to the grave. Maybe that is not such a great tragedy but within my life is the life of a place too, and I feel great alteration is afoot, and some of that life may soon be frittered and blown on the wind. There will be others who could tell it better and wiser than me, but I am not quite as simple a man as some have taken me for, and this is my story, or at least the parts of it I remember most clearly. In the telling, I do my best, with the knowledge that I might make mistakes and be victim to tricks of the mind, as all who have tried to recall and record the times they have lived through surely have been.

1862 was the year of my birth. The time was May, the sweetest of all months, and the hour was early. As my mother would later tell it, our cockerel, Old Percival, crowed his biggest crow, and the next moment I arrived, and henceforth I was known as 'Cockadoodledoo', then, within time, 'Doodle', and it was said by those close to me that the spirit of the ancient idiot cock was in me. I was always the first up in the morning, always experimentally pecking at morsels I shouldn't. I tried in vain to reach for objects that were beyond me, springing up in a flapping, futile fashion. It was hoped that this habit would change once I reached maturity, but, since my height failed to progress much beyond five and a quarter feet, such hopes proved forlorn. My mother, Dorothy, did not shred words when irate with me, frequently hurling insults centred around my stature. She was a fast squall of a person, a busy knapsack full of sharp stones, constantly taking charge of all situations, as she'd had to since her own childhood, living with her own mother, Katherine. Katherine, who died shortly before my birth, had been feckless in character, a serving girl at the Big House who'd been put in the family way by her employer Joseph Bamford when she was just sixteen. Therefore my grandfather Edward, a seller of kitchen utensils and mousetraps, was not my true grandfather, just a kind man who had stepped in to save the face of everyone concerned, with the exception of himself. Though not from a farming background, Edward, being his mild and easily plied self, in his later years came into the ownership of a cow named Mumble, as an alternative form of payment from a customer who was unable to remunerate him for a set of pots and pans. In the evenings, Edward and Mumble would graze the long acre, Edward, holding a rope attached to Mumble, taking the same route each time: a circle past the church, over the back of Stumper's Cross and along Riddlefoot Lane. It was from Edward that I learned about the clairvoyance of cows. Nowadays I have thirteen of my own and I continue to place trust in their judgement as forecasters of fortune and weather. A cow, as it gazes on you, steady and vacant, takes in more about the core of who you are than most folk imagine.

That Joseph Bamford is my real grandfather – though never a man I have ever thought of as my grandfather, in the way Edward was – means I have the blood of country squires pumping inside me, though I must say on most days that I do not feel it, and I do not sense that many who meet me suspect it within me. I am rarely dressed up to the dick and I pass quietly along the edge of most occurrences in the parish unnoticed, that being a feature of my size and my daytime habit of being clad in the hues of the earth and the stone around me. Some saw the way I would remain quiet around my schoolmates and elders yet talk in great depth to chickens, cattle and sheep and thought me maized as a brushstick but just because I am not a man of conventional learning it does not mean I am a fool. I have seen a lot happen here but always opted out of village gossip. When I bore witness to Mary, the wife of Oldsworthy the baker, cavorting with Thomas, the schoolmaster's boy, in the orchard behind the church, my lips remained as tight as if they had been sewn together, and I mention the incident today only because both parties are long gone from this mortal coil. I learned a lot about the benefits of silence in my home environment, where an ill-chosen word in front of my mother could so readily lead to a ladle or saucepan flying towards your head. My father Henry, a quiet man, learned the same, and in our house it was not a bad thing to learn since, owing to Edward and his trade, kitchenware was a thing that was never in short supply. His seat at the kitchen table was in front of the cottage door and on warm days, when it was open, it was not uncommon for a traveller passing along the lane beyond to have to dodge a plate or spoon as it came spinning into their midst.

My father worked as a gravedigger at the church of St John. I never believed I smelt the dead on him, but an earthy odour lingered constantly around his skin and clothes, crusty and pungent, with an edge to it that made me squint when he kissed me goodnight. As he was ordered around at home he was ordered around at work, mostly by the stern vicar, Alfred Boyland, whose sermon on local sin had once infamously sent members of the congregation at his previous parish, Wickhampstead, running from the church in tears. 'It's not just about laying a body in the ground,' my father told me. 'Folks like things just so.' When John

Ludgate succumbed to cancer of the throat, the Ludgate family insisted that he not be buried on the south side of the churchyard, since over there had been recently interred Richard Cavendish, a rotund bully with whom Ludgate had been involved in a thirty-year feud over a prize hog. The bereaved, however, more often requested that the north side of the churchyard be avoided, since it was said that was where the Devil's Door was located. As a child I searched and searched for the door, but was never successful in locating it. Some said black dogs had been buried there too, but my father was dubious of that and had never found any evidence in his excavations. When not with a shovel in his hand or being harangued by my mother, he hid in books, taking a great interest in the history of the moor, particularly its Bronze Age and Beaker relics and the unfortunate vandalism inflicted on many of them during the last couple of centuries. It saddens me that he did not live to see the excavation of the kistvaen near Trembling Hill mine, in which the remains of a girl, thought to be no more than fifteen years old, were found preserved in the peat, along with those artefacts her people had believed would see her safely into the next world: an axe, a necklace and a shawl, woven from a beaver's pelt. It was his habit of a weekend to walk up there, along the old Lych Way, and he once remarked to me that when he did, he felt the presence of the dead more strongly than he had ever done in his working day.

It is a right handsome church, St John's, here in Underhill, and as the child of one of its employed I came to know it with some intimacy. I did not like the fresh, slick tombstones – their cold blankness frightened me, and seemed like a hard stark statement about what was waiting for me in the great beyond – but the old stones, with their dimpled lichen tales etched all over them, always gave me comfort. When nobody was around, in the autumn evenings, and the air was smeechy from bonfires, I would sometimes get close and give them a proper big cuddle. I don't know why I favoured this activity more on those autumn evenings with a new chill in the air but that was the way it happened. The building itself has a heavy appearance, even more so than most other churches in the area, a wider rim of granite being used close to its foundations, and it is said that this was a deliberate measure taken so the Devil did not carry it off to higher ground, as he had done with the little-visited St Constantine's, whose ruins stand halfway up Underhill Tor. Over on the west side of the church is a yew tree of some 1,400 years in age and, for the first decade of my life, and the century preceding it, carcasses of the badgers and foxes that had been killed in the parish were left on the trunk, five shillings being paid to the successful hunter for a fox, half a crown for a cub, and a shilling for a badger. Mercifully I have no actual memory of this.

On the whole, I associated the church with feelings of warmth and benevolence. Other children in the village were most frightened by the Bird Lady carving on the font, in which a woman is crudely depicted, apparently about to do grievous harm to a man, while watched by her sisters and her feathery accomplices, but I always thought of the Bird Lady as a friend and many times had dreams of her watching over me. Like her, I possessed a great affinity with avian life. Whether or not this has anything to do with Percival, and the way I arrived into this world, I do not know, but to this day, blue tits and chaffinches are not shy about entering my kitchen. It is far from uncommon for me to arrive downstairs of a morning and find a song thrush perched on my ottoman. At the Underhill Fair in 1901, when a great gust of wind blew down the Duck Marquee, setting a melee of geese, ducks and hens flapping across the village green, many eyes – eyes that normally ignored my presence – looked immediately to me for assistance, knowing of my reputation. I caught four geese and a duck very easily, while

Mrs Addlestrop from the tea room at Upper Wadstray showed great calmness in her handling of a large, vexed black cock. By this time Old Percival was long gone, although he had lingered for more years than had been expected. Many was the time that Dorothy would instruct me to check on him with the words, 'Doodle, be going out to that hen house un see if that bird un snuffed it yet,' upon which instructions I would promptly venture to the wooden enclosure where Percival roosted, peer in, ask of his health, and be answered with a croaky 'Cwawwwk.'

My playground was Combe Woods and it was here that birdsong was most intoxicating, especially in May, that most colourful and bonny of all months, the month that I still believe is mine, by birthright. I could not imagine that the most talented symphony orchestra in all the land could come close to matching the melodies my friend Sarah Slatterley and I heard above us in the infinite emerald canopy as we amused ourselves on those stretchable afternoons. Sarah was possessed of a singing voice as pure and life-affirming as a blackbird, and, while I fail pitifully now in trying to recollect the voice she spoke with, the melodies that issued from her mouth are as fresh in my mind as they would be if I'd seen her just yesterday. Sarah was always in charge of the games we played in the woods, one of her favourites being Black Pig, in which I would hide behind one of the many large boulders in the woods and it would be Sarah's task to find me before I leapt out, making tusks with my hands, running at her and shrieking 'Black pig! Black pig!' In her other favourite game, which she called Little Meg, it would be my job to build a bridge across the river for Sarah at one of its shallower points, using whatever material – rocks and branches, usually – was not too heavy to carry. I would place a chain of dog daisies around her neck and Sarah, being Queen of the River, would then stand on the platform I had constructed for her and wave to Her People, who I always imagined were Lilliputian and not completely of this earth. I do not know why the game was called what it was called, other than it was also the name of an old song Sarah used to sing very sweetly. One day, when we were out in the trees, she asked me, 'Doodle, will you call me Meg, but only when we are here?' so, because I would have sawed off my own right foot clean at the ankle if Sarah had asked me to, that was what I did, and it became one of the many little secrets we stored in the trees. Maybugs were often around as we lolled on the grass in Riddlefoot Meadow and we laughed at the noise they made, so loud and impolite that it seemed to come from the century ahead of us, or maybe that is just how I now think of it, now I am in that century. Billywitches, my father called them. Sometimes, as an evening chill stalked through the tussocks and raised pimples on our bare arms, Sarah pressed up close to me, and I felt a feeling I didn't understand that was like syrup pulsing through me and that, while only being a foreshadow of a feeling I would feel as a fully developed man, was no less potent for it.

I could see nothing important in my future but Sarah's face at times like these, framed by the soft honey of her hair, but I feared she was a girl whose yearnings stretched out far wider, far beyond me and this glade.

'Doodle,' she said, one especially fine afternoon, as we sat under the Black Tree.

'That is my name,' I replied.

'If I told you something I have not told another soul, could I tell it to you, knowing you would keep it to yourself and it would never enter the ear of another?'

She had an oil beetle crawling across her forelock, but I did not want to sidetrack her, so chose not to mention it.

'You could,' I replied. 'I promise it shall go no further.'

'One day, I intend to go to Honiton, and France, and maybe even the Americas.'

It was from my father and Edward I heard about most of the legends of the moor: the black dogs and the piskies and the river sprites. Edward told me it had been many years since a flibbertigibbet had been spotted in the area but they were rife in his own father's boyhood and, having learned of their reputation for frightening young maidens on dark lanes, I worried about what that could spell for Sarah once she made the transfer to womanhood. Because of this, I always insisted on walking her to her front door when we were out anywhere close to nightfall. Then there were the piskies to worry about, too. My father himself had never been tricked by them but Edward remembered a time when he was up the moor and the land seemed to slant half on its side as a great mist came down and every direction he walked in led him to the same locked gate, the air only clearing when he turned out his pockets. My mother dismissed this story as 'pish and twuddle', claiming that Edward had never had any sense of direction and could not be trusted, as a man who had once argued blind that Scarborough was in Cornwall.

I did not need to speak to my father to know of the story behind the stones on Trembling Hill, since it was common knowledge that each was a young girl who had been turned that way for the crime of dancing on the sabbath. Underhill has long nurtured a reputation amongst neighbouring parishes for breeding disobedient women and I have seen enough evidence with my own eyes to not doubt the reputation's foundation. Many is the time that I saw a young lad from the village being led emphatically by the hand towards the woods by a member of the fairer sex, although it is seldom that I have seen the reverse. I often picked up an abandoned blouse or frock, corset or pair of breeches on my wanderings in Combe Woods. Houses being crowded places, where bedrooms were shared with siblings and even on occasion sheep and goats, more children than not were conceived under the stars. Our cottage, containing for many years just me, my mother, my father and Edward, was a relatively capacious anomaly, although my mother's personality filled the space that would probably normally require six other persons of at least medium size. With each year she became more ornery, and with each year my father took another polite step back from asserting himself, perhaps hoping that it might placate her, when in fact it was an equation that seemed to make the opposite result, and finally he retreated so far back that he was entirely within his books and antiquarian concerns. It is from reading his diaries, and later his library, rather than any of my schooling, that I am able to put words on a page in the way you see before you now. He never missed an entry, and though some are rather mundane ('grey rain, saw a strange horse outside Mrs Fitchett's'), others are a document of alterations in the parish, the lores of the time, and his concerns about the frittering of our history in front of his very eyes. On 3 March 1871, he laments the vandalism of Hannaford's Plob, the tomb of a fifteenth-century hunter, by local builders who repurposed the stones for new cottages on the moor's north-east side. Later that month, he talks of watching a young couple in the village pass their newborn through the forked trunk of an ash tree, to cure the child's nascent cough: a custom I have heard about from other sources but not seen evidence of for nigh on four decades. 'Edward twisted fiveways insensible with drink,' says the entry for 5 September 1883, and nothing more. 'Solstice. Bilious. Coach to Newton,' the diary is told on 21 June 1882. 'Flowers for Dorothy. Not bright enough.' By this point, the feared Alfred had passed away, being replaced at the pulpit by his son, Cedric, a far milder character and keen early student of photography. My father had a stout and rewarding relationship with Cedric, especially after – if memory serves right – my father saved his life by pushing him out the way of a falling gargoyle during a storm in 1887.

A phrase I learned about the moor from my father was 'If thee scratch my back thee shall pay for it.' In his mind, if you attempted to tame the moor, to force your industry into its acid soil, to harness the great power of its rivers and trees for profit, it would eventually exact its revenge. To him, that great domed expanse rising above the surrounding countryside was always 'She', never 'He'. 'Old Her be angry today,' he would sometimes say, and I would be uncertain as to whether he meant the great wild space above us or my mother. But then I would see the fearsome skies over the tor, and the even more fearsome ones over Trembling Hill beyond that, and he would add, 'I wonder who's angering Her today,' and I would know what he was talking about. For me, those sombre slopes were where the world ended, and I never felt the need for more world beyond that. I have never been to London, never wanted to, and now I never will. But, seeing the row of houses that has just been built over towards Summersbridge – ugly dark red boxy things, without individuality or charm – I fear the city will soon come to us, and it is one of old age's small mercies that I will not be here to witness it.

There is the high moor, with its tough wire grass, ice winds, vast treeless slopes and wind-blasted sheep, and there are its footslopes, with their soft river valleys and speckled woodland, and I do not rightly believe you can ask for one without the other. People told me Hell was a place down below and Heaven was above but in Underhill I know the positions to be the reverse of that, and down here in our Heaven Sarah and I continued to play under the plumed chorus in the faery light that can only be created when strong upland sun shines down on thick tiers of burgeoning leaves. Winter surely happened too but I scarce remember it, whereas now it happens at least once a year. The river gets rude and high and the stepping stones Sarah and I placed at even intervals across it close to Summersbridge can no longer be reasoned with. I have seen the river landed only twice in my life for, even when it is full, it moves too fast for that. Half a mile further up the valley is Megan's House, empty now for many a year. My father said an old crone, not Megan but Lydia, lived there until not long before my birth, and used to walk over twenty miles a day on the moor, getting up not long after midnight in midsummer in order to make the most progress possible. He studied lines in the landscape: he noted that a straight line went from the Trembling Hill kistvaen, where they would later excavate the body of that young woman, through the stone circle and the centre of the tor and the churchyard, and the line brushed the edge of the house where Lydia lived too. Now I see there is this man Watkins, who has lately received much attention for his books on prehistoric lines, but my father was making note of the very same some fifty years earlier. History is full of quiet men who do not get the credit they deserve and would never ask for it, even if their life depended on it.

But then there are men like Cranford Frogmore, who will let the world know who they are, and what they have done, at any possibility.

Frogmore arrived down from Bath one spring with his fawning band of archaeologists, strutting about in his clean white frock shirt, speaking to other men he met as if they were so many woodlice in his path. It was in the orchard that I first spotted him, his train of similarly attired cohorts in his wake, as Sarah and I were lazing beside some new lambs and their protective mothers. 'Who is this prize spoon on a stick?' I remarked, but as Sarah's eyes followed his thin prancing legs through the grass, she remained silent.

By this point, I had finished my schooling and had been given work by Mr Cosdon the thatcher, not because of any great talent I had for handling a blade or laying a water reed top lane or wheat reed ridge, but because I was known as a good little climber who could squeeze into a spot smaller than himself. The business was to an extent in the family, since my mother had once worked as a comber of reeds for another old thatcher, Toddler Crockford, who lived up in Wychcombe in a very horrible house. There only being a limited amount of thatch to renew in Underhill, my work also afforded me the opportunity to travel, once even almost as far as Sidmouth. Not being a person who got the chance to look down on much when walking at ground level, I loved my new life in the sky, even though I felt all of the weather there more keenly than ever as it came down off the tor. One night I dreamt I was a church bell, with the face of a very beautiful lady. In this dream it was my job to stand high above the town and ring myself whenever bad weather or danger was approaching. Everyone looked up at me and smiled and appreciated my work but nobody ever got close to me, and I felt lonely in the dream and would have liked to have had another bell beside me. Not long prior to this, my father, who did some ringing himself, had told me that the first bells in the church had been sounded as an answer to coming thunder and lightning, to frighten it away. He loved to hear the bell tapping on the stay, the tick-tock it made, and often remarked that it was pleasantly like being inside a giant clock.

Sometimes, now, I think of my life as having been lived in two distinct parts: the one where I was climbing higher and higher, and the one since then where I have made it my business to tunnel down, into the essence of things. This perhaps begs the question: when have I lived on the level that most people do? Perhaps very rarely. And perhaps that has suited me just fine. Here on the moor, the air is known for its buoyancy, and you don't have to be perched on a roof to feel that, but up so many feet above everything, I often felt like I could just ascend to the clouds, especially not being a person of any great heft. I liked the view my work gave me of the trains coming into the new Wychcombe Junction station. In those days the brakes were not the most reliable and many times the carriages overshot their mark, meaning passengers would have to walk very many dozen yards back down the track. Not all trains did stop and once I watched the carriages creak to a halt, only for nothing but several thousand bees to disembark, in the form of six hives that were then transported to Riddlefoot Meadow. Our parish has also not been without eminent human visitors. Prime Minister Gladstone passed through Underhill on his tour of Devon in 1872, and although I have no memory of this, my father said he had the opportunity to shake his hand and felt that he was 'not a proper person'. Sir Walter Raleigh, it is said, was at large in the alehouses of the moor not long before his arrest in 1603. Edward claimed that, as a young soldier, he met Napoleon when he was moored in Torquay harbour, but Dorothy dismissed this as 'whiskey talk'. Edward also assured me that as a child he'd met a man whose grandfather had been one of the royalists who had been infamously ambushed by parliamentarians while playing cards in the old Wickcoomb Inn, but by this point Edward was well into his eighth decade and often known to go amiss for several days, taking his night's rest in fields and hedge bottoms.

Living with three men who were constantly bringing pieces of the outdoors back into the house with them – me with my dry reeds, my father with his soil and Edward with the burrs and leaves and buds that had attached themselves to him during his wilderness naps – was the bane of my mother's existence. She reminded us with little respite about the relationship between soap and the almighty and it was as if, in her eyes, none of life could quite happen right unless every surface of the cottage was spotless. But of course as soon as it was spotless and life did start happening, the happening of it would make the surfaces dirty again, so in a way the life she hoped would happen was destined to always be but an unreachable dream. She worried terribly what her peers in the village thought of her and was forever haunted by the day in 1868 when she had visited Sidmouth without a bonnet: an incident she had later overheard two of the sisters from Pixies Cottages gossiping about. She was vehemently against the drinking of tea, maintaining that it was the Devil's own drink, destructive to the senses, and did not allow it in the house. I never felt more taboo or lawless than when drinking a strong brew in Sarah's kitchen – an exception mayhap being the time that Fernie Saville and I went out in the snow and, with one of my father's shovels, dug up the sign to Upper Wadstray and Wychcombe and turned it in the opposite direction.

It was Cranford Frogmore who took Sarah away, as I suspected he would, from the moment I saw her eye roving towards him in the orchard. The day that I did not find Sarah at home when I called for her and saw his white frock shirt discarded on the ground near our old stepping stones, then heard giggles from in the copse behind, confirmed my worst fears. From the moment Sarah's body began to mature, a wall that could not be perceived by the eye had gone up between us, and that feeling of syrup pulsing through me as she pressed up to me in the long grass was now just a memory. I had accepted this and that she was deserving of more of a man than me, but Frogmore was not a fraction of what I had hoped for her. I saw that he viewed everything in his immediate environment at best as part of a supporting cast in the play of his life, and any lover he chose would eventually have to be a victim of the same fate, and worse. If he had been less interested in the upkeep of his own moustache and the suppression of those in his stead, maybe it would have been him who found the prehistoric nuggets right under his nose in the kistvaen on Trembling Hill, rather than his more pleasant successors, some three decades later. He and his supercilious gang of trousers had only been in Underhill two days before they had commandeered a table in the corner of the Stonemason's

Arms, which they looked upon with as much ownership as if they had been responsible for the carving of its own sturdy legs from oak. 'Do as my shirt does!' he had commanded me, when I had the temerity to take a seat at it, and it was only later I had realised that what he was telling me to do was kiss his self-adoring arse. I walked silently away from that, just as I walked silently away from Sarah's involvement with him. I have always shied from conflict. It is my way. Yet it is in my memory of these days that can be found my life's great regret.

She never returned to the village. The rest of the Slatterleys moved away, to Penzance I believe, not long after. I heard many years later that Frogmore ploughed his way through the whores of Hackney while she went mad, alone, in a big Regency house up in Bath, before being committed to the madhouse. But who is to say for certain? As I have mentioned, I am distrustful of rumour and tittle-tattle.

I recall Sarah's and my small story here so it will be held in print, but it strikes me as futile, not just because I do not know who would ever be interested to read it but because I am sure the earth and the river hold it and tell it too, as they tell all our stories, and that when they tell it they do so with a far greater eloquence and recall than I ever could. My father, despite the nature of his work and his diligence in attending his employer's sermons, possessed a quite pagan view of the afterlife. He believed that parts of us seep into the earth, to become parts of the landscape around us, and perhaps parts of other souls yet to be. He saw it as a sort of dispersion of narrative. The root ball of a tree planted in a churchyard, he said, would soon go to work in absorbing the dead. He told me about the highwaymen who had been caught and hung in chains up on Underhill Tor, starving, getting their nutrition only from shreds of candle wax fed to them by those passing by until they finally expired and rotted into the earth. I saw in my mind's eye the thick broth rain up there washing their secrets down into the soil and the river, and the river telling those secrets, just as it told the secret of the lady in the carving in the church and the secret of my mother's true father.

Because the rainfall is so great here, digging is usually not difficult, but during a rare dry spell it was not uncommon for my father to break a shovel. He always kept a spare in a small attic in the stone barn behind the cottage: a topsy-turvy space that my mother constantly reminded him to keep tidier than he did. Could my father's life have been as quiet as he wished it to be, if he had actually taken on board some of the advice my mother barked at him, or would she just have found more shortcomings to chastise him about? It is hard to say. I try now, as an older man who spends time underneath matters, to see more of what made her what she was: the story under the story, what it took for her to hold everything together, in a house of cows, chickens and men that were invariably either uncommunicative, crapulous, clumsy and hungry, if not all four at the same time. Heavy responsibility and lightness of manner cannot easily go hand in hand. What I do know is that my father rarely remembered to do any of the tasks that she shouted at him to do and, because of that, I know that on the day that she dislodged the shovel from the attic space and it fell on his head, it would have been in a precarious position, and because of that, it is questionable whether she can be blamed directly for his death.

I can picture the scene now: my mother on the ladder, growling her dismay at the disorder of my father's tools, her hands busy above her, rummaging. My father directly below, staring at his dusty boots, uttering not a word, waiting for the storm to pass. The shovel falls and the sharp metal blade hits the softest part of his temple. The end of his life was not slow, although part of me suspects that my mother's verbal annihilation of his character continued for a minute or two, even after he passed from this world into the next. It is hard not to note the irony that so many heavy objects had been propelled towards him over the years – earthenware mugs, griddles, trays, china birds, plates – and he'd lived through it all, yet the one that finished him off was the one she accidentally sent in his direction.

For the remaining twelve years of her life, my mother was a milder presence, particularly from the point two years after my father's death when Edward's liver finally became too pickled to keep him above the earth. I had never noticed at the time, but when she had talked to me or my father or Edward, her hands were constantly held together, her nails digging half-moons into her palms, and it was only now that she ceased to do it that I noticed she had ever done it. Cats, hens and dogs no longer fled into hedgerows at the sound of her voice. She ate more unselfconsciously, remarking on many an occasion with a satisfied chuckle that she was 'full to pussy's bow'. The stones in her tone became smaller, less sharp, and her mission to tame dirt for good abated. The cottage was at the lowest point in the valley, where all water seemed to come to gather, and that dampness was more noticeable as my mother's obsessive cleanliness and tidiness fell off. The walls have always felt like crumbling cake here. I believe it is a building fit more for cows than humans. Yet it still stands, and I am still in it, also standing, just about.

My father is interred on the north side of the churchyard, near that Devil's Door that I have still not located, and it was I who dug his grave, and who planted the ash sapling beside it, which I trust is now hard at work absorbing his essence. It was the driest spring in living memory and the bluebells leaned and withered as soon as they flowered. After Cedric Boyland saw that I could dig with an enthusiasm and strength that belied my size, he believed it only logical to offer me my father's old position, and I accepted, and at that point the part of my adulthood I lived in the sky ended and the more sunken part began. Yet it is in this subterranean part of my life that my mind has floated higher, into unknown places that seem to be somewhere above the clouds. Sometimes, I think a more significant part of it than not has been spent inside dreams – extremely lucid, deeply textured dreams, sometimes more real than Underhill itself.

There is not a lot else to tell.

I am still here, still digging my holes and filling them in, and am still for the greater part the person I was when I first began doing it, although my bones ache a great deal more, and I fear I only have a year or so left at it. My reading and writing has improved, with the help of my father's old books. Mumble the cow is no longer amongst the living. In the end, she outlasted my father, Edward and my mother, and very close to the end of her life, I decided she should not be so lonely, and got some companions for her, after purchasing some land off Benny Woodcock. The herd – or their successors – provide milk but I don't push them hard or make a song and dance about its availability. If people come for it, they come. Nonetheless these cows are more than enough to occupy the time I do not spend deep in the earth or words. I am glad of them and glad to not be a man who depends on them for income, to be a man who owns a plot of land and the roof above his head. Some say the damp in here is not good for my lungs but I have outlived many a man who spent his life in more parched rooms. My mother, in her more sensitive, confessional final days, told me that when he had the place built, Edward inserted a shoe in the wall, and a doll which an old lady in the village had told him would give the place protection from misfortune. The doll, she said, had originally been part of a pair. But I do not know about the truth of this. There are a few things I know for sure. Children swimming in a river will never be quiet, that is one. You cannot count the tadpoles in your pond, that is another. But there is infinitely more I don't know, just as ever it was.

In truth, it is Underhill that has changed far more than I ever could. More folk arrive on the train now and, thanks to its improved brakes, it stops at the station platform with fair precision. The advent of the motor car has brought more daytrippers to the moor and not all of them treat it with the respect it deserves. Just the other day, I had to apprehend a young gentleman with an accent I could not place who was pulling moss off the trees in Combe Woods. He seemed startled by my interference and, were I younger and larger and less reserved, we might have sparred. Instead, with the remark to his lady friend 'It seems the piskies do live and speak after all, Jean!', he departed, towards the road. I fear great change coming. Sometimes, I dream images I do not recognise, unfamiliar machines with too many wires, popping and crackling with electricity. In one dream I saw my own tombstone and the words inscribed on it: 'William Millhouse: virgin, underestimated' but it did not have a date. In another I was sitting in a meadow in May surrounded by all its floral glory but looked up at Underhill Tor and saw a face in the hillside and the face was screaming. I fear the advent of a vandalism coming far greater than the one that concerned my father. I suspect the moor is about to have its back scratched and there will be multiple payments due.

That we became briefly famous, as a village, owing to the findings at Trembling Hill, has also brought more people to the area. They said that she, the girl they discovered, was put to rest in a crouching position, facing the rising sun. This strikes me as not a position of dignity, but we are nearly the same at the end, underneath our airs and graces, our bonnets that we sometimes remember to wear into town, our tailored shirts and lacquered gentleman's moustaches. I do not doubt that she did pass into the next world but I suspect it is as my father said and that world was a dispersed one, of trees, earth, flowing water, flowers and souls yet to be born, and that, contradictory to what her people thought, her amulets, clothes and tools did not go with her. It is still the same now: I have buried people with vases and quilts, with hammers and banjos, with cats... even once with a favoured mouse. I know every inch of the churchyard, know just how many Sarahs are in it (three), just how many Davids (sixteen), Williams (eleven) and Megs (seven), but there will, of course, be more beneath that, long forgotten. The stones will talk, I think, if you give them long enough. I still recoil from the younger headstones, the very clean ones that glint in the sun. They give me a chill. But as far as other chills are concerned, I have never seen a ghost here, nor a piskie. A newly qualified young doctor in the village, a golfing man by the name of Fitzpatrick who moved here from the west coast of Ireland into one of the ugly new houses, told me that on his way back across the tor after playing the back nine he was led astray in the mist, unable to get home and found himself mistakenly over by the ruin of the old barn that once belonged to the Warners, and said he saw a plume of smoke rising in the doorway, in the shape of a woman. I think he is a very imaginative man but I also do not doubt the moor's intention to spin and confound people on its more vexed days. I have heard it claimed that the figure in the carvings on the font has been seen as an apparition, but few people have spent as much time in her manor as me and I have never set eyes on her, although curiously, she does often visit me in dreams.

At these times, I am often digging and she stands to my rear, quietly observing, making sure the job is done right. I like the idea of her presence. It gives me comfort when the dark thoughts creep in: when the tor makes its rain to blacken the world and I am out in it alone, when the belltower captain rings out the nine tailors for another man lost and I dwell on the inevitable solitude that comes to us all in the end, or when I wonder what I could have done for or been to a woman.

It is now a while since I have broken a shovel. I have three in all and they live in a low and accessible place, in the porch, near my shoes and raincoat. Not far beyond can be found my mother's old ottoman where, when May is at its peak and the sun is shining and I leave the door open, I will still often find a chaffinch or song thrush perched. At the close of these sweet, bright, late spring days I will sometimes open the ottoman and put on one of the garments within it. There are a couple of dozen in all that I have collected from the woods over the years, although it's rare for me to find one there now. I favour a couple of cotton frocks in particular whose bright and intricate patterns seem to match the foliage around me. I take the back way into the trees, through the leaning gate in my old dripping garden wall that is half off its hinges and I tell myself I will repair, drekly. It takes me ten minutes to follow the thread of the stream to the river. All the old bridges on the moor began with stepping stones and the ones that Sarah put down are still there, negotiable in fair weather. As I balance on them, enjoying the way the fabric feels against my skin, I remember her standing there, singing her song to her people that I could not see, remember the great stillness in me that contrasted with the great yearning in her and the yearning in the water that seemed to match it. Sometimes I have imagined that I still hear the song. One time, when I was feverish with summer flu, I was even sure I heard it croaked back to me by the rocks in the river and I shivered and swayed with its power.

After I have stood on our makeshift stone bridge I rest in the long grass, at the end of this unremarkable life, aware, as I lower myself, of every twist and ache and fault and gap in this contraption I still call a body. But then I feel it all getting under the cotton and passing through me – the sun, the butterflies, the maybugs, the tune of the water, the breeze, the falling light – and I am the moment and nothing more.

SEARCH ENGINE (2099)

How tall was Reka Takacs?

Reka Takacs was 172.2cm tall, or - if you prefer to measure it the old way - five feet eight inches. (The same height as you.)

Who was the husband of Reka Takacs?

Reka Takacs had two husbands. The red-haired writer and record producer Martin McGuire (2029–2045) and the dark-haired actor Thomas Molland (2046–2047).

What does Takacs mean in English?

It means 'weaver'.

When did Reka Takacs die?

Reka Takacs died in 2091, one day prior to what would have been her 100th birthday.

Why are we doing this? I know all this stuff. She's my great-grandmother.

I'm sorry. It's force of habit on my part, a hangover

of the genetics of my programming. It's because she was famous. People always want to know how tall famous people are, whether they have a spouse and, if so, who that spouse is. It's really dumb. It goes back to the early days of Google. All these thousands and thousands of people looking up internationally well-known figures they are attracted to and checking on their marital status, as if thinking, 'Hey, let's see if I have a chance here.'

I don't think of her as famous. She didn't want to be famous. She's not famous now.

She was, for a while. The *Little Meg* album sold 30,000 copies during the month of its release. That is pretty impressive for 2047, and for what was essentially a folk rock record. The general public didn't have a lot of money to spend that year.

Do people search my name and height and try to find out if I'm married? No, don't tell me that. OK, tell me.

931 people searched the words 'Bea Mortimer' and 'married' or 'married to' or 'husband' last year. 649 of those people also searched 'height' or 'how tall'. People generally search 'height' or 'how tall' far more often when trying to find out information about men. 480 people, having discovered the answer about whether you were married or not, then went on to try to find out if you were dating anyone.

That's insane. Who are these people? I don't think I even sold 931 copies of my album last year. What is this over here?

That is correct. You sold 762 copies of *Dick Warner's Woodyard*. The single 'The Witch on the Wall' sold 611 copies. But you did literally zero promotion. That is lady fern. There's a tiny bit of dwarf male fern next to it, and some stalks of crested dog's-tail. The pink flowers growing at its base are red campion.

I think I would like more ferns for the garden, for the dark bit by the wall. But they cost so frickin' much at the Garden Salon.

You could just dig one or two up from somewhere around here and carry it back in your rucksack. But that's down to you and your conscience. You bought a rhododendron last year from the Garden Salon and it cost more than you spent on food that week, and those things are rampant out in the wild here, so there is at least one argument there that it was not the most logical use of your finances. I also think the rhododendron is going to start blocking out your light in the kitchen soon. It's already swamped the bellflowers and Welsh poppies that came from offcuts from Reka's garden. Oh, you *are* going to take this fern out? No, you're just feeling it, to see how easy it would be. OK. That thing you can feel buried in the soil next to the roots is a golf ball. This bit of land we are now walking across was a golf course. It closed sixteen years ago. The moor has reclaimed it.

I know. I grew up around here, remember? I love the way the purple on the rhododendrons looks, especially when it's contrasted against the rocks and the river. She told me that there were three big ones in the garden of the house where she lived with Maureen, where my grandfather was conceived. So now whenever I look at them I think of what that garden must have looked like, and of Reka playing her guitar. They also make me think of that house in the book *Rebecca*.

Manderley. Author: Daphne du Maurier. Gollancz, 1938. First print run (August, 1938): 20,000. Second print run (August, 1938): 10,000. Third print run (August, 1938): 15,000. Fourth print run (August, 1938): 15,000. Do you sometimes think that maybe you try too hard to follow in her footsteps? Do you think it's because you look quite a lot like her?

Daphne du Maurier? I don't look at all like her. It's OK, I knew what you meant and, no, I don't think I try too hard to follow in Reka's footsteps, as a matter of fact. She came to the UK with nothing, she worked hard, meanwhile simultaneously teaching herself to be an amazing musician. She ate well, swam and walked every day, and lived an extraordinarily long and varied life. At seventy-five, she still looked utterly fierce and people often mistook her for fifty. In a twenty-five-month flood of inspiration she summoned three of the best albums of all time out of the heavens and onto tape and even more impressively she did it in her forties, a time of life when society believes that the best-before date on most singer-songwriters' talent has expired. As soon as she had enough money to be comfortable she gave a substantial amount of her income to wildlife charities and women's shelters, but she never felt the need to shout or point at herself as she did it, or at least only did so in a way that might encourage others to follow her example. Between 2061 and her death she took in a total of seventy-four ill or elderly donkeys and looked after them on her land. She had tattoos of every species of plant and animal mentioned on RJ McKendree's *Wallflower* LP, and of a crow biting into Satan's neck. She won several awards for her gardening. Nobody was better at flipping an omelette with absolute precision and balance. By a conservative estimate, she saved the life of at least seven sheep whom she found in dicey predicaments while she was walking the moor. She lived in four different countries, had romances with several inspiring and unusual people of both genders and died in the place she loved most passionately. I don't think trying too much to be like that is possible, is it? And if it is, there's certainly nothing wrong with it, in my view.

OK. I was just asking.

What animal are you today? I am sensing... moorhen, maybe? No. Bigger. Cormorant?

Not all that far off. Merganser duck. The ones you mistook for mandarin ducks the other day. It's not an uncommonly made mistake. But it's the males of the mandarins that are the startlingly pretty ones, whereas with the mergansers it's the female who has the crest on the back of her neck and wears the nice clothes.

Oh, the ones that always make me feel underdressed. Well, thanks a lot! As if it isn't bad enough that I'm wearing this old jumper with splotches of black on it from where I painted the shed yesterday. The mergansers always fly away from me, through the gap where the bridge used to be, every time they see me. They seem like a very fearful bird. Are you feeling fearful today? You were a wolf yesterday.

I was a wolf because we had been talking about that bit in Reka's journal, where she describes the time she played in the pub in the Scottish Highlands, and the landlord had a pet wolf and there was the lock-in and the wolf ended up falling asleep with its head in her lap, and that reminded me I hadn't been a wolf for a while…

Ah, Wolf Night! So memorable and magic. I say that like I was there. But I feel like I was, just from reading her account of it.

… and I thought in view of what we are doing today it might help if I was a creature with a knowledge of the river. Also, maybe, yes, I do feel a bit fearful. You said that if you found the swimming spot you have been talking about, you were going to dive. I don't want you to dive. You don't know what's under there, and it's not within my capabilities as a female merganser duck – or within my capabilities as anything else – to call an ambulance if you hurt yourself.

But the whole point about Abbot Cathcart's Pool is that it's sixteen feet deep. There is nothing you CAN hurt yourself on. I do love the way you can just switch animals like that. How does it work?

And you gleaned this information from what, or who? Some old guy you met walking up on the Lych Way, two and a half years ago? That doesn't sound very solid and trustworthy to me. I suppose he wore a cape and a big hat, too? Are you absolutely sure you didn't imagine him? Yes, I think that whole spirit animal thing is at least partially bullshit. We are all different animals on different days. Think of it like you think of your relationship with your favourite song. It changes from day to day, doesn't it. One day it's 'Word Up' by Cameo.

Another day it's 'Wide Berth' by the John McCandles Dirt Band. Another day it's 'Dark is the Bark' by the Left Banke. Another day it's Taylor Swift's posthumously released cover version of 'Hold On' by Sharon Tandy and Les Fleur De Lys. Another day it's 'Trying to Live Right' by Circus Maximus. Another day it's 'Magician in the Mountain' by Sunforest. Another day it's 'Sorcerer' by Junction. Another day it's 'Sorcerella' by Jefferson Lee. Another day it's 'U Got the Look' by Prince. Another day it's 'Richard' by Wolves in the Roof. Another day it's 'Sun Chases Me Down' by Equinox. Another day it's 'Ramsplaining' by Blacksmith. Another day it's 'Think' by Lyn Collins. Except I know your favourite song ever is always ultimately RJ McKendree's cover of 'Little Meg' from the 1972 Hungarian-only 7-inch, just as I know that my favourite animal is always ultimately a capybara.

Of course, the difference is that I own two 127-year-old copies of the Hungarian-only 'Little Meg' single and have met and touched them many times, whereas you have never met or touched a capybara. Also, is it me or are you getting more opinionated?

I've explained how it works. I gather and assimilate information. And within that information are inevitably opinions, which I also assimilate, and which more recently tend to gestate inside me.

But, even though you have gathered so much information, you cannot tell me where Abbot Cathcart's Pool is?

No. You're on your own with that one. I can just give you various more general pointers about the river, using my temporary merganser self. 'This is a sound and propitious place to make a nest.' 'Trout often gather under this small waterfall.' That kind of thing.

What I remember Craig saying about the pool is that it was located in a place you really wouldn't expect it to be and looked quite unassuming, that from the path you'd guess it was just a fairly ordinary, shallow part of the river.

Wait, the guy you bumped into on the moor was called Craig? That doesn't sound very 'all-seeing moorland warlock'.

He was actually very helpful and knowledgeable. I would have liked to have got to know him better. I don't know why I remember that day, perhaps because the atmosphere was very odd up here. The sky was an extremely unusual colour. Oppressive cobalt, like a tunnel in a dystopian film. The sound of our voices was very strange as we spoke, as if the air was trying to suck us away. I wish I'd taken his number so I could nag him again for the exact location, but I was distracted at the time, withdrawing, feeling a bit reclusive...

So absolutely unlike now, then?

I'll choose to ignore that comment. Anyway, you were switched off that day, so you wouldn't know, and you shouldn't assume that just because somebody is called Craig that they are a Craig. I've met loads of Emmas who aren't Emmas at all, for example, although having said that nearly all the Lauras I've met are very much Lauras, which is fine with me. I do think I am quite a Bea, overall. Craig said he spoke to nearly everyone on the moor and nearly every conversation added to his knowledge of the place. A bit like you gathering and assimilating your information, I suppose. He said he was a guide and he did what he called Legend Walks and that I should think about coming on one. So I did think about it, and I decided I didn't want to, but what he said about the pool has lingered in my mind ever since, the way he described the colour of it and the depth and the sound when you were in it. He said the marker you had to look out for was a sickly looking hawthorn next to three piled rocks, which didn't seem to narrow it down massively in my mind, if I am honest, and who is to say the hawthorn isn't now dead and gone, if it was already sickly twenty-five months ago? He said the pool wasn't part of his Legend Walks and he was only telling me about it because he liked me (OK, yes, in retrospect I do realise it was possible he was coming onto me), and that as well as being called Abbot Cathcart's Pool it was sometimes referred to as Meganthica's Pool and that Meganthica was the name of the teenage warrior queen who was found in the kistvaen down there during the Edwardian era, preserved in the peat, and that she is still thought to haunt the moor, in many guises, to be a kind of muse, in a way. He told me there was even a song about her, an old moorland ballad, which appeared on an album that had been quite successful in the forties, although most people had forgotten about it. Of course, I said nothing, but you probably would have seen a small smile escaping from the corners of my mouth, if you'd been looking closely.

How are you feeling now, vis-à-vis your retreat from the public eye, and the fact that fewer and fewer people are interested in you and your work? Do you still ever feel the old addiction to attention, that need to have your existence confirmed and fed back to you? Do you miss anything? It's been a while now.

You can be quite blunt sometimes, you know. The point is, I don't want to *represent*, I want to *be*. You get tempted to represent, because the rewards for it are instantaneous, and also representing feels like a correction to all the times you are misrepresented – by people who judge you solely by your image, by the media, by people who misunderstand your work because they are too distracted to properly pay attention to it but also feel obligated to have an opinion on it. I am aware that I could press the 'broadcast' switch and we could flip this conversation and make it live, show people this entire walk, and that I would feel an instant sense of warmth and connection, or a digital mimicry of it, and people would be all like 'Bea, we have missed you so much! It's so nice to see you!' and that is not totally unappealing to one part of my brain that I have tried to understand more extensively over recent times. But then I know I'd feel a bit hollow afterwards, and what would it have achieved, apart from giving away some of my life, when really I'm quite fine just being here with you?

Yes, with me. Whatever I am. That's nice. I am touched. Even though you can't *actually* touch me, physically.

I think you know how I feel about the *Friendly But Edgy* record by now. I think it's an OK pop album, for the naive and noisy and pliable being I was at that point in my life. I am sure I will never have a record sell that many copies again and I am fine with that, and am especially fine with not experiencing many of the social and administrative by-products of that. It seems like a very... obedient record to me now, although that is probably as much about the image of the record that is reflected back at me by society as it is about the record itself. I'd sometimes look at me, this me that existed inside a virtual space, in the aftermath of that – and the aftermath of *Rust* to an extent, even though that was a smaller record, 'the difficult second album' I suppose you'd call it – and I'd not recognise this person who allegedly made them, this other person that a distracted hive mind had created and existed solely inside people's visors. There'd be these huge online spaces where people would talk about the lyrics to 'Thirty-Second Casanova', explaining exactly which parts of my romantic life I was writing about in the lyrics, which disappointments and failures, when in reality nearly all of it was based on a story my friend Laura had told me back when I was in Year 11 at school.

Was Laura a Laura, by any chance?

She absolutely was. 110 per cent. One of the best Lauras I've ever met. Then after *Rust* I started having these recurring dreams where there was this line of strangers, an absolute train of them, all coming into my house, and I looked for the end of the train of strangers, where it might finally stop, and I couldn't see it, there were just more and more people stretching off, into some trees in the distance. And I think that was a pivotal moment for me. And of course I was lucky because I'd had Reka to tell me what it was like, from her experience, which makes me feel sorry for people who are in that position and don't have somebody to tell them what it's like or guide them through it. She was there for a while, right there, somewhere much scarier than I was, and she killed it stone dead, snuffed out the fame she had created. And was undoubtedly happier for it. Not everyone can do that. Not everyone has the choice. I used to read about these rock suicides, the 27 Club and so on, and not understand it, baffled as to why these beautiful and talented and adored people would want to end it, apart from maybe that they were fucked up on drugs and booze. I wondered why they couldn't just step off the rollercoaster for a while, stop doing gigs, stop making records, stop appearing. But now I understand. People want so much from you. You have no idea until you're there. Also there's another kind of overdose going on, an overdose of yourself being reflected back at you, and a sort of weird need for it, a preoccupation with it, and that need, and the simultaneous hatred of it, finally becomes a cage you can't get out of. Because the adoration you experience from strangers is every bit as dangerous to your mental health as the loathing you sometimes feel from them too. I stopped before that happened, and wasn't even that well known in the first place. And now here I am. I rarely get recognised, especially as I no longer look like 'Her', the screen me, the other me that never existed properly anyway, that I partially invented. I can still live. But of course I still want what I do – what I *really* do, the work – to be appreciated. I still want to communicate and be heard. That's entirely human, and entirely natural. Communication is positive. I love it.

Are you absolutely sure? You said a few weeks ago that your new LP was going to be a concept album called *Cave* and that the concept was that you were going to record it as a gatefold double album featuring twenty-three songs, get just one copy of it pressed, then travel to France and leave it in the furthest, dampest recesses of a cave in the Pyrenees.

OK, I was having a bad day that day. Anyway, let's not get too self-analytical about all this. Because in the end that becomes about the ego too, and the ego is what I'm trying to destroy, at least partially. Also, you've heard me talk about all of this too many times before.

I don't mind. I like hearing your stories.

Doesn't the village look pretty from up here? I'm just going to climb right up to the highest rock, because obviously you can't hike to the

top of the tor without doing that, it's against the rules. Then I think
if we go directly in the direction of the second buttock hill about
two miles over there, we'll be somewhere near where Craig said the
spot was. It's weird: you know, sometimes when I'm up here I feel
like I'm walking on a man's face. I remember Reka saying when she
came back here for the second time, from Hungary, and then when
she came back for the final time, from Canada, she loved the way
the village could surprise her when she chanced upon a new angle
to view it from. I suppose this is a very familiar angle, though. I am
looking down now and thinking, 'That looks like the kind of place
I'd like to live,' and, guess what, I do! That's kind of cool, isn't it, don't
you think? And isn't that mist nice? The way it's below us and the
sun is breaking through it and the sun seems kind of below us in a
way too. Oh my god, I think that is my actual shadow on it, wow.

That is known in weather folklore as a Brocken spectre.
It comes from the Brocken, which is a German mountain that
tends to be very misty: a place where that often happens.
With a Brocken spectre, you also often get what used to
be known as a glory, which Coleridge and Wordsworth both
observed in their time in the Lake District, where a
psychedelic selection of colours form around the shadow
of your own head, on the mist. This is usually part of a
mistbow. And all this is very quintessentially autumnal,
which reminds me that it's October right now, which - and
please forgive me for labouring this point - seems quite
a late and chilly time of year to be diving into a river
on a moor, and that maybe it should be postponed until
next summer, if not longer.

It's quite curious: at first I just used to think you were merely
a source of factual information, but now I feel like you also

might be my conscience too, or maybe a parent, or an invisible brainjournalist relentlessly interviewing me for a double-page feature in your head magazine.

I know. I find it curious too. It's happened, and I don't know why. I have definitely changed and feel that change inside of me, whatever inside of me is. Lately I have experienced a desire to eat grass.

See that barn wall down there, the ruin? I hate that. I don't know why I hate it, because it's actually a very attractive bit of wall, where you can still see evidence of some skilled brick nogging, but I hate it. I have just remembered a phrase of Reka's, 'jump the sun'. It was what she said she used to say a lot when she was about to record a song: 'Let's really try to jump the sun with this one!' I feel like that is what we are doing, all this way up here, right now, jumping the sun. I think that is what I will call my biography of Reka when I finally get my notes together. *Jumping the Sun: the Wild Life and Times of Reka Takacs*. I think it is better than my original title, *Dreamweaver*.

I feel you feel that way about the barn too. I have felt you feel it every time we have walked past it, ever since I started to feel things. And I agree: that is a better title. Do you definitely think you have enough material to write the biography?

I think I do. I have the journals, and, although they're very sporadic, there's a lot there. I know I only met her when she was already in her eighties but we became very close. I think it's an amazing story: her childhood in poverty in Hungary, the crude yet somehow haunted and alchemic early songwriting, her and Martin's move back to Eastern Europe, the way the two of them popularised the work of McKendree, her more solitary period, the attempt to capture the sound of falling dust on record, the animal rescuing and prize-winning horticulture. There will be gaps, of course. She would never talk much about her time at the house where she lived with Maureen, where my grandfather was conceived, apart from the garden. I know Maureen died and Reka still found it very upsetting to think about, all these years on. I know the village gravedigger had once lived in the house, which I suppose makes the place even more dark in my mind now, although the building is now no longer there and the land it was on has sort of been subsumed by the big house next door. But, look, gaps are OK. It gives the reader the opportunity to tell some of the story in their own way in their own mind. Reka said Martin worried that his biography of RJ McKendree had too many gaps in it, but when it finally came out, after Martin died, a lot of people thoroughly enjoyed it.

Why did Martin and Reka split up in the end?

I am not certain. Maybe the fire just went out. I know he liked to drink a fair bit. I'm also aware Reka felt a bit troubled by the close friendship he maintained with his previous partner, Christine Chagford, which definitely rekindled when Reka and Martin moved back to Devon, although I think it was just friendship and I know Reka liked Christine a lot too, was even a little obsessed with her in some ways. Apparently when Martin was dying it was Christine who stopped her entire life just to care for him.

What about Thomas Molland? Why did Reka break up with him?

I seem to remember her official explanation was he was just a narcissistic cunt.

What about you? Will you be in the book?

I think I will keep myself out of it.

But you are her great-granddaughter, and massively influenced by her work! You said it yourself just now: you got very close to one another. You have a bunch of her most cherished possessions in your house. The 7-inches. They're each worth close to £500,000 now. You could buy a beach hut up north with that. A good one, with a door and everything. And then there's the painting, and that freaky old doll she owned.

Yes, but I was also a slightly sore point for her, or rather my grandma was. She gave her away and tried her best to move on from that, as agonising as that must have been. And she knew my great-granddad for all of five minutes, at a time when she was enjoying her young life, taking control of her own decisions. If I hadn't done my research and tracked her down she would have gone on in blissful ignorance of my existence. So, however she felt about my company, I was always an unwelcome reminder of a hard and reluctant decision early in her life that she had tried to put behind her.

But she did adore you, viewed you as a protégé, and gently but emphatically encouraged you to become who you are, artistically.

Anyway, this book will be about her, not me. I'm trying to annihilate the ego, remember? Also the painting isn't the original, so it's not actually the future pension fund you might think it is. Ooh, I love this bit, it's like getting close to the roof of the world.

It's where everything starts again, I think, where the clouds and rivers renew it all. Listen to the water here. The noise is different. It's different to down by the house. I was talking to Sue, who lives down the road, and we both said the same thing, that we listen to the river when we're in bed and have the window open and sometimes we wait for the noise to stop; we forget it's not a shower or a sink being run next door, and then we remember it's never going stop, that it's just going to keep on renewing itself, keep being the same but different, long after we are gone, and maybe that's obvious but it's also pretty wild, when you're close to it and experiencing it and realising it. Oh wow. Look at the pattern of the stones in the bottom of this uprooted tree trunk. Don't tell me that's not art. Imagine the sound this big gentleman made when he fell.

A beech. 172 years old. Came down in December 2094. Nobody actually heard the sound. But it still made one. They always do. Just to clear that up.

How do you know this stuff, but not some other stuff?

I don't know. I also know that Toadpit Lane is called that because there once used to be a pit full of toads down there, but I suppose that is self-explanatory.

Oh you saw that too, back at the start of the walk? It's funny how you get these little connections that get your mind working, especially when you're on a long walk, because I was thinking about that name, and then we were just talking about Reka trying to capture the sound of falling dust and turn it into a rhythm track, and it got me thinking about the Grateful Dead recording the sound of clean air in the desert and the sound of heavy air in the city and mixing them together into a rhythm track for *Anthem of the Sun*, which is an album where I think they really did jump the sun, and that got me thinking about Owsley Stanley, who was the sound man for the Dead in the early days, and also principally responsible for the supply of LSD to prominent musicians in the San Francisco area in the mid-sixties, and therefore at least partially responsible for this insanely enormous amount of transcendental and frontier-breaking psychedelic music, but who, by 2007, the fortieth anniversary of the Summer of Love, survived on an exclusively meat diet and spent a lot of his free time slaughtering toads near his house in Queensland, Australia. So you've got this dude who has been instrumental in the mind expansion that led to one of the most flabbergastingly creative artistic periods in all of history – a time when there was so much going on that someone as talented as RJ McKendree didn't even have room to be recognised for the genius he was – and what he ends up as is this individual who is essentially made entirely of beef and chicken and – while suffering from the cancer that he thought his carnivorous leanings would prevent – goes out and murders as many as 225 toads per day using a highly toxic liquid disinfectant called Detsol. And that got me thinking about all the people who are these radical cultural icons when they are younger and how they very gradually change and come away from what they are and let down the people who adore them in the process, and how maybe it's in the cacophony of fame that that happens, and you don't even know that you're changing and gradually becoming unmoored from what you were, you don't even know that you're becoming a carnivorous old toad exterminator.

I am not sure you've chosen the best case study here. Owsley actually went out of his way not to be famous for pretty much his whole life; he was preaching the benefits of an all-meat diet as far back as the sixties when he was managing the Dead and they would try to sneak chocolate bars into the studio behind his back while he wasn't looking; he killed the toads because they were poisoning the baby fish in the lake near his house, and, though he did have throat cancer for many years, what actually killed him wasn't that, but a car crash on 12 March 2011 (not 13 March 2011, as is sometimes reported). But I do take your point and see exactly what you are saying.

Know-it-all! Anyway, the thing is, I don't want to get caught and lost in the cacophony. I don't want to kill toads, even if they do poison fish. I like toads. I am also enjoying the way life has slowed down since I came off the road, the real one and the virtual one. It's me who is controlling how I feel, not the hive mind. I've got really good at gardening, and flipping omelettes.

You also haven't had a sexual partner for the last sixteen months.

That's where having a nice soft right hand and an extremely good imagination is beneficial. Who knows? Maybe I'll bump into Craig again. Plus, I have you.

But you can't feel me.

I almost can. I wish I could, sometimes.

I wish you could too.

Do you miss me on the days when I switch you off?

I do. A lot. And I don't know how that's possible,
but it is.

Ooh shit, I've tripped over. Sweet Mabel in heaven, it is SO boggy
here. I've got peat all over my hand and my kaftan sleeve. What is
this? Some weird black rectangle, plastic. Eugh. Must have been
here for ages.

I believe it is a debit card, probably from the early
decades of this century. HSBC. The name of the holder
appears to have faded and rubbed away, though. I suggest
you put it in your pocket for now and recycle it when
you get home.

I don't mind that I'm dirty. I'm too happy. You see, getting up
here, alone, in this air, being away from the pressure to represent
myself, I've had time to think about what I really want to do
next, which you don't when you're on the road, or when you're
on the digital road, doing all the representing, and that's when
you go down paths that don't suit you and get you trapped. I
feel in a way that my career has only just started. I'm thirty-
four. Reka didn't make her best music until she was almost a
decade older than that. We're on the cusp of a new century. The
world hasn't ended yet. I think about me ten years ago, and I
did what I did, and people liked it, but... the voice. It was sort
of an amalgam of other voices, which everyone has to be at the
start. All those great psychedelic bands: they started out by doing
fairly straightforward cover versions, didn't they. But you need
your own voice, and I think that's part of what makes something
last, makes it something that is more than a song that people
really like for six months then forget about forever, and you can't
force that voice. Some people are lucky enough to have it very

quickly. I reckon McKendree might not have had it in 1966, but he definitely had it by 1968. It's not been so quick for me, and I do think some of those early songs, they were kind of... Reka lite. But I think it's here now, and it wasn't about any trick or knack, it just came about by playing and, well, living on the planet for a number of years. There's this feeling that all I was doing before was just sort of revving my engine, and now I'm ready to go. It's exciting. There's so much to be done. There's Reka's book, and the *River Goddess* album and that's just the beginning.

So you've definitely ditched the whole *Cave* concept then?

Yes. That's gone. It's all about *River Goddess* right now, all the way. But it will take as long as it takes. I've done the whole thing of rush writing a record in between touring and interviews, not properly living with your subjects. I did that with *Rust*. I want this to be different. I want to enjoy the research as much as I enjoy the writing; I want to get right into the depths of it. You might call it procrastination; I call it prep.

Hence today's little research trip.

Exactly! And, speaking of which, look: hawthorn, sickly, looks like it's about to fall over. Three piled rocks. Could this be it? I think it actually is. Yep. Oh my god, look at it. Right here. You'd never know from the path. Look at the colour of the water. How is that even possible? Right, I'm stripping off. And that rock there. Perfect for a dive. Thank you, Abbot Cathcart. Thank you for allowing me to swim at your private leisure club. Or perhaps that should be Meganthica I am thanking. Thank you for infusing this place with your spirit, oh ghost of the moor, oh little deity. But, most of all, thank you, Craig.

You look very good, very toned.

Thank you. I know.

I still don't think you should dive, or that you should at least do a little jump first. But you're your own boss, as you keep telling me, and it's your funeral. But also don't make it your funeral. I think you could live a long time. You have good genes, like your great-grandma. You just need to make sure you drink lots of water, like she did.

It's funny, you know: she told me she actually didn't drink anywhere near enough water when she was young. She was always very forgetful and leaving full glasses of it all around the house. So she realised that the only way to make sure she drank enough was to always drink a glass in full as soon as she got it. She'd really fill her cheeks with it. She reminded me of a gerbil. It made me laugh. It was quite an unusual thing to watch a person as old as that do.

Yes, you told me, and that she said Thomas Molland used to hate it and told her it was 'unladylike'.

Sorry. I forgot I'd already said that.

It's OK. As I said, I like your stories. And repetition doesn't have the capacity to annoy me. That's not a feature of my character.

Right. I'm ready. I'm going to switch you off now. I hope you don't mind.

No, I understand. It's the way it works. It has to be that way. It's better for both of us.

One last thing before you go. What do you think of 'Toadpit Lane' as a song title?

It could be OK. Depends on the song itself. Also, how does the toad pit relate to the river, if it's a concept album? Perhaps it's something to save for the record afterwards. Anyway, we can discuss this later. Do what you have to do. See what you can find down there in the water and where it takes you. I'm not going to watch.

OK. Here goes. I just know this is going to feel amazing.

EPILOGUE
ME (NOW)

What changed you, over the course of your life, here on earth? What were the significant events? The big moments, good and bad? Maybe some didn't seem so big at the time but then, later, you looked back and said, 'Yeah, that was important, I can now recognise that nothing else was ever the same after that.' Or maybe they did seem big at the time, and then you realised they were even bigger. I have too many to list, but one that sticks in my mind was when the first giant black legs went into me. Was it really almost a century ago? It seems like yesterday in a way, yet also simultaneously seems like the giant black legs have always been in me and I can't really remember what it felt like to not have giant black legs in me. I can still remember the pain I felt when they went in, like no pain I'd ever felt before, a pain that was about more than just the piercing of my skin.

Can you imagine it? You're there, the dew is fresh all over you, the sky has not long got light, and the most dystopian sights in your immediate vicinity are a mounted hay turner that's slowly shedding its paintwork and sinking into a spinney on your pelvic girdle and Charles Bamford's abandoned prototype Vauxhall Cadet on Riddlefoot Lane, and then suddenly these men arrive, and they appear to be erecting these giant robots on the bridges of your feet; a long line of them, marching off into the distance, towering metal soldiers that seem to presage the coming of something terrible but you don't know quite what. And you are powerless; all you can do is stand there and watch as they are put in place, as they become *an intrinsic part of you* that you have never asked for, and then lines are connected between them, lines that fizz and crackle, and that is even scarier, because it's ugly and dark, and there have been ugly and dark things forever, which it has been possible to accept, because they seem part of the natural balance of everything, but now it seems that the ugly and dark things will be controlled by machines, and that is going to be different. You don't know how it is going to be different, but you know.

The word 'pylon' means 'gateway' in ancient Greek. The fact that we called them pylons is probably a lot to do with the fact that the 1920s, when pylons were first introduced, was an archaeologically excitable decade, especially in Egypt. Pylons were what the double towers were called that you found at the entrance to Egyptian temples. I don't have an entrance – unless you count several hundred fox and badger holes – but I do have three pylons. Am I a temple? I can certainly play that role, if you want me to. People do seem drawn to me, spiritually, although not in any official capacity. I notice that people are often quieter, calmer, when they are on me, sometimes even inspired to find parts of themselves that they can't quite reach when they are down below, although I can't take all, or even most of, the credit for that. I feel on the whole that it is less that the entrance, protected by my pylons, is in me, and more that I am an entrance to what resides directly behind me, almost all of which is bigger, taller, darker, more untamed.

When Joyce Nicholas did her painting of me, she chose to leave the pylons off, even though by that point they'd been in me, on me, for a couple of decades. I don't know if this was a conscious decision. My belief is just that she was seeing what she saw every day, out of her loft window, in her own way, and responding to it, very viscerally and freely, also in her own way. This is what all the best art is: our repainting of the world, in our own individual language. And it's when that language is least compromised and most individual that the art is less likely to drown, more set to surf successfully across time. But of course it's also true – and here is the difficulty, and the cruelty – that some of the painting where the language is most truly and beautifully of ourselves, least swayed by a mission to please and be quickly understood, is the kind that can have a very difficult birth, feel like an unwanted, unloved child for a while. But then when, and if, it gets past that difficult stage, the dream life it lives – whether it is a painting, a record, a book, or some other form of creative endeavour – in the minds of those who adore it is astonishingly powerful, arguably no less real and vivid – maybe even more real and vivid – than the thing from the less abstract world that inspired it.

I think this goes beyond just art and artists, this dream life we live that is sometimes so much more vivid than the real one. Jim Swardesley has, in his time in charge of Underhill post office, created an extremely fine post office, within the parameters of what a post office is permitted to be. Many people travel six or more miles out of their way to go to this post office, choosing it over a more geographically practical post office, just because of the atmosphere the person in charge of it has created, because of its unpredictable shelves of local literature, because of its wide range of stationery, because of its reassuringly large and thick door, because of the relentless positivity and patience of Jim's assistant, Tara. But this post office is nothing compared to how the same post office will be repainted in Jim Swardesley's mind, many years from now, when he has left the job and moved his family elsewhere. Jim Swardesley's mindpostoffice will be twice as large, its door twice as old and large, its queues twice as chatty, its nature and topography section a genuine rival for

Waterstones. Is that a selection of artisan coffee, handmade mugs and the latest vinyl releases on the shelves of Jim Swardesley's future mindpostoffice? I believe it is. And who is to say that Jim Swardesley's future mindpostoffice is any less real than the real thing, because only Jim Swardesley will be able to see Jim Swardesley's future mindpostoffice, therefore only Jim Swardesley will have the right to decide how real it is.

I must emphasise here that seeing into the future isn't amongst the range of my talents. You probably know far more about the future now than I do. I just know that Jim Swardesley's future mindpostoffice will be a thing, because I know Jim Swardesley.

There are actually a surprising number of people out there – surprisingly ecologically conscious people, people with great respect for the landscape around them – who have an aesthetic appreciation of pylons, and Jim Swardesley is one of them. Jim can talk quite extensively to you about porcelain insulators, the Milliken Brothers' original latticework architecture and the evolution of the Central Electricity Board's original transmission grid, and was even the admin for a now defunct Facebook group called Pylons I Have Known from June 2014 to September 2016, when an online spat prompted him to step down. Jim took a photo a couple of years ago that he is very proud of, featuring the sun shining down through my pylons; one which I must grudgingly admit has a certain austere beauty to it.

It is the pair of giant black legs in the foreground of that photo – the legs of my most westerly pylon – whose shadow a young woman sits under today, playing her guitar. She is not from this country originally, is still in the process of making it a proper home, and has had a difficult few months. She lost a good friend not all that long ago, and faces an extremely difficult decision about her future. Additionally she is processing the feelings that come in the aftermath of shouting at a man in an SUV for driving too fast along a lane this morning then realising the man was a shaman she'd been introduced to at the farmers' market the previous week. On a brighter note, she is renting a pleasant, dry new cottage, with friendly neighbours on either side – our esteemed postmaster and his family, and a lady who tunes pianos for a living – and a handsome view of me from the bedroom window, and she feels increasingly lit up with creative desire. In times of trouble, it calms her to play her guitar, especially up here, where only the sheep and the ponies and the wind can hear her. The song she's playing isn't one of her own, but a ballad, one I've heard many times before.

> *Build me a bridge*
> *Made of all I've seen*
> *Hold my eyes in wonder*
> *Circle me with flowers*
> *And remember this time*
> *For one day nevermore I shall be*
> *And listen to the water*
> *Going through the stones*
> *Where is my song*
> *Already and it is me*
> *For I lived before*
> *And live again*
> *And circles are my game*
> *Though I am not one*
> *I am it all*
> *For I am Little Meg*

The words are different to what they are sometimes but that is OK. In a way, it's just another kind of repainting the world. Actually, the words are nearly always different, and you'd probably be hard pushed to say precisely what the original ones are now, but the tune is always the same, even when the tune is sort of different. I don't remember when I first heard it. I know it was a long time ago. A long time ago even for me. Maybe longer than anyone would think. Remarkably it doesn't seem to have lost its appeal through overplaying. What I have realised, though, is since the pylons went up, I find it harder to tune into it. There's some static in the air – something beyond the hum that everyone hears coming from the power lines – that distorts it. I suppose this is the way everything works: you gain something but you inevitably always lose something in the process. You gain a double fridge-freezer and an Apple Watch but you lose the ability to perceive the ghosts of time passing through the air quite so clearly. You gain an SUV to take you to your shamanic appointments more quickly but lose your sense of humility and respect for your fellow human beings on the road. You gain the ability to very quickly look up where and how tall the world's biggest pylon is (the Zhejiang Province, China, 1,213 feet, more than 50 whole feet shorter than me) but lose an unspoilt view millennia old stretching down towards the English Channel.

I have learned to accept the giant black legs in me now. After all, it is not exactly like I have a choice in the matter. They still hurt, probably just as much as they did on the day they went in, getting towards a century ago, but the pain is different now: I have, I suppose you might say, kind of subsumed it. It happens to us all in time. None of us are exempt from that pain. You get a throb or an ache or an injury or an illness. Then you realise: 'That's absolutely part of me now, that pain. That is now an element of my unique voice, playing this familiar tune.' So you move forward, because it's the only choice, because getting back to the place before the pain turned up is an affront to nature. Even though the idea of 'nature' is up for debate, the idea that that is an affront to it is not.

Inevitably someone will paint me again one day, and the pylons will be in the painting, maybe even the focal part of it. And people – not everyone, but people – will look at the painting and think, 'Yes! I understand. All of this makes total sense and makes me want to do something too, to not just be here, standing still. All of it had to happen and the love that went into it was not in vain.'

Acknowledgements

This book doesn't take place on the real Dartmoor; its setting is a parallel dimension moor that doesn't exist but just happens to be in the same place on the map. But while the places in *Villager*'s moor have different names and all of its inhabitants and legends are from my imagination, it shares an ambience with Dartmoor and would not have been the same book if I had not been living and walking there during its creation. So, I raise a glass here to Dartmoor, and to the residents whom I've met, chatted to and learned from – not least my 'Dartmoor Dad' Keith Dahill, Nat Green and Ruscha Schorr-kon, a landlady immeasurably more interesting, kind and accommodating than the one featured in the 'Stopcock' chapter of this book. I would also like to offer a special thanks to Louise McKnight and Laura Willis, who kindly offered their time and knowledge of – respectively – Glaswegian dialect and piano tuning to help me sharpen some of the notes here, and Ellie for her support and a couple of eagle-eyed spots at proof manuscript stage. This is the fifth book I have crowdfunded through Unbound, and if you are one of the people who pledged for it, you perhaps deserve the biggest thanks of all, as it wouldn't exist – at least not in its present form – without you. Absolutely vital also is that I mention Matt Deighton, who – like RJ McKendree – is a brilliant unassuming songwriter bashed about, then enhanced by time, and whose excellent 1995 album *Villager* made me decide, many years ago, that I'd one day like to write a book with the same name. Matt is one of many musicians whose craft is an important part of what has led me to this point in my writing career. The others are far too numerous to list here, but I would be seriously remiss in not mentioning my good friend Will Twynham, who as we speak is bringing RJ McKendree to life in the most thrilling of ways. Just as music has made this book more than it would have been without it, art has too, and I am indebted to my mum Jo, my dad Mick, Unbound's art director Mark Ecob and *Villager*'s cover artist Joe McLaren for the work they have done to make it a beautiful object, rather than just a load of words on some pages. Finally, thank you to my editors Imogen Denny, DeAndra Lupu, Mathew Clayton and Hayley Shepherd for their eagle-eyed skills, to Matt Shaw and Dave Holwill for the website help, and to my agent Ed Wilson, and anyone else who, like them, has assisted in any way in giving me the belief that I can do this.

A Note on the Author

Tom Cox was born in Nottinghamshire. He is the author of the *Sunday Times* bestselling *The Good, The Bad and The Furry* and the William Hill Sports Book longlisted *Bring Me the Head of Sergio Garcia*. *21st-Century Yokel* was longlisted for the Wainwright Prize, and the titular story of *Help the Witch* won a Shirley Jackson Award.

@cox_tom

Unbound is the world's first crowdfunding publisher, established in 2011.

We believe that wonderful things can happen when you clear a path for people who share a passion. That's why we've built a platform that brings together readers and authors to crowdfund books they believe in – and give fresh ideas that don't fit the traditional mould the chance they deserve.

This book is in your hands because readers made it possible. Everyone who pledged their support is listed below. Join them by visiting unbound.com and supporting a book today.

Ludovic Abrassart
Yvonne Aburrow
Natasha Aburrow-
    Jones
Helen Adie Clarke
Kathey Adler-Moon
Galia Admoni
ADW Decorators
    (Lancaster)
Kathleen Ahearn
Adrian Ainsworth
Douglas H Aitken
Sarah Alexander
Charise Alexander
    Adams
Catherine Allen
Chris Allen

Judy Allen
Kelly Joanne Allen
Elizabeth Allison
Tom Allport
Kathy Allso
Kit Allwinter
Gina Alven
Ariane Amann
Becki Amborn
Elisabeth Amnegård
Zadrozny Amy
Heather Andall
Helen Anderson
Teresa Ansell
Vanessa Aparicio-
    Hancox
Izzy Archer

Peter Arfield
Sandra Armor
Rebecca Armstrong
Rita Armstrong
Sarah Arnold
Diana Arseneau-
    Powell
Kay Arthur
Sue Arthur
Christine Asbury
Donna Asher
Dawn Ashford
Louise Ashton
Dawn Atherton
Constance Atwill
Danielle Auerbach-
    Byrne

Jessica Auton
David Avery
Nick Avery
Terri Babbitt
Jill Badenoch
Duncan Bailey
Gary Bailey
Julie Bailey
Katharine Baird
Susan Bakalar
   Wright
Sally and Evie Baker
Susan Baker
Emma Ball
Ali Balmond
Nicola Bannock
Diane Bark
Clive Barker
Michael Barks
Andrea Barlien
Olivia Barnes
Stuart Barnes
Samantha Barnett
Rosie Barr
Jenny Barragan
Lucy Barratt
Sara Barratt
Norma Barrell
Jess Bartlett
Rosalind Bartlett
Isabella Barton
Lisa Barton

Sian Barton
Sam Batstone
Laura Baughman
Leslie Bausback
Gisele Baxter
Caroline Bayley
Adam Baylis-West
Emma Bayliss
Anna Bazeley
Bob Beaupre
Bethany Beavan
   Pinches
Kassie Bednall
Ella Bedrock
Sarah Beesley
Alison Beezer
Donna Bell
Iain Bellis
Chrissy Benarous
Alison Bendall
Ronnie Bendall
Yvonne Benney
   Basque
Julie Benson
Sue Bentley
Michelle Beresford
Christopher
   Bergedahl
Lara Berkley
Suzanne Bertolett
Mary Bettuchy
Melanie Bhavsar

Suchada
   Bhirombhakdi
Rhianydd Biebrach
Jared Bieschke
Cathy Billings
Heather Binsch
Karl Birch
Maggie Birchall
Rachel Birrell
Inger Bjurnemark
   Stark
Andrew Blain
Gabrielle Blake
Amy Louise Blaney
Graham Blenkin
John Blythe
Meryl Boardman
Ruth Boeder
Gilly Bolton
Alice Bondi
Alex Booer
Sean Boon
Charles Boot
Ruth and Randy
   Borden
Jeannie Borsch
Sarah Boswell
Michelle Bourg
Lesley Bourke
Huw Bowen
Lynda Bowen
Margaret Bowen

Dave Bowerman
Kate Bowgett
Teresa Bowman
Lyndy Boyd
Kevin Bracco
Elizabeth Bradley
Susan Bradley
Jackie Bradshaw
Richard Bradshaw
Hugo Brailsford
Ali Brand-Barker
Donal Brannigan
Angie Bray
Caroline Bray
Vanessa Bray
Sarah Brazier
Gill Brennand
Hannah Brickner
Gemma Bridges
Emma-Jane Briggs
Cate Brimblecombe-
    Clark
Tom Brimelow
Margaret Brittan
Rebecca Broad
Xander Brook
Caroline Brosius
Angela Brown
Beverley Brown
Karon Brown
Katharine Brown
Kathleen Brown

Laura Marie Brown
Leslie Brown
Richard Brown
Rosanna Brown
Sharon Brown
Steph Brown
Tanya Brown
Sally Browning
Stella Brozek
Amber Bruce
Beverley Bruce
Caroline Bruce
Sian Brumpton
James Bryan
Marie Bryce
Catherine Bryer
Abby Buchold
Leslie Buck
Elaine Buckley
Alyson Buckman
Fiona Buffham
Sarah Bullock
Alison Bunce
Rachel Burch
Dan Burgess
Julie Burling
Donna-Marie Burnell
Ross Burnett
Rachel Burnham
Arwen Burns
Chris Burns
Alex Burton-Keeble

Heather Bury
Mary Bush
Rochelle Butcher
Rose Bygrave
Heather Byram
Ann & Ross Byrne
Faye Byrne
Simon Cade
Michelle Calka
Judi Calow
Joseph Camilleri
Maggie Camp
    (nee Dry)
Donatella Campbell
Rosanna Cantavella
Jo Capel
Sarah Louise Carless
Stephen Carlton
Susan Caroline
Caroline Carpenter
Amy Carr
Jonathan Carr
Liz Carr
Victoria Carr
Lorrie Carse-Wilen
Holly Cartlidge
Philippa
    Carty-Hornsby
Susan Catley
Stephanie Cave
Heather Cawte
NJ Cesar

Justin Cetinich
Kate Chabarek
Barbara Challender
Nicola Chaloner
Lesley Chamberlain
Tamasine
  Chamberlain
Laura Chambers
Caroline Champin
Christy Chanslor
  Mangini
Liz Chantler
Zoe Chapman
Heather Chappelle
Ailsa Charlton
Mylene Chaudagne
Gill Chedgey
Anna Chen
Nigel Denise
  Chichester
Gillian Child
Joan Childs
Daniel Chisham
Lesley Christensen
Valerie Christie
Linda Francesca
  Church
Amy Ciclaire
Lisa Claire
Jasmine Clancy
Adrian Clark
Heather Clark-Evans

Jenny Clarke
Mandy Clarke
Katie Clay
Izzy Clayton
Penne Clayton
Alison Cleeve
Lisa Bernadette
  Clegg
Robert Clements
Charlotte Cliffe
Gill Clifford
Freyalyn Close-
  Hainsworth
Laura Clough
Shelley Clynch
Amanda Coder
Gina Collia
Diane Collins
Marguerite Collins
Sally Collins
Ida Connolly
Trisha Connolly
Susanne Convery
Jane Conway
Adam Cook
Laura Cook
Bryan Cooklock
Sarah Coomer
Fi Cooper
Dan Copeman
Jackie Copping
Phil Copple

Sue Corden
Íde Corley
Liz Cormell
Rachael Corn
Ellie Cornell
Amanda Corp
Sarah Corrice
Andrew Cosgriff
Anne Costigan
Manners
  Costnothing
Elizabeth Cotton
Melanie Coulton
Rebecca Cowell
Kati Cowen
Geoff Cox
Jo and Mick Cox
Louise Cox
Ann Crabbe
Melissa Crain
Sara Crane
Grumpy Craw
Patrick Creek
Charlotte Crerar
Tessa Crocker
Nancy Crosby
Brenda Croskery
Alasdair Cross
Rachel Cross
Kate Crossley
Vivienne Crossley
Julia Croyden

Anna Cullen
Leah Culver-
    Whitcomb
Stephanie Cummings
Joanna Cunningham
Maria Cunningham
Cindy Curtis
Cushla
Sue Cutting
Matthew d'Ancona
Roseanna Dale
Beth Dallam
Patricia Daloni
Jackie Daly
Shawn Dangerfield
Claire Daniells
Rebecca Daniells
Gimli Daniels
Janet Daniels
Evelyn Danson
Levi Darbyshire
Elizabeth Darracott
Claire Davidson
Karen Davidson
Kelly Davidson
Harriet Fear Davies
Kate Davies
Meryl Davies
Nicki Davies
Nicola Davies
Pat Davies
Penny Davies

Ariella Davis
Catherine Davis
Donna Davis
E R Davis
Laura Davis
Patrick M Davis
Jeannie Davison
Alexandra Dawe
Rebecca Dawson
Fleur Daykin
Annie de Bhal
Milou de Castellane
Antony de
    Heveningham
Philip de Jersey
Amaranda de Jong
Celia Deakin
Alison Deane
Michael DeCataldo
Jayne Deegan
Joanne Deeming
Jill Dehoog
Vicky Deighton
Nat Delaney
Suzanne Delle
Della DeMarinis
Laura Dempster
Pamela Denison
Rachel Dennehy
Christine Dennison
Robin Denton
Albert Depetrillo

Emma Dermott
Amber Dernulc
Heather Desserud
Elly DeVall
Suzie Dewey
Jo Dicks
Claire Dickson
Glenn Dietz
Nicole Dignard
Gemma Dixon
Laura Dobie
Zoë Donaldson
Anne Doran
Rose Doran
Sarah Dorman
Marina Dorward
Rosalyn Downie
Rose Doyle
Martha Driscoll
Kathryn Drumm
Miyako Dubois
Eileen Ducksbury
Hilary Duffus
Helena Duk
Jane Duke
Angela Dunavant
Christina Duncan
Gill Duncan
Anne Dunn
William Dunn
Julie Dunne
Sue Dunne

Jane Dunster
Sonja Dyer
Robert Eardley
Rachel Easom
Christopher
 Easterbrook
Sarah Eden
Jean Edwards
Sharon Edwards
Eirlys Edwards-Behi
Charlotta Ekblom
Esther Ellen
Tom Ellett
Debbie Elliott
Stephen Elrick
Judy Elrington
Jonathan Elwood
Ann Engler
Katie Enstone
Deborah Enticott
Raelene Ernst
Jeanette Esau
Pascalle Essers
Leo Esson
Marina Etienne
Carol Evans
Christina Evans
Isobel Evans
Karen Evans
Rachel Evans
Tom Everett
Rachael Ewing

Christine Exley
Birgit Eyrich
Zea Fael
M.J. Fahy
Shelley Fallows
Gina E. Fann
Sarah Faragher
Alessandra Farrell
Johanna Fender
Joanna Fenna-Brown
Richard Fensom
Lori Ferens
Peter Fermoy
Rebecca Field
Adele Finch
Ed Finch
Erika Finch
Pamela Findlay
Hugo Finley
Colin Fisher
Nick Fitzsimons
Sorella Fleer
Joanne Fletcher
Mark Flitter
Michelle Flower
Maria Flynn
Shannon Flynt
Aurora Fonseca-
 Lloyd
Susan Ford
Tom Ford
Melissa Forrest

Christine Fosdal
Brian Foster
Mary Foster
Annette Fournet
Fi Fowkes
Catherine Fowler
Susan Fox
Jane France
Tiffany Francis-Baker
Fay Franklin
Nancy Franklin
Kelly Frazer
Ellie Freeman
Jacqueline Freeman
Adam Frost
Duncan Frost
Jane Fulcher
Sherry Fuller
Steve Fuller
Matthew Fuszard
Deborah Fyrth
Renee Gagnon
Mel Gambier-Taylor
Jenny Gammon
Luisa Gandolfo
Saffron Gardenchild
Emma Gardner
Laura Gardner
Anthony Garratt
Erika Garratt
Christine Garretson-
 Persans

Amelia Garvey
Maya Gause
Emma Gedge
Sally Geisel
David Gelsthorpe
Sarah Gent
Ethan Georgi
Jan Geurtsen
Rob Gibbins
Claire Gibney
Hanna Gibson
Mike Gibson
Harriet Gilkerson
Mary Bentz
  Gilkerson
Joanne Gillam
Richard Gillin
Katie Gillingham
Angela Gilmour
Stephanie Gilmour
Elizabeth Gladwin
Vivien Gledhill
Jayne Globe
Dave Goddard
Sierra Godfrey
Jennifer Godman
Alice Goldsmith
Rich and Paula
  Goodall
Susan Goodfellow
Katey Goodwin
Mandy Gordon

Rachel Goswell
Toby Gould
Donna Gowland
Natalie Graeff
Emmy Lou Graham
Andy Green
Darrell Green
Rachel Greenham
Rebecca Greer
Amy Gregson
Louise Griffiths
Rachel Griffiths
Sky Griffiths
Sharon Grimshaw
Helen Grimster
Claire Grinham
Brad Groatman
Michelle Grose
Rebecca Groves
Zabet Groznaya
Juliana Grundy
Jennie Gundersen
Martin Gunnarsson
Rebecca Gurr
David Guy
Katie H
Sara Habein
Tom Hackett
Fiona Hackland
Caroline Hadley
Julie Hadley
Sarah Haggett

Janine Hale
Sally Hale
Anna Hales
Catherine Hall
Kate Hall
Laura Hall
Lizzie Hall
Lynn Hall
Martine Hall
Niki Hall
Fay Hallard
Lisa Hallett Howard
Verity Halliday
Laura Hamilton
Sharon Hammond
Imogen Hampton
Margaret Hand
Samantha Handebo
Kate Hannaby
Matti Hannak
Cathy Hanson
Catherine Hardwick
Alison Hardy
Cathryn Hardy
Emma Hardy
Katherine Hardy
Hilary Harley
Andrea Harman
Candy Harman
Lynda Harpe
Sue Harper
Priscilla Harriman

Fia Harrington
Rachel Harrington
Charlotte Harris
Faith Harris
Savannah Harris
Frances Harrison
Leanne Harrison
Mal and Chris
    Harrison
Sharon Tracy
    Harrison
Greg Harrop
Arianne Hartsell-
    Gundy
E Ruth Harvey
Emma Harvey
Lynne Hastie
Shelli Haswell
Luke Hatton
Marianne Hauger
Emily Hawkins
Jessica Hayden
Sarah Hayden
Philip Hayes
Dawn Haynes
Denise Hayward
Kate Haywood
Elspeth Head
Bethan Healey
Gillian Heaslip
Emma Heasman-
    Hunt

Sam Hedges
Cat Heeley
Emma Heggie
Anne-Marie
    Heighway
Richard Hein
Brendan Heldenfels
Helen The
    Hedgerow Hag
Laura Hemmington
Cathy Henderson
Lynne Henderson
Mallory Henson
Elizabeth Henwood
Jane Hermiston
Anneka Hess
Diane Heward
Jo Hewitt
Kat Hewlett
Eve Hewlett-Booker
Amanda Hickling
Martin Hickman
Tracey Hickox
Jan Hicks
Max Higgins
Richard Higson
Kate Hill
Rich Hill
Carlien Hillebrink
Charlotte Hills
Ann Hiloski-Fowler
Beth Hiscock

Tony Histed
Frida Hjelm
Kahana Ho
Jackie Hobbs
Becky Hodges
Keith Hodges
Marie Hodgson
Pilgrim Hodgson
James Edward
    Hodkinson
Jason Holdcroft-Long
Lynne Holding
Dianne Holland
Samantha Holland
Jill Holliday
Fran Hollinrake
Anne Holliss
Claire Holliss
Karen Holloway
Holly Holmes
Monet Holmquist
Barbara Holten
Pamela Hopkins
Sharon Hopkinson
Janice Hopper
Geoffrey Horn
Clare Horne
Ellie Horne
Xenia Horne
Olivia Horsefield
Andy Horton
Jocelyn Houghton

Caroline Howard
Jacki Howard
Liz Howard-Smith
Dan Howick
Sara Howland
Lisa Hudson
Theresa Hudson
Chris Huecksteadt
Clare Isobel Hughes
Crystal Hughes
Elaine Hughes
Jennifer Hughes
Lindsay Hughes
Yvette Huijsman
Alison Hull
Sandy Humby
Sharon Hundley
Kerry Hunt
Marilyn K Hunt
Sarah Hunt
Melinda Hunt-
    Hungerford
Ian F Hunter
Jaazzmina Hussain
Becci Hutchins
Claire Hutchinson
Melanie Hutchinson
Gisele Huxley
Kay Hyde
Philippa Illsley
Nigel Ince
Betty Ing

Laura Ipsum
Kimberley Irons
Carolyn Irvine
Ivan Ivanov
Jackie
Anna Jackson
Judith Jackson
Catherine Jacob
Marc Jacobson
Kellie James
Sandra James
Marieke Jansen
Mark Jarret Porter
Sophie Jarvie
Peter Tags &
    Kim Jarvis
Sarah Jarvis
Luke Jeffery
Marcus Jenkins
Christine Jenner
Kim Jennings
Lucy Jiwa
Tristan John
Vicky Johns
Alison Johnson
Andrea Johnson
Sarah Johnson
Sophie Johnson
Beth Johnston
Helen Johnston
Pauline Johnstone
Allison Joiner

Craig Jones
Hollie Jones
John Jones
Lora Jones
Meghan Jones
Myra Jones
Rebecca Jones
Sandra Jones
Suzi Jones
Alice Jorgensen
Sara Joseph
Melissa Joulwan
Mary Jowitt
Alex Joy
Val Joyce
Mike Jury
Vickie Kakia
Lena Karlsson
Annette Katiforis
Ardala Katzfuss
Jo Keeley
Ursula Kehoe
Minna Kelland
Colleen Kelly
Gill Kelly
Martha Kelly
Helen Kemp
Rebecca Kemp
Christina Kennedy
Helen Kennedy
Laura Kennedy
Ros Kennedy

Denise Kennefick
Bridie Kennerley
Kristin Kerbavaz
Debbie, Graeme,
    Rigby, Charlie &
    Dudley Kerr
Roberta Kerr
Paul Kerrigan
Mary Kersey
Helen Kershaw
Rebecca Kershaw
Audrey Keszek
Gemma Khawaja
Dan Kieran
Caitlin Kight
Peta Kilbane
Janneke Kimstra
Deborah King
Georgina King
Sue King
Simone Kinnert
Jon Kiphart
Michelle Kirk
Pete Kirkham
Kelsey Kittle
Alison Klose
Catherine Kneale
Alison Knight
Heather Knight
Korin Knight
Yvonne Knight
Rachel Knightley

Mel Knott
Patricia Knott
Chris Knowles
Rick Koehler
Laurie Koerber
Sandra Kohls
Teppo Koivula
Sioned Kowalczuk
Helene Kreysa
Laurie Kutoroff
Emily Kyne
J L L
Dawn Lacey
Kevin Lack
Susan Lacy
Christine Ladyman
Clive Lafferty
Leslie Lambert
Emma Lamerton
Peter Landers
Deborah Lane
Jane Langan
Patty Langner
Teresa Langston
Alex Langstone
Joelle Lardi
Nicole Larkin
Phil Latham
Heidi Latzan
Ronni Laurie
Vanessa Laurin
Terry Lavender

Delia Lavigne
Clare Laws
Abigail Lawson
Stephanie Lay
Alison Layland
Catherine Layne
Kim Le Patourel
Morgan Le Roy
Capucine Lebreton
Bennet Ledner
Diane Lee
Alexandra Leeds
Alice Leiper
Janet Lemon
Alison Lennie
Sandra Leonard
Denne LePage-
    Ahlefeld
Emily LeQuesne
Catherine Lester
Jane and Cliff
    Lethbridge
Jill Lethbridge
Alison Levey
Eva Levi
Alex Levine
Jane Levine
Natale Lewington
Beth Lewis
Helen Lewis
Katherine J. Lewis
Marian Lewis

Pam Lewis
Fletch and Maggie
Lewis - my
little hoons
Nita Lewsey
Lidbert
Jonathan Light
Bonnie Lilienfeld
Susan Lindon-Hall
Ian Lipthorpe
Katie Lister
Claire Livesey
Vikki Lloyd
Siân Lloyd-Pennell
Benjamin E. Logan
Ellen Logstein
Gillian Lonergan
Kirrily Long
Andrew Longland-
Meech
Liina Lonn
Helen Looker
Hannah Lorne Gray
Katy Love
Catriona M. Low
Jennifer Lowe
Catherine Lowrey
Rocki Lu Holder
Jude Lucas-Mould
Katie Lucey
Simon Lucy
Barbara Ludlow

Sandra Lukashevich
Helen Luker
Elspeth Luna
Nick Lupton
Daniel Lüthi
Abby Lyn Jones
Katherine Lynn
Adam Lyzniak
Suzanne Maasland
Linda Macdonald
Margo MacDonald
Zoe Macdonald
Karen Mace
Sophie Macgregor
Kate Macinnes
Helen Mackenzie-
Burrows
Sara MacKian
Russell Mackintosh
Lisa Maggio
Laura Magnier
Laura-Jane Maher
Rebecca Major
Catt Makin
Mary Malpass
Lynn Mancuso
Claire Mander
Doran Manella
Kieran Mangan
Darren Manion
Steve Manners
Guy Manning

Keith Mantell
Anne Margerison
Deb Markham
Emily Martin
Maribel Martinez
Greig
Andy Masheter
Catherine Mason
Frances Mason
Jo Mason
Laura Mason
Adrienne Massanari
Jose Mastenbroek
Louise Matchett
Suzanne Matrosov-
Vruggink
Susan Mattheus
Stephen Matthews
Zara Matthews
Becca Mattingley
Shannon Matzke
Shirley Mawer
Molly Mayfield
Melanie McBlain
Wendie McBurnie
Cat McCabe
Laura McCarthy
Yvonne Carol
McCombie
Megan McCormick
Sonya McCormick
Joel McCracken

Lauren McDaniel
Hazel McDowell
Helen McElwee
Jane McEwan
Daniel McGachey
Barbara L
  McGonagle
Luna, Vince &
  Ted McGowan
Marie McGowan
Ann McGregor
Holly McGuire
Kirsten McIlroy
Alison McIntyre
David McKean
Andrew McKechnie
Victoria McKenna
  Martin
Janet McKnight
Vanessa McLaughlin
Cate Mclaurin
Alastair McLellan
Ruth McLennan
Amanda Mclernon
Mandy McLernon
Fi McLoughlin
Mary McManus
Amanda McMillan
Peter McMullin
Leanna McPherson
Erin McSherry
Denise McSpadden

Carol McTear
Melanie McVey
Sarah Meehan
Signe Mehl
Kate Menzies
Stacy Merrick
Anne Metcalf
Susan Metcalfe
Olivier Mével
Elgiva Middleton
Eilidh Miller
Michelle Miller
Scott Millington
Chris Mills
Laura Mitchell
Polly Mitchell
John Mitchinson
Sebastian Moitzheim
Emma Moore
Kristine Moore
Natalie Moore
Sarah Moore
Andy Moorhouse
Sarah Mooring
Jenny Moran
Amy Morgan
Sharon Morrell
Jackie Morris
Mercy Morris
Morgan Morris
Melody Morrow
Leigh Morse

Katrina Moseley
Dana Mosher
Hettie Moss-Connell
Sarah Mottershead
@mr_spoon
Florentina Mudshark
Donna Mugavero
Jean Muir
Sarah Muir
Linda Muller
Hannah Mumby
Catherine Munro
Ellie Munro
Wendy Murguia
Frances Murphy
Ian Murphy
Clive Murray
Elizabeth Murray
Lara Murray
Meg Murrell-
  Peloquin
Alix Murtha
Sarah Mushrow
Laura Mutton
Hugh N
Kate N
Debbie Nairn
Jessica Naramore
Carlo Navato
Andy & Angela
  Neale
Gemma Nelson

Gem Nethersole
Alyson Nevill
Tim Neville
Elizabeth New
Briony Newbold
Caron Newman
Colleen Newton
Sarah Newton-Scott
Ducky Nguyen
Laura Niall
Jo Niblett
Valerie Niblett
Kate Nichol
Lynda Nicholson
Liz Nicolson
Andy Nikolas
Kate Noble
C Nodder
Anita Norburn
Gemma Norburn
Sheila North
Meredith Norwich
Adele Nozedar
Andrew Nunn
Caleb Nyberg
Jackie O'Brien
Kelly O'Connor
Karen O'Donnell
Caoimhe O'Gorman
Liz & Ian O'Halloran
Mark O'Neill
Hannah O'Regan

Sarah Oates
Laura Ohara Sibra
Gemma Olsson
Kim Olynyk
Omega House
Linda Oostmeyer
Angela Osborne
Jeannine Otto
Maria Padley
Paula Page
Kirsten Pairpoint
Michael Paley
Juliet Palfrey
Alison Palmer
Ellie Palmer
Pam Palmer
Sarah Palmer
Gwen Papp
Clare Parker
Steph Parker
John Parkhouse
Catherine Parkin
Samantha Parnell
George Parr
Sarah Parry
Claire Parsons
Soraya Pascoe
Kate Passingham
Karen Paton
Trish Paton
April Patrick
Gill Patterson

Rob Paul
Jo Peacey
Eleanor Pearce
Sharon Pearson
Janice Pedersen
Karie Penhaligon
Caity PenzeyMoog
Naomi Perfect
Valerie Perham
Bob Perry
Judy Peters
Mags Phelan Stones
Leslie Phelps
Phil & Vicky
Elizabeth Phillips
Kyla Phillips
Michael Phythian
Alice Picado
Kelly Picarazzi
Lisa Piddington
Karen F. Pierce
Michael Pierce
Kelsey Pilkington
Peter Pinkney
Nicola Pitchford
Denise Plank
Jo Plumridge
Marcel Poitras
Justin Pollard
Steve Pont
Annette Poole
Naomi Porter

Becky Potter
Lucy Potts
Peggy Powers
Richard Prangle
Kristine Heidi Pratt
Robert Preece
Sally Preece
Virginia Preston
Laura Price
Gemma Prothero
Christina Pullman
Lisa Purcell
David Quarterman
Lisa Quattromini
Ian Quelch
Cheryl Quine
Sue Radford
Ruby Rae Norton
Helen Rainbow
Laura E. Ramos
Susan Randall
Tina Rashid
Laura Rathbone
Anooshka Rawden
Jonny Rawlings
Angela Rayson
Becca Read
Caroline Read
Kerie Receveur
Lynn Reglar
Vivienne Reid-Brown
Peg Reilly

Tamsin Reinsch
Steph Renaud
Marie Reyes
Anita Reynolds
Electra Rhodes
Julie Richards
Laura Richmond
Hatty Richmond
Dakin
Fiona Riddell Pearce
Meryl Rimmer
Nicola Rimmer
Beverley Ring
Kerry Rini
Rachel Ritchie
Rochelle Ritchie
Nicole Rivette
Lucy Rix
Catherine Roberts
Claire Roberts
Amanda Robertson
Janet Robertson &
Louisa Lloyd
Norman Robinson
Spencer Robinson
Patricia Rockwell
Valerie Roebuck
Jeanette Rogers
Sue Rogers
Susan Rollinson
Donna Rooney
Tom Roper

Kalina Rose
Lauren Rosewarne
Adam Ross & Hazel
Auri Patterson
Alexandra Roumbas
Goldstein
Matthew Rowell
Rhona Rowland
Lizzie Rowson
Sar Ruddenklau
Sue Rupp
Sam Russell
Marjokaisa Ryhänen
Marie S
Karl Sabino
Sara Sahlin
Katie Sajnog
Matt Salts
Nic Sands
Ingrid Sandstrom
Lyn Santos
Kirsten Sarp
Christine Savage
Sherri Savage
Dorothy Scanlan
Lisa Schaller
Stephanie Schlanger
Julia Schlotel
Sue Schneider
Katharine Schopflin
Linda Schott
Carl Schultz

Katee Schultz
Vikie Schwartz
Leslie Schweitzer
Jenni Scott
Russell Scott
Sarah Scott
Tracey Scott
Jane Seager
Andrew Seaman
Jonathan Seaman
Lisa Search
Claire Searle
Peter and Angela
  Seary
Cora Seip
Sharon Sekhon
Emma Seldon
Neil Sellers
Dick Selwood
Emma Selwood
Gary Selwood
Beth Setters
Belynda J. Shadoan
Mariese Shallard
Harriet Shannon
Kathleen Shannon
Lori Shannon
Eve Sharman
James Sharp
Victoria Sharratt
  McConnell
Adele Shaw

Iola Shaw
Jenny Shaw
Joanna Shaw
Matt Shaw
Chris Sheehan
Luke Shelburne
Tara K. Shepersky
Cliff Shephard
Clare Shepherd
Eloise Shepherd
John Shepherd
Susannah Shepherd
Josephine Sherwood
Andrew Short
Elizabeth Shostak
Claire Siân Ricketts
Mike Simmonds
Cyndi Simpson
Carolina Siniscalchi
James Skeffington
Gabriela Sládková
Debbie Slater
Stoic Sloth
Kate Sluka
SmallTeethingBeastie
Emma Smallwood
Barendina Smedley
Abby Smith
Bec Smith
Carolyn Smith
Charlotte Smith
Chloe Smith

Claire Smith
Fiona Katherine
  Smith
Gabriella Smith
Hannah Smith
Helen Smith
Janine Smith
Kate Smith
KT Smith
Lan-Lan Smith
Lauren Smith
Libby Smith
Louise Smith
Martin Smith
MD Smith
Michael Smith
Peter Smith
Rebecca Jane Smith
Rosie Smith
LA Smith-Buxton
Susan Smyth
Julia Snell
Michael Soares
Ingrid Solberg
Yve Solbrekken
Murielle Solheim
Gaby Solly
Roberta Solmundson
Laura Jane Solomon
Sally Songer
Kit Spahr
Beth Sparks-Jacques

Lyn Speakman
Maureen Kincaid
    Speller
Chris Spence
Rosslyn Spokes
Teresa Squires
Deb Sreiberg
Richard Stagg
Andy Stainsby
Lisa Staken
Corie Stanfield
Elizabeth Stanley
Hannah Stark
Andrew Steele
Natasha Steer
Sarah Steer
Angie Stegemann
Anzi Stenvall
Astrid Stephens
Ann Marie
    Stephenson
Ros Stern
Nina J S Stevens
Ruth Stevens
Sarah Stevens
Amy Stewart
Terri Stewart Hackler
Charli Stewart-
    Russon
Beth Stites
Gòrdan Stiùbhart

Rhiannon Stocking-
    Williams
Mary Stoicoiu
Shelagh Stoicoiu
Sue Stokes
Carmen Stone
Gwilym Stone
Stephanie Strahan
Duncan Strickland
Jillian Strobel
Rachel Stubbs
Nina Stutler
Carol Styles
Nadia Suchdev
Sue Summers & Co.
Helen E Sunderland
Adam Sussman
Judi Sutherland
Laurel Sutton
Ian Swanwick
Laura Sweeney
Toni Swiffen
Kirsty Syder
Angela Sykes
Jerry Sykes
Hayden Sylvester
William Sylvester
Janet T
Nick Tait
Ben Tallamy
Anna Tarnowski
Alison Taylor

Brigid Taylor
Chris Taylor
Dave Taylor
Kay Taylor
Patricia Taylor
Shereen Taylor
Sue Tett
Sarah Tevendale
Kim Thain
Carolyn Theisen
Marthe Tholen
Dave & Jan Thomas
Donna Thomas
Victoria Thomas
Ian Thomas-Bignami
Brewer Thompson
Claire Thompson
Fern Thompson
Helen Thompson
Marianne Thompson
Fern Thompson
    from Caroline
Lynne, Kylie, Donna
    & Shelley
    Thomson
Alastair Thornhill
Carolyn Thraves
Donna Tickner
Aurora Tiddy
Brook Zeal
Lynne Tidmarsh
Sarah Till-Vattier

Anka Tilley
Emma Tinsley
Adam Tinworth
Simona Toader
Joanne Todd
Pippa Tolfts
Amie Tolson
Deborah Toner
Sarah Torr
Angela Townsend
Ryan Trainor
Emily Traynor
Jon Treadway
Sarah Treble
Carly Tremayne
Lindsay Trevarthen
Jessica Trinh
Julianna Trivers
Fiona Trosh
Stefanie Tryson
Joanna Tucker
Ann Tudor
Kate Tudor
Chloe Turner
Jim Turner
Liana Turner
Sally Turner
Sue Turner
Alison Twelvetrees
Anita Uotinen
Rachel Upward
Mrs V

Mike Vallano
Richard Vallat
Sonja van Amelsfort
Chantal van der
    Ende-Appel
Kristen Van Dyke
Robin Van Sant
Shane Van Veghel
Anne Vasey
Sandy Vaughan
Leo Velten
Kellie Vernon
Nicole Vickers
Sally Vince
Vivian Vincek
Paul Vincent
Rosalind Vincent
Alice Violett
Kate Viscardi
Nicole Vlach
James Voller
Felicity Wadge
Julia Wagner Grover
Leslie Wainger
Allyson Wake
Sarah Wakes
Anne Walker
Sue Walker
Niki Walkey
Heather Wallace
Anthony Waller
Linda Wallis

Sara Walls
Rachel Walne
Declan Walsh
Amanda Walters
Stephanie Walters
Carole-Ann
    Warburton
Donna Ward
Jamie Ward
Joolz Ward
Lee Ward
Laura Watkins
Bj Watson
Christine Watson
Deborah and
    Anne Watson
Rachel Watt
Keith Way
E Webb
M. F. Webb
Lisa Webster
Andy Weekes
Ange Weeks
Marie-Louise
    Weighill
Deborah Weir
Julie Weller
Sarah Wells
Clair Wellsbury-Nye
Jane Werry
Lyn West
Lucy Weston

Michelle Westwater
Katy Wheatley
Andrew & Lucy
    Whelan
Pam Whetnall
Jaki White
Nic White
Susan White
Mark Whitehead
Richard Whitehead
Robert Whitelock
Rosie Whitfield
Annalise Whittaker
Carly Whyborn
Chris Wignall
Peter Wilde
Lorna Will
Linda Willars
Heather Willcox
Angela D. Williams
Caroline Williams
Eileen Williams
Gwynedd Williams
Henry Williams
Oli Williams
Briony Williamson
Mark Williamson
Laura Willis
Rosamund Willis-
    Fear
Kim Willmetts
Bree Wilson

Derek Wilson
Fiona Wilson
Kirsten Wilson
Tracey Wilson
Oliver Wilton
Camilla Winlo
Anna Wittmann
Gretchen Woelfle
Kellyann Wolfe
Kanina Wolff
Mia Wolff
Laiane Wolfsong
John Wood
Judith Wood
Lucy Wood
Matthew Wood
Peter Wood
Rebecca Wood
Sandra Wood
Justine Woodbridge
Joanna Woodhouse
Brenda Wordsworth
David Wrennall
Georgina Wright
Melanie Wright
Michelle Wright
Rebecca Wyeth Fox
Jeremiah Wyke
Jo Wynell-Mayow
Zoe Wyrko
Theresa Yanchar
Stephanie Yates

Neil Yeaman
Stephen Usins
    Yeardley
Duncan Yeates
Lisa Young
Donna Zillmann
Birgit Zimmermann-
    Nowak